2007–2008

60th edition

Editors: Glenda Rollin and
Jack Rollin

headline

First published in 2007
by HEADLINE PUBLISHING GROUP

1

Cover photographs Front and spine: Aaron Lennon (Tottenham Hotspur) – *Getty Images Sport/Clive Rose*; back: Dirk Kuyt (Liverpool) – *Sportsphoto.*

ISBN 978 0 7553 1662 5

Typeset by Wearset Ltd, Boldon, Tyne and Wear

Printed and bound in Great Britain by Clays Ltd, St Ives plc

Headline's policy is to use papers that are natural, renewable and recyclable products and made from wood grown in sustainable forests. The logging and manufacturing processes are expected to conform to the environmental regulations of the country of origin.

HEADLINE PUBLISHING GROUP
An Hachette Livre UK Company
338 Euston Road
London NW1 3BH

www.headline.co.uk
www.hodderheadline.com

CONTENTS

European and International Football

Other Football

Information and Records

EDITORIAL

There really has to be a better method of deciding cup games than a penalty shoot-out. Naturally the disappointment which followed England Under-21s' exit from the European Championship highlighted the problem, but even had we been successful, the fact remained this is not the answer.

There are now a number of different interpretations of cup competitions in this country alone. The FA Cup still retains replays, but does not include away goals counting double at the end of the second game if aggregate scores are level.

The Carling Cup has abandoned replays in recent years and goes into penalties after extra time. The competition for the Associate Members which last season was sponsored as the Johnstone's Paint Trophy has no extra time and instant penalties.

The Football League even toyed with the idea of introducing penalties at the end of drawn fixtures! Perhaps the game is becoming so lacklustre that the shoot-out will become its sole excitement.

But such is the need to complete the shoot-out in the quickest possible time, the usual rules which apply to a penalty kick are quietly forgotten. Goalkeepers are prancing on and off the line and only on rare occasions is a kick retaken.

Morally the penalty shoot-out has no defence. During open play the spot kick is awarded as a punishment for an infringement in the penalty area. This has been turned into a circus act gaining access to a reward and in some instances, a substantial one particularly in the play-offs and the prize of many millions of pounds.

England's 32 kick marathon with Holland emphasised the farcical nature of the entire concept. Had the goalkeepers waited until the kick had been taken, they would have saved at least half a dozen shots, simply because the ball entered within handling distance in the centre of the goal.

So, what to do for a solution to the problems, given that the prospect of replays returning is out of the question with the calendar full to capacity? Why not scrap extra time completely and simply play on until a goal is scored? The players would still be fresh and there would be no psychological block with the comfort zone of the penalty shoot-out to follow.

Teams clearly are content to face losing on the spot rather than during open play. The stigma of defeat is softened it seems by this pathetic outcome.

Thus the mindset must be changed and with the knowledge that there is no alternative but to go for the winner, we might even see some attacking football and not the half-an-hour of inertia which invariably unfolds in extra time.

An experiment might be worthwhile in a domestic cup competition, with incentives for the winning team. Surely a sponsor could be found promoting attacking football.

So much for competition; now to the serious matter of abuse to referees by spectators, players and managers. This has to stop. Refereeing standards have fallen largely because of the poor recruitment figures of such officials. Only the determined, dedicated and some might add deranged are prepared to run the gauntlet of trying to control matches.

The days of getting referees and managers round the table for a chat at the local hostelry are gone but there has to be a move to eradicate bad behaviour as previously outlined. Also the fourth official has to take on more responsibility.

For a start he should be in charge of the time keeping. The referee has enough on his hands without looking at his watch. This could also prevent the awful time added on for injuries. The sign of the board being raised with up to five minutes or so being added is invariably the signal for remaining substitutes to be shuffled onto the pitch to waste even more time.

If the managers and players were unaware of how much longer was to be played, we might even get more playing time to satisfy us.

Of course if managers and coaches were treated as spectators in that they had to sit down, the confrontation between the benches would be ended. Why are such people elevated to a position where their conduct is excused while those who pay to watch are denied the same standing rights?

Moreover the unfortunate spectators who sit in close proximity to the dugouts must be highly unhappy with the scenario which punctures their viewing of the proceedings. It was a sad day when FIFA sanctioned freedom of movement for those in charge of players.

CLUB AND OTHER RECORDS DURING 2006–2007

Arsenal	Thierry Henry becomes the club's most capped player with 81 of his 92 caps for France. He also tops his 250th Premier League outing.
Bolton W	Gary Speed milestones: his 500th Premier League appearance and his 750th overall career club game.
Bournemouth	Steve Fletcher extends record club League appearances to 466.
Chelsea	Andriy Shevchenko scores his 59th goal in Europe leaving him second only to Gerd Muller in the goalscoring lists.
Cheltenham Town	Jamie Victory extends record club League appearances to 258 and Grant McCann adds to his caps for Northern Ireland.
Crewe Alexandra	Long serving manager Dario Gradi completes his 1,296th match in charge of the club.
Fulham	Matthew Briggs youngest Premier League goalscorer at 16 years 65 days. Moritz Volz scores the 15,000th Premier League goal.
Grimsby Town	John McDermott extends record club League appearances to 647.
Huddersfield Town	Gary Taylor-Fletcher hits the 500,000th goal since the start of League football in 1888.
Liverpool	Steven Gerrard beats Ian Rush's record with his 15th European Cup goal on the same day as Jamie Carragher eclipses Phil Neal's appearances in his 58th match.
Manchester U	Paul Scholes reaches his 500th club match.
Portsmouth	David James completes 142 Premier League clean sheets beating David Seaman's record.
Rangers	Kris Boyd scores his 100th Scottish Premier League goal.
Scunthorpe United	Dave Mulligan becomes the club's first full international capped for New Zealand.
Stockport Co	Establish all-time Football League record with nine wins in succession without conceding a goal.
Walsall	Most League points 89 a club record.
West Ham United	Teddy Sheringham becomes the oldest Premier League goalscorer at the age of 40 years 268 days.
Wigan Athletic	Lee McCulloch becomes the club's most capped player with 11 appearances for Scotland.
Yeovil Town	Terry Skiverton extends record club League appearances to 139.
England	Michael Owen's 23rd competitive international goal scored against Estonia is a record for his country.
Champions League	Fastest goal Roy Makaay 10 secs for Bayern Munich v Real Madrid 7 March 2007.
Euro 2008	San Marino 0 Germany 13 record score in the competition.
Northern Ireland	Play their 200th international.

LEAGUE REVIEW AND CLUB SECTION

Chelsea's hope of three Premiership titles in a row foundered and perhaps losing only their second League game of the season 2-1 at Middlesbrough where they had faltered much later the previous campaign, might have had the wiseacres nodding ominously. But the reality was somewhat different, though Manchester United's triumph was well deserved.

In fact Chelsea lost only three League games, were undefeated in the last 14 and had they wrested more points from the last five draws, could still have made it. In contrast United lost five times. The difference was in the number of drawn matches, just five to Chelsea's 11. Three points for a win is a huge advantage over a division of the spoils.

When United slipped up, Chelsea were indecisive. The Blues' last opportunity came after the events of 7 April. Manchester United were beaten 2-1 with a Rio Ferdinand own goal at Portsmouth while Chelsea were winning 1-0 against Tottenham Hotspur at Stamford Bridge.

With six games remaining for each team Chelsea had cut the deficit to three points with United still due to visit the Bridge. However, Chelsea still needed Sir Alex Ferguson's team to drop at least two more points in a draw because the Reds had a far superior goal difference.

Two weeks later it seemed the chance had fallen Chelsea's way as Middlesbrough – of all teams – drew 1-1 at Old Trafford. The following day Chelsea were away at Newcastle United but could only draw themselves and then it seemed their grip on the title was finally loosened. It was not over until 6 May when Chelsea in drawing mood by then failed to win at Arsenal.

With Cristiano Ronaldo, the double PFA Player and Young Player of the Year, in scintillating form and Wayne Rooney finding some of his former danger as a lethal striker, United had the two most potent forces in the Premier League next to Chelsea's dogged dangerman Didier Drogba, the top scorer in the League with 20 goals.

Such was the domination by these two clubs that there never appeared to be a serious challenge from anywhere else. Ultimately only goal difference gave Liverpool third place above Arsenal and then came an eight point gap before Tottenham Hotspur despite a hectic run-in at the end of the season climbed to fifth place, their best in the entire term.

Of the promoted teams Reading did extremely well, just failing to get into Europe. Alas Watford found the step up a problem as eventually did Sheffield United even though they were as high as 14th just before Christmas.

Charlton Athletic joined them in relegation after failing to win one of their last seven games. However, West Ham United survived if in controversial circumstances after being fined a record £5.5m instead of a points deduction for signing irregularities over Carlos Tevez, who ironically was the goalscorer in the Hammers' crucial last day victory at Manchester United, which actually gave them the double over the champions.

Previously Charlton and West Ham had exchanged managers, Alan Pardew taking the Addicks, Alan Curbishley moving to Upton Park and guiding them to safety.

The Championship was remarkable for Sunderland who lost their first four League games, appointed Roy Keane as manager and never looked back until taking the title. Birmingham City took the other automatic slot.

Relegated were Southend United, Luton Town and Leeds United who took administration and a ten-point deduction once all was lost for them. Scunthorpe United and Bristol City moved up.

At the bottom of League One, Chesterfield, Bradford City, Rotherham United and Brentford were demoted. Up automatically from League Two were Walsall, Hartlepool United and Swindon Town.

Losing their League place after close on 80 years were Torquay United accompanied by Boston United. Up from the Conference came Dagenham & Redbridge, who ironically had lost the chance of elevation when Boston were promoted with a points penalty which would have prevented them entering the Football League. The other newcomers are Morecambe.

The Championship play-offs saw West Bromwich Albion and Derby County dispute the lucrative prize of entry into the Premier League. This £60 million affair was decided when Stephen Pearson scored the only goal to put Derby back into the top echelon. The attendance at the new Wembley was 74,993.

Blackpool overcame Yeovil Town in the League One race, again the venue attracting 59,313 and Bristol Rovers made it a happy West Country occasion for the city beating Shrewsbury Town, viewed by 61,589.

FA Barclays Premiership

		Home						Away					Total						
		P	W	D	L	F	A	W	D	L	F	A	W	D	L	F	A	Gd	Pts
1	Manchester U	38	15	2	2	46	12	13	3	3	37	15	28	5	5	83	27	56	89
2	Chelsea	38	12	7	0	37	11	12	4	3	27	13	24	11	3	64	24	40	83
3	Liverpool	38	14	4	1	39	7	6	4	9	18	20	20	8	10	57	27	30	68
4	Arsenal	38	12	6	1	43	16	7	5	7	20	19	19	11	8	63	35	28	68
5	Tottenham H	38	12	3	4	34	22	5	6	8	23	32	17	9	12	57	54	3	60
6	Everton	38	11	4	4	33	17	4	9	6	19	19	15	13	10	52	36	16	58
7	Bolton W	38	9	5	5	26	20	7	3	9	21	32	16	8	14	47	52	–5	56
8	Reading	38	11	2	6	29	20	5	5	9	23	27	16	7	15	52	47	5	55
9	Portsmouth	38	11	5	3	28	15	3	7	9	17	27	14	12	12	45	42	3	54
10	Blackburn R	38	9	3	7	31	25	6	4	9	21	29	15	7	16	52	54	–2	52
11	Aston Villa	38	7	8	4	20	14	4	9	6	23	27	11	17	10	43	41	2	50
12	Middlesbrough	38	10	3	6	31	24	2	7	10	13	25	12	10	16	44	49	–5	46
13	Newcastle U	38	7	7	5	23	20	4	3	12	15	27	11	10	17	38	47	–9	43
14	Manchester C	38	5	6	8	10	16	6	3	10	19	28	11	9	18	29	44	–15	42
15	West Ham U	38	8	2	9	24	26	4	3	12	11	33	12	5	21	35	59	–24	41
16	Fulham	38	7	7	5	18	18	1	8	10	20	42	8	15	15	38	60	–22	39
17	Wigan Ath	38	5	4	10	18	30	5	4	10	19	29	10	8	20	37	59	–22	38
18	Sheffield U	38	7	6	6	24	21	3	2	14	8	34	10	8	20	32	55	–23	38
19	Charlton Ath	38	7	5	7	19	20	1	5	13	15	40	8	10	20	34	60	–26	34
20	Watford	38	3	9	7	19	25	2	4	13	10	34	5	13	20	29	59	–30	28

LEADING GOALSCORERS 2006–07

FA BARCLAYS PREMIERSHIP

Players in this competition scoring eleven or more League goals are listed. Other leading scorers classified by total number of goals in all competitions.

	League	Carling Cup	FA Cup	Other	Total
Didier Drogba *(Chelsea)*	20	4	3	6	33
Benny McCarthy *(Blackburn R)*	18	0	3	3	24
Cristiano Ronaldo *(Manchester U)*	17	0	3	3	23
Wayne Rooney *(Manchester U)*	14	0	5	4	23
Mark Viduka *(Middlesbrough)*	14	0	5	0	19
Kevin Doyle *(Reading)*	13	0	0	0	13
Dimitar Berbatov *(Tottenham H)*	12	1	3	7	23
Ayegbeni Yakubu *(Middlesbrough)*	12	0	4	0	16
Dirk Kuyt *(Liverpool)*	12	0	1	1	14
Robbie Keane *(Tottenham H)*	11	1	5	5	22
Frank Lampard *(Chelsea)*	11	3	6	1	21
Obi Martins *(Newcastle U)*	11	0	0	6	17
Robin Van Persie *(Arsenal)*	11	0	0	2	13
Nicolas Anelka *(Bolton W)*	11	1	0	0	12
Andrew Johnson *(Everton)*	11	0	1	0	12
Bobby Zamora *(West Ham U)*	11	0	0	0	11
In order of total goals:-					
Peter Crouch *(Liverpool)*	9	1	0	8	18
Andriy Shevchenko *(Chelsea)*	4	3	3	4	14

Other matches consist of European games, J Paint Trophy, Community Shield and Football League play-offs. Players listed in order of League goals total.

Coca-Cola Football League Championship

			Home					Away					Total						
		P	*W*	*D*	*L*	*F*	*A*	*W*	*D*	*L*	*F*	*A*	*W*	*D*	*L*	*F*	*A*	*Gd*	*Pts*
1	Sunderland	46	15	4	4	38	18	12	3	8	38	29	27	7	12	76	47	29	88
2	Birmingham C	46	15	5	3	37	18	11	3	9	30	24	26	8	12	67	42	25	86
3	Derby Co	46	13	6	4	33	19	12	3	8	29	27	25	9	12	62	46	16	84
4	WBA	46	14	4	5	51	24	8	6	9	30	31	22	10	14	81	55	26	76
5	Wolverhampton W	46	12	5	6	33	28	10	5	8	26	28	22	10	14	59	56	3	76
6	Southampton	46	13	6	4	36	20	8	6	9	41	33	21	12	13	77	53	24	75
7	Preston NE	46	15	4	4	38	17	7	4	12	26	36	22	8	16	64	53	11	74
8	Stoke C	46	12	8	3	35	16	7	8	8	27	25	19	16	11	62	41	21	73
9	Sheffield W	46	10	6	7	38	36	10	5	8	32	30	20	11	15	70	66	4	71
10	Colchester U	46	15	4	4	46	19	5	5	13	24	37	20	9	17	70	56	14	69
11	Plymouth Arg	46	10	8	5	36	26	7	8	8	27	36	17	16	13	63	62	1	67
12	Crystal Palace	46	12	3	8	33	22	6	8	9	26	29	18	11	17	59	51	8	65
13	Cardiff C	46	11	7	5	33	18	6	6	11	24	35	17	13	16	57	53	4	64
14	Ipswich T	46	13	2	8	40	29	5	6	12	24	30	18	8	20	64	59	5	62
15	Burnley	46	10	6	7	35	23	5	6	12	17	26	15	12	19	52	49	3	57
16	Norwich C	46	10	5	8	29	25	6	4	13	27	46	16	9	21	56	71	–15	57
17	Coventry C	46	11	4	8	30	25	5	4	14	17	37	16	8	22	47	62	–15	56
18	QPR	46	9	6	8	31	29	5	5	13	23	39	14	11	21	54	68	–14	53
19	Leicester C	46	6	8	9	26	31	7	6	10	23	33	13	14	19	49	64	–15	53
20	Barnsley	46	9	4	10	27	29	6	1	16	26	56	15	5	26	53	85	–32	50
21	Hull C	46	8	3	12	33	32	5	7	11	18	35	13	10	23	51	67	–16	49
22	Southend U	46	6	6	11	29	38	4	6	13	18	42	10	12	24	47	80	–33	42
23	Luton T	46	7	5	11	33	40	3	5	15	20	41	10	10	26	53	81	–28	40
24	Leeds U*	46	10	4	9	27	30	3	3	17	19	42	13	7	26	46	72	–26	36

**Deducted 10 points for breach of rule.*

COCA-COLA FOOTBALL LEAGUE CHAMPIONSHIP

	League	*Carling Cup*	*FA Cup*	*Other*	*Total*
Players in this competition scoring 13 or more League goals are listed.					
Jamie Cureton *(Colchester U)*	23	0	1	0	24
Michael Chopra *(Cardiff C)*	22	0	0	0	22
Diomansy Kamara *(WBA)*	20	0	2	1	23
Robert Earnshaw *(Norwich C)*	19	0	0	0	19
Grzegorz Rasiak *(Southampton)*	18	0	2	1	21
Chris Iwelumo *(Colchester U)*	18	0	0	0	18
Alan Lee *(Ipswich T)*	16	0	1	0	17
Kevin Phillips *(WBA)*	16	0	3	3	22
Steve Howard *(Derby Co)*	16	1	0	2	19
Dave Nugent *(Preston NE)*	15	0	2	0	17
Gary McSheffrey *(Birmingham C)*	14	2	1	0	17
(Includes 1 League goal for Coventry C).					
Kenwyne Jones *(Southampton)*	14	1	1	0	16
Andy Gray *(Burnley)*	14	0	0	0	14
Iain Hume *(Leicester C)*	13	1	0	0	14
Dexter Blackstock *(QPR)*	13	0	1	0	14
Barry Hayles *(Plymouth Arg)*	13	0	1	0	14
David Connolly *(Sunderland)*	13	0	0	0	13

Coca-Cola Football League Division 1

			Home					*Away*					*Total*						
		P	*W*	*D*	*L*	*F*	*A*	*W*	*D*	*L*	*F*	*A*	*W*	*D*	*L*	*F*	*A*	*Gd*	*Pts*
1	Scunthorpe U	46	15	6	2	40	17	11	7	5	33	18	26	13	7	73	35	38	91
2	Bristol C	46	15	5	3	35	20	10	5	8	28	19	25	10	11	63	39	24	85
3	Blackpool	46	12	6	5	40	25	12	5	6	36	24	24	11	11	76	49	27	83
4	Nottingham F	46	14	5	4	37	17	9	8	6	28	24	23	13	10	65	41	24	82
5	Yeovil T	46	14	3	6	22	12	9	7	7	33	27	23	10	13	55	39	16	79
6	Oldham Ath	46	13	4	6	36	18	8	8	7	33	29	21	12	13	69	47	22	75
7	Swansea C	46	12	6	5	36	20	8	6	9	33	33	20	12	14	69	53	16	72
8	Carlisle U	46	12	5	6	35	24	7	6	10	19	31	19	11	16	54	55	–1	68
9	Tranmere R	46	13	5	5	33	22	5	8	10	25	31	18	13	15	58	53	5	67
10	Millwall	46	11	8	4	33	19	8	1	14	26	43	19	9	18	59	62	–3	66
11	Doncaster R	46	8	10	5	30	23	8	5	10	22	24	16	15	15	52	47	5	63
12	Port Vale	46	12	3	8	35	26	6	3	14	29	39	18	6	22	64	65	–1	60
13	Crewe Alex	46	11	4	8	39	38	6	5	12	27	34	17	9	20	66	72	–6	60
14	Northampton T	46	8	5	10	27	28	7	9	7	21	23	15	14	17	48	51	–3	59
15	Huddersfield T	46	9	8	6	37	33	5	9	9	23	36	14	17	15	60	69	–9	59
16	Gillingham	46	14	2	7	29	24	3	6	14	27	53	17	8	21	56	77	–21	59
17	Cheltenham T	46	8	6	9	25	27	7	3	13	24	34	15	9	22	49	61	–12	54
18	Brighton & HA	46	5	7	11	23	34	9	4	10	26	24	14	11	21	49	58	–9	53
19	Bournemouth	46	10	5	8	28	27	3	8	12	22	37	13	13	20	50	64	–14	52
20	Leyton Orient	46	6	10	7	30	32	6	5	12	31	45	12	15	19	61	77	–16	51
21	Chesterfield	46	9	5	9	29	22	3	6	14	16	31	12	11	23	45	53	–8	47
22	Bradford C	46	5	9	9	27	31	6	5	12	20	34	11	14	21	47	65	–18	47
23	Rotherham U	46	8	4	11	37	39	5	5	13	21	36	13	9	24	58	75	–17	38
24	Brentford	46	5	8	10	24	41	3	5	15	16	38	8	13	25	40	79	–39	37

COCA-COLA FOOTBALL LEAGUE DIVISION 1

	League	*Carling Cup*	*FA Cup*	*Other*	*Total*
Billy Sharp *(Scunthorpe U)*	30	1	1	0	32
Leon Constantine *(Port Vale)*	22	2	0	2	26
Chris Porter *(Oldham Ath)*	21	0	1	0	22
Lee Trundle *(Swansea C)*	19	0	1	0	20
Luke Varney *(Crewe Alex)*	17	1	0	7	25
Chris Greenacre *(Tranmere R)*	17	0	2	0	19
Andy Morrell *(Blackpool)*	16	0	3	1	20
Nicky Maynard *(Crewe Alex)*	16	2	0	1	19
Darren Byfield *(Millwall)*	16	0	0	0	16
Will Hoskins *(Rotherham U)* *(now Watford).*	15	1	0	0	16
Luke Beckett *(Huddersfield T)*	15	0	0	0	15
Grant Holt *(Nottingham F)*	14	0	1	4	19
Akpo Sodje *(Port Vale)*	14	1	1	0	16
Keigan Parker *(Blackpool)*	13	0	1	2	16

Coca-Cola Football League Division 2

			Home					Away					Total						
		P	W	D	L	F	A	W	D	L	F	A	W	D	L	F	A	Gd	Pts
1	Walsall	46	16	4	3	39	13	9	10	4	27	21	25	14	7	66	34	32	89
2	Hartlepool U	46	14	5	4	34	17	12	5	6	31	23	26	10	10	65	40	25	88
3	Swindon T	46	15	4	4	34	17	10	6	7	24	21	25	10	11	58	38	20	85
4	Milton Keynes D	46	14	4	5	41	26	11	5	7	35	32	25	9	12	76	58	18	84
5	Lincoln C	46	12	4	7	36	28	9	7	7	34	31	21	11	14	70	59	11	74
6	Bristol R	46	13	5	5	27	14	7	7	9	22	28	20	12	14	49	42	7	72
7	Shrewsbury T	46	11	7	5	38	23	7	10	6	30	23	18	17	11	68	46	22	71
8	Stockport Co	46	14	4	5	41	25	7	4	12	24	29	21	8	17	65	54	11	71
9	Rochdale	46	9	6	8	33	20	9	6	8	37	30	18	12	16	70	50	20	66
10	Peterborough U	46	10	6	7	48	36	8	5	10	22	25	18	11	17	70	61	9	65
11	Darlington	46	10	6	7	28	30	7	8	8	24	26	17	14	15	52	56	–4	65
12	Wycombe W	46	8	11	4	23	14	8	3	12	29	33	16	14	16	52	47	5	62
13	Notts Co	46	8	6	9	29	25	8	8	7	26	28	16	14	16	55	53	2	62
14	Barnet	46	12	5	6	35	30	4	6	13	20	40	16	11	19	55	70	–15	59
15	Grimsby T	46	11	4	8	33	32	6	4	13	24	41	17	8	21	57	73	–16	59
16	Hereford U	46	9	7	7	23	17	5	6	12	22	36	14	13	19	45	53	–8	55
17	Mansfield T	46	10	4	9	38	31	4	8	11	20	32	14	12	20	58	63	–5	54
18	Chester C	46	7	9	7	23	23	6	5	12	17	25	13	14	19	40	48	–8	53
19	Wrexham	46	8	8	7	23	21	5	4	14	20	44	13	12	21	43	65	–22	51
20	Accrington S	46	10	6	7	42	33	3	5	15	28	48	13	11	22	70	81	–11	50
21	Bury	46	4	7	12	22	35	9	4	10	24	26	13	11	22	46	61	–15	50
22	Macclesfield T	46	8	7	8	36	34	4	5	14	19	43	12	12	22	55	77	–22	48
23	Boston U*	46	9	5	9	29	32	3	5	15	22	48	12	10	24	51	80	–29	36
24	Torquay U	46	5	8	10	19	22	2	6	15	17	41	7	14	25	36	63	–27	35

**Deducted 10 points for breach of rule.*

COCA-COLA FOOTBALL LEAGUE DIVISION 2

	League	Carling Cup	FA Cup	Other	Total
Richard Barker *(Hartlepool U)*	21	1	2	0	24
(Includes 12 League goals, 1 Carling Cup and 2 FA Cup matches for Mansfield T).					
Izale McLeod *(Milton Keynes D)*	21	1	2	0	24
Glenn Murray *(Rochdale)*	19	0	0	0	19
(Includes 3 League goals on loan to Stockport Co).					
Jamie Forrester *(Lincoln C)*	18	0	0	0	18
Clive Platt *(Milton Keynes D)*	18	0	0	0	18
Jermaine Easter *(Wycombe W)*	17	6	1	0	24
Chris Dagnall *(Rochdale)*	17	0	0	1	18
Anthony Elding *(Stockport Co)*	16	0	0	0	16
(Includes 5 League goals for Boston U).					
Andy Bishop *(Bury)*	15	1	5	0	21
Mark Stallard *(Lincoln C)*	15	1	0	1	17
Jason Lee *(Notts Co)*	15	1	0	0	16
Paul Mullin *(Accrington S)*	14	1	0	1	16
Dean Keates *(Walsall)*	13	0	0	0	13

FA BARCLAYS PREMIERSHIP

HOME TEAM	Arsenal	Aston Villa	Blackburn R	Bolton W	Charlton Ath	Chelsea	Everton	Fulham	Liverpool	Manchester C
Arsenal	—	1-1	6-2	2-1	4-0	1-1	1-1	3-1	3-0	3-1
Aston Villa	0-1	—	2-0	0-1	2-0	0-0	1-1	1-1	0-0	1-3
Blackburn R	0-2	1-2	—	0-1	4-1	0-2	1-1	2-0	1-0	4-2
Bolton W	3-1	2-2	1-2	—	1-1	0-1	1-1	2-1	2-0	0-0
Charlton Ath	1-2	2-1	1-0	2-0	—	0-1	1-1	2-2	0-3	1-0
Chelsea	1-1	1-1	3-0	2-2	2-1	—	1-1	2-2	1-0	3-0
Everton	1-0	0-1	1-0	1-0	2-1	2-3	—	4-1	3-0	1-1
Fulham	2-1	1-1	1-1	1-1	2-1	0-2	1-0	—	1-0	1-3
Liverpool	4-1	3-1	1-1	3-0	2-2	2-0	0-0	4-0	—	1-0
Manchester C	1-0	0-2	0-3	0-2	0-0	0-1	2-1	3-1	0-0	—
Manchester U	0-1	3-1	4-1	4-1	2-0	1-1	3-0	5-1	2-0	3-1
Middlesbrough	1-1	1-3	0-1	5-1	2-0	2-1	2-1	3-1	0-0	0-2
Newcastle U	0-0	3-1	0-2	1-2	0-0	0-0	1-1	1-2	2-1	0-1
Portsmouth	0-0	2-2	3-0	0-1	0-1	0-2	2-0	1-1	2-1	2-1
Reading	0-4	2-0	1-2	1-0	2-0	0-1	0-2	1-0	1-2	1-0
Sheffield U	1-0	2-2	0-0	2-2	2-1	0-2	1-1	2-0	1-1	0-1
Tottenham H	2-2	2-1	1-1	4-1	5-1	2-1	0-2	0-0	0-1	2-1
Watford	1-2	0-0	2-1	0-1	2-2	0-1	0-3	3-3	0-3	1-1
West Ham U	1-0	1-1	2-1	3-1	3-1	1-4	1-0	3-3	1-2	0-1
Wigan Ath	0-1	0-0	0-3	1-3	3-2	2-3	0-2	0-0	0-4	4-0

2006–2007 RESULTS

Manchester U	Middlesbrough	Newcastle U	Portsmouth	Reading	Sheffield U	Tottenham H	Watford	West Ham U	Wigan Ath
2-1	1-1	1-1	2-2	2-1	3-0	3-0	3-0	0-1	2-1
0-3	1-1	2-0	0-0	2-1	3-0	1-1	2-0	1-0	1-1
0-1	2-1	1-3	3-0	3-3	2-1	1-1	3-1	1-2	2-1
0-4	0-0	2-1	3-2	1-3	1-0	2-0	1-0	4-0	0-1
0-3	1-3	2-0	0-1	0-0	1-1	0-2	0-0	4-0	1-0
0-0	3-0	1-0	2-1	2-2	3-0	1-0	4-0	1-0	4-0
2-4	0-0	3-0	3-0	1-1	2-0	1-2	2-1	2-0	2-2
1-2	2-1	2-1	1-1	0-1	1-0	1-1	0-0	0-0	0-1
0-1	2-0	2-0	0-0	2-0	4-0	3-0	2-0	2-1	2-0
0-1	1-0	0-0	0-0	0-2	0-0	1-2	0-0	2-0	0-1
—	1-1	2-0	3-0	3-2	2-0	1-0	4-0	0-1	3-1
1-2	—	1-0	0-4	2-1	3-1	2-3	4-1	1-0	1-1
2-2	0-0	—	1-0	3-2	0-1	3-1	2-1	2-2	2-1
2-1	0-0	2-1	—	3-1	3-1	1-1	2-1	2-0	1-0
1-1	3-2	1-0	0-0	—	3-1	3-1	0-2	6-0	3-2
1-2	2-1	1-2	1-1	1-2	—	2-1	1-0	3-0	1-2
0-4	2-1	2-3	2-1	1-0	2-0	—	3-1	1-0	3-1
1-2	2-0	1-1	4-2	0-0	0-1	0-0	—	1-1	1-1
1-0	2-0	0-2	1-2	0-1	1-0	3-4	0-1	—	0-2
1-3	0-1	1-0	1-0	1-0	0-1	3-3	1-1	0-3	—

COCA-COLA FOOTBALL LEAGUE

HOME TEAM	Barnsley	Birmingham C	Burnley	Cardiff C	Colchester U	Coventry C	Crystal Palace	Derby Co	Hull C	Ipswich T
Barnsley	—	1-0	1-0	1-2	0-3	0-1	2-0	1-2	3-0	1-0
Birmingham C	2-0	—	0-1	1-0	2-1	3-0	2-1	1-0	2-1	2-2
Burnley	4-2	1-2	—	2-0	1-2	1-2	1-1	0-0	2-0	1-0
Cardiff C	2-0	2-0	1-0	—	0-0	1-0	0-0	2-2	0-1	2-2
Colchester U	1-2	1-1	0-0	3-1	—	0-0	0-2	4-3	5-1	1-0
Coventry C	4-1	0-1	1-0	2-2	2-1	—	2-4	1-2	2-0	1-2
Crystal Palace	2-0	0-1	2-2	1-2	1-3	1-0	—	2-0	1-1	2-0
Derby Co	2-1	0-1	1-0	3-1	5-1	1-1	1-0	—	2-2	2-1
Hull C	2-3	2-0	2-0	4-1	1-1	0-1	1-1	1-2	—	2-5
Ipswich T	5-1	1-0	1-1	3-1	3-2	2-1	1-2	2-1	0-0	—
Leeds U	2-2	3-2	1-0	0-1	3-0	2-1	2-1	0-1	0-0	1-1
Leicester C	2-0	1-2	0-1	0-0	0-0	3-0	1-1	1-1	0-1	3-1
Luton T	0-2	3-2	0-2	0-0	1-1	3-1	2-1	0-2	1-2	0-2
Norwich C	5-1	1-0	1-4	1-0	1-1	1-1	0-1	1-2	1-1	1-1
Plymouth Arg	2-4	0-1	0-0	3-3	3-0	3-2	1-0	3-1	1-0	1-1
Preston NE	1-0	1-0	2-0	2-1	1-0	1-1	0-0	1-2	2-1	1-0
QPR	1-0	0-2	3-1	1-0	1-0	0-1	4-2	1-2	2-0	1-3
Sheffield W	2-1	0-3	1-1	0-0	2-0	2-1	3-2	1-2	1-2	2-0
Southampton	5-2	4-3	0-0	2-2	1-2	2-0	1-1	0-1	0-0	1-0
Southend U	1-3	0-4	1-0	0-3	0-3	2-3	0-1	0-1	2-3	1-3
Stoke C	0-1	0-0	0-1	3-0	3-1	1-0	2-1	2-0	1-1	0-0
Sunderland	2-0	0-1	3-2	1-2	3-1	2-0	0-0	2-1	2-0	1-0
WBA	7-0	1-1	3-0	1-0	2-1	5-0	2-3	1-0	2-0	2-0
Wolverhampton W	2-0	2-3	2-1	1-2	1-0	1-0	1-1	0-1	3-1	1-0

CHAMPIONSHIP 2006–2007 RESULTS

Leeds U	Leicester C	Luton T	Norwich C	Plymouth Arg	Preston NE	QPR	Sheffield W	Southampton	Southend U	Stoke C	Sunderland	WBA	Wolverhampton W
3-2	0-1	1-2	1-3	2-2	0-1	2-0	0-3	2-2	2-0	2-2	0-2	1-1	1-0
1-0	1-1	2-2	0-1	3-0	3-1	2-1	2-0	2-1	1-3	1-0	1-1	2-0	1-1
2-1	0-1	0-0	3-0	4-0	3-2	2-0	1-1	2-3	0-0	0-1	2-2	3-2	0-1
1-0	3-2	4-1	1-0	2-2	4-1	0-1	1-2	1-0	0-1	1-1	0-1	1-1	4-0
2-1	1-1	4-1	3-0	0-1	1-0	2-1	4-0	2-0	3-0	3-0	3-1	1-2	2-1
1-0	0-0	1-0	3-0	0-1	0-4	0-1	3-1	2-1	1-1	0-0	2-1	0-1	2-1
1-0	2-0	2-1	3-1	0-1	3-0	3-0	1-2	0-2	3-1	0-1	1-0	0-2	2-2
2-0	1-0	1-0	0-0	1-0	1-1	1-1	1-0	2-2	3-0	0-2	1-2	2-1	0-2
1-2	1-2	0-0	1-2	1-2	2-0	2-1	2-1	2-4	4-0	0-2	0-1	0-1	2-0
1-0	0-2	5-0	3-1	3-0	2-3	2-1	0-2	2-1	0-2	0-1	3-1	1-5	0-1
—	1-2	1-0	1-0	2-1	2-1	0-0	2-3	0-3	2-0	0-4	0-3	2-3	0-1
1-1	—	1-1	1-2	2-2	0-1	1-3	1-4	3-2	1-0	2-1	0-2	1-1	1-4
5-1	2-0	—	2-3	1-2	2-0	2-3	3-2	0-2	0-0	2-2	0-5	2-2	2-3
2-1	3-1	3-2	—	1-3	2-0	1-0	1-2	0-1	0-0	1-0	1-0	1-2	0-1
1-2	3-0	1-0	3-1	—	2-0	1-1	1-2	1-1	2-1	1-1	0-2	2-2	1-1
4-1	0-1	3-0	2-1	3-0	—	1-1	0-0	3-1	2-3	3-2	4-1	1-0	0-1
2-2	1-1	3-2	3-3	1-1	1-0	—	1-1	0-2	2-0	1-1	1-2	1-2	0-1
0-1	2-1	0-1	3-2	1-1	1-3	3-2	—	3-3	3-2	1-1	2-4	3-1	2-2
1-0	2-0	2-1	2-1	1-0	1-1	1-2	2-1	—	4-1	1-0	1-2	0-0	2-0
1-1	2-2	1-3	3-3	1-1	0-0	5-0	0-0	2-1	—	1-0	3-1	3-1	0-1
3-1	4-2	0-0	5-0	1-1	1-1	1-0	1-2	2-1	1-1	—	2-1	1-0	1-1
2-0	1-1	2-1	1-0	2-3	0-1	2-1	1-0	1-1	4-0	2-2	—	2-0	2-1
4-2	2-0	3-2	0-1	2-1	4-2	3-3	0-1	1-1	1-1	1-3	1-2	—	3-0
1-0	1-2	1-0	2-2	2-2	1-3	2-0	2-2	0-6	3-1	2-0	1-1	1-0	—

COCA-COLA FOOTBALL LEAGUE

HOME TEAM	Blackpool	Bournemouth	Bradford C	Brentford	Brighton & HA	Bristol C	Carlisle U	Cheltenham T	Chesterfield	Crewe Alex
Blackpool	—	2-0	4-1	1-3	0-0	0-1	2-1	2-1	1-1	2-1
Bournemouth	1-3	—	1-1	1-0	1-0	0-1	0-1	2-1	0-3	1-0
Bradford C	1-3	0-0	—	1-1	2-3	2-1	1-1	2-2	1-0	0-1
Brentford	1-0	0-0	2-1	—	1-0	1-1	0-0	0-2	2-1	0-4
Brighton & HA	0-3	2-2	0-1	2-2	—	0-2	1-2	2-1	1-2	1-4
Bristol C	2-4	2-2	2-3	1-0	1-0	—	1-0	0-1	3-1	2-1
Carlisle U	2-0	3-1	1-0	2-0	3-1	1-3	—	2-0	0-0	0-2
Cheltenham T	1-2	1-0	1-2	2-0	1-1	2-2	0-1	—	0-0	1-1
Chesterfield	2-0	0-1	3-0	3-1	0-1	1-3	0-0	1-0	—	2-1
Crewe Alex	1-2	2-0	0-3	3-1	1-1	0-1	5-1	3-1	2-2	—
Doncaster R	0-0	1-1	3-3	3-0	1-0	0-1	1-2	0-2	1-0	3-1
Gillingham	2-2	1-1	1-0	2-1	0-1	1-0	2-0	2-1	2-1	1-0
Huddersfield T	0-2	2-2	2-0	0-2	0-3	2-1	2-1	2-0	1-1	1-2
Leyton Orient	0-1	3-2	1-2	1-1	1-4	1-1	1-1	2-0	0-0	1-1
Millwall	0-0	1-0	2-0	1-1	0-1	1-0	2-0	2-0	2-1	2-2
Northampton T	1-1	3-1	0-0	0-1	0-2	1-3	3-2	2-0	1-0	1-2
Nottingham F	1-1	3-0	1-0	2-0	2-1	1-0	0-0	3-0	4-0	0-0
Oldham Ath	0-1	1-2	2-0	3-0	1-1	0-3	0-0	0-2	1-0	1-0
Port Vale	2-1	2-1	0-1	1-0	2-1	0-2	0-2	1-1	3-2	3-0
Rotherham U	1-0	0-2	4-1	2-0	0-1	1-1	0-1	2-4	0-1	5-1
Scunthorpe U	1-3	3-2	2-0	1-1	1-2	1-0	3-0	1-0	1-0	2-2
Swansea C	3-6	4-2	1-0	2-0	2-1	0-0	5-0	1-2	2-0	2-1
Tranmere R	2-0	1-0	1-1	3-1	2-1	1-0	0-2	2-2	2-0	1-0
Yeovil T	0-1	0-0	0-0	1-0	2-0	2-1	2-1	0-1	1-0	2-0

DIVISION 1 2006–2007 RESULTS

Doncaster R	Gillingham	Huddersfield T	Leyton Orient	Millwall	Northampton T	Nottingham F	Oldham Ath	Port Vale	Rotherham U	Scunthorpe U	Swansea C	Tranmere R	Yeovil T
3-1	1-1	3-1	3-0	0-1	4-1	0-2	2-2	2-1	0-1	3-1	1-1	3-2	1-1
2-0	1-1	1-2	5-0	1-0	0-0	2-0	3-2	0-4	1-3	1-1	2-2	2-0	0-2
0-1	4-2	0-1	0-2	2-2	1-2	2-2	1-1	2-0	1-1	0-1	2-2	2-0	0-2
0-4	2-2	2-2	2-2	1-4	0-1	2-4	2-2	4-3	0-1	0-2	0-2	1-1	1-2
0-2	1-0	0-0	4-1	0-1	1-1	2-1	1-2	0-0	0-0	1-1	3-2	0-1	1-3
1-0	3-1	1-1	2-1	1-0	1-0	1-1	0-0	2-1	3-1	1-0	0-0	3-2	2-0
1-0	5-0	1-1	3-1	1-2	1-1	1-0	1-1	3-2	1-1	0-2	1-2	1-0	1-4
0-2	1-1	2-1	2-1	3-2	0-2	0-2	1-2	0-1	2-0	1-1	2-1	1-0	1-2
1-1	0-1	0-0	0-1	5-1	0-0	1-2	2-1	3-0	2-1	0-1	2-3	0-2	1-1
2-1	4-3	2-0	0-4	1-0	2-2	1-4	2-1	2-1	1-0	1-3	1-3	1-1	2-3
—	1-2	3-0	0-0	1-2	2-2	1-0	1-1	1-0	3-2	2-2	2-2	0-0	0-0
0-2	—	2-1	2-1	2-1	0-1	0-1	0-3	3-2	1-0	0-2	3-1	2-0	0-2
0-0	3-1	—	3-1	4-2	1-1	1-1	0-3	2-2	3-0	1-1	3-2	2-2	2-3
1-1	3-3	1-0	—	2-0	0-2	1-3	2-2	2-1	2-3	2-2	0-1	3-1	0-0
2-2	4-1	0-0	2-5	—	0-1	1-0	1-0	1-1	4-0	0-1	2-0	2-2	1-1
0-2	1-1	1-1	0-1	3-0	—	0-1	2-3	0-2	3-0	2-1	1-0	1-3	1-1
0-1	1-0	5-1	1-3	3-1	1-0	—	0-2	3-0	1-1	0-4	3-1	1-1	1-0
4-0	4-1	1-1	3-3	1-2	3-0	5-0	—	0-1	2-1	1-0	1-0	1-0	1-0
1-2	2-0	1-2	3-0	2-0	1-0	1-1	3-0	—	1-3	0-0	0-2	2-3	4-2
0-0	3-2	2-3	2-2	2-3	1-2	1-1	2-3	1-5	—	2-1	1-2	2-1	3-2
2-0	3-1	2-0	3-1	3-0	1-0	1-1	1-1	3-0	1-0	—	2-2	1-1	1-0
2-0	2-0	1-2	0-0	2-0	2-1	0-0	0-1	3-0	1-1	0-2	—	0-0	1-1
1-0	2-3	2-2	3-0	3-1	1-1	0-0	1-0	1-2	2-1	0-2	0-2	—	2-1
1-0	2-0	3-1	2-1	0-1	0-0	0-1	1-0	1-0	1-0	0-2	1-0	0-2	—

COCA-COLA FOOTBALL LEAGUE

HOME TEAM	Accrington S	Barnet	Boston U	Bristol R	Bury	Chester C	Darlington	Grimsby T	Hartlepool U	Hereford U
Accrington S	—	2-1	2-1	1-1	1-1	0-1	0-2	4-1	1-2	2-0
Barnet	1-2	—	3-3	1-1	2-1	1-0	2-1	0-1	2-1	3-0
Boston U	1-0	2-1	—	2-1	0-1	1-0	4-1	0-6	0-1	1-1
Bristol R	4-0	2-0	1-0	—	2-0	0-0	1-2	1-0	0-2	2-1
Bury	2-2	2-2	2-1	0-2	—	1-3	1-1	3-0	0-1	2-2
Chester C	2-0	2-0	3-1	2-0	1-0	—	1-1	0-2	2-1	1-1
Darlington	2-1	2-0	2-0	1-1	1-0	1-0	—	2-2	0-3	1-0
Grimsby T	2-0	5-0	3-2	4-3	2-0	0-2	0-1	—	1-4	2-1
Hartlepool U	1-0	0-1	2-1	1-2	2-0	3-0	0-0	2-0	—	3-2
Hereford U	1-0	2-0	3-0	0-0	1-0	2-0	1-1	0-1	3-1	—
Lincoln C	3-1	1-0	2-1	1-0	0-2	2-0	1-3	2-0	2-0	1-4
Macclesfield T	3-3	2-3	2-3	0-1	2-3	1-1	1-1	2-1	0-0	3-0
Mansfield T	2-2	2-1	1-2	0-1	0-2	2-1	1-0	1-2	0-1	4-1
Milton Keynes D	3-1	3-1	3-2	2-0	2-1	1-2	1-0	1-2	0-0	1-3
Notts Co	3-2	1-1	2-0	1-2	0-1	1-2	0-1	2-0	0-1	0-1
Peterborough U	4-2	1-1	1-1	4-1	0-1	0-2	1-3	2-2	3-5	3-0
Rochdale	4-2	0-2	4-0	0-1	1-3	0-0	0-0	1-0	2-0	1-1
Shrewsbury T	2-1	0-1	5-0	0-0	1-3	2-1	2-2	2-2	1-1	3-0
Stockport Co	1-1	2-0	2-0	2-1	0-0	2-0	5-2	3-0	3-3	0-2
Swindon T	2-0	2-1	1-1	2-1	2-1	1-0	1-1	3-0	0-1	1-2
Torquay U	0-2	1-1	0-1	0-0	2-2	2-2	0-1	4-1	0-1	0-0
Walsall	3-2	4-1	1-1	2-2	0-1	1-0	1-0	2-0	2-0	1-0
Wrexham	1-3	1-1	3-1	2-0	1-1	0-0	1-0	3-0	1-1	1-0
Wycombe W	1-1	1-1	0-0	0-1	3-0	1-0	1-0	1-1	0-1	0-0

DIVISION 2 2006–2007 RESULTS

Lincoln C	Macclesfield T	Mansfield T	Milton Keynes D	Notts Co	Peterborough U	Rochdale	Shrewsbury T	Stockport Co	Swindon T	Torquay U	Walsall	Wrexham	Wycombe W
2-2	3-2	3-2	3-4	1-2	3-2	1-1	3-3	0-1	1-1	1-0	1-2	5-0	2-1
0-5	1-0	2-1	3-3	2-3	1-0	3-2	0-0	3-1	1-0	0-1	1-1	1-2	2-1
1-0	4-1	1-1	0-1	3-3	0-1	0-3	0-3	2-1	1-3	1-1	1-1	4-0	0-1
0-0	0-0	1-0	1-1	2-0	3-2	0-0	1-0	2-1	1-0	1-0	1-2	0-1	1-2
2-2	1-1	1-1	0-2	0-1	0-3	0-1	1-2	2-0	0-1	0-1	1-2	1-0	0-4
4-1	0-3	1-1	0-3	0-0	1-1	0-1	0-0	1-1	0-2	1-1	0-0	1-2	0-1
1-1	4-0	0-2	1-0	0-1	3-1	0-5	1-2	0-5	1-2	1-1	0-0	1-1	3-2
0-0	1-1	1-1	1-3	0-2	0-2	0-4	2-1	0-1	1-0	2-0	2-1	2-1	2-2
1-1	3-2	2-0	1-0	1-1	1-0	1-0	0-3	1-1	0-1	1-1	3-1	3-0	2-0
1-2	1-0	1-3	0-0	3-2	0-0	0-0	0-1	0-2	0-0	1-1	0-1	2-0	1-2
—	2-1	1-2	2-3	1-1	1-0	7-1	1-1	0-0	2-3	1-0	2-2	0-3	1-0
2-1	—	2-3	1-2	1-1	2-1	1-0	2-2	2-0	2-1	3-3	0-2	2-0	0-2
2-4	1-2	—	2-1	2-2	0-2	1-2	1-1	1-1	2-0	5-0	2-1	3-0	3-2
2-2	3-0	1-1	—	3-2	0-2	2-1	2-0	2-0	0-1	3-2	1-1	2-1	3-1
3-1	1-2	0-0	2-2	—	0-0	1-2	1-1	1-0	1-1	5-2	1-2	2-1	1-0
1-2	3-1	2-0	4-0	2-0	—	3-3	2-1	0-3	1-1	5-2	0-2	3-0	3-3
2-0	5-0	2-0	5-0	0-1	0-1	—	1-1	1-3	0-0	2-0	0-1	2-2	0-2
0-1	2-1	2-2	2-1	2-0	2-1	3-0	—	4-2	1-2	1-0	1-1	0-1	0-0
2-0	1-1	1-0	1-2	2-0	0-1	2-7	0-3	—	3-0	1-0	1-0	5-2	2-0
0-1	2-0	2-0	2-1	1-1	0-1	1-0	2-1	2-0	—	2-1	1-1	2-1	2-1
1-2	0-1	1-0	0-2	0-1	1-1	1-0	0-0	1-0	0-1	—	1-2	1-1	3-0
1-2	2-0	4-0	0-0	2-1	5-0	1-1	1-0	2-0	0-2	1-0	—	1-0	2-0
2-1	0-0	0-0	1-2	0-1	0-0	1-2	1-3	0-1	2-1	1-0	1-1	—	0-2
1-3	3-0	1-0	0-2	0-0	2-0	1-1	1-1	2-0	1-1	2-0	0-0	1-1	—

ACCRINGTON STANLEY — FL CHAMPIONSHIP 2

Player	*Ht*	*Wt*	*Birthplace*	*D.O.B.*	*Source*
Boco Romuald (M)	5 10	10 12	Bernay	8 7 85	Niort
Brown David (F)	5 10	12 07	Bolton	2 10 78	Hereford U
Cavanagh Peter (D)	5 11	11 09	Liverpool	14 10 81	Liverpool
Dunbavin Ian (G)	6 2	10 10	Knowsley	27 5 80	Scarborough
Edwards Phil (D)	5 8	11 03	Kirkby	8 11 85	Wigan Ath
Grant Anthony (M)	5 10	10 02	Liverpool	14 11 74	Crewe Alex
Harris James (M)	5 7	11 06	Liverpool	15 4 87	Everton
Mangan Andrew (F)	5 9	10 03	Liverpool	30 8 86	Blackpool
McGivern Leighton (F)	5 8	11 01	Liverpool	2 6 84	Waterloo Dock
Mullin Paul (F)	6 0	12 01	Bury	16 3 74	Radcliffe Borough
Proctor Andy (M)	6 0	12 04	Lancashire	13 3 83	Gt Harwood T
Richardson Leam (D)	5 8	11 04	Blackpool	19 11 79	Leeds
Todd Andy (M)	6 0	11 03	Nottingham	22 2 79	Burton Alb
Whalley Shaun (M)	5 9	10 07	Prescot	7 8 87	Witton Alb
Williams Robbie (D)	5 10	12 00	Liverpool	12 4 79	St Dominics

League Appearances: Almeida, M. 5; Antwi-Birago, G. 9; Bains, R. 2(1); Boco, R. 28(4); Brown, D. 8(9); Byrom, J. (1); Cavanagh, P. 26; Craney, I. 18; Doherty, S. 14(6); Dugdale, A. 2; Dunbavin, I. 22(1); Edwards, P. 29(4); Elliot, R. 7; Fleetwood, S. 3; Grant, R. 1; Grant, T. 6; Harris, J. 26(6); Jacobson, J. 6; Kazimierczak, P. 7(1); Mangan, A. 6(28); Mannix, D. 1; Martin, D. 10; McGivern, L. 3(4); McGrail, C. (2); Mullin, P. 46; N'Da, J. (3); Proctor, A. 38(5); Richardson, L. 34(4); Roberts, G. 14; Rogers, A. 6; Todd, A. 44(2); Ventre, D. 4(2); Welch, M. 25(6); Whalley, S. 13(7); Williams, R. 43.
Goals – League (70): Mullin 14, Todd 10 (4 pens), Roberts 8 (2 pens), Brown 5, Craney 5, Cavanagh 4, Mangan 4, Boco 3, Proctor 3, Welch 3, Williams 3, Harris 2, Whalley 2, Doherty 1, Edwards 1, Jacobson 1, McGivern 1.
Carling Cup (1): Mullin 1.
FA Cup (0).
J Paint Trophy (5): Craney 1, Mullin 1, Todd 1, Williams 1, own goal 1.
Ground: The Fraser Eagle Stadium, Livingstone Road, Accrington, Lancashire BB5 5BX. Telephone: 01254 356 950.
Record Attendance: 4368 v Colchester U, FA Cup 1st rd, 3 January 2004.
Capacity: 5,057.
Manager: John Coleman.
Secretary: Hannah Bailey.
Most League Goals: 96, Division 3 (N) 1954–55.
Highest League Scorer in Season: George Stewart, 35, 1955–56 Division 3(N); George Hudson, 35, 1960–61, Division 4.
Most League Goals in Total Aggregate: George Stewart 136, 1954–58.
Most Capped Player: Romuald Boco, (17), Benin.
Most League Appearances: Jim Armstrong, 260, 1927–34.
Colours: Red shirts, white shorts, red stockings.

ARSENAL — FA PREMIERSHIP

Player	Ht	Wt	Birthplace	D.O.B.	Source
Adebayor Emmanuel (F)	6 4	11 08	Lome	26 2 84	Monaco
Aliadiere Jeremie (F)	6 0	11 00	Rambouillet	30 3 83	Scholar
Almunia Manuel (G)	6 3	13 00	Pamplona	19 5 77	Celta Vigo
Baptista Julio (M)	6 0	13 05	Sao Paulo	1 10 81	Real Madrid
Bendtner Nicklas (F)	6 2	13 00	Copenhagen	16 1 88	Scholar
Clichy Gael (D)	5 9	10 04	Toulouse	26 7 85	Cannes
Connolly Matthew (D)	6 1	11 03	Barnet	24 9 87	Scholar
Denilson (M)	5 10	11 00	Sao Paulo	16 2 88	Sao Paulo

Diaby Vassirki (M)	6 2	12 04	Paris	11 5 86	Auxerre
Djourou Johan (D)	6 3	13 01	Ivory Coast	18 1 87	Scholar
Eboue Emmanuel (D)	5 10	10 03	Abidjan	4 6 83	Beveren
Fabregas Francesc (M)	5 11	11 01	Vilessoc de Mar	4 5 87	Barcelona
Flamini Mathieu (M)	5 11	11 10	Marseille	7 3 84	Marseille
Gallas William (D)	5 11	12 10	Asnieres	17 8 77	Chelsea
Gilbert Kerrea (D)	5 6	11 03	Willesden	28 2 87	Scholar
Henry Thierry (F)	6 2	13 05	Paris	17 8 77	Juventus
Hleb Aleksandr (M)	5 10	11 07	Minsk	1 5 81	Stuttgart
Hoyte Justin (D)	5 11	11 00	Waltham Forest	20 11 84	Scholar
Lehmann Jens (G)	6 4	13 05	Essen	10 11 69	Borussia Dortmund
Ljungberg Frederik (M)	5 9	11 00	Vittsjo	16 4 77	Halmstad
Lupoli Arturo (F)	5 9	10 07	Brescia	24 6 87	Parma
Mannone Vito (G)	6 0	11 08	Desio	2 3 88	Atalanta
Parisio Carl (D)			Cannes	7 8 89	Scholar
Perez Fran Merida (M)	5 11	13 00	Barcelona	4 3 90	Scholar
Poom Mart (G)	6 4	14 02	Tallinn	3 2 72	Sunderland
Randall Mark (M)	6 0	12 12	Milton Keynes	28 9 89	Scholar
Rosicky Tomas (M)	5 11	11 06	Prague	4 10 80	Borussia Dortmund
Senderos Philippe (D)	6 1	13 10	Geneva	14 2 85	Servette
Silva Gilberto (M)	6 3	12 04	Lagoa da Prata	7 10 76	Atletico Mineiro
Song Bilong Alexandre (M)	6 4	12 07	Douala	9 9 87	Bastia
Toure Kolo (D)	5 10	13 08	Ivory Coast	19 3 81	ASEC Mimosas
Traore Armand (D)	6 1	12 12	Paris	8 10 89	Monaco
Van den Berg Vincent (M)			Holland	19 1 89	Heerenveen
Van Persie Robin (F)	6 0	11 00	Rotterdam	6 8 83	Feyenoord
Walcott Theo (F)	5 9	11 01	Compton	16 3 89	Southampton

League Appearances: Adebayor, E. 21(8); Aliadiere, J. 4(7); Almunia, M. 1; Baptista, J. 11(13); Clichy, G. 26(1); Denilson, 4(6); Diaby, V. 9(3); Djourou, J. 18(3); Eboue, E. 23(1); Fabregas, F. 34(4); Flamini, M. 9(11); Gallas, W. 21; Henry, T. 16(1); Hleb, A. 27(6); Hoyte, J. 18(4); Lehmann, J. 36; Ljungberg, F. 16(2); Poom, M. 1; Rosicky, T. 22(4); Senderos, P. 9(5); Silva, G. 34; Song Billong, A.. 1(1); Toure, K. 35; Van Persie, R. 17(5); Walcott, T. 5(11).
Goals – League (63): Van Persie 11 (1 pen), Henry 10 (3 pens), Silva 10 (5 pens), Adebayor 8 (1 pen), Baptista 3, Flamini 3, Gallas 3, Rosicky 3, Toure 3, Fabregas 2, Hleb 2, Diaby 1, Hoyte 1, own goals 3.
Carling Cup (15): Julio Baptista 6, Aliadiere 4 (1 pen), Adebayor 2, Song Billong 1, Walcott 1, own goal 1.
FA Cup (7): Adebayor 2, Rosicky 2, Henry 1, Ljungberg 1, Toure 1.
Champions League (13): Fabregas 2, Van Persie 2, Eboue 1, Flamini 1, Henry 1, Hleb 1, Julio Baptista 1, Ljungberg 1, Rosicky 1, Silva 1 (pen), own goal 1.
Ground: Emirates Stadium, Drayton Park, London N5 1BU. Telephone (020) 7704 4000.
Record Attendance: 73,295 v Sunderland, Div 1, 9 March 1935. **Capacity:** 60,432.
Manager: Arsène Wenger.
Secretary: David Miles.
Most League Goals: 127, Division 1, 1930–31.
Highest League Scorer in Season: Ted Drake, 42, 1934–35.
Most League Goals in Total Aggregate: Thierry Henry, 174, 1999–2007.
Most Capped Player: Thierry Henry, 81 (92), France.
Most League Appearances: David O'Leary, 558, 1975–93.
Honours – FA Premier League: Champions – 1997–98, 2001–02, 2003–04. **Football League:** Division 1 Champions – 1930–31, 1932–33, 1933–34, 1934–35, 1937–38, 1947–48, 1952–53, 1970–71, 1988–89, 1990–91. **FA Cup:** Winners – 1929–30, 1935–36, 1949–50, 1970–71, 1978–79, 1992–93, 1997–98, 2001–02, 2002–03, 2004–05. **Football League Cup:** Winners – 1986–87, 1992–93. **European Competitions: European Cup-Winners' Cup:** Winners – 1993–94. **Fairs Cup:** Winners – 1969–70.
Colours: Red shirts with white sleeves, white shorts and stockings.

Agbonlahor Gabriel (F)	5 11	12 05	Birmingham	13 10 86	Scholar
Barry Gareth (D)	5 11	12 06	Hastings	23 2 81	Trainee
Bellon Varela Damien (M)	5 8	11 05	St Gallen	28 8 89	Scholar
Bellon Varela Yago (M)	5 8	10 11	St Gallen	28 8 89	Scholar
Berger Patrik (M)	6 1	12 06	Prague	10 11 73	Portsmouth
Bouma Wilfred (D)	5 10	13 01	Helmond	15 6 78	PSV Eindhoven
Boyle Lee (M)	5 11	10 08	Donegal	22 1 88	Scholar
Bridges Scott (D)	5 7	13 08	Oxford	3 5 88	Scholar
Cahill Gary (D)	6 2	12 06	Dronfield	19 12 85	Trainee
Carew John (F)	6 5	15 00	Lorenskog	5 9 79	Lyon
Davis Steven (M)	5 7	9 07	Ballymena	1 1 85	Scholar
Djemba-Djemba Eric (M)	5 9	11 13	Douala	4 5 81	Manchester U
Gardner Craig (M)	5 10	11 13	Solihull	25 11 86	Scholar
Hughes Aaron (D)	6 0	11 02	Cookstown	8 11 79	Newcastle U
Laursen Martin (D)	6 2	12 05	Silkeborg	26 7 77	AC Milan
Lund Eric (D)	6 1	12 00	Gothemberg	6 11 88	Scholar
Maloney Shaun (M)	5 7	10 01	Sarawak	24 1 83	Celtic
McCann Gavin (M)	5 11	11 00	Blackpool	10 1 78	Sunderland
McGurk Adam (F)	5 9	12 13	St Helier	24 1 89	Scholar
Mellberg Olof (D)	6 1	12 10	Amncharad	3 9 77	Santander
Mikaelsson Tobias (F)	6 3	11 04	Jorlanda	17 11 88	Scholar
Moore Luke (F)	5 11	11 13	Birmingham	13 2 86	Trainee
O'Halloran Stephen (D)	6 0	11 07	Cork	29 11 87	Scholar
Osbourne Isaiah (M)	6 2	12 07	Birmingham	5 11 87	Scholar
Petrov Stilian (M)	5 11	13 05	Montana	5 7 79	Celtic
Ridgewell Liam (D)	5 10	10 03	Bexley	21 7 84	Scholar
Sorensen Thomas (G)	6 4	13 10	Fredericia	12 6 76	Sunderland
Stiever Zoltan (M)	5 8	9 10	Savar	16 10 88	Scholar
Taylor Stuart (G)	6 5	13 07	Romford	28 11 80	Arsenal
Williams Sam (M)	5 11	10 08	London	9 6 87	Scholar
Young Ashley (F)	5 6	9 06	Stevenage	9 7 85	Watford

League Appearances: Agathe, D. (5); Agbonlahor, G. 37(1); Angel, J. 18(5); Bardsley, P. 13; Baros, M. 10(7); Barry, G. 35; Berger, P. 5(8); Bouma, W. 23(2); Cahill, G. 19(1); Carew, J. 11; Davis, S. 17(11); Djemba-Djemba, E. (1); Gardner, C. 11(2); Hendrie, L. (1); Hughes, A. 15(4); Kiraly, G. 5; Laursen, M. 12(2); Maloney, S. 5(3); McCann, G. 28(2); Mellberg, O. 38; Moore, L. 7(6); Osbourne, I. 6(5); Petrov, S. 30; Ridgewell, L. 19(2); Samuel, J. 2(2); Sorensen, T. 29; Sutton, C. 6(2); Taylor, S. 4(2); Whittingham, P. 2(1); Young, A. 11(2).
Goals – League (43): Agbonlahor 9, Barry 8 (5 pens), Angel 4 (1 pen), Moore 4, Carew 3, Berger 2, Gardner 2, Petrov 2, Young 2, Baros 1, Maloney 1, McCann 1, Mellberg 1, Ridgewell 1, Sutton 1, own goal 1.
Carling Cup (5): Angel 3, Agbonlahor 1, Barry 1 (pen).
FA Cup (1): Baros 1.
Ground: Villa Park, Trinity Road, Birmingham B6 6HE. Telephone (0871) 423 8102.
Record Attendance: 76,588 v Derby Co, FA Cup 6th rd, 2 March 1946.
Capacity: 42,551.
Manager: Martin O'Neill.
Secretary: Sharon Barnhurst.
Most League Goals: 128, Division 1, 1930–31.
Highest League Scorer in Season: 'Pongo' Waring, 49, Division 1, 1930–31.
Most League Goals in Total Aggregate: Harry Hampton, 215, 1904–15.
Most Capped Player: Steve Staunton 64 (102), Republic of Ireland.
Most League Appearances: Charlie Aitken, 561, 1961–76.

Honours – Football League: Division 1 Champions – 1893–94, 1895–96, 1896–97, 1898–99, 1899–1900, 1909–10, 1980–81. Division 2 Champions – 1937–38, 1959–60. Division 3 Champions – 1971–72. **FA Cup:** Winners – 1887, 1895, 1897, 1905, 1913, 1920, 1957. **Football League Cup:** Winners – 1961, 1975, 1977, 1994, 1996. **European Competitions: European Cup:** Winners – 1981–82. **European Super Cup:** Winners – 1982–83. **Intertoto Cup:** Winners – 2001.
Colours: Claret body, blue sleeve shirts, white shorts, sky blue stockings with claret turnover.

BARNET — FL CHAMPIONSHIP 2

Bailey Nicky (M)	5 10	12 08	Putney	10 6 84	Sutton U
Birchall Adam (F)	5 6	10 09	Maidstone	2 12 84	Mansfield T
Devera Joe (D)	6 2	12 00	Southgate	6 2 87	Scholar
Grazioli Guiliano (F)	5 10	12 00	Marylebone	23 3 75	Bristol R
Hatch Liam (F)	6 4	13 01	Hitchin	3 4 82	Gravesend & Northfleet
Hendon Ian (D)	6 1	13 05	Ilford	5 12 71	Peterborough U
King Simon (D)	6 0	13 00	Oxford	11 4 83	Oxford U
Nicolau Nicky (D)	5 8	11 00	Camden	12 10 83	Swindon T
Puncheon Jason (M)	5 10	11 02	Croydon	26 6 86	Milton Keynes D
Sinclair Dean (M)	5 10	11 00	St Albans	17 12 84	Norwich C
Yakubu Ishmail (D)	6 1	12 09	Nigeria	8 4 85	Scholar

League Appearances: Allen, O. 7(7); Bailey, N. 43(1); Birchall, A. 22(1); Burch, R. 6; Charles, A. 13(4); Cogan, B. 33(6); Devera, J. 23(3); Flitney, R. 12(3); Graham, R. 22(12); Grazioli, G. 7(10); Gross, A. 27; Harrison, L. 28; Hatch, L. 18(13); Hendon, I. 25(1); Hessenthaler, A. 19(5); Ioannou, N. 1(1); Kandol, T. 14(2); King, S. 43; Lewis, S. 2(2); Nicolau, N. 17(5); Norville, J. 1(2); Puncheon, J. 34(3); Sinclair, D. 42; Vieira, M. 8(13); Warhurst, P. 11(8); Yakubu, I. 28(1).
Goals – League (55): Birchall 6, Kandol 6, Sinclair 6 (1 pen), Bailey 5, Puncheon 5, Allen 4, Hendon 4 (4 pens), Cogan 3, Hatch 3, Vieira 3, Graham 2, Grazioli 2, King 2, Gross 1, Hessenthaler 1, Nicolau 1, Yakubu 1.
Carling Cup (3): Kandol 2, Vieira 1.
FA Cup (9): Kandol 2 (1 pen), Sinclair 2, Birchall 1, Hendon 1 (pen), Puncheon 1, Vieira 1, Yakubu 1.
J Paint Trophy (3): Kandol 3.
Ground: Underhill Stadium, Barnet Lane, Barnet, Herts EN5 2DN. Telephone 0208 441 6932.
Record Attendance: 11,026 v Wycombe Wanderers, FA Amateur Cup 4th Round 1951–52. **Capacity:** 5,300.
Manager: Paul Fairclough.
Secretary: Andrew Adie.
Most League Goals: 81, Division 4, 1991–92
Highest League Scorer in Season: Dougie Freedman, 24, Division 3, 1994–95.
Most League Goals in Total Aggregate: Sean Devine, 47, 1995–99.
Most Capped Player: Ken Charlery, 4, St. Lucia.
Most League Appearances: Paul Wilson, 263, 1991–2000.
Honours – Football League: GMVC: Winners – 1990–91. **Football Conference:** Winners – 2004–05. **FA Amateur Cup:** Winners 1945–46.
Colours: Old gold and black striped shirts, black shorts, Old gold and black stockings.

BARNSLEY

FL CHAMPIONSHIP

Atkinson Rob (M)	6 1	12 00	North Ferriby	29 4 87	Scholar
Colgan Nick (G)	6 1	13 06	Drogheda	19 9 73	Hibernian
Coulson Michael (F)	5 10	10 00	Scarborough	29 4 87	Scarborough
Devaney Martin (M)	5 11	12 00	Cheltenham	1 6 80	Watford
Ferenczi Istvan (F)	6 2	13 10	Gyor	14 9 77	Zalaegerszeg
Harban Thomas (D)	6 0	11 09	Barnsley	12 11 85	Scholar
Hassell Bobby (D)	5 10	12 00	Derby	4 6 80	Mansfield T
Hayes Paul (F)	6 0	12 12	Dagenham	20 9 83	Scunthorpe U
Heckingbottom Paul (D)	6 0	13 01	Barnsley	17 7 77	Sheffield W
Heslop Simon (M)	5 11	11 00	York	1 5 87	Scholar
Howard Brian (M)	5 8	11 00	Winchester	23 1 83	Swindon T
Joynes Nathan (M)	6 1	12 00	Hoyland	7 8 85	Scholar
Letheren Kyle (G)	6 2	12 00	Swansea	26 12 87	Swansea C
Mattis Dwayne (M)	6 1	12 00	Huddersfield	31 7 81	Bury
McCann Grant (M)	5 11	13 00	Belfast	14 4 80	Cheltenham T
McGrory Scott (D)	5 11	10 11	Edinburgh	5 4 87	Scholar
Meynell Rhys (D)	5 11	12 03	Barnsley	17 8 88	Scholar
Nardiello Daniel (F)	5 11	11 04	Coventry	22 10 82	Manchester U
Rajczi Peter (F)	6 0	12 07	Llenyeakoti	3 4 81	Ujpest
Reid Paul (D)	6 2	11 08	Carlisle	18 2 82	Northampton T
Togwell Sam (M)	5 11	12 04	Beaconsfield	14 10 84	Crystal Palace
Williams Robbie (D)	5 10	11 13	Pontefract	2 10 84	Scholar

League Appearances: Atkinson, R. 6; Austin, N. 21(3); Colgan, N. 43(1); Coulson, M. (2); Devaney, M. 37(4); Eckersley, A. 6; Ferenczi, I. 14(2); Hassell, B. 37(2); Hayes, P. 25(5); Healy, C. (8); Heckingbottom, P. 28(3); Heslop, S. (1); Howard, B. 42; Jones, R. 1(3); Kay, A. 31(1); Knight, L. 6(3); Lucas, D. 2(1); Mannone, V. 1(1); Mattis, D. 3; McCann, G. 17(5); McIndoe, M. 18; Nardiello, D. 19(11); Nyatanga, L. 10; Potter, L. 1; Rajczi, P. 8(7); Reid, K. 12(14); Reid, P. 36(1); Richards, M. 22(9); Togwell, S. 44; Tonge, D. 2(4); Wallwork, R. 2; Williams, R. 8(7); Wright, T. 4(13); Wroe, N. (3).
Goals – League (53): Nardiello 9 (1 pen), Howard 8, Richards 6, Devaney 5, Ferenczi 5, Hayes 5 (1 pen), McIndoe 4, Hassell 2, Rajczi 2, Reid K 2, Kay 1, McCann 1, Nyatanga 1, Togwell 1, Wright 1.
Carling Cup (3): Devaney 1, McIndoe 1, Williams 1 (pen).
FA Cup (1): Coulson 1.
Ground: Oakwell Stadium, Grove St, Barnsley S71 1ET. Telephone (01226) 211 211.
Record Attendance: 40,255 v Stoke C, FA Cup 5th rd, 15 February 1936. **Capacity:** 23,186.
Manager: Simon Davey.
Secretary: A. D. Rowing.
Most League Goals: 118, Division 3 (N), 1933–34.
Highest League Scorer in Season: Cecil McCormack, 33, Division 2, 1950–51.
Most League Goals in Total Aggregate: Ernest Hine, 123, 1921–26 and 1934–38.
Most Capped Player: Gerry Taggart, 35 (50), Northern Ireland.
Most League Appearances: Barry Murphy, 514, 1962–78.
Honours – Football League: Division 3 (N) Champions – 1933–34, 1938–39, 1954–55. **FA Cup:** Winners – 1912.
Colours: Red shirts, white shorts, red stockings.

Aluko Sone (F)	5 8	9 11	Hounslow	19 2 89	Scholar
Burge Ryan (M)	5 10	10 03	Cheltenham	12 10 88	Scholar
Campbell Dudley (F)	5 10	11 00	London	12 11 81	Brentford
Clemence Stephen (M)	6 0	12 09	Liverpool	31 3 78	Tottenham H
Danns Neil (M)	5 9	12 03	Liverpool	23 11 82	Colchester U
Doyle Colin (G)	6 5	14 05	Cork	12 8 85	Scholar
Forssell Mikael (F)	5 10	10 10	Steinfourt	15 3 81	Chelsea
Hall Asa (M)	6 2	11 09	Dudley	29 11 86	Scholar
Howland David (M)	5 11	10 08	Ballynahinch	17 9 86	Scholar
Jaidi Radhi (D)	6 2	14 00	Gabes	30 8 75	Bolton W
Jerome Cameron (F)	6 1	13 06	Huddersfield	14 8 86	Cardiff C
Johnson Damien (M)	5 9	11 09	Lisburn	18 11 78	Blackburn R
Kelly Stephen (D)	6 0	12 13	Dublin	6 9 83	Tottenham H
Kilkenny Neil (M)	5 8	10 08	Middlesex	19 12 85	Arsenal
Krysiak Artur (G)	6 1	12 08	Lodz	11 8 89	UKS Lodz
Larsson Sebastian (M)	5 10	11 00	Eskilstuna	6 6 85	Arsenal
Legzdins Adam (G)	6 2	14 02	Stafford	22 11 86	Scholar
McPike James (F)	5 10	11 02	Birmingham	4 10 88	Scholar
McSheffrey Gary (M)	5 8	10 06	Coventry	13 8 82	Coventry C
Muamba Fabrice (M)	6 2	12 04	DR Congo	6 4 88	Arsenal
N'Gotty Bruno (D)	6 1	13 07	Lyon	10 6 71	Bolton W
Nafti Mehdi (M)	5 9	11 03	Toulouse	20 11 78	Santander
Oji Samuel (D)	6 0	14 05	Westminster	9 10 85	
Pearce Kaystian (D)	6 1	13 05	Birmingham	5 1 90	Scholar
Sadler Matthew (D)	5 11	11 08	Birmingham	26 2 85	Scholar
Taylor Maik (G)	6 4	14 02	Hildeshein	4 9 71	Fulham
Taylor Martin (D)	6 4	15 00	Ashington	9 11 79	Blackburn R
Tebily Oliver (D)	6 0	13 05	Abidjan	19 12 75	Celtic
Vine Rowan (F)	6 1	11 12	Basingstoke	21 9 82	Luton T
Wright Nick (M)	6 2	12 08	Birmingham	25 11 87	Scholar

League Appearances: Bendtner, N. 38(4); Campbell, D. 15(17); Clemence, S. 31(3); Cole, A. 5; Danns, N. 11(18); Doyle, C. 19; Dunn, D. 9(2); Forssell, M. 3(5); Gray, J. 2(5); Jaidi, R. 38; Jerome, C. 20(18); Johnson, D. 24(2); Kelly, S. 35(1); Kilkenny, N. (8); Larsson, S. 27(16); McSheffrey, G. 40; Muamba, F. 30(4); N'Gotty, B. 25; Nafti, M. 18(14); Painter, M. 1; Sadler, M. 36; Taylor, Maik 27; Taylor, Martin 29(2); Tebily, O. 5(1); Upson, M. 8(1); Vine, R. 10(7).
Goals – League (67): McSheffrey 13 (1 pen), Bendtner 11, Campbell 9, Jerome 7, Jaidi 6, Clemence 4, Larsson 4, Danns 3, Upson 2, Cole 1, Dunn 1, Forssell 1 (pen), Johnson 1, N'Gotty 1, Vine 1, own goals 2.
Carling Cup (9): Bendtner 2, Jerome 2, Larsson 2, McSheffrey 2, Campbell 1.
FA Cup (9): Larsson 3, Campbell 2, McSheffrey 1, N'Gotty 1, Martin Taylor 1, own goal 1.
Ground: St Andrews Stadium, Birmingham B9 4NH. Telephone (0871) 226 1875.
Record Attendance: 66,844 v Everton, FA Cup 5th rd, 11 February 1939. **Capacity:** 30,079 (all seated).
Manager: Steve Bruce.
Secretary: Julia Shelton.
Most League Goals: 103, Division 2, 1893–94 (only 28 games).
Highest League Scorer in Season: Joe Bradford, 29, Division 1, 1927–28.
Most League Goals in Total Aggregate: Joe Bradford, 249, 1920–35.
Most Capped Player: Kenny Cunningham, 32 (72), Republic of Ireland.
Most League Appearances: Frank Womack, 491, 1908–28.
Honours – Football League: Division 2 Champions – 1892–93, 1920–21, 1947–48,

1954–55, 1994–95. **Football League Cup:** Winners – 1963. **Leyland Daf Cup:** Winners – 1991. **Auto Windscreens Shield:** Winners – 1995.
Colours: Royal blue shirts, white shorts, white stockings.

BLACKBURN ROVERS — FA PREMIERSHIP

Name	Ht	Wt	Birthplace	Birthdate	Source
Bentley David (F)	5 10	11 03	Peterborough	27 8 84	Arsenal
Berner Bruno (M)	6 1	12 13	Zurich	21 11 77	Basle
Brown Jason (G)	5 11	13 03	Southwark	18 5 82	Gillingham
De Vita Raffaele (F)	6 0	11 09	Rome	23 9 87	Scholar
Derbyshire Matt (F)	5 10	11 01	Gt Harwood	14 4 86	Great Harwood T
Dunn David (M)	5 9	12 03	Gt Harwood	27 12 79	Birmingham C
Emerton Brett (M)	6 1	13 05	Bankstown	22 2 79	Feyenoord
Enckelman Peter (G)	6 2	12 05	Turku	10 3 77	Aston Villa
Fielding Frank (G)	5 11	12 00	Blackburn	4 4 88	Scholar
Friedel Brad (G)	6 3	14 00	Lakewood	18 5 71	Liverpool
Gallagher Paul (F)	6 1	12 00	Glasgow	9 8 84	Trainee
Garner Joseph (F)	5 10	11 02	Blackburn	12 4 88	Scholar
Griffiths Rostyn (M)	6 2	12 08	Stoke	10 3 88	Scholar
Henchoz Stephane (D)	6 1	12 08	Billens	7 9 74	Wigan Ath
Hodge Bryan (M)	5 10	12 02	Hamilton	23 9 87	Scholar
Jeffers Francis (F)	5 10	10 07	Liverpool	25 1 81	Charlton Ath
Jones Zak (G)	5 11	12 08	Darwen	24 11 88	Scholar
Kane Tony (D)	5 11	11 00	Belfast	29 8 87	Scholar
Khizanishvili Zurab (D)	6 1	12 08	Tbilisi	6 10 81	Rangers
McCarthy Benny (F)	6 0	12 08	Cape Town	12 11 77	Porto
Mokoena Aaron (D)	6 2	14 00	Johannesburg	25 11 80	Genk
Nelsen Ryan (D)	5 11	14 02	New Zealand	18 10 77	DC United
Nolan Eddie (D)	6 0	13 05	Waterford	5 8 88	Scholar
O'Keefe Josh (M)	6 1	11 05	Whalley	22 12 88	Scholar
Olsson Martin (D)			Sweden	17 5 88	Hogaborg
Ooijer Andre (D)	6 0	12 00	Amsterdam	11 7 74	PSV Eindhoven
Pedersen Morten (F)	5 11	11 00	Vadso	8 9 81	Tromso
Peter Sergio (M)	5 8	11 00	Ludwigshafen	12 10 86	Scholar
Reid Steven (M)	6 0	12 07	Kingston	10 3 81	Millwall
Roberts Jason (F)	6 1	13 06	Park Royal	25 1 78	Wigan Ath
Samba Christopher (D)	6 5	13 03	Creteil	28 3 84	Hertha Berlin
Savage Robbie (M)	5 11	11 00	Wrexham	18 10 74	Birmingham C
Taylor Andy (D)	5 11	11 07	Blackburn	14 3 86	Scholar
Todd Andy (D)	5 11	13 04	Derby	21 9 74	Charlton Ath
Treacy Keith (M)	5 11	11 11	Dublin	13 9 88	Scholar
Tugay Kerimoglu (M)	5 9	11 07	Istanbul	24 8 70	Rangers
Warnock Stephen (D)	5 7	11 09	Ormskirk	12 12 81	Liverpool

League Appearances: Bentley, D. 36; Berner, B. 1; Brown, J. (1); Derbyshire, M. 8(14); Dunn, D. 7(4); Emerton, B. 32(2); Friedel, B. 38; Gallagher, P. 2(14); Gray, M. 10(1); Henchoz, S. 10(2); Jeffers, F. 3(7); Khizanishvili, Z. 17(1); Kuqi, S. (1); McCarthy, B. 36; McEveley, J. 3(1); Mokoena, A. 18(9); Neill, L. 20; Nelsen, R. 12; Nonda, S. 17(9); Ooijer, A. 20; Pedersen, M. 36; Peter, S. 1(8); Reid, S. 3; Roberts, J. 9(9); Samba, C. 13(1); Savage, R. 21; Todd, A. 6(3); Tugay, K. 26(4); Warnock, S. 13.
Goals – League (52): McCarthy 18 (4 pens), Nonda 7 (1 pen), Pedersen 6, Derbyshire 5, Bentley 4, Roberts 4, Samba 2, Gallagher 1, Tugay 1, Warnock 1, own goals 3.
Carling Cup (0).

FA Cup (12): Derbyshire 4, McCarthy 3, Pedersen 2, Gallagher 1, Mokoena 1, Roberts 1.
UEFA Cup (12): Bentley 3, McCarthy 3, Savage 2, Jeffers 1 (pen), Neill 1, Nonda 1, Tugay 1.
Ground: Ewood Park, Blackburn BB2 4JF. Telephone (0870) 111 3232.
Record Attendance: 62,522 v Bolton W, FA Cup 6th rd, 2 March 1929. **Capacity:** 31,154.
Manager: Mark Hughes.
Secretary: Andrew Pincher.
Most League Goals: 114, Division 2, 1954–55.
Highest League Scorer in Season: Ted Harper, 43, Division 1, 1925–26.
Most League Goals in Total Aggregate: Simon Garner, 168, 1978–92.
Most Capped Player: Henning Berg, 58 (100), Norway.
Most League Appearances: Derek Fazackerley, 596, 1970–86.
Honours – FA Premier League: Champions – 1994–95. **Football League:** Division 1 Champions – 1911–12, 1913–14. Division 2 Champions – 1938–39. Division 3 Champions – 1974–75. **FA Cup:** Winners – 1884, 1885, 1886, 1890, 1891, 1928. **Football League Cup:** Winners – 2002. **Full Members' Cup:** Winners – 1986–87.
Colours: Blue and white halved shirts.

BLACKPOOL — FL CHAMPIONSHIP

Player	Ht	Wt	Birthplace	Birthdate	Source
Barker Shaun (D)	6 2	12 08	Nottingham	19 9 82	Rotherham U
Bean Marcus (M)	5 11	11 06	Hammersmith	2 11 84	QPR
Blinkhorn Matthew (F)	5 11	10 10	Blackpool	2 3 85	Scholar
Burgess Ben (F)	6 3	14 04	Buxton	9 11 81	Hull C
Coid Danny (D)	5 11	11 07	Liverpool	3 10 81	Trainee
Doughty Phil (D)	6 2	13 02	Kirkham	6 9 86	Scholar
Edge Lewis (G)	6 1	12 10	Lancaster	12 1 87	Scholar
Evans Rhys (G)	6 1	13 12	Swindon	27 1 82	Swindon T
Evatt Ian (D)	6 3	13 12	Coventry	19 11 81	QPR
Forbes Adrian (F)	5 8	11 10	Greenford	23 1 79	Swansea C
Fox David (M)	5 9	11 08	Leek	13 12 83	Manchester U
Gorkss Kaspars (D)	6 3	13 05	Riga	6 11 81	Ventspils
Hoolahan Wes (M)	5 6	10 03	Dublin	10 8 83	Livingston
Jackson Mike (D)	6 0	13 08	Runcorn	4 12 73	Tranmere R
Jorgensen Claus (M)	5 10	10 06	Holstebro	27 4 76	Coventry C
Kay Matty (M)	5 9	11 00	Blackpool	12 10 89	Scholar
Morrell Andy (F)	5 11	12 00	Doncaster	28 9 74	Coventry C
Parker Keigan (F)	5 7	10 05	Livington	8 6 82	St Johnstone
Southern Keith (M)	5 10	12 06	Gateshead	24 4 81	Everton
Tierney Paul (D)	5 10	12 05	Salford	15 9 82	Livingston
Vernon Scott (F)	6 1	11 06	Manchester	13 12 83	Oldham Ath
Wiles Simon (M)	5 11	11 04	Preston	22 4 85	Scholar

League Appearances: Barker, S. 45; Bean, M. 2(4); Blinkhorn, M. (2); Brandon, C. 4(1); Burgess, B. 13(14); Coid, D. 15(3); Dickinson, C. 7; Edge, L. 1; Evans, R. 32; Evatt, I. 42(2); Farrelly, G. (1); Fernandez, V. (1); Forbes, A. 26(8); Fox, D. 33(4); Gillett, S. 20(11); Gorkss, K. 8(2); Graham, D. 1(3); Hart, J. 5; Hoolahan, W. 37(5); Jackson, M. 42(1); Jorgensen, C. 21(10); Joseph, M. 3(5); Morrell, A. 34(6); Parker, K. 24(21); Prendergast, R. 3(2); Rachubka, P. 8; Southern, K. 37(2); Tierney, P. 8(2); Vernon, S. 21(17); Wilkinson, A. 5(2); Williams, R. 9.
Goals – League (76): Morrell 16, Parker 13, Vernon 11, Hoolahan 8 (5 pens), Southern 5, Fox 4, Williams 4, Barker 3, Brandon 2, Burgess 2, Jorgensen 2, Forbes 1, Gillett 1, Graham 1, Jackson 1, own goals 2.
Carling Cup (2): Vernon 2.

FA Cup (10): Morrell 3, Barker 1, Burgess 1 (pen), Evatt 1, Hoolahan 1 (pen), Jackson 1, Parker 1, Vernon 1.
J Paint Trophy (4): Burgess 2 (1 pen), Barker 1, Gillett 1.
Play-Offs (7): Parker 2, Barker 1, Hoolahan 1, Morrell 1, Southern 1, Williams 1.
Ground: Bloomfield Road, Seasiders Way, Blackpool FY1 6JJ. Telephone (0870) 443 1953.
Record Attendance: 38,098 v Wolverhampton W, Division 1, 17 September 1955.
Capacity: 9,612.
Manager: Simon Grayson.
Secretary: Matt Williams.
Most League Goals: 98, Division 2, 1929–30.
Highest League Scorer in Season: Jimmy Hampson, 45, Division 2, 1929–30.
Most League Goals in Total Aggregate: Jimmy Hampson, 246, 1927–38.
Most Capped Player: Jimmy Armfield, 43, England.
Most League Appearances: Jimmy Armfield, 568, 1952–71.
Honours – Football League: Division 2 Champions – 1929–30. **FA Cup:** Winners – 1953. **Anglo-Italian Cup:** Winners – 1971. **LDV Vans Trophy:** Winners – 2002, 2004.
Colours: Tangerine shirts, white shorts, tangerine stockings.

BOLTON WANDERERS — FA PREMIERSHIP

Name	Ht	Wt	Birthplace	DOB	Source
Al-Habsi Ali (G)	6 4	12 06	Oman	30 12 81	Lyn
Anelka Nicolas (F)	6 1	13 03	Versailles	14 3 79	Fenerbahce
Augustyn Blazej (M)	6 3	13 00	Strzelin	26 1 88	Scholar
Ben Haim Tal (D)	5 11	11 09	Rishon Le Zion	31 3 82	Maccabi Tel Aviv
Campo Ivan (M)	6 1	12 10	San Sebastian	21 2 74	Real Madrid
Davies Kevin (F)	6 0	12 10	Sheffield	26 3 77	Southampton
Diouf El Hadji (F)	5 11	11 11	Dakar	15 1 81	Liverpool
Faye Aboulaye (M)	6 2	13 10	Dakar	26 2 78	Istres
Fojut Jaroslaw (D)	6 2	13 00	Legionowo	17 10 87	Scholar
Gardner Ricardo (D)	5 9	11 00	St Andrews	25 9 78	Harbour View
Giannakopoulos Stelios (M)	5 8	11 00	Athens	12 7 74	Olympiakos
Howarth Chris (G)	6 2	12 10	Bolton	23 5 86	Scholar
Hunt Nicky (D)	6 1	13 08	Westhoughton	3 9 83	Scholar
Jaaskelainen Jussi (G)	6 3	12 10	Mikkeli	19 4 75	VPS
Kazimierczak Prezemek (G)	6 0	12 02	Lodz	22 2 88	Scholar
Meite Abdoulaye (D)	6 1	12 13	Paris	6 10 80	Marseille
Michalik Lubomir (D)	6 4	13 00	Cadca	13 8 83	Senec
Nolan Kevin (M)	6 0	14 00	Liverpool	24 6 82	Scholar
O'Brien Joey (M)	6 0	10 13	Dublin	17 2 86	Scholar
Sissons Robert (M)	5 8	11 02	Stockport	29 9 88	Scholar
Smith Johann (M)	5 11	12 06	Hartford	25 4 87	Scholar
Speed Gary (M)	5 10	12 11	Deeside	8 9 69	Newcastle U
Tal Idan (M)	5 10	10 13	Petah Tikva	13 9 75	Maccabi Haifa
Teimourian Andranik (M)	5 11	11 07	Tehran	6 3 83	Aboo Moslem
Vaz Te Ricardo (F)	6 2	12 07	Lisbon	1 10 86	Scholar
Walker Ian (G)	6 2	13 01	Watford	31 10 71	Leicester C

League Appearances: Anelka, N. 35; Ben Haim, T. 30(2); Campo, I. 31(3); Davies, K. 30; Diagne-Faye, A. 29(3); Diouf, E. 32(1); Fortune, Q. 5(1); Gardner, R. 13(5); Giannakopoulos, S. 11(12); Hunt, N. 32(1); Jaaskelainen, J. 38; Martin, C. (1); Meite, A. 35; Michalik, L. 3(1); Nolan, K. 31; Pedersen, H. 10(8); Sinclair, J. (2); Smith, J. (1); Speed, G. 38; Tal, I. 4(12); Teimourian, A. 6(11); Thompson, D. 3(5); Vaz Te, R. 2(23).
Goals – League (47): Anelka 11, Davies 8, Speed 8 (5 pens), Diouf 5 (1 pen), Campo 4, Nolan 3, Diagne-Faye 2, Teimourian 2, Michalik 1, Pedersen 1, own goals 2.

Carling Cup (3): Anelka 1, Campo 1, Nolan 1.
FA Cup (6): Teimourian 2, Davies 1, Meite 1, Nolan 1, Tal 1.
Ground: Reebok Stadium, Burnden Way, Bolton BL6 6JW. Telephone Bolton (01204) 673 673.
Record Attendance: 69,912 v Manchester C, FA Cup 5th rd, 18 February 1933.
Capacity: 28,101.
Manager: Sammy Lee.
Secretary: Simon Marland.
Most League Goals: 100, Division 1, 1996–97.
Highest League Scorer in Season: Joe Smith, 38, Division 1, 1920–21.
Most League Goals in Total Aggregate: Nat Lofthouse, 255, 1946–61.
Most Capped Player: Mark Fish, 34 (62), South Africa.
Most League Appearances: Eddie Hopkinson, 519, 1956–70.
Honours – Football League: Division 1 Champions – 1996–97. Division 2 Champions – 1908–09, 1977–78. Division 3 Champions – 1972–73. **FA Cup:** Winners – 1923, 1926, 1929, 1958. **Sherpa Van Trophy:** Winners – 1989.
Colours: White shirts, white shorts, white stockings.

BOSTON UNITED — BLUE SQUARE NORTH

Albrighton Mark (D)	6 1	12 07	Nuneaton	6 3 76	Doncaster R
Ellender Paul (D)	6 1	12 07	Scunthorpe	21 10 74	Scarborough
Greaves Mark (D)	6 1	13 00	Hull	22 1 75	Hull C
Green Francis (F)	5 9	11 04	Nottingham	25 4 80	Lincoln C
Marriott Andy (G)	6 2	13 07	Sutton-in-Ashfield	11 10 70	Torquay U
Nunn Ben (D)	5 8	10 00	Cambridge	25 10 89	Scholar
Rowntree Adam (F)	5 7	11 02	Lincoln	23 11 88	Scholar
Ryan Richie (M)	5 10	10 07	Kilkenny	6 1 85	Scunthorpe U
Stevens Jamie (D)	5 11	11 05	Holbeach	25 2 89	Scholar
Talbot Stewart (M)	6 0	13 07	Birmingham	14 6 73	Brentford

League Appearances: Albrighton, M. 12; Benjamin, T. 2(1); Broughton, D. 25; Canoville, L. 15(1); Clarke, J. 30(7); Cooksey, E. 11(5); Cotton, D. (2); Cryan, C. 15; Davidson, R. 3(6); Elding, A. 18(1); Ellender, P. 40(2); Farrell, D. 23(16); Forbes, L. (1); Galbraith, D. 21(9); Greaves, M. 38(1); Green, F. 35(4); Holland, C. 12(2); Jarrett, A. 5; Joachim, J. 3; Joynes, N. 9(1); Kennedy, J. 13; Marriott, A. 46; Maylett, B. 4(17); Miller, I. 12; N'Guessan, D. 13(10); Nicholson, S. 5(1); Nunn, B. (1); Richards, J. 3; Rowntree, A. (3); Rowson, D. 6; Rusk, S. 2(1); Ryan, R. 9(4); Ryan, T. 23; Stevens, J. 11(1); Tait, P. 9(5); Talbot, S. 16(2); Thomas, B. 11; Vaughan, S. 6(1).
Goals – League (51): Broughton 8, Elding 5, N'Guessan 5, Green 4, Ryan T 4 (4 pens), Greaves 3, Joachim 3, Clarke 2 (1 pen), Galbraith 2, Jarrett 2 (1 pen), Stevens 2, Tait 2, Thomas 2, Ellender 1, Farrell 1, Joynes 1, Kennedy 1, Talbot 1, own goals 2.
Carling Cup (0).
FA Cup (0).
J Paint Trophy (0).
Ground: York Street Ground, York Street, Boston, Lincolnshire PE21 6HJ. Telephone (01205) 364 406.
Record Attendance: 10,086 v Corby Town, Friendly, 1955.
Capacity: 6,300.
Manager: TBC.
Secretary: John Blackwell.
Most League Appearances: Paul Ellender, 174, 2002–.
Most Capped Player: Andy Kirk, 1(8), Northern Ireland.
Honours – Conference: Champions – 2001–02. **Dr. Martens:** Champions – 1999–2000. Runners-up – 1998–99. **Northern Premier League:** Champions –

1972–73, 1973–74, 1976–77, 1977–78. **Northern Premier League Cup:** Winners – 1974, 1976. **Northern Premier League Challenge Shield:** Winners – 1974, 1975, 1977, 1978. **Lincolnshire Senior Cup:** Winners – 1935, 1937, 1938, 1946, 1950, 1955, 1956, 1960, 1977, 1979, 1986, 1988, 1989. **Non-League Champions of Champions Cup:** Winners – 1973, 1977. **East Anglian Cup:** – Winners 1961. **Central Alliance League:** Champions – 1961–62. **United Counties League:** Champions – 1965–66. **West Midlands League:** Champions – 1966–67, 1967–68. **Eastern Professional Floodlit Cup:** Winners – 1972.
Colours: Amber and black shirts, black shorts, black stockings.

AFC BOURNEMOUTH FL CHAMPIONSHIP 1

Anderton Darren (M)	6 2	13 04	Southampton	3 3 72	Wolverhampton W
Cooper Shaun (D)	5 10	10 05	Newport (IW)	5 10 83	Portsmouth
Cummings Warren (D)	5 9	11 08	Aberdeen	15 10 80	Chelsea
Foley-Sheridan Steven (M)	5 4	9 00	Dublin	10 2 86	Aston Villa
Gowling Josh (D)	6 3	12 08	Coventry	29 11 83	Herfolge
Hayter James (F)	5 9	10 13	Sandown (IW)	9 4 79	Trainee
Hollands Danny (M)	6 0	12 00	Ashford	6 11 85	Chelsea
Moss Neil (G)	6 2	13 10	New Milton	10 5 75	Southampton
Pitman Brett (M)	6 0	11 00	Jersey	31 1 88	St Paul's, Jersey
Purches Stephen (M)	5 11	11 09	Ilford	14 1 80	West Ham U
Stewart Gareth (G)	6 0	12 08	Preston	3 2 80	Blackburn R
Vokes Sam (F)	6 1	13 10	Southampton	21 10 89	Scholar
Young Neil (D)	5 9	12 00	Harlow	31 8 73	Tottenham H

League Appearances: Ainsworth, L. 2(5); Anderton, D. 28; Bertrand, R. 5; Best, L. 12(3); Broadhurst, K. 25(2); Browning, M. 17(4); Claridge, S. 1; Connolly, M. 3(2); Cooke, S. 6(4); Cooper, S. 29(4); Cork, J. 7; Cummings, W. 26(5); Fletcher, S. 32(9); Foley-Sheridan, S. 15(3); Gillett, S. 7; Gowling, J. 25(8); Hart, C. 8; Hayter, J. 41(1); Hollands, D. 14(19); Howe, E. 14(1); Lawson, J. 2(2); Maher, S. 5(2); McGoldrick, D. 12; McQuoid, J. (2); Moss, N. 26; Pitman, B. 8(21); Purches, J. 38(5); Songo'o, F. 3(1); Standing, M. (1); Stewart, G. 20; Summerfield, L. 5(3); Vidarsson, B. 4(2); Vokes, S. 8(5); Walker, J. 5(1); Wilson, M. 19; Young, N. 34.
Goals – League (50): Hayter 10 (2 pens), Anderton 6, McGoldrick 6, Pitman 5 (1 pen), Vokes 4, Best 3, Wilson 3, Browning 2, Connolly 1, Cooke 1, Fletcher 1, Foley-Sheridan 1, Gillett 1, Gowling 1, Hollands 1, Howe 1, Purches 1, Summerfield 1, Vidarsson 1.
Carling Cup (1): Fletcher 1.
FA Cup (5): Fletcher 2, Hayter 2, Hollands 1.
J Paint Trophy (0).
Ground: The Fitness First Stadium at Dean Court, Bournemouth BH7 7AF. Telephone (01202) 726 300.
Record Attendance: 28,799 v Manchester U, FA Cup 6th rd, 2 March 1957.
Capacity: 10,375.
Manager: Kevin Bond.
Secretary: K. R. J. MacAlister.
Most League Goals: 88, Division 3 (S), 1956–57.
Highest League Scorer in Season: Ted MacDougall, 42, 1970–71.
Most League Goals in Total Aggregate: Ron Eyre, 202, 1924–33.
Most Capped Player: Gerry Peyton, 7 (33), Republic of Ireland.
Most League Appearances: Steve Fletcher, 466, 1992–2007.
Honours – Football League: Division 3 Champions – 1986–87. **Associate Members' Cup:** Winners – 1984.
Colours: Red shirts with three black stripes front and back, black shorts, black stockings.

BRADFORD CITY — FL CHAMPIONSHIP 2

Ainge Simon (D)	6 1	12 02	Bradford	18 2 88	Scholar
Bentham Craig (D)	5 9	11 06	Bingley	7 3 85	Scholar
Bower Mark (D)	5 10	11 00	Bradford	23 1 80	Trainee
Clarke Matthew (D)	6 3	12 07	Leeds	18 12 80	Darlington
Colbeck Joe (M)	5 10	10 12	Bradford	29 11 86	Scholar
Daley Omar (M)	5 7	10 03	Jamaica	25 4 81	Charleston Battery
Johnson Eddie (F)	5 10	13 05	Chester	20 9 84	Manchester U
Penford Thomas (M)	5 10	11 03	Leeds	5 1 85	Scholar
Ricketts Donovan (G)	6 1	11 05	St James	6 7 77	Village U
Wetherall David (D)	6 3	13 12	Sheffield	14 3 71	Leeds U
Windass Dean (F)	5 10	12 03	North Ferriby	1 4 69	Sheffield U

League Appearances: Ainge, S. 5(4); Ashikodi, M. 8; Barrau, X. 1(2); Bentham, C. 12(6); Black, T. 4; Bower, M. 46; Bridge-Wilkinson, M. 39; Brown, J. 1(5); Clarke, M. 5(3); Colbeck, J. 14(18); Daley, O. 13(1); Doyle, N. 25(3); Dyer, B. 2(3); Edghill, R. 20(4); Graham, D. 17(5); Healy, C. 2; Hibbert, D. 4(4); Holmes, L. 16; Johnson, E. 17(15); Johnson, J. 26(1); Logan, C. 3(1); Muirhead, B. 1(3); Osborne, L. (1); Parker, B. 35(4); Paynter, B. 15; Penford, T. 1(2); Ricketts, D. 46; Rogers, A. 4(4); Schumacher, S. 44; Swift, J. 1(1); Weir-Daley, S. 2(3); Wetherall, D. 41; Windass, D. 25; Youga, K. 11.
Goals – League (47): Windass 11 (2 pens), Schumacher 6 (1 pen), Bridge-Wilkinson 4, Johnson J 4, Paynter 4, Bower 3, Graham 3, Johnson E 3, Ashikodi 2, Barrau 2, Daley 2, Dyer 1, Weir-Daley 1, Wetherall 1.
Carling Cup (1): Johnson E 1.
FA Cup (4): Bridge-Wilkinson 1, Schumacher 1, Windass 1, own goal 1.
J Paint Trophy (1): Brown 1.
Ground: Intersonic Stadium, Valley Parade, Bradford BD8 7DY. Telephone 0870 822 0000.
Record Attendance: 39,146 v Burnley, FA Cup 4th rd, 11 March 1911. **Capacity:** 25,136.
Manager: Stuart McCall.
Secretary: Jon Pollard.
Most League Goals: 128, Division 3 (N), 1928–29.
Highest League Scorer in Season: David Layne, 34, Division 4, 1961–62.
Most League Goals in Total Aggregate: Bobby Campbell, 121, 1981–84, 1984–86.
Most Capped Player: Jamie Lawrence, (42), Jamaica.
Most League Appearances: Cec Podd, 502, 1970–84.
Honours – Football League: Division 2 Champions – 1907–08. Division 3 Champions – 1984–85. Division 3 (N) Champions – 1928–29. **FA Cup:** Winners – 1911.
Colours: Claret and amber.

BRENTFORD — FL CHAMPIONSHIP 2

Brooker Paul (M)	5 8	10 00	Hammersmith	25 11 76	Reading
Carder-Andrews Karle (M)	5 11	10 08	Isleworth	13 3 89	Scholar
Charles Darius (M)	5 11	11 10	Ealing	10 12 87	Scholar
Dark Lewis (D)	5 8	11 06	Harlow	10 4 89	Scholar
Frampton Andrew (D)	5 11	10 10	Wimbledon	3 9 79	Crystal Palace
Heywood Matt (D)	6 3	14 00	Chatham	26 8 79	Bristol C
Ide Charlie (M)	5 8	10 06	Sunbury	10 5 88	Scholar
Masters Clark (G)	6 3	13 12	Hastings	31 5 87	Scholar
Montague Ross (F)	6 0	12 11	Isleworth	1 11 88	Scholar

Mousinho John (D)	6 1	12 07	Buckingham	30 4 86	Univ of Notre Dame
O'Connor Kevin (F)	5 11	12 00	Blackburn	24 2 82	Trainee
Osborne Karleigh (M)	6 2	12 08	Southall	19 3 88	Scholar
Osei-Kuffour Jo (F)	5 8	11 11	Edmonton	17 11 81	Torquay U
Peters Ryan (F)	5 8	10 08	London	21 8 87	Scholar
Rhodes Alex (F)	5 9	10 04	Cambridge	23 1 82	Newmarket T
Tillen Sam (D)	5 10	11 09	Newbury	16 4 85	Chelsea

League Appearances: Abbey, N. 16; Brooker, P. 24(10); Carder-Andrews, K. 2(3); Charles, D. 9(8); Cox, S. 11(2); Dark, L. 2(1); Frampton, A. 32; Griffiths, A. 32(5); Heywood, M. 25(3); Ide, C. 24(2); Keith, J. 17(1); Leary, M. 17; Masters, C. 11; Montague, R. (4); Moore, C. 8(8); Mousinho, J. 29(5); Nelson, S. 19; O'Connor, K. 38(1); Onibuje, F. (2); Osborne, K. 17(4); Osei-Kuffour, J. 38(1); Owusu, L. 4(3); Partridge, D. 3; Peters, R. (13); Pinault, T. 24(3); Rhodes, A. 8(7); Richards, G. 10; Shipperley, N. 11; Skulason, O. 10; Taylor, S. 3(3); Tillen, S. 28(6); Tomlin, G. 6(6); Wijnhard, C. 7(2); Willock, C. 18(10); Wilson, C. 3.
Goals – League (40): Osei-Kuffour 12, Ide 7, O'Connor 6 (4 pens), Willock 3, Keith 2 (1 pen), Moore 2, Charles 1, Frampton 1, Griffiths 1, Heywood 1, Pinault 1, Richards 1, Skulason 1, Tillen 1.
Carling Cup (2): O'Connor 1, Osei-Kuffour 1.
FA Cup (0).
J Paint Trophy (1): Osei-Kuffour 1.
Ground: Griffin Park, Braemar Road, Brentford, Middlesex TW8 0NT. Telephone (0845) 3456 442.
Record Attendance: 38,678 v Leicester C, FA Cup 6th rd, 26 February 1949.
Capacity: 12,500.
Manager: Terry Butcher.
Secretary: Lisa Hall.
Most League Goals: 98, Division 4, 1962–63.
Highest League Scorer in Season: Jack Holliday, 38, Division 3 (S), 1932–33.
Most League Goals in Total Aggregate: Jim Towers, 153, 1954–61.
Most Capped Player: John Buttigieg, 22 (98), Malta.
Most League Appearances: Ken Coote, 514, 1949–64.
Honours – Football League: Division 2 Champions – 1934–35. Division 3 Champions – 1991–92, 1998–99. Division 3 (S) Champions – 1932–33. Division 4 Champions – 1962–63.
Colours: Red and white striped shirts, black shorts, red and black stockings.

BRIGHTON & HOVE ALBION FL CHAMPIONSHIP 1

Bertin Alexis (M)	5 7	12 00	Le Havre	13 5 80	Le Havre
Butters Guy (D)	6 1	15 05	Hillingdon	30 10 69	Gillingham
Chamberlain Scott (M)	5 9	10 08	Eastbourne	15 1 88	Scholar
Cox Dean (M)	5 4	9 08	Haywards Heath	12 8 87	Scholar
El-Abd Adam (D)	5 10	13 05	Brighton	11 9 84	Scholar
Elder Nathan (F)	6 1	13 12	Hornchurch	5 4 85	Billericay T
Elphick Tommy (M)	5 11	11 07	Brighton	7 9 87	Scholar
Fogden Wes (F)	5 8	10 04	Brighton	12 4 88	Scholar
Fraser Tom (M)	5 10	11 00	Brighton	5 12 87	Scholar
Frutos Alexandre (M)	5 9	10 03	Vitry-le-Francois	23 4 82	Metz
Gatting Joe (D)	5 11	12 04	Brighton	25 11 87	Scholar
Hammond Dean (M)	6 1	11 02	Hastings	7 3 83	Scholar
Hart Gary (F)	5 9	12 07	Harlow	21 9 76	Stansted
Hinshelwood Adam (D)	5 11	13 00	Oxford	8 1 84	Scholar
Kuipers Michels (G)	6 2	15 00	Amsterdam	26 6 74	Bristol R
Loft Doug (M)	6 0	12 01	Maidstone	25 12 86	Hastings U

Lynch Joel (D)	6 1	12 10	Eastbourne	3 10 87	Scholar
Mayo Kerry (D)	5 9	13 10	Cuckfield	21 9 77	Trainee
Oatway Charlie (M)	5 7	11 11	Hammersmith	28 11 73	Brentford
Reid Paul (M)	5 8	12 09	Sydney	6 7 79	Bradford C
Rents Sam (D)	5 9	11 03	Brighton	22 6 87	Scholar
Revell Alexander (F)	6 2	13 02	Cambridge	7 7 83	Braintree T
Robinson Jake (F)	5 7	10 10	Brighton	23 10 86	Scholar
Savage Bas (F)	6 3	13 00	London	7 1 82	Gillingham
Sullivan John (M)	5 10	11 04	Brighton	8 3 88	Scholar

League Appearances: Bertin, A. 15(1); Bowditch, D. 1(2); Butters, G. 31; Carpenter, R. 13(2); Cox, D. 40(2); El-Abd, A. 39(3); Elder, N. 1(12); Elphick, T. 2(1); Flinders, S. 12; Fraser, T. 18(10); Frutos, A. 5(5); Gatting, J. 10(13); Hammond, D. 37; Hart, G. 18(7); Henderson, W. 20; Hinshelwood, A. 10(1); John, A. 1(3); Kazim-Richards, C. (1); Kuipers, M. 14; Loft, D. 5(6); Lynch, J. 34(5); Mayo, K. 28(2); Molango, M. (1); O'Cearuill, J. 6(2); Rehman, Z. 8; Reid, P. 10; Rents, S. 19(6); Revell, A. 34(4); Robinson, J. 28(10); Santos, G. 7(4); Savage, B. 14(1); Stokes, T. 5(1); Ward, N. 6(2); Whing, A. 12; Williams, S. 3.
Goals – League (49): Hammond 8 (3 pens), Revell 7, Cox 6, Robinson 6, Savage 6, Gatting 4, Hart 2, Bowditch 1, El-Abd 1, Elder 1, Fraser 1, Loft 1, Reid 1, Ward 1, Williams 1, own goals 2.
Carling Cup (3): Cox 1, El- Abd 1, Reid 1.
FA Cup (11): Robinson 4, Cox 2, Revell 2, Gatting 1, Hammond 1, Rents 1.
J Paint Trophy (7): Hammond 2, Revell 2, Robinson 2, Cox 1.
Ground: Withdean Stadium, Tongdean Lane, Brighton. East Sussex BN1 5JD. Telephone (01273) 695 400 (admin offices 44 North Road, Brighton).
Record Attendance: 36,747 v Fulham, Division 2, 27 December 1958 (at Goldstone Ground).
Capacity: 8,850.
Manager: Dean Wilkins.
Secretary: Derek J. Allan.
Most League Goals: 112, Division 3 (S), 1955–56.
Highest League Scorer in Season: Peter Ward, 32, Division 3, 1976–77.
Most League Goals in Total Aggregate: Tommy Cook, 114, 1922–29.
Most Capped Player: Steve Penney, 17, Northern Ireland.
Most League Appearances: 'Tug' Wilson, 509, 1922–36.
Honours – Football League: Division 2 Champions – 2001–02. Division 3 Champions – 2000–01. Division 3 (S) Champions – 1957–58. Division 4 Champions – 1964–65.
Colours: Blue and white striped shirts, white shorts, white stockings.

BRISTOL CITY — FL CHAMPIONSHIP

Artus Frankie (M)	6 0	11 02	Bristol	27 9 88	Scholar
Basso Adriano (G)	6 1	11 07	Jundiai	18 4 75	Woking
Betsy Kevin (M)	6 1	12 00	Seychelles	20 3 78	Wycombe W
Brooker Stephen (F)	5 11	13 13	Newport Pagnell	21 5 81	Port Vale
Carey Louis (D)	5 10	12 09	Bristol	20 1 77	Trainee
Fontaine Liam (D)	5 11	11 09	Beckenham	7 1 86	Fulham
Jevons Phil (F)	5 11	12 00	Liverpool	1 8 79	Yeovil T
Johnson Lee (M)	5 6	10 07	Newmarket	7 6 81	Hearts
Keogh Richard (M)	6 0	11 02	Harlow	11 8 86	Stoke C
McAllister Jamie (D)	5 10	11 00	Glasgow	26 4 78	Hearts
McCombe Jamie (D)	6 5	12 05	Scunthorpe	1 1 83	Lincoln C
Murray Scott (M)	5 8	11 02	Aberdeen	26 5 74	Reading
Myrie-Williams Jennison (F)	5 11	12 08	Lambeth	17 5 88	Scholar
Noble David (M)	6 0	12 04	Hitchin	2 2 82	Boston U

Orr Bradley (M)	6 0	11 11	Liverpool	1 11 82	Newcastle U
Partridge David (D)	6 1	13 06	Westminster	26 11 78	Motherwell
Ribeiro Christian (D)	5 11	12 02	Neath	14 12 89	Scholar
Russell Alex (M)	5 10	11 07	Crosby	17 3 73	Torquay U
Showunmi Enoch (F)	6 5	14 09	Kilburn	21 4 82	Luton T
Skuse Cole (M)	6 1	11 05	Bristol	29 3 86	Scholar
Weale Chris (G)	6 2	13 01	Chard	9 2 82	Yeovil T
Wilson Brian (D)	5 10	11 00	Manchester	9 5 83	Cheltenham T
Wilson James (D)	6 2	11 05	Newport	26 2 89	Scholar

League Appearances: Andrews, W. 3(4); Basso, A. 45; Betsy, K. 16(1); Brooker, S. 19(4); Brown, S. 12(3); Carey, L. 36(2); Corr, B. 1(2); Cotterill, D. 3(2); Fontaine, L. 23(7); Jevons, P. 31(10); Johnson, L. 41(1); Keogh, R. 20(11); McAllister, J. 29(2); McCombe, J. 38(3); Murray, S. 21(7); Myrie-Williams, J. 15(10); Noble, D. 18(8); Orr, B. 29(6); Ruddy, J. 1; Russell, A. 20(8); Showunmi, E. 28(5); Skuse, C. 31(11); Smith, A. 3(7); Weale, C. (1); Wilson, B. 17(2); Woodman, C. 5(6); Wright, N. 1(3).
Goals – League (63): Jevons 11 (4 pens), Showunmi 10 (1 pen), Murray 7, Johnson 5, Brown 4, McCombe 4, Orr 4 (1 pen), Noble 3, Andrews 2, Brooker 2, Carey 2, Keogh 2, Myrie-Williams 2, Russell 2, Betsy 1, Cotterill 1 (pen), McAllister 1.
Carling Cup (1): Cotterill 1.
FA Cup (14): Jevons 4, Showunmi 3, McCombe 2, Murray 2, Brooker 1, Keogh 1, Noble 1.
J Paint Trophy (7): Jevons 2, Showunmi 2, Andrews 1, Corr 1, Keogh 1.
Ground: Ashton Gate Stadium, Bristol BS3 2EJ. Telephone (0117) 9630 630.
Record Attendance: 43,335 v Preston NE, FA Cup 5th rd, 16 February 1935.
Capacity: 21,497.
Manager: Gary Johnson.
Secretary: Michelle McDonald.
Most League Goals: 104, Division 3 (S), 1926–27.
Highest League Scorer in Season: Don Clark, 36, Division 3 (S), 1946–47.
Most League Goals in Total Aggregate: John Atyeo, 314, 1951–66.
Most Capped Player: Billy Wedlock, 26, England.
Most League Appearances: John Atyeo, 597, 1951–66.
Honours – Football League: Division 2 Champions – 1905–06. Division 3 (S) Champions – 1922–23, 1926–27, 1954–55. **Welsh Cup:** Winners – 1934. **Anglo-Scottish Cup:** Winners – 1977–78. **Freight Rover Trophy:** Winners – 1985–86. **LDV Vans Trophy:** Winners – 2002–03.
Colours: Red shirts, white shorts, white and red stockings.

BRISTOL ROVERS — FL CHAMPIONSHIP 1

Anthony Byron (D)	6 1	11 02	Newport	20 9 84	Cardiff C
Campbell Stuart (M)	5 10	10 00	Corby	9 12 77	Grimsby T
Carruthers Chris (M)	5 10	12 00	Kettering	19 8 83	Northampton T
Disley Craig (M)	5 10	10 13	Worksop	24 8 81	Mansfield T
Elliott Steve (D)	6 1	14 00	Derby	29 10 78	Blackpool
Green Mike (G)	6 1	13 01	Bristol	23 07 89	Scholar
Green Ryan (D	5 7	10 10	Cardiff	20 10 80	Hereford U
Haldane Lewis (F)	6 0	11 03	Trowbridge	13 3 85	Scholar
Hinton Craig (D)	6 0	12 00	Wolverhampton	26 11 77	Kidderminster H
Igoe Sammy (M)	5 6	10 00	Staines	30 9 75	Millwall
Lambert Ricky (F)	6 2	14 08	Liverpool	16 2 82	Rochdale
Lescott Aaron (M)	5 8	10 09	Birmingham	2 12 78	Stockport Co
Lines Chris (M)	6 2	12 00	Bristol	30 11 85	Filton College
Palmer James (M)	5 7	11 04	Bristol	30 3 88	Scholar
Parrinello Tom (D)	5 6	10 07	Parkway	11 11 89	Scholar

Phillips Steve (G)	6 1	11 10	Bath	6 5 78	Bristol C
Rigg Sean (F)	5 9	12 01	Bristol	1 10 88	Scholar
Sandell Andy (M)	5 11	11 09	Swindon	8 9 83	Bath C
Walker Richard (F)	6 0	12 04	Sutton Coldfield	8 11 77	Oxford U

League Appearances: Agogo, J. 3; Anthony, B. 20(3); Campbell, S. 35(6); Carruthers, C. 33(5); Disley, C. 42(3); Easter, J. 1(2); Elliott, S. 39; Green, R. 29(4); Haldane, L. 32(13); Hinton, C. 28(2); Hunt, J. 12(2); Igoe, S. 35(5); Jacobson, J. 9(2); Lambert, R. 28(8); Lescott, A. 30(4); Lines, C. 4(3); Nicholson, S. 12(10); Oji, S. 5; Phillips, S. 44; Rigg, S. 1(17); Sandell, A. 20(16); Shearer, S. 2; Walker, J. 3(1); Walker, R. 39(7).
Goals – League (49): Walker R 12 (2 pens), Lambert 8 (1 pen), Haldane 6, Nicholson 6, Elliott 5, Disley 4, Sandell 3, Campbell 1, Hunt 1, Igoe 1, Rigg 1, Walker J 1.
Carling Cup (1): Walker R 1.
FA Cup (6): Walker R 4 (2 pens), Anthony 1, Disley 1.
J Paint Trophy (8): Igoe 2, Walker R 2 (1 pen), Anthony 1, Easter 1, Lambert 1, Nicholson 1.
Play-Offs (10): Walker R 4, Igoe 2, Campbell 1, Disley 1, Lambert 1, Rigg 1.
Ground: The Memorial Stadium, Filton Avenue, Horfield, Bristol BS7 0BF. Telephone (0117) 909 6648.
Record Attendance: 9,464 v Liverpool, FA Cup 4th rd, 8 February 1992 (Twerton Park). 38,472 v Preston NE, FA Cup 4th rd, 30 January 1960 (Eastville). 11,433 v Sunderland, Worthington Cup 3rd rd, 31 October 2000 (Memorial Stadium). **Capacity:** 11,626.
Manager: Paul Trollope.
Secretary: Rod Wesson.
Most League Goals: 92, Division 3 (S), 1952–53.
Highest League Scorer in Season: Geoff Bradford, 33, Division 3 (S), 1952–53.
Most League Goals in Total Aggregate: Geoff Bradford, 242, 1949–64.
Most Capped Player: Vitalijs Astafjevs, 31 (133), Latvia.
Most League Appearances: Stuart Taylor, 546, 1966–80.
Honours – Football League: Division 3 (S) Champions – 1952–53. Division 3 Champions – 1989–90.
Colours: Blue and white quartered shirts, blue shorts, white stockings.

BURNLEY — FL CHAMPIONSHIP

Akinbiyi Ade (F)	6 1	13 08	Hackney	10 10 74	Sheffield U
Caldwell Steve (D)	5 11	11 05	Stirling	12 9 80	Sunderland
Duff Michael (D)	6 3	12 10	Belfast	11 1 78	Cheltenham T
Elliott Wade (M)	5 10	10 03	Southampton	14 12 78	Bournemouth
Foster Stephen (D)	5 11	12 05	Warrington	18 9 80	Crewe Alex
Gray Andy (F)	6 1	13 00	Harrogate	15 11 77	Sunderland
Gudjohnsson Joey (M)	5 9	12 04	Akranes	25 5 80	AZ
Harley Jon (D)	5 8	10 03	Maidstone	26 9 79	Sheffield U
Jensen Brian (G)	6 4	16 09	Copenhagen	8 6 75	WBA
Jones Steve (F)	5 10	10 05	Derry	25 10 76	Crewe Alex
Lafferty Kyle (F)	6 4	11 02	Belfast	21 7 87	Scholar
Mahon Alan (M)	5 8	12 03	Dublin	4 4 78	Wigan Ath
McCann Chris (M)	6 1	11 11	Dublin	21 7 87	Scholar
O'Connor Gareth (M)	5 10	11 00	Dublin	10 11 78	Bournemouth
O'Connor James (M)	5 8	11 06	Dublin	1 9 79	WBA
Spicer John (M)	5 11	11 07	Romford	13 9 83	Bournemouth
Thomas Wayne (D)	6 2	14 12	Gloucester	17 5 79	Stoke C

League Appearances: Akinbiyi, A. 15(5); Branch, G. (5); Caldwell, S. 16(1); Coughlan, G. 1(1); Coyne, D. 12; Djemba-Djemba, E. 13(2); Duff, M. 42(2);

Elliott, W. 40(2); Foster, S. 7(10); Gray, A. 34(1); Gudjonsson, J. 9(2); Harley, J. 44(1); Hyde, M. 19(4); Jensen, B. 30(1); Jones, S. 37(4); Lafferty, K. 15(20); Mahon, A. 10(15); McCann, C. 24(14); McGreal, J. 21(1); McVeigh, P. 6(2); Noel-Williams, G. 19(4); O'Connor, G. (8); O'Connor, J. 39(4); Pollitt, M. 4; Sinclair, F. 16(3); Spicer, J. (11); Thomas, M. 33.
Goals – League (52): Gray 14 (1 pen), Jones 5, McCann 5, Noel-Williams 5, Elliott 4, Lafferty 4, McVeigh 3, O'Connor J 3, Akinbiyi 2, Duff 2, Mahon 2, Harley 1, Spicer 1, own goal 1.
Carling Cup (0).
FA Cup (2): Akinbiyi 1, O'Connor G 1.
Ground: Turf Moor, Harry Potts Way, Burnley, Lancashire BB10 4BX. Telephone (0870) 443 1882.
Record Attendance: 54,775 v Huddersfield T, FA Cup 3rd rd, 23 February 1924.
Capacity: 22,619.
Manager: Steve Cotterill.
Secretary: Cathy Pickup.
Most League Goals: 102, Division 1, 1960–61.
Highest League Scorer in Season: George Beel, 35, Division 1, 1927–28.
Most League Goals in Total Aggregate: George Beel, 178, 1923–32.
Most Capped Player: Jimmy McIlroy, 51 (55), Northern Ireland.
Most League Appearances: Jerry Dawson, 522, 1907–28.
Honours – Football League: Division 1 Champions – 1920–21, 1959–60. Division 2 Champions – 1897–98, 1972–73. Division 3 Champions – 1981–82. Division 4 Champions – 1991–92. **FA Cup:** Winners – 1913–14. **Anglo-Scottish Cup:** Winners – 1978–79.
Colours: Claret shirts, white shorts, white stockings.

BURY — FL CHAMPIONSHIP 2

Adams Nicky (F)	5 10	11 00	Bolton	16 10 86	Scholar
Baker Richie (M)	5 7	11 10	Burnley	29 12 87	Preston NE
Barry-Murphy Brian (M)	6 1	13 01	Cork	27 7 78	Sheffield W
Bishop Andy (F)	6 0	11 00	Stone	19 10 82	York C
Buchanan David (M)	5 8	10 08	Rochdale	6 5 86	Scholar
Challinor Dave (D)	6 1	12 06	Chester	2 10 75	Stockport Co
Grundy Aaron (G)	6 1	12 07	Bolton	21 1 88	Scholar
Hurst Glynn (F)	5 10	11 05	Barnsley	17 1 76	Shrewsbury T
Parrish Andy (D)	6 0	11 00	Bolton	22 6 88	
Pugh Marc (M)	5 11	11 04	Burnley	2 4 87	Burnley
Scott Paul (D)	5 11	12 00	Wakefield	5 11 79	Huddersfield T
Warrington Andy (G)	6 3	12 13	Sheffield	10 6 76	Doncaster R

League Appearances: Adams, N. 11(8); Baker, R. 34(5); Barry-Murphy, B. 8(6); Bedeau, A. 2(2); Bishop, A. 43; Blinkhorn, M. 1(9); Brass, C. 20(2); Buchanan, D. 36(5); Challinor, D. 43; Edge, L. 1; Fettis, A. 9; Fitzgerald, J. 20(3); Flitcroft, D. 3(1); Goodfellow, M. 2(2); Grundy, A. (1); Hurst, G. 32(3); Jones, L. 2; Kempson, D. 12; Kennedy, J. 12; Kennedy, T. 35(2); Mattis, D. 22; Mocquet, W. 9; Parrish, A. 6(3); Pittman, J. 5(4); Pugh, M. 27(8); Rouse, D. (2); Schmeichel, K. 14; Scott, P. 45(1); Speight, J. (13); Stephens, D. 2(1); Taylor, D. 1(3); Turnbull, S. 4(1); Warrington, A. 20; Woodthorpe, C. 12(4); Worrall, D. (1); Wroe, N. 4(1); Youngs, T. 9(10).
Goals – League (46): Bishop 15 (6 pens), Hurst 11, Baker 5 (1 pen), Youngs 4, Fitzgerald 3, Pugh 3, Scott 2, Adams 1, Mattis 1, Pittman 1.
Carling Cup (2): Bishop 1, Fitzgerald 1.
FA Cup (11): Bishop 5, Mattis 3, Baker 1, Hurst 1, Pugh 1.
J Paint Trophy (0).
Ground: Gigg Lane, Bury BL9 9HR. Telephone (0161) 764 4881.

Record Attendance: 35,000 v Bolton W, FA Cup 3rd rd, 9 January 1960. **Capacity:** 11,669.
Manager: Chris Casper.
Secretary: Mrs Jill Neville.
Most League Goals: 108, Division 3, 1960–61.
Highest League Scorer in Season: Craig Madden, 35, Division 4, 1981–82.
Most League Goals in Total Aggregate: Craig Madden, 129, 1978–86.
Most Capped Player: Bill Gorman, 11 (13), Repubiic of Ireland and (4), Northern Ireland.
Most League Appearances: Norman Bullock, 506, 1920–35.
Honours – Football League: Division 2 Champions – 1894–95, 1996–97. Division 3 Champions – 1960–61. **FA Cup:** Winners – 1900, 1903.
Colours: Royal blue shirts, white shorts.

CARDIFF CITY — FL CHAMPIONSHIP

Barker Chris (D)	6 2	13 08	Sheffield	2 3 80	Barnsley
Blake Darcy (M)	5 10	12 05	New Tredegar	13 12 88	Scholar
Byrne Jason (F)	5 11	11 11	Dublin	23 2 79	Shelbourne
Chopra Michael (F)	5 8	11 02	Newcastle	23 12 83	Newcastle U
Cooper Kevin (M)	5 8	10 04	Derby	8 2 75	Wolverhampton W
Flood Willo (M)	5 7	10 05	Dublin	10 4 85	Manchester C
Forde David (G)	6 2	13 06	Galway	20 12 79	Derry C
Green Matthew (F)	5 11	11 06	Bath	2 1 87	Newport Co
Gunter Chris (D)	5 11	11 02	Newport	21 7 89	Scholar
Jacobson Joe (D)	5 11	12 06	Cardiff	17 11 86	Scholar
Johnson Roger (D)	6 3	12 02	Ashford	24 4 83	Wycombe W
Ledley Joe (M)	6 0	11 07	Cardiff	23 1 87	Scholar
Loovens Glenn (D)	6 2	14 00	Rotterdam	22 10 83	Feyenoord
McNaughton Kevin (D)	5 10	10 06	Dundee	28 8 82	Aberdeen
McPhail Steve (M)	5 10	13 03	Westminster	9 12 79	Barnsley
Parry Paul (M)	5 11	12 12	Newport	19 8 80	Hereford U
Purse Darren (D)	6 2	12 08	Stepney	14 2 77	WBA
Scimeca Riccardo (D)	6 1	12 09	Leamington Spa	13 6 75	WBA
Thompson Steven (F)	6 2	12 05	Paisley	14 10 78	Rangers
Whittingham Peter (M)	5 10	11 06	Nuneaton	8 9 84	Aston Villa

League Appearances: Alexander, N. 39; Blake, D. 3(7); Byrne, J. 2(8); Campbell, K. 4(15); Chambers, J. 7; Chopra, M. 42; Cooper, K. (4); Feeney, W. 4(2); Ferretti, A. (1); Flood, W. 5(20); Forde, D. 7; Gilbert, K. 21(3); Glombard, L. 1(5); Green, M. (6); Gunter, C. 9(6); Johnson, R. 26(6); Kamara, M. 3(12); Ledley, J. 46; Loovens, G. 30; McNaughton, K. 39(3); McPhail, S. 43; Parry, P. 41(1); Purse, D. 31; Ramsey, A. (1); Redan, I. (2); Scimeca, R. 35; Thompson, S. 39(4); Walton, S. 5(1); Whittingham, P. 18(1); Wright, A. 6(1).
Goals – League (57): Chopra 22 (2 pens), Parry 6, Thompson 6, Scimeca 5, Purse 4 (2 pens), Whittingham 4, Johnson 2, Ledley 2, Byrne 1, Flood 1, Kamara 1, Loovens 1, own goals 2.
Carling Cup (0).
FA Cup (0).
Ground: Ninian Park, Cardiff CF11 8SX. Telephone (029) 2022 1001.
Record Attendance: 62,634, Wales v England, 17 October 1959. **Capacity:** 20,340.
Manager: Dave Jones.
Secretary: Jason Turner.
Most League Goals: 95, Division 3, 2000–01.
Highest League Scorer in Season: Robert Earnshaw, 31, Division 2, 2002–03.
Most League Goals in Total Aggregate: Len Davies, 128, 1920–31.
Most Capped Player: Alf Sherwood, 39 (41), Wales.

Most League Appearances: Phil Dwyer, 471, 1972–85.
Honours – Football League: Division 3 (S) Champions – 1946–47; Division 3 Champions – 1992–93. **FA Cup:** Winners – 1926–27 (only occasion the Cup has been won by a club outside England). **Welsh Cup:** Winners – 22 times. **Charity Shield:** Winners 1927.
Colours: Royal blue shirts, white shorts, royal blue stockings.

CARLISLE UNITED — FL CHAMPIONSHIP 1

Aranalde Zigor (D)	6 1	13 03	Ibarra	28 2 73	Sheffield W
Arnison Paul (D)	5 10	10 12	Hartlepool	18 9 77	Hartlepool U
Bradley Adam (G)	6 0	12 06	Carlisle	25 8 88	Scholar
Gall Kevin (F)	5 9	10 08	Merthyr	4 2 82	Yeovil T
Hackney Simon (M)	5 8	9 13	Stockport	5 2 84	Woodley Sports
Joyce Luke (M)	5 11	12 03	Bolton	9 7 87	Wigan Ath
Kirkup Dan (D)	6 3	12 07	Hexham	19 5 88	Scholar
Livesey Danny (D)	6 3	12 10	Salford	31 12 84	Bolton W
Lumsdon Chris (M)	5 11	10 06	Newcastle	15 12 79	Barnsley
McDermott Neale (M)	5 9	10 11	Newcastle	8 3 85	Fulham
Raven David (D)	6 0	11 04	Birkenhead	10 3 85	Liverpool
Smith Jeff (M)	5 11	11 10	Middlesbrough	28 6 80	Port Vale
Thirlwell Paul (M)	5 11	11 04	Springwell Village	13 2 79	Derby Co
Westwood Keiren (G)	6 1	13 10	Manchester	23 10 84	Manchester C

League Appearances: Aranalde, Z. 43; Arnison, P. 6(5); Beckford, J. 4; Billy, C. 16(4); Bridges, M. 5; Gall, K. 44(1); Garner, J. 17(1); Graham, D. 11; Grand, S. 1(3); Gray, K. 27(4); Hackney, S. 14(4); Harper, K. 7; Hawley, K. 30(2); Hindmarch, S. (7); Holmes, D. 8(28); Joyce, L. 7(9); Krause, J. 3; Livesey, D. 29(2); Lumsdon, C. 36(3); McDermott, N. 6(9); Murphy, P. 40; Murray, G. (1); Murray, P. 14; Raven, D. 36; Smith, Jeff 17; Smith, Johann 9(5); Thirlwell, P. 29(1); Vipond, S. 1(3); Westwood, K. 46.
Goals – League (54): Hawley 12 (1 pen), Gall 8, Graham 7 (2 pens), Garner 5, Gray 3, Holmes 3, McDermott 3, Hackney 2, Lumsdon 2, Murphy 2, Aranalde 1, Beckford 1, Joyce 1, Livesey 1, Murray P 1, Jeff Smith 1, Johann Smith 1.
Carling Cup (1): Holmes 1.
FA Cup (1): Gray 1.
J Paint Trophy (1): Holmes 1.
Ground: Brunton Park, Warwick Road, Carlisle CA1 1LL. Telephone (01228) 526 237.
Record Attendance: 27,500 v Birmingham C, FA Cup 3rd rd, 5 January 1957 and v Middlesbrough, FA Cup 5th rd, 7 February 1970. **Capacity:** 16,982.
Manager: Neil McDonald.
Secretary: Mrs Sarah McKnight.
Most League Goals: 113, Division 4, 1963–64.
Highest League Scorer in Season: Jimmy McConnell, 42, Division 3 (N), 1928–29.
Most League Goals in Total Aggregate: Jimmy McConnell, 126, 1928–32.
Most Capped Player: Eric Welsh, 4, Northern Ireland.
Most League Appearances: Allan Ross, 466, 1963–79.
Honours – Football League: Division 3 Champions – 1964–65, 1994–95; Championship 2 Champions – 2005–06. **Auto Windscreen Shield:** Winners 1997.
Colours: Blue shirts, white shorts, blue stockings.

CHARLTON ATHLETIC — FL CHAMPIONSHIP

Ambrose Darren (M)	6 0	11 00	Harlow	29 2 84	Newcastle U
Bent Darren (F)	5 11	12 07	Wandsworth	6 2 84	Ipswich T

Bent Marcus (F)	6 2	13 03	Hammersmith	19 5 78	Everton
Bougherra Madjid (D)	6 2	14 02	Dijon	7 10 82	Sheffield W
Diawara Soulemane (D)	6 1	13 12	Gabou	24 12 78	Sochaux
Dickson Christopher (F)			East Dulwich	28 12 84	Dulwich H
Elliot Rob (G)	6 3	14 10	Chatham	30 4 86	Scholar
Faye Amady (M)	6 0	12 03	Dakar	12 3 77	Newcastle U
Fortune Jon (D)	6 2	12 12	Islington	23 8 80	Trainee
Gibbs Cory (D)	6 3	12 12	Fort Lauderdale	14 1 80	Feyenoord
Holland Matt (M)	5 10	12 03	Bury	11 4 74	Ipswich T
Hreidarsson Hermann (D)	6 3	12 12	Reykjavik	11 7 74	Ipswich T
Hughes Bryan (M)	5 10	11 08	Liverpool	19 6 76	Birmingham C
Randolph Darren (G)	6 2	14 00	Dublin	12 5 87	Scholar
Reid Andy (M)	5 7	12 08	Dublin	29 7 82	Tottenham H
Rommedahl Dennis (F)	5 9	11 08	Copenhagen	22 7 78	PSV Eindhoven
Sam Lloyd (F)	5 8	10 00	Leeds	27 9 84	Scholar
Sankofa Osei (D)	6 0	12 04	London	19 3 85	Scholar
Staunton Mark (D)	5 11	12 00	Glasgow	30 1 89	Celtic
Thatcher Ben (D)	5 11	12 07	Swindon	30 11 75	Manchester C
Thomas Jerome (M)	5 9	11 09	Brent	23 3 83	Arsenal
Varney Luke (F)	5 11	12 00	Leicester	28 9 82	Crewe Alex
Walker James (F)	5 10	11 10	Hackney	25 11 87	Scholar
Walton Simon (M)	6 1	13 05	Leeds	13 9 87	Leeds U
Youga Kelly (D)	5 11	12 06	Bangui	22 9 85	Lyon
Young Luke (D)	6 0	12 04	Harlow	19 7 79	Tottenham H

League Appearances: Ambrose, D. 21(5); Bent, D. 32; Bent, M. 17(13); Bougherra, M. 2(3); Carson, S. 36; Diawara, S. 18(5); El Karkouri, T. 36; Faye, A. 25(3); Fortune, J. 6(2); Hasselbaink, J. 11(14); Holland, M. 27(6); Hreidarsson, H. 30(1); Hughes, B. 15(9); Kishishev, R. 6(8); Lisbie, K. 1(7); Myhre, T. 1; Pouso, O. 1; Randolph, D. 1; Reid, A. 15(1); Rommedahl, D. 19(9); Sam, L. 3(4); Sankofa, O. 9; Song Billong, A. 12; Sorondo, G. (1); Thatcher, B. 10(1); Thomas, J. 16(4); Traore, D. 11; Young, L. 29; Zheng-Zhi, 8(4).
Goals – League (34): Bent D 13 (3 pens), Ambrose 3, El Karkouri 3, Thomas 3 (1 pen), Hasselbaink 2, Reid 2, Bent M 1, Faye 1, Holland 1, Hughes 1, Young 1, Zheng-Zhi 1, own goals 2.
Carling Cup (5): Bent D 2, Hasselbaink 2, Bent M 1.
FA Cup (0).
Ground: The Valley, Floyd Road, Charlton, London SE7 8BL. Telephone (020) 8333 4000.
Record Attendance: 75,031 v Aston Villa, FA Cup 5th rd, 12 February 1938 (at The Valley). **Capacity:** 27,113.
Manager: Alan Pardew.
Secretary: Chris Parkes.
Most League Goals: 107, Division 2, 1957–58.
Highest League Scorer in Season: Ralph Allen, 32, Division 3 (S), 1934–35.
Most League Goals in Total Aggregate: Stuart Leary, 153, 1953–62.
Most Capped Player: Jonatan Johansson, 41 (70), Finland.
Most League Appearances: Sam Bartram, 583, 1934–56.
Honours – Football League: Division 1 Champions – 1999–2000. Division 3 (S) Champions – 1928–29, 1934–35. **FA Cup:** Winners – 1947.
Colours: Red shirts, white shorts, red stockings.

CHELSEA — FA PREMIERSHIP

Ballack Michael (M)	6 2	13 05	Gorlitz	26 12 76	Bayern Munich
Bertrand Ryan (D)	5 10	11 00	Southwark	5 8 89	Scholar
Boulahrouz Khalid (D)	6 0	12 11	Maassluis	28 12 81	Hamburg

Bridge Wayne (D)	5 10	12 13	Southampton	5 8 80	Southampton
Cech Petr (G)	6 5	14 03	Plzen	20 5 82	Rennes
Cole Ashley (D)	5 8	10 08	Stepney	20 12 80	Arsenal
Cole Joe (M)	5 9	11 07	Islington	8 11 81	West Ham U
Cork Jack (D)	6 0	10 12	Carshalton	25 6 89	Scholar
Crespo Hernan (F)	6 0	12 13	Florida	5 7 75	Internazionale
Cudicini Carlo (G)	6 1	12 06	Milan	6 9 73	Castel di Sangro
Diarra Lassana (M)	5 8	11 02	Paris	10 3 85	Le Havre
Drogba Didier (F)	6 2	13 08	Abidjan	11 3 78	Marseille
Elmer Jonas (D)			Zurich	28 2 88	Scholar
Essien Michael (M)	5 10	13 06	Accra	3 12 82	Lyon
Fabio Ferreira (M)			Barreiro	3 5 89	Sporting Lisbon
Fernandes Ricardo (M)			Portugal	20 4 78	Scholar
Geremi (M)	5 9	13 05	Bafoussam	20 12 78	Real Madrid
Grant Anthony (M)	5 11	11 03	Lambeth	4 6 87	Scholar
Hilario Henrique (G)	6 2	13 08	Sao Pedro de Cova	21 10 75	Porto
Hutchinson Sam (D)	6 0	11 07	Slough	3 8 89	Scholar
Johnson Glen (D)	6 0	12 13	Greenwich	23 8 84	West Ham U
Kalou Salomon (F)	6 0	12 02	Oume	5 8 85	Feyenoord
Lampard Frank (M)	6 0	14 01	Romford	20 6 78	West Ham U
Ma Kalambay Yves (G)	6 5	14 10	Brussels	31 1 86	PSV Eindhoven
Makelele Claude (M)	5 7	10 08	Kinshasa	18 2 73	Real Madrid
Mancienne Michael (D)	6 0	11 09	Isleworth	8 1 88	Scholar
Mikel John Obi (M)	6 0	13 05	Jos	22 4 87	Lyn
Nuno Morais (D)	6 0	12 04	Penafiel	29 1 84	Penafiel
Paulo Ferreira (D)	6 0	11 13	Cascais	18 1 79	Porto
Pettigrew Adrian (D)	6 0	13 01	Hackney	12 11 86	Scholar
Ricardo Carvalho (D)	6 0	12 06	Amarante	18 5 78	Porto
Robben Arjen (M)	5 11	12 08	Groningen	23 1 84	PSV Eindhoven
Sahar Ben (F)	5 10	12 05	Holon	10 8 89	Hapoel Tel Aviv
Sarki Emmanuel (M)			Nigeria	26 12 87	
Shevchenko Andriy (F)	5 11	13 03	Yagotyn	29 9 76	AC Milan
Simmonds James (M)	5 10	11 03	Hammersmith	3 12 87	Scholar
Sinclair Scott (F)	5 10	10 00	Bath	26 3 89	Bristol R
Smith Jimmy (M)	6 0	10 03	Newham	7 1 87	Scholar
Terry John (D)	6 1	13 08	Barking	7 12 80	Trainee
Weihrauch Per (F)			Copenhagen	3 7 88	Ajax
Worley Harry (D)	6 3	13 00	Warrington	25 11 88	Scholar
Wright-Phillips Shaun (F)	5 5	10 01	Lewisham	25 10 81	Manchester C
Younghusband Phil (F)	5 10	10 08	Ashford	4 8 87	Scholar

League Appearances: Ballack, M. 23(3); Boulahrouz, K. 10(3); Bridge, W. 17(5); Cech, P. 20; Cole, A. 21(2); Cole, J. 3(10); Cudicini, C. 7(1); Diarra, L. 7(3); Drogba, D. 32(4); Essien, M. 33; Geremi, 15(4); Hilario, 11; Hutchinson, S. (1); Kalou, S. 19(14); Lampard, F. 36(1); Makelele, C. 26(3); Mikel, J. 10(12); Nuno Morais, (2); Paulo Ferreira, 18(6); Ricardo Carvalho, 31; Robben, A. 16(5); Sahar, B. (3); Shevchenko, A. 22(8); Sinclair, S. 1(1); Terry, J. 27(1); Wright-Phillips, S. 13(14).

Goals – League (64): Drogba 20, Lampard 11 (3 pens), Kalou 7, Ballack 5, Shevchenko 4, Ricardo Carvalho 3, Essien 2, Robben 2, Wright-Phillips 2, Geremi 1, Makelele 1, Terry 1, own goals 5.

Carling Cup (14): Drogba 4, Lampard 3, Shevchenko 3, Bridge 1, Cole J 1, Essien 1, Kalou 1.

FA Cup (21): Lampard 6 (1 pen), Drogba 3, Shevchenko 3, Wright-Phillips 3, Mikel 2, Ballack 1, Essien 1, Kalou 1, Ricardo Carvalho 1.

Champions League (17): Drogba 6, Shevchenko 3, Ballack 2 (1 pen), Essien 2, Cole J 1, Lampard 1, Robben 1, Wright-Phillips 1.

Community Shield (1): Shevchenko 1.
Ground: Stamford Bridge, London SW6 1HS. Telephone (0870) 300 1212 (UK), 0044 207 386 9373 (INTL).
Record Attendance: 82,905 v Arsenal, Division 1, 12 October 1935.
Capacity: 42,055.
Manager: José Mourinho.
Secretary: David Barnard.
Most League Goals: 98, Division 1, 1960–61.
Highest League Scorer in Season: Jimmy Greaves, 41, 1960–61.
Most League Goals in Total Aggregate: Bobby Tambling, 164, 1958–70.
Most Capped Player: Marcel Desailly, 67 (116), France.
Most League Appearances: Ron Harris, 655, 1962–80.
Honours – FA Premier League: Champions – 2004–05, 2005–06. **Football League:** Division 1 Champions – 1954–55. Division 2 Champions – 1983–84, 1988–89. **FA Cup:** Winners – 1970, 1997, 2000, 2007. **Football League Cup:** Winners – 1964–65, 1997–98, 2004–05, 2006–07. **Full Members' Cup:** Winners – 1985–86. **Zenith Data Systems Cup:** Winners – 1989–90. **European Cup-Winners' Cup:** Winners – 1970–71, 1997–98. **Super Cup:** Winners – 1999.
Colours: Blue.

CHELTENHAM TOWN — FL CHAMPIONSHIP 1

Armstrong Craig (M)	5 11	12 09	South Shields	23 5 75	Bradford C
Bird David (M)	5 9	12 00	Gloucester	26 12 84	Cinderford T
Brown Scott (G)	6 2	13 01	Wolverhampton	26 4 85	Bristol C
Brown Scott (M)	5 9	10 03	Runcorn	8 5 85	Bristol C
Caines Gavin (D)	6 1	12 00	Birmingham	20 9 83	Scholar
Connolly Adam (M)	5 9	12 04	Manchester	10 4 86	Scholar
Connor Paul (F)	6 2	11 08	Bishop Auckland	12 1 79	Leyton Orient
Duff Shane (D)	6 1	12 10	Wroughton	2 4 82	Juniors
Finnigan John (M)	5 8	10 09	Wakefield	29 3 76	Lincoln C
Foley Sam (M)	6 0	10 08	Upton-on-Severn	17 10 86	Scholar
Gallinagh Andy (D)	5 8	11 08	Sutton Coldfield	16 3 85	Stratford T
Gill Jeremy (D)	5 11	12 00	Clevedon	8 9 70	Northampton T
Gillespie Steven (F)	5 9	11 02	Liverpool	4 6 84	Bristol C
Higgs Shane (G)	6 3	14 06	Oxford	13 5 77	Bristol R
Melligan John (M)	5 9	11 02	Dublin	11 2 82	Wolverhampton W
Odejayi Kayode (F)	6 2	12 02	Ibadon	21 2 82	Bristol C
Puddy Will (G)	5 10	11 07	Salisbury	4 10 87	Scholar
Spencer Damien (F)	6 1	14 00	Ascot	19 9 81	Bristol C
Townsend Michael (D)	6 1	13 12	Walsall	17 5 86	Wolverhampton W
Vincent Ashley (F)	5 10	11 08	Oldbury	26 5 85	Wolverhampton W
Wylde Michael (M)	6 2	13 02	Birmingham	6 1 87	Scholar
Yao Sosthene (M)	5 4	11 09	Ivory Coast	7 8 87	West Ham U

League Appearances: Armstrong, C. 42; Bell, M. 5(2); Bird, D. 26(5); Brown, S. 10(1); Brown, S. 4; Caines, G. 26(13); Connolly, A. 6(2); Connor, P. 9(6); Duff, S. 34; Elvins, R. (5); Finnigan, J. 40; Gallinagh, A. (1); Gill, J. 38(1); Gillespie, S. 13(10); Guinan, S. 17(2); Higgs, S. 36; Lowe, K. 14(2); McCann, G. 15; Melligan, J. 38(5); O'Leary, K. 5; Odejayi, K. 38(7); Reid, C. (6); Rosa, D. 3(1); Smith, A. 2; Spencer, D. 23(4); Townsend, M. 27(3); Victory, J. 7(3); Vincent, A. (5); Wilson, B. 22(3); Wylde, M. 4(3); Yao, S. 2(13).
Goals – League (49): Odejayi 13, Finnigan 7 (3 pens), Melligan 7, Gillespie 5, McCann 5 (1 pen), Spencer 3, Bird 2, Wilson 2, Connor 1, Lowe 1, O'Leary 1, Townsend 1, Victory 1.
Carling Cup (3): Guinan 1, Odejayi 1, Wilson 1.

FA Cup (0).
J Paint Trophy (5): McCann 2 (1 pen), Finnigan 1, Mulligan 1, Odejayi 1.
Ground: Whaddon Road, Cheltenham, Gloucester GL52 5NA. Telephone (01242) 573 558.
Record Attendance: at Whaddon Road: 8,326 v Reading, FA Cup 1st rd, 17 November 1956; at Cheltenham Athletic Ground: 10,389 v Blackpool, FA Cup 3rd rd, 13 January 1934.
Capacity: 7,013.
Manager: John Ward.
Secretary: Paul Godfrey.
Most League Goals: 66, Division 3, 2001–02.
Highest League Scorer in Season: Julian Alsop, 20, Division 3, 2001–02.
Most League Goals in Total Aggregate: Martin Devaney, 38, 1999–2005.
Most Capped Player: Grant McCann, 7 (15), Northern Ireland.
Most League Appearances: Jamie Victory, 258, 1999–.
Honours – Football Conference: Champions – 1998–99. **FA Trophy:** Winners – 1997–98.
Colours: Red and white striped shirts, white shorts, red stockings.

CHESTER CITY — FL CHAMPIONSHIP 2

Bennett Dean (M)	5 11	11 00	Wolverhampton	13 12 77	Wrexham
Bolland Phil (D)	6 4	13 03	Liverpool	26 8 76	Peterborough U
Broughton Drewe (F)	6 3	12 01	Hitchin	25 10 78	Rushden & D
Cronin Glenn (M)	5 8	10 08	Dublin	14 9 81	Exeter C
Danby John (G)	6 2	14 06	Stoke	20 9 83	Kidderminster H
Hand Jamie (M)	6 0	11 08	Uxbridge	7 2 84	Fisher Ath
Hessey Sean (D)	6 1	12 09	Liverpool	19 9 78	Blackpool
Holroyd Chris (F)	5 11	12 03	Macclesfield	24 10 86	Crewe Alex
Kelly Shaun (D)	6 1	11 04	Southampton	4 7 86	Scholar
Linwood Paul (D)	6 2	13 03	Birkenhead	24 10 83	Tranmere R
Marples Simon (D)	5 10	11 00	Sheffield	30 7 75	Doncaster R
Marsh-Evans Robert (D)	6 3	12 08	Abergele	13 10 86	Ruthin T
Roberts Kevin (D)	6 2	14 00	Chester	10 3 87	
Rutherford Paul (M)	5 9	11 07	Moreton	10 7 87	Greenleas
Sandwith Kevin (D)	5 11	12 05	Workington	30 4 78	Macclesfield T
Steele Lee (F)	5 8	12 05	Liverpool	7 12 73	Leyton Orient
Vaughan James (D)	5 10	12 09	Liverpool	6 12 86	Tranmere R
Westwood Ashley (D)	6 0	12 09	Bridgnorth	31 8 76	Northampton T
Wilson Laurence (M)	5 10	10 09	Huyton	10 10 86	Everton
Yeo Simon (F)	5 10	11 08	Stockport	20 10 73	Peterborough U

League Appearances: Allen, G. 2(1); Artell, D. 42(1); Bennett, D. 27(5); Blundell, G. 21(6); Bolland, P. 23(3); Broughton, D. 9(5); Brownlie, R. 3(1); Cronin, G. 1(3); Danby, J. 46; Hand, J. 43; Hessey, S. 22(4); Holroyd, C. 7(15); Kearney, A. 4(2); Kelly, S. (2); Linwood, P. 33(4); Marples, S. 24(6); Martinez, R. 31; Maylett, B. 3(2); McSporran, J. (1); Meechan, A. 2(6); Ravenhill, R. 1(2); Rutherford, P. 6(3); Sandwith, K. 27(5); Semple, R. (3); Steele, L. 11(9); Vaughan, J. 5(1); Vaughan, S. 20; Walters, J. 24(2); Westwood, A. 21; Wilson, L. 34(7); Yeo, S. 14(1).
Goals – League (40): Walters 9, Blundell 6 (2 pens), Yeo 4 (1 pen), Martinez 3, Westwood 3, Broughton 2, Hand 2, Sandwith 2, Artell 1, Bennett 1, Bolland 1, Linwood 1, Maylett 1, Steele 1, Wilson 1, own goals 2.
Carling Cup (0).
FA Cup (7): Steele 2, Wilson 2, Blundell 1, Hand 1, Walters 1.
J Paint Trophy (7): Blundell 2, Wilson 2, Bolland 1, Hand 1, Linwood 1.
Ground: Saunders Honda Stadium, Bumpers Lane, Chester CH1 4LT. Telephone (01244) 371 376.

Record Attendance: 20,500 v Chelsea, FA Cup 3rd rd (replay), 16 January 1952 (at Sealand Rd).
Capacity: 6,012.
Manager: Bobby Williamson.
Secretary: Tony Allan.
Most League Goals: 119, Division 4, 1964–65.
Highest League Scorer in Season: Dick Yates, 36, Division 3 (N), 1946–47.
Most League Goals in Total Aggregate: Stuart Rimmer, 135, 1985–88, 1991–98.
Most Capped Player: Angus Eve, 35 (117), Trinidad & Tobago.
Most League Appearances: Ray Gill, 406, 1951–62.
Honours – Conference: Champions – 2003–04. **Welsh Cup:** Winners – 1908, 1933, 1947. **Debenhams Cup:** Winners 1977.
Colours: Blue and white striped shirts, blue shorts, blue stockings.

CHESTERFIELD — FL CHAMPIONSHIP 2

Allison Wayne (F)	6 0	15 00	Huddersfield	16 10 68	Sheffield U
Allott Mark (M)	6 0	11 10	Manchester	3 10 77	Oldham Ath
Davies Gareth (M)	6 0	12 00	Chesterfield	4 2 83	Trainee
Downes Aaron (D)	6 3	13 00	Mudgee	15 5 85	Frickley C
Hall Paul (M)	5 8	12 00	Manchester	3 7 72	Tranmere R
Jackson Jamie (F)	5 6	10 04	Sheffield	1 11 86	Scholar
Jordan Michael (G)	6 2	13 02	Cheshunt	7 4 86	Arsenal
Kovacs Janos (D)	6 4	14 10	Budapest	11 9 85	MTK
Larkin Colin (F)	5 9	11 07	Dundalk	27 4 82	Mansfield T
Lowry Jamie (D)	6 0	12 04	Newquay	18 3 87	Scholar
Niven Derek (M)	6 0	12 02	Falkirk	12 12 83	Bolton W
O'Hare Alan (D)	6 2	12 08	Drogheda	31 7 82	Bolton W
Picken Phil (D)	5 9	10 08	Droylsden	12 11 85	Manchester U
Roche Barry (G)	6 5	14 08	Dublin	6 4 82	Nottingham F
Shaw Paul (F)	5 11	12 04	Burnham	4 9 73	Rotherham U
Smith Adam (M)	5 11	12 00	Huddersfield	20 2 85	Scholar
Ward Jamie (F)	5 6	9 04	Birmingham	12 5 86	Torquay U

League Appearances: Allison, W. 13(23); Allott, M. 39; Bailey, A. 25(5); Boertien, P. 4; Critchell, K. 6(4); Daniels, C. 2; Davies, G. 6(8); Downes, A. 45; Folan, C. 19(4); Grimaldi, S. 8; Hall, P. 40(6); Hazell, R. 39; Holmes, P. 10; Hughes, M. 2; Hurst, K. 25; Jackson, J. 1(13); Jordan, M. 6; Kovacs, J. 5(2); Larkin, C. 27(12); Lowry, J. 6(2); Meredith, J. 1; Nicholson, S. (2); Niven, D. 45; O'Hare, A. 16(1); Picken, P. 38(1); Rizzo, N. 2(2); Roche, B. 40; Shaw, P. 23(7); Smith, A. 5(8); Ward, J. 8(1).
Goals – League (45): Folan 8, Hall 5 (1 pen), Allison 4, Larkin 4, Shaw 4, Downes 3, Hurst 3, Niven 3, Ward 3, Hazell 2, O'Hare 2, Holmes 1, Hughes 1, Picken 1, own goal 1.
Carling Cup (7): Folan 3, Larkin 2, Allison 1, Niven 1.
FA Cup (0).
J Paint Trophy (7): Downes 2, Folan 1, Hall 1, Niven 1, Shaw 1, Smith 1.
Ground: The Recreation Ground, Chesterfield S40 4SX. Telephone (01246) 209 765.
Record Attendance: 30,968 v Newcastle U, Division 2, 7 April 1939. **Capacity:** 8,502.
Manager: Lee Richardson.
Secretary: Alan Walters.
Most League Goals: 102, Division 3 (N), 1930–31.
Highest League Scorer in Season: Jimmy Cookson, 44, Division 3 (N), 1925–26.
Most League Goals in Total Aggregate: Ernie Moss, 161, 1969–76, 1979–81 and 1984–86.

Most Capped Player: Walter McMillen, 4 (7), Northern Ireland; Mark Williams, 4 (30), Northern Ireland.
Most League Appearances: Dave Blakey, 613, 1948–67.
Honours – Football League: Division 3 (N) Champions – 1930–31, 1935–36. Division 4 Champions – 1969–70, 1984–85. **Anglo-Scottish Cup:** Winners – 1980–81.
Colours: Royal blue shirts, white shorts, royal blue stockings.

COLCHESTER UNITED FL CHAMPIONSHIP

Baldwin Pat (D)	6 3	12 07	City of London	12 11 82	Chelsea
Brown Wayne (D)	6 0	12 06	Barking	20 8 77	Watford
Cousins Mark (G)	6 1	11 03	Chelmsford	9 1 87	Scholar
Cureton Jamie (F)	5 7	10 10	Bristol	28 8 75	Swindon T
Davison Aidan (G)	6 1	13 12	Sedgefield	11 5 68	Grimsby T
Duguid Karl (M)	5 11	11 06	Hitchin	21 3 78	Trainee
Elokobi George (D)	5 10	13 02	Cameroon	31 1 86	Dulwich Hamlet
Garcia Richard (F)	5 11	12 01	Perth	4 9 81	West Ham U
Gerken Dean (G)	6 1	12 08	Rochford	22 5 85	Scholar
Guy Jamie (M)	6 1	13 00	Barking	1 8 87	Scholar
Iwelumo Chris (F)	6 3	15 03	Coatbridge	1 8 78	Aachen
Izzet Kem (M)	5 7	10 05	Mile End	29 9 80	Charlton Ath
Jackson Johnnie (M)	6 0	12 08	Camden	15 8 82	Tottenham H
King Robbie (M)	5 11	12 05	Chelmsford	1 10 86	Scholar
McLeod Kevin (F)	5 11	12 13	Liverpool	12 9 80	Swansea C
Richards Garry (D)	6 3	13 00	Romford	11 6 86	Scholar
Watson Kevin (M)	6 0	12 06	Hackney	3 1 74	Reading
White John (M)	5 10	12 01	Maldon	26 7 86	Scholar

League Appearances: Baldwin, P. 35(3); Barker, C. 38; Brown, W. 46; Cureton, J. 44; Davison, A. 19; Duguid, K. 42(1); Elokobi, G. 8(2); Ephraim, H. 5(16); Garcia, R. 33(3); Gerken, D. 27; Guy, J. 1(31); Halford, G. 28; Iwelumo, C. 41(5); Izzet, K. 45; Jackson, J. 24(8); Jones, R. (6); McLeod, K. 13(11); Mills, M. 8(1); Richards, G. 3(2); Watson, K. 38(2); White, J. 8(8).
Goals – League (70): Cureton 23 (2 pens), Iwelumo 18 (7 pens), Garcia 7, Duguid 5, Guy 3, Halford 3, McLeod 3, Jackson 2, Baldwin 1, Brown 1, Ephraim 1, Izzet 1, Richards 1, Watson 1.
Carling Cup (0).
FA Cup (1): Cureton 1.
Ground: Layer Road Ground, Colchester CO2 7JJ. Telephone (0871) 226 2161.
Record Attendance: 19,072 v Reading, FA Cup 1st rd, 27 November, 1948. **Capacity:** 6,300.
Manager: Geraint Williams.
Secretary: Miss Caroline Pugh.
Most League Goals: 104, Division 4, 1961–62.
Highest League Scorer in Season: Bobby Hunt, 38, Division 4, 1961–62.
Most League Goals in Total Aggregate: Martyn King, 130, 1956–64.
Most Capped Player: None.
Most League Appearances: Micky Cook, 613, 1969–84.
Honours – GM Vauxhall Conference: Winners – 1991–92. **FA Trophy:** Winners: 1991–92.
Colours: Blue and white striped shirts, royal blue shorts, white with blue hoop stockings.

COVENTRY CITY — FL CHAMPIONSHIP

Adebola Dele (F)	6 3	15 00	Lagos	23 6 75	Crystal Palace
Andrews Wayne (F)	5 10	11 06	Paddington	25 11 77	Crystal Palace
Birchall Chris (M)	5 7	13 05	Stafford	5 5 84	Port Vale
Davis Liam (M)	5 9	11 07	Wandsworth	23 11 86	Scholar
Doyle Micky (M)	5 8	11 00	Dublin	8 7 81	Celtic
Giddings Stuart (M)	6 0	11 08	Coventry	27 3 86	Scholar
Gooding Andy (M)	5 7	10 05	Coventry	30 4 88	Scholar
Hall Marcus (D)	6 1	12 02	Coventry	24 3 76	Stoke C
Hawkins Colin (D)	6 1	12 06	Galway	17 8 77	Shelbourne
Hughes Stephen (M)	5 9	12 12	Wokingham	18 9 76	Charlton Ath
Kyle Kevin (F)	6 3	12 00	Stranraer	7 6 81	Sunderland
Marshall Andy (G)	6 3	14 08	Bury St Edmunds	14 4 75	Millwall
McKenzie Leon (F)	5 11	12 11	Croydon	17 5 78	Norwich C
McNamee David (D)	5 11	11 02	Glasgow	10 10 80	Livingston
Mifsud Michael (F)	5 6	9 11	Pieta	17 4 81	Lillestrom
Osbourne Isaac (M)	5 9	11 11	Birmingham	22 6 86	Scholar
Page Robert (D)	6 0	13 10	Llwynpia	3 9 74	Cardiff C
Tabb Jay (M)	5 7	10 00	Tooting	21 2 84	Brentford
Thornton Kevin (M)	5 7	11 00	Drogheda	9 7 86	Scholar
Turner Ben (D)	6 4	14 04	Birmingham	21 1 88	Scholar
Ward Elliot (D)	6 2	13 00	Harrow	19 1 85	West Ham U

League Appearances: Adebola, D. 28(12); Andrews, W. (3); Birchall, C. 17(11); Bischoff, M. 2(1); Cameron, C. 16(8); Clarke, C. 12; Currie, D. 6(2); Davis, L. 1(2); Doyle, M. 40; Duffy, R. 13; El Idrissi, F. (1); Fadiga, K. 1(5); Giddings, S. (1); Hall, M. 38(2); Hawkins, C. 13; Heath, M. 7; Hildreth, L. (1); Hughes, S. 36(1); Hutchison, D. 3(11); John, S. 19(4); Kyle, K. 18(13); Marshall, A. 41; McKenzie, L. 23(8); McNamee, D. 16; McSheffrey, G. 3; Mifsud, M. 12(7); Osbourne, I. 16(3); Page, R. 28(1); Steele, L. 5; Tabb, J. 22(9); Thornton, K. 5(6); Turner, B. 1; Virgo, A. 10(5); Ward, E. 39; Whing, A. 15(1).
Goals – League (47): Adebola 8, McKenzie 7, John 5, Mifsud 4, Doyle 3 (1 pen), Kyle 3, Tabb 3, Ward 3, Birchall 2, Cameron 2 (2 pens), Andrews 1, Hughes 1, McSheffrey 1, Thornton 1, Virgo 1, own goals 2.
Carling Cup (1): Adebola 1.
FA Cup (3): Cameron 1, John 1, McKenzie 1.
Ground: Ricoh Arena, Phoenix Way, Foleshill, Coventry CV6 6GE. Telephone (0870) 421 1987.
Record Attendance: 51,455 v Wolverhampton W, Division 2, 29 April 1967 (at Highfield Road). **Capacity:** 32,609.
Manager: Iain Dowie.
Secretary: Roger Brinsford.
Most League Goals: 108, Division 3 (S), 1931–32.
Highest League Scorer in Season: Clarrie Bourton, 49, Division 3 (S), 1931–32.
Most League Goals in Total Aggregate: Clarrie Bourton, 171, 1931–37.
Most Capped Player: Magnus Hedman, 44 (58), Sweden.
Most League Appearances: Steve Ogrizovic, 507, 1984–2000.
Honours – Football League: Division 2 Champions – 1966–67. Division 3 Champions – 1963–64. Division 3 (S) Champions 1935–36. **FA Cup:** Winners – 1986–87.
Colours: Sky blue.

CREWE ALEXANDRA — FL CHAMPIONSHIP 1

Bailey Matt (F)	6 4	11 06	Crewe	12 3 86	Northwich Vic
Baudet Julien (D)	6 2	13 07	Grenoble	13 1 79	Notts Co
Carrington Mark (M)	6 0	11 00	Warrington	4 5 87	Scholar
Cox Neil (D)	5 11	13 08	Scunthorpe	8 10 71	Cardiff C
Higdon Michael (M)	6 2	11 05	Liverpool	2 9 83	School
Jones Billy (D)	5 11	13 00	Shrewsbury	24 3 87	Scholar
Lowe Ryan (F)	5 10	12 08	Liverpool	18 9 78	Chester C
Maynard Nicky (F)	5 11	11 00	Winsford	11 12 86	Scholar
Miller Shaun (F)	5 10	11 08	Alsager	25 9 87	Scholar
O'Connor Michael (M)	6 1	11 08	Belfast	6 10 87	Scholar
Pope Tom (F)	6 3	11 03	Stoke	27 8 85	Lancaster C
Rix Ben (M)	5 9	11 05	Wolverhampton	11 12 82	Scholar
Roberts Gary (M)	5 8	10 05	Chester	4 2 87	Scholar
Tomlinson Stuart (G)	6 1	11 02	Chester	10 5 85	Scholar
Vaughan David (M)	5 7	11 00	Abergele	18 2 83	Scholar
Williams Ben (G)	6 0	13 01	Manchester	27 8 82	Manchester U
Williams Owain Fon (G)	6 1	12 09	Gwynedd	17 3 87	Scholar
Woodards Danny (M)	5 11	11 01	Forest Gate	7 10 83	Exeter C

League Appearances: Baudet, J. 42; Bignot, P. 9(2); Carrington, M. (3); Coo, C. (1); Cox, N. 29(2); Flynn, C. (1); Grant, T. 3(1); Higdon, M. 13(12); Jack, R. 19(11); Jones, B. 41; Kempson, D. 6(1); Lowe, R. 31(6); Matthews, L. (10); Maynard, N. 27(4); McNamee, A. 5; Miller, S. 2(5); Moss, D. 18(4); O'Connor, M. 25(4); O'Donnell, D. 21(4); Osbourne, I. 2; Otsemobor, J. 27; Pope, T. (4); Rix, B. 24(7); Roberts, G. 41(2); Rodgers, L. 5(7); Suhaj, P. (2); Taylor, A. 4; Tomlinson, S. 7; Varney, L. 31(3); Vaughan, D. 26(3); Williams, B. 39; Woodards, D. 9(2).
Goals – League (66): Varney 17, Maynard 16, Lowe 8 (1 pen), Vaughan 4, Higdon 3, Miller 3, Roberts 3 (2 pens), Rodgers 3 (2 pens), Moss 2, Rix 2, Baudet 1, Cox 1, Jack 1, Jones 1, O'Donnell 1.
Carling Cup (6): Maynard 2, Jack 1, Lowe 1 (pen), O'Connor 1, Varney 1.
FA Cup (0).
J Paint Trophy (13): Varney 7, Lowe 3 (1 pen), Jack 1, Maynard 1, Moss 1.
Ground: Alexandra Stadium, Gresty Road, Crewe CW2 6EB. Telephone (01270) 213 014.
Record Attendance: 20,000 v Tottenham H, FA Cup 4th rd, 30 January 1960.
Capacity: 10,109.
Manager: Steve Holland.
Secretary: Alison Bowler.
Most League Goals: 95, Division 3 (N), 1931–32.
Highest League Scorer in Season: Terry Harkin, 35, Division 4, 1964–65.
Most League Goals in Total Aggregate: Bert Swindells, 126, 1928–37.
Most Capped Player: Clayton Ince, 38(63), Trinidad & Tobago.
Most League Appearances: Tommy Lowry, 436, 1966–78.
Honours – Welsh Cup: Winners – 1936, 1937.
Colours: Red shirts, white shorts, red stockings.

CRYSTAL PALACE — FL CHAMPIONSHIP

Borrowdale Gary (D)	6 0	12 01	Sutton	16 7 85	Scholar
Butterfield Danny (D)	5 10	11 06	Boston	21 11 79	Grimsby T
Cort Leon (D)	6 3	13 00	Bermondsey	11 7 79	Hull C
Fletcher Carl (M)	5 10	11 07	Camberley	6 4 80	West Ham U
Flinders Scott (G)	6 4	13 00	Rotherham	12 6 86	Barnsley

Fray Arron (D)	5 11	11 02	Beckenham	1 5 87	Scholar
Grabban Lewis (F)	6 0	11 03	Croydon	12 1 88	Scholar
Green Stuart (M)	5 10	11 00	Whitehaven	15 6 81	Hull C
Hall Ryan (M)	5 10	10 04	Dulwich	4 1 88	Scholar
Hudson Mark (D)	6 1	12 01	Guildford	30 3 82	Fulham
Ifill Paul (M)	6 0	12 08	Brighton	20 10 79	Sheffield U
Kennedy Mark (M)	5 11	11 09	Dublin	15 5 76	Wolverhampton W
Kuqi Shefki (F)	6 2	13 13	Kosova	10 11 76	Blackburn R
Lawrence Matthew (D)	6 1	12 10	Northampton	14 6 74	Millwall
Martin David (M)	5 9	10 12	Sidcup	3 6 85	Dartford
McAnuff Jobi (M)	5 11	11 05	Edmonton	9 11 81	Cardiff C
Morrison Clinton (F)	6 0	12 00	Tooting	14 5 79	Birmingham C
Scowcroft James (F)	6 2	12 12	Bury St Edmunds	15 11 75	Coventry C
Sheringham Charlie (F)	6 1	11 06	Chingford	17 4 88	Ipswich T
Soares Tom (M)	6 0	11 04	Reading	10 7 86	Scholar
Spence Lewis (M)	5 9	11 02	Lambeth	29 10 87	Scholar
Speroni Julian (G)	6 0	11 00	Buenos Aires	18 5 79	Dundee
Ward Darren (D)	6 3	11 04	Kenton	13 9 78	Millwall
Watson Ben (M)	5 10	10 11	Camberwell	9 7 85	Scholar
Wiggins Rhoys (D)	5 8	11 05	Hillingdon	4 11 87	Scholar
Wilkinson David (G)	5 11	12 00	Croydon	17 4 88	Scholar

League Appearances: Borrowdale, G. 24(1); Butterfield, D. 25(3); Cort, L. 37; Fletcher, C. 33(4); Flinders, S. 7(1); Freedman, D. 11(23); Grabban, L. (8); Granville, D. 15; Green, S. 5(9); Hudson, M. 38(1); Hughes, M. 12(4); Ifill, P. 6(7); Kennedy, M. 34(4); Kiraly, G. 29; Kuqi, S. 24(11); Lawrence, M. 31(3); Macken, J. 1; Martin, D. (5); McAnuff, J. 31(3); Morrison, C. 31(10); Reich, M. 4(2); Scowcroft, J. 26(9); Soares, T. 32(5); Spence, L. 1(1); Speroni, J. 5; Turner, I. 5; Ward, D. 20; Watson, B. 19(6).
Goals – League (59): Morrison 12, Cort 7, Kuqi 7, McAnuff 5, Scowcroft 5, Hudson 4, Fletcher 3, Freedman 3, Soares 3, Watson 3 (2 pens), Green 2, Ifill 2, Grabban 1, Kennedy 1, own goal 1.
Carling Cup (1): Hughes 1.
FA Cup (2): Kuqi 1, McAnuff 1.
Ground: Selhurst Park Stadium, Whitehorse Lane, London SE25 6PU. Telephone (020) 8768 6000.
Record Attendance: 51,482 v Burnley, Division 2, 11 May 1979. **Capacity:** 26,225.
Manager: Peter Taylor.
Secretary: Christine Dowdeswell.
Most League Goals: 110, Division 4, 1960–61.
Highest League Scorer in Season: Peter Simpson, 46, Division 3 (S), 1930–31.
Most League Goals in Total Aggregate: Peter Simpson, 153, 1930–36.
Most Capped Player: Aleksandrs Kolinko, 23 (76), Latvia.
Most League Appearances: Jim Cannon, 571, 1973–88.
Honours – Football League: Division 1 – Champions 1993–94. Division 2 Champions – 1978–79. Division 3 (S) 1920–21. **Zenith Data Systems Cup:** Winners – 1991.
Colours: Red and royal blue striped shirts, red shorts, red stockings.

DAGENHAM & REDBRIDGE FL CHAMPIONSHIP 2

Akurang Cliff (F)	6 2	12 06	London	27 2 81	Thurrock
Batt Shane (F)	6 3	12 06	Hoddesdon	22 2 87	
Benson Paul (F)	6 1	11 01	Rochford	12 10 79	White Notley
Boardman Jon (D)	6 1	12 01	Reading	27 1 81	Rochdale
Bruce Paul (M)	5 10	12 08	London	18 2 78	QPR
Cole Tim (D)	6 1	13 04	London	9 10 76	Leyton Pennant
Foster Danny (D)	5 11	13 02	Enfield	23 9 84	Tottenham H

Goodwin Lee (D)	6 1	13 12	London	5 9 78	West Ham U
Griffiths Scott (D)	5 9	11 08	London	27 11 85	Aveley
Moore Chris (F)	6 0	11 12	London	13 1 80	Brentford
Rainford David (M)	6 1	12 08	London	21 4 79	Bishop's Stortford
Roberts Tony (G)	6 0	14 11	Bangor	4 8 69	QPR
Saunders Sam (M)	5 8	11 06	London	29 10 82	Thurrock
Southam Glen (M)	5 9	11 06	Enfield	27 8 80	Bishop's Stortford
Strevens Ben (F)	6 0	12 02	Edgware	24 5 80	Barnet
Uddin Anwar (D)	6 1	13 07	London	1 11 81	Bristol R
Vernazza Paolo (M)	5 11	12 03	London	11 1 79	Watford

League Appearances: Akurang, 10+17; Arber, 6; Atieno, 0+3; Batt, 0+4; Benson, 45+1; Blackett, 17; Boardman, 9; Bruce, 1+12; Cole, 3+1; Eyre, 1; Foster, 45; Griffiths, 44+1; Hogan, 0+1; Lawson, 0+3; Leberl, 28+9; Lettejallon, 0+3; Mackail-Smith, 27+1; Moore, 6+9; Olayle, 2; Rainford, 40; Roberts, 45; Saunders, 37+5; Sloma, 40+4; Southam, 42+1; Strevens, 10+10; Taylor, 2+2; Uddin, 42+1; Vernazza, 4+6; Wallis, 0+2.
Goals – League (93): Benson 28, Mackail-Smith 15, Rainford 11 (3 pens), Sloma 8, Southam 7 (2 pens), Strevens 6, Akurang 3 (1 pen), Boardman 3, Moore 3 (1 pen), Saunders 3, Uddin 3, Taylor 1, own goals 2.
FA Cup (0).
Trophy (4): Benson 2, Mackail-Smith 1, Sloma 1.
Ground: The London Borough of Barking and Dagenham Stadium, Dagenham, Essex, RM10 7XL Telephone (0208) 592 1549.
Record Attendance: 5,949 v Ipswich T, FA Cup 3rd rd, 5 January 2002. **Capacity:** 6,087.
Manager: John L. Still.
Secretary: Derek P. Almond.
Most League Goals: 97, Ryman Premier, 1999–2000.
Highest League Scorer in Season: Paul Benson, 28 Conference 2006–07.
Most League Goals in Total Aggregate: 105, Danny Shipp, 1997–2004.
Most League Appearances: Jason Broom, 462, 1992–2003.
Honours – Conference: Champions – 2006–07. **Isthmian League (Premier)**: Champions 1999–2000.
Colours: Red and blue striped shirts, white shorts, blue stockings.

DARLINGTON — FL CHAMPIONSHIP 2

Blundell Gregg (F)	5 10	11 00	Liverpool	1 1 76	Chester C
Burgess Kevin (D)	6 0	12 00	Eston	8 1 88	Middlesbrough
Collins Patrick (D)	6 2	12 08	Oman	4 2 85	Sheffield W
Cummins Michael (M)	6 0	13 06	Dublin	1 6 78	Port Vale
Joachim Julian (F)	5 6	12 02	Boston	20 9 74	Boston U
Keltie Clark (M)	6 0	11 08	Newcastle	31 8 83	Shildon
Ravenhill Ricky (M)	5 10	11 00	Doncaster	16 1 82	Grimsby T
Reay Sean (F)	6 1	12 00	Seaham	17 6 89	Scholar
Russell Sam (G)	6 0	11 00	Middlesbrough	4 10 82	Middlesbrough
Ryan Tim (D)	5 10	11 00	Stockport	10 12 74	Boston U
Smith Martin (F)	5 11	12 07	Sunderland	13 11 74	Northampton T
Stockdale David (G)	6 3	13 04	Leeds	20 9 85	York C
Wainwright Neil (M)	6 0	12 00	Warrington	4 11 77	Sunderland
Wright Tommy (F)	6 0	12 02	Leicester	28 9 84	Barnsley

League Appearances: Albrighton, M. 3; Armstrong, A. 16(13); Blundell, G. 14(1); Burgess, K. (1); Clarke, M. 2; Close, B. 26(1); Collins, P. 28(3); Conlon, B. 12(7); Cummins, M. 38(1); Duke, D. 4(9); Giallanza, G. 12(2); Griffith, A. 2(2); Hardman, L. (1); Holloway, D. 14(7); Horwood, E. 20; Hutchinson, J. 13; James, C.

22(1); Joachim, J. 26(10); Johnson, S. 8(16); Jones, L. 9; Keltie, C. 25(2); Logan, C. (9); Martis, S. 2; McLeod, M. 2; Miller, I. 7; Ngoma, K. 15(3); Phillips, M. 7(1); Prendergast, R. 5(3); Ravenhill, R. 13(2); Reay, S. 1(2); Rowson, D. 20(4); Russell, S. 31; Ryan, T. 4(1); Smith, M. 30(4); Stockdale, D. 6; Vaisanen, V. 5; Wainwright, N. 30(11); Wheater, D. 15; Wiseman, S. 10; Wright, J. (1); Wright, T. 9(4).
Goals – League (52): Joachim 7, Conlon 6 (2 pens), Smith 5, Wainwright 5, Cummins 4, Wright T 4 (1 pen), Blundell 3 (1 pen), Giallanza 3, Armstrong 2, Johnson 2, Rowson 2, Wheater 2, Holloway 1, Keltie 1 (pen), Miller 1, Ngoma 1, Ravenhill 1, Ryan 1, own goal 1.
Carling Cup (5): Joachim 3, Johnson 1 (pen), Logan 1.
FA Cup (5): Smith 3, Collins 1, Ngoma 1.
J Paint Trophy (2): Giallanza 1 (pen), Smith 1.
Ground: 96.6 TFM Darlington Arena, Neasham Road, Hurworth Moor, Darlington DL2 1DL. Telephone (01325) 387 000.
Record Attendance: 21,023 v Bolton W, League Cup 3rd rd, 14 November 1960.
Capacity: 25,000.
Manager: Dave Penney.
Secretary: Lisa Charlton.
Most League Goals: 108, Division 3 (N), 1929–30.
Highest League Scorer in Season: David Brown, 39, Division 3 (N), 1924–25.
Most League Goals in Total Aggregate: Alan Walsh, 90, 1978–84.
Most Capped Player: Jason Devos, 3 (49), Canada and Adrian Webster, 3, New Zealand.
Most League Appearances: Ron Greener, 442, 1955–68.
Honours – Football League: Division 3 (N) Champions – 1924–25. Division 4 Champions – 1990–91. **GM Vauxhall Conference:** Champions – 1989–90.
Colours: Black and white.

DERBY COUNTY — FA PREMIERSHIP

Addison Miles (D)	6 2	13 03	Newham	7 1 89	Scholar
Barnes Giles (M)	6 0	12 10	Barking	5 8 88	Scholar
Bywater Stephen (G)	6 2	12 08	Manchester	7 6 81	West Ham U
Camara Mo (D)	5 11	11 09	Guinea	25 6 75	Celtic
Camp Lee (G)	5 11	11 11	Derby	22 8 84	Scholar
Cumberworth Tom (M)	5 8	12 02	Dagenham	12 1 88	Scholar
Edworthy Marc (D)	5 10	11 11	Barnstaple	24 12 72	Norwich C
Fagan Craig (F)	5 11	11 11	Birmingham	11 12 82	Hull C
Holmes Lee (M)	5 8	10 06	Sutton-in-Ashfield	2 4 87	Scholar
Howard Steven (F)	6 3	14 05	Durham	10 5 76	Luton T
Jackson Richard (D)	5 8	12 10	Whitby	18 4 80	Scarborough
Johnson Michael (D)	5 11	11 12	Nottingham	4 7 73	Birmingham C
Jones David (M)	5 11	10 00	Southport	4 11 84	Manchester U
Leacock Dean (D)	6 2	12 04	Croydon	10 6 84	Fulham
Macken Jon (F)	5 10	12 04	Manchester	7 9 77	Crystal Palace
Malcolm Bob (M)	5 11	11 02	Glasgow	12 11 80	Rangers
McEveley James (D)	6 1	13 13	Liverpool	11 2 85	Blackburn R
Meredith James (D)	6 0	11 09	New South Wales	4 4 88	Scholar
Moore Darren (D)	6 2	15 07	Birmingham	22 4 74	WBA
Nyatanga Lewin (D)	6 2	12 08	Burton	18 8 88	Scholar
Oakley Matt (M)	5 10	11 00	Peterborough	17 8 77	Southampton
Pearson Stephen (M)	6 1	11 11	Lanark	2 10 82	Celtic
Richards Matthew (M)	5 9	11 07	Derby	1 12 89	Scholar
Smith Ryan (F)	5 9	10 06	Islington	10 11 86	Arsenal
Teale Gary (M)	5 9	11 04	Glasgow	21 7 78	Wigan Ath

League Appearances: Barnes, G. 31(8); Bisgaard, M. 17(15); Boertien, P. 10(1); Bolder, A. 9(4); Bywater, S. 37; Camara, M. 19; Camp, L. 3; Currie, D. 4(3); Edworthy, M. 38; Fagan, C. 12(5); Grant, L. 6(1); Howard, S. 43; Idiakez, I. 4(1); Jackson, R. 3(2); Johnson, M. 22(7); Johnson, S. 21(6); Jones, D. 27(1); Leacock, D. 36(2); Lupoli, A. 18(17); Macken, J. 4(4); Malcolm, B. 6(3); McEveley, J. 15; Mears, T. 8(5); Moore, D. 28(7); Nyatanga, L. 5(2); Oakley, M. 36(1); Pearson, S. 6(3); Peschisolido, P. 3(11); Smith, R. 5(10); Smith, T. 4(1); Stead, J. 15(2); Teale, G. 11(5).
Goals – League (62): Howard 16 (4 pens), Barnes 8, Lupoli 7, Jones 6, Oakley 6, Peschisolido 3, Stead 3, Bisgaard 2, Moore 2, Currie 1, Fagan 1, Johnson M 1, Johnson S 1, Mears 1, Nyatanga 1, Smith T 1 (pen), Teale 1, own goal 1.
Carling Cup (4): Howard 1, Johnson M 1, Lupoli 1, Moore 1.
FA Cup (4): Lupoli 3, Peschisolido 1.
Play-Offs (5): Howard 2 (1 pen), Moore 1, Pearson 1, own goal 1.
Ground: Pride Park Stadium, Derby DE24 8XL. Telephone (0870) 444 1884.
Record Attendance: Pride Park: 33, 475 Derby Co Legends v Rangers 9 in a row Legends, 1 May 2006 (Ted McMinn Benefit). Baseball Ground: 41,826 v Tottenham H, Division 1, 20 September 1969. **Capacity:** 33,597.
Manager: Billy Davies.
Secretary: Marian McMinn.
Most League Goals: 111, Division 3 (N), 1956–57.
Highest League Scorer in Season: Jack Bowers, 37, Division 1, 1930–31; Ray Straw, 37 Division 3 (N), 1956–57.
Most League Goals in Total Aggregate: Steve Bloomer, 292, 1892–1906 and 1910–14.
Most Capped Players: Deon Burton, 41 (49), Jamaica and Mart Poom, 41 (104), Estonia.
Most League Appearances: Kevin Hector, 486, 1966–78 and 1980–82.
Honours – Football League: Division 1 Champions – 1971–72, 1974–75. Division 2 Champions – 1911–12, 1914–15, 1968–69, 1986–87. Division 3 (N) Champions – 1956–57. **FA Cup:** Winners – 1945–46. **Texaco Cup:** Winners 1972.
Colours: White shirts, black shorts, white stockings.

DONCASTER ROVERS — FL CHAMPIONSHIP 1

Coppinger James (F)	5 7	10 03	Middlesbrough	10 1 81	Exeter C
Dyer Bruce (F)	6 0	11 05	Ilford	13 4 75	Sheffield U
Green Paul (M)	5 10	12 00	Pontefract	10 4 83	Trainee
Griffith Anthony (M)	5 10	12 00	Huddersfield	28 10 86	Scholar
Guy Lewis (F)	5 10	10 07	Penrith	27 8 85	Newcastle U
Heffernan Paul (F)	5 10	11 00	Dublin	29 12 81	Bristol C
Horlock Kevin (M)	6 0	12 00	Erith	1 11 72	Ipswich T
Lee Graeme (D)	6 2	13 07	Middlesbrough	31 5 78	Sheffield W
Lockwood Adam (D)	6 0	12 07	Wakefield	26 10 81	Yeovil T
McCammon Mark (F)	6 5	14 05	Barnet	7 8 78	Brighton & HA
McDaid Sean (D)	5 6	9 08	Harrogate	6 3 86	Leeds U
Nelthorpe Craig (M)	5 10	11 00	Doncaster	10 6 87	Scholar
O'Connor James (D)	5 10	12 05	Birmingham	20 11 84	Bournemouth
Price Jamie (D)	5 10	11 00	Normanton	27 10 81	Trainee
Roberts Gareth (D)	5 8	12 00	Wrexham	6 2 78	Tranmere R
Roberts Steve (D)	6 1	11 02	Wrexham	24 2 80	Wrexham
Smith Ben (G)	6 0	13 00	Newcastle	5 9 86	Stockport Co
Stock Brian (M)	5 11	11 02	Winchester	24 12 81	Preston NE
Wilson Mark (M)	5 11	12 00	Scunthorpe	9 2 79	Dallas

League Appearances: Blayney, A. 8; Budtz, J. 6(1); Cadamarteri, D. 6; Coppinger, J. 34(5); Di Piedi, M. 1(2); Dyer, B. 9(6); Filan, J. 3; Forte, J. 31(10); Gilbert, P. 4; Green, L. (2); Green, P. 36(5); Griffith, A. 2; Guy, L. 19(17); Heffernan, P. 23(6);

Hird, S. (5); Horlock, K. 2; Lee, G. 36(3); Lockwood, A. 42(2); McCammon, M. 14(8); McDaid, S. 16(4); Nelthorpe, C. 2(4); O'Connor, J. 39(1); Price, J. 19(12); Roberts, G. 28(2); Roberts, S. 15(6); Smith, B. 13; Stock, B. 35(1); Streete, T. 2(4); Sullivan, N. 16; Thornton, B. 15(15); Wilson, M. 17(5); Worley, H. 10; Wright, A. 3.
Goals – League (52): Heffernan 11 (2 pens), Price 6, Forte 5, Coppinger 4, Guy 4 (1 pen), Lee 4, Stock 3, Green P 2, Lockwood 2, McCammon 2, Cadamarteri 1, Dyer 1, Horlock 1, Nelthorpe 1, O'Connor 1, Roberts G 1, Streete 1, Wilson 1, own goal 1.
Carling Cup (8): Forte 3, McCammon 2, Coppinger 1, Stock 1, own goal 1.
FA Cup (4): Guy 1, Heffernan 1, McCammon 1, Stock 1.
J Paint Trophy (18): Heffernan 9 (2 pens), Price 4, Forte 1, Guy 1, Lee 1, Stock 1, Thornton 1.
Ground: Keepmoat Stadium, Stadium Way, Lakeside, Doncaster DN4 5JW. Telephone (01302) 764 664.
Record Attendance: 37,149 v Hull C, Division 3 (N), 2 October 1948. **Capacity:** 15,269.
Manager: Sean O'Driscoll.
Secretary: Jenny Short.
Most League Goals: 123, Division 3 (N), 1946–47.
Highest League Scorer in Season: Clarrie Jordan, 42, Division 3 (N) 1946–47.
Most League Goals in Total Aggregate: Tom Keetley, 180, 1923–29.
Most Capped Player: Len Graham, 14, Northern Ireland.
Most League Appearances: Fred Emery, 417, 1925–36.
Honours – Football League: Division 3 Champions – 2003–04. Division 3 (N) Champions – 1934–35, 1946–47, 1949–50. Division 4 Champions – 1965–66, 1968–69. **J Paint Trophy:** Winners – 2006–07. **Football Conference:** Champions – 2002–03.
Colours: Red and white hooped shirt, black shorts, black stockings.

EVERTON — FA PREMIERSHIP

Agard Kieran (F)			Newham	10 10 89	Scholar
Anderson (M)	6 2	12 10	Sao Paulo	28 8 82	Santander
Anichebe Victor (F)	6 1	13 00	Nigeria	23 4 88	Scholar
Arteta Mikel (M)	5 9	10 08	San Sebastian	26 3 82	Real Sociedad
Beattie James (F)	6 1	13 06	Lancaster	27 2 78	Southampton
Boyle Patrick (D)	6 0	12 09	Glasgow	20 3 87	Scholar
Cahill Tim (M)	5 10	10 12	Sydney	6 12 79	Millwall
Carsley Lee (M)	5 10	12 04	Birmingham	28 2 74	Coventry C
Dennehy Darren (D)	6 3	11 11	Republic of Ireland	21 9 88	Scholar
Downes Aiden (F)	5 8	11 07	Republic of Ireland	24 7 88	Scholar
Harpur Ryan (M)	5 9	11 11	Craigavon	1 12 88	Scholar
Hibbert Tony (D)	5 9	11 05	Liverpool	20 2 81	Trainee
Howard Tim (G)	6 3	14 12	North Brunswick	6 3 79	Manchester U
Irving John (M)	5 10	11 00	Liverpool	17 9 88	Scholar
Johnson Andrew (F)	5 7	10 09	Bedford	10 2 81	Crystal Palace
Jutkiewicz Lukas (F)	6 1	12 11	Southampton	20 3 89	Swindon T
Kissock John (M)			Fazackerley	1 12 89	Scholar
Lescott Jolean (D)	6 2	13 00	Birmingham	16 8 82	Wolverhampton W
McFadden James (M)	6 0	12 11	Glasgow	14 4 83	Motherwell
Molyneux Lee (D)	5 10	11 07	Liverpool	24 2 89	Scholar
Morrison Steven (M)	6 0	10 13	Southport	10 9 88	Scholar
Naysmith Gary (D)	5 9	12 01	Edinburgh	16 11 78	Hearts
Neville Phil (M)	5 11	12 00	Bury	21 1 77	Manchester U
Nuno Valente (D)	6 0	12 03	Lisbon	12 9 74	Porto
Osman Leon (F)	5 8	10 09	Billinge	17 5 81	Trainee

Ruddy John (G)	6 3	12 07	St Ives	24 10 86	Cambridge U
Spencer Scott (F)			Oldham	1 1 89	Scholar
Stubbs Alan (D)	6 2	13 12	Kirkby	6 10 71	Celtic
Stubhaug Lars (G)			Haugesund	18 4 90	Vard
Turner Iain (G)	6 3	12 10	Stirling	26 1 84	Trainee
Van der Meyde Andy (M)	5 10	12 04	Arnhem	30 9 79	Internazionale
Vaughan James (F)	5 11	12 08	Birmingham	14 7 88	Scholar
Vidarsson Bjarni (M)	6 1	11 08	Iceland	5 3 88	Scholar
Yobo Joseph (D)	6 1	13 00	Kano	6 9 80	Marseille

League Appearances: Anderson, (1); Anichebe, V. 5(14); Arteta, M. 35; Beattie, J. 15(18); Cahill, T. 17(1); Carsley, L. 38; Davies, S. 13(2); Fernandes, M. 8(1); Hibbert, T. 12(1); Howard, T. 36; Hughes, M. (1); Johnson, A. 32; Kilbane, K. 2; Lescott, J. 36(2); McFadden, J. 6(13); Naysmith, G. 10(5); Neville, P. 35; Nuno Valente, 10(4); Osman, L. 31(3); Stubbs, A. 23; Turner, I. 1; Van der Meyde, A. 5(3); Vaughan, J. 7(7); Weir, D. 2(3); Wright, R. 1; Yobo, J. 38.
Goals – League (52): Johnson 11 (1 pen), Arteta 9 (5 pens), Cahill 5, Vaughan 4, Anichebe 3, Osman 3, Beattie 2 (2 pens), Fernandes 2, Lescott 2, McFadden 2, Stubbs 2, Yobo 2, Carsley 1, Naysmith 1, Neville 1, own goals 2.
Carling Cup (6): Cahill 2, Anichebe 1, McFadden 1, own goals 2.
FA Cup (1): Johnson 1 (pen).
Ground: Goodison Park, Liverpool L4 4EL. Telephone (0870) 442 1878.
Record Attendance: 78,299 v Liverpool, Division 1, 18 September 1948. **Capacity:** 40,394.
Manager: David Moyes.
Secretary: David Harrison.
Most League Goals: 121, Division 2, 1930–31.
Highest League Scorer in Season: William Ralph 'Dixie' Dean, 60, Division 1, 1927–28 (All-time League record).
Most League Goals in Total Aggregate: William Ralph 'Dixie' Dean, 349, 1925–37.
Most Capped Player: Neville Southall, 92, Wales.
Most League Appearances: Neville Southall, 578, 1981–98.
Honours – Football League: Division 1 Champions – 1890–91, 1914–15, 1927–28, 1931–32, 1938–39, 1962–63, 1969–70, 1984–85, 1986–87. Division 2 Champions – 1930–31. **FA Cup:** Winners – 1906, 1933, 1966, 1984, 1995. **European Competitions: European Cup-Winners' Cup:** Winners – 1984–85.
Colours: Blue shirts, white shorts, white stockings.

FULHAM — FA PREMIERSHIP

Batista Ricardo (G)	6 2	12 06	Portugal	19 11 86	Vitoria Setubal
Bocanegra Carlos (D)	5 11	12 07	Alta Loma	25 5 79	Chicago Fire
Brooks-Meade Corrin (G)			London	19 3 88	Scholar
Brown Michael (M)	5 9	12 04	Hartlepool	25 1 77	Tottenham H
Brown Wayne (M)			Surrey	6 8 88	Scholar
Bullard Jimmy (M)	5 10	11 05	Newham	23 10 78	Wigan Ath
Christanval Philippe (D)	6 2	12 10	Paris	31 8 78	Marseille
Collins Matthew (M)			Merthyr	31 3 86	Scholar
Davies Simon (M)	5 10	11 07	Haverfordwest	23 10 79	Everton
Dempsey Clinton (M)	6 1	12 02	Nacogdoches	9 3 83	New England R
Diop Papa Bouba (M)	6 4	14 12	Dakar	28 1 78	Lens
Ehui Ismael (F)	5 7	10 10	Lille	10 12 86	Scholar
Elliott Simon (M)	6 0	13 02	Wellington	10 6 74	Columbus Crew
Elrich Ahmed (M)	5 11	12 00	Sydney	30 5 81	Busan Icons
Helguson Heidar (F)	5 10	12 09	Akureyri	22 8 77	Watford
James Chris (M)	5 8	10 12	New Zealand	4 7 87	Scholar
John Collins (F)	5 11	12 13	Zwandru	17 10 85	Twente

Knight Zat (D)	6 6	15 02	Solihull	2 5 80	Rushall Olympic
McBride Brian (F)	6 0	12 08	Chicago	19 6 72	Columbus Crew
Milsom Robert (D)			Redhill	2 1 87	Scholar
Moncur Tom (D)			Hackney	23 9 87	Scholar
Niemi Antti (G)	6 1	12 04	Oulu	31 5 72	Southampton
Omozusi Elliot (D)			Hackney	15 12 88	Scholar
Pearce Ian (D)	6 3	15 06	Bury St Edmunds	7 5 74	West Ham U
Queudrue Franck (D)	6 1	12 01	Paris	27 8 78	Middlesbrough
Rosenior Liam (M)	5 9	11 05	Wandsworth	9 7 84	Bristol C
Runstrom Bjorn (F)	6 1	12 08	Stockholm	1 3 84	Hammarby
Smertin Alexei (M)	5 9	10 10	Barnaul	1 5 75	Dynamo Moscow
Timlin Michael (M)	5 9	11 10	Lambeth	19 3 85	Trainee
Volz Moritz (D)	5 8	11 07	Siegen	21 1 83	Arsenal
Warner Tony (G)	6 4	15 06	Liverpool	11 5 74	Cardiff C
Watts Adam (D)	6 1	11 09	London	4 3 88	Scholar
Zakuani Gabriel (D)	6 1	12 13	DR Congo	31 5 86	Leyton Orient

League Appearances: Boa Morte, L. 12(3); Bocanegra, C. 26(4); Briggs, M. (1); Brown, M. 34; Bullard, J. 4; Christanval, P. 19(1); Davies, S. 14; Dempsey, C. 1(9); Diop, P. 20(3); Helguson, H. 16(14); Jensen, C. 10(2); John, C. 9(14); Knight, Z. 22(1); Lastuvka, J. 7(1); McBride, B. 34(4); Montella, V. 3(7); Niemi, A. 31; Pearce, I. 22; Queudrue, F. 28(1); Radzinski, T. 25(10); Rosenior, L. 38; Routledge, W. 13(11); Runstrom, B. (1); Smertin, A. 6(1); Volz, M. 24(5).
Goals – League (38): McBride 9, Bocanegra 5, Helguson 4 (1 pen), Bullard 2 (1 pen), Davies 2, Jensen 2, Knight 2, Montella 2 (1 pen), Radzinski 2, Volz 2, Christanval 1, Dempsey 1, John 1, Pearce 1, Queudrue 1, own goal 1.
Carling Cup (1): Helguson 1.
FA Cup (9): McBride 3, Montella 3, Radzinski 1, Routledge 1, Volz 1.
Ground: Craven Cottage, Stevenage Road, London SW6 6HH. Telephone: (0870) 442 1222.
Record Attendance: 49,335 v Millwall, Division 2, 8 October 1938. **Capacity:** 24,590.
Manager: Lawrie Sanchez.
Secretary: Darren Preston.
Most League Goals: 111, Division 3 (S), 1931–32.
Highest League Scorer in Season: Frank Newton, 43, Division 3 (S), 1931–32.
Most League Goals in Total Aggregate: Gordon Davies, 159, 1978–84, 1986–91.
Most Capped Player: Johnny Haynes, 56, England.
Most League Appearances: Johnny Haynes, 594, 1952–70.
Honours – Football League: Division 1 Champions – 2000–01. Division 2 Champions – 1948–49, 1998–99. Division 3 (S) Champions – 1931–32. **European Competitions: Intertoto Cup:** Winners – 2002.
Colours: White shirts, black shorts, white stockings.

GILLINGHAM — FL CHAMPIONSHIP 1

Bentley Mark (M)	6 2	13 07	Hertford	7 1 78	Southend U
Clohessy Sean (D)	5 11	12 07	Croydon	12 12 86	Arsenal
Cox Ian (D)	6 1	12 05	Croydon	25 3 71	Burnley
Crofts Andrew (D)	5 10	11 13	Chatham	29 5 84	Trainee
Flynn Michael (M)	5 10	12 10	Newport	17 10 80	Wigan Ath
Jack Kelvin (G)	6 3	16 03	Trinidad	29 4 76	Dundee
Jackman Danny (D)	5 4	10 00	Worcester	3 1 83	Stockport Co
Jarvis Matthew (M)	5 7	11 05	Middlesbrough	22 5 86	Scholar
Jupp Duncan (D)	6 1	13 09	Hazelmere	25 1 75	Southend U
McDonald Dean (F)	5 6	12 12	Lambeth	19 2 86	Ipswich T
Mulligan Gary (F)	6 1	12 01	Dublin	23 4 85	Sheffield U

Ndumbu-Nsungu Guylain (F)	6 2	13 00	Kinshasa	26 12 82	Cardiff C
Southall Nicky (M)	5 11	12 04	Stockton	28 1 72	Nottingham F
Spiller Danny (M)	5 8	10 12	Maidstone	10 10 81	Trainee
Stone Craig (M)	6 0	10 05	Gravesend	29 12 88	Scholar

League Appearances: Bastians, F. 5; Bentley, M. 41; Brill, D. 8; Chorley, B. 24(3); Clohessy, S. 3(3); Collin, F. (3); Cox, I. 33; Crofts, A. 43; Cumbers, L. (1); Easton, C. 26(6); Flinders, S. 9; Flynn, M. 44(1); Howell, L. (1); Jack, K. 9; Jackman, D. 30(1); Jarvis, M. 34(1); Johnson, L. 23(1); Jupp, D. 26(1); Larrieu, R. 14; McDonald, D. 16(10); Mulligan, G. 37(1); N'Dumbu Nsungu, G. 14(18); Pouton, A. 3(5); Pugh, A. (3); Randolph, D. 3; Royce, S. 3; Sancho, B. 19(7); Savage, B. 8(6); Southall, N. 15; Spiller, D. 11(14); Stone, C. 2(1); Tonge, D. 3.
Goals – League (56): Flynn 10 (3 pens), Crofts 8, Mulligan 7, Jarvis 6, McDonald 6, Bentley 4, Cox 3, N'Dumbu Nsungu 3 (1 pen), Bastians 1, Chorley 1, Easton 1, Jackman 1, Johnson 1, Pouton 1, Savage 1, own goals 2.
Carling Cup (1): Crofts 1.
FA Cup (7): Bentley 2, Flynn 2 (1 pen), Ndumbu-Nsungu 2, Mulligan 1.
J Paint Trophy (1): Mulligan 1.
Ground: Priestfield Stadium, Redfern Avenue, Gillingham ME7 4DD. Telephone (01634) 300 000.
Record Attendance: 23,002 v QPR, FA Cup 3rd rd, 10 January 1948. **Capacity:** 11,400.
Manager: Ronnie Jepson.
Secretary: Mrs Gwen E. Poynter.
Most League Goals: 90, Division 4, 1973–74.
Highest League Scorer in Season: Ernie Morgan, 31, Division 3 (S), 1954–55; Brian Yeo, 31, Division 4, 1973–74.
Most League Goals in Total Aggregate: Brian Yeo, 135, 1963–75.
Most Capped Player: Mamady Sidibe 7, Mali.
Most League Appearances: John Simpson, 571, 1957–72.
Honours – Football League: Division 4 Champions – 1963–64.
Colours: Blue with white insert.

GRIMSBY TOWN — FL CHAMPIONSHIP 2

Barnes Phil (G)	6 1	11 01	Sheffield	2 3 79	Sheffield U
Bennett Ryan (D)	6 0	13 02	London	4 8 85	Scholar
Bolland Paul (M)	5 10	10 12	Bradford	23 12 79	Notts Co
Bore Peter (M)	5 11	11 04	Grimsby	4 11 87	Scholar
Boshell Danny (M)	5 11	11 09	Bradford	30 5 81	Stockport Co
Cohen Gary (F)	5 11	11 02	Ilford	20 1 84	Gretna
Fenton Nick (D)	6 0	10 02	Preston	23 11 79	Doncaster R
Harkins Gary (M)	6 2	12 10	Greenock	2 1 85	Blackburn R
Hegarty Nick (M)	5 10	11 00	Hemsworth	25 6 86	Scholar
Jones Gary (F)	6 3	15 02	Chester	10 5 75	Tranmere R
Murray Robert (M)	5 8	9 00	Leamington Spa	11 7 88	Scholar
Newey Tom (D)	5 10	10 02	Sheffield	31 10 82	Leyton Orient
North Danny (F)	5 9	12 08	Grimsby	7 9 87	Scholar
Rankin Isaiah (F)	5 10	11 00	London	22 5 78	Brentford
Taylor Andy (M)	6 2	13 00	Grimsby	30 10 88	Scholar
Till Peter (M)	5 11	11 04	Birmingham	7 9 85	Birmingham C
Toner Ciaran (M)	6 1	12 02	Craigavon	30 6 81	Lincoln C
Whittle Justin (D)	6 1	13 00	Derby	18 3 71	Hull C

League Appearances: Barnes, P. 46; Beagrie, P. 6(3); Bennett, R. 3(2); Bloomer, M. 5(4); Bolland, P. 37(2); Bore, P. 21(11); Boshell, D. 23(6); Butler, A. 4; Croft, G. 26(2); Fenton, N. 37(1); Futcher, B. 3(1); Grand, S. 4(3); Harkins, G. 11(6); Hegarty, N. 9(6); Hunt, J. 15; James, K. 2; Jones, G. 29(10); Lawson, J. (1); McDer-

mott, J. 20(3); McIntosh, M. 4; Newey, T. 42(1); North, D. 12(8); Paterson, M. 15; Pulis, A. 9; Rankin, I. 15(5); Ravenhill, R. 15(2); Reddy, M. 4(6); Rizzo, N. 1; Taylor, A. 2(9); Thorpe, T. 5(1); Till, P. 17(5); Toner, C. 31(2); Whittle, J. 33(4).
Goals – League (57): Bore 8, Jones 8, Toner 8 (2 pens), North 6 (1 pen), Paterson 6, Bolland 5, Fenton 4, Boshell 2, Hunt 2, Rankin 2, Ravenhill 2, Taylor 2, Newey 1, Whittle 1.
Carling Cup (0).
FA Cup (0).
J Paint Trophy (0).
Ground: Blundell Park, Cleethorpes, North-East Lincolnshire DN35 7PY. Telephone (01472) 605 050.
Record Attendance: 31,651 v Wolverhampton W, FA Cup 5th rd, 20 February 1937. **Capacity:** 10,033.
Manager: Alan Buckley.
Chief Executive: Ian Fleming.
Most League Goals: 103, Division 2, 1933–34.
Highest League Scorer in Season: Pat Glover, 42, Division 2, 1933–34.
Most League Goals in Total Aggregate: Pat Glover, 180, 1930–39.
Most Capped Player: Pat Glover, 7, Wales.
Most League Appearances: John McDermott, 647, 1987–2007.
Honours – Football League: Division 2 Champions – 1900–01, 1933–34. Division 3 (N) Champions – 1925–26, 1955–56. Division 3 Champions – 1979–80. Division 4 Champions – 1971–72. **League Group Cup:** Winners – 1981–82. **Auto Windscreens Shield:** Winners – 1997–98.
Colours: Black and white striped shirts, black shorts, white stockings with black trim.

HARTLEPOOL UNITED — FL CHAMPIONSHIP 1

Barker Richard (F)	6 0	14 06	Sheffield	30 5 75	Mansfield T
Barron Micky (D)	5 11	11 10	Lumley	22 12 74	Middlesbrough
Boland Willie (M)	5 9	11 02	Ennis	6 8 75	Cardiff C
Brown James (F)	5 11	11 00	Newcastle	3 1 87	Cramlington J
Bullock Lee (M)	6 0	11 04	Stockton	22 5 81	Cardiff C
Clark Ben (D)	6 1	13 11	Shotley Bridge	24 1 83	Sunderland
Foley David (F)	5 4	8 09	South Shields	12 5 87	Scholar
Gibb Ali (M)	5 9	11 06	Salisbury	17 2 76	Bristol R
Humphreys Richie (M)	5 11	12 07	Sheffield	30 11 77	Cambridge U
Konstantopoulos Dimitrios (G)	6 4	14 02	Kalamata	29 11 78	Farense
Liddle Gary (D)	6 1	12 06	Middlesbrough	15 6 86	Middlesbrough
Mackay Michael (F)	6 0	11 08	Durham	11 10 82	Consett
Maidens Michael (M)	5 11	11 04	Middlesbrough	7 5 87	Scholar
Monkhouse Andrew (M)	6 2	12 06	Leeds	23 10 80	Swindon T
Nelson Michael (D)	6 2	13 03	Gateshead	15 3 82	Bury
Porter Joel (F)	5 9	11 13	Adelaide	25 12 78	Sydney Olympic
Provett Jim (G)	6 0	13 04	Stockton	22 12 82	Trainee
Rae Michael (F)	5 10	12 04	North Cleveland	23 10 87	Scholar
Robson Matty (D)	5 10	11 02	Durham	23 1 85	Scholar
Sweeney Anthony (M)	6 0	11 07	Stockton	5 9 83	Scholar
Turnbull Stephen (M)	5 10	11 00	South Shields	7 1 87	Scholar

League Appearances: Barker, R. 18; Barron, M. 26(3); Boland, W. 25(2); Brackstone, J. 6(2); Brown, J. 29(7); Bullock, L. 8(17); Clark, B. 40; Daly, J. 14(5); Duffy, D. 10; Foley, D. 4(21); Gibb, A. 12(13); Hignett, C. (2); Humphreys, R. 37(1); Konstantopoulos, D. 46; Liddle, G. 42; MacKay, M. (1); Maidens, M. (4); Monkhouse, A. 26; Nelson, M. 42; Porter, J. 14(8); Proctor, M. 1(1); Robson, M. 18(2);

Strachan, G. 2(2); Sweeney, A. 31(4); Tinkler, M. 4(2); Williams, D. 19(7); Williams, E. 32(8).
Goals – League (65): Barker 9 (3 pens), Daly 9 (2 pens), Monkhouse 7, Brown 6, Williams E 6, Duffy 5, Porter 5, Sweeney 4, Clark 3, Humphreys 3, Liddle 3, Robson 2, Bullock 1, Nelson 1, own goal 1.
Carling Cup (1): Porter 1 (pen).
FA Cup (2): Brown 1, own goal 1.
J Paint Trophy (4): Bullock 1, Foley 1, Humphreys 1, Liddle 1.
Ground: Victoria Park, Clarence Road, Hartlepool TS24 8BZ. Telephone (01429) 272 584.
Record Attendance: 17,426 v Manchester U, FA Cup 3rd rd, 5 January 1957.
Capacity: 7,629.
Manager: Danny Wilson.
Secretary: Maureen Smith.
Most League Goals: 90, Division 3 (N), 1956–57.
Highest League Scorer in Season: William Robinson, 28, Division 3 (N), 1927–28; Joe Allon, 28, Division 4, 1990–91.
Most League Goals in Total Aggregate: Ken Johnson, 98, 1949–64.
Most Capped Player: Ambrose Fogarty, 1 (11), Republic of Ireland.
Most League Appearances: Wattie Moore, 447, 1948–64.
Honours – Nil.
Colours: Blue and white striped shirts, blue shorts, white stockings.

HEREFORD UNITED — FL CHAMPIONSHIP 2

Player	Ht	Wt	Birthplace	D.O.B.	Source
Beckwith Dean (D)	6 3	13 01	Southwark	18 9 83	Gillingham
Brown Wayne (G)	6 0	13 11	Southampton	14 1 77	Chester C
Connell Alan (F)	6 0	12 00	Enfield	5 2 83	Torquay U
Fitzpatrick Jordan (M)	6 0	12 00	Stourbridge	15 6 88	Wolverhampton W
Gulliver Phil (D)	6 2	13 05	Bishop Auckland	12 9 82	Rushden & D
Gwynne Sam (M)	5 9	11 11	Hereford	17 12 87	Scholar
McClenahan Trent (D)	5 11	12 00	Sydney	4 2 85	West Ham U
Mkandawire Tamika (D)	6 0	12 03	Malawi	28 5 83	WBA
Palmer Marcus (F)	6 0	11 07	Gloucester	22 12 88	Cheltenham T
Purdie Rob (F)	5 8	11 02	Leicester	28 9 82	Leicester C
Rose Richard (D)	6 0	12 04	Pembury	8 9 82	Gillingham
Sills Tim (F)	6 1	14 00	Romsey	10 9 79	Oxford U
Smith Ben (M)	5 9	11 09	Chelmsford	23 11 78	Weymouth
Travis Simon (D)	5 10	11 00	Preston	22 3 77	Stevenage B
Webb Luke (M)	6 0	12 01	Nottingham	12 9 86	Coventry C
Williams Andy (F)	5 11	11 02	Hereford	14 8 86	Scholar

League Appearances: Beckwith, D. 32; Brown, W. 39; Connell, A. 33(11); Eustace, J. 8; Ferrell, A. 15(6); Fitzpatrick, J. (1); Fleetwood, S. 21(6); Giles, M. 11(2); Guinan, S. 16; Gulliver, P. 24(2); Harrison, P. (1); Jeannin, A. 11(1); Jennings, S. 11; MacKenzie, N. 7; McClenahan, T. 24(2); Mkandawire, T. 39; Osborn, S. (1); Palmer, M. 1(2); Purdie, R. 43(1); Rose, R. 29(4); Sheldon, G. 3(5); Sills, T. 22(14); Smith, B. 18; Thomas, D. 15; Travis, S. 34(2); Tynan, S. 7; Wallis, J. (2); Webb, L. 13(8); Williams, A. 30(11).
Goals – League (45): Connell 9, Williams 8, Guinan 7, Purdie 6 (6 pens), Fleetwood 3, Mkandawire 2, Sills 2, Thomas 2, Jeannin 1, McClenahan 1, Rose 1, Sheldon 1, Smith 1, own goal 1.
Carling Cup (4): Fleetwood 3, Purdie 1 (pen).
FA Cup (6): Purdie 2 (1 pen), Webb 2, Connell 1, Ferrell 1.
J Paint Trophy (1): Williams 1.
Ground: Edgar Street, Hereford, Herefordshire HR4 9JU. Telephone: (01432) 276 666.

Record Attendance: 18,114 v Sheffield Wed., FA Cup 3rd rd, 4 January 1958.
Capacity: 7,873.
Manager: Graham Turner.
Secretary: Mrs Joan Fennessey.
Most League Goals: 86, Division 3, 1975–76.
Highest League Scorer in Season: Dixie McNeil, 35, 1975–76.
Most League Goals in Total Aggregate: Stewart Phillips, 93, 1980–88, 1990–91.
Most Capped Player: Brian Evans, 1 (7) Wales.
Most League Appearances: Mel Pejic, 412, 1980–92.
Honours – Football League: Division 3 Champions – 1975–76. **Welsh Cup:** Winners – 1990.
Colours: White shirts, black shorts, black stockings.

HUDDERSFIELD TOWN — FL CHAMPIONSHIP 1

Akins Lucas (F)	5 10	11 07	Huddersfield	25 2 89	Scholar
Beckett Luke (F)	5 11	14 01	Sheffield	25 11 76	Sheffield U
Berrett James (M)	5 10	10 13	Halifax	13 1 89	Scholar
Booth Andy (F)	6 1	13 00	Huddersfield	6 12 73	Sheffield W
Brandon Chris (M)	5 8	10 13	Bradford	7 4 76	Chesterfield
Clarke Nathan (D)	6 2	12 00	Halifax	30 11 83	Scholar
Clarke Tom (D)	5 11	12 02	Halifax	21 12 87	Scholar
Collins Michael (M)	6 0	10 12	Halifax	30 4 86	Scholar
Eastwood Simon (G)	6 2	12 09	Luton	26 6 89	Scholar
Glennon Matthew (G)	6 2	13 11	Stockport	8 10 78	St Johnstone
Hardy Aaron (M)	5 8	11 04	South Elmsall	26 5 86	Scholar
Holdsworth Andy (D)	5 9	11 02	Pontefract	29 1 84	Scholar
Mirfin David (M)	6 2	14 05	Sheffield	18 4 85	Scholar
Racchi Danny (M)	5 8	10 04	Halifax	22 11 88	Scholar
Schofield Danny (F)	5 11	12 00	Doncaster	10 4 80	Brodsworth
Skarz Joe (D)	5 11	13 00	Huddersfield	13 7 89	Scholar
Smithies Alex (G)	6 1	10 01	Huddersfield	25 3 90	Scholar
Taylor-Fletcher Gary (F)	6 0	11 00	Liverpool	4 6 81	Lincoln C
Worthington Jon (M)	5 9	11 05	Dewsbury	16 4 83	Scholar
Young Matthew (M)	5 8	11 03	Leeds	25 10 85	Scholar

League Appearances: Abbott, P. 8(10); Adams, D. 23; Ahmed, A. 4(5); Akins, L. (2); Beckett, L. 32(9); Berrett, J. (2); Booth, A. 29(5); Brandon, C. 17(6); Clarke, N. 16; Clarke, T. 6(3); Collins, M. 39(4); Glennon, M. 46; Hand, J. (1); Hardy, A. 5(4); Hayes, P. 4; Holdsworth, A. 35; Hudson, M. 30(2); McAliskey, J. 3(5); McCombe, J. 5(2); McIntosh, M. 24(2); Mirfin, D. 38; Racchi, D. (3); Schofield, D. 25(10); Sinclair, F. 13; Skarz, J. 15(2); Taylor, A. 7(1); Taylor-Fletcher, G. 39; Worthington, J. 27(1); Young, M. 16(13).
Goals – League (60): Beckett 15 (3 pens), Taylor-Fletcher 11, Booth 7, Abbott 5 (1 pen), Schofield 5 (1 pen), Collins 4, Hudson 3, Holdsworth 2, Worthington 2, Young 2, Brandon 1, Hayes 1, McAliskey 1, Mirfin 1.
Carling Cup (0).
FA Cup (0).
J Paint Trophy (1): Booth 1.
Ground: The Galpharm Stadium, Stadium Way, Leeds Road, Huddersfield HD1 6PX. Telephone 0870 4444 677.
Record Attendance: 67,037 v Arsenal, FA Cup 6th rd, 27 February 1932 (at Leeds Road); 23,678 v Liverpool, FA Cup 3rd rd, 12 December 1999 (at Alfred McAlpine Stadium).
Capacity: 24,500.
Manager: Andy Ritchie.
Secretary: J. Ann Hough.

Most League Goals: 101, Division 4, 1979–80.
Highest League Scorer in Season: Sam Taylor, 35, Division 2, 1919–20; George Brown, 35, Division 1, 1925–26.
Most League Goals in Total Aggregate: George Brown, 142, 1921–29; Jimmy Glazzard, 142, 1946–56.
Most Capped Player: Jimmy Nicholson, 31 (41), Northern Ireland.
Most League Appearances: Billy Smith, 520, 1914–34.
Honours – Football League: Division 1 Champions – 1923–24, 1924–25, 1925–26. Division 2 Champions – 1969–70. Division 4 Champions – 1979–80. **FA Cup:** Winners – 1922.
Colours: Blue and white striped shirts, white shorts, white stockings.

HULL CITY — FL CHAMPIONSHIP

Ashbee Ian (M)	6 1	13 07	Birmingham	6 9 76	Cambridge U
Aspden Curtis (G)	6 1	11 12	Blackburn	16 11 87	Scholar
Atkinson William (M)	5 10	10 07	Beverley	14 10 88	Scholar
Barmby Nick (M)	5 7	11 03	Hull	11 2 74	Leeds U
Bennett James (M)	5 10	12 03	Beverley	4 9 88	Scholar
Bridges Michael (F)	6 1	10 11	North Shields	5 8 78	Carlisle U
Coles Danny (D)	6 1	11 05	Bristol	31 10 81	Bristol C
Collins Sam (D)	6 2	14 03	Pontefract	5 6 77	Port Vale
Dawson Andy (D)	5 10	11 02	Northallerton	20 10 78	Scunthorpe U
Delaney Damien (D)	6 3	14 00	Cork	20 7 81	Leicester C
Doyle Nathan (M)	5 11	12 06	Derby	12 1 87	Derby Co
Duffy Darryl (F)	5 11	12 01	Glasgow	16 4 84	Falkirk
Duke Matt (G)	6 5	13 04	Sheffield	16 7 77	Sheffield U
Elliott Stuart (M)	5 10	11 09	Belfast	23 7 78	Motherwell
Featherstone Nicky (F)	5 7	11 03	Goole	22 9 89	Scholar
Forster Nicky (F)	5 9	11 05	Caterham	18 9 73	Ipswich T
France Ryan (M)	5 11	11 11	Sheffield	13 12 80	Alfreton T
Livermore David (M)	5 11	12 07	Edmonton	20 5 80	Leeds U
Marney Dean (M)	6 0	11 05	Barking	31 1 84	Tottenham H
McPhee Stephen (F)	5 7	10 08	Glasgow	5 6 81	Beira Mar
Myhill Boaz (G)	6 3	14 06	Modesto	9 11 82	Aston Villa
Parkin Jon (F)	6 4	13 07	Barnsley	30 12 81	Macclesfield T
Plummer Matthew (D)	6 1	12 01	Hull	18 1 89	Scholar
Ricketts Sam (D)	6 1	12 01	Aylesbury	11 10 81	Swansea C
Turner Michael (D)	6 4	13 05	Lewisham	9 11 83	Brentford
Welsh John (M)	5 7	12 02	Liverpool	10 1 84	Liverpool
Wilkinson Ben (M)	5 11	12 01	Sheffield	25 4 87	Scholar

League Appearances: Andrews, K. (3); Ashbee, I. 35; Barmby, N. 7(13); Bridges, M. 8(7); Burgess, B. (3); Coles, D. 16(5); Collins, S. 6; Dawson, A. 38; Delaney, D. 36(1); Doyle, N. 1; Duffy, D. 4(5); Duke, M. (1); Elliott, S. 20(12); Fagan, C. 27; Featherstone, N. (2); Forster, N. 26(9); France, R. 13(11); Jarrett, J. 3; Livermore, D. 24(1); Marney, D. 26(11); McPhee, S. 9(3); Mills, D. 9; Myhill, B. 46; Parkin, J. 22(7); Parlour, R. 14(1); Peltier, L. 5(2); Ricketts, S. 40; Thelwell, A. 2; Turner, M. 42(1); Vaz Te, R. 1(5); Welsh, J. 9(9); Windass, D. 15(3); Yeates, M. 2(3).
Goals – League (51): Windass 8 (2 pens), Fagan 6 (1 pen), Parkin 6 (1 pen), Elliott 5, Forster 5, Barmby 4, Livermore 4, Turner 3, Bridges 2, Dawson 2, Marney 2, Ashbee 1, Delaney 1, Ricketts 1, Welsh 1.
Carling Cup (3): Barmby 1, Burgess 1, Duffy 1.
FA Cup (4): Dawson 2, Forster 1, Parkin 1 (pen).
Ground: KC Stadium, The Circle, Walton Street, Anlaby Road, Hull HU3 6HU. Telephone (0870) 837 0003.

Record Attendance: 55,019 v Manchester U, FA Cup 6th rd, 26 February 1949 (Boothferry Park); 23,495 v Huddersfield T, Division 3, 24 April 2004 (KC Stadium).
Capacity: 25,104.
Manager: Phil Brown.
Secretary: Phil Hough.
Most League Goals: 109, Division 3, 1965–66.
Highest League Scorer in Season: Bill McNaughton, 39, Division 3 (N), 1932–33.
Most League Goals in Total Aggregate: Chris Chilton, 195, 1960–71.
Most Capped Player: Theo Whitmore, Jamaica.
Most League Appearances: Andy Davidson, 520, 1952–67.
Honours – Football League: Division 3 (N) Champions – 1932–33, 1948–49. Division 3 Champions – 1965–66.
Colours: Amber shirts, black shorts, black stockings.

IPSWICH TOWN — FL CHAMPIONSHIP

Barron Scott (D)	5 9	9 08	Preston	2 9 85	Scholar
Bowditch Dean (F)	5 11	10 08	Bishop's Stortford	15 6 86	Trainee
Bruce Alex (D)	6 0	11 06	Norwich	28 9 84	Birmingham C
Casement Chris (M)	6 0	12 02	Belfast	12 1 88	Scholar
Clarke Billy (F)	5 7	10 01	Cork	13 12 87	Scholar
De Vos Jason (D)	6 4	13 07	London, Can	2 1 74	Wigan Ath
Garvan Owen (M)	6 0	10 07	Dublin	29 1 88	Scholar
Harding Dan (D)	6 0	11 11	Gloucester	23 12 83	Leeds U
Haynes Danny (F)	5 11	12 04	Peckham	19 1 88	Scholar
Lee Alan (F)	6 2	13 09	Galway	21 8 78	Cardiff C
Legwinski Sylvain (M)	6 1	11 07	Clermont-Ferrand	6 10 73	Fulham
Miller Ian (M)	6 2	12 02	Colchester	23 11 83	Bury T
Moore Sammy (M)	5 8	9 00	Dover	7 9 87	Scholar
Naylor Richard (D)	6 1	13 07	Leeds	28 2 77	Trainee
O'Callaghan George (M)	6 1	10 11	Cork	5 9 79	Cork C
Peters Jaime (M)	5 7	10 12	Toronto	4 5 87	Moor Green
Price Lewis (G)	6 3	13 06	Poole	19 7 84	Academy
Richards Matt (D)	5 8	10 10	Harlow	26 12 84	Scholar
Roberts Gary (M)	5 10	11 09	Liverpool	18 3 84	Accrington S
Sito (D)	5 8	11 07	Coruna	21 5 80	Racing Ferrol
Supple Shane (G)	5 11	11 07	Dublin	4 5 87	Scholar
Trotter Liam (M)	6 2	12 02	Ipswich	24 8 88	Scholar
Upson Edward (M)	5 10	11 07	Bury St Edmunds	21 11 89	Scholar
Walters Jon (F)	6 0	12 06	Birkenhead	20 9 83	Chester C
Williams Gavin (M)	5 10	11 05	Pontypridd	20 6 80	West Ham U
Wilnis Fabian (D)	5 8	12 06	Paramaribo	23 8 70	De Graafschap
Wright David (D)	5 11	11 01	Warrington	1 5 80	Wigan Ath

League Appearances: Bates, M. 2; Bowditch, D. 3(6); Bruce, A. 40(1); Clarke, B. 10(17); Currie, D. 6(7); De Vos, J. 39; Forster, N. 4; Garvan, O. 24(3); Harding, D. 40(2); Haynes, D. 4(27); Jeffers, F. 7(2); Lee, A. 38(3); Legwinski, S. 31(1); Macken, J. 13(1); Miller, I. (1); Moore, S. (1); Naylor, R. 21(4); Noble, M. 12(1); O'Callaghan, G. 3(8); Parkin, S. (2); Peters, J. 20(3); Pollitt, M. 1; Price, L. 34; Richards, M. 20(8); Roberts, G. 30(3); Sito, 6(2); Supple, S. 11(1); Walters, J. 11(5); Walton, S. 13(6); Williams, G. 25(4); Wilnis, F. 19(2); Wright, D. 19.
Goals – League (64): Lee 16 (3 pens), Haynes 7 (1 pen), Legwinski 5, Jeffers 4, Macken 4 (2 pens), Walters 4, Clarke 3, Walton 3 (2 pens), De Vos 2, Peters 2, Richards 2, Roberts 2, Williams 2, Bowditch 1, Currie 1, Forster 1, Garvan 1, Noble 1, O'Callaghan 1, Wright 1, own goal 1.
Carling Cup (2): Clarke 1, De Vos 1.

FA Cup (2): Lee 1 (pen), Richards 1.
Ground: Portman Road, Ipswich, Suffolk IP1 2DA. Telephone (01473) 400 500.
Record Attendance: 38,010 v Leeds U, FA Cup 6th rd, 8 March 1975.
Capacity: 30,311.
Manager: Jim Magilton.
Secretary: Sally Webb.
Most League Goals: 106, Division 3 (S), 1955–56.
Highest League Scorer in Season: Ted Phillips, 41, Division 3 (S), 1956–57.
Most League Goals in Total Aggregate: Ray Crawford, 203, 1958–63 and 1966–69.
Most Capped Player: Allan Hunter, 47 (53), Northern Ireland.
Most League Appearances: Mick Mills, 591, 1966–82.
Honours – Football League: Division 1 Champions – 1961–62. Division 2 Champions – 1960–61, 1967–68, 1991–92. Division 3 (S) Champions – 1953–54, 1956–57. **FA Cup:** Winners – 1977–78. **European Competitions: UEFA Cup:** Winners – 1980–81.
Colours: Blue shirts, white shorts, blue stockings.

LEEDS UNITED — FL CHAMPIONSHIP 1

Bayly Robert (M)	5 8	11 00	Dublin	22 2 88	Scholar
Beckford Jermaine (F)	6 2	13 02	Ealing	9 12 83	Wealdstone
Blake Robbie (F)	5 9	12 00	Middlesbrough	4 3 76	Birmingham C
Carole Sebastien (M)	5 7	11 02	Pontoise	8 9 82	Brighton & HA
Cresswell Richard (F)	6 0	11 08	Bridlington	20 9 77	Preston NE
Delph Fabian (M)	5 8	10 00	Bradford	21 11 89	Scholar
Derry Shaun (M)	5 10	13 02	Nottingham	6 12 77	Crystal Palace
Douglas Jonathan (M)	6 0	12 06	Monaghan	22 11 81	Blackburn R
Einarsson Gylfi (M)	6 0	12 00	Iceland	27 10 78	Lille
Gardner Scott (M)			Luxembourg	1 4 88	Scholar
Healy David (F)	5 8	11 07	Downpatrick	5 8 79	Preston NE
Howson Jonathan (M)	5 11	12 01	Leeds	21 5 88	Scholar
Kandol Tresor (F)	6 1	11 05	Banga	20 8 81	Barnet
Lewis Eddie (M)	5 10	11 02	Cerritos	17 5 74	Preston NE
Madden Simon (D)			Dublin	1 5 88	Shelbourne
Nicholls Kevin (M)	5 9	11 13	Newham	2 1 79	Luton T
Parker Ben (D)	5 11	11 06	Pontefract	8 11 87	Scholar
Richardson Frazer (D)	5 11	12 04	Rotherham	29 10 82	Trainee
Rothery Gavin (F)			Morley	22 9 87	Scholar
Thompson Alan (M)	6 0	12 08	Newcastle	22 12 73	Celtic
Westlake Ian (M)	5 11	11 00	Clacton	10 11 83	Ipswich T

League Appearances: Ankergren, C. 14; Armando Sa, M. 6(5); Bakke, E. 2(1); Bayly, R. 1; Beckford, J. 1(4); Blake, R. 27(9); Butler, P. 16; Carole, S. 7(10); Crainey, S. 18(1); Cresswell, R. 18(4); Delph, F. (1); Derry, S. 23; Douglas, J. 34(1); Ehiogu, U. 6; Einarsson, G. (3); Elliott, R. 5(2); Elliott, T. (3); Flo, T. 1; Foxe, H. 12(6); Gray, M. 6; Gregan, S. 1; Healy, D. 31(10); Heath, M. 26; Horsfield, G. 11(3); Howson, J. 6(3); Johnson, A. 4(1); Johnson, J. 3(2); Kandol, T. 11(7); Kelly, G. 16; Kilgallon, M. 18(1); Kishishev, R. 10; Lewis, E. 40(1); Michalik, L. 7; Moore, I. 14(19); Nicholls, K. 12(1); Richardson, F. 19(3); Rui Marques, M. 14(3); Stack, G. 12; Stone, S. 5(5); Sullivan, N. 7; Thompson, A. 9(2); Warner, T. 13; Westlake, I. 19(8); Wright, A. 1.
Goals – League (46): Healy 10 (3 pens), Blake 8 (1 pen), Cresswell 4, Heath 3, Lewis 3, Horsfield 2, Moore 2, Thompson 2, Butler 1, Derry 1, Douglas 1, Ehiogu 1, Flo 1, Foxe 1, Howson 1, Kandol 1, Michalik 1, Stone 1, own goals 2.
Carling Cup (5): Moore 3, Bakke 1, Blake 1.
FA Cup (1): own goal 1.
Ground: Elland Road, Leeds LS11 0ES. Telephone (0113) 367 6000.
Record Attendance: 57,892 v Sunderland, FA Cup 5th rd (replay), 15 March 1967.

Capacity: 39,4619.
Manager: Dennis Wise.
Most League Goals: 98, Division 2, 1927–28.
Highest League Scorer in Season: John Charles, 42, Division 2, 1953–54.
Most League Goals in Total Aggregate: Peter Lorimer, 168, 1965–79 and 1983–86.
Most Capped Player: Lucas Radebe, 58 (70), South Africa.
Most League Appearances: Jack Charlton, 629, 1953–73.
Honours – Football League: Division 1 Champions – 1968–69, 1973–74, 1991–92. Division 2 Champions – 1923–24, 1963–64, 1989–90. **FA Cup:** Winners – 1972. **Football League Cup:** Winners – 1967–68. **European Competitions: European Fairs Cup:** Winners – 1967–68, 1970–71.
Colours: White shirts, white shorts, white stockings all with royal blue trim and yellow piping.

LEICESTER CITY — FL CHAMPIONSHIP

Cisak Aleksander (G)	6 3	14 11	Krakow	19 5 89	Scholar
De Vries Mark (F)	6 3	12 01	Surinam	24 8 75	Hearts
Dodds Louis (F)	5 10	12 04	Leicester	8 10 86	Scholar
Douglas Rab (G)	6 3	14 12	Lanark	24 4 72	Celtic
Fryatt Matty (F)	5 10	11 00	Nuneaton	5 3 86	Walsall
Gerrbrand Patrik (D)	6 2	12 06	Stockholm	27 4 81	Hammarby
Gradel Max (M)	5 8	12 03	Ivory Coast	30 9 87	
Hammond Elvis (F)	5 10	11 02	Accra	6 10 80	Fulham
Henderson Paul (G)	6 1	12 06	Sydney	22 4 76	Bradford C
Hughes Stephen (M)	5 11	9 06	Motherwell	14 11 82	Rangers
Hume Iain (F)	5 7	11 02	Brampton	31 10 83	Tranmere R
Kenton Darren (D)	5 10	12 10	Wandsworth	13 9 78	Southampton
Kisnorbo Patrick (D)	6 1	11 11	Melbourne	24 3 81	Hearts
Logan Conrad (G)	6 0	14 09	Letterkenny	18 4 86	Scholar
Mattock Joe (D)	5 11	11 04	Leicester	15 5 90	Scholar
Maybury Alan (D)	5 8	11 08	Dublin	8 8 78	Hearts
McAuley Gareth (D)	6 4	13 12	Larne	5 12 79	Lincoln C
McCarthy Patrick (D)	6 2	13 07	Dublin	31 5 83	Manchester C
Odhiambo Eric (F)	5 9	11 00	Oxford	12 5 89	Scholar
Porter Levi (F)	5 4	10 05	Leicester	6 4 87	Scholar
Sheehan Alan (D)	5 11	11 02	Athlone	14 9 86	Scholar
Stearman Richard (D)	6 2	10 08	Wolverhampton	19 8 87	Scholar
Wesolowski James (D)	5 8	11 11	Sydney	25 8 87	Scholar

League Appearances: Cadamarteri, D. (9); Fryatt, M. 21(11); Glombard, L. (1); Hammond, E. 17(14); Henderson, P. 28; Horsfield, G. 9(4); Hughes, S. 34(7); Hume, I. 39(6); Jarrett, J. 13; Johansson, N. 36; Johnson, A. 21(1); Kenton, D. 20(3); Kisnorbo, P. 40; Logan, C. 18; Low, J. 12(4); Mattock, J. 3(1); Maybury, A. 25(2); McAuley, G. 27(3); McCarthy, P. 20(2); Newton, S. 9; O'Grady, C. 6(4); Porter, L. 26(8); Stearman, R. 23(12); Sylla, M. 3(3); Tiatto, D. 24(1); Welsh, A. 4(3); Wesolowski, J. 11(8); Williams, G. 12(2); Yeates, M. 5(4).
Goals – League (49): Hume 13 (2 pens), Hammond 5, Kisnorbo 5, Fryatt 3, Hughes 3, McAuley 3, Porter 3, Horsfield 2, Kenton 2, Johansson 1, Johnson 1, McCarthy 1, Newton 1, Stearman 1, Tiatto 1, Williams 1, Yeates 1, own goals 2.
Carling Cup (7): Stearman 2, Hammond 1, Hume 1 (pen), Kisnorbo 1, McCarthy 1, O'Grady 1.
FA Cup (5): Cadamarteri 1, Fryatt 1, Kisnorbo 1, McAuley 1, Wesolowski 1.
Ground: The Walkers Stadium, Filbert Way, Leicester LE2 7FL. Telephone (0870) 040 6000.
Record Attendance: 47,298 v Tottenham H, FA Cup 5th rd, 18 February 1928.
Capacity: 32,500.

Head Coach: Martin Allen.
Secretary: Andrew Neville.
Most League Goals: 109, Division 2, 1956–57.
Highest League Scorer in Season: Arthur Rowley, 44, Division 2, 1956–57.
Most League Goals in Total Aggregate: Arthur Chandler, 259, 1923–35.
Most Capped Player: John O'Neill, 39, Northern Ireland.
Most League Appearances: Adam Black, 528, 1920–35.
Honours – Football League: Division 2 Champions – 1924–25, 1936–37, 1953–54, 1956–57, 1970–71, 1979–80. **Football League Cup:** Winners – 1964, 1997, 2000.
Colours: Blue shirts, blue shorts, blue stockings.

LEYTON ORIENT — FL CHAMPIONSHIP 1

Alexander Gary (F)	6 0	12 00	Lambeth	15 8 79	Hull C
Chambers Adam (M)	5 10	11 08	Sandwell	20 11 80	Kidderminster H
Corden Wayne (M)	5 9	11 02	Leek	1 11 75	Scunthorpe U
Demetriou Jason (M)	5 11	10 08	Newham	18 11 87	Scholar
Easton Craig (M)	5 11	11 03	Airdrie	26 2 79	Dundee U
Echanomi Efe (M)	5 7	11 07	Nigeria	27 9 86	Scholar
Fortune Clayton (D)	6 3	14 00	Forest Gate	10 11 82	Bristol C
Garner Glyn (G)	6 2	13 11	Pontypool	9 12 76	Bury
Guttridge Luke (M)	5 6	10 05	Barnstaple	12 3 82	Southend U
Ibehre Jabo (F)	6 1	12 10	Islington	28 1 83	Trainee
Lockwood Matt (D)	6 0	11 06	Rochford	17 10 76	Bristol R
Morris Glenn (G)	5 11	11 00	Woolwich	20 12 83	Scholar
Palmer Aiden (M)	5 8	10 04	Enfield	2 1 87	Scholar
Saah Brian (M)	6 1	11 05	Rush Green	16 12 86	Scholar
Tann Adam (D)	6 0	11 05	Fakenham	12 5 82	Notts Co
Thelwell Alton (D)	6 0	12 05	London	5 9 80	Hull C

League Appearances: Alexander, G. 42(2); Barnard, D. 9(10); Chambers, A. 36(2); Connor, P. 5(13); Corden, W. 36(6); Demetriou, J. 2(13); Duncan, D. (3); Easton, C. 29(1); Echanomi, E. (3); Fortune, C. 9; Garner, G. 43; Guttridge, L. 15(2); Hooper, G. 2(2); Ibehre, J. 12(18); Jarvis, R. 14; Keith, J. 8(3); Lockwood, M. 41; Mackie, J. 33(2); McMahon, D. 3(5); Miller, J. 28(3); Morris, G. 3; Mulryne, P. 1(1); Page, J. (1); Palmer, A. 6; Partridge, D. 1; Saah, B. 30(2); Shields, S. (1); Simpson, M. 15; Steele, L. 9(2); Tann, A. 13(8); Thelwell, A. 20(2); Till, P. 4; Tudor, S. 28(5); Walker, J. 9(5).
Goals – League (61): Alexander 12, Lockwood 11 (6 pens), Jarvis 6, Chambers 4, Ibehre 4, Steele 4, Corden 3, Connor 2, Demetriou 2, Hooper 2, Miller 2, Tudor 2, Walker 2, Easton 1, Guttridge 1, Simpson 1, Tann 1, Thelwell 1.
Carling Cup (0).
FA Cup (4): Corden 2, Miller 1, Walker 1.
J Paint Trophy (1): Duncan 1.
Ground: Matchroom Stadium, Brisbane Road, Leyton, London E10 5NE. Telephone 0871 310 1881.
Record Attendance: 34,345 v West Ham U, FA Cup 4th rd, 25 January 1964.
Capacity: 7,872 (rising to approx 9,000 by 2007).
Manager: Martin Ling.
Secretary: Lindsey Freeman.
Most League Goals: 106, Division 3 (S), 1955–56.
Highest League Scorer in Season: Tom Johnston, 35, Division 2, 1957–58.
Most League Goals in Total Aggregate: Tom Johnston, 121, 1956–58, 1959–61.
Most Capped Players: Tunji Banjo, 7 (7), Nigeria; John Chiedozie, 7 (9), Nigeria; Tony Grealish, 7 (45), Eire.
Most League Appearances: Peter Allen, 432, 1965–78.

Honours – Football League: Division 3 Champions – 1969–70. Division 3 (S) Champions – 1955–56.
Colours: All red with white trim.

LINCOLN CITY — FL CHAMPIONSHIP 2

Amoo Ryan (M)	5 10	9 12	Leicester	11 10 83	Northampton T
Beevers Lee (D)	6 1	13 00	Doncaster	4 12 83	Boston U
Brown Nat (F)	6 2	12 05	Sheffield	15 6 81	Huddersfield T
Clarke Shane (D)	6 1	13 03	Lincoln	7 11 87	Scholar
Duffy Ayden (M)	5 8	10 12	Kettering	16 11 86	Scholar
Forrester Jamie (F)	5 7	11 00	Bradford	1 11 74	Bristol R
Frecklington Lee (M)	5 8	11 00	Lincoln	8 9 85	Scholar
Green Paul (D)	5 8	10 04	Birmigham	15 4 87	Aston Villa
Hughes Jeff (D)	6 1	11 00	Larne	29 5 85	Larne
Kerr Scott (M)	5 9	10 07	Leeds	11 12 81	Scarborough
Marriott Alan (G)	6 0	12 04	Bedford	3 9 78	Tottenham H
Mayo Paul (D)	5 11	11 09	Lincoln	13 10 81	Watford
Morgan Paul (D)	6 0	11 03	Belfast	23 10 78	Preston NE
Moses Adi (D)	5 11	13 01	Doncaster	4 5 75	Crewe Alex
N'Guessan Dany (M)	6 0	12 13	Ivry-sur-Seine	11 8 87	Boston U
Ryan Oliver (M)	5 9	11 00	Boston	26 9 85	Scholar
Semple Ryan (M)	5 11	10 11	Belfast	4 7 85	Peterborough U
Stallard Mark (F)	6 0	13 09	Derby	24 10 74	Shrewsbury T
Warlow Owain (M)	6 0	12 00	Treforest	3 7 88	Scholar
Watt Phil (F)	5 11	11 04	Rotherham	10 1 88	Scholar

League Appearances: Amoo, R. 35(8); Bacon, D. 1; Beevers, L. 42(2); Birley, M. 3(1); Brown, N. 26(2); Cryan, C. (4); Eaden, N. 32(1); Forrester, J. 39(2); Frecklington, L. 38(4); Green, P. 11(5); Gritton, M. 5(12); Holmes, P. 5; Hughes, J. 37(4); Kerr, S. 44; Marriott, A. 46; Mayo, P. 28(6); Mendes, J. 4(5); Mettam, L. 1(3); Morgan, P. 27(6); Moses, A. 26(6); N'Guessan, D. 4(5); Nicholson, S. 7(1); Ryan, O. (7); Semple, R. (4); Stallard, M. 41; Warlow, O. (5); Weir-Daley, S. 4(7).
Goals – League (70): Forrester 18 (7 pens), Stallard 15, Frecklington 8, Hughes 6, Beevers 5, Weir-Daley 5, Kerr 3, Amoo 2, Gritton 2, Brown N 1, Green 1, Mayo 1, Mettam 1, Morgan 1, Moses 1.
Carling Cup (3): Beevers 1, Frecklington 1, Stallard 1.
FA Cup (1): Frecklington 1.
J Paint Trophy (0).
Play-Offs (4): Hughes 3, Stallard 1.
Ground: Sincil Bank Stadium, Sincil Bank, Lincoln LN5 8LD. Telephone (0870) 899 2005.
Record Attendance: 23,196 v Derby Co, League Cup 4th rd, 15 November 1967.
Capacity: 10,055.
Head Coach: John Schofield.
Secretary: Fran Martin.
Most League Goals: 121, Division 3 (N), 1951–52.
Highest League Scorer in Season: Allan Hall, 41, Division 3 (N), 1931–32.
Most League Goals in Total Aggregate: Andy Graver, 144, 1950–55 and 1958–61.
Most Capped Player: Gareth McAuley, 5, Northern Ireland.
Most League Appearances: Grant Brown, 407, 1989–2002.
Honours – Football League: Division 3 (N) Champions – 1931–32, 1947–48, 1951–52. Division 4 Champions – 1975–76. **GM Vauxhall Conference:** Champions – 1987–88.
Colours: Red and white.

Name	Ht	Wt	Birthplace	Birthdate	Source
Agger Daniel (D)	6 2	12 06	Hvidovre	12 12 84	Brondby
Ajdarevic Astrit (M)			Kosovo	20 9 90	Falkenberg
Anderson Paul (M)	5 9	10 04	Leicester	23 7 88	Hull C
Antwi-Birago Godwin (D)	6 1	13 09	Tafu	7 6 88	San Gregorio
Arbeloa Alvaro (D)	6 0	12 06	Salamanca	17 1 83	La Coruna
Barnett Charlie (M)			Liverpool	19 9 88	Scholar
Bellamy Craig (F)	5 9	10 12	Cardiff	13 7 79	Blackburn R
Brouwer Jordy (F)			Den Haag	26 2 88	Ajax
Carragher Jamie (D)	5 9	12 01	Liverpool	28 1 78	Trainee
Carson Scott (G)	6 3	13 12	Whitehaven	3 9 85	Leeds U
Cisse Djibril (F)	6 0	13 00	Arles	12 8 81	Auxerre
Crouch Peter (F)	6 7	13 03	Macclesfield	30 1 81	Southampton
Darby Stephen (D)			Liverpool	6 10 88	Scholar
Duran Vazquez Fransisco (M)			Malaga	28 4 88	Malaga
El Zhar Nabil (F)	5 9	11 05	Rabat	27 8 86	St Etienne
Fabio Aurelio (M)	5 10	11 11	Sao Carlos	24 9 79	Valencia
Finnan Steve (M)	6 0	12 03	Limerick	24 4 76	Fulham
Flynn Ryan (M)	5 8	10 00	Scotland	4 9 88	Falkirk
Gerrard Steven (M)	6 0	12 05	Whiston	30 5 80	Trainee
Gonzalez Jose Miguel (M)	5 9	12 08	Malaga	15 11 79	Real Sociedad
Guthrie Danny (M)	5 9	11 06	Shrewsbury	18 4 87	Scholar
Hammill Adam (M)			Liverpool	25 1 88	Scholar
Hobbs Jack (D)	6 3	13 05	Portsmouth	18 8 88	Lincoln C
Huth Ronald (D)			Asuncion	30 10 89	Tacuary
Hyypia Sami (D)	6 3	13 09	Porvoo	7 10 73	Willem II
Idrizaj Bezian (F)	6 2	12 02	Austria	12 10 87	LASK Linz
Kewell Harry (M)	5 9	12 06	Sydney	22 9 78	Leeds U
Kuyt Dirk (F)	6 0	12 02	Katwijk	22 7 80	Feyenoord
Le Tallec Anthony (M)	6 0	12 00	Hennebont	3 10 84	Le Havre
Lindfield Craig (F)	6 0	10 05	Wirral	7 9 88	Scholar
Luis Garcia (M)	5 6	10 05	Badalona	24 6 78	Barcelona
Martin David (G)	6 1	13 04	Romford	22 1 86	Milton Keynes D
Mascherano Javier (M)	5 10	12 02	San Lorenzo	8 6 84	West Ham U
O'Donnell Daniel (D)	6 2	11 11	Liverpool	10 3 86	Scholar
Paletta Gabriel (D)	6 1	13 07	Longchamps	15 2 86	Banfield
Peltier Lee (F)	5 10	12 00	Liverpool	11 12 86	Scholar
Pennant Jermaine (M)	5 8	10 01	Nottingham	15 1 83	Birmingham C
Reina Jose (G)	6 2	14 06	Madrid	31 8 82	Villarreal
Riise John Arne (M)	6 1	14 00	Molde	24 9 80	Monaco
Roque Miguel (M)	6 2	12 03	Tremp	8 7 88	UE Lleida
Ryan James (M)			Maghull	6 9 88	Scholar
Sinama-Pongolle Florent (F)	5 7	11 05	Saint-Pierre	20 10 84	Le Havre
Sissoko Mohamed (M)	6 2	12 08	Rouen	21 1 85	Valencia
Smith James (M)	5 11	12 06	Liverpool	17 10 85	Scholar
Spearing Jay (D)			Wirral	25 11 88	Scholar
Threlfall Robbie (D)	5 11	11 00	Liverpool	25 11 88	Scholar
Xabi Alonso (M)	6 0	12 02	Tolosa	25 11 81	Real Sociedad

League Appearances: Agger, D. 23(4); Alonso, X. 29(3); Arbeloa, A. 8(1); Bellamy, C. 23(4); Carragher, J. 34(1); Crouch, P. 19(13); Dudek, J. 2; El Zhar, N. (3); Fabio Aurelio, 10(7); Finnan, S. 32(1); Fowler, R. 6(10); Gerrard, S. 35(1); Gonzalez, J. 14(11); Guthrie, D. (3); Hyypia, S. 23; Insua, E. 2; Kewell, H. (2); Kromkamp, J. 1; Kuyt, D. 27(7); Luis Garcia, 11(6); Mascherano, J. 7; Padelli, D. 1; Paletta, G. 2(1); Pennant, J. 20(14); Reina, J. 35; Riise, J. 29(4); Sissoko, M. 15(1);

Warnock, S. 1; Zenden, B. 9(7).
Goals – League (57): Kuyt 12, Crouch 9, Bellamy 7, Gerrard 7 (1 pen), Alonso 4 (1 pen), Fowler 3 (3 pens), Luis Garcia 3, Agger 2, Gonzalez 2, Hyypia 2, Arbeloa 1, Carragher 1, Kewell 1 (pen), Pennant 1, Riise 1, own goal 1.
Carling Cup (8): Fowler 2, Agger 1, Crouch 1, Gerrard 1, Hyypia 1, Paletta 1, Riise 1.
FA Cup (1): Kuyt 1.
Champions League (22): Crouch 7, Gerrard 3, Luis Garcia 3, Bellamy 2, Fowler 2, Riise 2, Agger 1, Gonzalez 1, Kuyt 1.
Community Shield (2): Crouch 1, Riise 1.
Ground: Anfield, Anfield Road, Liverpool L4 0TH. Telephone (0151) 263 2361.
Record Attendance: 61,905 v Wolverhampton W, FA Cup 4th rd, 2 February 1952.
Capacity: 45,362.
Manager: Rafael Benitez.
Secretary: William Bryce Morrison.
Most League Goals: 106, Division 2, 1895–96.
Highest League Scorer in Season: Roger Hunt, 41, Division 2, 1961–62.
Most League Goals in Total Aggregate: Roger Hunt, 245, 1959–69.
Most Capped Player: Ian Rush, 67 (73), Wales.
Most League Appearances: Ian Callaghan, 640, 1960–78.
Honours – Football League: Division 1 – Champions 1900–01, 1905–06, 1921–22, 1922–23, 1946–47, 1963–64, 1965–66, 1972–73, 1975–76, 1976–77, 1978–79, 1979–80, 1981–82, 1982–83, 1983–84, 1985–86, 1987–88, 1989–90 (Liverpool have a record number of 18 League Championship wins). Division 2 Champions – 1893–94, 1895–96, 1904–05, 1961–62. **FA Cup**: Winners – 1965, 1974, 1986, 1989, 1992, 2001, 2006. **League Cup:** Winners – 1981, 1982, 1983, 1984, 1995, 2001, 2003. **League Super Cup:** Winners 1985–86. **European Competitions: European Cup:** Winners – 1976–77, 1977–78, 1980–81, 1983–84. **Champions League:** Winners – 2004–05. **UEFA Cup:** Winners – 1972–73, 1975–76, 2001. **Super Cup:** Winners – 1977, 2005.
Colours: Red shirts, red shorts, red stockings.

LUTON TOWN — FL CHAMPIONSHIP 1

Andrew Calvin (F)	6 0	12 11	Luton	19 12 86	Scholar
Barnett Leon (D)	6 0	12 04	Stevenage	30 11 85	Scholar
Barrett Zac (G)	6 2	13 03	Stevenage	26 5 88	Scholar
Bell David (M)	5 10	11 05	Kettering	21 1 84	Rushden & D
Beresford Marlon (G)	6 1	13 05	Lincoln	2 9 69	Barnsley
Boyd Adam (F)	5 9	10 12	Hartlepool	25 5 82	Hartlepool U
Brill Dean (G)	6 2	14 05	Luton	2 12 85	Scholar
Brkovic Ahmet (M)	5 8	11 11	Dubrovnik	23 9 74	Leyton Orient
Coyne Chris (D)	6 2	13 12	Brisbane	20 12 78	Dundee
Davis Sol (D)	5 8	11 13	Cheltenham	4 9 79	Swindon T
Emanuel Lewis (D)	5 8	12 01	Bradford	14 10 83	Bradford C
Feeney Warren (F)	5 10	11 03	Belfast	17 1 81	Stockport Co
Foley Kevin (M)	5 10	11 02	London	1 11 84	Scholar
Keane Keith (M)	5 9	11 02	Luton	20 11 86	Scholar
Langley Richard (M)	6 0	11 04	Harlesden	27 12 79	QPR
Morgan Dean (M)	5 11	13 00	Enfield	3 10 83	Reading
O'Leary Stephen (M)	6 0	11 09	Barnet	12 2 85	Scholar
Parkin Sam (F)	6 2	13 00	Roehampton	14 3 81	Ipswich T
Perrett Russell (D)	6 1	12 06	Barton-on-Sea	18 6 73	Cardiff C
Robinson Steve (M)	5 9	11 02	Lisburn	10 12 74	Preston NE
Spring Matthew (M)	5 11	12 05	Harlow	17 11 79	Watford
Talbot Drew (F)	5 11	11 00	Barnsley	19 7 86	Sheffield W
Underwood Paul (M)	5 11	12 11	Wimbledon	16 8 73	Rushden & D

League Appearances: Andrew, C. 5(2); Barnett, L. 39; Bell, D. 28(6); Beresford, M. 26; Boyd, A. 5(14); Brill, D. 9(2); Brkovic, A. 14(6); Carlisle, C. 4(1); Coyne, C. 11(7); Davis, S. 20(4); Edwards, C. 26; Emanuel, L. 39(1); Feeney, W. 15(14); Foley, K. 38(1); Heikkinen, M. 37; Holmes, P. 3(2); Idrizaj, B. 3(4); Keane, K. 17(2); Kiely, D. 11; Langley, R. 18(11); Morgan, D. 21(15); O'Leary, S. 5(2); Parkin, S. 7(1); Perrett, R. 8(2); Robinson, S. 37(1); Runstrom, B. 7(1); Spring, M. 14; Talbot, D. 13(2); Vine, R. 26.
Goals – League (53): Vine 12 (2 pens), Edwards 6, Morgan 4, Barnett 3, Bell 3 (1 pen), Brkovic 3, Talbot 3, Emanuel 2, Feeney 2, Runstrom 2, Andrew 1, Boyd 1, Coyne 1, Heikkinen 1, Idrizaj 1, Keane 1, Langley 1 (pen), O'Leary 1, Parkin 1, Perrett 1, Spring 1, own goals 2.
Carling Cup (4): Boyd 1, Feeney 1, Morgan 1, Vine 1.
FA Cup (3): Feeney 1, Vine 1, own goal 1.
Ground: Kenilworth Stadium, 1 Maple Road, Luton, Beds LU4 8AW. Telephone (01582) 411 622.
Record Attendance: 30,069 v Blackpool, FA Cup 6th rd replay, 4 March 1959.
Capacity: 10,260.
Manager: Kevin Blackwell.
Secretary: Cherry Newbery.
Most League Goals: 103, Division 3 (S), 1936–37.
Highest League Scorer in Season: Joe Payne, 55, Division 3 (S), 1936–37.
Most League Goals in Total Aggregate: Gordon Turner, 243, 1949–64.
Most Capped Player: Mal Donaghy, 58 (91), Northern Ireland.
Most League Appearances: Bob Morton, 494, 1948–64.
Honours – Football League: Championship 1: Winners – 2004–05. Division 2 Champions – 1981–82. Division 4 Champions – 1967–68. Division 3 (S) Champions – 1936–37. **Football League Cup:** Winners – 1987–88.
Colours: White shirts, black shorts, white stockings.

MACCLESFIELD TOWN FL CHAMPIONSHIP 2

Blackman Nick (M)	6 2	11 08	Whitefield	11 11 89	Scholar
Brain Jonny (G)	6 3	13 05	Carlisle	11 2 83	Port Vale
Brightwell Ian (D)	5 10	12 08	Lutterworth	9 4 68	Port Vale
Doyle Robert (F)	5 9	12 00	Bray	15 4 82	Bray W
Hadfield Jordan (M)	5 10	11 04	Swinton	12 8 87	Stockport Co
Jennings James (M)	5 9	12 02	Leeds	2 9 87	Scholar
Lee Tommy (G)	6 2	12 00	Keighley	3 1 86	Manchester U
McDonald Marvin (F)	5 7	10 00	Wythenshawe	24 8 86	Scholar
McIntyre Kevin (M)	5 11	12 00	Liverpool	23 12 77	Chester C
McNeil Matthew (F)	6 5	14 03	Macclesfield	14 7 76	Hyde U
McNulty Jim (D)	6 1	12 00	Liverpool	13 2 85	Wrexham
Miles John (F)	5 10	12 09	Fazackerley	28 9 81	Crewe Alex
Morley Dave (D)	6 3	13 00	St Helens	25 9 77	Doncaster R
Murphy John (F)	6 2	14 00	Whiston	18 10 76	Blackpool
Murray Adam (M)	5 8	10 12	Birmingham	30 9 81	Torquay U
Navarro Alan (M)	5 10	11 07	Liverpool	31 5 81	Accrington S
Regan Carl (D)	5 11	11 12	Liverpool	14 1 80	Chester C
Reid Izak (M)	5 5	10 05	Sheffield	08 7 87	Scholar
Swailes Danny (D)	6 3	13 07	Bolton	1 4 79	Bury
Teague Andrew (D)	6 2	12 00	Preston	5 2 86	Scholar
Tolley Jamie (M)	6 1	11 03	Ludlow	12 5 83	Shrewsbury T

League Appearances: Begovic, A. 2(1); Benjamin, R. (3); Blackman, N. (1); Brain, J. 9; Brightwell, I. 4; Bullock, M. 38(5); D'Laryea, N. 1; Doyle, R. (2); Hadfield, J. 30(7); Heath, C. 16(9); Holgate, A. 2(4); Ince, P. (1); Jennings, J. 5(4); Lee, T. 34;

McIntyre, K. 43(1); McNeil, M. 29(6); McNulty, J. 15; Miles, J. 23(7); Morley, D. 35; Murphy, J. 25(4); Murray, A. 8(3); Navarro, A. 28(4); Rankin, I. 1(3); Regan, C. 36(2); Reid, I. 2(6); Robinson, M. 5; Rouse, D. 1; Scott, R. 22(4); Swailes, D. 38; Teague, A. 10(3); Tipton, M. 15(17); Tolley, J. 22(1); Weir-Daley, S. 5(2); Wiles, S. 2(5).
Goals – League (55): McIntyre 9 (8 pens), Murphy 7, McNeil 5, Bullock 4, Heath 4 (1 pen), Miles 4, Tipton 4, Morley 3, Swailes 3, Navarro 2, Regan 2, Scott 2, Weir-Daley 2, Hadfield 1, Holgate 1, Teague 1, Tolley 1.
Carling Cup (0).
FA Cup (4): Murphy 2, McIntyre 1 (pen), McNulty 1.
J Paint Trophy (0).
Ground: Moss Rose Ground, London Road, Macclesfield, Cheshire SK11 0DQ. Telephone (01625) 264 686.
Record Attendance: 9,008 v Winsford U, Cheshire Senior Cup 2nd rd, 4 February 1948. **Capacity:** 6,141.
Manager: Ian Brightwell.
Secretary: Diane Hehir.
Most League Goals: 66, Division 3, 1999–2000.
Highest League Scorer in Season: Jon Parkin, 22, League 2, 2004–05.
Most League Goals in Total Aggregate: Matt Tipton, 45, 2002–05; 2006–07.
Most Capped Player: George Abbey, 10(16), Nigeria.
Most League Appearances: Darren Tinson, 263, 1997–2003.
Honours – None.
Colours: All blue.

MANCHESTER CITY — FA PREMIERSHIP

Ball Michael (D)	5 10	12 02	Liverpool	2 10 79	PSV Eindhoven
Barton Joey (M)	5 11	11 09	Huyton	2 9 82	Scholar
Corradi Bernardo (F)	6 0	13 10	Siena	30 3 76	Valencia
Dabo Ousmane (M)	6 1	13 10	Laval	8 2 77	Lazio
Dickov Paul (F)	5 6	10 09	Livingston	1 11 72	Blackburn R
Distin Sylvain (D)	6 3	14 08	Bagnolet	16 12 77	Newcastle U
Dunne Richard (D)	6 2	15 12	Dublin	21 9 79	Everton
Etuhu Calvin (F)	6 0	12 09	Nigeria	30 5 88	Scholar
Grimes Ashley (F)	5 11	11 07	Salford	9 12 86	Scholar
Hamann Dietmar (M)	6 3	13 01	Waldasson	27 8 73	Liverpool
Hart Joe (G)	6 5	14 05	Shrewsbury	19 4 87	Shrewsbury T
Ireland Stephen (F)	5 8	10 07	Cobh	22 8 86	Scholar
Isaksson Andreas (G)	6 6	13 07	Smygehamn	3 10 81	Rennes
Jihai Sun (D)	5 9	12 02	Dalian	30 9 77	Dalian Wanda
Johnson Michael (M)	6 0	12 07	Urmston	3 3 88	Scholar
Laird Marc (M)	6 1	10 07	Edinburgh	23 1 86	Scholar
Logan Shaleum (D)	5 8	10 01	Manchester	29 1 88	Scholar
Miller Ishmael (F)	6 3	14 00	Manchester	5 3 87	Scholar
Mills Danny (D)	5 11	12 06	Norwich	18 5 77	Leeds U
Mills Matthew (D)	6 3	12 12	Swindon	14 7 86	Southampton
Mpenza Emile (F)	5 10	11 06	Brussels	4 7 78	Al Rayyan
Onuoha Nedum (D)	6 2	12 04	Warri	12 11 86	Scholar
Richards Micah (D)	5 11	13 00	Birmingham	24 6 88	Scholar
Samaras Georgios (F)	6 3	13 07	Heraklion	21 2 85	Heerenveen
Schmeichel Kasper (G)	6 1	13 00	Copenhagen	5 11 86	Scholar
Sturridge Danny (F)	5 11	12 02	Birmingham	1 9 89	Scholar
Vassell Darius (F)	5 9	13 00	Birmingham	13 6 80	Aston Villa
Weaver Nick (G)	6 4	14 07	Sheffield	2 3 79	Mansfield T
Williamson Sam (D)	5 8	11 09	Macclesfield	15 10 87	Scholar

League Appearances: Ball, M. 12; Barton, J. 33; Beasley, D. 11(7); Corradi, B. 19(6); Dabo, O. 10(3); Dickov, P. 9(7); Distin, S. 37; Dunne, R. 38; Hamann, D. 12(4); Hart, J. 1; Ireland, S. 14(10); Isaksson, A. 12(2); Jihai, S. 10(3); Johnson, M. 10; Jordan, S. 12(1); Miller, I. 3(13); Mills, D. (1); Mills, M. 1; Mpenza, E. 9(1); Onuoha, N. 15(3); Reyna, C. 12(3); Richards, M. 28; Samaras, G. 16(20); Sinclair, T. 14(4); Sturridge, D. (2); Thatcher, B. 11; Trabelsi, H. 16(4); Vassell, D. 28(4); Weaver, N. 25.
Goals – League (29): Barton 6 (1 pen), Samaras 4 (1 pen), Beasley 3, Corradi 3, Mpenza 3, Vassell 3, Distin 2, Dunne 1, Ireland 1, Richards 1, Trabelsi 1, own goal 1.
Carling Cup (1): Samaras 1.
FA Cup (9): Ireland 2, Vassell 2, Ball 1, Barton 1, Beasley 1, Samaras 1 (pen), own goal 1.
Ground: The City of Manchester Stadium, SportCity, Manchester M11 3FF. Telephone (0870) 062 1894.
Record Attendance: (at Maine Road) 85,569 v Stoke C, FA Cup 6th rd, 3 March 1934 (British record for any game outside London or Glasgow). **Capacity:** 47,715.
Manager: Sven-Göran Eriksson.
Secretary: J. B. Halford.
Most League Goals: 108, Division 2, 1926–27, 108, Division 1, 2001–02.
Highest League Scorer in Season: Tommy Johnson, 38, Division 1, 1928–29.
Most League Goals in Total Aggregate: Tommy Johnson, 158, 1919–30.
Most Capped Player: Colin Bell, 48, England.
Most League Appearances: Alan Oakes, 565, 1959–76.
Honours – Football League: Division 1 Champions – 1936–37, 1967–68, 2001–02. Division 2 Champions – 1898–99, 1902–03, 1909–10, 1927–28, 1946–47, 1965–66. **FA Cup:** Winners – 1904, 1934, 1956, 1969. **Football League Cup:** Winners – 1970, 1976. **European Competitions: European Cup-Winners' Cup:** Winners – 1969–70.
Colours: Sky blue shirts, white shorts, sky blue stockings.

MANCHESTER UNITED — FA PREMIERSHIP

Bardsley Phillip (D)	5 11	11 08	Salford	28 6 85	Scholar
Barnes Michael (M)	5 10	11 05	Chorley	24 6 88	Scholar
Brandy Febian (F)	5 5	10 00	Manchester	4 2 89	Scholar
Brown Wes (D)	6 1	13 11	Manchester	13 10 79	Scholar
Campbell Frazier (F)	5 11	12 04	Huddersfield	13 9 87	Scholar
Carrick Michael (M)	6 2	13 03	Wallsend	28 7 81	Tottenham H
Cathcart Craig (D)	6 2	11 06	Belfast	6 2 89	Scholar
Dong Fangzhuo (F)	6 0	12 07	Liaoning	23 1 85	Dalian Shide
Eagles Chris (M)	6 0	10 08	Hemel Hempstead	19 11 85	Scholar
Eckersley Adam (D)	5 9	11 13	Worsley	7 9 85	Scholar
Evans Jonny (D)	6 2	12 02	Belfast	3 1 88	Scholar
Evans Sean (F)	5 9	11 02	Ludlow	25 9 87	Scholar
Evra Patrice (D)	5 8	11 10	Dakar	15 5 81	Monaco
Fagan Chris (F)	5 8	10 05	Dublin	11 5 89	Scholar
Ferdinand Rio (D)	6 2	13 12	Peckham	7 11 78	Leeds U
Fletcher Darren (M)	6 0	13 01	Edinburgh	1 2 84	Scholar
Foster Ben (G)	6 2	12 08	Leamington Spa	3 4 83	Stoke C
Gibson Darron (M)	6 0	12 04	Londonderry	25 10 87	Scholar
Giggs Ryan (F)	5 11	11 00	Cardiff	29 11 73	School
Gray David (F)	5 11	11 02	Edinburgh	4 5 88	Scholar
Heaton Tom (G)	6 1	13 12	Chester	15 4 86	Scholar
Heinze Gabriel (D)	5 10	12 04	Crespo	19 4 78	Paris St Germain
Jones Richie (M)	6 0	11 00	Manchester	26 9 86	Scholar
Lee Kieran (D)	5 9	10 07	Tameside	22 6 88	Scholar
Martin Lee (M)	5 10	10 03	Taunton	9 2 87	Scholar

Neville Gary (D)	5 11	12 04	Bury	18 2 75	Scholar
O'Shea John (D)	6 3	12 10	Waterford	30 4 81	Waterford
Park Ji-Sung (M)	5 9	11 06	Seoul	25 2 81	PSV Eindhoven
Pique Gerard (D)	6 3	12 10	Barcelona	2 2 87	Scholar
Richardson Kieran (M)	5 8	11 00	Greenwich	21 10 84	Scholar
Ronaldo Cristiano (M)	6 1	12 04	Funchal	5 2 85	Sporting Lisbon
Rooney Wayne (F)	5 10	12 04	Liverpool	24 10 85	Everton
Rossi Giuseppe (F)	5 9	11 03	New Jersey	1 2 87	Scholar
Saha Louis (F)	6 1	12 06	Paris	8 8 78	Fulham
Scholes Paul (M)	5 7	11 00	Salford	16 11 74	Scholar
Shawcross Ryan (D)	6 3	13 13	Chester	4 10 87	Scholar
Silvestre Mikael (D)	6 0	13 01	Chambray les Tours	9 8 77	Internazionale
Simpson Danny (D)	5 9	11 05	Salford	4 1 87	Scholar
Smith Alan (F)	5 10	12 01	Leeds	28 10 80	Leeds U
Solskjaer Ole Gunnar (F)	5 10	11 11	Kristiansund	26 2 73	Molde
Van der Sar Edwin (G)	6 5	14 11	Voorhout	29 10 70	Fulham
Vidic Nemanja (D)	6 1	13 02	Uzice	21 10 81	Spartak Moscow
Zieler Ron-Robert (G)	6 1	11 07	Cologne	12 2 89	Scholar

League Appearances: Brown, W. 17(5); Carrick, M. 29(4); Dong Fangshou, 1; Eagles, C. 1(1); Evra, P. 22(2); Ferdinand, R. 33; Fletcher, D. 16(8); Giggs, R. 25(5); Heinze, G. 17(5); Kuszczak, T. 6; Larsson, H. 5(2); Lee, K. 1; Neville, G. 24; O'Shea, J. 16(16); Park, J. 8(6); Richardson, K. 8(7); Ronaldo, C. 31(3); Rooney, W. 33(2); Saha, L. 18(6); Scholes, P. 29(1); Silvestre, M. 6(8); Smith, A. 6(3); Solskjaer, O. 9(10); Van der Sar, E. 32; Vidic, N. 25.
Goals – League (83): Ronaldo 17 (3 pens), Rooney 14, Saha 8 (2 pens), Solskjaer 7, Scholes 6, Park 5, Giggs 4, O'Shea 4, Carrick 3, Fletcher 3, Vidic 3, Eagles 1, Evra 1, Ferdinand 1, Larsson 1, Richardson 1, Silvestre 1, own goals 3.
Carling Cup (2): Lee 1, Solskjaer 1.
FA Cup (15): Rooney 5, Ronaldo 3 (2 pens), Solskjaer 2, Carrick 1, Heinze 1, Larsson 1, Richardson 1, Saha 1.
Champions League (23): Rooney 4, Saha 4 (1 pen), Ronaldo 3, Carrick 2, Giggs 2, Evra 1, Larsson 1, O'Shea 1, Richardson 1, Scholes 1, Smith 1, Solskjaer 1, Vidic 1.
Ground: Old Trafford, Sir Matt Busby Way, Manchester M16 0RA. Telephone (0161) 868 8000.
Record Attendance: 76,962 Wolverhampton W v Grimsby T, FA Cup semi-final. 25 March 1939. **Club record:** 76,098 v Blackburn R, Premier League, 31 March 2007. **Capacity:** 76,212.
Manager: Sir Alex Ferguson CBE.
Secretary: Ken Ramsden.
Most League Goals: 103, Division 1, 1956–57 and 1958–59.
Highest League Scorer in Season: Dennis Viollet, 32, 1959–60.
Most League Goals in Total Aggregate: Bobby Charlton, 199, 1956–73.
Most Capped Player: Bobby Charlton, 106, England.
Most League Appearances: Bobby Charlton, 606, 1956–73.
Honours – FA Premier League: Champions – 1992–93, 1993–94, 1995–96, 1996–97, 1998–99, 1999–2000, 2000–01, 2002–03, 2006–07. **Football League:** Division 1 Champions – 1907–8, 1910–11, 1951–52, 1955–56, 1956–57, 1964–65, 1966–67. Division 2 Champions – 1935–36, 1974–75. **FA Cup:** Winners – 1909, 1948, 1963, 1977, 1983, 1985, 1990, 1994, 1996, 1999, 2004. **Football League Cup:** Winners – 1991–92, 2006. **European Competitions: European Cup:** Winners – 1967–68. **Champions League:** Winners – 1998–99. **European Cup-Winners' Cup:** Winners – 1990–91. **Super Cup:** Winners – 1991. **Inter-Continental Cup:** Winners – 1999.
Colours: Red shirts, white shorts, black stockings.

MANSFIELD TOWN — FL CHAMPIONSHIP 2

Arnold Nathan (F)	5 8	10 07	Mansfield	26 7 87	Scholar
Boulding Rory (F)	6 0	12 02	Sheffield	21 7 88	Ilkeston T
Brown Simon (F)	5 10	11 05	West Bromwich	18 9 83	WBA
Buxton Jake (D)	6 1	13 05	Sutton-in-Ashfield	4 3 85	Scholar
Coke Gilles (M)	6 0	11 11	London	3 6 86	Kingstonian
D'Laryea Jonathan (M)	5 10	12 02	Manchester	3 9 85	Manchester C
Dawson Stephen (M)	5 6	11 01	Dublin	4 12 85	Leicester C
Hamshaw Matthew (M)	5 10	11 09	Rotherham	1 1 82	Stockport Co
Jelleyman Gareth (D)	5 10	11 05	Holywell	14 11 80	Peterborough U
John-Baptiste Alex (D)	5 11	11 11	Sutton-in-Ashfield	31 1 86	Scholar
Kitchen Ashley (D)	5 11	11 06	Edwinstowe	10 10 88	Scholar
McGhee Jamie (M)	5 8	10 07	Grantham	28 9 89	Scholar
Muggleton Carl (G)	6 2	13 03	Leicester	13 9 68	Chesterfield
Mullins Johnny (D)	5 11	12 06	Hampstead	6 11 85	Scholar
Reet Danny (F)	6 1	14 02	Sheffield	31 1 87	Sheffield W
Sleath Danny (D)	5 8	10 00	Derby	14 12 86	Scholar
Trimmer Lewis (F)	5 7	10 00	Norwich	30 10 89	
White Jason (G)	6 2	12 13	Mansfield	28 1 83	Trainee
Wood Chris (M)	6 0	10 11	Worksop	24 1 87	Scholar

League Appearances: Arnold, N. 6(16); Barker, R. 24; Beardsley, C. 3(7); Birchall, A. 1(4); Boulding, M. 25(14); Boulding, R. (9); Brown, S. 30(4); Buxton, J. 27(3); Charlton, A. 3(1); Coke, G. 15(6); Conlon, B. 16(1); D'Laryea, J. 37; Dawson, S. 32(2); Gritton, M. 14(5); Hamshaw, M. 38(2); Hjelde, J. 25(3); Hodge, B. 9; Jelleyman, G. 39(1); John-Baptiste, A. 46; Kitchen, A. 4; Lloyd, C. 6(13); McGhee, J. (2); Muggleton, C. 16; Mullins, J. 39(4); Reet, D. 8(13); Sheehan, A. 9(1); Sleath, D. 3(4); Trimmer, L. (1); White, J. 30; Wood, C. 1.
Goals – League (58): Barker 12 (4 pens), Conlon 6 (1 pen), Gritton 6 (1 pen), Reet 6, Boulding M 5, Brown 5, Hamshaw 4, Arnold 3, John-Baptiste 3, Mullins 2, Buxton 1, Coke 1, D'Laryea 1, Dawson 1, Hjelde 1, own goal 1.
Carling Cup (3): Barker 1, Boulding M 1, Reet 1.
FA Cup (2): Barker 2 (2 pens).
J Paint Trophy (3): Beardsley 2, own goal 1.
Ground: Field Mill Ground, Quarry Lane, Mansfield, Nottinghamshire NG18 5DA. Telephone (0870) 756 3160.
Record Attendance: 24,467 v Nottingham F, FA Cup 3rd rd, 10 January 1953.
Capacity: 9,365.
Manager: Billy Dearden.
Secretary: Sharon Roberts.
Most League Goals: 108, Division 4, 1962–63.
Highest League Scorer in Season: Ted Harston, 55, Division 3 (N), 1936–37.
Most League Goals in Total Aggregate: Harry Johnson, 104, 1931–36.
Most Capped Player: John McClelland, 6 (53), Northern Ireland.
Most League Appearances: Rod Arnold, 440, 1970–83.
Honours – Football League: Division 3 Champions – 1976–77. Division 4 Champions – 1974–75. **Freight Rover Trophy:** Winners – 1986–87.
Colours: Amber shirts with royal blue trim, royal blue shorts with amber side stripe, amber stockings.

MIDDLESBROUGH — FA PREMIERSHIP

Arca Julio (M)	5 9	11 13	Quilmes	31 1 81	Sunderland
Bates Matthew (D)	5 10	12 03	Stockton	10 12 86	Scholar
Boateng George (M)	5 9	12 06	Nkawkaw	5 9 75	Aston Villa

Cattermole Lee (M)	5 10	11 13	Stockton	21 3 88	Scholar
Craddock Tom (F)	5 11	12 00	Darlington	14 10 86	Scholar
Davies Andrew (D)	6 3	14 08	Stockton	17 12 84	Scholar
Downing Stewart (M)	5 11	10 04	Middlesbrough	22 7 84	Scholar
Euell Jason (F)	5 11	11 13	Lambeth	6 2 77	Charlton Ath
Goulon Herold (M)	6 4	14 07	Paris	12 6 88	Lyon
Hines Sebastian (M)	6 2	12 04	Wetherby	29 5 88	Scholar
Hutchinson Ben (D)	5 11	12 07	Nottingham	27 11 87	Arnold T
Huth Robert (D)	6 3	14 07	Berlin	18 8 84	Chelsea
Johnson Adam (M)	5 9	9 11	Sunderland	14 7 87	Scholar
Jones Brad (G)	6 3	12 01	Armidale	19 3 82	Trainee
Kennedy Jason (M)	6 1	11 10	Stockton	11 9 86	Scholar
Knight David (G)	6 0	11 07	Houghton-le-Spring	15 1 87	Scholar
Lee Dong-Gook (F)	6 1	12 07	Pohang	29 4 79	Pohang S
McMahon Anthony (D)	5 10	11 04	Bishop Auckland	24 3 86	Scholar
Mendieta Gaizka (M)	5 9	11 02	Bilbao	27 3 74	Barcelona
Morrison James (M)	5 10	10 06	Darlington	25 5 86	Trainee
Pogatetz Emanuel (D)	6 2	13 05	Steinbock	16 1 83	Graz
Riggott Chris (D)	6 2	13 09	Derby	1 9 80	Derby Co
Rochemback Fabio (M)	6 0	13 01	Soledade	10 12 81	Sporting Lisbon
Schwarzer Mark (G)	6 4	14 07	Sydney	6 10 72	Bradford C
Taylor Andrew (D)	5 10	11 04	Hartlepool	1 8 86	Trainee
Turnbull Ross (G)	6 4	15 00	Bishop Auckland	4 1 85	Trainee
Viduka Mark (F)	6 2	15 01	Melbourne	9 10 75	Leeds U
Walker Josh (M)	5 11	11 13	Newcastle	21 2 89	Scholar
Wheater David (D)	6 4	12 12	Redcar	14 2 87	Scholar
Williams Rhys (D)			Perth	14 7 88	Scholar
Yakubu Ayegbeni (F)	6 0	14 07	Benin City	22 11 82	Portsmouth

League Appearances: Arca, J. 18(3); Bates, M. (1); Boateng, G. 35; Cattermole, L. 22(9); Christie, M. 4(9); Davies, A. 21(2); Downing, S. 34; Euell, J. 9(8); Graham, D. (1); Huth, R. 8(4); Johnson, A. 3(9); Jones, B. 2; Lee, D. 3(6); Maccarone, M. 1(6); Mendieta, G. 4(3); Morrison, J. 15(13); Parnaby, S. 9(9); Pogatetz, E. 35; Riggott, C. 5(1); Rochemback, F. 17(3); Schwarzer, M. 36; Taylor, A. 34; Viduka, M. 22(7); Wheater, D. 1(1); Woodgate, J. 30; Xavier, A. 14; Yakubu, A. 36(1).
Goals – League (44): Viduka 14, Yakubu 12 (4 pens), Arca 2, Downing 2, Morrison 2, Pogatetz 2, Rochemback 2, Boateng 1, Cattermole 1, Christie 1, Huth 1, Maccarone 1, Wheater 1, Xavier 1, own goal 1.
Carling Cup (0).
FA Cup (14): Viduka 5, Yakubu 4 (2 pens), Arca 1, Boateng 1, Cattermole 1, Christie 1, Hines 1.
Ground: Riverside Stadium, Middlesbrough, TS3 6RS. Telephone (0844) 499 6789.
Record Attendance: Ayresome Park: 53,536 v Newcastle U, Division 1, 27 December 1949. Riverside Stadium: 34,814 v Newcastle U, FA Premier League, 5 March 2003. **Capacity:** 35,041.
Manager: Gareth Southgate.
Secretary: Karen Nelson.
Most League Goals: 122, Division 2, 1926–27.
Highest League Scorer in Season: George Camsell, 59, Division 2, 1926–27 (Second Division record).
Most League Goals in Total Aggregate: George Camsell, 325, 1925–39.
Most Capped Player: Wilf Mannion, 26, England.
Most League Appearances: Tim Williamson, 563, 1902–23.
Honours – Football League: Division 1 Champions 1994–95. Division 2 Champions 1926–27, 1928–29, 1973–74. **Football League Cup:** Winners – 2004. **Amateur Cup:** Winners – 1895, 1898. **Anglo-Scottish Cup:** Winners – 1975–76.
Colours: Red shirts with white trim, red shorts, red stockings.

Ardley Neal (M)	5 9	11 09	Epsom	1 9 72	Cardiff C
Bakayogo Zoumana (D)	5 9	11 03	Paris	17 8 86	Paris St Germain
Brammer David (M)	5 10	12 00	Bromborough	28 2 75	Stoke C
Brighton Tom (F)	5 11	11 10	Irvine	28 3 84	Clyde
Byfield Darren (F)	5 11	11 11	Birmingham	29 9 76	Gillingham
Craig Tony (D)	6 0	10 03	Greenwich	20 4 85	Scholar
Day Chris (G)	6 2	13 06	Whipps Cross	28 7 75	Oldham Ath
Dunne Alan (D)	5 10	10 13	Dublin	23 8 82	Trainee
Edwards Preston (G)	6 0	12 07	Edmonton	5 9 89	Scholar
Elliott Marvin (M)	6 0	12 02	Wandsworth	15 9 84	Scholar
Fuseini Ali (M)	5 6	9 10	Ghana	7 12 88	Scholar
Gaynor Ross (F)	5 10	11 12	Drogheda	9 9 87	Scholar
Grant Gavin (F)	5 11	11 00	Wembley	27 3 84	Gillingham
Hackett Chris (M)	6 0	11 06	Oxford	1 3 83	Hearts
Harris Neil (F)	5 11	12 09	Orsett	12 7 77	Nottingham F
Hubertz Poul (F)	6 5	15 02	Viborg	21 9 76	Herfolge
Mawene Samy (M)	6 0	12 04	Caen	12 11 84	Caen
May Ben (F)	6 3	12 12	Gravesend	10 3 84	Juniors
Morais Filipe (F)	5 9	11 07	Lisbon	21 11 85	Chelsea
Phillips Mark (D)	6 2	11 00	Lambeth	27 1 82	Scholar
Pidgeley Lenny (G)	6 3	13 09	Isleworth	7 2 84	Chelsea
Robinson Paul (D)	6 1	11 09	Barnet	7 1 82	Scholar
Senda Danny (D)	5 10	10 02	Harrow	17 4 81	Wycombe W
Shaw Richard (D)	5 9	12 08	Brentford	11 9 68	Crystal Palace
Whitbread Zak (D)	6 2	11 04	Houston	10 1 84	Liverpool
Williams Marvin (M)	5 11	11 06	Sydenham	12 8 87	Scholar
Zebroski Chris (F)	6 1	11 08	Swindon	29 10 86	Plymouth Arg

League Appearances: Ardley, N. 15(5); Bakayogo, Z. 3(2); Brammer, D. 17; Braniff, K. 5(2); Brighton, T. 13(3); Byfield, D. 28(3); Craig, T. 30; Day, C. 4(1); Dunne, A. 29(3); Elliott, M. 40(2); Fuseini, A. 5(2); Grant, G. 1(3); Hackett, C. 21(12); Harris, N. 21; Haynes, D. 5; Hubertz, P. 14(20); Lee, C. 4(1); Mawene, S. 4; May, B. 7(6); McInnes, D. 7(6); Morais, F. 8(4); Morris, J. 1(3); Phillips, M. 8(4); Pidgeley, L. 42; Robinson, P. 37(1); Ross, M. 14(1); Senda, D. 34(2); Shaw, R. 41; Smith, R. 5(1); Trotter, L. 1(1); Whitbread, Z. 13(1); Williams, M. 19(10); Zebroski, C. 10(15).
Goals – League (59): Byfield 16 (4 pens), Hubertz 9, Dunne 6, Harris 5 (1 pen), Hackett 3, Robinson 3, Williams 3, Zebroski 3, Haynes 2 (1 pen), May 2, Brammer 1, Braniff 1, Brighton 1, Craig 1, McInnes 1, Morais 1, own goal 1.
Carling Cup (2): Braniff 1, Hubertz 1.
FA Cup (3): Dunne 1, May 1, own goal 1.
J Paint Trophy (3): Hackett 1, May 1, Robinson 1.
Ground: The Den, Zampa Road, London SE16 3LN. Telephone (020) 7232 1222.
Record Attendance: 20,093 v Arsenal, FA Cup 3rd rd, 10 January 1994. **Capacity:** 20,146.
Manager: Willie Donachie.
Secretary: Yvonne Haines.
Most League Goals: 127, Division 3 (S), 1927–28.
Highest League Scorer in Season: Richard Parker, 37, Division 3 (S), 1926–27.
Most League Goals in Total Aggregate: Teddy Sheringham, 93, 1984–91 and Neil Harris, 98, 1995–2004; 2006–07.
Most Capped Player: Eamonn Dunphy, 22 (23), Republic of Ireland.
Most League Appearances: Barry Kitchener, 523, 1967–82.
Honours – Football League: Division 2 Champions – 1987–88, 2000–01. Division 3 (S) Champions – 1927–28, 1937–38. Division 4 Champions – 1961–62. **Football League Trophy:** Winners – 1982–83.
Colours: Blue shirts, white shorts, blue stockings.

MILTON KEYNES DONS — FL CHAMPIONSHIP 2

Andrews Keith (M)	6 0	12 04	Dublin	13 9 80	Hull C
Baldock Sam (F)	5 7	10 07	Buckingham	15 3 89	Scholar
Bankole Ademola (G)	6 3	12 13	Lagos	9 9 69	Brentford
Diallo Drissa (D)	6 1	11 13	Nouadhibou	4 1 73	Sheffield W
Dyer Lloyd (M)	5 8	10 02	Birmingham	13 9 82	Millwall
Edds Gareth (D)	5 11	11 01	Sydney	3 2 81	Bradford C
Hastings John (F)	6 1	11 11	London	9 5 84	Tooting & M
Knight Leon (F)	5 5	9 06	Hackney	16 9 82	Swansea C
Lewington Dean (D)	5 11	11 07	Kingston	18 5 84	Scholar
McGovern Jon-Paul (M)	5 10	12 02	Glasgow	3 10 80	Sheffield W
McLeod Izale (F)	6 1	11 02	Perry Bar	15 10 84	Derby Co
Mitchell Paul (M)	5 9	12 01	Manchester	26 8 81	Scholar
Murphy Kieron (D)	5 11	10 12	Kingston	21 12 87	
O'Hanlon Sean (D)	6 1	12 05	Southport	2 1 83	Swindon T
Page Sam (D)	6 4	13 02	Croydon	30 10 87	Scholar
Platt Clive (F)	6 4	12 07	Wolverhampton	27 10 77	Peterborough U
Stirling Jude (D)	6 2	11 12	Enfield	29 6 82	Peterborough U
Taylor Scott (F)	5 10	11 04	Chertsey	5 5 76	Plymouth Arg
Wilbraham Aaron (F)	6 3	12 04	Knutsford	21 10 79	Hull C

League Appearances: Andrews, K. 34; Baines, A. 19; Baldock, S. (1); Bankole, A. 5(1); Blizzard, D. 8; Butler, P. 17; Chorley, B. 12(1); Crooks, L. 3(9); Diallo, D. 40; Dyer, L. 39(2); Edds, G. 26(9); Harper, L. 22; Hastings, J. (7); Hayes, J. (11); Jarrett, A. 2(3); Knight, L. 7(9); Lewington, D. 45; McGovern, J. 40(4); McLeod, I. 33(1); Mitchell, P. 13(7); Morgan, C. 3; O'Hanlon, S. 33(3); Page, S. (1); Platt, C. 37(5); Rizzo, N. (3); Smith, G. 9(14); Smith, J. 16(1); Stirling, J. 5(11); Taylor, S. 6(22); Tillen, J. (1); Watts, A. 1(1); Wilbraham, A. 31(1).
Goals – League (76): McLeod 21 (5 pens), Platt 18, Wilbraham 7, Andrews 6 (2 pens), Dyer 5, O'Hanlon 4, McGovern 3, Edds 2, Taylor 2, Chorley 1 (pen), Knight 1, Lewington 1, Smith G 1, Stirling 1, own goals 3.
Carling Cup (3): Wilbraham 2, McLeod 1.
FA Cup (2): McLeod 2 (1 pen).
J Paint Trophy (1): Page 1.
Play-Offs (1): Andrews 1.
Ground: The National Hockey Stadium, Silbury Boulevard, Milton Keynes, Buckinghamshire MK9 1FA. Telephone (01908) 607 090.
Record Attendance: 30,115 v Manchester U, FA Premier League, 9 May 1993 (at Selhurst Park). **Capacity:** 8,836.
Manager: Paul Ince.
Head of Football Operations: Kirstine Nicholson.
Most League Goals: 97, Division 3, 1983–84.
Highest League Scorer in Season: Alan Cork, 29, 1983–84.
Most League Goals in Total Aggregate: Alan Cork, 145, 1977–92.
Most Capped Player: Kenny Cunningham, 40 (72), Republic of Ireland.
Most League Appearances: Alan Cork, 430, 1977–92.
Honours – Football League: Division 4 Champions – 1982–83. **FA Cup:** Winners – 1987–88.
Colours: All white.

MORECAMBE — FL CHAMPIONSHIP 2

Adams Danny (D)	6 1	14 00	Altrincham	3 1 76	Huddersfield T
Bentley Jim (D)	6 1	12 00	Liverpool	11 6 76	Telford U

Blackburn Chris (D)	6 0	12 13	Crewe	2 8 82	Northwich Vic
Brannan Jed (M)	6 0	13 06	Prescot	15 1 72	Radcliffe Borough
Burns Jamie (M)	5 9	10 11	Blackpool	6 3 84	Blackpool
Carlton Danny (F)	5 11	11 05	Leeds	22 12 83	Scholar
Curtis Wayne (F)	6 0	14 05	Barrow	6 3 80	Holker Old Boys
Davies Scott (G)			Blackpool	27 2 87	Scholar
Drench Steven (G)	5 10	11 05	Manchester	11 9 85	Blackburn R
Howard Michael (D)	5 7	10 10	Birkenhead	2 12 78	Swansea C
Hunter Garry (M)	5 7	10 03	Morecambe	1 1 85	Scholar
Lloyd Paul (M)			Preston	25 3 87	Scholar
McLachlan Fraser (M)	5 11	12 11	Manchester	9 11 82	Mansfield T
McNiven David (F)	5 10	11 06	Leeds	27 5 78	Scarborough
Meadowcroft Danny (D)	6 2	12 08	Macclesfield	22 5 85	Mossley
Sorvel Neil (M)	5 10	11 07	Whiston	3 5 73	Shrewsbury T
Stanley Craig (M)	6 0	12 06	Coventry	3 3 83	Hereford U
Thompson Gary (F)	6 0	14 02	Kendal	24 11 80	Scholar
Twiss Michael (F)	5 11	13 05	Salford	26 12 77	Chester C
Walmsley Kieron (D)	5 10	12 07	Preston	11 12 83	Scholar
Yates Adam (D)	5 11	13 10	Stoke	28 5 83	Leek T

League Appearances: Adams, 16; Bentley, 31; Blackburn, 39+1; Blinkhorn, 12; Brannan, 17+14; Burns, 4+10; Carlton, 27+5; Curtis, 28+2; Davies, 1+2; Drench, 41; Howard, 31+1; Hunter, 27+7; Lloyd, 4+4; McLachlan, 10+5; McNiven, D. 13+14; Meadowcroft, 7+5; Perkins, 20; Platt, 1+3; Rigoglioso, 7+3; Robinson, 4; Shaw, 0+4; Sorvel, 19; Stanley, 37+6; Thompson, 35; Twiss, 30; Walker, 1+4; Walmsley, 0+1; Watt, 1+2; Yates, 43+1.
Goals – League (64): Thompson 11 (1 pen), Twiss 10, Blinkhorn 8, Carlton 7, Curtis 6 (1 pen), Blackburn 3, Lloyd 3, McNiven D 3, Sorvel 2, Stanley 2, Yates 2, Bentley 1, McLachlan 1, Meadowcroft 1, own goals 4.
FA Cup (4): Curtis 1 (pen), McNiven 1, Stanley 1, Twiss 1.
Trophy (8): Twiss 3, Curtis 1, Howard 1, Hunter 1, Thompson 1 (pen), Walker 1.
Play-Offs (4): Curtis 2, Carlton 1, Thompson 1.
Ground: Christie Park, Morecambe LA4 5TJ. Telephone (01524) 411 797.
Record Attendance: 9,383 v Weymouth FA Cup 3rd rd, 6 January 1962.
Capacity: 6,030.
Manager: Sammy McIlroy.
Secretary: Neil Marsdin.
Most League Goals: 86, Conference 2002–03.
Highest League Scorer in Season: Justin Jackson, 29, 1999–2000.
Most League Goals in Total Aggregate: 100, John Norman, 1994–99; 2000–02.
Most League Appearances: 209, Dave McKeanney, 1995–2004.
Honours – Conference: Promoted to Football League (play-offs) 2006–07. **Presidents Cup:** Winners – 1991–92. **FA Trophy:** Winners 1973–74. **Lancs Senior Cup:** Winners 1967–68. **Lancs Combination:** Champions – 1924–25, 1961–62, 1962–63, 1967–68. **Lancs Combination Cup:** Winners – 1926–27, 1945–46, 1964–65, 1966=67, 1967–68. **Lancs Junior Cup:** Winners – 1927, 1928, 1962, 1963, 1969, 1986, 1987, 1994, 1996, 1999, 2004.
Colours: Red shirts, white shorts, white stockings.

NEWCASTLE UNITED — FA PREMIERSHIP

Ameobi Foluwashola (F)	6 3	11 13	Zaria	12 10 81	Scholar
Babayaro Celestine (D)	5 9	12 06	Kaduna	29 8 78	Chelsea
Butt Nicky (M)	5 10	11 05	Manchester	21 1 75	Manchester U
Carr Stephen (D)	5 9	12 02	Dublin	29 8 76	Tottenham H
Carroll Andy (F)	6 3	13 08	Newcastle	6 1 89	Scholar
Duff Damien (M)	5 9	12 06	Ballyboden	2 3 79	Chelsea

Dyer Kieron (M)	5 8	10 00	Ipswich	29 12 78	Ipswich T
Edgar David (D)	6 2	12 13	Ontario	19 5 87	Scholar
Emre Belezoglu (M)	5 8	10 10	Istanbul	7 9 80	Internazionale
Given Shay (G)	6 0	13 03	Lifford	20 4 76	Blackburn R
Harper Steve (G)	6 2	13 10	Easington	14 3 75	Seaham Red Star
Huntington Paul (D)	6 3	12 08	Carlisle	17 9 87	Scholar
Krul Tim (G)	6 2	11 08	Den Haag	3 4 88	Den Haag
Luque Alberto (F)	6 0	11 11	Barcelona	11 3 78	La Coruna
Martins Obafemi (F)	5 10	11 06	Lagos	28 10 84	Internazionale
Milner James (M)	5 10	11 00	Leeds	4 1 86	Leeds U
N'Zogbia Charles (M)	5 9	11 00	Le Havre	28 5 86	Le Havre
O'Brien Alan (M)	5 10	10 10	Dublin	20 2 85	Scholar
Owen Michael (F)	5 8	10 12	Chester	14 12 79	Liverpool
Parker Scott (M)	5 9	11 10	Lambeth	13 10 80	Chelsea
Pattison Matt (M)	5 9	11 00	Johannesburg	27 10 86	Scholar
Ramage Peter (D)	6 1	11 03	Whitley Bay	22 11 83	Scholar
Shanks Chris (D)	6 0	11 00	Ashington	16 10 86	Scholar
Solano Nolberto (M)	5 8	10 07	Callao	12 12 74	Aston Villa
Taylor Steven (D)	6 1	13 01	Greenwich	23 1 86	Scholar
Troisi James (F)	5 10	11 03	Adelaide	3 7 88	Scholar

League Appearances: Ameobi, F. 9(3); Babayaro, C. 12; Bramble, T. 17; Butt, N. 27(4); Carr, S. 23; Carroll, A. (4); Duff, D. 20(2); Dyer, K. 20(2); Edgar, D. 2(1); Emre, B. 21(3); Given, S. 22; Harper, S. 15(3); Huntington, P. 10(1); Luque, A. (7); Martins, O. 32(1); Milner, J. 31(4); Moore, C. 17; N'Zogbia, C. 10(12); O'Brien, A. 1(1); Onyewu, O. 7(4); Owen, M. 3; Parker, S. 28(1); Pattison, M. 2(5); Ramage, P. 20(1); Rossi, G. 3(8); Sibierski, A. 14(12); Solano, N. 25(3); Srnicek, P. 1(1); Taylor, S. 26(1).
Goals – League (38): Martins 11 (1 pen), Dyer 5, Ameobi 3 (1 pen), Milner 3, Parker 3, Sibierski 3, Emre 2 (1 pen), Solano 2 (2 pens), Taylor 2, Butt 1, Duff 1, Edgar 1, Huntington 1.
Carling Cup (5): Solano 2, Parker 1, Rossi 1, Sibierski 1.
FA Cup (3): Dyer 1, Milner 1, Taylor 1.
Inter-Toto (4): Ameobi 2, Emre 1, Luque 1.
UEFA Cup (16): Martins 6 (1 pen), Sibierski 4, Bramble 1, Dyer 1, Luque 1, Taylor 1, own goals 2.
Ground: St James' Park, Newcastle-upon-Tyne NE1 4ST. Telephone (0191) 201 8400.
Record Attendance: 68,386 v Chelsea, Division 1, 3 Sept 1930. **Capacity:** 52,387.
Manager: Sam Allardyce.
Most League Goals: 98, Division 1, 1951–52.
Highest League Scorer in Season: Hughie Gallacher, 36, Division 1, 1926–27.
Most League Goals in Total Aggregate: Jackie Milburn, 177, 1946–57.
Most Capped Player: Shay Given, 71 (80), Republic of Ireland.
Most League Appearances: Jim Lawrence, 432, 1904–22.
Honours – Football League: Division 1 – Champions 1904–05, 1906–07, 1908–09, 1926–27, 1992–93. Division 2 Champions – 1964–65. **FA Cup:** Winners – 1910, 1924, 1932, 1951, 1952, 1955. **Texaco Cup:** Winners – 1973–74, 1974–75. **European Competitions: European Fairs Cup:** Winners – 1968–69. **Anglo-Italian Cup:** Winners – 1973. **Intertoto Cup:** Winners – 2006.
Colours: Black and white striped shirts, black shorts, black stockings.

NORTHAMPTON TOWN — FL CHAMPIONSHIP 1

Aiston Sam (M)	6 2	12 00	Newcastle	21 11 76	Tranmere R
Bunn Mark (G)	6 0	12 02	Camden	16 11 84	Scholar
Burnell Joe (M)	5 9	11 09	Bristol	10 10 80	Wycombe W

Crowe Jason (D)	5 9	10 09	Sidcup	30 9 78	Grimsby T
Doig Chris (D)	6 2	12 06	Dumfries	13 2 81	Nottingham F
Dolman Liam (D)	6 0	14 05	Brixworth	26 9 87	Scholar
Dunn Chris (G)	6 5	13 11	Essex	23 10 87	Scholar
Gilligan Ryan (M)	5 10	11 07	Swindon	18 1 87	Watford
Holt Andy (D)	6 1	12 07	Stockport	21 4 78	Wrexham
Hughes Mark (D)	6 1	13 10	Liverpool	9 12 86	Everton
Johnson Brad (M)	6 0	12 10	Hackney	28 4 87	Cambridge U
Johnson Brett (D)	6 1	13 00	Hammersmith	15 8 85	Aldershot T
Kirk Andy (F)	5 11	11 07	Belfast	29 5 79	Boston U
May Danny (D)	5 11	11 08	Northampton	19 11 88	Scholar
Quinn James (F)	6 2	12 10	Coventry	15 12 74	Peterborough U

League Appearances: Aiston, S. 14(7); Bojic, P. 19(7); Bunn, M. 42; Burnell, J. 24; Chambers, L. 29; Cole, M. 6(2); Cox, S. 6(2); Crowe, J. 43; Deuchar, K. 14(3); Doig, C. 39; Dolman, L. 1; Dyche, S. 20(1); Gilligan, R. 14(10); Harper, L. 4; Holt, A. 33(2); Hughes, M. 17; Hunt, D. 20(9); Jess, E. 22(4); Johnson, Brad 21(6); Johnson, Brett 2(2); Kirk, A. 29(15); Laird, M. 2(4); May, D. 2(1); McGleish, S. 24(1); Pearce, A. 15; Quinn, J. 5(13); Robertson, J. 9(8); Taylor, I. 26(7); Watt, J. 2(8); Wright, N. 2(2).
Goals – League (48): McGleish 12 (2 pens), Kirk 7, Brad Johnson 5, Cox 3, Crowe 3, Deuchar 3, Robertson 3, Holt 2, Hughes 2, Burnell 1, Chambers 1, Cole 1, Jess 1, Pearce 1, Quinn 1, Taylor 1, own goal 1.
Carling Cup (2): Kirk 1, Watt 1.
FA Cup (3): Burnell 1, McGleish 1, own goal 1.
J Paint Trophy (0).
Ground: Sixfields Stadium, Upton Way, Northampton NN5 5QA. Telephone 0870 822 1997.
Record Attendance: (at County Ground): 24,523 v Fulham, Division 1, 23 April 1966; (at Sixfields Stadium): 7,557 v Manchester C, Division 2, 26 September 1998.
Capacity: 7,653.
Manager: Stuart Gray.
Secretary: Norman Howells.
Most League Goals: 109, Division 3, 1962–63 and Division 3 (S), 1952–53.
Highest League Scorer in Season: Cliff Holton, 36, Division 3, 1961–62.
Most League Goals in Total Aggregate: Jack English, 135, 1947–60.
Most Capped Player: Edwin Lloyd Davies, 12 (16), Wales.
Most League Appearances: Tommy Fowler, 521, 1946–61.
Honours – Football League: Division 3 Champions – 1962–63. Division 4 Champions – 1986–87.
Colours: Claret shirts, white shorts, claret stockings.

NORWICH CITY — FL CHAMPIONSHIP

Brown Chris (F)	6 3	13 03	Doncaster	11 12 84	Sunderland
Cave-Brown Andrew (D)	5 10	12 02	Gravesend	5 8 88	Scholar
Chadwick Luke (M)	5 11	11 08	Cambridge	18 11 80	Stoke C
Colin Jurgen (D)	5 10	11 10	Utrecht	20 1 81	PSV Eindhoven
Croft Lee (D)	5 11	12 12	Wigan	21 6 85	Manchester C
Doherty Gary (D)	6 2	13 04	Carndonagh	31 1 80	Tottenham H
Drury Adam (D)	5 10	11 08	Cottenham	29 8 78	Peterborough U
Dublin Dion (F)	6 2	12 07	Leicester	22 4 69	Celtic
Eagle Robert (M)	5 7	10 08	Ipswich	23 2 87	Scholar
Earnshaw Robert (F)	5 6	9 09	Mulfulira	6 4 81	WBA
Etuhu Dickson (M)	6 2	13 04	Kano	8 6 82	Preston NE
Fotheringham Mark (M)	5 10	11 04	Dundee	22 10 83	Aarau
Gallacher Paul (G)	6 0	12 00	Glasgow	16 8 79	Dundee U

Halliday Matthew (D)	6 2	12 05	Norwich	21 1 87	Scholar
Huckerby Darren (F)	5 10	12 02	Nottingham	23 4 76	Manchester C
Hughes Andy (M)	5 11	12 01	Stockport	2 1 78	Reading
Jarvis Rossi (D)	5 11	11 12	Fakenham	11 3 88	Scholar
Jarvis Ryan (F)	6 0	11 05	Fakenham	11 7 86	Scholar
Lappin Simon (M)	5 9	10 10	Glasgow	25 1 83	St Mirren
Lewis Joe (G)	6 5	11 12	Bury St Edmunds	6 10 87	Scholar
Martin Chris (F)	6 2	12 06	Norwich	4 11 88	Scholar
Safri Youseff (M)	5 8	11 00	Casablanca	13 1 77	Coventry C
Shackell Jason (D)	6 3	12 09	Hitchin	27 9 83	Scholar
Spillane Michael (M)	5 9	11 10	Cambridge	23 3 89	Scholar

League Appearances: Ashdown, J. 2; Boyle, P. 3; Brown, C. 3(1); Camp, L. 3; Chadwick, L. 1(3); Colin, J. 30(3); Croft, L. 33(3); Doherty, G. 34; Drury, A. 39; Dublin, D. 22(11); Eagle, R. 3(7); Earnshaw, R. 28(2); Etuhu, D. 42(1); Fleming, C. 4(6); Fotheringham, M. 9(5); Gallacher, P. 26(1); Henderson, I. (2); Huckerby, D. 40; Hughes, A. 28(8); Jarvis, Ryan 1(4); Lappin, S. 14; Marshall, D. 2; Martin, C. 13(5); McKenzie, L. (4); McVeigh, P. 6(15); Renton, K. 1(2); Robinson, C. 26(1); Safri, Y. 30(5); Shackell, J. 42(1); Smart, B. (1); Spillane, M. 4(1); Thorne, P. 4(11); Warner, T. 13.
Goals – League (56): Earnshaw 19 (4 pens), Huckerby 8, Etuhu 6, Dublin 5, Martin 4, Croft 3, Shackell 3, Robinson 2, Chadwick 1, Lappin 1, Safri 1, own goals 3.
Carling Cup (6): Ryan Jarvis 2, Etuhu 1, Fleming 1, McKenzie 1, Thorne 1.
FA Cup (8): Huckerby 5, Dublin 2, Martin 1.
Ground: Carrow Road, Norwich NR1 1JE. Telephone (01603) 760 760.
Record Attendance: 43,984 v Leicester C, FA Cup 6th rd, 30 March 1963.
Capacity: 26,034.
Manager: Peter Grant.
Secretary: Kevan Platt.
Most League Goals: 99, Division 3 (S), 1952–53.
Highest League Scorer in Season: Ralph Hunt, 31, Division 3 (S), 1955–56.
Most League Goals in Total Aggregate: Johnny Gavin, 122, 1945–54, 1955–58.
Most Capped Player: Mark Bowen, 35 (41), Wales.
Most League Appearances: Ron Ashman, 592, 1947–64.
Honours – Football League: Division 1 Champions – 2003–04. Division 2 Champions – 1971–72, 1985–86. Division 3 (S) Champions – 1933–34. **Football League Cup:** Winners – 1962, 1985.
Colours: Yellow shirts, green shorts, yellow stockings.

NOTTINGHAM FOREST — FL CHAMPIONSHIP 1

Agogo Junior (F)	5 10	11 07	Accra	1 8 79	Bristol R
Bastians Felix (M)	6 2	12 00	Bochum	9 5 88	Scholar
Bencherif Hamza (D)	5 9	12 03	France	9 2 88	Scholar
Bennett Julian (D)	6 1	13 00	Nottingham	17 12 84	Walsall
Breckin Ian (D)	6 2	13 05	Rotherham	24 2 75	Wigan Ath
Byrne Mark (M)			Dublin	9 11 78	Crumlin
Chambers Luke (D)	6 1	11 13	Kettering	28 9 85	Northampton T
Clingan Sammy (M)	5 11	11 06	Belfast	13 1 84	Wolverhampton W
Commons Kris (M)	5 6	9 08	Nottingham	30 8 83	Stoke C
Dobie Scott (F)	6 1	12 05	Workington	10 10 78	Millwall
Gamble Paddy (G)			Nottingham	1 9 88	Scholar
Heath Joseph (D)			Birkenhead	4 10 88	Scholar
Holt Grant (F)	6 1	14 02	Carlisle	12 4 81	Rochdale
Moloney Brendan (M)	6 1	11 02	Enfield	18 1 89	Scholar
McGugan Lewis (M)	5 9	11 06	Long Eaton	25 10 88	Scholar
Morgan Wes (D)	6 2	14 00	Nottingham	21 1 84	Scholar

Newbold Adam (F)			Nottingham	16 11 89	Scholar
Perch James (D)	5 11	11 05	Mansfield	29 9 85	Scholar
Power Alan (M)	5 7	11 06	Dublin	23 1 88	Scholar
Redmond Shane (G)			Dublin	23 3 89	Scholar
Roberts Dale (M)	6 3	11 06	Horden	22 10 86	Scholar
Smith Paul (G)	6 3	14 00	Epsom	17 12 79	Southampton
Staples Reece (M)			Nottingham	10 9 89	Scholar
Tyson Nathan (F)	5 10	10 02	Reading	4 5 82	Wycombe W
Weir-Daley Spencer (F)	5 9	10 11	Leicester	5 9 85	Scholar

League Appearances: Agogo, J. 20(9); Bastians, F. (2); Bennett, J. 24(6); Breckin, I. 46; Chambers, L. 10(4); Clingan, S. 25(3); Commons, K. 28(4); Cullip, D. 19(1); Curtis, J. 38(3); Dobie, S. 2(17); Harris, N. 11(8); Henry, J. (1); Holt, Gary 30(9); Holt, Grant 34(11); Hughes, R. (2); Lester, J. 24(11); McGugan, L. 11(2); Moloney, B. (1); Morgan, W. 31(7); Pedersen, R. 1; Perch, J. 43(3); Prutton, D. 11(1); Smith, P. 45; Southall, N. 26(1); Thompson, J. 6(8); Tyson, N. 12(12); Weir-Daley, S. (1); Wright, A. 9.
Goals – League (65): Grant Holt 14 (4 pens), Commons 9, Agogo 7 (1 pen), Tyson 7 (1 pen), Lester 6, Perch 5, Southall 5, Breckin 3, Bennett 2, McGugan 2, Prutton 2, Harris 1, Holt Gary 1, own goal 1.
Carling Cup (0).
FA Cup (10): Agogo 3 (1 pen), Commons 3, Tyson 2, Grant Holt 1, Southall 1.
J Paint Trophy (6): Grant Holt 3, Lester 1, Morgan 1, Southall 1.
Play-Offs (4): Commons 1 (pen), Dobie 1, Grant Holt 1, Perch 1 (pen).
Ground: The City Ground, Nottingham NG2 5FJ. Telephone (0115) 982 4444.
Record Attendance: 49,946 v Manchester U, Division 1, 28 October 1967.
Capacity: 30,602.
Manager: Colin Calderwood.
Football Administrator: Jane Carnelly.
Most League Goals: 110, Division 3 (S), 1950–51.
Highest League Scorer in Season: Wally Ardron, 36, Division 3 (S), 1950–51.
Most League Goals in Total Aggregate: Grenville Morris, 199, 1898–1913.
Most Capped Player: Stuart Pearce, 76 (78), England.
Most League Appearances: Bob McKinlay, 614, 1951–70.
Honours – Football League: Division 1 – Champions 1977–78, 1997–98. Division 2 Champions – 1906–07, 1921–22. Division 3 (S) Champions – 1950–51. **FA Cup:** Winners – 1898, 1959. **Football League Cup:** Winners – 1977–78, 1978–79, 1988–89, 1989–90. **Anglo-Scottish Cup:** Winners – 1976–77. **Simod Cup:** Winners – 1989. **Zenith Data Systems Cup:** Winners – 1991–92. **European Competitions: European Cup:** Winners – 1978–79, 1979–80. **Super Cup:** Winners – 1979–80.
Colours: Red shirts, white shorts, red stockings.

NOTTS COUNTY — FL CHAMPIONSHIP 2

Dudfield Lawrie (F)	6 1	13 11	Southwark	7 5 80	Boston U
Edwards Mike (D)	6 1	13 01	North Ferriby	25 4 80	Grimsby T
Frost Stef (M)	6 2	11 05	Eastwood	3 7 89	Scholar
Hunt Steve (D)	6 1	13 05	Southampton	11 11 84	Colchester U
Lee Jason (F)	6 3	14 09	Forest Gate	9 5 71	Northampton T
McCann Austin (D)	5 9	13 03	Clydebank	21 1 80	Boston U
Mendes Junior (F)	5 10	12 02	Ballam	15 9 76	Grimsby T
Parkinson Andy (M)	5 8	10 12	Liverpool	27 5 79	Grimsby T
Pilkington Kevin (G)	6 1	13 00	Hitchin	8 3 74	Mansfield T
Pipe David (M)	5 10	12 04	Caerphilly	5 11 83	Coventry C
Silk Gary (D)	5 9	11 11	Newport	13 7 84	Portsmouth
Smith Jay (M)	5 7	10 01	London	25 9 81	Southend U
Somner Matt (M)	6 0	13 03	Isleworth	8 12 82	Aldershot T

League Appearances: Byron, M. 2(1); Curtis, T. (2); Deeney, S. 7; Dudfield, L. 29(12); Edwards, M. 44(1); Gleeson, D. 16(1); Hunt, S. 24(8); Lee, J. 37(1); Martin, D. 12(17); McCann, A. 43; McMahon, L. 3(4); Mendes, J. 22(15); N'Toya, T. 4(17); Needham, L. (1); Parkinson, A. 40(5); Pilkington, K. 39; Pipe, D. 39; Ross, I. 26(10); Sheridan, J. (3); Silk, G. 24(6); Smith, J. 25(2); Somner, M. 35(3); Walker, J. 2(6); Weston, M. 1(3); White, A. 32(3).
Goals – League (55): Lee 15, Dudfield 7 (1 pen), Mendes 5, Parkinson 5, White A. 5, Martin 4, Smith 4 (1 pen), Edwards 3, Hunt 1, N'Toya 1, Ross 1, Somner 1, own goals 3.
Carling Cup (5): Dudfield 1, Edwards 1, Lee 1, Martin 1, N'Toya 1.
FA Cup (1): Dudfield 1.
J Paint Trophy (0).
Ground: Meadow Lane Stadium, Meadow Lane, Nottingham NG2 3HJ. Telephone (0115) 952 9000.
Record Attendance: 47,310 v York C, FA Cup 6th rd, 12 March 1955. **Capacity:** 20,300.
Manager: Steve Thompson.
Secretary: Tony Cuthbert.
Most League Goals: 107, Division 4, 1959–60.
Highest League Scorer in Season: Tom Keetley, 39, Division 3 (S), 1930–31.
Most League Goals in Total Aggregate: Les Bradd, 125, 1967–78.
Most Capped Player: Kevin Wilson, 15 (42), Northern Ireland.
Most League Appearances: Albert Iremonger, 564, 1904–26.
Honours – Football League: Division 2 Champions – 1896–97, 1913–14, 1922–23. Division 3 Champions – 1997–98. Division 3 (S) Champions – 1930–31, 1949–50. Division 4 Champions – 1970–71. **FA Cup:** Winners – 1893–94. **Anglo-Italian Cup:** Winners – 1995.
Colours: Black and white striped shirts, black shorts, black stockings.

OLDHAM ATHLETIC — FL CHAMPIONSHIP 1

Eardley Neal (D)	5 11	11 10	Llandudno	6 11 88	Scholar
Gregan Sean (D)	6 2	15 00	Billingham	29 3 74	Leeds U
Hall Chris (F)	6 1	11 04	Manchester	27 11 86	Scholar
Liddell Andy (F)	5 7	11 11	Leeds	28 6 73	Sheffield U
Lomax Kelvin (D)	5 10	12 03	Bury	12 11 86	Scholar
McDonald Gary (M)	6 1	12 05	Irvine	10 4 82	Kilmarnock
Owen Gareth (D)	6 1	11 07	Stoke	21 9 82	Stoke C
Pearson Michael (M)	5 11	11 01	Bangor	19 1 88	Scholar
Pogliacomi Les (G)	6 4	13 04	Sydney	3 5 76	Blackpool
Porter Chris (F)	6 1	12 09	Wigan	12 12 83	Bury
Rocastle Craig (M)	6 2	13 05	Lewisham	17 8 81	Sheffield W
Taylor Chris (M)	5 11	11 00	Oldham	20 12 86	Scholar
Trotman Neal (D)	6 3	13 08	Manchester	11 3 87	Burnley
Wolfenden Matthew (M)	5 9	11 01	Oldham	23 7 87	Scholar
Wood Neil (M)	5 10	13 00	Manchester	4 1 83	Blackpool

League Appearances: Aljofree, H. 5; Blayney, A. 2(1); Charlton, S. 34; Clarke, L. 5; Cywka, T. (4); Eardley, I. 36; Edwards, P. 10(16); Glombard, L. 3(5); Grabban, L. 1(8); Gregan, S. 27; Haining, W. 44; Hall, C. 2(17); Howarth, C. 2(1); Knight, D. 2; Liddell, A. 44(2); Lomax, K. 3(6); McDonald, G. 39(4); Molango, M. 3(2); Pearson, M. (1); Pogliacomi, L. 40; Porter, C. 34(1); Rocastle, C. 17(18); Roque, M. 1(3); Smalley, D. (2); Smith, T. (1); Stam, S. 19(3); Swailes, C. 4; Taylor, C. 40(4); Tierney, M. 1(4); Trotman, N. (1); Turner, B. 1; Warne, P. 42(4); Wellens, R. 42; Wolfenden, M. (6); Wood, N. 3(2).
Goals – League (69): Porter 21, Liddell 10 (7 pens), Warne 9, McDonald 7, Taylor 4, Wellens 4, Clarke 3 (1 pen), Eardley 2, Haining 2, Rocastle 2, Charlton 1, Glombard 1, Hall C 1, Molango 1, Stam 1.

Carling Cup (1): Rocastle 1.
FA Cup (8): Hall 3, Warne 2, Gregan 1, Porter 1, Trotman 1.
J Paint Trophy (0).
Play-Offs (2): Liddell 1 (pen), Wolfenden 1.
Ground: Boundary Park, Furtherwood Road, Oldham OL1 2PA. Telephone (0871) 226 2235.
Record Attendance: 46,471 v Sheffield W, FA Cup 4th rd. 25 January 1930.
Capacity: 13,595.
Manager: John Sheridan.
Chief Executive/Secretary: Alan Hardy.
Most League Goals: 95, Division 4, 1962–63.
Highest League Scorer in Season: Tom Davis, 33, Division 3 (N), 1936–37.
Most League Goals in Total Aggregate: Roger Palmer, 141, 1980–94.
Most Capped Player: Gunnar Halle, 24 (64), Norway.
Most League Appearances: Ian Wood, 525, 1966–80.
Honours – Football League: Division 2 Champions – 1990–91, Division 3 (N) Champions – 1952–53. Division 3 Champions – 1973–74.
Colours: Royal blue shirts with white piping, blue shorts, white stockings.

PETERBOROUGH UNITED FL CHAMPIONSHIP 2

Benjamin Trevor (F)	6 2	13 07	Kettering	8 2 79	Coventry C
Blackett Shane (D)	6 0	12 11	Luton	3 10 82	Dagenham & R
Blanchett Danny (M)	5 11	11 12	Derby	12 3 88	Cambridge C
Boyd George (M)	5 10	11 07	Stevenage	2 10 85	Stevenage B
Branston Guy (D)	6 1	14 00	Leicester	9 1 79	Oldham Ath
Butcher Richard (M)	6 0	13 00	Northampton	22 1 81	Lincoln C
Crow Danny (F)	5 10	11 00	Great Yarmouth	26 1 86	Norwich C
Day Jamie (M)	5 9	10 06	Wycombe	7 5 86	Scholar
Ferguson Darren (M)	5 10	11 10	Glasgow	9 2 72	Wrexham
Futcher Ben (D)	6 7	12 05	Bradford	4 6 81	Grimsby T
Gain Peter (M)	5 9	11 07	Hammersmith	11 11 76	Lincoln C
Huke Shane (M)	5 11	12 07	Reading	2 10 85	Scholar
Hyde Micah (M)	5 10	11 02	Newham	10 11 74	Burnley
Jalal Shwan (G)	6 2	14 00	Baghdad	14 8 83	Woking
Low Josh (M)	6 0	14 00	Bristol	15 2 79	Leicester C
Mackail-Smith Craig (F)	6 3	12 04	Hertford	25 2 84	Dagenham & R
McLean Aaron (F)	5 8	10 03	Hammersmith	25 5 83	Grays Ath
Morgan Craig (D)	6 0	11 00	Asaph	16 6 85	Milton Keynes D
Newton Adam (M)	5 10	11 00	Ascot	4 12 80	West Ham U
Richards Justin (F)	6 0	11 10	Sandwell	16 10 80	Woking
Smith Adam (D)	5 7	10 05	Lingwood	11 9 85	Kings Lynn
Strachan Gavin (M)	5 10	11 07	Aberdeen	23 12 78	Hartlepool U
Tyler Mark (G)	5 11	12 00	Norwich	2 4 77	Trainee

League Appearances: Arber, M. 31(3); Benjamin, T. 15(12); Blackett, S. 12(1); Blanchett, D. (3); Boyd, G. 19(1); Branston, G. 23(1); Butcher, R. 35(8); Carden, P. 1(1); Crow, D. 22(13); Davis, L. 7; Day, J. 17(7); Futcher, B. 22(3); Gain, P. 26(8); Ghaichem, J. 1(1); Holden, D. 20(1); Huke, S. 9(9); Hyde, M. 18; Jalal, S. 1; Low, J. 17(2); Mackail-Smith, C. 13(2); McLean, A. 16; Morgan, C. 22(1); Newton, A. 43; Opara, L. 6(5); Plummer, C. 7; Rachubka, P. 4; Richards, J. 4(9); Smith, A. 5(4); Stirling, J. 14(8); Strachan, G. 13(3); Turner, B. 7(1); Tyler, M. 41; White, A. 7; Yeo, S. 8(5).
Goals – League (70): Mackail-Smith 8 (1 pen), Benjamin 7 (1 pen), McLean 7, Boyd 6, Crow 6, Gain 6, Butcher 4, Futcher 3, Strachan 3, White 3, Yeo 2, Arber 1, Blanchett 1, Day 1, Holden 1, Huke 1, Low 1, Morgan 1, Newton 1, Opara 1, Richards 1, Smith 1, own goals 4.

Carling Cup (3): Branston 2, Benjamin 1 (pen).
FA Cup (7): Crow 3, McLean 3, Butcher 1.
J Paint Trophy (1): Crow 1.
Ground: London Road Stadium, Peterborough PE2 8AL. Telephone (01733) 563 947.
Record Attendance: 30,096 v Swansea T, FA Cup 5th rd, 20 February 1965.
Capacity: 15,460.
Manager: Darren Ferguson.
Secretary: Mary Faxon.
Most League Goals: 134, Division 4, 1960–61.
Highest League Scorer in Season: Terry Bly, 52, Division 4, 1960–61.
Most League Goals in Total Aggregate: Jim Hall, 122, 1967–75.
Most Capped Player: James Quinn, 9 (50), Northern Ireland.
Most League Appearances: Tommy Robson, 482, 1968–81.
Honours – Football League: Division 4 Champions – 1960–61, 1973–74.
Colours: Blue shirts, blue shorts, blue stockings.

PLYMOUTH ARGYLE — FL CHAMPIONSHIP

Name	Ht	Wt	Birthplace	D.O.B.	Source
Aljofree Hasney (D)	6 0	12 03	Manchester	11 7 78	Dundee U
Barnes Ashley (F)	6 0	12 00	Bath	30 10 89	Paulton R
Bouzsaky Akos (M)	5 11	11 09	Hungary	7 5 82	MTK
Chadwick Nick (F)	5 11	10 09	Stoke	26 10 82	Everton
Connolly Paul (D)	6 0	11 10	Liverpool	29 9 83	Scholar
Dickson Ryan (M)	5 10	11 05	Saltash	14 12 86	Scholar
Djordjic Bojan (M)	5 10	11 01	Belgrade	6 2 82	Rangers
Doumbe Stephen (D)	6 1	12 05	Paris	28 0 79	Hibernian
Ebanks-Blake Sylvan (F)	5 10	13 04	Cambridge	29 3 86	Manchester U
Fallon Rory (F)	6 2	11 09	Gisborne	20 3 82	Swansea C
Gosling Daniel (M)	6 0	11 00	Brixham	2 2 90	Scholar
Hayles Barry (F)	5 9	13 00	Lambeth	17 4 72	Millwall
Hodges Lee (M)	6 0	12 01	Epping	4 9 73	Reading
Laird Scott (D)	5 11	11 05	Taunton	15 5 88	Scholar
Larrieu Romain (G)	6 2	13 00	Mont-de-Marsan	31 8 76	ASOA Valence
McCormick Luke (G)	6 0	13 12	Coventry	15 8 83	Scholar
Nalis Lilian (M)	6 1	11 00	Nogent sur Marne	29 9 71	Sheffield U
Norris David (M)	5 7	11 06	Peterborough	22 2 81	Bolton W
Reid Reuben (F)	6 0	12 00	Bristol	26 7 88	Scholar
Samba Cherno (F)	5 10	10 01	Gambia	10 1 85	Cadiz
Sawyer Gary (D)	6 0	11 08	Bideford	5 7 85	Scholar
Seip Marcel (D)	6 0	12 04	Wenschoten	5 4 82	Heerenveen
Summerfield Luke (M)	6 0	11 00	Ivybridge	6 12 87	Scholar
Wotton Paul (D)	5 11	11 01	Plymouth	17 8 77	Scholar

League Appearances: Aljofree, H. 22(3); Barness, A. 1; Buzsaky, A. 27(9); Capaldi, T. 30(1); Chadwick, N. 9(7); Connolly, P. 38; Dickson, R. (2); Djordjic, B. 8(9); Doumbe, S. 29; Ebanks-Blake, S. 30(11); Fallon, R. 5(10); Gallen, K. 6(7); Gosling, D. 8(4); Halmosi, P. 14(2); Hayles, B. 37(2); Hodges, L. 11(4); Larrieu, R. 6; McCormick, L. 40; Nalis, L. 39(3); Norris, D. 41; Reid, R. 1(5); Samba, C. 1(12); Sawyer, G. 19(3); Seip, M. 36(1); Sinclair, S. 8(7); Summerfield, L. 11(12); Timar, K. 8(1); Wotton, P. 21(1).
Goals – League (63): Hayles 13, Ebanks-Blake 10 (3 pens), Norris 6, Halmosi 4, Nalis 4, Wotton 4 (3 pens), Buzsaky 3, Djordjic 3, Chadwick 2, Gosling 2, Seip 2, Sinclair 2, Fallon 1, Gallen 1, Samba 1, Summerfield 1, Timar 1, own goals 3.
Carling Cup (0).
FA Cup (7): Aljofree 2 (2 pens), Sinclair 2, Gallen 1 (pen), Hayles 1, Norris 1.
Ground: Home Park, Plymouth, Devon PL2 3DQ. Telephone (01752) 562 561.

Record Attendance: 43,596 v Aston Villa, Division 2, 10 October 1936.
Capacity: 21,118.
Manager: Ian Holloway.
Secretary: Mrs Carole Rowntree.
Most League Goals: 107, Division 3 (S), 1925–26 and 1951–52.
Highest League Scorer in Season: Jack Cock, 32, Division 3 (S), 1926–27.
Most League Goals in Total Aggregate: Sammy Black, 180, 1924–38.
Most Capped Player: Moses Russell, 20 (23), Wales.
Most League Appearances: Kevin Hodges, 530, 1978–92.
Honours – Football League: Division 2 Champions – 2003–04. Division 3 (S) Champions – 1929–30, 1951–52. Division 3 Champions – 1958–59, 2001–02.
Colours: Green shirts, white shorts, green stockings.

PORTSMOUTH — FA PREMIERSHIP

Ashdown Jamie (G)	6 1	13 05	Reading	30 11 80	Reading
Begovic Asmir (G)	6 6	13 01	Trebinje	20 6 87	La Louviere
Campbell Sol (D)	6 2	14 05	Newham	18 9 74	Arsenal
Cole Andy (F)	5 9	12 11	Nottingham	15 10 71	Manchester C
Davis Sean (M)	5 10	12 00	Clapham	20 9 79	Tottenham H
Duffy Richard (D)	5 10	9 05	Swansea	30 8 85	Swansea C
Griffin Andy (D)	5 9	10 10	Billinge	7 3 79	Newcastle U
Hughes Richard (M)	6 0	13 03	Glasgow	25 6 79	Bournemouth
James David (G)	6 4	14 13	Welwyn	1 8 70	Manchester C
Kanu Nwankwo (F)	6 5	13 00	Owerri	1 8 76	WBA
Kranjcar Niko (M)	6 1	12 08	Zagreb	13 8 84	Hajduk Split
Lauren (D)	5 11	11 02	Londi Kribi	19 1 77	Arsenal
Lua-Lua Lomano (F)	5 8	12 00	Kinshasa	28 12 80	Newcastle U
Mbesuma Collins (F)	6 0	12 04	Luanshya	3 2 84	Kaizer Chiefs
Mwaruwari Benjamin (F)	6 2	12 03	Harare	13 8 78	Auxerre
O'Brien Andy (D)	6 2	11 13	Harrogate	29 6 79	Newcastle U
O'Neil Gary (M)	5 10	11 00	Beckenham	18 5 83	Trainee
Pamarot Noe (D)	5 11	13 07	Fontenay-sous-Bois	14 4 79	Tottenham H
Pearce Jason (D)	5 11	12 00	Hampshire	6 12 87	Scholar
Pedro Mendes (M)	5 9	12 04	Guimaraes	26 2 79	Tottenham H
Primus Linvoy (D)	5 10	12 04	Forest Gate	14 9 73	Reading
Songo'o Frank (M)	6 2	12 06	Yaounde	14 5 87	Barcelona
Stefanovic Dejan (D)	6 2	13 01	Belgrade	28 10 74	Vitesse
Taylor Matthew (D)	5 11	12 03	Oxford	27 11 81	Luton T
Todorov Svetoslav (F)	6 0	12 02	Dobrich	30 8 78	West Ham U
Traore Djimi (D)	6 3	12 04	Laval	1 3 80	Charlton Ath
Wilson Marc (M)	6 2	12 07	Belfast	17 8 87	Scholar

League Appearances: Campbell, S. 32; Cole, A. 5(13); Davis, S. 29(2); Douala, R. 1(6); Fernandes, M. 7(3); Hughes, R. 11(7); James, D. 38; Johnson, G. 25(1); Kanu, N. 32(4); Koroman, O. (1); Kranjcar, N. 11(13); Lauren, E. 9(1); Lua-Lua, L. 8(14); Mvuemba, A. 1(6); Mwaruwari, B. 25(6); O'Brien, A. 1(2); O'Neil, G. 35; Pamarot, N. 21(2); Pedro Mendes, 25(1); Primus, L. 36; Stefanovic, D. 20; Taylor, M. 30(5); Thompson, D. 5(7); Todorov, S. 1(3); Traore, D. 10.
Goals – League (45): Kanu 10, Taylor 8 (1 pen), Mwaruwari 6, Cole 3, Kranjcar 2, Lua-Lua 2 (1 pen), Pamarot 2, Pedro Mendes 2, Primus 2, Todorov 2, Campbell 1, Mvuemba 1, O'Neil 1, own goals 3.
Carling Cup (2): Fernandes 1, Taylor 1.
FA Cup (3): Kanu 2, Cole 1.
Ground: Fratton Park, Frogmore Road, Portsmouth, Hampshire PO4 8RA. Telephone (02392) 731 204.
Record Attendance: 51,385 v Derby Co, FA Cup 6th rd, 26 February 1949.
Capacity: 20,328.
Manager: Harry Redknapp.

Secretary: Paul Weld.
Most League Goals: 97, Division 1, 2002–03.
Highest League Scorer in Season: Guy Whittingham, 42, Division 1, 1992–93.
Most League Goals in Total Aggregate: Peter Harris, 194, 1946–60.
Most Capped Player: Jimmy Dickinson, 48, England.
Most League Appearances: Jimmy Dickinson, 764, 1946–65.
Honours – Football League: Division 1 Champions – 1948–49, 1949–50, 2002–03. Division 3 (S) Champions – 1923–24. Division 3 Champions – 1961–62, 1982–83.
FA Cup: Winners – 1939.
Colours: Blue shirts, white shorts, red stockings.

PORT VALE — FL CHAMPIONSHIP 1

Anyon Joe (G)	6 1	12 11	Poulton-le-Fylde	29 12 86	Scholar
Cardle Joe (M)	5 8	9 05	Blackpool	27 2 87	Scholar
Gardner Matthew (M)	5 8	11 12	South Shields	15 2 85	Nottingham F
Goodlad Mark (G)	6 2	14 00	Barnsley	9 9 79	Nottingham F
Harsley Paul (M)	5 8	11 09	Scunthorpe	29 5 78	Macclesfield T
McGregor Mark (D)	5 11	11 05	Chester	16 2 77	Blackpool
Miles Colin (D)	6 0	13 06	Edmonton	6 9 78	Yeovil T
Pilkington George (D)	5 11	12 00	Rugeley	7 11 81	Everton
Prosser Luke (M)	6 3	10 05	Hertfordshire	28 5 88	Scholar
Rodgers Luke (F)	5 6	11 00	Birmingham	1 1 82	Crewe Alex
Sodje Akpo (F)	6 3	12 00	Greenwich	31 1 81	Darlington
Sonner Danny (M)	6 0	12 06	Wigan	9 1 72	Peterborough U
Talbot Jason (D)	5 9	10 08	Manchester	30 9 85	Mansfield T
Walker Richard (D)	6 3	14 00	Bolton	17 9 80	Crewe Alex
Whitaker Danny (M)	5 11	10 12	Manchester	14 11 80	Macclesfield T

League Appearances: Abbey, G. 18(6); Anyon, J. 21(1); Cardle, J. 1(6); Constantine, L. 41(1); Fortune, C. 11(2); Gardner, R. 12(4); Goodlad, M. 25; Harsley, P. 29(3); Hulbert, R. 16(4); Humphreys, R. 5(2); Husbands, M. 3(20); Kamara, M. 14(4); Lowndes, N. 1(11); McGregor, M. 26(6); Miles, C. 23(6); Moore, S. 8(4); Pilkington, G. 46; Rodgers, L. 6(2); Smith, C. (1); Smith, J. 24(3); Sodje, A. 38(5); Sonner, D. 33; Talbot, J. 18(4); Walker, R. 12(4); Walsh, M. 16(2); Weston, R. 15; Whitaker, D. 44(1).
Goals – League (64): Constantine 22 (4 pens), Sodje 14 (1 pen), Whitaker 7, Pilkington 6, Rodgers 3, Smith J. 3, Abbey 1, Gardner 1, Harsley 1, Hulbert 1, Husbands 1, Kamara 1, Moore 1, Sonner 1, own goal 1.
Carling Cup (6): Constantine 2, Smith J. 1, Sodje 1, Walker 1, Whitaker 1.
FA Cup (2): Sodje 1, Whitaker 1.
J Paint Trophy (2): Constantine 2.
Ground: Vale Park, Hamil Road, Burslem, Stoke-on-Trent ST6 1AW. Telephone (01782) 655 800.
Record Attendance: 49,768 v Aston Villa, FA Cup 5th rd, 20 February 1960.
Capacity: 18,982.
Manager: Martin Foyle.
Secretary: Bill Lodey.
Most League Goals: 110, Division 4, 1958–59.
Highest League Scorer in Season: Wilf Kirkham 38, Division 2, 1926–27.
Most League Goals in Total Aggregate: Wilf Kirkham, 154, 1923–29, 1931–33.
Most Capped Player: Chris Birchall, 22 (26), Trinidad & Tobago.
Most League Appearances: Roy Sproson, 761, 1950–72.
Honours – Football League: Division 3 (N) Champions – 1929–30, 1953–54. Division 4 Champions – 1958–59. **Autoglass Trophy:** Winners – 1993. **LDV Vans Trophy:** Winners – 2001
Colours: White shirts with black and gold trim, black shorts with white and gold trim.

Agyemang Patrick (F)	6 1	13 10	Walthamstow	29 9 80	Gillingham
Alexander Graham (D)	5 10	12 02	Coventry	10 10 71	Luton T
Anyinsah Joe (M)	5 8	11 00	Bristol	8 10 84	Bristol C
Chilvers Liam (D)	6 2	12 08	Chelmsford	6 11 81	Colchester U
Davidson Callum (D)	5 10	11 00	Stirling	25 6 76	Leicester C
Henderson Wayne (G)	5 11	12 02	Dublin	16 9 83	Brighton & HA
Hibbert Dave (F)	6 2	12 00	Eccleshall	28 1 86	Port Vale
Hill Matt (D)	5 8	11 13	Bristol	26 3 81	Bristol C
Jarrett Jason (M)	6 0	13 04	Bury	14 9 79	Leicester C
Lonergan Andrew (G)	6 2	13 00	Preston	19 10 83	Scholar
Mawene Youl (D)	6 1	13 00	Caen	16 7 79	Derby Co
McKenna Paul (M)	5 8	11 00	Eccleston	20 10 77	Trainee
Mellor Neil (F)	6 0	14 00	Sheffield	4 11 82	Liverpool
Nash Carlo (G)	6 3	15 03	Bolton	13 9 73	Middlesbrough
Neal Chris (G)	6 2	12 04	St Albans	23 10 85	Scholar
Neal Lewis (M)	5 10	11 02	Leicester	14 7 81	Stoke C
Nowland Adam (M)	5 11	11 06	Preston	6 7 81	Nottingham F
Nugent Dave (F)	5 11	12 00	Liverpool	2 5 85	Bury
Ormerod Brett (F)	5 11	11 12	Blackburn	18 10 76	Southampton
Pugh Danny (M)	6 0	12 10	Manchester	19 10 82	Leeds U
Sedgwick Chris (M)	6 0	12 01	Sheffield	28 4 80	Rotherham U
Soley Seyfo (D)	6 3	13 12	Lamin	16 2 80	Genk
St Ledger-Hall Sean (D)	6 0	11 09	Birmingham	28 12 84	Peterborough U
Whaley Simon (M)	5 10	11 11	Bolton	7 6 85	Bury
Wilson Kelvin (D)	6 2	12 00	Nottingham	3 9 85	Notts Co

League Appearances: Agyemang, P. 10(21); Alexander, G. 42; Anyinsah, J. (3); Chilvers, L. 45; Davidson, C. 12(3); Dichio, D. 16(14); Henderson, W. 4; Hill, M. 37(1); Jarrett, J. 4(1); Lonergan, A. 13; McCormack, A. (3); McKenna, P. 32(1); Mellor, N. 2(3); Miller, T. 4(3); Nash, C. 29; Neal, L. 3(21); Nowland, A. (1); Nugent, D. 43(1); Ormerod, B. 16(13); Pergl, P. 6; Pugh, D. 45; Ricketts, M. 7(7); Sedgwick, C. 41(2); Soley, S. 6; Songo'o, F. 4(2); St Ledger-Hall, S. 40(1); Stock, B. 1(1); Whaley, S. 31(9); Wilson, K. 13(8).
Goals – League (64): Nugent 15, Ormerod 8, Agyemang 7, Alexander 6 (6 pens), Whaley 6, Dichio 5, Pugh 4, Chilvers 2, McKenna 2, Mellor 1, Neal 1, Pergl 1, Ricketts 1, Sedgwick 1, St Ledger-Hall 1, Wilson 1, own goals 2.
Carling Cup (1): Whaley 1.
FA Cup (4): Nugent 2, Ormerod 1, Wilson 1.
Ground: Sir Tom Finney Way, Deepdale, Preston PR1 6RU. Telephone (0870) 442 1964.
Record Attendance: 42,684 v Arsenal, Division 1, 23 April 1938. **Capacity:** 20,600.
Manager: Paul Simpson.
Secretary: Janet Parr.
Most League Goals: 100, Division 2, 1927–28 and Division 1, 1957–58.
Highest League Scorer in Season: Ted Harper, 37, Division 2, 1932–33.
Most League Goals in Total Aggregate: Tom Finney, 187, 1946–60.
Most Capped Player: Tom Finney, 76, England.
Most League Appearances: Alan Kelly, 447, 1961–75.
Honours – Football League: Division 1 Champions – 1888–89 (first champions), 1889–90. Division 2 Champions – 1903–04, 1912–13, 1950–51, 1999–2000. Division 3 Champions – 1970–71, 1995–96. **FA Cup:** Winners – 1889, 1938.
Colours: White shirts, blue shorts, white stockings.

QUEENS PARK RANGERS FL CHAMPIONSHIP

Ainsworth Gareth (M)	5 10	12 05	Blackburn	10 5 73	Cardiff C
Baidoo Shabazz (M)	5 8	10 07	Hackney	13 4 88	Scholar
Bailey Stefan (M)	5 11	12 08	London	10 11 87	Scholar
Bignot Marcus (D)	5 7	11 04	Birmingham	22 8 74	Rushden & D
Blackstock Dexter (F)	6 2	13 03	Oxford	20 5 86	Southampton
Bolder Adam (M)	5 9	10 08	Hull	25 10 80	Derby Co
Cole Jake (G)	6 2	13 00	Hammersmith	11 9 85	Scholar
Cook Lee (M)	5 8	11 10	Hammersmith	3 8 82	Watford
Cullip Danny (D)	6 0	12 08	Bracknell	17 9 76	Nottingham F
Doherty Tom (M)	5 8	10 06	Bristol	17 3 79	Bristol C
Howell Andrew (D)	5 11	12 01	Gt Yarmouth	18 3 89	Scholar
Jones Ray (F)	6 4	14 05	East Ham	28 8 88	Scholar
Kanyuka Patrick (D)	6 0	12 06	Kinshasa	19 7 87	Juniors
Moore Stefan (F)	5 10	10 12	Birmingham	28 9 83	Aston Villa
Nygaard Marc (F)	6 5	14 05	Copenhagen	1 9 76	Brescia
Rehman Zesh (D)	6 2	12 08	Birmingham	14 10 83	Fulham
Rowlands Martin (M)	5 9	10 10	Hammersmith	8 2 79	Brentford
Shimmin Dominic (D)	6 0	12 06	Bermondsey	13 10 87	Arsenal
Stewart Damion (D)	6 3	13 08	Kingston	8 8 80	Harbour View
Thomas Sean (G)	6 1	12 03	Edgware	5 9 87	Scholar
Timoska Sampsa (D)	6 1	11 11	Kokemaki	12 2 79	MyPa
Ward Nick (M)	6 0	12 02	Perth	24 3 85	Perth Glory

League Appearances: Ainsworth, G. 18(4); Baidoo, S. 2(7); Bailey, S. 7(3); Bignot, M. 32(1); Bircham, M. 12(5); Blackstock, D. 37(2); Bolder, A. 16; Camp, L. 11; Cole, J. 3; Cook, L. 37; Cullip, D. 13; Czerkas, A. 2(1); Donnelly, S. (3); Furlong, P. 9(13); Gallen, K. 9(9); Idiakez, I. 4(1); Jones, P. 12; Jones, R. 17(14); Kanyuka, P. 7(4); Lomas, S. 26(8); Mancienne, M. 26(2); Milanese, M. 14; Moore, S. 3; Nygaard, M. 17(6); Oliseh, E. 2; Rehman, Z. 23(2); Ricketts, R. (2); Rose, M. 10(1); Rowlands, M. 27(2); Royce, S. 20; Shimmin, D. 1; Smith, J. 22(7); Stewart, D. 45; Timoska, S. 11(3); Ward, N. 11(8).
Goals – League (54): Blackstock 13 (1 pen), Rowlands 10 (4 pens), Smith 6, Jones R 5, Cook 3, Gallen 3 (1 pen), Nygaard 3 (1 pen), Furlong 2, Lomas 2, Ainsworth 1, Baidoo 1, Idiakez 1, Stewart 1, Ward 1, own goals 2.
Carling Cup (5): Cook 1, Gallen 1, Jones R 1, Nygaard 1, Stewart 1.
FA Cup (2): Baidoo 1, Blackstock 1.
Ground: Loftus Road Stadium, South Africa Road, Shepherds Bush, London W12 7PA. Telephone (020) 8740 2602, (020) 8740 2541 (press office).
Record Attendance: 35,353 v Leeds U, Division 1, 27 April 1974. **Capacity:** 18,420.
Manager: John Gregory.
Secretary: Mrs Sheila Marson.
Most League Goals: 111, Division 3, 1961–62.
Highest League Scorer in Season: George Goddard, 37, Division 3 (S), 1929–30.
Most League Goals in Total Aggregate: George Goddard, 172, 1926–34.
Most Capped Player: Alan McDonald, 52, Northern Ireland.
Most League Appearances: Tony Ingham, 519, 1950–63.
Honours – Football League: Division 2 Champions – 1982–83. Division 3 (S) Champions – 1947–48. Division 3 Champions – 1966–67. **Football League Cup:** Winners – 1966–67.
Colours: Blue and white hooped shirts.

READING FA PREMIERSHIP

Andersen Mikkel (G)	6 5	12 08	Herlev	17 12 88	AB Copenhagen
Bennett Alan (D)	6 2	12 08	Kilkenny	4 10 81	Cork C
Bozanic Oliver (M)	6 0	12 00	Melbourne	8 1 89	Central Coast M
Brown Aaron (D)	6 4	14 07	Birmingham	23 6 83	Tamworth
Convey Bobby (M)	5 9	11 04	Philadelphia	27 5 83	DC United
Cox Simon (M)	5 10	10 12	Reading	28 4 87	Scholar
Davies Scott (M)	5 11	12 00	Dublin	10 3 88	Wycombe W
De La Cruz Ulises (D)	5 9	11 09	Piqulucho	8 2 74	Aston Villa
Doyle Kevin (F)	5 11	12 06	Adamstown	18 9 83	Cork C
Duberry Michael (D)	6 1	13 10	Enfield	14 10 75	Leeds U
Federici Adam (G)	6 2	14 02	Nowra	31 1 85	
Golbourne Scott (M)	5 8	11 08	Bristol	29 2 88	Bristol C
Gunnarsson Brynjar (M)	6 1	12 01	Reykjavik	16 10 75	Watford
Hahnemann Marcus (G)	6 3	16 04	Seattle	15 6 72	Fulham
Halford Greg (D)	6 4	12 11	Chelmsford	8 12 84	Colchester U
Halls John (M)	6 0	11 11	Islington	14 2 82	Stoke C
Hamer Ben (G)	5 11	12 04	Reading	20 11 87	Crawley T
Harper James (M)	5 10	11 02	Chelmsford	9 11 80	Arsenal
Henry James (M)	6 1	11 11	Woodley	10 6 89	Scholar
Hunt Steve (M)	5 9	10 10	Port Laoise	1 8 80	Brentford
Ingimarsson Ivar (D)	6 0	12 07	Reykjavik	20 8 77	Wolverhampton W
Kitson Dave (F)	6 3	13 00	Hitchin	21 1 80	Cambridge U
Lita Leroy (F)	5 7	11 12	DR Congo	28 12 84	Bristol C
Little Glen (M)	6 3	13 00	Wimbledon	15 10 75	Burnley
Long Shane (F)	5 10	11 02	Kilkenny	22 1 87	Cork C
Murty Graeme (D)	5 10	11 10	Saltburn	13 11 74	York C
Osano Curtis (M)	5 11	11 04	Nakuru	8 3 87	Scholar
Oster John (M)	5 9	10 08	Boston	8 12 78	Burnley
Pearce Alex (D)	6 0	11 10	Reading	9 11 88	Scholar
Seol Ki-Hyeon (M)	6 0	11 07	South Korea	8 1 79	Wolverhampton W
Shorey Nicky (D)	5 9	10 10	Romford	19 2 81	Leyton Orient
Sidwell Steven (M)	5 10	11 00	Wandsworth	14 12 82	Arsenal
Sodje Sam (D)	6 0	12 00	Greenwich	29 5 79	Brentford
Sonko Ibrahima (D)	6 3	13 07	Bignola	22 1 81	Brentford
Stack Graham (G)	6 2	12 07	Hampstead	26 9 81	Arsenal

League Appearances: Bikey, A. 7(8); Convey, B. 8(1); De la Cruz, U. 9; Doyle, K. 28(4); Duberry, M. 8; Federici, A. (2); Gunnarsson, B. 10(13); Hahnemann, M. 38; Halford, G. 2(1); Harper, J. 36(2); Hunt, S. 28(7); Ingimarsson, I. 38; Kitson, D. 9(4); Lita, L. 22(11); Little, G. 18(6); Long, S. 9(12); Murty, G. 23; Oster, J. 6(19); Seol, K. 22(5); Shorey, N. 37; Sidwell, S. 35; Sodje, S. 2(1); Sonko, I. 23.
Goals – League (52): Doyle 13 (3 pens), Lita 7, Hunt 4, Seol 4, Sidwell 4, Gunnarsson 3, Harper 3, Ingimarsson 2, Kitson 2, Long 2, De la Cruz 1, Oster 1, Shorey 1, Sonko 1, own goals 4.
Carling Cup (6): Lita 3, Bikey 1, Long 1, Mate 1.
FA Cup (9): Lita 4, Kitson 2, Gunnarsson 1, Long 1, Sodje 1.
Ground: Madejski Stadium, Junction 11, M4, Reading, Berkshire RG2 0FL. Telephone (0118) 968 1100.
Record Attendance: Elm Park: 33,042 v Brentford, FA Cup 5th rd, 19 February 1927; Madejski Stadium: 24,122 v Aston villa, Premiership, 10 February 2007.
Capacity: 24,225.
Manager: Steve Coppell.
Secretary: Sue Hewett.
Most League Goals: 112, Division 3 (S), 1951–52.

Highest League Scorer in Season: Ronnie Blackman, 39, Division 3 (S), 1951–52.
Most League Goals in Total Aggregate: Ronnie Blackman, 158, 1947–54.
Most Capped Player: Jimmy Quinn, 17 (46), Northern Ireland.
Most League Appearances: Martin Hicks, 500, 1978–91.
Honours – Football League: Championship Champions – 2005–06. Division 2 Champions – 1993–94. Division 3 Champions – 1985–86. Division 3 (S) Champions – 1925–26. Division 4 Champions – 1978–79. **Simod Cup:** Winners – 1987–88.
Colours: Blue and white hooped shirts, blue shorts, blue stockings.

ROCHDALE — FL CHAMPIONSHIP 2

Brown Gary (D)	5 6	10 00	Darwen	29 10 85	Scholar
Comyn-Platt Charlie (D)	6 2	12 04	Manchester	2 10 85	Swindon T
Crooks Lee (D)	6 2	13 07	Wakefield	14 1 78	Bradford C
Dagnall Chris (F)	5 8	12 03	Liverpool	15 4 86	Tranmere R
Doolan John (M)	6 1	13 00	Liverpool	7 5 74	Blackpool
Gilks Matthew (G)	6 3	13 09	Rochdale	4 6 82	Scholar
Jones Gary (M)	5 11	12 05	Birkenhead	3 6 77	Barnsley
McArdle Rory (D)	6 1	11 05	Sheffield	1 5 87	Sheffield W
Murray Glenn (F)	6 0	12 08	Whitehaven	25 9 83	Carlisle U
Perkins David (M)	5 6	11 06	St Asaph	21 6 82	Morecambe
Prendergast Rory (M)	5 8	12 00	Pontefract	6 4 78	Blackpool
Ramsden Simon (D)	6 0	12 06	Bishop Auckland	17 12 81	Grimsby T
Rundle Adam (M)	5 8	11 01	Durham	8 7 84	Mansfield T
Stanton Nathan (D)	5 9	13 00	Nottingham	6 5 81	Scunthorpe U
Thompson Joe (M)	6 0	9 07	Rochdale	5 3 89	Scholar
Warburton Callum (M)	5 9	11 00	Stockport	25 2 89	Scholar

League Appearances: Barker, K. 11(1); Bates, T. (2); Boardman, J. 3(1); Brown, G. 14(7); Christie, I. 4(1); Clarke, D. 5(7); Cooksey, E. 10(9); Crooks, L. 26(5); Dagnall, C. 32(5); Dodds, L. 6(6); Doolan, J. 40; Etuhu, C. 3(1); Gilks, M. 46; Goodall, A. 46; Jackson, M. 8(4); Jones, G. 26(1); Lambert, R. 3; Le Fondre, A. 7; McArdle, R. 25; Mocquet, W. 6(1); Moyo-Modise, C. 1(18); Muirhead, B. 12; Murray, G. 29(2); Perkins, D. 14(4); Poole, G. 1(5); Prendergast, R. 4(1); Ramsden, S. 32(2); Reet, D. (6); Reid, R. (2); Rundle, A. 20(9); Sako, M. 14(3); Sharp, J. 12; Stanton, N. 35; Thompson, J. 5(8); Turnbull, S. 2(2); Warburton, C. 4.
Goals – League (70): Dagnall 17 (1 pen), Murray 16, Le Fondre 4 (2 pens), Rundle 4 (1 pen), Doolan 3, Goodall 3, Jones 3 (2 pens), Muirhead 3, Ramsden 3, Sako 3, Dodds 2, Etuhu 2, Clarke 1, Mocquet 1, Moyo-Modise 1, Prendergast 1, Sharp 1, own goals 2.
Carling Cup (2): Doolan 1, Rundle 1.
FA Cup (1): Doolan 1.
J Paint Trophy (2): Barker 1, Dagnall 1.
Ground: Spotland Stadium, Sandy Lane, Rochdale OL11 5DS. Telephone (0870) 822 1907.
Record Attendance: 24,231 v Notts Co, FA Cup 2nd rd, 10 December 1949.
Capacity: 10,208.
Manager: Keith Hill.
Chief Executive/Secretary: Colin Garlick.
Most League Goals: 105, Division 3 (N), 1926–27.
Highest League Scorer in Season: Albert Whitehurst, 44, Division 3 (N), 1926–27.
Most League Goals in Total Aggregate: Reg Jenkins, 119, 1964–73.
Most Capped Player: Leo Bertos, 6 (7), New Zealand.
Most League Appearances: Graham Smith, 317, 1966–74.
Honours – None.
Colours: Black and white striped shirts, white shorts, black stockings.

ROTHERHAM UNITED — FL CHAMPIONSHIP 2

Brogan Stephen (D)	5 7	10 04	Rotherham	12 4 88	Scholar
Cochrane Justin (M)	5 11	11 07	Hackney	26 1 82	Crewe Alex
Duncum Sam (M)	5 9	11 02	Sheffield	18 2 87	Scholar
Facey Delroy (F)	6 0	12 10	Huddersfield	22 4 80	Tranmere R
Fleming Craig (D)	6 0	11 07	Halifax	6 10 71	Norwich C
Hurst Paul (D)	5 5	10 03	Sheffield	25 9 74	Trainee
Kerr Natt (D)	6 0	10 10	Manchester	31 10 87	Crewe Alex
King Liam (D)	5 9	10 02	Rainworth	3 12 87	Scholar
Mills Pablo (D)	5 11	11 04	Birmingham	27 5 84	Derby Co
Newsham Mark (M)	5 10	9 11	Hatfield	24 3 87	Scholar
O'Grady Chris (F)	6 1	12 06	Nottingham	25 1 86	Leicester C
Partridge Richie (M)	5 8	10 10	Dublin	12 9 80	Sheffield W
Sharps Ian (D)	6 3	13 05	Warrington	23 10 80	Tranmere R
Streete Theo (D)	5 5	9 13	Birmingham	23 11 87	Derby Co
Taylor Ryan (F)	6 2	10 10	Rotherham	4 5 88	Scholar
Woods Martin (M)	5 9	10 09	Bellshill	1 1 86	Sunderland
Yates Jamie (F)	5 7	10 11	Sheffield	24 12 88	Scholar

League Appearances: Bopp, E. 24(5); Brogan, S. 19(4); Cochrane, J. 29(2); Cutler, N. 41; Diagouraga, T. 4(3); Duncum, S. (2); Facey, D. 37(3); Fleming, C. 17; Henderson, I. 18; Hibbert, D. 12(9); Hoskins, W. 22(2); Hurst, P. 11(1); Jarvis, R. 10; Keane, M. 16(6); Kerr, N. 1(2); King, L. 4(2); Mills, P. 27(4); Montgomery, G. 5(1); Murdock, C. 4; Newsham, M. 3(13); O'Grady, C. 11(2); Partridge, R. 30(3); Robertson, G. 16(2); Sharps, I. 38; Streete, T. 4; Taylor, R. 1(9); Williamson, L. 17(2); Wilson, C. 5(1); Wiseman, S. 9(9); Woods, M. 31(5); Worrell, D. 38(3); Yates, J. 2(1).
Goals – League (58): Hoskins 15 (2 pens), Facey 10, Bopp 5, Williamson 5 (2 pens), O'Grady 4 (1 pen), Woods 4, Newsham 3, Partridge 3, Hibbert 2, Sharps 2, Cochrane 1, Henderson 1, Mills 1, Wiseman 1, own goal 1.
Carling Cup (5): Hoskins 1, Keane 1, Partridge 1, Sharps 1, Williamson 1 (pen).
FA Cup (0).
J Paint Trophy (1): Facey 1.
Ground: Millmoor Ground, Rotherham S60 1HR. Telephone (01709) 512 434.
Record Attendance: 25,170 v Sheffield U, Division 2, 13 December 1952. **Capacity:** 8,287.
Manager: Mark Robins.
Chief Operating Officer/Secretary: Paul Douglas.
Most League Goals: 114, Division 3 (N), 1946–47.
Highest League Scorer in Season: Wally Ardron, 38, Division 3 (N), 1946–47.
Most League Goals in Total Aggregate: Gladstone Guest, 130, 1946–56.
Most Capped Player: Shaun Goater, 14 (19), Bermuda.
Most League Appearances: Danny Williams, 459, 1946–62.
Honours – Football League: Division 3 Champions – 1980–81. Division 3 (N) Champions – 1950–51. Division 4 Champions – 1988–89. **Auto Windscreens Shield:** Winners – 1996.
Colours: Red shirts with white band on sleeves and white sides, white shorts, red stockings.

SCUNTHORPE UNITED — FL CHAMPIONSHIP

Baraclough Ian (M)	6 1	12 02	Leicester	4 12 70	Notts Co
Butler Andy (D)	6 2	14 02	Doncaster	4 11 83	Scholar
Byrne Cliff (D)	6 0	12 11	Dublin	27 4 82	Sunderland

Crosby Andy (D)	6 2	13 07	Rotherham	3 3 73	Oxford U
Foster Stephen (D)	6 1	13 00	Mansfield	3 12 74	Doncaster R
Goodwin Jim (M)	5 9	12 01	Waterford	20 11 81	Stockport Co
Hinds Richard (D)	6 2	12 02	Sheffield	22 8 80	Hull C
Lillis Joshua (G)	6 2	12 09	Scunthorpe	24 6 87	Scholar
McBreen Daniel (F)	6 1	13 01	Newcastle, Aus	23 4 77	Falkirk
Morris Ian (M)	6 0	11 05	Dublin	27 2 87	Leeds U
Mulligan Dave (D)	5 8	10 02	Bootle	24 3 82	Doncaster R
Murphy Joe (G)	6 2	13 06	Dublin	21 8 81	Sunderland
Ridley Lee (D)	5 9	11 09	Scunthorpe	5 12 81	Scholar
Sharp Billy (F)	5 9	11 00	Sheffield	5 2 86	Sheffield U
Sparrow Matt (M)	5 11	11 06	Wembley	3 10 81	Scholar
Taylor Cleveland (M)	5 8	10 07	Leicester	9 9 83	Bolton W
Williams Marcus (D)	5 10	10 07	Doncaster	8 4 86	Scholar

League Appearances: Baraclough, I. 25(8); Beckford, J. 17(1); Butler, A. 4(7); Byrne, C. 18(6); Crosby, A. 36(3); Ferretti, A. (4); Foster, S. 44; Foy, R. 1(4); Goodwin, J. 25(6); Hinds, R. 37(7); Hurst, K. 11(2); Keogh, A. 25(3); Lillis, J. 1; MacKenzie, N. 10(14); McBreen, D. 1(6); Morris, I. 18(10); Mulligan, D. 20(4); Murphy, J. 45; Ridley, L. 15(3); Sharp, B. 45; Sparrow, M. 27(2); Talbot, D. 2(1); Taylor, C. 42(3); Torpey, S. 5(9); Williams, M. 32(3).
Goals – League (73): Sharp 30 (1 pen), Beckford 8, Keogh 7, Crosby 5 (4 pens), Sparrow 4, Morris 3, Taylor 3, Hinds 2, MacKenzie 2, Baraclough 1, Butler 1, Goodwin 1, Mulligan 1, Talbot 1, Torpey 1, own goals 3.
Carling Cup (5): Baraclough 1, Mulligan 1, Paul 1, Sharp 1, Torpey 1.
FA Cup (2): Baraclough 1, Sharp 1.
J Paint Trophy (2): Foy 1, Goodwin 1 (pen).
Ground: Glanford Park, Doncaster Road, Scunthorpe DN15 8TD. Telephone (0871) 2211 899.
Record Attendance: Old Showground: 23,935 v Portsmouth, FA Cup 4th rd, 30 January 1954. Glanford Park: 8,906 v Nottingham F, FL 1, 10 March 2007.
Capacity: 9,182.
Manager: Nigel Adkins.
General Manager: Jamie Hammond.
Most League Goals: 88, Division 3 (N), 1957–58.
Highest League Scorer in Season: Barrie Thomas, 31, Division 2, 1961–62.
Most League Goals in Total Aggregate: Steve Cammack, 110, 1979–81, 1981–86.
Most Capped Player: Dave Mulligan, 1(12), New Zealand.
Most League Appearances: Jack Brownsword, 595, 1950–65.
Honours – Football League: FL 1 Champions – 2006–07; Division 3 (N) Champions – 1957–58.
Colours: Claret and blue.

SHEFFIELD UNITED — FL CHAMPIONSHIP

Annerson Jamie (G)	6 2	13 02	Sheffield	21 6 88	Scholar
Armstrong Chris (D)	5 9	11 00	Newcastle	5 8 82	Oldham Ath
Bennett Ian (G)	6 0	12 10	Worksop	10 10 71	Leeds U
Binnion Travis (M)	5 10	11 02	Derby	10 11 86	Scholar
Bromby Leigh (D)	6 0	12 04	Dewsbury	2 6 80	Sheffield W
Davis Claude (D)	6 3	12 08	Kingston	6 3 79	Preston NE
Fathi Ahmed (M)	5 8	11 07	Cairo	10 11 84	Ismaily
Forte Jonathan (M)	6 0	12 06	Sheffield	25 7 86	Scholar
Geary Derek (D)	5 6	10 08	Dublin	19 6 80	Sheffield W
Gillespie Keith (M)	5 10	11 03	Larne	18 2 75	Leicester C
Horsfield Geoff (F)	6 0	11 07	Barnsley	1 11 73	WBA
Horwood Evan (D)	6 0	10 06	Billingham	10 3 86	Scholar

Hulse Rob (F)	6 1	12 04	Crewe	25 10 79	Leeds U
Hurst Kevan (M)	5 10	11 07	Chesterfield	27 8 85	Scholar
Jagielka Phil (D)	5 11	14 00	Manchester	17 8 82	Scholar
Kazim-Richards Colin (F)	6 1	10 10	Leyton	26 8 86	Brighton & HA
Kenny Paddy (G)	6 0	15 10	Halifax	17 5 78	Bury
Kerry Lloyd (M)	6 2	12 04	Chesterfield	22 1 88	Scholar
Kilgallon Matt (D)	6 2	12 11	York	8 1 84	Leeds U
Law Nicky (M)	5 10	11 06	Nottingham	29 3 88	Scholar
Leigertwood Mikele (M)	6 2	12 03	Enfield	12 11 82	Crystal Palace
Li Tie (M)	6 0	11 00	Liaoning	18 9 77	Everton
Lucketti Chris (D)	6 0	13 06	Littleborough	28 9 71	Preston NE
Montgomery Nick (M)	5 8	12 08	Leeds	28 10 81	Scholar
Morgan Chris (D)	6 0	13 06	Barnsley	9 11 77	Barnsley
Nade Christian (F)	6 1	12 08	Montmorency	18 9 84	Troyes
Oliver Dean (F)	6 0	12 05	Derby	4 12 87	Scholar
Quinn Alan (M)	5 9	11 09	Dublin	13 6 79	Sheffield W
Quinn Stephen (M)	5 6	9 08	Dublin	4 4 86	Scholar
Robertson Jordan (F)	6 0	12 06	Sheffield	12 2 88	Scholar
Ross Ian (M)	5 10	11 00	Sheffield	13 1 86	Scholar
SeckMamadou (D)	6 4	12 13	Rufisgue	23 8 79	Le Havre
Shelton Luton (F)	5 11	11 11	Kingston	11 11 85	Harbour View
Sommeil David (D)	5 10	12 12	Ponte-a-Pitre	10 8 74	Manchester C
Stead Jon (F)	6 3	12 00	Huddersfield	7 4 83	Sunderland
Tonge Michael (M)	5 10	12 06	Manchester	7 4 83	Scholar
Travis Nicky (M)	6 0	12 01	Sheffield	12 3 87	Scholar
Webber Danny (F)	5 10	11 04	Manchester	28 12 81	Watford

League Appearances: Akinbiyi, A. 2(1); Armstrong, C. 24(3); Bennett, I. 2; Bromby, L. 12(5); Davis, C. 18(3); Fathi, A. 2(1); Geary, D. 26; Gerrard, P. 2; Gillespie, K. 27(4); Hulse, R. 28(1); Ifill, P. 3; Jagielka, P. 38; Kabba, S. (7); Kazim-Richards, C. 15(12); Kenny, P. 34; Kilgallon, M. 6; Kozluk, R. 17(2); Law, N. 2(2); Leigertwood, M. 16(3); Lucketti, C. 8; Montgomery, N. 22(4); Morgan, C. 21(3); Nade, C. 7(18); Quinn, A. 11(8); Quinn, S. 15; Shelton, L. 2(2); Sommeil, D. 4(1); Stead, J. 12(2); Tonge, M. 23(4); Unsworth, D. 5; Webber, D. 13(9); Wright, A. 1.
Goals – League (32): Hulse 8, Stead 5, Jagielka 4 (2 pens), Nade 3, Webber 3, Gillespie 2, Quinn S 2, Tonge 2, Kazim-Richards 1, Morgan 1, own goal 1.
Carling Cup (3): Akinbiyi 1, Montgomery 1, Nade 1.
FA Cup (0).
Ground: Bramall Lane Ground, Cherry Street, Bramall Lane, Sheffield S2 4SU. Telephone (0870) 787 1960.
Record Attendance: 68,287 v Leeds U, FA Cup 5th rd, 15 February 1936.
Capacity: 32,609.
Manager: Bryan Robson.
Secretary: Donna Fletcher.
Most League Goals: 102, Division 1, 1925–26.
Highest League Scorer in Season: Jimmy Dunne, 41, Division 1, 1930–31.
Most League Goals in Total Aggregate: Harry Johnson, 205, 1919–30.
Most Capped Player: Billy Gillespie, 25, Northern Ireland.
Most League Appearances: Joe Shaw, 629, 1948–66.
Honours – Football League: Division 1 Champions – 1897–98. Division 2 Champions – 1952–53. Division 4 Champions – 1981–82. **FA Cup:** Winners – 1899, 1902, 1915, 1925.
Colours: Red and white stripes.

SHEFFIELD WEDNESDAY — FL CHAMPIONSHIP

Beevers Mark (D)	6 4	13 00	Barnsley	21 11 89	Scholar
Boden Luke (F)	6 1	12 00	Sheffield	26 11 88	Scholar
Bowman Matthew (F)	5 8	11 11	Barnsley	31 1 90	Scholar

Brunt Chris (M)	6 1	13 02	Belfast	14 12 84	Middlesbrough
Bullen Lee (D)	6 1	12 08	Edinburgh	29 3 71	Dunfermline Ath
Burton Deon (F)	5 9	11 09	Ashford	25 10 76	Rotherham U
Clarke Leon (F)	6 2	14 02	Birmingham	10 2 85	Wolverhampton W
Coughlan Graham (D)	6 2	13 07	Dublin	18 11 74	Plymouth Arg
Folly Yoann (M)	5 10	11 00	Paris	6 6 85	Southampton
Gilbert Peter (D)	5 11	12 00	Newcastle	31 7 83	Leicester C
Graham David (F)	5 10	11 02	Edinburgh	6 10 78	Wigan Ath
Johnson Jermaine (M)	6 0	12 08	Kingston	25 6 80	Bradford C
Lekaj Rocky (M)	5 10	10 05	Kosovo	12 10 89	Scholar
Lunt Kenny (M)	5 9	11 00	Runcorn	20 11 79	Crewe Alex
MacLean Steve (F)	5 10	12 01	Edinburgh	23 8 82	Scunthorpe U
McAllister Sean (M)	5 8	10 07	Bolton	15 8 87	Scholar
McClements David (M)	5 7	10 01	Ballymoney	14 1 89	Scholar
O'Brien Burton (M)	5 10	11 09	South Africa	10 6 81	Livingston
Simek Frankie (D)	6 0	11 06	St Louis	13 10 84	Arsenal
Small Wade (M)	5 7	11 00	Croydon	23 4 84	Milton Keynes D
Spurr Tommy (D)	6 1	11 05	Leeds	13 9 87	Scholar
Tudgay Marcus (F)	5 10	12 04	Worthing	3 2 83	Derby Co
Whelan Glenn (M)	5 11	12 07	Dublin	13 1 84	Manchester C
Wood Richard (D)	6 3	12 03	Ossett	5 7 85	Scholar

League Appearances: Adams, S. 2(1); Adamson, C. 3(1); Andrews, W. 7(2); Beevers, M. 2; Boden, L. (1); Bougherra, M. 28; Brunt, C. 42(2); Bullen, L. 33(5); Burton, D. 35(7); Clarke, L. 3(7); Corr, B. (1); Coughlan, G. 14(4); Crossley, M. 17; Folly, Y. 20(9); Gilbert, P. 5(1); Graham, D. (4); Hills, J. 15(1); Johnson, J. 5(2); Jones, B. 15; Lekaj, R. (2); Lunt, K. 30(7); MacLean, S. 20(21); McAllister, S. (6); McArdle, R. (1); O'Brien, B. 13(9); Sam, L. 4; Simek, F. 41; Small, W. 13(7); Spurr, T. 31(5); Talbot, D. 2(6); Tudgay, M. 37(3); Turner, I. 11; Watson, S. 11; Whelan, G. 35(3); Wood, R. 12.
Goals – League (70): Burton 12 (1 pen), MacLean 12 (4 pens), Brunt 11 (2 pens), Tudgay 11, Whelan 7, Bougherra 2, Johnson 2, Small 2, Andrews 1, Clarke 1, Coughlan 1, Crossley 1, McAllister 1, O'Brien 1, Simek 1, own goals 4.
Carling Cup (1): Whelan 1.
FA Cup (2): Bullen 1, MacLean 1.
Ground: Hillsborough, Sheffield S6 1SW. Telephone 0870 999 1867.
Record Attendance: 72,841 v Manchester C, FA Cup 5th rd, 17 February 1934.
Capacity: 39,812.
Manager: Brian Laws.
Chief Executive: Kaven B. Walker.
Company Secretary: Paul D. Johnson.
Most League Goals: 106, Division 2, 1958–59.
Highest League Scorer in Season: Derek Dooley, 46, Division 2, 1951–52.
Most League Goals in Total Aggregate: Andrew Wilson, 199, 1900–20.
Most Capped Player: Nigel Worthington, 50 (66), Northern Ireland.
Most League Appearances: Andrew Wilson, 501, 1900–20.
Honours – Football League: Division 1 Champions – 1902–03, 1903–04, 1928–29, 1929–30. Division 2 Champions – 1899–1900, 1925–26, 1951–52, 1955–56, 1958–59. **FA Cup:** Winners – 1896, 1907, 1935. **Football League Cup:** Winners – 1990–91.
Colours: Blue and white stripes.

SHREWSBURY TOWN — FL CHAMPIONSHIP 2

Asamoah Derek (F)	5 6	10 04	Ghana	1 5 81	Chester C
Ashton Neil (M)	5 8	12 04	Liverpool	15 1 85	Tranmere R
Cooke Andy (F)	6 0	12 07	Shrewbury	20 1 74	Bradford C
Davies Ben (M)	5 10	12 08	Birmingham	27 5 81	Chester C

Drummond Stewart (M)	6 1	13 05	Preston	11 12 75	Chester C
Edwards Dave (M)	5 11	11 05	Shrewsbury	3 2 86	Trainee
Esson Ryan (G)	6 1	12 09	Aberdeen	19 3 80	Aberdeen
Hall Danny (D)	6 2	13 04	Ashton-under-Lyne	14 11 83	Oldham Ath
Herd Ben (D)	5 9	10 12	Welwyn	21 6 85	Watford
Humphrey Chris (M)	5 10	10 08	Walsall	19 9 87	WBA
Jones Luke (D)	6 1	12 12	Blackburn	10 4 87	Blackburn R
Langmead Kelvin (F)	6 1	12 00	Coventry	23 3 85	Preston NE
Leslie Steve (M)	5 11	12 10	Shrewsbury	5 11 87	Scholar
MacKenzie Chris (G)	6 0	12 06	Northampton	14 5 72	Chester C
Symes Michael (F)	6 3	12 04	Yarmouth	31 10 83	Bradford C
Tierney Marc (D)	5 11	12 04	Bury	23 8 85	Oldham Ath

League Appearances: Asamoah, D. 34(5); Ashton, N. 42(1); Burton, S. 26(2); Canoville, L. 6(1); Cooke, A. 21(13); Cowan, G. 3(1); Davies, B. 43; Drummond, S. 43(1); Edwards, D. 39(6); Esson, R. 6; Fortune-West, L. 10(9); Hall, D. 21(6); Herd, B. 29(2); Hogg, S. (1); Hope, R. 33; Humphrey, C. (12); Jones, L. 4(3); Jones, M. 3(10); Keith, J. 1; Langmead, K. 45; Leslie, S. 1(4); MacKenzie, C. 20; Shearer, S. 20; Sorvel, N. 15(3); Symes, M. 20(13); Thomas, D. 3(3); Tierney, M. 18; Williams, D. (2).
Goals – League (68): Davies 12 (5 pens), Asamoah 10 (1 pen), Cooke 10, Symes 9 (1 pen), Fortune-West 7, Edwards 5, Drummond 4, Langmead 3, Ashton 2, Burton 1, Herd 1, Jones M 1, Sorvel 1, own goals 2.
Carling Cup (0).
FA Cup (0).
J Paint Trophy (7): Symes 4, Asamoah 1, Edwards 1, own goal 1.
Play-Offs (3): Cooke 2, Drummond 1.
Ground: Oteley Road, Shrewsbury, Shropshire SY2 6ST. Telephone (01743) 360 111.
Record Attendance: 18,917 v Walsall, Division 3, 26 April 1961. **Capacity:** 10,000.
Manager: Gary Peters.
Secretary: John Howarth.
Most League Goals: 101, Division 4, 1958–59.
Highest League Scorer in Season: Arthur Rowley, 38, Division 4, 1958–59.
Most League Goals in Total Aggregate: Arthur Rowley, 152, 1958–65 (completing his League record of 434 goals).
Most Capped Player: Jimmy McLaughlin, 5 (12), Northern Ireland; Bernard McNally, 5, Northern Ireland.
Most League Appearances: Mickey Brown, 418, 1986–91; 1992–94; 1996–2001.
Honours – Football League: Division 3 Champions – 1978–79, 1993–94. **Welsh Cup:** Winners – 1891, 1938, 1977, 1979, 1984, 1985.
Colours: Blue and amber.

SOUTHAMPTON — FL CHAMPIONSHIP

Baird Chris (D)	5 10	11 11	Ballymoney	25 2 82	Scholar
Bale Gareth (D)	6 0	11 09	Cardiff	16 7 89	Scholar
Best Leon (F)	6 1	13 03	Nottingham	19 9 86	Scholar
Bialkowski Bartosz (G)	6 3	12 10	Braniewo	6 7 87	Gornik Zabrze
Condesso Feliciano (M)	6 0	11 13	Congo	6 4 87	Scholar
Cranie Martin (D)	6 1	12 09	Yeovil	23 9 86	Scholar
Davis Kelvin (G)	6 1	14 09	Bedford	29 9 76	Sunderland
Dutton-Black Josh (M)			Oxford	29 12 87	Scholar
Dyer Nathan (M)	5 5	9 00	Trowbridge	29 11 87	Scholar
Giallombardo Andrew (M)	5 9	12 02	New York	15 3 89	Scholar
Gillett Simon (M)	5 6	11 07	Oxford	6 11 85	Scholar
Idiakez Inigo (M)	6 0	12 08	San Sebastian	8 11 73	Derby Co

James Lloyd (M)	5 11	11 01	Bristol	16 2 88	Scholar
Jones Kenwyne (F)	6 2	13 06	Trinidad & Tobago	5 10 84	W Connection
Lallana Adam (M)			Southampton	10 5 88	Scholar
Lancashire Oliver (D)	6 1	11 10	Basingstoke	13 12 88	Scholar
Licka Mario (M)	5 9	12 03	Ostrava	30 4 82	Slovacko
Lundekvam Claus (D)	6 3	13 05	Austevoll	22 2 73	Brann
Makin Chris (D)	5 10	13 07	Manchester	8 5 73	Reading
McGoldrick David (F)	6 1	11 10	Nottingham	29 11 87	Notts Co
Mills Joseph (F)	5 9	11 00	Swindon	30 10 89	Scholar
Ostlund Alexander (D)	5 11	11 13	Akersborg	2 11 78	Feyenoord
Pele (D)	6 2	13 12	Albufeira	2 5 78	Belenenses
Poke Michael (G)	6 1	13 12	Staines	21 11 85	Trainee
Powell Darren (D)	6 2	13 07	Hammersmith	10 3 76	Crystal Palace
Rasiak Grzegorz (F)	6 2	13 10	Szczecin	12 1 79	Tottenham H
Skacel Rudi (M)	5 10	12 10	Trutnov	17 7 79	Hearts
Surman Andrew (M)	6 0	11 09	Johannesburg	20 8 86	Trainee
Thomson Jake (M)	5 11	11 05	Southsea	12 5 89	Scholar
Viafara John (M)	6 1	12 12	Robles	27 10 78	Portsmouth
White Jamie (F)	5 8	10 07	Southampton	21 9 89	Scholar
Wright Jemaine (M)	5 10	12 13	Greenwich	12 10 75	Leeds U
Wright-Phillips Bradley (F)	5 10	11 00	Lewisham	12 3 85	Manchester C

League Appearances: Baird, C. 44; Bale, G. 38; Belmadi, D. 9(5); Best, L. 6(3); Bialkowski, B. 8; Cranie, M. (1); Davis, K. 38; Dyer, N. 10(8); Fuller, R. 1; Guthrie, D. 8(2); Idiakez, I. 12(2); Jones, K. 25(9); Lallana, A. 1; Licka, M. 7(8); Lundekvam, C. 33; Makin, C. 19(3); McGoldrick, D. 1(8); Ostlund, A. 17(3); Pele, 34(3); Powell, D. 8; Prutton, D. 1(2); Rasiak, G. 32(7); Saganowski, M. 11(2); Skacel, R. 32(5); Surman, A. 26(11); Viafara, J. 29(7); Wright, J. 41(1); Wright-Phillips, B. 15(24).
Goals – League (77): Rasiak 18 (3 pens), Jones 14 (1 pen), Saganowski 10, Wright-Phillips 8, Bale 5, Best 4, Surman 4 (1 pen), Baird 3, Skacel 3, Viafara 2, Idiakez 1, Licka 1, Pele 1, Prutton 1, Wright 1, own goal 1.
Carling Cup (9): Wright-Phillips 3, Belmadi 1, Dyer 1, Jones 1, McGoldrick 1, Skacel 1, own goal 1.
FA Cup (3): Rasiak 2, Jones 1.
Play-Offs (4): Viafara 2, Rasiak 1, Surman 1.
Ground: St Mary's Stadium, Britannia Road, Southampton SO14 5FP. Telephone (0845) 688 9448.
Record Attendance: 32,104 v Liverpool, FA Premier League, 18 January 2003.
Capacity: 32,689.
Manager: George Burley.
Secretary: Liz Coley.
Most League Goals: 112, Division 3 (S), 1957–58.
Highest League Scorer in Season: Derek Reeves, 39, Division 3, 1959–60.
Most League Goals in Total Aggregate: Mike Channon, 185, 1966–77, 1979–82.
Most Capped Player: Peter Shilton, 49 (125), England.
Most League Appearances: Terry Paine, 713, 1956–74.
Honours – Football League: Division 3 (S) Champions – 1921–22. Division 3 Champions – 1959–60. **FA Cup:** Winners – 1975–76.
Colours: Red and white striped shirts, black shorts, white with red stockings.

SOUTHEND UNITED — FL CHAMPIONSHIP 1

Ademeno Charles (F)	5 10	11 13	Milton Keynes	12 12 88	Scholar
Barrett Adam (D)	6 1	12 09	Dagenham	29 11 79	Bristol R
Bradbury Lee (F)	6 0	12 07	Isle of Wight	3 7 75	Oxford U
Campbell-Ryce Jamal (M)	5 5	10 02	Wembley	6 4 83	Charlton Ath

Clarke Peter (D)	6 0	12 10	Southport	3 1 82	Blackpool
Collis Steve (G)	6 2	13 05	Barnet	18 3 81	Yeovil T
Eastwood Freddy (F)	5 11	12 00	Epsom	29 10 83	Grays Ath
Flahavan Darryl (G)	5 11	12 06	Southampton	28 11 78	Woking
Foran Richie (F)	5 11	12 03	Dublin	16 6 80	Motherwell
Francis Simon (D)	6 3	14 00	Nottingham	16 2 85	Sheffield U
Gower Mark (M)	5 8	12 02	Edmonton	5 10 78	Barnet
Hammell Steven (D)	5 9	12 07	Rutherglen	18 2 82	Motherwell
Harrold Matt (F)	6 2	13 07	Walthamstow	25 7 84	Yeovil T
Hooper Gary (M)	5 10	12 07	Harlow	26 1 88	Grays Ath
Hunt Lewis (D)	5 11	12 09	Birmingham	25 8 82	Derby Co
Maher Kevin (M)	6 0	12 00	Ilford	17 10 76	Tottenham H
McCormack James (M)	5 9	11 09	Dublin	10 1 84	Preston NE
Moussa Franck (M)	5 8	10 08	Brussels	24 9 87	Scholar
Paynter Billy (F)	6 0	13 12	Liverpool	13 7 84	Hull C
Wilson Che (D)	5 9	12 01	Ely	17 1 79	Cambridge C

League Appearances: Ademeno, C. (1); Arnau, C. 1(1); Barrett, A. 26(2); Bradbury, L. 28(3); Campbell-Ryce, J. 38(5); Clarke, P. 34(4); Cole, M. 1(3); Collis, S. (1); Eastwood, F. 41(1); Flahavan, D. 46; Foran, R. 9(6); Francis, S. 32(8); Gower, M. 43; Guttridge, L. 15(2); Hammell, S. 38(1); Harrold, M. 13(23); Hooper, G. 3(16); Hunt, L. 30(5); Lawson, J. (2); Maher, K. 41; McCormack, A. 20(2); Moussa, F. 2(2); Paynter, B. 5(4); Prior, S. 15(2); Ricketts, M. (2); Sam, L. (2); Sodje, E. 23(1); Wilson, C. 2.
Goals – League (47): Eastwood 11 (2 pens), Gower 8, Maher 5, Bradbury 4, Barrett 3, Harrold 3, McCormack 3, Campbell-Ryce 2, Clarke 2, Hunt 2, Foran 1, Francis 1, Hammell 1, Sodje 1.
Carling Cup (10): Eastwood 4 (1 pen), Hooper 2, Gower 1, Hammell 1 (pen), Hunt 1, Paynter 1.
FA Cup (4): Bradbury 1, Eastwood 1 (pen), Gower 1, Maher 1.
Ground: Roots Hall, Victoria Avenue, Southend-on-Sea SS2 6NQ. Telephone (01702) 304 050.
Record Attendance: 31,090 v Liverpool FA Cup 3rd rd, 10 January 1979. **Capacity:** 12,260.
Manager: Steve Tilson.
Secretary: Mrs Helen Norbury.
Most League Goals: 92, Division 3 (S), 1950–51.
Highest League Scorer in Season: Jim Shankly, 31, 1928–29; Sammy McCrory, 1957–58, both in Division 3 (S).
Most League Goals in Total Aggregate: Roy Hollis, 122, 1953–60.
Most Capped Player: George Mackenzie, 9, Eire.
Most League Appearances: Sandy Anderson, 452, 1950–63.
Honours – Football League: Championship 1 Champions – 2005–06. Division 4 Champions – 1980–81.
Colours: Navy blue shirts with white piping, navy blue shorts.

STOCKPORT COUNTY — FL CHAMPIONSHIP 2

Bowler Michael (M)	5 11	12 00	Manchester	8 9 87	Scholar
Briggs Keith (M)	6 0	11 05	Glossop	11 12 81	Norwich C
Coward Chris (F)	6 1	11 07	Manchester	23 7 89	Scholar
Crowther Ryan (M)	5 11	11 00	Stockport	17 9 88	Scholar
Dickinson Liam (F)	6 4	11 07	Salford	4 10 85	Woodley Sports
Dinning Tony (M)	6 0	13 05	Wallsend	12 4 75	Port Vale
Elding Anthony (F)	5 9	11 00	Boston	16 4 82	Boston U
Ellis Dan (M)	5 10	12 07	Stockport	18 11 88	Scholar
Griffin Adam (D)	5 7	10 04	Salford	26 8 84	Oldham Ath

Havern Gianluca (F)	6 1	13 00	Manchester	24 9 88	Scholar
Le Fondre Adam (F)	5 9	11 04	Stockport	2 12 86	Scholar
Pilkington Anthony (M)	5 11	12 00	Manchester	3 11 87	Atherton CW
Poole David (M)	5 8	12 00	Manchester	25 11 84	Yeovil T
Proudlock Adam (F)	6 0	13 07	Wellington	9 5 81	Ipswich T
Raynes Michael (M)	6 2	12 02	Wythenshawe	15 10 87	Scholar
Rose Michael (D)	5 11	12 04	Salford	28 7 82	Yeovil T
Rowe Tommy (M)	5 11	12 11	Manchester	1 5 89	Scholar
Spencer James (G)	6 3	15 04	Stockport	11 4 85	Trainee
Tansey Greg (M)	6 1	12 03	Huyton	21 11 88	Scholar
Taylor Jason (M)	6 1	11 03	Ashton-under-Lyne	28 1 87	Oldham Ath
Tunnicliffe James (D)	6 4	12 03	Denton	17 1 89	Scholar
Turnbull Paul (F)	5 10	11 07	Stockport	23 1 89	Scholar
Williams Ashley (D)	6 0	11 02	Wolverhampton	23 8 84	Hednesford T

League Appearances: Allen, D. 1(6); Blizzard, D. 7; Bowler, M. 5(3); Bramble, T. 19(12); Briggs, K. 16(4); Clare, R. 29(1); Crowther, R. 1; Dickinson, L. 11(22); Dinning, T. 27(5); Elding, A. 20; Ellis, D. (2); Gleeson, S. 14; Griffin, A. 29(13); Hennessey, W. 15; Kane, T. 4; Le Fondre, A. 14(7); Lewis, J. 5; Malcolm, M. 10(8); Murray, G. 11; Nolan, E. 2(2); Owen, G. 39; Pilkinton, A. 18(6); Poole, D. 30(1); Proudlock, A. 14(9); Raynes, M. 7(2); Robinson, M. 11(2); Rose, M. 22(3); Rowe, T. 1(3); Ruddy, J. 11; Spencer, J. 15; Tansey, G. 2(1); Taylor, J. 44(1); Treacy, K. 2(2); Tunnicliffe, J. 4(1); Williams, A. 46.
Goals – League (65): Elding 11 (1 pen), Dickinson 7, Le Fondre 7 (1 pen), Bramble 6, Pilkinton 5, Poole 4, Griffin 3, Murray 3, Proudlock 3, Rose 3, Briggs 2, Dinning 2, Gleeson 2, Malcolm 2, Robinson 2 (2 pens), Taylor 1, Williams 1, own goal.
Carling Cup (0).
FA Cup (5): Proudlock 3 (1 pen), Bramble 1, Poole 1.
J Paint Trophy (1): Malcolm 1.
Ground: Edgeley Park, Hardcastle Road, Edgeley, Stockport, Cheshire SK3 9DD. Telephone (0161) 286 8888.
Record Attendance: 27,833 v Liverpool, FA Cup 5th rd, 11 February 1950.
Capacity: 10,641.
Manager: Jim Gannon.
Chief Executive/Secretary: Kevan Taylor.
Most League Goals: 115, Division 3 (N), 1933–34.
Highest League Scorer in Season: Alf Lythgoe, 46, Division 3 (N), 1933–34.
Most League Goals in Total Aggregate: Jack Connor, 132, 1951–56.
Most Capped Player: Jarkko Wiss, 9 (43), Finland.
Most League Appearances: Andy Thorpe, 489, 1978–86, 1988–92.
Honours – Football League: Division 3 (N) Champions – 1921–22, 1936–37. Division 4 Champions – 1966–67.
Colours: Blue shirts with white chestband, blue shorts, white stockings.

STOKE CITY — FL CHAMPIONSHIP

Bangoura Sambegou (F)	6 0	12 02	Guinea	3 4 82	Standard Liege
Broomes Marlon (D)	6 0	12 12	Birmingham	28 11 77	Preston NE
Buxton Lewis (D)	6 1	13 10	Newport (IW)	10 12 83	Portsmouth
Delap Rory (M)	6 0	11 10	Sutton Coldfield	6 7 76	Sunderland
Diao Salif (M)	6 1	13 03	Kedougou	10 2 77	Liverpool
Dickinson Carl (D)	6 0	12 00	Swadlincote	31 3 87	Scholar
Eustace John (M)	5 11	11 12	Solihull	3 11 79	Coventry C
Fuller Ricardo (F)	6 3	13 03	Kingston	31 10 79	Southampton
Garret Robert (M)	5 6	10 04	Belfast	5 5 88	Scholar
Hazley Matthew (M)	5 10	12 03	Banbridge	30 12 87	Scholar
Higginbotham Danny (D)	6 1	12 03	Manchester	29 12 78	Southampton

Hill Clint (D)	6 0	11 06	Liverpool	19 10 78	Oldham Ath
Hoefkens Carl (D)	6 1	12 13	Lier	6 10 78	Beerschot
Lawrence Liam (M)	5 11	11 03	Retford	14 12 81	Sunderland
Matteo Dominic (D)	6 1	12 06	Dumfries	28 4 74	Blackburn R
Paterson Martin (M)	5 9	11 05	Tunstall	13 5 87	Scholar
Pericard Vincent (F)	6 1	13 08	Efko	3 10 82	Portsmouth
Pulis Anthony (M)	5 10	11 10	Bristol	21 7 84	Portsmouth
Rooney Adam (F)	5 10	12 03	Dublin	21 4 87	Scholar
Russell Darel (M)	6 0	11 09	Mile End	22 10 80	Norwich C
Sidibe Mamady (F)	6 4	12 02	Bamako	18 12 79	Gillingham
Simonsen Steve (G)	6 2	12 00	South Shields	3 4 79	Everton
Sweeney Peter (M)	6 0	12 11	Glasgow	25 9 84	Millwall
Wilkinson Andy (D)	5 11	11 00	Stone	6 8 84	Scholar

League Appearances: Bangoura, S. 1(3); Berger, P. 1(6); Brammer, D. 11(11); Buxton, L. 1; Chadwick, L. 13(2); Delap, R. 2; Diao, S. 27; Dickinson, C. 5(8); Duberry, M. 29; Eustace, J. 7(8); Fortune, J. 14; Fuller, R. 25(5); Griffin, A. 32(1); Harper, K. (3); Hendrie, L. 26(2); Higginbotham, D. 44; Hill, C. 15(3); Hoefkens, C. 42(3); Lawrence, L. 27; Martin, L. 4(9); Matteo, D. 9; Parkin, J. 5(1); Paterson, M. (9); Pericard, V. 17(12); Pulis, A. (1); Rooney, A. (10); Russell, D. 40(3); Sidibe, M. 42(1); Sigurdsson, H. (2); Simonsen, S. 46; Sweeney, P. 10(3); Whitley, J. (3); Wilkinson, A. 2(2); Zakuani, G. 9.
Goals – League (62): Fuller 10 (1 pen), Sidibe 9, Higginbotham 7 (4 pens), Russell 7, Lawrence 5, Chadwick 3, Hendrie 3, Parkin 3, Griffin 2, Hill 2, Hoefkens 2, Pericard 2, Fortune 1, Martin 1, Matteo 1, Paterson 1, Sweeney 1, own goals 2.
Carling Cup (1): Pericard 1.
FA Cup (2): Fuller 1, own goal 1.
Ground: Britannia Stadium, Stanley Matthews Way, Stoke-on-Trent ST4 4EG. Telephone (01782) 592 222.
Record Attendance: 51,380 v Arsenal, Division 1, 29 March 1937 (at Victoria Ground). **Capacity:** 28,218.
Manager: Tony Pulis.
Football Administrator: Eddie Harrison.
Most League Goals: 92, Division 3 (N), 1926–27.
Highest League Scorer in Season: Freddie Steele, 33, Division 1, 1936–37.
Most League Goals in Total Aggregate: Freddie Steele, 142, 1934–49.
Most Capped Player: Gordon Banks, 36 (73), England.
Most League Appearances: Eric Skeels, 506, 1958–76.
Honours – Football League: Division 2 Champions – 1932–33, 1962–63, 1992–93. Division 3 (N) Champions – 1926–27. **Football League Cup:** Winners – 1971–72. **Autoglass Trophy:** Winners – 1992. **Auto Windscreens Shield:** Winners – 2000.
Colours: Red and white striped shirts, white shorts, white stockings.

SUNDERLAND — FA PREMIERSHIP

Arnau (M)	5 8	11 09	Manacor	1 10 81	Barcelona
Carson Trevor (G)	6 0	14 11	Downpatrick	5 3 88	Scholar
Clarke Clive (D)	5 11	12 08	Dublin	14 1 80	West Ham U
Collins Danny (D)	6 2	12 00	Buckley	6 8 80	Chester C
Connolly David (F)	5 7	11 09	Willesden	6 6 77	Wigan Ath
Dennehy Billy (F)	5 8	11 10	Tralee	17 2 87	Scholar
Edwards Carlos (M)	5 8	11 02	Port of Spain	24 10 78	Luton T
Elliott Stephen (F)	5 8	11 08	Dublin	6 1 84	Manchester C
Fulop Marton (G)	6 6	14 07	Budapest	3 5 83	Tottenham H
Hartley Peter (D)	6 0	12 06	Hartlepool	3 4 88	Scholar
Hysen Tobias (M)	5 10	11 11	Gothenburg	9 3 82	Djurgaarden
John Stern (F)	6 1	12 13	Tunapuna	30 10 76	Coventry C

Kavanagh Graham (M)	5 10	13 03	Dublin	2 12 73	Wigan Ath
Leadbitter Grant (M)	5 9	11 06	Sunderland	7 1 86	Trainee
Miller Liam (M)	5 7	10 05	Cork	13 2 81	Manchester U
Mocquet William (M)	5 10	10 07	Valognes	23 1 83	Louhans-Cuiseaux
Murphy Daryl (F)	6 2	13 12	Waterford	15 3 83	Waterford
Nosworthy Nayron (D)	6 0	12 08	Brixton	11 10 80	Gillingham
Richardson Jake (M)	5 8	10 00	Watford	22 10 88	Scholar
Stokes Anthony (F)	5 11	11 06	Dublin	25 7 88	Arsenal
Varga Stanislav (D)	6 5	14 09	Lipany	8 10 72	Celtic
Wallace Ross (M)	5 6	9 12	Dundee	23 5 85	Celtic
Ward Darren (G)	6 0	13 09	Worksop	11 5 74	Norwich C
Whitehead Dean (M)	5 11	12 06	Oxford	12 1 82	Oxford U
Wright Stephen (D)	6 0	12 00	Liverpool	8 2 80	Liverpool
Yorke Dwight (M)	5 10	12 04	Canaan	3 11 71	Sydney

League Appearances: Alnwick, B. 11; Arnau, C. (1); Brown, C. 10(6); Caldwell, S. 11; Clarke, C. 2(2); Collins, D. 36(2); Collins, N. 6(1); Connolly, D. 30(6); Cunningham, K. 11; Delap, R. 6; Edwards, C. 15; Elliott, R. 7; Elliott, S. 15(9); Evans, J. 18; Fulop, M. 5; Hartley, P. (1); Hysen, T. 15(11); John, S. 10(5); Kavanagh, G. 10(4); Kyle, K. (2); Lawrence, L. 10(2); Leadbitter, G. 24(20); Miller, L. 24(6); Miller, T. 3(1); Murphy, D. 27(11); Nosworthy, N. 27(2); Nyatanga, L. 9(2); Simpson, D. 13(1); Stead, J. 1(4); Stokes, A. 7(7); Varga, S. 20; Wallace, R. 20(12); Ward, D. 30; Whitehead, D. 43(2); Wright, S. 2(1); Yorke, D. 28(4).
Goals – League (76): Connolly 13 (2 pens), Murphy 10, Leadbitter 7, Wallace 6, Edwards 5, Elliott S 5, Yorke 5, Hysen 4, John 4, Whitehead 4, Brown 3, Miller L 2, Stokes 2, Collins N 1, Evans 1, Kavanagh 1, Stead 1, Varga 1, own goal 1.
Carling Cup (0).
FA Cup (0).
Ground: Stadium of Light, Sunderland, Tyne and Wear SR5 1SU. Telephone (0191) 551 5000.
Record Attendance: 75,118 v Derby Co, FA Cup 6th rd replay, 8 March 1933 (Roker Park). 48,353 v Liverpool, FA Premier League, 13 April 2002 (Stadium of Light). **Capacity:** 49,000.
Manager: Roy Keane.
Club Secretary: Margaret Byrne.
Most League Goals: 109, Division 1, 1935–36.
Highest League Scorer in Season: Dave Halliday, 43, Division 1, 1928–29.
Most League Goals in Total Aggregate: Charlie Buchan, 209, 1911–25.
Most Capped Player: Charlie Hurley, 38 (40), Republic of Ireland.
Most League Appearances: Jim Montgomery, 537, 1962–77.
Honours – Football League: Championship – Winners – 2004–05, 2006–07. Division 1 Champions – 1891–92, 1892–93, 1894–95, 1901–02, 1912–13, 1935–36, 1995–96, 1998–99. Division 2 Champions – 1975–76. Division 3 Champions – 1987–88. **FA Cup:** Winners – 1937, 1973.
Colours: Red and white striped shirts, black shorts, black and red stockings.

SWANSEA CITY — FL CHAMPIONSHIP 1

Abbott Pawel (F)	6 2	13 10	York	5 5 82	Huddersfield T
Akinfenwa Adebayo (F)	5 11	13 07	Nigeria	10 5 82	Torquay U
Amankwaah Kevin (D)	6 1	12 12	Harrow	19 5 82	Yeovil T
Austin Kevin (D)	6 2	15 00	Hackney	12 2 73	Bristol R
Britton Leon (M)	5 6	10 00	Merton	16 9 82	West Ham U
Butler Thomas (M)	5 7	12 00	Dublin	25 4 81	Hartlepool U
Craney Ian (M)	5 10	12 00	Bootle	21 7 82	Accrington S
Evans Scott (M)	6 0	11 07	Swansea	6 1 89	Manchester C
Gueret Willy (G)	6 2	14 01	Saint Claude	3 8 73	Millwall

Iriekpen Ezomo (D)	6 1	12 02	East London	14 5 82	West Ham U
Jones Chris (F)	5 9	11 00	Swansea	12 9 89	Scholar
Lawrence Dennis (D)	6 7	11 13	Trinidad	1 8 74	Wrexham
MacDonald Shaun (M)	6 1	11 04	Swansea	17 6 88	Scholar
Monk Garry (D)	6 1	13 00	Bedford	6 3 79	Barnsley
O'Leary Kristian (M)	6 0	12 09	Port Talbot	30 8 77	Trainee
Painter Marcos (D)	5 11	12 04	Solihull	17 8 86	Birmingham C
Pratley Darren (M)	6 1	11 00	Barking	22 4 85	Fulham
Robinson Andy (M)	5 8	11 04	Birkenhead	3 11 79	Cammell Laird
Tate Alan (D)	6 1	13 05	Easington	2 9 82	Manchester U
Trundle Lee (F)	6 0	13 03	Liverpool	10 10 76	Wrexham
Tudur-Jones Owain (M)	6 2	12 00	Bangor	15 10 84	Bangor C
Watt Steven (D)	6 2	12 09	Aberdeen	1 5 85	Chelsea
Way Darren (M)	5 7	11 00	Plymouth	21 11 79	Yeovil T

League Appearances: Abbott, P. 9(9); Akinfenwa, A. 12(13); Allen, J. (1); Amankwaah, K. 23(6); Austin, K. 26(4); Britton, L. 39(2); Butler, T. 17(13); Craney, I. 24(3); Duffy, D. 5(3); Duffy, R. 8(3); Fallon, R. 22(2); Gueret, W. 42; Iriekpen, E. 31(1); Jones, C. (7); Knight, L. 10(1); Lawrence, D. 37(2); Macdonald, S. 3(5); McLeod, K. 2(2); Meslien, S. (1); Monk, G. 2; O'Leary, K. 19(4); Oakes, A. 4; Painter, M. 22(1); Pratley, D. 25(3); Robinson, A. 33(6); Tate, A. 36(2); Trundle, L. 31(3); Tudur Jones, O. 3(1); Watt, S. (1); Way, D. 4(5); Williams, T. 17(12).
Goals – League (69): Trundle 19 (4 pens), Fallon 8, Knight 7, Robinson 7 (1 pen), Akinfenwa 5, Duffy D 5, Lawrence 5, Iriekpen 4, Britton 2, Abbott 1, Butler 1, O'Leary 1, Pratley 1, Tate 1, own goals 2.
Carling Cup (2): Pratley 1, own goal 1.
FA Cup (9): Britton 3 (1 pen), Butler 2, Akinfenwa 1, Iriekpen 1, Robinson 1, Trundle 1.
J Paint Trophy (1): Tudur-Jones 1.
Ground: Liberty Stadium, Landore, Swansea SA1 2FA. Telephone (01792) 616 600.
Record Attendance: 32,796 v Arsenal, FA Cup 4th rd, 17 February 1968 (at Vetch Field). **Capacity:** 20,520.
Manager: Roberto Martinez.
Secretary: Jackie Rockey.
Most League Goals: 90, Division 2, 1956–57.
Highest League Scorer in Season: Cyril Pearce, 35, Division 2, 1931–32.
Most League Goals in Total Aggregate: Ivor Allchurch, 166, 1949–58, 1965–68.
Most Capped Player: Ivor Allchurch, 42 (68), Wales.
Most League Appearances: Wilfred Milne, 585, 1919–37.
Honours – Football League: Division 3 Champions – 1999–2000. Division 3 (S) Champions – 1924–25, 1948–49. **Autoglass Trophy:** Winners – 1994, 2006. **Football League Trophy:** Winners – 2006. **Welsh Cup:** Winners – 11 times.
Colours: All white.

SWINDON TOWN — FL CHAMPIONSHIP 1

Brezovan Peter (G)	6 6	15 04	Bratislava	9 12 79	Brno
Caton Andy (M)	6 0	12 03	Oxford	3 12 87	Scholar
Ifil Jerel (D)	6 1	12 11	Wembley	27 6 82	Watford
Peacock Lee (F)	6 0	12 08	Paisley	9 10 76	Sheffield W
Pook Michael (M)	5 11	11 10	Swindon	22 10 85	Scholar
Roberts Chris (F)	5 9	13 02	Cardiff	22 10 79	Bristol C
Smith Jack (D)	5 11	11 05	Hemel Hempsted	14 10 83	Watford
Smith Phil (G)	6 0	15 02	Harrow	14 12 79	Crawley T
Vincent Jamie (D)	5 11	11 13	Wimbledon	18 6 75	Yeovil T
Weston Curtis (M)	5 11	11 09	Greenwich	24 1 87	Millwall

Whalley Gareth (M)	5 10	11 06	Manchester	19 12 73	Wigan Ath
Williams Ady (D)	6 1	13 02	Reading	16 8 71	Coventry C
Zaaboub Sofiane (M)	5 10	11 11	Melun	23 1 83	FC Brussels

League Appearances: Brezovan, P. 14; Brown, A. 13(17); Brownlie, R. 6(8); Caton, A. 3(2); Comyn-Platt, C. 2; Corr, B. 8; Evans, P. 11(4); Grimes, A. (4); Holgate, A. (1); Ifil, J. 40; Ince, P. 2(1); James, K. (2); Jutkiewicz, L. 13(20); Lonergan, A. 1; Monkhouse, A. 9(1); Nicholas, A. 30(5); Noubissie, P. 1(2); Onibuje, F. 6(8); Peacock, L. 40(2); Pook, M. 32(6); Rhodes, A. (4); Roberts, C. 39(3); Shakes, R. 26(6); Smith, J. 41; Smith, P. 31; Sturrock, B. 7(12); Timlin, M. 18(6); Vincent, J. 34; Wells, B. (1); Weston, C. 21(6); Westwood, A. 8(1); Williams, A. 27; Zaaboub, S. 23(4).
Goals – League (58): Peacock 10, Roberts 10 (3 pens), Jutkiewicz 5, Corr 3, Evans 3 (1 pen), Smith J 3 (3 pens), Sturrock 3, Brown 2, Brownlie 2, Monkhouse 2, Nicholas 2, Onibuje 2, Pook 2, Shakes 2, Ifil 1, Timlin 1, Weston 1, Zaaboub 1, own goals 3.
Carling Cup (2): Evans 1, Nicholas 1.
FA Cup (5): Roberts 3 (1 pen), Ifil 1, own goal 1.
J Paint Trophy (0).
Ground: County Ground, County Road, Swindon SN1 2ED. Telephone (0870) 443 1969.
Record Attendance: 32,000 v Arsenal, FA Cup 3rd rd, 15 January 1972. **Capacity:** 14,800 (approx).
Manager: Paul Sturrock.
Secretary: Louise Fletcher.
Most League Goals: 100, Division 3 (S), 1926–27.
Highest League Scorer in Season: Harry Morris, 47, Division 3 (S), 1926–27.
Most League Goals in Total Aggregate: Harry Morris, 216, 1926–33.
Most Capped Player: Rod Thomas, 30 (50), Wales.
Most League Appearances: John Trollope, 770, 1960–80.
Honours – Football League: Division 2 Champions – 1995–96. Division 4 Champions – 1985–86. **Football League Cup:** Winners – 1968–69. **Anglo-Italian Cup:** Winners – 1970.
Colours: Red shirts, red shorts, red stockings.

TORQUAY UNITED — BLUE SQUARE PREMIER

Andrews Lee (D)	5 11	11 06	Carlisle	23 4 83	Carlisle U
Hill Kevin (F)	5 11	11 00	Exeter	6 3 76	Torrington
Hockley Matthew (D)	5 10	12 07	Paignton	5 6 82	Trainee
Horsell Martin (G)	6 2	11 02	Torbay	10 12 86	Bristol R
Mansell Lee (M)	5 10	11 05	Gloucester	23 9 82	Oxford U
McPhee Chris (F)	6 0	13 03	Eastbourne	20 3 83	Brighton & HA
Robertson Chris (D)	6 3	11 08	Dundee	11 10 85	Sheffield U
Thorpe Lee (F)	6 0	12 08	Wolverhampton	14 12 75	Swansea C
Woods Steve (D)	6 0	12 05	Northwich	15 12 76	Chesterfield

League Appearances: Abbey, N. 24; Andrews, L. 46; Angus, S. 33(3); Baxter, D. (1); Cooke, S. 9(4); Critchell, K. 6(1); Dickson, R. 7(2); Easter, J. 8(2); Evans, M. 14; Fortune-West, L. 2(3); Garner, D. 8; Gordon, D. 8; Graham, D. 7; Halliday, M. 3; Hapgood, L. (1); Hill, K. 24(12); Hockley, M. 25(12); Horsell, M. 5(1); Jarvis, R. 2(2); John, A. 6(1); Kerry, L. 6(1); Leary, M. (2); Mansell, L. 43(2); McKoy, N. 1(3); McPhee, C. 11(26); Miller, K. 7; Motteram, C. 1(6); Murray, A. 21; Oliver, D. (1); Phillips, M. 10(4); Rayner, S. 10; Reed, S. 10(5); Reid, R. 4(3); Robertson, C. 9; Robertson, J. 5(4); Robinson, M. 18; Smith, P. 5(3); Taylor, C. 11(2); Thorpe, L. 39(2); Villis, M. 3(3); Ward, J. 21(4); Williams, M. 2; Woods, S. 32.

Goals – League (36): Ward 9 (2 pens), Thorpe 8 (4 pens), Mansell 4, Reid 2, Robertson J 2, Angus 1, Cooke 1, Dickson 1, Evans 1, Garner 1, Hill 1, Kerry 1, Phillips 1, Robertson C 1, Taylor 1, Williams 1.
Carling Cup (0).
FA Cup (5): Robertson J 2, Ward 2 (1 pen), McPhee 1.
J Paint Trophy (0).
Ground: Plainmoor Ground, Torquay, Devon TQ1 3PS. Telephone (01803) 328 666.
Record Attendance: 21,908 v Huddersfield T, FA Cup 4th rd, 29 January 1955.
Capacity: 6,117.
Manager: Paul Buckle.
Secretary: Deborah Hancox.
Most League Goals: 89, Division 3 (S), 1956–57.
Highest League Scorer in Season: Sammy Collins, 40, Division 3 (S), 1955–56.
Most League Goals in Total Aggregate: Sammy Collins, 204, 1948–58.
Most Capped Player: Rodney Jack (71) St Vincent.
Most League Appearances: Dennis Lewis, 443, 1947–59.
Honours – None.
Colours: Yellow shirts, yellow shorts, yellow stockings.

TOTTENHAM HOTSPUR — FA PREMIERSHIP

Name	Ht	Wt	Birthplace	D.O.B.	Source
Alnwick Ben (G)	6 0	12 09	Prudhoe	1 1 87	Sunderland
Assou-Ekotto Benoit (D)	5 10	11 00	Douala	24 3 84	Lens
Barcham Andy (F)	5 8	11 10	Basildon	16 12 86	Scholar
Barnard Lee (F)	5 10	10 10	Romford	18 7 84	Trainee
Berbatov Dimitar (F)	6 2	12 06	Sofia	30 1 81	Leverkusen
Button David (G)	6 3	13 00	Stevenage	27 2 89	Scholar
Chimbonda Pascal (D)	5 11	11 11	Les Abymes	21 2 79	Wigan Ath
Daniels Charlie (M)	6 1	12 12	Harlow	7 9 86	Scholar
Davis Jamie (M)	5 7	10 10	Braintree	25 10 88	Scholar
Dawkins Simon (F)	5 10	11 01	Edgware	1 12 87	Scholar
Dawson Michael (D)	6 2	12 02	Northallerton	18 11 83	Nottingham F
Defendi Rodrigo (D)	6 2	13 01	Ribeirao Preto	16 6 86	Cruzeiro
Defoe Jermain (F)	5 7	10 04	Beckton	7 10 82	West Ham U
Dervite Dorian (D)			Lille	25 7 88	
Forecast Tommy (G)	6 6	11 10	Newham	15 10 86	Scholar
Gardner Anthony (D)	6 3	14 00	Stafford	19 9 80	Port Vale
Ghali Hossam (M)	5 11	12 04	Cairo	15 12 81	Feyenoord
Hallfredsson Emil (M)	6 1	13 01	Iceland	29 6 84	FH
Hamed Radwan (F)				19 12 88	Scholar
Huddlestone Tom (M)	6 2	11 02	Nottingham	28 12 86	Derby Co
Ifil Phil (D)	5 9	10 08	Willesden	18 11 86	Scholar
Jenas Jermaine (M)	5 11	11 00	Nottingham	18 2 83	Newcastle U
Keane Robbie (F)	5 9	12 06	Dublin	8 7 80	Leeds U
King Ledley (D)	6 2	14 05	Bow	12 10 80	Trainee
Lee Young-Pyo (D)	5 8	10 10	Hong Chung	23 4 77	PSV Eindhoven
Lennon Aaron (M)	5 6	10 03	Leeds	16 4 87	Leeds U
Maghoma Jacques (M)	5 9	11 06	Lubumbashi	23 10 87	Scholar
Malbranque Steed (M)	5 8	11 12	Mouscron	6 1 80	Fulham
Martin Joe (M)	6 0	12 13	Dagenham	29 11 88	Scholar
McKenna Kieran (M)	5 10	10 07	London	14 5 86	Academy
Mido (F)	6 2	14 09	Cairo	23 2 83	Roma
Mills Leigh (D)	6 2	13 00	Winchester	8 2 88	Scholar
Murphy Danny (M)	5 10	11 09	Chester	18 3 77	Charlton Ath
O'Hara Jamie (M)	5 11	12 04	Dartford	25 9 86	Scholar
Pekhart Tomas (F)			Susice	26 5 89	

Riley Chris (D)			London	2 2 88	Scholar
Robinson Paul (G)	6 4	15 07	Beverley	15 10 79	Leeds U
Rocha Ricardo (D)	6 0	12 08	Braga	3 10 78	Benfica
Routledge Wayne (M)	5 6	11 02	Sidcup	7 1 85	Crystal Palace
Stalteri Paul (D)	5 11	11 13	Toronto	18 10 77	Werder Bremen
Tainio Teemu (M)	5 9	11 09	Tornio	27 11 79	Auxerre
Yeates Mark (F)	5 9	10 07	Dublin	11 1 85	Trainee
Ziegler Reto (M)	6 0	12 06	Nyon	16 1 86	Grasshoppers
Zokora Didier (M)	5 11	12 04	Abidjan	14 12 80	St Etienne

League Appearances: Assou-Ekotto, B. 16; Berbatov, D. 30(3); Chimbonda, P. 33; Davenport, C. 8(2); Davids, E. 6(3); Dawson, M. 37; Defoe, J. 20(14); Gardner, A. 6(2); Ghaly, H. 17(4); Huddlestone, T. 15(6); Ifil, P. 1; Jenas, J. 24(1); Keane, R. 18(9); King, L. 21; Lee, Y. 20(1); Lennon, A. 22(4); Malbranque, S. 18(7); Mido, 7(5); Murphy, D. 5(7); Ricardo Rocha, 9; Robinson, P. 38; Stalteri, P. 1(5); Taarabt, A. (2); Tainio, T. 20(1); Ziegler, R. (1); Zokora, D. 26(5).
Goals – League (57): Berbatov 12, Keane 11 (3 pens), Defoe 10 (3 pens), Jenas 6, Lennon 3, Malbranque 2, Tainio 2, Chimbonda 1, Davenport 1, Dawson 1, Ghaly 1, Huddlestone 1, Mido 1, Murphy 1, Robinson 1, Stalteri 1, own goals 2.
Carling Cup (12): Defoe 4, Mido 3, Huddlestone 2, Berbatov 1, Keane 1, own goal 1.
FA Cup (15): Keane 5 (1 pen), Berbatov 3, Defoe 1, Ghaly 1, Jenas 1, Lennon 1, Malbranque 1, Mido 1, own goal 1.
UEFA Cup (20): Berbatov 7, Keane 5, Defoe 3, Málbranque 2, Ghaly 1, Jenas 1, Lennon 1.
Ground: White Hart Lane, Bill Nicholson Way, 748 High Road, Tottenham, London N17 0AP. Telephone (0870) 420 5000.
Record Attendance: 75,038 v Sunderland, FA Cup 6th rd, 5 March 1938. **Capacity:** 36,310.
Manager: Martin Jol.
Secretary: John Alexander.
Most League Goals: 115, Division 1, 1960–61.
Highest League Scorer in Season: Jimmy Greaves, 37, Division 1, 1962–63.
Most League Goals in Total Aggregate: Jimmy Greaves, 220, 1961–70.
Most Capped Player: Pat Jennings, 74 (119), Northern Ireland.
Most League Appearances: Steve Perryman, 655, 1969–86.
Honours – Football League: Division 1 Champions – 1950–51, 1960–61. Division 2 Champions – 1919–20, 1949–50. **FA Cup:** Winners – 1901 (as non-League club), 1921, 1961, 1962, 1967, 1981, 1982, 1991. **Football League Cup:** Winners – 1970–71, 1972–73, 1998–99. **European Competitions: European Cup-Winners' Cup:** Winners – 1962–63. **UEFA Cup:** Winners – 1971–72, 1983–84.
Colours: White shirts, white shorts, white stockings.

TRANMERE ROVERS — FL CHAMPIONSHIP 1

Achterberg John (G)	6 1	13 00	Utrecht	8 7 71	Eindhoven
Beahon Thomas (M)	5 8	10 02	Wirral	18 9 88	Scholar
Cansdell-Sheriff Shane (D)	6 0	12 00	Sydney	10 11 82	Aarhus
Curran Craig (F)	5 11	11 11	Liverpool	23 8 89	Scholar
Davies Steve (F)	6 0	12 00	Liverpool	29 12 87	Scholar
Ellison Kevin (M)	6 0	12 00	Liverpool	23 2 79	Hull C
Goodison Ian (D)	6 1	12 06	St James, Jam	21 11 72	Seba U
Greenacre Chris (F)	5 9	12 09	Halifax	23 12 77	Stoke C
Henry Paul (M)	5 8	11 06	Liverpool	28 1 88	Scholar
Jennings Steven (M)	5 7	11 07	Liverpool	28 10 84	Scholar
Johnston Michael (D)	5 9	12 03	Birkenhead	16 12 87	Scholar
Jones Mike (M)	5 11	12 04	Birkenhead	15 8 87	Scholar

McCready Chris (D)	6 1	12 02	Chester	5 9 81	Crewe Alex
McLaren Paul (M)	6 1	13 04	High Wycombe	17 11 76	Rotherham U
Mullin John (M)	5 10	11 00	Bury	11 8 75	Rotherham U
Shuker Chris (M)	5 5	9 03	Liverpool	9 5 82	Barnsley
Stockdale Robbie (D)	6 0	11 03	Redcar	30 11 79	Hull C
Taylor Gareth (F)	6 2	13 08	Weston-Super-Mare	25 2 73	Nottingham F
Tremarco Carl (D)	5 10	12 02	Liverpool	11 10 85	Scholar
Zola Makongo Calvin (F)	6 3	13 07	Kinshasa	31 12 84	Newcastle U

League Appearances: Achterberg, J. 3(1); Cansdell-Sheriff, S. 40(3); Curran, C. 2(2); Davies, S. 16(12); Ellison, K. 26(8); Goodison, I. 40; Greenacre, C. 39(5); Harrison, D. 7(5); Hart, J. 6; Hinchliffe, B. 1(1); Jennings, S. (2); McAteer, J. 10(8); McCready, C. 42; McLaren, P. 42; Mullin, J. 39(1); Shuker, C. 45(1); Stockdale, R. 35(1); Taylor, G. 36(1); Thompson, J. 12; Tremarco, C. 14(9); Ward, G. 36(2); Zola, C. 15(14).
Goals – League (58): Greenacre 17 (2 pens), Taylor 7, Shuker 6, Mullin 5 (1 pen), Zola 5, Curran 4, Ellison 4, Cansdell-Sheriff 3, Davies 1, Harrison 1, McCready 1, McLaren 1, Ward 1, own goals 2.
Carling Cup (1): Cansdell-Sheriff 1.
FA Cup (5): Greenacre 2, Taylor 2, Cansdell-Sheriff 1.
J Paint Trophy (2): Jennings 1, Shuker 1.
Ground: Prenton Park, Prenton Road West, Birkenhead, Merseyside CH42 9PY. Telephone (0870) 460 3333.
Record Attendance: 24,424 v Stoke C, FA Cup 4th rd, 5 February 1972.
Capacity: 16,567.
Manager: Ronnie Moore.
Chief Executive/Secretary: Mick Horton.
Most League Goals: 111, Division 3 (N), 1930–31.
Highest League Scorer in Season: Bunny Bell, 35, Division 3 (N), 1933–34.
Most League Goals in Total Aggregate: Ian Muir, 142, 1985–95.
Most Capped Player: John Aldridge, 30 (69), Republic of Ireland.
Most League Appearances: Harold Bell, 595, 1946–64 (incl. League record 401 consecutive appearances).
Honours – Football League: Division 3 (N) Champions – 1937–38. **Welsh Cup:** Winners – 1935. **Leyland Daf Cup:** Winners – 1990.
Colours: White.

WALSALL — FL CHAMPIONSHIP 1

Bedeau Tony (F)	5 10	12 00	Hammersmith	24 3 79	Torquay U
Bossu Bertrand (G)	6 6	14 00	Calais	14 10 80	Darlington
Bradley Mark (D)	6 0	11 05	Dudley	14 1 88	Scholar
Butler Martin (F)	5 11	11 07	Dudley	15 9 74	Rotherham U
Dann Scott (D)	6 2	12 00	Liverpool	14 2 87	Scholar
Deeney Troy (F)	5 11	12 00	Birmingham	29 6 88	Chelmsley T
Demontagnac Ishmel (F)	5 10	11 05	Newham	15 6 88	Charlton Ath
Dobson Michael (M)	6 0	13 05	Isleworth	9 4 81	Brentford
Fox Daniel (D)	5 11	12 06	Winsford	29 5 86	Everton
Gerrard Anthony (D)	6 2	13 07	Liverpool	6 2 86	Everton
Gilmartin Rene (G)	6 5	13 06	Islington	31 5 87	St Patrick's BC
Ince Clayton (G)	6 3	13 02	Trinidad	13 7 72	Coventry C
McDermott David (M)	5 5	10 00	Stourbridge	6 2 88	Scholar
McKeown James (G)	6 1	13 07	Birmingham	24 7 89	Scholar
Nicholls Alex (F)	5 10	11 00	Stourbridge	19 12 87	Scholar
Picken Allan (D)	6 2	13 12	Sydney	17 9 81	Newcastle Jets
Roper Ian (D)	6 3	14 00	Nuneaton	20 6 77	Trainee

Sansara Netan (D)	6 0	12 00	Walsall	3 8 89	Scholar
Smith Emmanuel (D)	6 2	12 03	Birmingham	8 11 88	Scholar
Wrack Darren (M)	5 9	12 02	Cleethorpes	5 5 76	Grimsby T

League Appearances: Bedeau, A. 8(10); Benjamin, T. 8; Bossu, B. 1; Bradley, M. (1); Butler, M. 44; Cederqvist, P. 3(8); Constable, J. 2(4); Cooper, K. 8; Dann, S. 24(6); Deeney, T. (1); Demontagnac, I. 2(17); Dobson, M. 39; Fangueiro, C. 2(3); Fox, D. 44; Gerrard, A. 31(4); Harper, K. 10; Ince, C. 45; Keates, D. 36(3); Kinsella, M. 8(3); Pead, C. 26(15); Picken, A. 1(1); Roper, I. 27; Sam, H. 28(14); Smith, E. 1(2); Taylor, K. 27(8); Westwood, C. 38(2); Wrack, D. 7(11); Wright, M. 31(6); Wright, T. 5(1).
Goals – League (66): Keates 13 (4 pens), Butler 11, Sam 7, Dann 4, Harper 4, Roper 4, Dobson 3, Fox 3, Wright M 3, Benjamin 2, Westwood 2, Wright T 2, Bedeau 1, Demontagnac 1, Fangueiro 1, Gerrard 1, Kinsella 1, Taylor K 1, Wrack 1, own goal 1.
Carling Cup (2): Butler 1, Dann 1.
FA Cup (0).
J Paint Trophy (1): Wrack 1.
Ground: Banks's Stadium, Bescot Crescent, Walsall WS1 4SA. Telephone (0870) 221 0442.
Record Attendance: 11,037 v Wolverhampton W, Division 1, 11 January 2003.
Capacity: 11,300.
Manager: Richard Money.
Chief Executive/Secretary: Roy Whalley.
Most League Goals: 102, Division 4, 1959–60.
Highest League Scorer in Season: Gilbert Alsop, 40, Division 3 (N), 1933–34 and 1934–35.
Most League Goals in Total Aggregate: Tony Richards, 184, 1954–63; Colin Taylor, 184, 1958–63, 1964–68, 1969–73.
Most Capped Player: Mick Kearns, 15 (18), Republic of Ireland.
Most League Appearances: Colin Harrison, 467, 1964–82.
Honours – Football League: FL 2 Champions – 2006–07. Division 4 Champions – 1959–60.
Colours: White shirts with red band, red shorts, red stockings.

WATFORD — FL CHAMPIONSHIP

Ashikodi Moses (F)	5 10	10 07	Lagos	27 6 87	Rangers
Avinel Cedric (D)	6 2	13 03	Paris	11 9 86	Creteil
Bangura Al Hassan (M)	5 8	10 07	Sierra Leone	24 1 88	Scholar
Bouazza Hameur (F)	5 11	12 01	Evry	22 2 85	Scholar
Campana Alex (M)	5 11	12 01	Harrow	11 10 88	Scholar
Carlisle Clarke (D)	6 2	14 11	Preston	14 10 79	Leeds U
Cavalli Johan (M)	5 5	9 02	Ajaccio	12 9 81	Istres
Chambers James (D)	5 10	12 05	Sandwell	20 11 80	WBA
DeMerit Jay (D)	6 1	13 05	Wisconsin	4 12 79	Northwood
Diagouraga Toumani (M)	6 2	11 05	Paris	10 6 87	Scholar
Doyley Lloyd (D)	5 10	12 05	Whitechapel	1 12 82	Scholar
Francis Fran (M)	6 2	14 03	Jamaica	18 1 87	Stoke C
Henderson Darius (F)	6 3	14 03	Sutton	7 9 81	Gillingham
Hoskins Will (F)	5 9	11 11	Nottingham	6 5 86	Rotherham U
Kabba Steve (F)	5 10	11 03	Lambeth	7 3 81	Sheffield U
King Marlon (F)	5 10	12 10	Dulwich	26 4 80	Nottingham F
Lee Richard (G)	6 0	13 03	Oxford	5 10 82	Scholar
Loach Scott (G)	6 1	13 01	Nottingham	27 5 88	Lincoln C
Mackay Malky (D)	6 2	14 07	Bellshill	19 2 72	West Ham U
Mahon Gavin (M)	6 0	13 00	Birmingham	2 1 77	Brentford

Mariappa Adrian (D)	5 10	11 12	Harrow	3 10 86	Scholar
McNamee Anthony (M)	5 6	9 11	Lambeth	13 7 84	Scholar
Osborne Junior (M)	5 10	12 03	Watford	12 2 88	Scholar
Parkes Jordan (D)	6 0	12 00	Watford	26 7 89	Scholar
Prisken Tamas (F)	6 1	11 07	Komarno	27 6 86	Gyor
Robinson Theo (M)	5 11	11 00	Birmingham	22 1 89	Scholar
Shittu Dan (D)	6 3	15 00	Lagos	2 9 80	QPR
Smith Tommy (M)	5 8	11 04	Hemel Hempstead	22 5 80	Derby Co
Stewart Jordan (D)	6 0	12 09	Birmingham	3 3 82	Leicester C
Williams Gareth (M)	5 11	12 08	Glasgow	16 12 81	Leicester C
Williamson Lee (M)	5 10	10 04	Derby	7 6 82	Rotherham U

League Appearances: Ashikodi, M. (2); Avinel, C. 1; Bangura, A. 12(4); Bouazza, H. 27(5); Carlisle, C. 4; Cavalli, J. 2(1); Chamberlain, A. (1); Chambers, J. 8(4); DeMerit, J. 29(3); Doyley, L. 17(4); Foster, B. 29; Francis, D. 28(4); Henderson, D. 24(11); Hoskins, W. 4(5); Jarrett, A. (1); Kabba, S. 6(5); King, M. 12(1); Lee, R. 9(1); MacKay, M. 13(1); Mahon, G. 33(1); Mariappa, A. 17(2); McNamee, A. 4(3); Powell, C. 9(6); Priskin, T. 7(9); Rinaldi, D. 6(1); Robinson, T. (1); Shittu, D. 27(3); Smith, T. 32; Spring, M. 2(4); Stewart, J. 30(1); Williams, G. 2(1); Williamson, L. 4(1); Young, A. 20.
Goals – League (29): Bouazza 6 (1 pen), Francis 3, King 4 (1 pen), Henderson 3 (1 pen), Young 3, DeMerit 2, Priskin 2, Mahon 1, Rinaldi 1, Shittu 1, Smith 1, own goals 2.
Carling Cup (4): Francis 1, Priskin 1, Shittu 1, Young 1.
FA Cup (8): Bouazza 2, Mackay 2, Ashikodi 1, Francis 1, McNamee 1, Smith 1.
Ground: Vicarage Road Stadium, Vicarage Road, Watford, Herts WD18 0ER. Telephone (0870) 111 1881.
Record Attendance: 34,099 v Manchester U, FA Cup 4th rd (replay), 3 February 1969. **Capacity:** 19,920.
Manager: Aidy Boothroyd.
Secretary: Michelle Ives.
Most League Goals: 92, Division 4, 1959–60.
Highest League Scorer in Season: Cliff Holton, 42, Division 4, 1959–60.
Most League Goals in Total Aggregate: Luther Blissett, 148, 1976–83, 1984–88, 1991–92.
Most Capped Player: John Barnes, 31 (79), England and Kenny Jackett, 31, Wales.
Most League Appearances: Luther Blissett, 415, 1976–83, 1984–88, 1991–92.
Honours – Football League: Division 2 Champions – 1997–98. Division 3 Champions – 1968–69. Division 4 Champions – 1977–78.
Colours: Yellow shirts, red shorts, red stockings.

WEST BROMWICH ALBION FL CHAMPIONSHIP

Albrechtsen Martin (D)	6 1	12 13	Copenhagen	30 3 80	FC Copenhagen
Carter Darren (M)	6 2	12 11	Solihull	18 12 83	Birmingham C
Chaplow Richard (M)	5 9	9 03	Accrington	2 2 85	Burnley
Clement Neil (D)	6 0	12 03	Reading	3 10 78	Chelsea
Daniels Luke (G)	6 1	12 10	Bolton	5 1 88	Manchester U
Davies Curtis (D)	6 2	11 13	Waltham Forest	15 3 85	Luton T
Ellington Nathan (F)	5 10	13 01	Bradford	2 7 81	Wigan Ath
Gera Zoltan (M)	6 0	11 11	Pecs	22 4 79	Ferencvaros
Greening Jonathan (M)	5 11	11 00	Scarborough	2 1 79	Middlesbrough
Hartson John (F)	6 1	14 06	Neath	5 4 75	Celtic
Hodgkiss Jared (M)	5 6	11 02	Stafford	15 11 86	Scholar
Kamara Diomansy (F)	6 0	11 05	Paris	8 11 80	Portsmouth
Kiely Dean (G)	6 1	12 05	Salford	10 10 70	Portsmouth
Koren Robert (M)	5 9	11 03	Ljubljana	20 9 80	Lillestrom

Koumas Jason (M)	5 10	11 02	Wrexham	25 9 79	Tranmere R
Kuszczak Tomasz (G)	6 3	13 03	Krosno Odrzansia	20 3 82	Hertha Berlin
McShane Paul (D)	6 0	11 05	Co Wicklow	6 1 86	Manchester U
Nardiello Michael (F)	5 10	11 09	Torquay	9 5 89	Liverpool
Nicholson Stuart (F)	5 10	11 09	Newcastle	3 2 86	Scholar
Perry Chris (D)	5 9	11 01	Carshalton	26 4 73	Charlton Ath
Phillips Kevin (F)	5 7	11 00	Hitchin	25 7 73	Aston Villa
Robinson Paul (D)	5 9	11 12	Watford	14 12 78	Watford
Steele Luke (G)	6 2	12 00	Peterborough	24 9 84	Manchester U
Wallwork Ronnie (M)	5 10	12 09	Manchester	10 9 77	Manchester U
Watson Steve (D)	6 0	12 07	North Shields	1 4 74	Everton

League Appearances: Albrechtsen, M. 26(5); Carter, D. 19(14); Chaplow, R. 16(12); Clement, N. 14(6); Davies, C. 32; Ellington, N. 19(15); Gera, Z. 28(12); Greening, J. 40(2); Hartson, J. 14(7); Hodgkiss, J. (5); Hoult, R. 14; Inamoto, J. (3); Kamara, D. 33(1); Kiely, D. 17; Koren, R. 15(3); Koumas, J. 34(5); MacDonald, S. (9); McShane, P. 31(1); Nicholson, S. (2); Perry, C. 23; Phillips, K. 31(5); Quashie, N. 17(3); Robinson, P. 42; Sodje, S. 7; Wallwork, R. 9(1); Watson, S. 10(2); Zuberbuhler, P. 15.
Goals – League (81): Kamara 20 (3 pens), Phillips 16 (1 pen), Ellington 9 (2 pens), Koumas 9, Gera 5, Hartson 5 (1 pen), Carter 3, Greening 2, McShane 2, Robinson 2, Albrechtsen 1, Chaplow 1, Clement 1, Koren 1, Sodje 1, Wallwork 1, own goals 2.
Carling Cup (6): Nicholson 2 (1 pen), Carter 1, Ellington 1 (pen), Greening 1, Wallwork 1.
FA Cup (9): Phillips 3, Kamara 2, Carter 1, Gera 1, Hartson 1, McShane 1.
Play-Offs (4): Phillips 3, Kamara 1.
Ground: The Hawthorns, West Bromwich, West Midlands B71 4LF. Telephone (0871) 271 1100
Record Attendance: 64,815 v Arsenal, FA Cup 6th rd, 6 March 1937. **Capacity:** 27,877.
Manager: Tony Mowbray.
Club Secretary: Darren Eales.
Most League Goals: 105, Division 2, 1929–30.
Highest League Scorer in Season: William 'Ginger' Richardson, 39, Division 1, 1935–36.
Most League Goals in Total Aggregate: Tony Brown, 218, 1963–79.
Most Capped Player: Stuart Williams, 33 (43), Wales.
Most League Appearances: Tony Brown, 574, 1963–80.
Honours – Football League: Division 1 Champions – 1919–20. Division 2 Champions – 1901–02, 1910–11. **FA Cup:** Winners – 1888, 1892, 1931, 1954, 1968. **Football League Cup:** Winners – 1965–66.
Colours: Navy blue and white striped shirts, white shorts, navy blue stockings.

WEST HAM UNITED — FA PREMIERSHIP

Ashton Dean (F)	6 2	14 07	Crewe	24 11 83	Norwich C
Benayoun Yossi (M)	5 10	11 00	Beer Sheva	6 6 80	Santander
Blackmore David (G)	6 1	13 00	Chelmsford	23 3 89	Scholar
Boa Morte Luis (F)	5 9	12 06	Lisbon	4 8 77	Fulham
Bowyer Lee (M)	5 9	10 12	Canning Town	3 1 77	Newcastle U
Carroll Roy (G)	6 2	13 12	Enniskillen	30 9 77	Manchester U
Cole Carlton (F)	6 3	14 02	Croydon	12 11 83	Chelsea
Collins James (D)	6 2	14 05	Newport	23 8 83	Cardiff C
Dailly Christian (D)	6 1	12 10	Dundee	23 10 73	Blackburn R
Davenport Calum (D)	6 4	14 00	Bedford	1 1 83	Tottenham H
Ephraim Hogan (F)	5 9	10 06	Islington	31 3 88	Scholar

Etherington Matthew (M)	5 10	10 12	Truro	14 8 81	Tottenham H
Ferdinand Anton (D)	6 2	11 00	Peckham	18 2 85	Trainee
Fitzgerald Lorcan (D)	5 9	10 09	Republic of Ireland	3 1 89	Scholar
Gabbidon Daniel (D)	6 0	13 05	Cwmbran	8 8 79	Cardiff C
Green Robert (G)	6 3	14 09	Chertsey	18 1 80	Norwich C
Harewood Marlon (F)	6 1	13 07	Hampstead	25 8 79	Nottingham F
Katan Yaniv (F)	6 1	12 13	Haifa	27 1 81	Maccabi Haifa
Konchesky Paul (D)	5 10	11 07	Barking	15 5 81	Charlton Ath
McCartney George (D)	5 11	11 02	Belfast	29 4 81	Sunderland
Mears Tyrone (D)	5 11	11 10	Stockport	18 2 83	Preston NE
Mullins Hayden (D)	5 11	11 12	Reading	27 3 79	Crystal Palace
Neill Lucas (D)	6 0	12 03	Sydney	9 3 78	Blackburn R
Noble Mark (M)	5 11	12 00	West Ham	8 5 87	Scholar
Pantsil John (D)	6 0	11 10	Berekum	15 6 81	Hapoel Tel Aviv
Quashie Nigel (M)	6 0	13 10	Peckham	20 7 78	WBA
Reid Kyel (M)	5 10	12 05	Deptford	26 11 87	Scholar
Reo-Coker Nigel (M)	5 8	12 03	Southwark	14 5 84	Wimbledon
Spector Jonathan (D)	6 0	12 08	Arlington	1 3 86	Manchester U
Stokes Tony (M)	5 10	11 10	Bethnal Green	7 1 87	Scholar
Tevez Carlos (F)	5 6	12 00	Buenos Aires	5 2 84	Corinthians
Tomkins James (D)	6 3	11 10	Basildon	29 3 89	Scholar
Upson Matthew (D)	6 1	11 04	Stowmarket	18 4 79	Birmingham C
Walker Jim (G)	5 11	13 04	Sutton-in-Ashfield	9 7 73	Walsall
Zamora Bobby (F)	6 1	11 11	Barking	16 1 81	Tottenham H

League Appearances: Benayoun, Y. 25(4); Boa Morte, L. 8(6); Bowyer, L. 18(2); Carroll, R. 12; Cole, C. 5(12); Collins, J. 16; Dailly, C. 10(4); Davenport, C. 5(1); Etherington, M. 24(3); Ferdinand, A. 31; Gabbidon, D. 18; Green, R. 26; Harewood, M. 19(13); Kepa, 1(7); Konchesky, P. 22; Mascherano, J. 3(2); McCartney, G. 16(6); Mears, T. 3(2); Mullins, H. 21(9); Neill, L. 11; Newton, S. (3); Noble, M. 10; Pantsil, J. 3(2); Quashie, N. 7; Reo-Coker, N. 35; Sheringham, T. 4(13); Spector, J. 17(8); Tevez, C. 19(7); Upson, M. 2; Zamora, B. 27(5).
Goals – League (35): Zamora 11, Tevez 7 (1 pen), Benayoun 3, Harewood 3, Cole 2, Mullins 2, Noble 2, Sheringham 2, Boa Morte 1, Kepa 1, Reo-Coker 1.
Carling Cup (1): Harewood 1.
FA Cup (3): Cole 1, Mullins 1, Noble 1.
UEFA Cup (0).
Ground: The Boleyn Ground, Upton Park, Green Street, London E13 9AZ. Telephone (020) 8548 2748.
Record Attendance: 42,322 v Tottenham H, Division 1, 17 October 1970. **Capacity:** 35,300.
Manager: Alan Curbishley.
Secretary: Peter Barnes.
Most League Goals: 101, Division 2, 1957–58.
Highest League Scorer in Season: Vic Watson, 42, Division 1, 1929–30.
Most League Goals in Total Aggregate: Vic Watson, 298, 1920–35.
Most Capped Player: Bobby Moore, 108, England.
Most League Appearances: Billy Bonds, 663, 1967–88.
Honours – Football League: Division 2 Champions – 1957–58, 1980–81. **FA Cup:** Winners – 1964, 1975, 1980. **European Competitions: European Cup-Winners' Cup:** Winners – 1964–65. **Intertoto Cup:** Winners – 1999.
Colours: Claret and blue shirts, white shorts, white stockings.

WIGAN ATHLETIC — FA PREMIERSHIP

Aghahowa Julius (F)	5 10	11 07	Benin City	12 2 82	Shakhtar Donetsk
Baines Leighton (D)	5 8	11 10	Liverpool	11 12 84	Trainee
Boyce Emmerson (D)	6 0	12 06	Aylesbury	24 9 79	Crystal Palace

Camara Henri (F)	5 9	10 08	Dakar	10 5 77	Wolverhampton W
Cotterill David (M)	5 10	11 04	Cardiff	4 12 87	Bristol C
Cywka Tomasz (M)	5 10	11 09	Gliwice	27 6 88	Gwarek Zabrze
Folan Caleb (F)	6 2	12 10	Leeds	26 10 82	Chesterfield
Hall Fitz (D)	6 3	13 09	Leytonstone	20 12 80	Crystal Palace
Heskey Emile (F)	6 2	13 08	Leicester	11 1 78	Birmingham C
Jackson Matt (D)	6 1	14 00	Leeds	19 10 71	Norwich C
Johansson Andreas (M)	5 11	12 05	Vanersborg	5 7 78	Djurgaarden
Kilbane Kevin (M)	6 1	12 08	Preston	1 2 77	Everton
Kirkland Chris (G)	6 5	14 05	Leicester	2 5 81	Liverpool
Kupisz Tomasz (M)			Radom	2 1 90	Piaseczno
Landzaat Denny (M)	5 10	12 04	Amsterdam	6 5 76	AZ
McCulloch Lee (F)	6 1	13 00	Bellshill	14 5 78	Motherwell
Pollitt Mike (G)	6 4	15 03	Farnworth	29 2 72	Rotherham U
Scharner Paul (D)	6 3	13 03	Prugstall	11 3 80	Brann
Skoko Josip (M)	5 9	12 02	Mount Gambier	10 12 75	Genclerbirligi
Taylor Ryan (M)	5 8	10 04	Liverpool	19 8 84	Tranmere R
Valencia Luis Antonio (M)	5 11	12 09	Lago Agrio	4 8 85	Villarreal
Webster Andrew (D)	6 2	13 07	Dundee	23 4 82	Hearts

League Appearances: Aghahowa, J. 3(3); Baines, L. 35; Boyce, E. 34; Camara, H. 18(5); Chimbonda, P. (1); Connolly, D. (2); Cotterill, D. 5(11); De Zeeuw, A. 21; Filan, J. 10; Folan, C. 8(5); Haestad, K. 1(1); Hall, F. 22(2); Heskey, E. 33(1); Jackson, M. 17(3); Johansson, A. 4(8); Kavanagh, G. (2); Kilbane, K. 26(5); Kirkland, C. 26; Landzaat, D. 29(4); McCulloch, L. 25(4); Pollitt, M. 2(1); Scharner, P. 22(3); Skoko, J. 24(4); Taylor, R. 12(4); Teale, G. 7(5); Todorov, S. 2(3); Unsworth, D. 6(4); Valencia, L. 17(5); Webster, A. 3(1); Wright, D. 6(6).
Goals – League (37): Heskey 8, Camara 6 (1 pen), McCulloch 4, Baines 3 (1 pen), Scharner 3, Folan 2, Landzaat 2, Cotterill 1, Jackson 1, Kilbane 1, Taylor 1, Unsworth 1 (pen), Valencia 1, own goals 3.
Carling Cup (0).
FA Cup (1): McCulloch 1.
Ground: JJB Stadium, Robin Park, Newtown, Wigan WN5 OUZ. Telephone (01942) 774 000.
Record Attendance: 27,526 v Hereford U, FA Cup 2nd rd, 12 December 1953 (at Springfield Park). **Capacity:** 25,138.
Manager: Chris Hutchings.
Secretary: Stuart Hayton.
Most League Goals: 84, Division 3, 1996–97.
Highest League Scorer in Season: Graeme Jones, 31, Division 3, 1996–97.
Most League Goals in Total Aggregate: Andy Liddell, 70, 1998–2004.
Most Capped Player: Lee McCulloch, 11, Scotland.
Most League Appearances: Kevin Langley, 317, 1981–86, 1990–94.
Honours – Football League: Division 2 Champions – 2002–03. Division 3 Champions – 1996–97. **Freight Rover Trophy:** Winners – 1984–85. **Auto Windscreens Shield:** Winners – 1998–99.
Colours: Blue and white striped shirts, blue shorts, white stockings.

WOLVERHAMPTON WANDERERS FL CHAMPIONSHIP

Bailey Matthew (M)	5 10	9 11	Birmingham	24 9 88	Scholar
Bennett Elliott (M)	5 9	10 13	Telford	18 12 88	Scholar
Bothroyd Jay (F)	6 3	13 00	Islington	7 5 82	Charlton Ath
Breen Gary (D)	6 1	12 06	Hendon	12 12 73	Sunderland
Clapham Jamie (D)	5 9	10 08	Lincoln	7 12 75	Birmingham C
Collins Lee (D)	6 1	11 10	Telford	23 9 83	Scholar
Collins Neill (D)	6 3	12 06	Irvine	2 9 83	Sunderland

Craddock Jody (D)	6 2	12 00	Bromsgrove	25 7 75	Sunderland
Davies Craig (F)	6 2	13 03	Burton-on-Trent	9 1 86	Verona
Davies Mark (M)	5 11	11 08	Willenhall	18 2 88	Scholar
Edwards Rob (D)	6 1	11 10	Telford	25 12 82	Aston Villa
Frankowski Tomasz (F)	5 8	10 01	Poland	16 8 74	Elche
Gleeson Stephen (M)	6 2	11 00	Dublin	3 8 88	Scholar
Gobern Lewis (M)	5 10	11 07	Birmingham	28 1 85	Scholar
Hennessey Wayne (G)	6 0	11 06	Anglesey	24 1 87	Scholar
Henry Karl (M)	6 0	11 02	Wolverhampton	26 11 82	Stoke C
Hughes Liam (F)	6 2	11 09	Gornal	11 9 88	Scholar
Ikeme Carl (G)	6 2	13 09	Sutton Coldfield	8 6 86	Scholar
Johnson Jemal (F)	5 8	11 09	New Jersey	3 5 85	Blackburn R
Jones Daniel (D)	6 2	13 00	Rowley Regis	14 7 86	Scholar
Keogh Andy (F)	6 0	11 00	Dublin	16 5 86	Scunthorpe U
Kightly Michael (F)	5 9	11 09	Basildon	24 1 86	Grays Ath
Lescott Jolean (D)	6 2	14 00	Birmingham	16 8 82	Trainee
Little Mark (D)	6 1	12 11	Worcester	20 8 88	Scholar
Lowe Keith (D)	6 2	13 03	Wolverhampton	13 9 85	Scholar
McIndoe Michael (M)	5 8	10 12	Edinburgh	2 2 79	Barnsley
Mulgrew Charlie (D)	6 2	13 02	Glasgow	6 3 86	Celtic
Murray Matt (G)	6 4	13 10	Solihull	2 5 81	Trainee
O'Connor Kevin (M)	5 11	12 02	Dublin	19 10 85	Scholar
Olofinjana Seyi (M)	6 2	13 05	Nigeria	30 6 80	Brann
Potter Darren (M)	6 1	11 05	Liverpool	21 12 84	Liverpool
Riley Martin (D)	6 0	12 01	Wolverhampton	5 12 86	Scholar
Rosa Denes (M)	5 8	10 05	Hungary	7 4 77	Ferencvaros
Salmon Mark (M)	5 10	10 07	Dublin	31 10 88	Scholar
Ward Stephen (F)	5 11	12 01	Dublin	20 8 85	Bohemians

League Appearances: Bothroyd, J. 19(14); Breen, G. 40; Budtz, J. 2(2); Clapham, J. 21(5); Clarke, L. 11(11); Clyde, M. 3; Collins, N. 20(2); Cort, C. 7(3); Craddock, J. 28(6); Davies, C. 6(17); Davies, M. (7); Edwards, R. 24(9); Fleming, C. 1; Gleeson, S. (3); Gobern, L. 6(6); Henry, K. 34; Ikeme, C. (1); Johnson, J. 14(6); Jones, D. 8; Keogh, A. 17; Kightly, M. 24; Little, M. 19(7); McIndoe, M. 25(2); McNamara, J. 19; Mulgrew, C. 5(1); Murray, M. 44; Naylor, L. 3; O'Connor, K. 3; Olofinjana, S. 41(3); Potter, D. 35(3); Ricketts, R. 15(4); Ward, S. 11(7); Wheater, D. 1.
Goals – League (59): Bothroyd 9, Kightly 8, Olofinjana 8, Clarke 5, Keogh 5 (1 pen), Craddock 4, Henry 3, Johnson 3, McIndoe 3, Ward 3, Collins 2, Gobern 2, Breen 1, own goals 3.
Carling Cup (0).
FA Cup (4): Davies C 2, Olofinjana 1, Potter 1.
Play-Offs (2): Craddock 1, Olofinjana 1.
Ground: Molineux, Waterloo Road, Wolverhampton WV1 4QR. Telephone (0870) 442 0123.
Record Attendance: 61,315 v Liverpool, FA Cup 5th rd, 11 February 1939.
Capacity: 29,277.
Manager: Mick McCarthy.
Secretary: Richard Skirrow.
Most League Goals: 115, Division 2, 1931–32.
Highest League Scorer in Season: Dennis Westcott, 38, Division 1, 1946–47.
Most League Goals in Total Aggregate: Steve Bull, 250, 1986–99.
Most Capped Player: Billy Wright, 105, England (70 consecutive).
Most League Appearances: Derek Parkin, 501, 1967–82.
Honours – Football League: Division 1 Champions – 1953–54, 1957–58, 1958–59. Division 2 Champions – 1931–32, 1976–77. Division 3 (N) Champions – 1923–24. Division 3 Champions – 1988–89. Division 4 Champions – 1987–88. **FA Cup:** Winners – 1893, 1908, 1949, 1960. **Football League Cup:** Winners – 1973–74, 1979–80. **Texaco Cup:** Winners – 1971. **Sherpa Van Trophy:** Winners – 1988.
Colours: Gold and black.

Carvill Michael (F)	5 10	10 10	Belfast	3 4 88	Charlton Ath
Crowell Matt (M)	5 11	10 10	Bridgend	3 7 84	Southampton
Done Matt (M)	5 10	10 04	Oswestry	22 6 88	Scholar
Evans Gareth (D)	6 1	12 12	Wrexham	10 1 87	Scholar
Evans Steve (D)	6 4	13 05	Wrexham	26 2 79	TNS
Johnson Josh (M)	5 9	10 09	Trinidad	16 4 81	San Juan
Jones Mark (M)	5 11	10 12	Wrexham	15 8 83	Scholar
Jones Michael (M)	6 3	13 00	Liverpool	3 12 87	Scholar
Llewellyn Chris (M)	6 0	11 12	Swansea	29 8 79	Hartlepool U
Mackin Levi (M)	6 1	12 00	Chester	4 4 86	Scholar
McEvilly Lee (F)	6 0	13 00	Liverpool	15 4 82	Accrington S
Pejic Shaun (D)	6 0	11 07	Hereford	16 11 82	Trainee
Reed Jamie (F)	6 0	12 07	Deeside	13 8 87	Scholar
Roberts Neil (F)	5 11	11 00	Wrexham	7 4 78	Doncaster R
Spender Simon (D)	5 11	11 00	Mold	15 11 85	Scholar
Ugarte Juan (F)	5 10	11 05	San Sebastian	7 11 80	Crewe Alex
Valentine Ryan (D)	5 10	11 05	Wrexham	19 8 82	Darlington
Williams Danny (M)	6 1	13 00	Wrexham	12 7 79	Bristol R
Williams Marc (F)	5 10	11 12	Colwyn Bay	27 7 88	Scholar
Williams Mike (D)	5 11	12 00	Colwyn Bay	27 10 86	Scholar

League Appearances: Barron, S. 3; Carvill, M. 1(5); Craddock, T. 1; Crowell, M. 10(5); Done, M. 27(7); Evans, G. 9(3); Evans, S. 34(1); Ferguson, D. 19(1); Fleming, A. 1(1); Garret, R. 10; Ingham, M. 31; Johnson, J. 10(12); Jones, Mark 29(1); Jones, Michael 1; Lawrence, D. 3; Llewellyn, C. 39; Mackin, L. 1(7); McAliskey, J. 3; McEvilly, L. 18(10); Mitchell, P. 5; Molango, M. 3; Morgan, C. 1; Newby, J. 2(9); Pejic, S. 33; Proctor, M. 9; Reed, J. (4); Roberts, N. 17(2); Roche, L. 26(2); Ruddy, J. 5; Samba, C. 1(2); Smith, K. 5(3); Spender, S. 23(2); Ugarte, J. (2); Valentine, R. 32(2); Walker, R. 3; Whitley, Jeff 11; Williams, D. 40; Williams, Marc 11(5); Williams, Mike 20(11); Williams, T. 9.
Goals – League (43): Llewellyn 9, McEvilly 7, Mark Jones 5, Roberts 3 (1 pen), Williams D 3, Evans S 2, Proctor 2, Spender 2, Valentine 2 (2 pens), Craddock 1, Done 1, Johnson 1, Smith K 1, Jeff Whitley 1, Marc Williams 1, own goals 2.
Carling Cup (5): Llewellyn 2, Done 1, Mark Jones 1, Roberts 1.
FA Cup (4): Mark Jones 1, McEvilly 1, Smith 1, Williams D 1.
J Paint Trophy (1): Crowell 1.
Ground: Racecourse Ground, Mold Road, Wrexham LL11 2AH. Telephone (01978) 262 129.
Record Attendance: 34,445 v Manchester U, FA Cup 4th rd, 26 January 1957.
Capacity: 15,500.
Manager: Brian Carey.
Secretary: Geraint Parry.
Most League Goals: 106, Division 3 (N), 1932–33.
Highest League Scorer in Season: Tom Bamford, 44, Division 3 (N), 1933–34.
Most League Goals in Total Aggregate: Tom Bamford, 175, 1928–34.
Most Capped Player: Joey Jones, 29 (72), Wales.
Most League Appearances: Arfon Griffiths, 592, 1959–61, 1962–79.
Honours – Football League: Division 3 Champions – 1977–78. **LDV Vans Trophy:** Winners – 2004–05. **Welsh Cup:** Winners – 22 times. **FAW Premier Cup:** Winners – 1998, 2000, 2001, 2003.
Colours: Red shirts, white shorts, white stockings.

WYCOMBE WANDERERS — FL CHAMPIONSHIP 2

Antwi Will (D)	6 2	12 08	Epsom	19 10 82	Aldershot T
Barnes-Homer Matthew (F)	5 11	12 05	Dudley	25 1 86	Willenhall T
Bloomfield Matt (M)	5 9	11 00	Ipswich	8 2 84	Ipswich T
Cadmore Tom (D)			Rickmansworth	26 1 88	Scholar
Christon Lewis (M)	6 0	12 02	Milton Keynes	21 1 89	Scholar
Crooks Leon (M)	6 0	11 12	Greenwich	21 11 85	Milton Keynes D
Easter Jermaine (F)	5 9	12 02	Cardiff	15 1 82	Stockport
Gregory Steven (D)	6 1	12 04	Haddenham	19 3 87	Scholar
Martin Russell (M)	6 0	11 08	Brighton	4 1 86	Lewes
Massey Alan (D)				11 1 89	Scholar
McGleish Scott (F)	5 9	11 09	Barnet	10 2 74	Northampton T
Mooney Tommy (F)	5 10	13 05	Billingham	11 8 71	Oxford U
Oakes Stefan (M)	6 1	13 07	Leicester	6 9 78	Notts Co
Onibuje Fola (F)	6 6	12 00	Lagos	25 9 84	Swindon T
Palmer Chris (M)	5 7	11 00	Derby	16 10 83	Notts Co
Stockley Sam (D)	6 0	12 08	Tiverton	5 9 77	Colchester U
Torres Sergio (M)	6 2	12 04	Mar del Plata	8 11 83	Basingstoke T
Williamson Mike (D)	6 4	13 03	Stoke	8 11 83	Southampton
Young Jamie (G)	5 11	13 00	Brisbane	25 8 85	Reading

League Appearances: Ainsworth, L. 3(4); Antwi, W. 25; Anya, I. 1(12); Barnes-Homer, M. (1); Batista, R. 29; Betsy, K. 29; Bloomfield, M. 39(2); Christon, L. 5(1); Crooks, L. 11; Dixon, J. 1(9); Doherty, T. 23(3); Easter, J. 30(8); Fernandez, V. 1; Golbourne, S. 31(3); Grant, A. 39(1); Gregory, S. (3); Martin, R. 32(10); McGleish, S. 11(3); McParland, A. 1(3); Mooney, T. 41(1); O'Halloran, S. 9(2); Oakes, S. 29(6); Onibuje, F. 1(4); Palmer, C. 22(10); Pettigrew, A. 1; Stockley, S. 33(1); Stonebridge, I. 1(8); Torres, S. 8(12); Williamson, M. 33; Young, J. 17(2).
Goals – League (52): Easter 17, Mooney 12 (1 pen), Betsy 5, McGleish 5, Bloomfield 4, Doherty 2, Martin 2, Antwi 1, Dixon 1, Golbourne 1, Stockley 1, Williamson 1.
Carling Cup (10): Easter 6, Oakes 2, Mooney 1 (pen), Williamson 1.
FA Cup (3): Antwi 1, Easter 1, Oakes 1.
J Paint Trophy (1): Stonebridge 1.
Ground: Adams Park, Hillbottom Road, Sands, High Wycombe HP12 4HJ. Telephone (01494) 472 100.
Record Attendance: 9,921 v Fulham, FA Cup 3rd rd, 9 January 2002.
Manager: Paul Lambert.
Secretary: Keith J. Allen.
Most League Goals: 72, Championship 2, 2005–06.
Highest League Goalscorer in Season: Sean Devine, 23, 1999–2000.
Most League Goals in Total Aggregate: Nathan Tyson, 42, 2005–06.
Most Capped Player: Mark Rogers, 7, Canada.
Most League Appearances: Steve Brown, 371, 1994–2004.
Honours – GM Vauxhall Conference: Winners – 1993. **FA Trophy:** Winners – 1991, 1993.
Colours: Light blue and dark blue quarters.

YEOVIL TOWN — FL CHAMPIONSHIP 1

Alcock Craig (D)	5 8	11 00	Truro	8 12 87	Scholar
Barry Anthony (M)	5 7	10 00	Liverpool	29 5 86	Accrington S
Behcet Darren (G)	6 2	13 00	London	18 10 86	West Ham U
Clarke Tom (F)	5 8	10 00	Worthing	2 1 89	Scholar

Cohen Chris (M)	6 1	13 05	Norwich	5 3 87	West Ham U
Davies Arron (M)	5 9	11 00	Cardiff	22 6 84	Southampton
Forbes Terrell (D)	5 11	12 09	Southwark	17 8 81	Oldham Ath
Gray Wayne (F)	5 11	13 10	London	7 11 80	Southend U
Guyett Scott (D)	6 2	13 06	Ascot	20 1 76	Chester C
Jones Nathan (M)	5 6	10 06	Rhondda	28 5 73	Brighton & HA
Lynch Mark (D)	6 0	11 10	Manchester	2 9 81	Hull C
Maher Stephen (M)	5 10	11 01	Dublin	3 3 88	Shelbourne
Mildenhall Stephen (G)	6 5	15 00	Swindon	13 5 78	Grimsby T
Rose Matthew (D)	5 11	11 04	Dartford	24 9 75	QPR
Skiverton Terry (D)	6 1	13 06	Mile End	26 6 75	Wycombe W
Stewart Marcus (F)	5 9	11 00	Bristol	8 11 72	Bristol C
Terry Paul (M)	5 10	12 06	Barking	3 4 79	Dagenham & R
Welsh Ishmael (F)	5 7	10 11	Leicester	4 9 87	West Ham U

League Appearances: Alcock, C. (1); Barry, A. 13(11); Best, L. 14(1); Brittain, M. 12(3); Clarke, T. 1; Cohen, C. 44; Cooper, K. 4; Cranie, M. 11(1); Davies, A. 34(5); Forbes, T. 46; Gray, W. 24(22); Guyett, S. 10(6); Harrold, M. 2(3); James, K. 2(4); Jones, N. 42; Kamudimba Kalala, J. 35(3); Knights, D. (4); Law, N. 5(1); Lindegaard, A. 12(2); Lynch, M. 17; Maher, S. (1); McCallum, G. (1); Mildenhall, S. 46; Morris, L. 23(10); Poole, D. 1(3); Rooney, A. 1(2); Rose, M. 7(2); Skiverton, T. 39; Stewart, M. 31; Sweeney, P. 5(3); Terry, P. 20; Tonkin, A. 1(4); Webb, D. (4); Welsh, I. 4(14).
Goals – League (55): Gray 11 (1 pen), Best 10, Stewart 8, Cohen 6, Davies 6, Morris 5, Skiverton 2, Terry 2, Jones 1, Kamudimba Kalala 1, Welsh 1, own goals 2.
Carling Cup (2): Gray 1, Harrold 1.
FA Cup (1): Cohen 1.
J Paint Trophy (1): Barry 1.
Play-Offs (5): Davies 2, Morris 1, Stewart 1, own goal 1.
Ground: Huish Park, Lufton Way, Yeovil, Somerset BA22 8YF. Telephone (01935) 423 662.
Record Attendance: 9,348 v Liverpool, FA Cup 3rd rd, 4 January 2004 (16,318 v Sunderland at Huish). **Capacity:** 9,665.
Manager: Russell Slade.
Secretary: Jean Cotton.
Most League Goals: 90, FL 2, 2004–05.
Highest League Goalscorer in Season: Phil Jevons, 27, 2004–05.
Most League Goals in Total Aggregate: Phil Jevons, 42, 2004–06.
Most Capped Player: Andrejs Stolcers, 1 (81), Latvia and Arron Davies, 1, Wales.
Most League Appearances: Terry Skiverton, 139, 2003–.
Honours – Football League: Championship 2 – Winners 2004–05. **Football Conference:** Champions – 2002–03. **FA Trophy:** Winners 2001–02.
Colours: Green and white hooped shirts, white shorts, white stockings.

LEAGUE POSITIONS: FA PREMIER from 1992–93 and DIVISION 1 1981–82 to 1991–92

	2005–06	2004–05	2003–04	2002–03	2001–02	2000–01	1999–2000	1998–99	1997–98	1996–97	1995–96	1994–95	1993–94
Arsenal	4	2	1	2	1	2	2	2	1	3	5	12	4
Aston Villa	16	10	6	16	8	8	6	6	7	5	4	18	10
Barnsley	–	–	–	–	–	–	–	–	19	–	–	–	–
Birmingham C	18	12	10	13	–	–	–	–	–	–	–	–	–
Blackburn R	6	15	15	6	10	–	–	19	6	13	7	1	2
Bolton W	8	6	8	17	16	–	–	–	18	–	20	–	–
Bradford C	–	–	–	–	–	20	17	–	–	–	–	–	–
Brighton & HA	–	–	–	–	–	–	–	–	–	–	–	–	–
Charlton Ath	13	11	7	12	14	9	–	18	–	–	–	–	–
Chelsea	1	1	2	4	6	6	5	3	4	6	11	11	14
Coventry C	–	–	–	–	–	19	14	15	11	17	16	16	11
Crystal Palace	–	18	–	–	–	–	–	–	20	–	–	19	–
Derby Co	–	–	–	–	19	17	16	8	9	12	–	–	–
Everton	11	4	17	7	15	16	13	14	17	15	6	15	17
Fulham	12	13	9	14	13	–	–	–	–	–	–	–	–
Ipswich T	–	–	–	–	18	5	–	–	–	–	–	22	19
Leeds U	–	–	19	15	5	4	3	4	5	11	13	5	5
Leicester C	–	–	18	–	20	13	8	10	10	9	–	21	–
Liverpool	3	5	4	5	2	3	4	7	3	4	3	4	8
Luton T	–	–	–	–	–	–	–	–	–	–	–	–	–
Manchester C	15	8	16	9	–	18	–	–	–	–	18	17	16
Manchester U	2	3	3	1	3	1	1	1	2	1	1	2	1
Middlesbrough	14	7	11	11	12	14	12	9	–	19	12	–	–
Millwall	–	–	–	–	–	–	–	–	–	–	–	–	–
Newcastle U	7	14	5	3	4	11	11	13	13	2	2	6	3
Norwich C	–	19	–	–	–	–	–	–	–	–	–	20	12
Nottingham F	–	–	–	–	–	–	–	20	–	20	9	3	–
Notts Co	–	–	–	–	–	–	–	–	–	–	–	–	–
Oldham Ath	–	–	–	–	–	–	–	–	–	–	–	–	21
Oxford U	–	–	–	–	–	–	–	–	–	–	–	–	–
Portsmouth	17	16	13	–	–	–	–	–	–	–	–	–	–
QPR	–	–	–	–	–	–	–	–	–	–	19	8	9
Sheffield U	–	–	–	–	–	–	–	–	–	–	–	–	20
Sheffield W	–	–	–	–	–	–	19	12	16	7	15	13	7
Southampton	–	20	12	8	11	10	15	17	12	16	17	10	18
Stoke C	–	–	–	–	–	–	–	–	–	–	–	–	–
Sunderland	20	–	–	20	17	7	7	–	–	18	–	–	–
Swansea C	–	–	–	–	–	–	–	–	–	–	–	–	–
Swindon T	–	–	–	–	–	–	–	–	–	–	–	–	22
Tottenham H	5	9	14	10	9	12	10	11	14	10	8	7	15
Watford	–	–	–	–	–	–	20	–	–	–	–	–	–
WBA	19	17	–	19	–	–	–	–	–	–	–	–	–
West Ham U	9	–	–	18	7	15	9	5	8	14	10	14	13
Wigan Ath	10	–	–	–	–	–	–	–	–	–	–	–	–
Wimbledon	–	–	–	–	–	–	18	16	15	8	14	9	6
Wolverhampton W	–	–	20	–	–	–	–	–	–	–	–	–	–

1992–93	1991–92	1990–91	1989–90	1988–89	1987–88	1986–87	1985–86	1984–85	1983–84	1982–83	1981–82	
10	4	1	4	1	6	4	7	7	6	10	5	Arsenal
2	7	17	2	17	–	22	16	10	10	6	11	Aston Villa
–	–	–	–	–	–	–	–	–	–	–	–	Barnsley
–	–	–	–	–	–	–	21	–	20	17	16	Birmingham C
4	–	–	–	–	–	–	–	–	–	–	–	Blackburn R
–	–	–	–	–	–	–	–	–	–	–	–	Bolton W
–	–	–	–	–	–	–	–	–	–	–	–	Bradford C
–	–	–	–	–	–	–	–	–	–	22	13	Brighton & HA
–	–	–	19	14	17	19	–	–	–	–	–	Charlton Ath
11	14	11	5	–	18	14	6	6	–	–	–	Chelsea
15	19	16	12	7	10	10	17	18	19	19	14	Coventry C
20	10	3	15	–	–	–	–	–	–	–	–	Crystal Palace
–	–	20	16	5	15	–	–	–	–	–	–	Derby Co
13	12	9	6	8	4	1	2	1	7	7	8	Everton
–	–	–	–	–	–	–	–	–	–	–	–	Fulham
16	–	–	–	–	–	–	20	17	12	9	2	Ipswich T
17	1	4	–	–	–	–	–	–	–	–	20	Leeds U
–	–	–	–	–	–	20	19	15	15	–	–	Leicester C
6	6	2	1	2	1	2	1	2	1	1	1	Liverpool
–	20	18	17	16	9	7	9	13	16	18	–	Luton T
9	5	5	14	–	–	21	15	–	–	20	10	Manchester C
1	2	6	13	11	2	11	4	4	4	3	3	Manchester U
21	–	–	–	18	–	–	–	–	–	–	22	Middlesbrough
–	–	–	20	10	–	–	–	–	–	–	–	Millwall
–	–	–	–	20	8	17	11	14	–	–	–	Newcastle U
3	18	15	10	4	14	5	–	20	14	14	–	Norwich C
22	8	8	9	3	3	8	8	9	3	5	12	Nottingham F
–	21	–	–	–	–	–	–	–	21	15	15	Notts Co
19	17	–	–	–	–	–	–	–	–	–	–	Oldham Ath
–	–	–	–	–	21	18	18	–	–	–	–	Oxford U
–	–	–	–	–	19	–	–	–	–	–	–	Portsmouth
5	11	12	11	9	5	16	13	19	5	–	–	QPR
14	9	13	–	–	–	–	–	–	–	–	–	Sheffield U
7	3	–	18	15	11	13	5	8	–	–	–	Sheffield W
18	16	14	7	13	12	12	14	5	2	12	7	Southampton
–	–	–	–	–	–	–	–	22	18	13	18	Stoke C
–	–	19	–	–	–	–	–	21	13	16	19	Sunderland
–	–	–	–	–	–	–	–	–	–	21	6	Swansea C
–	–	–	–	–	–	–	–	–	–	–	–	Swindon T
8	15	10	3	6	13	3	10	3	8	4	4	Tottenham H
–	–	–	–	–	20	9	12	11	11	2	–	Watford
–	–	–	–	–	–	–	22	12	17	11	17	WBA
–	22	–	–	19	16	15	3	16	9	8	9	West Ham U
–	–	–	–	–	–	–	–	–	–	–	–	Wigan Ath
12	13	7	8	12	7	6	–	–	–	–	–	Wimbledon
–	–	–	–	–	–	–	–	–	22	–	21	Wolverhampton W

LEAGUE POSITIONS: DIVISION 1 from 1992–93, CHAMPIONSHIP from 2004–05 and DIVISION 2 1981–82 to 1991–92

	2005–06	2004–05	2003–04	2002–03	2001–02	2000–01	1999–2000	1998–99	1997–98	1996–97	1995–96	1994–95	1993–94
Aston Villa	–	–	–	–	–	–	–	–	–	–	–	–	–
Barnsley	–	–	–	–	23	16	4	13	–	2	10	6	18
Birmingham C	–	–	–	–	5	5	5	4	7	10	15	–	22
Blackburn R	–	–	–	–	–	2	11	–	–	–	–	–	–
Bolton W	–	–	–	–	–	3	6	6	–	1	–	3	14
Bournemouth	–	–	–	–	–	–	–	–	–	–	–	–	–
Bradford C	–	–	23	19	15	–	–	2	13	21	–	–	–
Brentford	–	–	–	–	–	–	–	–	–	–	–	–	–
Brighton & HA	22	20	–	23	–	–	–	–	–	–	–	–	–
Bristol C	–	–	–	–	–	–	–	24	–	–	–	23	13
Bristol R	–	–	–	–	–	–	–	–	–	–	–	–	–
Burnley	17	13	19	16	7	7	–	–	–	–	–	22	–
Bury	–	–	–	–	–	–	–	22	17	–	–	–	–
Cambridge U	–	–	–	–	–	–	–	–	–	–	–	–	–
Cardiff C	11	16	13	–	–	–	–	–	–	–	–	–	–
Carlisle U	–	–	–	–	–	–	–	–	–	–	–	–	–
Charlton Ath	–	–	–	–	–	–	1	–	4	15	6	15	11
Chelsea	–	–	–	–	–	–	–	–	–	–	–	–	–
Coventry C	8	19	12	20	11	–	–	–	–	–	–	–	–
Crewe Alex	22	21	18	–	22	14	19	18	11	–	–	–	–
Crystal Palace	6	–	6	14	10	21	15	14	–	6	3	–	1
Derby Co	20	4	20	18	–	–	–	–	–	–	2	9	6
Fulham	–	–	–	–	–	1	9	–	–	–	–	–	–
Gillingham	–	22	21	11	12	13	–	–	–	–	–	–	–
Grimsby T	–	–	–	24	19	18	20	11	–	22	17	10	16
Huddersfield T	–	–	–	–	–	22	8	10	16	20	8	–	–
Hull C	18	–	–	–	–	–	–	–	–	–	–	–	–
Ipswich T	15	3	5	7	–	–	3	3	5	4	7	–	–
Leeds U	5	14	–	–	–	–	–	–	–	–	–	–	–
Leicester C	16	15	–	2	–	–	–	–	–	–	5	–	4
Leyton Orient	–	–	–	–	–	–	–	–	–	–	–	–	–
Luton T	10	–	–	–	–	–	–	–	–	–	24	16	20
Manchester C	–	–	–	–	1	–	2	–	22	14	–	–	–
Mansfield T	–	–	–	–	–	–	–	–	–	–	–	–	–
Middlesbrough	–	–	–	–	–	–	–	–	2	–	–	1	9
Millwall	23	10	10	9	4	–	–	–	–	–	22	12	3
Newcastle U	–	–	–	–	–	–	–	–	–	–	–	–	–
Norwich C	9	–	1	8	6	15	12	9	15	13	16	–	–
Nottingham F	–	23	14	6	16	11	14	–	1	–	–	–	2
Notts Co	–	–	–	–	–	–	–	–	–	–	–	24	7
Oldham Ath	–	–	–	–	–	–	–	–	–	23	18	14	–
Oxford U	–	–	–	–	–	–	–	23	12	17	–	–	23
Peterborough U	–	–	–	–	–	–	–	–	–	–	–	–	24
Plymouth Arg	14	17	–	–	–	–	–	–	–	–	–	–	–
Port Vale	–	–	–	–	–	–	23	21	19	8	12	17	–
Portsmouth	–	–	–	1	17	20	18	19	20	7	21	18	17
Preston NE	4	5	15	12	8	4	–	–	–	–	–	–	–
QPR	21	11	–	–	–	23	10	20	21	9	–	–	–
Reading	1	7	9	4	–	–	–	–	24	18	19	2	–

1992–93	1991–92	1990–91	1989–90	1988–89	1987–88	1986–87	1985–86	1984–85	1983–84	1982–83	1981–82	
–	–	–	–	–	2	–	–	–	–	–	–	Aston Villa
13	16	8	19	7	14	11	12	11	14	10	6	Barnsley
19	–	–	–	23	19	19	–	2	–	–	–	Birmingham C
–	6	19	5	5	5	12	19	5	6	11	10	Blackburn R
–	–	–	–	–	–	–	–	–	–	22	19	Bolton W
–	–	–	22	12	17	–	–	–	–	–	–	Bournemouth
–	–	–	23	14	4	10	13	–	–	–	–	Bradford C
22	–	–	–	–	–	–	–	–	–	–	–	Brentford
–	23	6	18	19	–	22	11	6	9	–	–	Brighton & HA
15	17	9	–	–	–	–	–	–	–	–	–	Bristol C
24	13	13	–	–	–	–	–	–	–	–	–	Bristol R
–	–	–	–	–	–	–	–	–	–	21	–	Burnley
–	–	–	–	–	–	–	–	–	–	–	–	Bury
23	5	–	–	–	–	–	–	–	22	12	14	Cambridge U
–	–	–	–	–	–	–	–	21	15	–	20	Cardiff C
–	–	–	–	–	–	–	20	16	7	14	–	Carlisle U
12	7	16	–	–	–	–	2	17	13	17	13	Charlton Ath
–	–	–	–	1	–	–	–	–	1	18	12	Chelsea
–	–	–	–	–	–	–	–	–	–	–	–	Coventry C
–	–	–	–	–	–	–	–	–	–	–	–	Crewe Alex
–	–	–	–	3	6	6	5	15	18	15	15	Crystal Palace
8	3	–	–	–	–	1	–	–	20	13	16	Derby Co
–	–	–	–	–	–	–	22	9	11	4	–	Fulham
–	–	–	–	–	–	–	–	–	–	–	–	Gillingham
9	19	–	–	–	–	21	15	10	5	19	17	Grimsby T
–	–	–	–	–	23	17	16	13	12	–	–	Huddersfield T
–	–	24	14	21	15	14	6	–	–	–	–	Hull C
–	1	14	9	8	8	5	–	–	–	–	–	Ipswich T
–	–	–	1	10	7	4	14	7	10	8	–	Leeds U
6	4	22	13	15	13	–	–	–	–	3	8	Leicester C
–	–	–	–	–	–	–	–	–	–	–	22	Leyton Orient
20	–	–	–	–	–	–	–	–	–	–	1	Luton T
–	–	–	–	2	9	–	–	3	4	–	–	Manchester C
–	–	–	–	–	–	–	–	–	–	–	–	Mansfield T
–	2	7	21	–	3	–	21	19	17	16	–	Middlesbrough
7	15	5	–	–	1	16	9	–	–	–	–	Millwall
1	20	11	3	–	–	–	–	–	3	5	9	Newcastle U
–	–	–	–	–	–	–	1	–	–	–	3	Norwich C
–	–	–	–	–	–	–	–	–	–	–	–	Nottingham F
17	–	4	–	–	–	–	–	20	–	–	–	Notts Co
–	–	1	8	16	10	3	8	14	19	7	11	Oldham Ath
14	21	10	17	17	–	–	–	1	–	–	–	Oxford U
10	–	–	–	–	–	–	–	–	–	–	–	Peterborough U
–	22	18	16	18	16	7	–	–	–	–	–	Plymouth Arg
–	24	15	11	–	–	–	–	–	–	–	–	Port Vale
3	9	17	12	20	–	2	4	4	16	–	–	Portsmouth
–	–	–	–	–	–	–	–	–	–	–	–	Preston NE
–	–	–	–	–	–	–	–	–	–	1	5	QPR
–	–	–	–	–	22	13	–	–	–	–	–	Reading

LEAGUE POSITIONS: DIVISION 1 from 1992–93, CHAMPIONSHIP from 2004–05 and DIVISION 2 1981–82 to 1991–92 (cont.)

	2005–06	2004–05	2003–04	2002–03	2001–02	2000–01	1999–2000	1998–99	1997–98	1996–97	1995–96	1994–95	1993–94
Rotherham U	–	24	17	15	21	–	–	–	–	–	–	–	–
Sheffield U	2	8	8	3	13	10	16	8	6	5	9	8	–
Sheffield W	19	–	–	22	20	17	–	–	–	–	–	–	–
Shrewsbury T	–	–	–	–	–	–	–	–	–	–	–	–	–
Southampton	12	–	–	–	–	–	–	–	–	–	–	–	–
Southend U	–	–	–	–	–	–	–	–	–	24	14	13	15
Stockport Co	–	–	–	–	24	19	17	16	8	–	–	–	–
Stoke C	13	12	11	21	–	–	–	–	23	12	4	11	10
Sunderland	–	1	3	–	–	–	–	1	3	–	1	20	12
Swansea C	–	–	–	–	–	–	–	–	–	–	–	–	–
Swindon T	–	–	–	–	–	–	24	17	18	19	–	21	–
Tranmere R	–	–	–	–	–	24	13	15	14	11	13	5	5
Walsall	–	–	22	17	18	–	22	–	–	–	–	–	–
Watford	3	18	16	13	14	9	–	5	–	–	23	7	19
WBA	–	–	2	–	2	6	21	12	10	16	11	19	21
West Ham U	–	6	4	–	–	–	–	–	–	–	–	–	–
Wigan Ath	–	2	7		–	–	–	–	–	–	–	–	–
Wimbledon	–	–	24	10	9	8	–	–	–	–	–	–	–
Wolverhampton W	7	9	–	5	3	12	7	7	9	3	20	4	8
Wrexham	–	–	–	–	–	–	–	–	–	–	–	–	–

LEAGUE POSITIONS: DIVISION 2 from 1992–93, LEAGUE 1 from 2004–05 and DIVISION 3 1981–82 to 1991–92

	2005–06	2004–05	2003–04	2002–03	2001–02	2000–01	1999–2000	1998–99	1997–98	1996–97	1995–96	1994–95	1993–94
Aldershot	–	–	–	–	–	–	–	–	–	–	–	–	–
Barnet	–	–	–	–	–	–	–	–	–	–	–	–	24
Barnsley	5	13	12	19	–	–	–	–	–	–	–	–	–
Birmingham C	–	–	–	–	–	–	–	–	–	–	–	1	–
Blackpool	19	16	14	13	16	–	22	14	12	7	3	12	20
Bolton W	–	–	–	–	–	–	–	–	–	–	–	–	–
Bournemouth	17	8	9	–	21	7	16	7	9	16	14	19	17
Bradford C	11	11	–	–	–	–	–	–	–	–	6	14	7
Brentford	3	4	17	16	3	14	17	–	21	4	15	2	16
Brighton & HA	–	–	4	–	1	–	–	–	–	–	23	16	14
Bristol C	9	7	3	3	7	9	9	–	2	5	13	–	–
Bristol R	–	–	–	–	–	21	7	13	5	17	10	4	8
Burnley	–	–	–	–	–	–	2	15	20	9	17	–	6
Bury	–	–	–	–	22	16	15	–	–	1	–	–	–
Cambridge U	–	–	–	–	24	19	19	–	–	–	–	20	10
Cardiff C	–	–	–	6	4	–	21	–	–	–	–	22	19
Carlisle U	–	–	–	–	–	–	–	–	23	–	21	–	–

1992–93	1991–92	1990–91	1989–90	1988–89	1987–88	1986–87	1985–86	1984–85	1983–84	1982–83	1981–82	
–	–	–	–	–	–	–	–	–	–	20	7	Rotherham U
–	–	–	2	–	21	9	7	18	–	–	–	Sheffield U
–	–	3	–	–	–	–	–	–	2	6	4	Sheffield W
–	–	–	–	22	18	18	17	8	8	9	18	Shrewsbury T
–	–	–	–	–	–	–	–	–	–	–	–	Southampton
18	12	–	–	–	–	–	–	–	–	–	–	Southend U
–	–	–	–	–	–	–	–	–	–	–	–	Stockport Co
–	–	–	24	13	11	8	10	–	–	–	–	Stoke C
21	18	–	6	11	–	20	18	–	–	–	–	Sunderland
–	–	–	–	–	–	–	–	–	21	–	–	Swansea C
5	8	21	4	6	12	–	–	–	–	–	–	Swindon T
4	14	–	–	–	–	–	–	–	–	–	–	Tranmere R
–	–	–	–	24	–	–	–	–	–	–	–	Walsall
16	10	20	15	4	–	–	–	–	–	–	2	Watford
–	–	23	20	9	20	15	–	–	–	–	–	WBA
2	–	2	7	–	–	–	–	–	–	–	–	West Ham U
–	–	–	–	–	–	–	–	–	–	–	–	Wigan Ath
–	–	–	–	–	–	–	3	12	–	–	–	Wimbledon
11	11	12	10	–	–	–	–	22	–	2	–	Wolverhampton W
–	–	–	–	–	–	–	–	–	–	–	21	Wrexham

1992–93	1991–92	1990–91	1989–90	1988–89	1987–88	1986–87	1985–86	1984–85	1983–84	1982–83	1981–82	
–	–	–	–	24	20	–	–	–	–	–	–	Aldershot
–	–	–	–	–	–	–	–	–	–	–	–	Barnet
–	–	–	–	–	–	–	–	–	–	–	–	Barnsley
–	2	12	7	–	–	–	–	–	–	–	–	Birmingham C
18	–	–	23	19	10	9	12	–	–	–	–	Blackpool
2	13	4	6	10	–	21	18	17	10	–	–	Bolton W
17	8	9	–	–	–	1	15	10	17	14	–	Bournemouth
10	16	8	–	–	–	–	–	1	7	12	–	Bradford C
–	1	6	13	7	12	11	10	13	20	9	8	Brentford
9	–	–	–	–	2	–	–	–	–	–	–	Brighton & HA
–	–	–	2	11	5	6	9	5	–	–	23	Bristol C
–	–	–	1	5	8	19	16	6	5	7	15	Bristol R
13	–	–	–	–	–	–	–	21	12	–	1	Burnley
–	21	7	5	13	14	16	20	–	–	–	–	Bury
–	–	1	–	–	–	–	–	24	–	–	–	Cambridge U
–	–	–	21	16	–	–	22	–	–	2	–	Cardiff C
–	–	–	–	–	–	22	–	–	–	–	2	Carlisle U

LEAGUE POSITIONS: DIVISION 2 from 1992–93, LEAGUE 1 from 2004–05 and DIVISION 3 1981–82 to 1991–92 (cont.)

	2005–06	2004–05	2003–04	2002–03	2001–02	2000–01	1999–2000	1998–99	1997–98	1996–97	1995–96	1994–95	1993–94
Cheltenham T	–	–	–	21	–	–	–	–	–	–	–	–	–
Chester C	–	–	–	–	–	–	–	–	–	–	–	23	–
Chesterfield	16	17	20	20	18	–	24	9	10	10	7	–	–
Colchester U	2	15	11	12	15	17	18	18	–	–	–	–	–
Crewe Alex	–	–	–	2	–	–	–	–	–	6	5	3	–
Darlington	–	–	–	–	–	–	–	–	–	–	–	–	–
Derby Co	–	–	–	–	–	–	–	–	–	–	–	–	–
Doncaster R	8	10	–	–	–	–	–	–	–	–	–	–	–
Exeter C	–	–	–	–	–	–	–	–	–	–	–	–	22
Fulham	–	–	–	–	–	–	–	1	6	–	–	–	21
Gillingham	14	–	–	–	–	–	3	4	8	11	–	–	–
Grimsby T	–	–	21	–	–	–	–	–	3	–	–	–	–
Hartlepool U	21	6	6	–	–	–	–	–	–	–	–	–	23
Huddersfield T	4	9	–	22	6	–	–	–	–	–	–	5	11
Hull C	–	2	–	–	–	–	–	–	–	–	24	8	9
Leyton Orient	–	–	–	–	–	–	–	–	–	–	–	24	18
Lincoln C	–	–	–	–	–	–	–	23	–	–	–	–	–
Luton T	–	1	10	9	–	22	13	12	17	3	–	–	–
Macclesfield T	–	–	–	–	–	–	–	24	–	–	–	–	–
Manchester C	–	–	–	–	–	–	–	3	–	–	–	–	–
Mansfield T	–	–	–	23	–	–	–	–	–	–	–	–	–
Middlesbrough	–	–	–	–	–	–	–	–	–	–	–	–	–
Millwall	–	–	–	–	–	1	5	10	18	14	–	–	–
Newport Co	–	–	–	–	–	–	–	–	–	–	–	–	–
Northampton T	–	–	–	24	20	18	–	22	4	–	–	–	–
Nottingham F	7	–	–	–	–	–	–	–	–	–	–	–	–
Notts Co	–	–	23	15	19	8	8	16	–	24	4	–	–
Oldham Ath	10	19	15	5	9	15	14	20	13	–	–	–	–
Oxford U	–	–	–	–	–	24	20	–	–	–	2	7	–
Peterborough U	–	23	18	11	17	12	–	–	–	21	19	15	–
Plymouth Arg	–	–	1	8	–	–	–	–	22	19	–	21	3
Portsmouth	–	–	–	–	–	–	–	–	–	–	–	–	–
Port Vale	13	18	7	17	14	11	–	–	–	–	–	–	2
Preston NE	–	–	–	–	–	–	1	5	15	15	–	–	–
QPR	–	–	2	4	8	–	–	–	–	–	–	–	–
Reading	–	–	–	–	2	3	10	11	–	–	–	–	1
Rotherham U	20	–	–	–	–	2	–	–	–	23	16	17	15
Rushden & D	–	–	22	–	–	–	–	–	–	–	–	–	–
Scunthorpe U	12	–	–	–	–	–	23	–	–	–	–	–	–
Sheffield U	–	–	–	–	–	–	–	–	–	–	–	–	–
Sheffield W	–	5	16	–	–	–	–	–	–	–	–	–	–
Shrewsbury T	–	–	–	–	–	–	–	–	–	22	18	18	–
Southend U	1	–	–	–	–	–	–	–	24	–	–	–	–
Stockport Co	–	24	19	14	–	–	–	–	–	2	9	11	4
Stoke C	–	–	–	–	5	5	6	8	–	–	–	–	–
Sunderland	–	–	–	–	–	–	–	–	–	–	–	–	–
Swansea C	6	–	–	–	–	23	–	–	–	–	22	10	13
Swindon T	23	12	5	10	13	20	–	–	–	–	1	–	–
Torquay U	–	21	–	–	–	–	–	–	–	–	–	–	–

1992–93	1991–92	1990–91	1989–90	1988–89	1987–88	1986–87	1985–86	1984–85	1983–84	1982–83	1981–82	
–	–	–	–	–	–	–	–	–	–	–	–	Cheltenham T
24	18	19	16	8	15	15	–	–	–	–	24	Chester C
–	–	–	–	22	18	17	17	–	–	24	11	Chesterfield
–	–	–	–	–	–	–	–	–	–	–	–	Colchester U
–	–	22	12	–	–	–	–	–	–	–	–	Crewe Alex
–	24	–	–	–	–	23	13	–	–	–	–	Darlington
–	–	–	–	–	–	–	3	7	–	–	–	Derby Co
–	–	–	–	–	24	13	11	14	–	23	19	Doncaster R
19	20	16	–	–	–	–	–	–	24	19	18	Exeter C
12	9	21	20	4	9	18	–	–	–	–	3	Fulham
–	–	–	–	23	13	5	5	4	8	13	6	Gillingham
–	–	3	–	–	22	–	–	–	–	–	–	Grimsby T
16	11	–	–	–	–	–	–	–	–	–	–	Hartlepool U
15	3	11	8	14	–	–	–	–	–	3	17	Huddersfield T
20	14	–	–	–	–	–	–	3	4	–	–	Hull C
7	10	13	14	–	–	–	–	22	11	20	–	Leyton Orient
–	–	–	–	–	–	–	21	19	14	6	4	Lincoln C
–	–	–	–	–	–	–	–	–	–	–	–	Luton T
–	–	–	–	–	–	–	–	–	–	–	–	Macclesfield T
–	–	–	–	–	–	–	–	–	–	–	–	Manchester C
22	–	24	15	15	19	10	–	–	–	–	–	Mansfield T
–	–	–	–	–	–	2	–	–	–	–	–	Middlesbrough
–	–	–	–	–	–	–	–	2	9	17	9	Millwall
–	–	–	–	–	–	23	19	18	13	4	16	Newport Co
–	–	–	22	20	6	–	–	–	–	–	–	Northampton T
–	–	–	–	–	–	–	–	–	–	–	–	Nottingham F
–	–	–	3	9	4	7	8	–	–	–	–	Notts Co
–	–	–	–	–	–	–	–	–	–	–	–	Oldham Ath
–	–	–	–	–	–	–	–	–	1	5	5	Oxford U
–	6	–	–	–	–	–	–	–	–	–	–	Peterborough U
14	–	–	–	–	–	–	2	15	19	8	10	Plymouth Arg
–	–	–	–	–	–	–	–	–	–	1	13	Portsmouth
3	–	–	–	3	11	12	–	–	23	–	–	Port Vale
21	17	17	19	6	16	–	–	23	16	16	14	Preston NE
–	–	–	–	–	–	–	–	–	–	–	–	QPR
8	12	15	10	18	–	–	1	9	–	21	12	Reading
11	–	23	9	–	21	14	14	12	18	–	–	Rotherham U
–	–	–	–	–	–	–	–	–	–	–	–	Rushden & D
–	–	–	–	–	–	–	–	–	21	–	–	Scunthorpe U
–	–	–	–	2	–	–	–	–	3	11	–	Sheffield U
–	–	–	–	–	–	–	–	–	–	–	–	Sheffield W
–	22	18	11	–	–	–	–	–	–	–	–	Shrewsbury T
–	–	2	–	21	17	–	–	–	22	15	7	Southend U
6	5	–	–	–	–	–	–	–	–	–	–	Stockport Co
1	4	14	–	–	–	–	–	–	–	–	–	Stoke C
–	–	–	–	–	1	–	–	–	–	–	–	Sunderland
5	19	20	17	12	–	–	24	20	–	–	–	Swansea C
–	–	–	–	–	–	3	–	–	–	–	22	Swindon T
–	23	–	–	–	–	–	–	–	–	–	–	Torquay U

LEAGUE POSITIONS: DIVISION 2 from 1992–93, LEAGUE 1 from 2004–05 and DIVISION 3 1981–82 to 1991–92 (cont.)

	2005–06	2004–05	2003–04	2002–03	2001–02	2000–01	1999–2000	1998–99	1997–98	1996–97	1995–96	1994–95	1993–94
Tranmere R	18	3	8	7	12	–	–	–	–	–	–	–	–
Walsall	24	14	–	–	–	4	–	2	19	12	11	–	–
Watford	–	–	–	–	–	–	–	–	1	13	–	–	–
WBA	–	–	–	–	–	–	–	–	–	–	–	–	–
Wigan Ath	–	–	–	1	10	6	4	6	11	–	–	–	–
Wimbledon	22†	20†	–	–	–	–	–	–	–	–	–	–	–
Wolverhampton W	–	–	–	–	–	–	–	–	–	–	–	–	–
Wrexham	–	22	13	–	23	10	11	17	7	8	8	13	12
Wycombe W	–	–	24	18	11	13	12	19	14	18	12	6	–
Yeovil T	15	–	–	–	–	–	–	–	–	–	–	–	–
York C	–	–	–	–	–	–	–	21	16	20	20	9	5

†As Milton Keynes D

LEAGUE POSITIONS: DIVISION 3 from 1992–93, LEAGUE 2 from 2004–05 and DIVISION 4 1981–82 to 1991–92

	2005–06	2004–05	2003–04	2002–03	2001–02	2000–01	1999–2000	1998–99	1997–98	1996–97	1995–96	1994–95	1993–94
Aldershot	–	–	–	–	–	–	–	–	–	–	–	–	–
Barnet	18	–	–	–	–	24	6	16	7	15	9	11	–
Blackpool	–	–	–	–	–	7	–	–	–	–	–	–	–
Bolton W	–	–	–	–	–	–	–	–	–	–	–	–	–
Boston U	11	16	11	15	–	–	–	–	–	–	–	–	–
Bournemouth	–	–	–	4	–	–	–	–	–	–	–	–	–
Bradford C	–	–	–	–	–	–	–	–	–	–	–	–	–
Brentford	–	–	–	–	–	–	–	1	–	–	–	–	–
Brighton & HA	–	–	–	–	–	1	11	17	23	23	–	–	–
Bristol C	–	–	–	–	–	–	–	–	–	–	–	–	–
Bristol R	12	12	15	20	23	–	–	–	–	–	–	–	–
Burnley	–	–	–	–	–	–	–	–	–	–	–	–	–
Bury	19	17	12	7	–	–	–	–	–	–	3	4	13
Cambridge U	–	24	13	12	–	–	–	2	16	10	16	–	–
Cardiff C	–	–	–	–	–	2	–	3	21	7	22	–	–
Carlisle U	1	–	23	22	17	22	23	23	–	3	–	1	7
Cheltenham T	5	14	14	–	4	9	8	–	–	–	–	–	–
Chester C	15	20	–	–	–	–	24	14	14	6	8	–	2
Chesterfield	–	–	–	–	–	3	–	–	–	–	–	3	8
Colchester U	–	–	–	–	–	–	–	–	4	8	7	10	17
Crewe Alex	–	–	–	–	–	–	–	–	–	–	–	–	3

*Record expunged

1992–93	1991–92	1990–91	1989–90	1988–89	1987–88	1986–87	1985–86	1984–85	1983–84	1982–83	1981–82	
–	–	5	4	–	–	–	–	–	–	–	–	Tranmere R
–	–	–	24	–	3	8	6	11	6	10	20	Walsall
–	–	–	–	–	–	–	–	–	–	–	–	Watford
4	7	–	–	–	–	–	–	–	–	–	–	WBA
23	15	10	18	17	7	4	4	16	15	18	–	Wigan Ath
–	–	–	–	–	–	–	–	–	2	–	21	Wimbledon
–	–	–	–	1	–	–	23	–	–	–	–	Wolverhampton W
–	–	–	–	–	–	–	–	–	–	22	–	Wrexham
–	–	–	–	–	–	–	–	–	–	–	–	Wycombe W
–	–	–	–	–	–	–	–	–	–	–	–	Yeovil T
–	–	–	–	–	23	20	7	8	–	–	–	York C

1992–93	1991–92	1990–91	1989–90	1988–89	1987–88	1986–87	1985–86	1984–85	1983–84	1982–83	1981–82	
–	*	23	22	–	–	6	16	13	5	18	16	Aldershot
3	7	–	–	–	–	–	–	–	–	–	–	Barnet
–	4	5	–	–	–	–	–	2	6	21	12	Blackpool
–	–	–	–	–	3	–	–	–	–	–	–	Bolton W
–	–	–	–	–	–	–	–	–	–	–	–	Boston U
–	–	–	–	–	–	–	–	–	–	–	4	Bournemouth
–	–	–	–	–	–	–	–	–	–	–	2	Bradford C
–	–	–	–	–	–	–	–	–	–	–	–	Brentford
–	–	–	–	–	–	–	–	–	–	–	–	Brighton & HA
–	–	–	–	–	–	–	–	–	4	14	–	Bristol C
–	–	–	–	–	–	–	–	–	–	–	–	Bristol R
–	1	6	16	16	10	22	14	–	–	–	–	Burnley
7	–	–	–	–	–	–	–	4	15	5	9	Bury
–	–	–	6	8	15	11	22	–	–	–	–	Cambridge U
1	9	13	–	–	2	13	–	–	–	–	–	Cardiff C
18	22	20	8	12	23	–	–	–	–	–	–	Carlisle U
–	–	–	–	–	–	–	–	–	–	–	–	Cheltenham T
–	–	–	–	–	–	–	2	16	24	13	–	Chester C
12	13	18	7	–	–	–	–	1	13	–	–	Chesterfield
10	–	–	24	22	9	5	6	7	8	6	6	Colchester U
6	6	–	–	3	17	17	12	10	16	23	24	Crewe Alex

LEAGUE POSITIONS: DIVISION 3 from 1992–93, LEAGUE 2 from 2004–05 and DIVISION 4 1981–82 to 1991–92 (cont.)

	2005–06	2004–05	2003–04	2002–03	2001–02	2000–01	1999–2000	1998–99	1997–98	1996–97	1995–96	1994–95	1993–94
Darlington	8	8	18	14	15	20	4	11	19	18	5	20	21
Doncaster R	–	–	1	–	–	–	–	–	24	19	13	9	15
Exeter C	–	–	–	23	16	19	21	12	15	22	14	22	–
Fulham	–	–	–	–	–	–	–	–	–	2	17	8	–
Gillingham	–	–	–	–	–	–	–	–	–	–	2	19	16
Grimsby T	4	18	–	–	–	–	–	–	–	–	–	–	–
Halifax T	–	–	–	–	24	23	18	10	–	–	–	–	–
Hartlepool U	–	–	–	2	7	4	7	22	17	20	20	18	–
Hereford U	–	–	–	–	–	–	–	–	–	24	6	16	20
Huddersfield T	–	–	4	–	–	–	–	–	–	–	–	–	–
Hull C	–	–	2	13	11	6	14	21	22	17	–	–	–
Kidderminster H	–	23	16	11	10	16	–	–	–	–	–	–	–
Leyton Orient	3	11	19	18	18	5	19	6	11	16	21	–	–
Lincoln C	7	6	7	6	22	18	15	–	3	9	18	12	18
Luton T	–	–	–	–	2	–	–	–	–	–	–	–	–
Macclesfield T	17	5	20	16	13	14	13	–	2	–	–	–	–
Maidstone U	–	–	–	–	–	–	–	–	–	–	–	–	–
Mansfield T	16	13	5	–	3	13	17	8	12	11	19	6	12
Newport Co	–	–	–	–	–	–	–	–	–	–	–	–	–
Northampton T	2	7	6	–	–	–	3	–	–	4	11	17	22
Notts Co	21	19	–	–	–	–	–	–	1	–	–	–	–
Oxford U	23	15	9	8	21	–	–	–	–	–	–	–	–
Peterborough U	9	–	–	–	–	–	5	9	10	–	–	–	–
Plymouth Arg	–	–	–	–	1	12	12	13	–	–	4	–	–
Port Vale	–	–	–	–	–	–	–	–	–	–	–	–	–
Preston NE	–	–	–	–	–	–	–	–	–	–	1	5	5
Reading	–	–	–	–	–	–	–	–	–	–	–	–	–
Rochdale	14	9	21	19	5	8	10	19	18	14	15	15	9
Rotherham U	–	–	–	–	–	–	2	5	9	–	–	–	–
Rushden & D	24	22	–	1	6	–	–	–	–	–	–	–	–
Scarborough	–	–	–	–	–	–	–	24	6	12	23	21	14
Scunthorpe U	–	2	22	5	8	10	–	4	8	13	12	7	11
Sheffield U	–	–	–	–	–	–	–	–	–	–	–	–	–
Shrewsbury T	10	21	–	24	9	15	22	15	13	–	–	–	1
Southend U	–	4	17	17	12	11	16	18	–	–	–	–	–
Stockport Co	22	–	–	–	–	–	–	–	–	–	–	–	–
Swansea C	–	3	10	21	20	–	1	7	20	5	–	–	–
Swindon T	–	–	–	–	–	–	–	–	–	–	–	–	–
Torquay U	20	–	3	9	19	21	9	20	5	21	24	13	6
Tranmere R	–	–	–	–	–	–	–	–	–	–	–	–	–
Walsall	–	–	–	–	–	–	–	–	–	–	–	2	10
Wigan Ath	–	–	–	–	–	–	–	–	–	1	10	14	19
Wimbledon	–	–	–	–	–	–	–	–	–	–	–	–	–
Wolverhampton W	–	–	–	–	–	–	–	–	–	–	–	–	–
Wrexham	13	–	–	3	–	–	–	–	–	–	–	–	–
Wycombe W	6	10	–	–	–	–	–	–	–	–	–	–	4
Yeovil T	–	1	8	–	–	–	–	–	–	–	–	–	–
York C	–	–	24	10	14	17	20	–	–	–	–	–	–

1992–93	1991–92	1990–91	1989–90	1988–89	1987–88	1986–87	1985–86	1984–85	1983–84	1982–83	1981–82	
15	–	1	–	24	13	–	–	3	14	17	13	Darlington
16	21	11	20	23	–	–	–	–	2	–	–	Doncaster R
–	–	–	1	13	22	14	21	18	–	–	–	Exeter C
–	–	–	–	–	–	–	–	–	–	–	–	Fulham
21	11	15	14	–	–	–	–	–	–	–	–	Gillingham
–	–	–	2	9	–	–	–	–	–	–	–	Grimsby T
22	20	22	23	21	18	15	20	21	21	11	19	Halifax T
–	–	3	19	19	16	18	7	19	23	22	14	Hartlepool U
17	17	17	17	15	19	16	10	5	11	24	10	Hereford U
–	–	–	–	–	–	–	–	–	–	–	–	Huddersfield T
–	–	–	–	–	–	–	–	–	–	2	8	Hull C
–	–	–	–	–	–	–	–	–	–	–	–	Kidderminster H
–	–	–	–	6	8	7	5	–	–	–	–	Leyton Orient
8	10	14	10	10	–	24	–	–	–	–	–	Lincoln C
–	–	–	–	–	–	–	–	–	–	–	–	Luton T
–	–	–	–	–	–	–	–	–	–	–	–	Macclesfield T
–	18	19	5	–	–	–	–	–	–	–	–	Maidstone U
–	3	–	–	–	–	–	3	14	19	10	20	Mansfield T
–	–	–	–	–	24	–	–	–	–	–	–	Newport Co
20	16	10	–	–	–	1	8	23	18	15	22	Northampton T
–	–	–	–	–	–	–	–	–	–	–	–	Notts Co
–	–	–	–	–	–	–	–	–	–	–	–	Oxford U
–	–	4	9	17	7	10	17	11	7	9	5	Peterborough U
–	–	–	–	–	–	–	–	–	–	–	–	Plymouth Arg
–	–	–	–	–	–	–	4	12	–	3	7	Port Vale
–	–	–	–	–	–	2	23	–	–	–	–	Preston NE
–	–	–	–	–	–	–	–	–	3	–	–	Reading
11	8	12	12	18	21	21	18	17	22	20	21	Rochdale
–	2	–	–	1	–	–	–	–	–	–	–	Rotherham U
–	–	–	–	–	–	–	–	–	–	–	–	Rushden & D
13	12	9	18	5	12	–	–	–	–	–	–	Scarborough
14	5	8	11	4	4	8	15	9	–	4	23	Scunthorpe U
–	–	–	–	–	–	–	–	–	–	–	1	Sheffield U
9	–	–	–	–	–	–	–	–	–	–	–	Shrewsbury T
–	–	–	3	–	–	3	9	20	–	–	–	Southend U
–	–	2	4	20	20	19	11	22	12	16	18	Stockport Co
–	–	–	–	–	6	12	–	–	–	–	–	Swansea C
–	–	–	–	–	–	–	1	8	17	8	–	Swindon T
19	–	7	15	14	5	23	24	24	9	12	15	Torquay U
–	–	–	–	2	14	20	19	6	10	19	11	Tranmere R
5	15	16	–	–	–	–	–	–	–	–	–	Walsall
–	–	–	–	–	–	–	–	–	–	–	3	Wigan Ath
–	–	–	–	–	–	–	–	–	–	1	–	Wimbledon
–	–	–	–	–	1	4	–	–	–	–	–	Wolverhampton W
2	14	24	21	7	11	9	13	15	20	–	–	Wrexham
–	–	–	–	–	–	–	–	–	–	–	–	Wycombe W
–	–	–	–	–	–	–	–	–	–	–	–	Yeovil T
4	19	21	13	11	–	–	–	–	1	7	17	York C

LEAGUE CHAMPIONSHIP HONOURS

FA PREMIER LEAGUE

Maximum points: 126

	First	*Pts*	*Second*	*Pts*	*Third*	*Pts*
1992–93	Manchester U	84	Aston Villa	74	Norwich C	72
1993–94	Manchester U	92	Blackburn R	84	Newcastle U	77
1994–95	Blackburn R	89	Manchester U	88	Nottingham F	77

Maximum points: 114

1995–96	Manchester U	82	Newcastle U	78	Liverpool	71
1996–97	Manchester U	75	Newcastle U*	68	Arsenal*	68
1997–98	Arsenal	78	Manchester U	77	Liverpool	65
1998–99	Manchester U	79	Arsenal	78	Chelsea	75
1999–00	Manchester U	91	Arsenal	73	Leeds U	69
2000–01	Manchester U	80	Arsenal	70	Liverpool	69
2001–02	Arsenal	87	Liverpool	80	Manchester U	77
2002–03	Manchester U	83	Arsenal	78	Newcastle U	69
2003–04	Arsenal	90	Chelsea	79	Manchester U	75
2004–05	Chelsea	95	Arsenal	83	Manchester U	77
2005–06	Chelsea	91	Manchester U	83	Liverpool	82
2006–07	Manchester U	89	Chelsea	83	Liverpool*	68

FOOTBALL LEAGUE CHAMPIONSHIP

Maximum points: 138

2004–05	Sunderland	94	Wigan Ath	87	Ipswich T††	85
2005–06	Reading	106	Sheffield U	90	Watford	81
2006–07	Sunderland	88	Birmingham C	86	Derby Co	84

DIVISION 1

Maximum points: 138

1992–93	Newcastle U	96	West Ham U*	88	Portsmouth††	88
1993–94	Crystal Palace	90	Nottingham F	83	Millwall††	74
1994–95	Middlesbrough	82	Reading††	79	Bolton W	77
1995–96	Sunderland	83	Derby Co	79	Crystal Palace††	75
1996–97	Bolton W	98	Barnsley	80	Wolverhampton W††	76
1997–98	Nottingham F	94	Middlesbrough	91	Sunderland††	90
1998–99	Sunderland	105	Bradford C	87	Ipswich T††	86
1999–00	Charlton Ath	91	Manchester C	89	Ipswich T	87
2000–01	Fulham	101	Blackburn R	91	Bolton W	87
2001–02	Manchester C	99	WBA	89	Wolverhampton W††	86
2002–03	Portsmouth	98	Leicester C	92	Sheffield U††	80
2003–04	Norwich C	94	WBA	86	Sunderland††	79

FOOTBALL LEAGUE CHAMPIONSHIP 1

Maximum points: 138

2004–05	Luton T	98	Hull C	86	Tranmere R††	79
2005–06	Southend U	82	Colchester U	79	Brentford††	76
2006–07	Scunthorpe U	91	Bristol C	85	Blackpool	83

DIVISION 2

Maximum points: 138

1992–93	Stoke C	93	Bolton W	90	Port Vale††	89
1993–94	Reading	89	Port Vale	88	Plymouth Arg††	85
1994–95	Birmingham C	89	Brentford††	85	Crewe Alex††	83

	First	Pts	Second	Pts	Third	Pts
1995–96	Swindon T	92	Oxford U	83	Blackpool††	82
1996–97	Bury	84	Stockport Co	82	Luton T††	78
1997–98	Watford	88	Bristol C	85	Grimsby T	72
1998–99	Fulham	101	Walsall	87	Manchester C	82
1999–00	Preston NE	95	Burnley	88	Gillingham	85
2000–01	Millwall	93	Rotherham U	91	Reading††	86
2001–02	Brighton & HA	90	Reading	84	Brentford*††	83
2002–03	Wigan Ath	100	Crewe Alex	86	Bristol C††	83
2003–04	Plymouth Arg	90	QPR	83	Bristol C††	82

FOOTBALL LEAGUE CHAMPIONSHIP 2

Maximum points: 138

2004–05	Yeovil T	83	Scunthorpe U*	80	Swansea C	80
2005–06	Carlisle U	86	Northampton T	83	Leyton Orient	81
2006–07	Walsall	89	Hartlepool U	88	Swindon T	85

DIVISION 3

Maximum points: 126

1992–93	Cardiff C	83	Wrexham	80	Barnet	79
1993–94	Shrewsbury T	79	Chester C	74	Crewe Alex	73
1994–95	Carlisle U	91	Walsall	83	Chesterfield	81

Maximum points: 138

1995–96	Preston NE	86	Gillingham	83	Bury	79
1996–97	Wigan Ath*	87	Fulham	87	Carlisle U	84
1997–98	Notts Co	99	Macclesfield T	82	Lincoln C	75
1998–99	Brentford	85	Cambridge U	81	Cardiff C	80
1999–00	Swansea C	85	Rotherham U	84	Northampton T	82
2000–01	Brighton & HA	92	Cardiff C	82	Chesterfield¶	80
2001–02	Plymouth Arg	102	Luton T	97	Mansfield T	79
2002–03	Rushden & D	87	Hartlepool U	85	Wrexham	84
2003–04	Doncaster R	92	Hull C	88	Torquay U*	81

** Won or placed on goal average (ratio)/goal difference.*
†† Not promoted after play-offs. ¶ 9 pts deducted for irregularities.

FOOTBALL LEAGUE

Maximum points: a 44; *b* 60

1888–89*a*	Preston NE	40	Aston Villa	29	Wolverhampton W	28
1889–90*a*	Preston NE	33	Everton	31	Blackburn R	27
1890–91*a*	Everton	29	Preston NE	27	Notts Co	26
1891–92*b*	Sunderland	42	Preston NE	37	Bolton W	36

DIVISION 1 to 1991–92

Maximum points: a 44; *b* 52; *c* 60; *d* 68; *e* 76; *f* 84; *g* 126; *h* 120; *k* 114.

1892–93*c*	Sunderland	48	Preston NE	37	Everton	36
1893–94*c*	Aston Villa	44	Sunderland	38	Derby Co	36
1894–95*c*	Sunderland	47	Everton	42	Aston Villa	39
1895–96*c*	Aston Villa	45	Derby Co	41	Everton	39
1896–97*c*	Aston Villa	47	Sheffield U*	36	Derby Co	36
1897–98*c*	Sheffield U	42	Sunderland	37	Wolverhampton W*	35
1898–99*d*	Aston Villa	45	Liverpool	43	Burnley	39
1899–1900*d*	Aston Villa	50	Sheffield U	48	Sunderland	41
1900–01*d*	Liverpool	45	Sunderland	43	Notts Co	40
1901–02*d*	Sunderland	44	Everton	41	Newcastle U	37

	First	*Pts*	*Second*	*Pts*	*Third*	*Pts*
1902–03*d*	The Wednesday	42	Aston Villa*	41	Sunderland	41
1903–04*d*	The Wednesday	47	Manchester C	44	Everton	43
1904–05*d*	Newcastle U	48	Everton	47	Manchester C	46
1905–06*e*	Liverpool	51	Preston NE	47	The Wednesday	44
1906–07*e*	Newcastle U	51	Bristol C	48	Everton*	45
1907–08*e*	Manchester U	52	Aston Villa*	43	Manchester C	43
1908–09*e*	Newcastle U	53	Everton	46	Sunderland	44
1909–10*e*	Aston Villa	53	Liverpool	48	Blackburn R*	45
1910–11*e*	Manchester U	52	Aston Villa	51	Sunderland*	45
1911–12*e*	Blackburn R	49	Everton	46	Newcastle U	44
1912–13*e*	Sunderland	54	Aston Villa	50	Sheffield W	49
1913–14*e*	Blackburn R	51	Aston Villa	44	Middlesbrough*	43
1914–15*e*	Everton	46	Oldham Ath	45	Blackburn R*	43
1919–20*f*	WBA	60	Burnley	51	Chelsea	49
1920–21*f*	Burnley	59	Manchester C	54	Bolton W	52
1921–22*f*	Liverpool	57	Tottenham H	51	Burnley	49
1922–23*f*	Liverpool	60	Sunderland	54	Huddersfield T	53
1923–24*f*	Huddersfield T*	57	Cardiff C	57	Sunderland	53
1924–25*f*	Huddersfield T	58	WBA	56	Bolton W	55
1925–26*f*	Huddersfield T	57	Arsenal	52	Sunderland	48
1926–27*f*	Newcastle U	56	Huddersfield T	51	Sunderland	49
1927–28*f*	Everton	53	Huddersfield T	51	Leicester C	48
1928–29*f*	Sheffield W	52	Leicester C	51	Aston Villa	50
1929–30*f*	Sheffield W	60	Derby Co	50	Manchester C*	47
1930–31*f*	Arsenal	66	Aston Villa	59	Sheffield W	52
1931–32*f*	Everton	56	Arsenal	54	Sheffield W	50
1932–33*f*	Arsenal	58	Aston Villa	54	Sheffield W	51
1933–34*f*	Arsenal	59	Huddersfield T	56	Tottenham H	49
1934–35*f*	Arsenal	58	Sunderland	54	Sheffield W	49
1935–36*f*	Sunderland	56	Derby Co*	48	Huddersfield T	48
1936–37*f*	Manchester C	57	Charlton Ath	54	Arsenal	52
1937–38*f*	Arsenal	52	Wolverhampton W	51	Preston NE	49
1938–39*f*	Everton	59	Wolverhampton W	55	Charlton Ath	50
1946–47*f*	Liverpool	57	Manchester U*	56	Wolverhampton W	56
1947–48*f*	Arsenal	59	Manchester U*	52	Burnley	52
1948–49*f*	Portsmouth	58	Manchester U*	53	Derby Co	53
1949–50*f*	Portsmouth*	53	Wolverhampton W	53	Sunderland	52
1950–51*f*	Tottenham H	60	Manchester U	56	Blackpool	50
1951–52*f*	Manchester U	57	Tottenham H*	53	Arsenal	53
1952–53*f*	Arsenal*	54	Preston NE	54	Wolverhampton W	51
1953–54*f*	Wolverhampton W	57	WBA	53	Huddersfield T	51
1954–55*f*	Chelsea	52	Wolverhampton W*	48	Portsmouth*	48
1955–56*f*	Manchester U	60	Blackpool*	49	Wolverhampton W	49
1956–57*f*	Manchester U	64	Tottenham H*	56	Preston NE	56
1957–58*f*	Wolverhampton W	64	Preston NE	59	Tottenham H	51
1958–59*f*	Wolverhampton W	61	Manchester U	55	Arsenal*	50
1959–60*f*	Burnley	55	Wolverhampton W	54	Tottenham H	53
1960–61*f*	Tottenham H	66	Sheffield W	58	Wolverhampton W	57
1961–62*f*	Ipswich T	56	Burnley	53	Tottenham H	52
1962–63*f*	Everton	61	Tottenham H	55	Burnley	54
1963–64*f*	Liverpool	57	Manchester U	53	Everton	52
1964–65*f*	Manchester U*	61	Leeds U	61	Chelsea	56
1965–66*f*	Liverpool	61	Leeds U*	55	Burnley	55
1966–67*f*	Manchester U	60	Nottingham F*	56	Tottenham H	56

	First	Pts	Second	Pts	Third	Pts
1967–68*f*	Manchester C	58	Manchester U	56	Liverpool	55
1968–69*f*	Leeds U	67	Liverpool	61	Everton	57
1969–70*f*	Everton	66	Leeds U	57	Chelsea	55
1970–71*f*	Arsenal	65	Leeds U	64	Tottenham H*	52
1971–72*f*	Derby Co	58	Leeds U*	57	Liverpool*	57
1972–73*f*	Liverpool	60	Arsenal	57	Leeds U	53
1973–74*f*	Leeds U	62	Liverpool	57	Derby Co	48
1974–75*f*	Derby Co	53	Liverpool*	51	Ipswich T	51
1975–76*f*	Liverpool	60	QPR	59	Manchester U	56
1976–77*f*	Liverpool	57	Manchester C	56	Ipswich T	52
1977–78*f*	Nottingham F	64	Liverpool	57	Everton	55
1978–79*f*	Liverpool	68	Nottingham F	60	WBA	59
1979–80*f*	Liverpool	60	Manchester U	58	Ipswich T	53
1980–81*f*	Aston Villa	60	Ipswich T	56	Arsenal	53
1981–82*g*	Liverpool	87	Ipswich T	83	Manchester U	78
1982–83*g*	Liverpool	82	Watford	71	Manchester U	70
1983–84*g*	Liverpool	80	Southampton	77	Nottingham F*	74
1984–85*g*	Everton	90	Liverpool*	77	Tottenham H	77
1985–86*g*	Liverpool	88	Everton	86	West Ham U	84
1986–87*g*	Everton	86	Liverpool	77	Tottenham H	71
1987–88*h*	Liverpool	90	Manchester U	81	Nottingham F	73
1988–89*k*	Arsenal*	76	Liverpool	76	Nottingham F	64
1989–90*k*	Liverpool	79	Aston Villa	70	Tottenham H	63
1990–91*k*	Arsenal†	83	Liverpool	76	Crystal Palace	69
1991–92*g*	Leeds U	82	Manchester U	78	Sheffield W	75

No official competition during 1915–19 and 1939–46; Regional Leagues operating.
** Won or placed on goal average (ratio)/goal difference.*
† 2 pts deducted

DIVISION 2 to 1991–92

Maximum points: a 44; *b* 56; *c* 60; *d* 68; *e* 76; *f* 84; *g* 126; *h* 132; *k* 138.

	First	Pts	Second	Pts	Third	Pts
1892–93*a*	Small Heath	36	Sheffield U	35	Darwen	30
1893–94*b*	Liverpool	50	Small Heath	42	Notts Co	39
1894–95*c*	Bury	48	Notts Co	39	Newton Heath*	38
1895–96*c*	Liverpool*	46	Manchester C	46	Grimsby T*	42
1896–97*c*	Notts Co	42	Newton Heath	39	Grimsby T	38
1897–98*c*	Burnley	48	Newcastle U	45	Manchester C	39
1898–99*d*	Manchester C	52	Glossop NE	46	Leicester Fosse	45
1899–1900*d*	The Wednesday	54	Bolton W	52	Small Heath	46
1900–01*d*	Grimsby T	49	Small Heath	48	Burnley	44
1901–02*d*	WBA	55	Middlesbrough	51	Preston NE*	42
1902–03*d*	Manchester C	54	Small Heath	51	Woolwich A	48
1903–04*d*	Preston NE	50	Woolwich A	49	Manchester U	48
1904–05*d*	Liverpool	58	Bolton W	56	Manchester U	53
1905–06*e*	Bristol C	66	Manchester U	62	Chelsea	53
1906–07*e*	Nottingham F	60	Chelsea	57	Leicester Fosse	48
1907–08*e*	Bradford C	54	Leicester Fosse	52	Oldham Ath	50
1908–09*e*	Bolton W	52	Tottenham H*	51	WBA	51
1909–10*e*	Manchester C	54	Oldham Ath*	53	Hull C*	53
1910–11*e*	WBA	53	Bolton W	51	Chelsea	49
1911–12*e*	Derby Co*	54	Chelsea	54	Burnley	52
1912–13*e*	Preston NE	53	Burnley	50	Birmingham	46
1913–14*e*	Notts Co	53	Bradford PA*	49	Woolwich A	49
1914–15*e*	Derby Co	53	Preston NE	50	Barnsley	47

	First	*Pts*	*Second*	*Pts*	*Third*	*Pts*
1919–20*f*	Tottenham H	70	Huddersfield T	64	Birmingham	56
1920–21*f*	Birmingham*	58	Cardiff C	58	Bristol C	51
1921–22*f*	Nottingham F	56	Stoke C*	52	Barnsley	52
1922–23*f*	Notts Co	53	West Ham U*	51	Leicester C	51
1923–24*f*	Leeds U	54	Bury*	51	Derby Co	51
1924–25*f*	Leicester C	59	Manchester U	57	Derby Co	55
1925–26*f*	Sheffield W	60	Derby Co	57	Chelsea	52
1926–27*f*	Middlesbrough	62	Portsmouth*	54	Manchester C	54
1927–28*f*	Manchester C	59	Leeds U	57	Chelsea	54
1928–29*f*	Middlesbrough	55	Grimsby T	53	Bradford PA*	48
1929–30*f*	Blackpool	58	Chelsea	55	Oldham Ath	53
1930–31*f*	Everton	61	WBA	54	Tottenham H	51
1931–32*f*	Wolverhampton W	56	Leeds U	54	Stoke C	52
1932–33*f*	Stoke C	56	Tottenham H	55	Fulham	50
1933–34*f*	Grimsby T	59	Preston NE	52	Bolton W*	51
1934–35*f*	Brentford	61	Bolton W*	56	West Ham U	56
1935–36*f*	Manchester U	56	Charlton Ath	55	Sheffield U*	52
1936–37*f*	Leicester C	56	Blackpool	55	Bury	52
1937–38*f*	Aston Villa	57	Manchester U*	53	Sheffield U	53
1938–39*f*	Blackburn R	55	Sheffield U	54	Sheffield W	53
1946–47*f*	Manchester C	62	Burnley	58	Birmingham C	55
1947–48*f*	Birmingham C	59	Newcastle U	56	Southampton	52
1948–49*f*	Fulham	57	WBA	56	Southampton	55
1949–50*f*	Tottenham H	61	Sheffield W*	52	Sheffield U*	52
1950–51*f*	Preston NE	57	Manchester C	52	Cardiff C	50
1951–52*f*	Sheffield W	53	Cardiff C*	51	Birmingham C	51
1952–53*f*	Sheffield U	60	Huddersfield T	58	Luton T	52
1953–54*f*	Leicester C*	56	Everton	56	Blackburn R	55
1954–55*f*	Birmingham C*	54	Luton T*	54	Rotherham U	54
1955–56*f*	Sheffield W	55	Leeds U	52	Liverpool*	48
1956–57*f*	Leicester C	61	Nottingham F	54	Liverpool	53
1957–58*f*	West Ham U	57	Blackburn R	56	Charlton Ath	55
1958–59*f*	Sheffield W	62	Fulham	60	Sheffield U*	53
1959–60*f*	Aston Villa	59	Cardiff C	58	Liverpool*	50
1960–61*f*	Ipswich T	59	Sheffield U	58	Liverpool	52
1961–62*f*	Liverpool	62	Leyton Orient	54	Sunderland	53
1962–63*f*	Stoke C	53	Chelsea*	52	Sunderland	52
1963–64*f*	Leeds U	63	Sunderland	61	Preston NE	56
1964–65*f*	Newcastle U	57	Northampton T	56	Bolton W	50
1965–66*f*	Manchester C	59	Southampton	54	Coventry C	53
1966–67*f*	Coventry C	59	Wolverhampton W	58	Carlisle U	52
1967–68*f*	Ipswich T	59	QPR*	58	Blackpool	58
1968–69*f*	Derby Co	63	Crystal Palace	56	Charlton Ath	50
1969–70*f*	Huddersfield T	60	Blackpool	53	Leicester C	51
1970–71*f*	Leicester C	59	Sheffield U	56	Cardiff C*	53
1971–72*f*	Norwich C	57	Birmingham C	56	Millwall	55
1972–73*f*	Burnley	62	QPR	61	Aston Villa	50
1973–74*f*	Middlesbrough	65	Luton T	50	Carlisle U	49
1974–75*f*	Manchester U	61	Aston Villa	58	Norwich C	53
1975–76*f*	Sunderland	56	Bristol C*	53	WBA	53
1976–77*f*	Wolverhampton W	57	Chelsea	55	Nottingham F	52
1977–78*f*	Bolton W	58	Southampton	57	Tottenham H*	56
1978–79*f*	Crystal Palace	57	Brighton & HA*	56	Stoke C	56
1979–80*f*	Leicester C	55	Sunderland	54	Birmingham C*	53

	First	Pts	Second	Pts	Third	Pts
1980–81*f*	West Ham U	66	Notts Co	53	Swansea C*	50
1981–82*g*	Luton T	88	Watford	80	Norwich C	71
1982–83*g*	QPR	85	Wolverhampton W	75	Leicester C	70
1983–84*g*	Chelsea*	88	Sheffield W	88	Newcastle U	80
1984–85*g*	Oxford U	84	Birmingham C	82	Manchester C	74
1985–86*g*	Norwich C	84	Charlton Ath	77	Wimbledon	76
1986–87*g*	Derby Co	84	Portsmouth	78	Oldham Ath††	75
1987–88*h*	Millwall	82	Aston Villa*	78	Middlesbrough	78
1988–89*k*	Chelsea	99	Manchester C	82	Crystal Palace	81
1989–90*k*	Leeds U*	85	Sheffield U	85	Newcastle U††	80
1990–91*k*	Oldham Ath	88	West Ham U	87	Sheffield W	82
1991–92*k*	Ipswich T	84	Middlesbrough	80	Derby Co	78

No official competition during 1915–19 and 1939–46; Regional Leagues operating.
** Won or placed on goal average (ratio)/goal difference.*
†† *Not promoted after play-offs.*

DIVISION 3 to 1991–92

Maximum points: 92; 138 from 1981–82.

	First	Pts	Second	Pts	Third	Pts
1958–59	Plymouth Arg	62	Hull C	61	Brentford*	57
1959–60	Southampton	61	Norwich C	59	Shrewsbury T*	52
1960–61	Bury	68	Walsall	62	QPR	60
1961–62	Portsmouth	65	Grimsby T	62	Bournemouth*	59
1962–63	Northampton T	62	Swindon T	58	Port Vale	54
1963–64	Coventry C*	60	Crystal Palace	60	Watford	58
1964–65	Carlisle U	60	Bristol C*	59	Mansfield T	59
1965–66	Hull C	69	Millwall	65	QPR	57
1966–67	QPR	67	Middlesbrough	55	Watford	54
1967–68	Oxford U	57	Bury	56	Shrewsbury T	55
1968–69	Watford*	64	Swindon T	64	Luton T	61
1969–70	Orient	62	Luton T	60	Bristol R	56
1970–71	Preston NE	61	Fulham	60	Halifax T	56
1971–72	Aston Villa	70	Brighton & HA	65	Bournemouth*	62
1972–73	Bolton W	61	Notts Co	57	Blackburn R	55
1973–74	Oldham Ath	62	Bristol R*	61	York C	61
1974–75	Blackburn R	60	Plymouth Arg	59	Charlton Ath	55
1975–76	Hereford U	63	Cardiff C	57	Millwall	56
1976–77	Mansfield T	64	Brighton & HA	61	Crystal Palace*	59
1977–78	Wrexham	61	Cambridge U	58	Preston NE*	56
1978–79	Shrewsbury T	61	Watford*	60	Swansea C	60
1979–80	Grimsby T	62	Blackburn R	59	Sheffield W	58
1980–81	Rotherham U	61	Barnsley*	59	Charlton Ath	59
1981–82	Burnley*	80	Carlisle U	80	Fulham	78
1982–83	Portsmouth	91	Cardiff C	86	Huddersfield T	82
1983–84	Oxford U	95	Wimbledon	87	Sheffield U*	83
1984–85	Bradford C	94	Millwall	90	Hull C	87
1985–86	Reading	94	Plymouth Arg	87	Derby Co	84
1986–87	Bournemouth	97	Middlesbrough	94	Swindon T	87
1987–88	Sunderland	93	Brighton & HA	84	Walsall	82
1988–89	Wolverhampton W	92	Sheffield U*	84	Port Vale	84
1989–90	Bristol R	93	Bristol C	91	Notts Co	87
1990–91	Cambridge U	86	Southend U	85	Grimsby T*	83
1991–92	Brentford	82	Birmingham C	81	Huddersfield T	78

** Won or placed on goal average (ratio)/goal difference.*

DIVISION 4 (1958–1992)

Maximum points: 92; 138 from 1981–82.

1958–59	Port Vale	64	Coventry C*	60	York C	60
1959–60	Walsall	65	Notts Co*	60	Torquay U	60
1960–61	Peterborough U	66	Crystal Palace	64	Northampton T*	60
1961–62†	Millwall	56	Colchester U	55	Wrexham	53
1962–63	Brentford	62	Oldham Ath*	59	Crewe Alex	59
1963–64	Gillingham*	60	Carlisle U	60	Workington	59
1964–65	Brighton & HA	63	Millwall*	62	York C	62
1965–66	Doncaster R*	59	Darlington	59	Torquay U	58
1966–67	Stockport Co	64	Southport*	59	Barrow	59
1967–68	Luton T	66	Barnsley	61	Hartlepools U	60
1968–69	Doncaster R	59	Halifax T	57	Rochdale*	56
1969–70	Chesterfield	64	Wrexham	61	Swansea C	60
1970–71	Notts Co	69	Bournemouth	60	Oldham Ath	59
1971–72	Grimsby T	63	Southend U	60	Brentford	59
1972–73	Southport	62	Hereford U	58	Cambridge U	57
1973–74	Peterborough U	65	Gillingham	62	Colchester U	60
1974–75	Mansfield T	68	Shrewsbury T	62	Rotherham U	59
1975–76	Lincoln C	74	Northampton T	68	Reading	60
1976–77	Cambridge U	65	Exeter C	62	Colchester U*	59
1977–78	Watford	71	Southend U	60	Swansea C*	56
1978–79	Reading	65	Grimsby T*	61	Wimbledon*	61
1979–80	Huddersfield T	66	Walsall	64	Newport Co	61
1980–81	Southend U	67	Lincoln C	65	Doncaster R	56
1981–82	Sheffield U	96	Bradford C*	91	Wigan Ath	91
1982–83	Wimbledon	98	Hull C	90	Port Vale	88
1983–84	York C	101	Doncaster R	85	Reading*	82
1984–85	Chesterfield	91	Blackpool	86	Darlington	85
1985–86	Swindon T	102	Chester C	84	Mansfield T	81
1986–87	Northampton T	99	Preston NE	90	Southend U	80
1987–88	Wolverhampton W	90	Cardiff C	85	Bolton W	78
1988–89	Rotherham U	82	Tranmere R	80	Crewe Alex	78
1989–90	Exeter C	89	Grimsby T	79	Southend U	75
1990–91	Darlington	83	Stockport Co*	82	Hartlepool U	82
1991–92§	Burnley	83	Rotherham U*	77	Mansfield T	77

* *Won or placed on goal average (ratio)/goal difference.*
†*Maximum points:* 88 owing to Accrington Stanley's resignation. ††*Not promoted after play-offs.*
§*Maximum points:* 126 owing to Aldershot being expelled.

DIVISION 3—SOUTH (1920–1958)

1920–21 Season as Division 3.
Maximum points: a 84; *b* 92.

1920–21*a*	Crystal Palace	59	Southampton	54	QPR	53
1921–22*a*	Southampton*	61	Plymouth Arg	61	Portsmouth	53
1922–23*a*	Bristol C	59	Plymouth Arg*	53	Swansea T	53
1923–24*a*	Portsmouth	59	Plymouth Arg	55	Millwall	54
1924–25*a*	Swansea T	57	Plymouth Arg	56	Bristol C	53
1925–26*a*	Reading	57	Plymouth Arg	56	Millwall	53
1926–27*a*	Bristol C	62	Plymouth Arg	60	Millwall	56
1927–28*a*	Millwall	65	Northampton T	55	Plymouth Arg	53
1928–29*a*	Charlton Ath*	54	Crystal Palace	54	Northampton T*	52
1929–30*a*	Plymouth Arg	68	Brentford	61	QPR	51

	First	Pts	Second	Pts	Third	Pts
1930–31*a*	Notts Co	59	Crystal Palace	51	Brentford	50
1931–32*a*	Fulham	57	Reading	55	Southend U	53
1932–33*a*	Brentford	62	Exeter C	58	Norwich C	57
1933–34*a*	Norwich C	61	Coventry C*	54	Reading*	54
1934–35*a*	Charlton Ath	61	Reading	53	Coventry C	51
1935–36*a*	Coventry C	57	Luton T	56	Reading	54
1936–37*a*	Luton T	58	Notts Co	56	Brighton & HA	53
1937–38*a*	Millwall	56	Bristol C	55	QPR*	53
1938–39*a*	Newport Co	55	Crystal Palace	52	Brighton & HA	49
1939–46	Competition cancelled owing to war.					
1946–47*a*	Cardiff C	66	QPR	57	Bristol C	51
1947–48*a*	QPR	61	Bournemouth	57	Walsall	51
1948–49*a*	Swansea T	62	Reading	55	Bournemouth	52
1949–50*a*	Notts Co	58	Northampton T*	51	Southend U	51
1950–51*b*	Nottingham F	70	Norwich C	64	Reading*	57
1951–52*b*	Plymouth Arg	66	Reading*	61	Norwich C	61
1952–53*b*	Bristol R	64	Millwall*	62	Northampton T	62
1953–54*b*	Ipswich T	64	Brighton & HA	61	Bristol C	56
1954–55*b*	Bristol C	70	Leyton Orient	61	Southampton	59
1955–56*b*	Leyton Orient	66	Brighton & HA	65	Ipswich T	64
1956–57*b*	Ipswich T*	59	Torquay U	59	Colchester U	58
1957–58*b*	Brighton & HA	60	Brentford*	58	Plymouth Arg	58

** Won or placed on goal average (ratio).*

DIVISION 3—NORTH (1921–1958)

Maximum points: a 76; *b* 84; *c* 80; *d* 92.

1921–22*a*	Stockport Co	56	Darlington*	50	Grimsby T	50
1922–23*a*	Nelson	51	Bradford PA	47	Walsall	46
1923–24*b*	Wolverhampton W	63	Rochdale	62	Chesterfield	54
1924–25*b*	Darlington	58	Nelson*	53	New Brighton	53
1925–26*b*	Grimsby T	61	Bradford PA	60	Rochdale	59
1926–27*b*	Stoke C	63	Rochdale	58	Bradford PA	55
1927–28*b*	Bradford PA	63	Lincoln C	55	Stockport Co	54
1928–29*g*	Bradford C	63	Stockport Co	62	Wrexham	52
1929–30*b*	Port Vale	67	Stockport Co	63	Darlington*	50
1930–31*b*	Chesterfield	58	Lincoln C	57	Wrexham*	54
1931–32*c*	Lincoln C*	57	Gateshead	57	Chester	50
1932–33*b*	Hull C	59	Wrexham	57	Stockport Co	54
1933–34*b*	Barnsley	62	Chesterfield	61	Stockport Co	59
1934–35*b*	Doncaster R	57	Halifax T	55	Chester	54
1935–36*b*	Chesterfield	60	Chester*	55	Tranmere R	55
1936–37*b*	Stockport Co	60	Lincoln C	57	Chester	53
1937–38*b*	Tranmere R	56	Doncaster R	54	Hull C	53
1938–39*b*	Barnsley	67	Doncaster R	56	Bradford C	52
1939–46	Competition cancelled owing to war.					
1946–47*b*	Doncaster R	72	Rotherham U	60	Chester	56
1947–48*b*	Lincoln C	60	Rotherham U	59	Wrexham	50
1948–49*b*	Hull C	65	Rotherham U	62	Doncaster R	50
1949–50*b*	Doncaster R	55	Gateshead	53	Rochdale*	51
1950–51*d*	Rotherham U	71	Mansfield T	64	Carlisle U	62
1951–52*d*	Lincoln C	69	Grimsby T	66	Stockport Co	59
1952–53*d*	Oldham Ath	59	Port Vale	58	Wrexham	56
1953–54*d*	Port Vale	69	Barnsley	58	Scunthorpe U	57

	First	Pts	Second	Pts	Third	Pts
1954–55*d*	Barnsley	65	Accrington S	61	Scunthorpe U*	58
1955–56*d*	Grimsby T	68	Derby Co	63	Accrington S	59
1956–57*d*	Derby Co	63	Hartlepools U	59	Accrington S*	58
1957–58*d*	Scunthorpe U	66	Accrington S	59	Bradford C	57

* *Won or placed on goal average (ratio).*

PROMOTED AFTER PLAY-OFFS

(Not accounted for in previous section)

1986–87 Aldershot to Division 3.
1987–88 Swansea C to Division 3.
1988–89 Leyton Orient to Division 3.
1989–90 Cambridge U to Division 3; Notts Co to Division 2; Sunderland to Division 1.
1990–91 Notts Co to Division 1; Tranmere R to Division 2; Torquay U to Division 3.
1991–92 Blackburn R to Premier League; Peterborough U to Division 1.
1992–93 Swindon T to Premier League; WBA to Division 1; York C to Division 2.
1993–94 Leicester C to Premier League; Burnley to Division 1; Wycombe W to Division 2.
1994–95 Huddersfield T to Division 1.
1995–96 Leicester C to Premier League; Bradford C to Division 1; Plymouth Arg to Division 2.
1996–97 Crystal Palace to Premier League; Crewe Alex to Division 1; Northampton T to Division 2.
1997–98 Charlton Ath to Premier League; Colchester U to Division 2.
1998–99 Watford to Premier League; Scunthorpe to Division 2.
1999–00 Peterborough U to Division 2.
2000–01 Walsall to Division 1; Blackpool to Division 2.
2001–02 Birmingham C to Premier League; Stoke C to Division 1; Cheltenham T to Division 2.
2002–03 Wolverhampton W to Premier League; Cardiff C to Division 1; Bournemouth to Division 2.
2003–04 Crystal Palace to Premier League; Brighton & HA to Division 1; Huddersfield T to Division 2.
2004–05 West Ham U to Premier League; Sheffield W to Football League Championship, Southend U to Football League Championship 1.
2005–06 Watford to Premier League; Barnsley to Football League Championship; Cheltenham T to Football League Championship 1.
2006–07 Derby Co to Premier League; Blackpool to Football League Championship; Bristol R to Football League Championship 1.

RELEGATED CLUBS

FA PREMIER LEAGUE TO DIVISION 1

1992–93 Crystal Palace, Middlesbrough, Nottingham F.
1993–94 Sheffield U, Oldham Ath, Swindon T.
1994–95 Crystal Palace, Norwich C, Leicester C, Ipswich T.
1995–96 Manchester C, QPR, Bolton W.
1996–97 Sunderland, Middlesbrough, Nottingham F.
1997–98 Bolton W, Barnsley, Crystal Palace.
1998–99 Charlton Ath, Blackburn R, Nottingham F.
1999–90 Wimbledon, Sheffield W, Watford.
2000–01 Manchester C, Coventry C, Bradford C.
2001–02 Ipswich T, Derby Co, Leicester C.
2002–03 West Ham U, WBA, Sunderland.
2003–04 Leicester C, Leeds U, Wolverhampton W.

FA PREMIER LEAGUE TO FOOTBALL LEAGUE CHAMPIONSHIP

2004–05 Crystal Palace, Norwich C, Southampton.
2005–06 Birmingham C, WBA, Sunderland.
2006–07 Sheffield U, Charlton Ath, Watford

DIVISION 1 TO DIVISION 2

1898–99 Bolton W and Sheffield W
1899–1900 Burnley and Glossop
1900–01 Preston NE and WBA
1901–02 Small Heath and Manchester C
1902–03 Grimsby T and Bolton W
1903–04 Liverpool and WBA
1904–05 League extended. Bury and Notts Co, two bottom clubs in First Division, re-elected.
1905–06 Nottingham F and Wolverhampton W
1906–07 Derby Co and Stoke C
1907–08 Bolton W and Birmingham C
1908–09 Manchester C and Leicester Fosse
1909–10 Bolton W and Chelsea
1910–11 Bristol C and Nottingham F
1911–12 Preston NE and Bury
1912–13 Notts Co and Woolwich Arsenal
1913–14 Preston NE and Derby Co
1914–15 Tottenham H and Chelsea*
1919–20 Notts Co and Sheffield W
1920–21 Derby Co and Bradford PA
1921–22 Bradford C and Manchester U
1922–23 Stoke C and Oldham Ath
1923–24 Chelsea and Middlesbrough
1924–25 Preston NE and Nottingham F
1925–26 Manchester C and Notts Co
1926–27 Leeds U and WBA
1927–28 Tottenham H and Middlesbrough
1928–29 Bury and Cardiff C
1929–30 Burnley and Everton
1930–31 Leeds U and Manchester U
1931–32 Grimsby T and West Ham U
1932–33 Bolton W and Blackpool
1933–34 Newcastle U and Sheffield U
1934–35 Leicester C and Tottenham H
1935–36 Aston Villa and Blackburn R
1936–37 Manchester U and Sheffield W
1937–38 Manchester C and WBA
1938–39 Birmingham C and Leicester C
1946–47 Brentford and Leeds U
1947–48 Blackburn R and Grimsby T
1948–49 Preston NE and Sheffield U
1949–50 Manchester C and Birmingham C
1950–51 Sheffield W and Everton
1951–52 Huddersfield T and Fulham
1952–53 Stoke C and Derby Co
1953–54 Middlesbrough and Liverpool
1954–55 Leicester C and Sheffield W
1955–56 Huddersfield T and Sheffield U
1956–57 Charlton Ath and Cardiff C
1957–58 Sheffield W and Sunderland
1958–59 Portsmouth and Aston Villa
1959–60 Luton T and Leeds U
1960–61 Preston NE and Newcastle U
1961–62 Chelsea and Cardiff C
1962–63 Manchester C and Leyton Orient
1963–64 Bolton W and Ipswich T
1964–65 Wolverhampton W and Birmingham C
1965–66 Northampton T and Blackburn R
1966–67 Aston Villa and Blackpool
1967–68 Fulham and Sheffield U
1968–69 Leicester C and QPR
1969–70 Sunderland and Sheffield W
1970–71 Burnley and Blackpool
1971–72 Huddersfield T and Nottingham F
1972–73 Crystal Palace and WBA

1973–74 Southampton, Manchester U, Norwich C
1974–75 Luton T, Chelsea, Carlisle U
1975–76 Wolverhampton W, Burnley, Sheffield U
1976–77 Sunderland, Stoke C, Tottenham H
1977–78 West Ham U, Newcastle U, Leicester C
1978–79 QPR, Birmingham C, Chelsea
1979–80 Bristol C, Derby Co, Bolton W
1980–81 Norwich C, Leicester C, Crystal Palace
1981–82 Leeds U, Wolverhampton W, Middlesbrough
1982–83 Manchester C, Swansea C, Brighton & HA
1983–84 Birmingham C, Notts Co, Wolverhampton W
1984–85 Norwich C, Sunderland, Stoke C
1985–86 Ipswich T, Birmingham C, WBA
1986–87 Leicester C, Manchester C, Aston Villa
1987–88 Chelsea**, Portsmouth, Watford, Oxford U
1988–89 Middlesbrough, West Ham U, Newcastle U
1989–90 Sheffield W, Charlton Ath, Millwall
1990–91 Sunderland and Derby Co
1991–92 Luton T, Notts Co, West Ham U
1992–93 Brentford, Cambridge U, Bristol R
1993–94 Birmingham C, Oxford U, Peterborough U
1994–95 Swindon T, Burnley, Bristol C, Notts Co
1995–96 Millwall, Watford, Luton T
1996–97 Grimsby T, Oldham Ath, Southend U
1997–98 Manchester C, Stoke C, Reading
1998–99 Bury, Oxford U, Bristol C
1999–00 Walsall, Port Vale, Swindon T
2000–01 Huddersfield T, QPR, Tranmere R
2001–02 Crewe Alex, Barnsley, Stockport Co
2002–03 Sheffield W, Brighton & HA, Grimsby T
2003–04 Walsall, Bradford C, Wimbledon

***Relegated after play-offs.*
**Subsequently re-elected to Division 1 when League was extended after the War.*

FOOTBALL LEAGUE CHAMPIONSHIP TO FOOTBALL LEAGUE CHAMPIONSHIP 1

2004–05 Gillingham, Nottingham F, Rotherham U.
2005–06 Crewe Alex, Millwall, Brighton & HA.
2006–07 Southend U, Luton T, Leeds U

DIVISION 2 TO DIVISION 3

1920–21 Stockport Co
1921–22 Bradford PA and Bristol C
1922–23 Rotherham Co and Wolverhampton W
1923–24 Nelson and Bristol C
1924–25 Crystal Palace and Coventry C
1925–26 Stoke C and Stockport Co
1926–27 Darlington and Bradford C
1927–28 Fulham and South Shields
1928–29 Port Vale and Clapton Orient
1929–30 Hull C and Notts Co
1930–31 Reading and Cardiff C
1931–32 Barnsley and Bristol C
1932–33 Chesterfield and Charlton Ath
1933–34 Millwall and Lincoln C
1934–35 Oldham Ath and Notts Co
1935–36 Port Vale and Hull C
1936–37 Doncaster R and Bradford C
1937–38 Barnsley and Stockport Co
1938–39 Norwich C and Tranmere R
1946–47 Swansea T and Newport Co
1947–48 Doncaster R and Millwall
1948–49 Nottingham F and Lincoln C
1949–50 Plymouth Arg and Bradford PA
1950–51 Grimsby T and Chesterfield
1951–52 Coventry C and QPR
1952–53 Southampton and Barnsley
1953–54 Brentford and Oldham Ath
1954–55 Ipswich T and Derby Co
1955–56 Plymouth Arg and Hull C
1956–57 Port Vale and Bury
1957–58 Doncaster R and Notts Co
1958–59 Barnsley and Grimsby T
1959–60 Bristol C and Hull C
1960–61 Lincoln C and Portsmouth
1961–62 Brighton & HA and Bristol R
1962–63 Walsall and Luton T
1963–64 Grimsby T and Scunthorpe U
1964–65 Swindon T and Swansea T
1965–66 Middlesbrough and Leyton Orient

1966–67 Northampton T and Bury
1967–68 Plymouth Arg and Rotherham U
1968–69 Fulham and Bury
1969–70 Preston NE and Aston Villa
1970–71 Blackburn R and Bolton W
1971–72 Charlton Ath and Watford
1972–73 Huddersfield T and Brighton & HA
1973–74 Crystal Palace, Preston NE, Swindon T
1974–75 Millwall, Cardiff C, Sheffield W
1975–76 Oxford U, York C, Portsmouth
1976–77 Carlisle U, Plymouth Arg, Hereford U
1977–78 Blackpool, Mansfield T, Hull C
1978–79 Sheffield U, Millwall, Blackburn R
1979–80 Fulham, Burnley, Charlton Ath
1980–81 Preston NE, Bristol C, Bristol R
1981–82 Cardiff C, Wrexham, Orient
1982–83 Rotherham U, Burnley, Bolton W
1983–84 Derby Co, Swansea C, Cambridge U
1984–85 Notts Co, Cardiff C, Wolverhampton W
1985–86 Carlisle U, Middlesbrough, Fulham
1986–87 Sunderland**, Grimsby T, Brighton & HA
1987–88 Huddersfield T, Reading, Sheffield U**
1988–89 Shrewsbury T, Birmingham C, Walsall
1989–90 Bournemouth, Bradford C, Stoke C
1990–91 WBA and Hull C
1991–92 Plymouth Arg, Brighton & HA, Port Vale
1992–93 Preston NE, Mansfield T, Wigan Ath, Chester C
1993–94 Fulham, Exeter C, Hartlepool U, Barnet
1994–95 Cambridge U, Plymouth Arg, Cardiff C, Chester C, Leyton Orient
1995–96 Carlisle U, Swansea C, Brighton & HA, Hull C
1996–97 Peterborough U, Shrewsbury T, Rotherham U, Notts Co
1997–98 Brentford, Plymouth Arg, Carlisle U, Southend U
1998–99 York C, Northampton T, Lincoln C, Macclesfield T
1999–00 Cardiff C, Blackpool, Scunthorpe U, Chesterfield
2000–01 Bristol R, Luton T, Swansea C, Oxford U
2001–02 Bournemouth, Bury, Wrexham, Cambridge U
2002–03 Cheltenham T, Huddersfield T, Mansfield T, Northampton T
2003–04 Grimsby T, Rushden & D, Notts Co, Wycombe W

FOOTBALL LEAGUE CHAMPIONSHIP 1 TO FOOTBALL LEAGUE CHAMPIONSHIP 2

2004–05 Torquay U, Wrexham, Peterborough U, Stockport Co.
2005–06 Hartlepool U, Milton Keynes D, Swindon T, Walsall.
2006–07 Chesterfield, Bradford C, Rotherham U, Brentford

DIVISION 3 TO DIVISION 4

1958–59 Rochdale, Notts Co, Doncaster R, Stockport Co
1959–60 Accrington S, Wrexham, Mansfield T, York C
1960–61 Chesterfield, Colchester U, Bradford C, Tranmere R
1961–62 Newport Co, Brentford, Lincoln C, Torquay U
1962–63 Bradford PA, Brighton & HA, Carlisle U, Halifax T
1963–64 Millwall, Crewe Alex, Wrexham, Notts Co
1964–65 Luton T, Port Vale, Colchester U, Barnsley
1965–66 Southend U, Exeter C, Brentford, York C
1966–67 Doncaster R, Workington, Darlington, Swansea T
1967–68 Scunthorpe U, Colchester U, Grimsby T, Peterborough U (demoted)
1968–69 Oldham Ath, Crewe Alex, Hartlepool, Northampton T
1969–70 Bournemouth, Southport, Barrow, Stockport Co
1970–71 Reading, Bury, Doncaster R, Gillingham

1971–72 Mansfield T, Barnsley, Torquay U, Bradford C
1972–73 Rotherham U, Brentford, Swansea C, Scunthorpe U
1973–74 Cambridge U, Shrewsbury T, Southport, Rochdale
1974–75 Bournemouth, Tranmere R, Watford, Huddersfield T
1975–76 Aldershot, Colchester U, Southend U, Halifax T
1976–77 Reading, Northampton T, Grimsby T, York C
1977–78 Port Vale, Bradford C, Hereford U, Portsmouth
1978–79 Peterborough U, Walsall, Tranmere R, Lincoln C
1979–80 Bury, Southend U, Mansfield T, Wimbledon
1980–81 Sheffield U, Colchester U, Blackpool, Hull C
1981–82 Wimbledon, Swindon T, Bristol C, Chester
1982–83 Reading, Wrexham, Doncaster R, Chesterfield
1983–84 Scunthorpe U, Southend U, Port Vale, Exeter C
1984–85 Burnley, Orient, Preston NE, Cambridge U
1985–86 Lincoln C, Cardiff C, Wolverhampton W, Swansea C
1986–87 Bolton W**, Carlisle U, Darlington, Newport Co
1987–88 Doncaster R, York C, Grimsby T, Rotherham U**
1988–89 Southend U, Chesterfield, Gillingham, Aldershot
1989–90 Cardiff C, Northampton T, Blackpool, Walsall
1990–91 Crewe Alex, Rotherham U, Mansfield T
1991–92 Bury, Shrewsbury T, Torquay U, Darlington

***Relegated after play-offs.*

LEAGUE STATUS FROM 1986–1987

	RELEGATED FROM LEAGUE	PROMOTED TO LEAGUE
1986–87	Lincoln C	Scarborough
1987–88	Newport Co	Lincoln C
1988–89	Darlington	Maidstone U
1989–90	Colchester U	Darlington
1990–91	—	Barnet
1991–92	—	Colchester U
1992–93	Halifax T	Wycombe W
1993–94	—	—
1994–95	—	—
1995–96	—	—
1996–97	Hereford U	Macclesfield T
1997–98	Doncaster R	Halifax T
1998–99	Scarborough	Cheltenham T
1999–2000	Chester C	Kidderminster H
2000–01	Barnet	Rushden & D
2001–02	Halifax T	Boston U
2002–03	Shrewsbury T, Exeter C	Yeovil T, Doncaster R
2003–04	Carlisle U, York C	Chester C, Shrewsbury T
2004–05	Kidderminster H, Cambridge U	Barnet, Carlisle U
2005–06	Oxford U, Rushden & D	Accrington S, Hereford U
2006–07	Boston U, Torquay U	Dagenham & R, Morecambe

LEAGUE TITLE WINS

FA PREMIER LEAGUE – Manchester U 9, Arsenal 3, Chelsea 2, Blackburn R 1.

FOOTBALL LEAGUE CHAMPIONSHIP – Sunderland 2, Reading 1.

LEAGUE DIVISION 1 – Liverpool 18, Arsenal 10, Everton 9, Sunderland 8, Aston Villa 7, Manchester U 7, Newcastle U 5, Sheffield W 4, Huddersfield T 3, Leeds U 3, Manchester C 3, Portsmouth 3, Wolverhampton W 3, Blackburn R 2, Burnley 2, Derby Co 2, Nottingham F 2, Preston NE 2, Tottenham H 2; Bolton W, Charlton Ath, Chelsea, Crystal Palace, Fulham, Ipswich T, Middlesbrough, Norwich C, Sheffield U, WBA 1 each.

FOOTBALL LEAGUE CHAMPIONSHIP 1 – Luton T 1, Scunthorpe U, Southend U 1.

LEAGUE DIVISION 2 – Leicester C 6, Manchester C 6, Birmingham C (one as Small Heath) 5, Sheffield W 5, Derby Co 4, Liverpool 4, Preston NE 4, Ipswich T 3, Leeds U 3, Middlesbrough 3, Notts Co 3, Stoke C 3, Aston Villa 2, Bolton W 2, Burnley 2, Bury 2, Chelsea 2, Fulham 2, Grimsby T 2, Manchester U 2, Millwall 2, Norwich C 2, Nottingham F 2, Tottenham H 2, WBA 2, West Ham U 2, Wolverhampton W 2; Blackburn R, Blackpool, Bradford C, Brentford, Brighton & HA, Bristol C, Coventry C, Crystal Palace, Everton, Huddersfield T, Luton T, Newcastle U, Plymouth Arg, QPR, Oldham Ath, Oxford U, Reading, Sheffield U, Sunderland, Swindon T, Watford, Wigan Ath 1 each.

FOOTBALL LEAGUE CHAMPIONSHIP 2 – Carlisle U 1, Walsall 1, Yeovil T 1.

LEAGUE DIVISION 3 – Brentford 2, Carlisle U 2, Oxford U 2, Plymouth Arg 2, Portsmouth 2, Preston NE 2, Shrewsbury T 2; Aston Villa, Blackburn R, Bolton W, Bournemouth, Bradford C, Brighton & HA, Bristol R, Burnley, Bury, Cambridge U, Cardiff C, Coventry C, Doncaster R, Grimsby T, Hereford U, Hull C, Leyton Orient, Mansfield T, Northampton T, Notts Co, Oldham Ath, QPR, Reading, Rotherham U, Rushden & D Southampton, Sunderland, Swansea C, Watford, Wigan Ath, Wolverhampton W, Wrexham 1 each.

LEAGUE DIVISION 4 – Chesterfield 2, Doncaster R 2, Peterborough U 2; Brentford, Brighton & HA, Burnley, Cambridge U, Darlington, Exeter C, Gillingham, Grimsby T, Huddersfield T, Lincoln C, Luton T, Mansfield T, Millwall, Northampton T, Notts Co, Port Vale, Reading, Rotherham U, Sheffield U, Southend U, Southport, Stockport Co, Swindon T, Walsall, Watford, Wimbledon, Wolverhampton W, York C 1 each.

DIVISION 3 (South) – Bristol C 3, Charlton Ath 2, Ipswich T 2, Millwall 2, Notts Co 2, Plymouth Arg 2, Swansea T 2; Brentford, Brighton & HA, Bristol R, Cardiff C, Coventry C, Crystal Palace, Fulham, Leyton Orient, Luton T, Newport Co, Norwich C, Nottingham F, Portsmouth, QPR, Reading, Southampton 1 each.

DIVISION 3 (North) – Barnsley 3, Doncaster R 3, Lincoln C 3, Chesterfield 2, Grimsby T 2, Hull C 2, Port Vale 2, Stockport Co 2; Bradford C, Bradford PA, Darlington, Derby Co, Nelson, Oldham Ath, Rotherham U, Scunthorpe U, Stoke C, Tranmere R, Wolverhampton W 1 each.

FOOTBALL LEAGUE PLAY-OFFS 2006–2007

CHAMPIONSHIP SEMI-FINALS FIRST LEG

Southampton	(1) 1	Derby Co	(1) 2
Wolverhampton W	(1) 2	WBA	(1) 3

CHAMPIONSHIP SEMI-FINALS SECOND LEG

Derby Co	(2) 2	Southampton	(2) 3
aet; Derby Co won 4-3 on penalties.			
WBA	(0) 1	Wolverhampton W	(0) 0

CHAMPIONSHIP FINAL Monday, 28 May 2007 *(at Wembley)*

Derby Co (0) 1 *(Pearson 61)*

WBA (0) 0 74,993

Derby Co: Bywater; Mears, McEveley, Oakley, Moore, Leacock, Fagan (Edworthy), Pearson, Howard, Peschisolido (Barnes), Johnson S (Jones).
WBA: Kiely; McShane (Ellington), Robinson, Koumas, Sodje (Clement), Perry, Gera (Carter), Koren, Phillips, Kamara, Greening.
Referee: G. Poll (Hertfordshire).

LEAGUE 1 SEMI-FINALS FIRST LEG

Yeovil T	(0) 0	Nottingham F	(1) 2
Oldham Ath	(0) 1	Blackpool	(0) 2

LEAGUE 1 SEMI-FINALS SECOND LEG

Nottingham F	(0) 2	Yeovil T	(1) 5
aet.			
Blackpool	(1) 3	Oldham Ath	(0) 1

LEAGUE 1 FINAL Sunday, 27 May 2007 *(at Wembley)*

Yeovil T (0) 0

Blackpool (1) 2 *(Williams 43, Parker 52)* 59,313

Yeovil T: Mildenhall; Lindegaard (Lynch), Gray, Cohen (Kamudimba Kalala), Guyett, Forbes, Barry, Davies, Gray, Stewart, Morris (Knights).
Blackpool: Rachubka; Evatt, Williams, Jorgensen, Jackson, Barker, Forbes (Fox), Southern, Morrell, Parker (Gillett), Hoolahan (Vernon).
Referee: A. D'Urso (Essex).

LEAGUE 2 SEMI-FINALS FIRST LEG

Bristol R	(1) 2	Lincoln C	(1) 1
Shrewsbury T	(0) 0	Milton Keynes D	(0) 0

LEAGUE 2 SEMI-FINALS SECOND LEG

Lincoln C	(2) 3	Bristol R	(3) 5
Milton Keynes D	(0) 1	Shrewsbury T	(0) 2

LEAGUE 2 FINAL Saturday, 26 May 2007 *(at Wembley)*

Bristol R (2) 3 *(Walker R 21, 35, Igoe 90)*

Shrewsbury T (1) 1 *(Drummond 3)* 61,589

Bristol R: Phillips; Green, Carruthers, Campbell, Anthony, Elliott, Igoe, Disley, Walker R, Lambert, Haldane (Rigg).
Shrewsbury T: MacKenzie; Herd (Burton), Tierney■, Drummond, Hope, Langmead, Hall, Cooke (Humphrey), Symes (Fortune-West), Asamoah, Ashton.
Referee: M. Jones (Cheshire).

LEAGUE ATTENDANCES 2006–2007

FA BARCLAYCARD PREMIERSHIP ATTENDANCES

	Average Gate			*Season 2006–07*	
	2005–06	2006–07	+/–%	Highest	Lowest
Arsenal	38,186	60,045	+57.24	60,132	59,912
Aston Villa	34,059	36,214	+6.33	42,551	27,450
Blackburn Rovers	21,015	21,275	+1.24	29,342	16,035
Bolton Wanderers	25,265	23,606	–6.57	27,229	21,140
Charlton Athletic	26,196	26,195	–0.00	27,111	23,423
Chelsea	41,902	41,542	–0.86	41,953	38,000
Everton	36,860	36,739	–0.33	40,004	32,968
Fulham	20,654	22,279	+7.87	24,554	17,000
Liverpool	44,236	43,563	–1.52	44,403	41,370
Manchester City	42,856	39,997	–6.67	47,244	35,776
Manchester United	68,765	75,826	+10.27	76,098	75,115
Middlesbrough	28,463	27,730	–2.58	32,013	23,638
Newcastle United	52,032	50,686	–2.59	52,305	48,145
Portsmouth	19,840	19,862	+0.11	20,223	19,105
Reading	20,207	23,829	+17.92	24,122	21,954
Sheffield United	23,650	30,512	+29.01	32,604	25,011
Tottenham Hotspur	36,074	35,739	–0.93	36,170	34,154
Watford	15,415	18,750	+21.63	19,830	13,760
West Ham United	33,743	34,719	+2.89	34,977	33,805
Wigan Athletic	20,610	18,159	–11.89	24,726	14,636

FOOTBALL LEAGUE CHAMPIONSHIP ATTENDANCES

	Average Gate			*Season 2006–07*	
	2005–06	2006–07	+/–%	Highest	Lowest
Barnsley	9,054	12,733	+40.6	21,253	9,479
Birmingham City	27,392	22,274	–18.7	29,431	15,854
Burnley	12,462	11,956	–4.1	15,061	9,681
Cardiff City	11,720	15,219	+29.9	20,109	11,549
Colchester United	3,969	5,466	+37.7	6,065	4,249
Coventry City	21,302	20,342	–4.5	27,212	16,178
Crystal Palace	19,457	17,541	–9.8	21,523	15,985
Derby County	24,166	25,945	+7.4	31,920	21,295
Hull City	19,841	18,758	–5.5	25,512	14,895
Ipswich Town	24,253	22,445	–7.5	28,355	19,337
Leeds United	22,355	21,613	–3.3	31,269	16,268
Leicester City	22,234	23,206	+4.4	30,457	18,677
Luton Town	9,139	8,580	–6.1	10,260	7,441
Norwich City	24,952	24,545	–1.6	25,476	23,311
Plymouth Argyle	13,776	13,012	–5.5	17,088	9,841
Preston North End	14,617	14,430	–1.3	19,603	11,601
Queens Park Rangers	13,441	12,936	–3.8	16,741	10,811
Sheffield Wednesday	24,853	23,638	–4.9	29,103	18,752
Southampton	23,614	23,556	–0.2	32,008	18,736
Southend United	8,053	10,024	+24.5	11,415	7,901
Stoke City	14,432	15,749	+9.1	23,017	11,626
Sunderland	33,904	31,887	–5.9	44,448	24,242
West Bromwich Albion	25,404	20,472	–19.4	26,606	17,417
Wolverhampton Wanderers	23,624	20,968	–11.2	28,016	16,772

Premiership and Football League attendance averages and highest crowd figures for 2006–07 are unofficial. The official Premiership total was 13,094,307.

FOOTBALL LEAGUE CHAMPIONSHIP 1 ATTENDANCES

	Average Gate			*Season 2006–07*	
	2005–06	2006–07	+/–%	Highest	Lowest
Blackpool	5,820	6,877	+18.2	9,482	4,600
AFC Bournemouth	6,458	6,028	–6.7	8,001	4,538
Bradford City	8,265	8,694	+5.2	14,925	7,134
Brentford	6,775	5,600	–17.3	7,023	4,296
Brighton & Hove Albion	6,802	6,048	–11.1	7,749	5,146
Bristol City	11,725	12,818	+9.3	19,517	9,726
Carlisle United	7,218	7,907	+9.5	12,031	6,087
Cheltenham Town	3,453	4,359	+26.2	6,554	3,036
Chesterfield	4,772	4,235	–11.3	6,641	3,341
Crewe Alexandra	6,732	5,462	–18.9	7,632	4,062
Doncaster Rovers	6,139	7,746	+26.2	14,470	5,190
Gillingham	6,671	6,282	–5.8	8,216	5,103
Huddersfield Town	13,058	10,573	–19.0	14,772	8,723
Leyton Orient	4,699	4,857	+3.4	7,206	3,529
Millwall	9,529	9,234	–3.1	12,547	6,251
Northampton Town	5,935	5,573	–6.1	7,172	4,564
Nottingham Forest	20,257	20,612	+1.8	27,875	16,785
Oldham Athletic	5,797	6,334	+9.3	10,207	4,652
Port Vale	4,657	4,725	+1.5	7,388	3,077
Rotherham United	5,306	4,763	–10.2	7,809	3,223
Scunthorpe United	5,171	5,669	+9.6	8,906	3,473
Swansea City	14,112	12,720	–9.9	18,903	9,675
Tranmere Rovers	7,211	6,930	–3.9	11,444	5,528
Yeovil Town	6,668	5,765	–13.5	9,009	4,709

FOOTBALL LEAGUE CHAMPIONSHIP 2 ATTENDANCES

	Average Gate			*Season 2006–07*	
	2005–06	2006–07	+/–%	Highest	Lowest
Accrington Stanley	1,895	2,260	+19.3	4,004	1,234
Barnet	2,578	2,279	–11.6	2,958	1,461
Boston United	2,519	2,152	–14.6	4,327	1,571
Bristol Rovers	5,989	5,480	–8.5	9,902	4,327
Bury	2,594	2,588	–0.2	5,075	1,775
Chester City	2,964	2,473	–16.6	4,206	1,527
Darlington	4,199	3,814	–9.2	9,987	2,321
Grimsby Town	5,151	4,379	–15.0	6,137	3,012
Hartlepool United	4,812	5,096	+5.9	7,629	3,659
Hereford United	2,793	3,328	+19.2	5,201	2,176
Lincoln City	4,739	5,176	+9.2	6,820	3,913
Macclesfield Town	2,275	2,863	+25.8	14,142	1,472
Mansfield Town	3,560	3,176	–10.8	6,182	2,023
Milton Keynes Dons	5,776	6,034	+4.5	8,102	4,564
Notts County	5,467	4,974	–9.0	10,034	3,010
Peterborough United	4,364	4,662	+6.8	8,405	3,193
Rochdale	2,808	2,898	+3.2	5,846	1,982
Shrewsbury Town	3,997	4,730	+18.3	7,782	3,369
Stockport County	4,772	5,514	+15.5	7,860	4,089
Swindon Town	5,951	7,419	+24.7	14,731	5,462
Torquay United	2,851	2,633	–7.6	4,047	1,588
Walsall	5,392	5,643	+4.7	8,345	4,070
Wrexham	4,478	5,030	+12.3	12,374	3,401
Wycombe Wanderers	5,445	4,983	–8.5	7,150	3,885

TRANSFERS 2006–2007

JUNE 2006	*From*	*To*
3 Baudet, Julien	Notts County	Crewe Alexandra
12 Bowyer, Lee D.	Newcastle United	West Ham United
26 Butcher, Richard T.	Oldham Athletic	Peterborough United
30 Cort, Leon	Hull City	Crystal Palace
27 Danns, Neil A.	Colchester United	Birmingham City
14 Davis, Claude	Preston North End	Sheffield United
13 Francis, Simon C.	Sheffield United	Southend United
2 Gray, Andrew D.	Sunderland	Burnley
30 Hall, Fitz	Crystal Palace	Wigan Athletic
2 Johnson, Andrew	Crystal Palace	Everton
15 Lescott, Joleon P.	Wolverhampton Wanderers	Everton
1 Lucketti, Christopher J.	Preston North End	Sheffield United
1 Lunt, Kenny V.	Crewe Alexandra	Sheffield Wednesday
3 McCombe, Jamie	Lincoln City	Bristol City
28 Morais, Filipe A.	Chelsea	Millwall
9 Pidgeley, Leonard J.	Chelsea	Millwall
1 Small, Wade K.	Milton Keynes Dons	Sheffield Wednesday
16 Spector, Jonathan M.	Manchester United	West Ham United
19 Ward, Elliot L.	West Ham United	Coventry City
13 Whitbread, Zak B.	Liverpool	Millwall

JULY 2006		
7 Barnes, Philip K.	Sheffield United	Grimsby Town
5 Beckett, Luke J.	Sheffield United	Huddersfield Town
7 Bellamy, Craig D.	Blackburn Rovers	Liverpool
27 Bennett, Ian M.	Leeds United	Sheffield United
31 Boyd, Adam M.	Hartlepool United	Luton Town
7 Cohen, Christopher D.	West Ham United	Yeovil Town
6 Cole, Carlton	Chelsea	West Ham United
6 Collins, Patrick	Sheffield Wednesday	Darlington
31 Croft, Lee	Manchester City	Norwich City
21 Davis, Kelvin G.	Sunderland	Southampton
6 Day, Christopher N.	Oldham Athletic	Millwall
26 Duff, Damien A.	Chelsea	Newcastle United
17 Ebanks-Blake, Sylvan	Manchester United	Plymouth Argyle
3 Ellison, Kevin	Hull City	Tranmere Rovers
29 Fletcher, Carl N.	West Ham United	Crystal Palace
13 Flinders, Scott L.	Barnsley	Crystal Palace
12 Folly, Yoann	Southampton	Sheffield Wednesday
13 Francis, Damien J.	Wigan Athletic	Watford
11 Hamann, Dietmar	Liverpool	Bolton Wanderers
12 Hamann, Dietmar	Bolton Wanderers	Manchester City
20 Hayles, Barrington	Millwall	Plymouth Argyle
14 Heskey, Emile I.	Birmingham City	Wigan Athletic
3 Horsfield, Geoffrey M.	West Bromwich Albion	Sheffield United
26 Hulse, Robert W.	Leeds United	Sheffield United
4 Kelly, Stephen M.	Tottenham Hotspur	Birmingham City
19 Leigertwood, Mikele B.	Crystal Palace	Sheffield United
21 Livermore, David	Millwall	Leeds United
18 Mansell, Lee R.S.	Oxford United	Torquay United
14 Marney, Dean E.	Tottenham Hotspur	Hull City
17 McIndoe, Michael	Doncaster Rovers	Barnsley
6 Mears, Tyrone	Preston North End	West Ham United
27 Nicholls, Kevin J.	Luton Town	Leeds United
4 Opara, Lloyd	Cheshunt	Peterborough United

27 Pennant, Jermaine	Birmingham City	Liverpool
20 Phillips, Steven J.	Bristol City	Bristol Rovers
28 Queudrue, Franck	Middlesbrough	Fulham
13 Raven, David H.	Liverpool	Carlisle United
4 Ricketts, Michael B.	Leeds United	Southend United
3 Roberts, Jason A.D.	Wigan Athletic	Blackburn Rovers
26 Scowcroft, James B.	Coventry City	Crystal Palace
27 Semple, Ryan D.	Peterborough United	Lincoln City
12 Seol, Ki-Hyeon	Wolverhampton Wanderers	Reading
11 Smith, Paul	Southampton	Nottingham Forest
14 Sodje, Samuel	Brentford	Reading
10 St Ledger-Hall, Sean P.	Peterborough United	Preston North End
19 Togwell, Samuel J.	Crystal Palace	Barnsley
5 Turner, Michael T.	Brentford	Hull City
10 Walton, Simon W.	Leeds United	Charlton Athletic
5 Wright-Phillips, Bradley E.	Manchester City	Southampton
12 Zakuani, Gabriel A.	Leyton Orient	Fulham

TEMPORARY TRANSFERS

27 Clarke, Darrell J. – Hartlepool United – Rochdale; 19 Forte, Jonathan – Sheffield United – Doncaster Rovers; 29 Graham, David – Sheffield Wednesday – Bradford City; 26 Grant, Anthony P.S. – Chelsea – Wycombe Wanderers; 14 Griffin, Charles – Wycombe Wanderers – Forest Green Rovers; 27 Heywood, Matthew S. – Bristol City – Brentford; 5 Howard, Timothy M. – Manchester United – Everton; 20 Hurst, Kevan – Sheffield United – Chesterfield; 11 Johnson, Glen M.C. – Chelsea – Portsmouth; 22 Kirkland, Christopher E. – Liverpool – Wigan Athletic; 31 Muamba, Fabrice – Arsenal – Birmingham City; 30 Nade, Raphael – Carlisle United – Weymouth; 3 Owen, Gareth J. – Oldham Athletic – Stockport County; 28 Parker, Ben B.C. – Leeds United – Bradford City; 27 Partridge, David W. – Bristol City – Leyton Orient; 28 Ravenhill, Richard J. – Doncaster Rovers – Chester City; 21 Roberts, Dale – Nottingham Forest – Alfreton Town; 17 Ross, Ian – Sheffield United – Notts County; 10 Wiseman, Scott N.K. – Hull City – Rotherham United

AUGUST 2006

29 Agogo, Manuel	Bristol Rovers	Nottingham Forest
9 Arca, Julio A.	Sunderland	Middlesbrough
2 Barker, Shaun	Rotherham United	Blackpool
7 Birchall, Chris	Port Vale	Coventry City
10 Blackstock, Dexter A.	Southampton	Queens Park Rangers
15 Boyce, Emmerson O.	Crystal Palace	Wigan Athletic
31 Bridges, Michael	Carlisle United	Hull City
3 Bruce, Alex	Birmingham City	Ipswich Town
31 Burgess, Benjamin K.	Hull City	Blackpool
29 Bywater, Stephen	West Ham United	Derby County
1 Carrick, Michael	Tottenham Hotspur	Manchester United
31 Chimbonda, Pascal	Wigan Athletic	Tottenham Hotspur
8 Clarke, Clive	West Ham United	Sunderland
2 Clarke, Peter M.	Blackpool	Southend United
11 Cogan, Barry	Millwall	Barnet
3 Cole, Andrew A.	Manchester City	Portsmouth
31 Connolly, David J.	Wigan Athletic	Sunderland
31 Cotterill, David	Bristol City	Wigan Athletic
31 Douglas, Jonathan	Blackburn Rovers	Leeds United
31 Euell, Jason J.	Charlton Athletic	Middlesbrough
10 Faye, Amdy M.	Newcastle United	Charlton Athletic

24 Fenton, Nicholas L.	Doncaster Rovers	Grimsby Town
31 Forster, Nicholas	Ipswich Town	Hull City
31 Fuller, Ricardo	Southampton	Stoke City
24 Futcher, Benjamin P.	Grimsby Town	Peterborough United
18 Green, Robert P.	Norwich City	West Ham United
31 Green, Stuart	Hull City	Crystal Palace
11 Griffin, Adam	Oldham Athletic	Stockport County
4 Harding, Daniel A.	Leeds United	Ipswich Town
31 Harrold, Matthew	Yeovil Town	Southend United
18 Heywood, Matthew S.	Bristol City	Brentford
3 Higginbotham, Daniel J.	Southampton	Stoke City
31 Idiakez-Barkaiztegi, Inigo	Derby County	Southampton
4 Jaidi, Radhi B.A.	Bolton Wanderers	Birmingham City
15 James, David B.	Manchester City	Portsmouth
16 Jarrett, Albert O.	Brighton & Hove Albion	Watford
15 Joachim, Julian K.	Boston United	Darlington
17 Johnson, Jemal J.	Blackburn Rovers	Wolverhampton Wanderers
31 Jorgensen, Claus B.	Coventry City	Blackpool
31 Kavanagh, Graham A.	Wigan Athletic	Sunderland
31 Kazim-Richards, Colin	Brighton & Hove Albion	Sheffield United
31 Kilbane, Kevin	Everton	Wigan Athletic
25 Kyle, Kevin	Sunderland	Coventry City
31 Lambert, Rickie L.	Rochdale	Bristol Rovers
17 Lawrence, Dennis W.	Wrexham	Swansea City
2 Lawrence, Matthew J.	Millwall	Crystal Palace
11 Leacock, Dean	Fulham	Derby County
18 Liddle, Gary D.	Middlesbrough	Hartlepool United
4 Llewellyn, Christopher M.	Hartlepool United	Wrexham
31 Lynch, Mark J.	Hull City	Yeovil Town
16 Makin, Christopher	Reading	Southampton
31 Malbranque, Steed	Fulham	Tottenham Hotspur
31 McKenzie, Leon M.	Norwich City	Coventry City
30 McLeod, Kevin A.	Swansea City	Colchester United
10 McShane, Paul D.	Manchester United	West Bromwich Albion
17 McSheffrey, Gary	Coventry City	Birmingham City
30 Mellor, Neil A.	Liverpool	Preston North End
31 Miller, Liam W.	Manchester United	Sunderland
16 Morrell, Andrew J.	Coventry City	Blackpool
31 Morris, Ian	Leeds United	Scunthorpe United
31 Murray, Adam D.	Carlisle United	Torquay United
25 Parkin, Sam	Ipswich Town	Luton Town
7 Paynter, William P.	Hull City	Southend United
22 Phillips, Kevin	Aston Villa	West Bromwich Albion
31 Ravenhill, Richard J.	Doncaster Rovers	Grimsby Town
8 Rehman, Zeshan	Fulham	Queens Park Rangers
17 Reid, Andrew M.	Tottenham Hotspur	Charlton Athletic
31 Robinson, Marvin L.S.C.	Macclesfield Town	Oxford United
7 Shittu, Daniel O.	Queens Park Rangers	Watford
4 Smith, Ryan C.M.	Arsenal	Derby County
10 Steele, Luke D.	Manchester United	West Bromwich Albion
31 Symes, Michael	Bradford City	Shrewsbury Town
3 Taylor, Jason J.F.	Oldham Athletic	Stockport County
11 Tolley, Jamie	Shrewsbury Town	Macclesfield Town
10 Traore, Djimi	Liverpool	Charlton Athletic
4 Viafara, John E.	Portsmouth	Southampton
4 Westlake, Ian J.	Ipswich Town	Leeds United

TEMPORARY TRANSFERS

3 Ainsworth, Lionel – Derby County – AFC Bournemouth; 11 Aspden, Curtis – Hull City – Scarborough; 25 Baldock, Samuel – Milton Keynes Dons – Arlesey Town; 31 Barker, Keith H.D. – Blackburn Rovers – Rochdale; 4 Bendtner, Nicklas – Arsenal – Birmingham City; 2 Best, Leon J. – Southampton – AFC Bournemouth; 10 Birch, Gary S. – Lincoln City – Tamworth; 5 Birchall, Chris – Port Vale – Coventry City; 11 Bonner, Tom E. – Northampton Town – Nuneaton Borough; 11 Bostwick, Michael – Millwall – Crawley Town; 18 Boulding, Rory J. – Mansfield Town – Ilkeston Town; 12 Bywater, Stephen – West Ham United – Derby County; 14 Carson, Scott P. – Liverpool – Charlton Athletic; 4 Batista, Ricardo – Fulham – Wycombe Wanderers; 31 Christie, Iyseden – Rochdale – Kidderminster Harriers; 10 Cowan, Gavin P. – Shrewsbury Town – Kidderminster Harriers; 18 Davison, Tony – Hartlepool United – Newcastle Blue Star; 31 Deakin, Graham – Walsall – Tamworth; 2 Doyle, Nathan – Derby County – Bradford City; 31 Eaden, Nicholas J. – Nottingham Forest – Lincoln City; 1 Edge, Lewis J.S. – Blackpool – Rochdale; 2 Elliot, Robert – Charlton Athletic – Accrington Stanley; 3 Evatt, Ian R. – Queens Park Rangers – Blackpool; 29 Federici, Adam – Reading – Bristol City; 30 Fernandez, Vincent – Nottingham Forest – Wycombe Wanderers; 25 Fitzgerald, Scott – Brentford – AFC Wimbledon; 10 Foster, Benjamin – Manchester United – Watford; 14 Fry, Adam G. – Peterborough United – Kettering Town; 24 Fry, Russell H. – Hull City – Halifax Town; 8 Gillett, Simon J. – Southampton – Blackpool; 18 Golbourne, Scott J. – Reading – Wycombe Wanderers; 17 Grabban, Lewis – Crystal Palace – Oldham Athletic; 1 Graham, Daniel A.W. – Middlesbrough – Blackpool; 31 Grant, Joel V. – Watford – Aldershot Town; 18 Hamer, Ben – Reading – Crawley Town; 31 Harding, Benjamin S. – Milton Keynes Dons – Aldershot Town; 31 Hennessey, Wayne R. – Wolverhampton Wanderers – Bristol City; 10 Henry, Leigh – Swindon Town – Weston-Super-Mare; 1 Hibbert, David J. – Preston North End – Rotherham United; 18 Hinchliffe, Ben – Preston North End – Kendal Town; 19 Hinshelwood, Paul – Brighton & Hove Albion – Burgess Hill Town; 2 Holmes, Lee D. – Derby County – Bradford City; 4 Horsfield, Geoffrey M. – Sheffield United – Leeds United; 4 Howarth, Christopher – Bolton Wanderers – Oldham Athletic; 25 Howe, Joe D.W. – Milton Keynes Dons – Walton & Hersham; 3 James, Kevin E. – Nottingham Forest – Yeovil Town; 4 Jones, Bradley – Middlesbrough – Sheffield Wednesday; 10 Kemp, Thomas J.R. – Lincoln City – Tamworth; 25 Knight, David – Middlesbrough – Oldham Athletic; 10 Kuszczak, Tomasz – West Bromwich Albion – Manchester United; 4 Larsson, Sebastien – Arsenal – Birmingham City; 1 Lowe, Keith S. – Wolverhampton Wanderers – Brighton & Hove Albion; 18 Lupoli, Arturo – Arsenal – Derby County; 22 Lynch, Mark J. – Hull City – Yeovil Town; 31 Macken, Jonathan P. – Crystal Palace – Ipswich Town; 18 Mannone, Vito – Arsenal – Barnsley; 10 Martin, Richard W. – Brighton & Hove Albion – Dorchester Town; 24 Matthews, Thomas M. – Hull City – Halifax Town; 23 McCallum, Gavin K. – Yeovil Town – Tamworth; 8 McCartney, George – Sunderland – West Ham United; 17 McIntosh, Martin W. – Huddersfield Town – Grimsby Town; 25 McShane, Luke – Peterborough United – Kettering Town; 4 Molango, Maheta – Brighton & Hove Albion – Oldham Athletic; 30 Moore, Stefan – Queens Park Rangers – Port Vale; 18 Murphy, Kieran – Milton Keynes Dons – Aylesbury United; 1 Murray, Glenn – Carlisle United – Stockport County; 18 Noble, Mark – West Ham United – Ipswich Town; 8 O'Donnell, Daniel – Liverpool – Crewe Alexandra; 18 Page, Sam T. – Milton Keynes Dons – Aylesbury United; 4 Paynter, William P. – Hull City – Southend United; 18 Pearce, Jason D. – Portsmouth – Bognor Regis Town; 4 Pittman, Jon P. – Nottingham Forest – Bury; 10 Pope, Thomas J. – Crewe Alexandra – Barrow; 15 Potter, Darren M. – Liverpool – Wolverhampton Wanderers; 18 Rae, Michael E. – Hartlepool United – Newcastle Blue Star; 18 Randolph, Darren E. – Charlton Athletic – Gillingham; 4 Roberts, Mark A. – Crewe Alexandra – Halifax Town; 31 Rossi, Giuseppe – Manchester United – Newcastle United; 31 Routledge, Wayne N.A. – Tottenham Hotspur – Fulham; 24 Sam, Lloyd E. – Charlton Athletic – Sheffield Wednesday;

24 Schmeichel, Kasper – Manchester City – Bury; 31 Sibierski, Antoine – Manchester City – Newcastle United; 4 Steele, Luke D. – Manchester United – Coventry City; 30 Stewart, Marcus P. – Bristol City – Yeovil Town; 3 Stokes, Tony – West Ham United – Brighton & Hove Albion; 9 Sutton, Richard A. – Crewe Alexandra – Stafford Rangers; 4 Symes, Michael – Bradford City – Shrewsbury Town; 23 Thomas, Bradley M. – Yeovil Town – Tamworth; 31 Tipton, Matthew – Bury – Macclesfield Town; 31 Todorov, Svetoslav – Portsmouth – Wigan Athletic; 31 Trotter, Liam – Ipswich Town – Millwall; 11 Wall, Stuart J. – Peterborough United – Alfreton Town; 18 Walton, Simon W. – Charlton Athletic – Ipswich Town; 18 Warlow, Adam T. – Crewe Alexandra – Witton Albion; 4 Warner, Anthony R. – Fulham – Leeds United; 18 Webb, Robert D. – Milton Keynes Dons – Thurrock; 31 Weir-Daley, Spencer J.A. – Nottingham Forest – Macclesfield Town; 1 Williams, Steven – Wycombe Wanderers – Forest Green Rovers; 10 Yeates, Mark – Tottenham Hotspur – Hull City

SEPTEMBER 2006

1 Cole, Ashley	Arsenal	Chelsea
1 Gallas, William	Chelsea	Arsenal
1 Huth, Robert	Chelsea	Middlesbrough
21 McCartney, George	Sunderland	West Ham United
23 Miller, Ian	Bury Town	Ipswich Town

TEMPORARY TRANSFERS

21 Bacon, Daniel S. – Lincoln City – Worksop Town; 22 Barker, Daniel G. – Yeovil Town – Clyst Rovers; 14 Boyle, Patrick – Everton – Norwich City; 12 Brooks, Alan – Millwall – Beckenham Town; 8 Camp, Lee M.J. – Derby County – Norwich City; 11 Carrington, Mark R. – Crewe Alexandra – Kidsgrove Athletic; 14 Cole, Mitchell J. – Southend United – Northampton Town; 11 Cox, Simon – Reading – Brentford; 15 Cross, Scott – Northampton Town – Bedford Town; 22 Davies, Scott – Reading – Yeading; 15 Davis, Liam L. – Coventry City – Peterborough United; 14 Doherty, Thomas – Queens Park Rangers – Wycombe Wanderers; 8 Duffy, Ayden – Lincoln City – Worksop Town; 5 Duncan, Derek – Leyton Orient – Lewes; 8 Elvins, Robert – West Bromwich Albion – Cheltenham Town; 8 Flinders, Scott L. – Crystal Palace – Gillingham; 29 Fortune-West, Leo P.D. – Rushden & Diamonds – Torquay United; 28 Fry, Adam G. – Peterborough United – Kings Lynn; 11 Gaynor, Ross – Millwall – Sutton United; 22 Green, Michael J. – Bristol Rovers – Mangotsfield United; 9 Griffin, Andrew – Portsmouth – Stoke City; 26 Haynes, Danny – Ipswich Town – Millwall; 29 Hendrie, Lee A. – Aston Villa – Stoke City; 11 Higgins, Ben – Grimsby Town – Eastwood Town; 8 Humphreys, Richie J. – Hartlepool United – Port Vale; 22 Hurst, Glynn – Shrewsbury Town – Bury; 11 Ide, Charles – Brentford – Sutton United; 1 Joseph-Dubois, Pierre – Reading – Tooting & Mitcham United; 28 Kirkup, Daniel – Carlisle United – Southport; 8 Laird, Scott – Plymouth Argyle – Tiverton Town; 22 Lawson, James P. – Southend United – Grimsby Town; 26 Ledgister, Joel – Southend United – Lewes; 29 Logan, Richard A. – Darlington – Gateshead; 8 Lowe, Keith S. – Wolverhampton Wanderers – Cheltenham Town; 19 McAliskey, John J. – Huddersfield Town – Wrexham; 1 McDonald, Marvin M. – Macclesfield Town – Mossley; 14 Mills, Daniel J. – Manchester City – Hull City; 22 Muckles, Neil – Hartlepool United – Newcastle Blue Star; 22 Neal, Christopher M. – Preston North End – Shrewsbury Town; 25 Page, Sam T. – Milton Keynes Dons – Hendon; 15 Poole, David A. – Yeovil Town – Stockport County; 12 Pooley, Dean – Millwall – Beckenham Town; 14 Ruddy, John T.G. – Everton – Stockport County; 8 Sheehan, Alan – Leicester City – Mansfield Town; 27 Smith, James D. – Chelsea – Queens Park Rangers; 12 Stock, Brian B. – Preston North End – Doncaster Rovers; 22 Streete, Theo – Derby County – Doncaster Rovers; 29 Stroud, David – Swindon Town – Basingstoke Town; 8 Thirlwell, Paul – Derby County – Carlisle United; 26 Thorpe, Anthony L. – Stevenage Borough – Grimsby Town; 15 Turner, Ben H. – Coventry City – Peterborough United; 15 Ujah, Curtis

– Reading – Slough Town; 27 Walker, James L.N. – Charlton Athletic – Bristol Rovers; 1 Watt, Philip A. – Lincoln City – Grantham Town; 29 Wells, Benjamin – Swindon Town – Basingstoke Town; 29 Wheater, David J. – Middlesbrough – Wolverhampton Wanderers; 14 Whittington, Michael J. – Cheltenham Town – Gloucester City; 29 Williams, Sam – Aston Villa – Brighton & Hove Albion

OCTOBER 2006

27 Kirkland, Christopher E. Liverpool Wigan Athletic

TEMPORARY TRANSFERS

13 Alcock, Craig – Yeovil Town – Weston-Super-Mare; 20 Ashdown, Jamie – Portsmouth – Norwich City; 17 Beattie, Warren S. – Preston North End – Kendal Town; 5 Beckford, Jermaine P. – Leeds United – Carlisle United; 10 Benyon, Elliot P. – Bristol City – St Albans City; 3 Bignot, Paul J. – Crewe Alexandra – Kidderminster Harriers; 27 Birch, Gary S. – Lincoln City – Hucknall Town; 9 Bowler, Michael – Stockport County – Witton Albion; 31 Brittain, Martin – Ipswich Town – Yeovil Town; 26 Broughton, Drewe O. – Chester City – Boston United; 6 Butler, Andrew P. – Scunthorpe United – Grimsby Town; 17 Byron, Michael J. – Hull City – Hinckley United; 10 Chamberlain, Miles – Grimsby Town – Eastwood Town; 14 Charles, Wesley D.D. – Brentford – Staines Town; 26 Chorley, Benjamin F. – Milton Keynes Dons – Gillingham; 6 Clapham, Joshua T. – Plymouth Argyle – Tiverton Town; 23 Clarke, Clive – Sunderland – Coventry City; 26 Clarke, Matthew P. – Bradford City – Darlington; 26 Corr, Barry – Sheffield Wednesday – Bristol City; 31 Cywka, Tomasz – Wigan Athletic – Oldham Athletic; 12 Delap, Rory J. – Sunderland – Stoke City; 12 Diao, Salif – Liverpool – Stoke City; 20 Dickinson, Carl – Stoke City – Blackpool; 9 Dodds, Louis – Leicester City – Northwich Victoria; 23 Duffy, Richard – Portsmouth – Coventry City; 2 Eaden, Nicholas J. – Nottingham Forest – Lincoln City; 13 Edge, Lewis J.S. – Blackpool – Bury; 13 Eustace, John M. – Stoke City – Hereford United; 5 Federici, Adam – Reading – Bristol City; 20 Ferris, Peter – Carlisle United – Workington; 6 Filan, John R. – Wigan Athletic – Doncaster Rovers; 5 Foster, Luke J. – Lincoln City – York City; 5 Gill, Benjamin D. – Watford – Cambridge United; 13 Gunn, Andrew P. – Oxford United – Didcot Town; 2 Harban, Thomas J. – Barnsley – Tamworth; 20 Harper, Kevin P. – Stoke City – Carlisle United; 27 Harper, Lee C.P. – Northampton Town – Milton Keynes Dons; 12 Horwood, Evan D. – Sheffield United – Darlington; 13 Hutchinson, Ben L.P. – Middlesbrough – Billingham Synthonia; 27 James, Kevin E. – Nottingham Forest – Grimsby Town; 16 Johnson, Adam – Middlesbrough – Leeds United; 27 Jones, Richard G. – Manchester United – Colchester United; 31 Keith, Joseph R. – Leyton Orient – Shrewsbury Town; 2 Laight, Ryan D. – Barnsley – Tamworth; 27 Legzdins, Adam R. – Birmingham City – Oldham Athletic; 12 Lloyd, Robert F. – Crewe Alexandra – Witton Albion; 26 MacKenzie, Neil – Scunthorpe United – Hereford United; 16 Mancienne, Michael I. – Chelsea – Queens Park Rangers; 9 Matthews, Thomas M. – Hull City – Halifax Town; 6 McCallum, Gavin K. – Yeovil Town – Tamworth; 31 McLean, Aaron – Grays Athletic – Peterborough United; 19 Meredith, James G. – Derby County – Cambridge United; 5 Moore, Stefan – Queens Park Rangers – Port Vale; 26 Mullings, Darren – Bristol Rovers – Clevedon Town; 27 Murphy, John J. – Blackpool – Macclesfield Town; 20 Murray, Glenn – Carlisle United – Rochdale; 9 Nelthorpe, Craig R. – Doncaster Rovers – Kidderminster Harriers; 19 Nyatanga, Lewin J. – Derby County – Sunderland; 20 O'Halloran, Stephen – Aston Villa – Wycombe Wanderers; 20 Osbourne, Isaac S. – Coventry City – Crewe Alexandra; 20 Paterson, Sean P. – Blackpool – Southport; 27 Pendleton, Chris – Luton Town – Hitchin Town; 12 Plummer, Christopher S. – Peterborough United – Grays Athletic; 20 Powell, Lewis – Bristol Rovers – Mangotsfield United; 2 Rae, Michael E. – Hartlepool United – Gateshead; 5 Reid, Reuben – Plymouth Argyle – Kidderminster Harriers; 10 Rhodes, Alexander – Brentford – Swindon Town; 17 Roberts, Gary – Accrington Stanley – Ipswich Town; 20 Schmeichel, Kasper – Manchester City –

Bury; 25 Shearer, Scott – Bristol Rovers – Shrewsbury Town; 2 Sherlock, James – Lincoln City – Ilkeston Town; 13 Sleath, Danny – Mansfield Town – Gresley Rovers; 20 Songo'o, Franck S. – Portsmouth – AFC Bournemouth; 27 Stack, Graham – Reading – Leeds United; 13 Stead, Jonathan – Sunderland – Derby County; 30 Steele, Lee A.J. – Leyton Orient – Chester City; 27 Tait, Paul – Boston United – Southport; 20 Taylor, Andrew – Blackburn Rovers – Crewe Alexandra; 21 Thelwell, Alton A. – Hull City – Leyton Orient; 6 Thomas, Bradley M. – Yeovil Town – Tamworth; 25 Thompson, John – Nottingham Forest – Tranmere Rovers; 6 Till, Peter – Birmingham City – Leyton Orient; 13 Tillen, Joseph E. – Milton Keynes Dons – Thurrock; 12 Ventre, Daniel – Accrington Stanley – Southport; 16 Welsh, Andrew P.D. – Sunderland – Leicester City; 7 Whing, Andrew J. – Coventry City – Brighton & Hove Albion; 31 Wiles, Simon P. – Blackpool – Macclesfield Town; 12 Wright, Alan – Sheffield United – Leeds United; 12 Wright, Nicholas – Birmingham City – Bristol City

NOVEMBER 2006

9 Sibierski, Antoine	Manchester City	Newcastle United

TEMPORARY TRANSFERS

23 Albrighton, Mark – Boston United – Darlington; 23 Andrews, Wayne M.A. – Coventry City – Sheffield Wednesday; 23 Arnau – Sunderland – Southend United; 14 Atkinson, Robert – Barnsley – Halifax Town; 3 Bacon, Daniel S. – Lincoln City – Worksop Town; 23 Bains, Rikki L. – Accrington Stanley – Leek Town; 23 Barlow, Matthew J. – Oldham Athletic – Stafford Rangers; 6 Barrett, Zach – Luton Town – Kettering Town; 2 Bastians, Felix – Nottingham Forest – Northwich Victoria; 17 Bates, Matthew D. – Middlesbrough – Ipswich Town; 15 Beechers, Billy J. – Oxford United – Oxford City; 23 Begovic, Asmir – Portsmouth – Macclesfield Town; 23 Berger, Patrik – Aston Villa – Stoke City; 3 Bertrand, Ryan D. – Chelsea – AFC Bournemouth; 23 Best, Leon J. – Southampton – Yeovil Town; 22 Birchall, Adam S. – Mansfield Town – Barnet; 23 Birley, Matthew – Birmingham City – Lincoln City; 16 Black, Thomas R. – Crystal Palace – Bradford City; 22 Blinkhorn, Matthew D. – Blackpool – Bury; 1 Bowditch, Dean – Ipswich Town – Brighton & Hove Albion; 16 Brown, David A. – Accrington Stanley – Burton Albion; 23 Burns, Jamie D. – Blackpool – Morecambe; 21 Butler, Paul J. – Leeds United – Milton Keynes Dons; 14 Chadwick, Luke H. – Stoke City – Norwich City; 2 Collins, Neill – Sunderland – Wolverhampton Wanderers; 23 Comyn-Platt, Charlie – Swindon Town – Grays Athletic; 23 Connolly, Matthew T. – Arsenal – AFC Bournemouth; 23 Constable, James A. – Walsall – Kidderminster Harriers; 3 Cork, Jack F.P. – Chelsea – AFC Bournemouth; 3 Cousins, Mark – Colchester United – Yeading; 17 Coutts, James R. – AFC Bournemouth – Grays Athletic; 22 Cox, Simon – Reading – Brentford; 8 Cranie, Martin J. – Southampton – Yeovil Town; 7 Critchell, Kyle A.R. – Southampton – Torquay United; 8 Crossley, Mark G. – Fulham – Sheffield Wednesday; 23 Currie, Darren – Ipswich Town – Coventry City; 17 Davies, Robert – West Bromwich Albion – Kidderminster Harriers; 23 Dillon, John G. – Crewe Alexandra – Leigh RMI; 22 Doherty, Sean – Accrington Stanley – Southport; 23 Donnelly, Ciaran – Blackpool – Southport; 22 Dubourdeau, Francois – Accrington Stanley – Southport; 3 Duffy, Darryl A. – Hull City – Hartlepool United; 23 Dugdale, Adam – Crewe Alexandra – Accrington Stanley; 23 Ehiogu, Ugochuku – Middlesbrough – Leeds United; 23 Ephraim, Hogan – West Ham United – Colchester United; 23 Fernandez, Vincent – Nottingham Forest – Blackpool; 10 Fitzgerald, Scott – Brentford – AFC Wimbledon; 23 Fortune, Clayton A. – Leyton Orient – Port Vale; 6 Fortune-West, Leo P.D. – Rushden & Diamonds – Shrewsbury Town; 23 Fulop, Marton – Tottenham Hotspur – Sunderland; 8 Gardner, Ross – Nottingham Forest – Port Vale; 22 Gillett, Simon J. – Southampton – AFC Bournemouth; 3 Gleeson, Stephen M. – Wolverhampton Wanderers – Stockport County; 8 Gregan, Sean M. – Leeds United – Oldham Athletic; 23 Griffiths, Anthony J. – Doncaster Rovers – Darlington; 23 Guttridge, Luke – Southend United – Leyton Orient; 3 Hannigan, Thomas J. – Notts County –

Alfreton Town; 9 Healy, Colin – Barnsley – Bradford City; 9 Heath, Matthew P. – Coventry City – Leeds United; 16 Heslop, Simon – Barnsley – Tamworth; 23 Hicks, Rodney D. – Peterborough United – Kings Lynn; 23 Hinchliffe, Ben – Preston North End – Kendal Town; 3 Howell, Luke A. – Gillingham – Folkestone Invicta; 3 Hughes, Mark A. – Thurrock – Chesterfield; 23 Jalal, Shwan S. – Woking – Sheffield Wednesday; 10 Janes, Alex – Darlington – Whitby Town; 2 Jarrett, Jason L. – Preston North End – Hull City; 23 John, Alistair A. – Charlton Athletic – Brighton & Hove Albion; 16 Johnson, Bradley – Northampton Town – Stevenage Borough; 17 Jones, David F.L. – Manchester United – Derby County; 14 Joynes, Nathan – Barnsley – Halifax Town; 23 Kamara, Sheku – Watford – Grays Athletic; 23 Kandol, Tresor O. – Barnet – Leeds United; 2 Kane, Anthony M. – Blackburn Rovers – Stockport County; 2 Kennedy, Jason – Middlesbrough – Boston United; 23 Kiely, Dean L. – Portsmouth – Luton Town; 16 Kightly, Michael J. – Grays Athletic – Wolverhampton Wanderers; 17 Kiraly, Gabor F. – Crystal Palace – West Ham United; 22 Kirkup, Daniel – Carlisle United – Southport; 22 Krause, James – Ipswich Town – Carlisle United; 18 Lawrence, Liam – Sunderland – Stoke City; 3 Leary, Michael – Luton Town – Torquay United; 16 Lee, Charlie – Tottenham Hotspur – Millwall; 2 Lonergan, Andrew – Preston North End – Swindon Town; 20 Mancienne, Michael I. – Chelsea – Queens Park Rangers; 23 Mannix, David – Liverpool – Accrington Stanley; 7 McArdle, Rory A. – Sheffield Wednesday – Rochdale; 23 McCallum, Gavin K. – Yeovil Town – Crawley Town; 23 McCann, Grant S. – Cheltenham Town – Barnsley; 17 McCormack, Alan – Preston North End – Southend United; 23 McIndoe, Michael – Barnsley – Wolverhampton Wanderers; 24 McLeod, Mark – Darlington – Workington; 13 McMahon, Daryl – Leyton Orient – Notts County; 3 McShane, Luke – Peterborough United – Worksop Town; 3 Miller, Ian – Ipswich Town – Boston United; 14 Miller, Thomas W. – Sunderland – Preston North End; 23 Mocquet, William – Sunderland – Rochdale; 23 Monkhouse, Andrew W. – Swindon Town – Hartlepool United; 23 Morgan, Craig – Milton Keynes Dons – Peterborough United; 10 Munday, John – Queens Park Rangers – Hendon; 17 Murphy, Kieran – Milton Keynes Dons – Maidenhead United; 16 Needham, Liam P. – Notts County – Gainsborough Trinity; 17 Nelthorpe, Craig R. – Doncaster Rovers – Gateshead; 23 Nicholson, Shane M. – Chesterfield – Lincoln City; 16 Nicholson, Stuart I. – West Bromwich Albion – Bristol Rovers; 10 Onibuje, Fola – Swindon Town – Brentford; 21 Paterson, Sean P. – Blackpool – Southport; 23 Patterson, Martin – Stoke City – Grimsby Town; 8 Pearce, Jason D. – Portsmouth – Bognor Regis Town; 15 Peters, Ryan V. – Brentford – Crawley Town; 3 Platt, Conal J. – AFC Bournemouth – Morecambe; 17 Plummer, Christopher S. – Peterborough United – Rushden & Diamonds; 23 Poke, Michael H. – Southampton – Woking; 15 Pollitt, Michael F. – Wigan Athletic – Ipswich Town; 23 Pulis, Anthony J. – Stoke City – Grimsby Town; 23 Reid, Kyel – West Ham United – Barnsley; 3 Richards, Justin D. – Peterborough United – Grays Athletic; 3 Robertson, Jordan – Sheffield United – Torquay United; 22 Rowson, David – Darlington – Boston United; 23 Semple, Ryan D. – Lincoln City – Chester City; 17 Slabber, Jamie – Grays Athletic – Oxford United; 3 Smith, Andrew W. – Preston North End – Cheltenham Town; 1 Smith, James D. – Chelsea – Queens Park Rangers; 16 Smith, Jay A. – Southend United – Notts County; 28 Sullivan, Neil – Leeds United – Doncaster Rovers; 23 Till, Peter – Birmingham City – Grimsby Town; 23 Timlin, Michael – Fulham – Swindon Town; 23 Treacy, Keith P. – Blackburn Rovers – Stockport County; 22 Turnbull, Stephen – Hartlepool United – Bury; 16 Turner, Iain R. – Everton – Crystal Palace; 23 Walker, James L.N. – Charlton Athletic – Leyton Orient; 3 Wallis, Jonathan – Hereford United – Dover Athletic; 23 Wallwork, Ronald – West Bromwich Albion – Barnsley; 9 Webb, Robert D. – Milton Keynes Dons – Fisher Athletic; 8 Whalley, Shaun – Witton Albion – Accrington Stanley; 3 Whittington, Michael J. – Cheltenham Town – Gloucester City; 23 Wilkinson, Andrew G. – Stoke City – Blackpool; 23 Wright, Nicholas – Birmingham City – Northampton Town; 23 Wright, Thomas – Barnsley – Walsall.

DECEMBER 2006

29 Elder, Nathan	Billericay Town	Brighton & Hove Albion

TEMPORARY TRANSFERS

29 Abbey, Nathanael – Torquay United – Brentford; 8 Allanson, Ashley G. – Scunthorpe United – Farsley Celtic; 8 Barnes, Oliver J.P. – Bristol Rovers – Gloucester City; 1 Beattie, Warren S. – Preston North End – Lancaster City; 1 Breach, Christopher B. – Brighton & Hove Albion – Bognor Regis Town; 8 Brill, Dean M. – Luton Town – Gillingham; 21 Cave-Brown, Andrew – Norwich City – King's Lynn; 30 Cecila Batista, Ricardo J. – Fulham – Wycombe Wanderers; 1 Coo, Cavell S. – Crewe Alexandra – Woodley Sports; 29 Cresswell, Ryan – Sheffield United – Ilkeston Town; 8 Cross, Scott – Northampton Town – Basingstoke Town; 28 Curtis, Thomas D. – Notts County – Nuneaton Borough; 1 Duffy, Ayden – Lincoln City – Worksop Town; 21 Fisk, Andrew – Norwich City – Kings Lynn; 5 Fry, Russell H. – Hull City – Hinckley United; 22 Green, Liam T. – Doncaster Rovers – Guiseley; 29 Hall, Ryan – Crystal Palace – Lewes; 7 Hendrie, Lee A. – Aston Villa – Stoke City; 30 Horwood, Evan D. – Sheffield United – Darlington; 8 Jones, Lee – Blackpool – Bury; 14 Kiraly, Gabor F. – Crystal Palace – Aston Villa; 16 Logan, Richard A. – Darlington – Durham City; 31 McParland, Anthony – Barnsley – Wycombe Wanderers; 15 Miller, Shaun R. – Crewe Alexandra – Witton Albion; 22 Murphy, Kieran – Milton Keynes Dons – Hendon; 20 Peacock, Anthony L. – Darlington – Blyth Spartans; 22 Rachubka, Paul S. – Huddersfield Town – Peterborough United; 29 Serrant, Ryan P. – Leeds United – Guiseley; 8 Smeeton, Jake – Yeovil Town – Chard Town; 1 Smith, Nicholas – Bradford City – Farsley Celtic; 22 Steele, Luke D. – West Bromwich Albion – Coventry City; 20 Thornton, Dean – Wycombe Wanderers – Banbury United; 29 Vaughan, James – Chester City – Droylsden; 7 Wilkinson, Alistair B. – Hull City – Harrogate Town; 8 Wilson, Lawrie – Colchester United – Welling United

JANUARY 2007

22 Abbott, Pawel T.H.	Huddersfield Town	Swansea City
3 Akinbiyi, Adeola P.	Sheffield United	Burnley
2 Alnwick, Ben	Sunderland	Tottenham Hotspur
5 Barker, Richard I.	Mansfield Town	Hartlepool United
31 Beardsley, Christopher K.	Mansfield Town	Rushden & Diamonds
27 Betsy, Kevin	Wycombe Wanderers	Bristol City
31 Billy, Christopher A.	Carlisle United	Halifax Town
4 Birchall, Adam S.	Mansfield Town	Barnet
18 Bisan-Etame Mayer, Laurean	Arsenal	Portsmouth
29 Blackett, Shane J.	Dagenham & Redbridge	Peterborough United
31 Blundell, Gregg	Chester City	Darlington
5 Boa Morte, Luis	Fulham	West Ham United
29 Bougherra, Madjid	Sheffield Wednesday	Charlton Athletic
8 Boyd, George	Stevenage Borough	Peterborough United
29 Brammer, David	Stoke City	Millwall
11 Brown, Christopher	Sunderland	Norwich City
30 Brown, Scott	Bristol City	Cheltenham Town
30 Burns, Jamie D.	Blackpool	Morecambe
31 Caldwell, Stephen	Sunderland	Burnley
30 Chambers, Luke	Northampton Town	Nottingham Forest
16 Clarke, Leon M.	Wolverhampton Wanderers	Sheffield Wednesday
26 Cole, Mitchell J.	Southend United	Stevenage Borough
5 Collins, Neill	Sunderland	Wolverhampton Wanderers
16 Connor, Paul	Leyton Orient	Cheltenham Town
30 Constable, James A.	Walsall	Kidderminster Harriers
9 Craney, Ian T.W.	Accrington Stanley	Swansea City
19 Critchell, Kyle A.R.	Southampton	Chesterfield

5 Crooks, Leon E.G.	Milton Keynes Dons	Wycombe Wanderers
18 Davenport, Calum R.P.	Tottenham Hotspur	West Ham United
24 Davies, Simon	Everton	Fulham
29 Delap, Rory J.	Sunderland	Stoke City
25 Diao, Salif	Liverpool	Stoke City
11 Dixon, Jonathan J.	Wycombe Wanderers	Aldershot Town
31 Doyle, Nathan	Derby County	Hull City
31 Duberry, Michael W.	Stoke City	Reading
17 Dunn, David J.I.	Birmingham City	Blackburn Rovers
2 Edwards, Akhenaton C.	Luton Town	Sunderland
3 Elding, Anthony L.	Boston United	Stockport County
3 Elliott, Robert J.	Sunderland	Leeds United
10 Fagan, Craig	Hull City	Derby County
19 Fallon, Rory M.	Swansea City	Plymouth Argyle
22 Ferguson, Darren	Wrexham	Peterborough United
31 Fleming, Craig	Norwich City	Rotherham United
26 Folan, Caleb C.	Chesterfield	Wigan Athletic
2 Fulop, Marton	Tottenham Hotspur	Sunderland
12 Grand, Simon	Carlisle United	Grimsby Town
31 Guttridge, Luke	Sheffield United	Leyton Orient
30 Halford, Gregory	Colchester United	Reading
9 Harris, Neil	Nottingham Forest	Millwall
31 Henderson, Wayne	Brighton & Hove Albion	Preston North End
31 Holland, Christopher J.	Boston United	Southport
8 Hoskins, William	Rotherham United	Watford
31 Hoult, Russell	West Bromwich Albion	Stoke City
31 Hughes, Mark A.	Everton	Northampton Town
3 Hurst, Glynn	Shrewsbury Town	Bury
11 Hyde, Micah A.	Burnley	Peterborough United
8 Ifill, Paul E.	Sheffield United	Crystal Palace
10 Jalal, Shwan S.	Woking	Peterborough United
29 John, Stern	Coventry City	Sunderland
30 Johnson, Jermaine	Bradford City	Sheffield Wednesday
3 Jones, David F.L.	Manchester United	Derby County
31 Jones, Lee	Blackpool	Darlington
25 Kabba, Steven	Sheffield United	Watford
4 Kandol, Tresor O.	Barnet	Leeds United
23 Keogh, Andrew D.	Scunthorpe United	Wolverhampton Wanderers
30 Kiely, Dean L.	Portsmouth	West Bromwich Albion
3 Kightly, Michael J.	Grays Athletic	Wolverhampton Wanderers
10 Kilgallon, Matthew	Leeds United	Sheffield United
22 Knight, Leon L.	Swansea City	Milton Keynes Dons
31 Larsson, Sebastien	Arsenal	Birmingham City
3 Lawrence, Liam	Sunderland	Stoke City
31 Lee-Barrett, Arran	Weymouth	Coventry City
5 Low, Joshua D.	Leicester City	Peterborough United
29 Mackail-Smith, Craig	Dagenham & Redbridge	Peterborough United
22 Martin, David	Dartford	Crystal Palace
19 Matteo, Dominic	Blackburn Rovers	Stoke City
11 Mattis, Dwayne A.	Bury	Barnsley
8 McArdle, Rory A.	Sheffield Wednesday	Rochdale
5 McCann, Grant S.	Cheltenham Town	Barnsley
3 McCormack, Alan	Preston North End	Southend United
29 McEveley, James	Blackburn Rovers	Derby County
26 McGleish, Scott	Northampton Town	Wycombe Wanderers
4 McIndoe, Michael	Barnsley	Wolverhampton Wanderers
1 McLean, Aaron	Grays Athletic	Peterborough United
29 McParland, Anthony	Barnsley	Wycombe Wanderers

12 Monkhouse, Andrew W.	Swindon Town	Hartlepool United
10 Murray, Adam D.	Torquay United	Macclesfield Town
4 Murray, Glenn	Carlisle United	Rochdale
23 Neill, Lucas E.	Blackburn Rovers	West Ham United
26 O'Grady, Christopher	Leicester City	Rotherham United
5 Onibuje, Fola	Swindon Town	Wycombe Wanderers
31 Painter, Marcos	Birmingham City	Swansea City
22 Perkins, David	Morecambe	Rochdale
3 Poole, David A.	Yeovil Town	Stockport County
19 Potter, Darren M.	Liverpool	Wolverhampton Wanderers
9 Quashie, Nigel F.	West Bromwich Albion	West Ham United
19 Ravenhill, Richard J.	Grimsby Town	Darlington
2 Roberts, Gareth M.	Accrington Stanley	Ipswich Town
17 Rodgers, Luke J.	Crewe Alexandra	Port Vale
9 Ryan, Tim J.	Boston United	Darlington
29 Smith, Jeff	Port Vale	Carlisle United
31 Southall, Leslie N.	Nottingham Forest	Gillingham
18 Spring, Matthew	Watford	Luton Town
11 Stead, Jonathan	Sunderland	Sheffield United
5 Steele, Lee A.J.	Leyton Orient	Chester City
9 Stirling, Jude B.	Peterborough United	Milton Keynes Dons
1 Stock, Brian B.	Preston North End	Doncaster Rovers
11 Stokes, Anthony	Arsenal	Sunderland
26 Tait, Paul	Boston United	Southport
26 Talbot, Andrew	Sheffield Wednesday	Luton Town
11 Teale, Gary	Wigan Athletic	Derby County
11 Thatcher, Benjamin D.	Manchester City	Charlton Athletic
3 Thelwell, Alton A.	Hull City	Leyton Orient
31 Thompson, David A.	Portsmouth	Bolton Wanderers
15 Tierney, Marc	Oldham Athletic	Shrewsbury Town
5 Till, Peter	Birmingham City	Grimsby Town
11 Traore, Djimi	Charlton Athletic	Portsmouth
5 Unsworth, David G.	Sheffield United	Wigan Athletic
31 Upson, Matthew J.	Birmingham City	West Ham United
19 Vaughan, Stephen J.	Chester City	Boston United
12 Vine, Rowan	Luton Town	Birmingham City
27 Walters, Jonathan R.	Chester City	Ipswich Town
31 Ward, Jamie J.	Torquay United	Chesterfield
23 Warnock, Stephen	Liverpool	Blackburn Rovers
10 Whalley, Shaun	Witton Albion	Accrington Stanley
11 Whittingham, Peter M.	Aston Villa	Cardiff City
31 Williams, Gareth J.G.	Leicester City	Watford
8 Williamson, Lee	Rotherham United	Watford
12 Wilson, Brian	Cheltenham Town	Bristol City
31 Woodards, Daniel M.	Exeter City	Crewe Alexandra
12 Wright, David	Wigan Athletic	Ipswich Town
19 Wright, Thomas	Barnsley	Darlington
31 Yeo, Simon J.	Peterborough United	Chester City
23 Young, Ashley	Watford	Aston Villa

TEMPORARY TRANSFERS

22 Ainsworth, Lionel – Derby County – Halifax Town; 31 Albrighton, Mark – Boston United – Rushden & Diamonds; 31 Andrews, Wayne M.H. – Coventry City – Bristol City; 11 Bailey, Matthew – Crewe Alexandra – Barrow; 25 Bakayoko, Zoumana – Millwall – Brighton & Hove Albion; 8 Bardsley, Phillip A. – Manchester United – Aston Villa; 7 Barnes, Oliver J.P. – Bristol Rovers – Gloucester City; 26 Bastians, Felix – Nottingham Forest – Halifax Town; 19 Beardsley, Christopher K. – Mansfield Town – Rushden & Diamonds;

19 Beckford, Jermaine P. – Leeds United – Scunthorpe United; 3 Bendtner, Niklas – Arsenal – Birmingham City; 25 Benyon, Elliot P. – Bristol City – Crawley Town; 18 Bertrand, Ryan D. – Chelsea – AFC Bournemouth; 2 Best, Leon J. – Southampton – Yeovil Town; 3 Blinkhorn, Matthew D. – Blackpool – Bury; 31 Brittain, Martin – Ipswich Town – Yeovil Town; 4 Broughton, Drewe O. – Chester City – Boston United; 12 Brown, Scott – Bristol City – Cheltenham Town; 26 Budtz, Jan – Doncaster Rovers – Wolverhampton Wanderers; 30 Burch, Robert K. – Tottenham Hotspur – Barnet; 5 Cadmore, Tom – Wycombe Wanderers – Yeading; 30 Canoville, Lee – Boston United – Shrewsbury Town; 10 Chorley, Benjamin F. – Milton Keynes Dons – Gillingham; 15 Connor, Paul – Leyton Orient – Cheltenham Town; 15 Cooke, Stephen L. – AFC Bournemouth – Torquay United; 29 Cork, Jack F.P. – Chelsea – AFC Bournemouth; 19 Coutts, James R. – AFC Bournemouth – Weymouth; 5 Crossley, Mark G. – Fulham – Sheffield Wednesday; 11 Dawson, Tony – Hartlepool United – Gateshead; 11 Diagouraga, Toumani – Watford – Rotherham United; 12 Dickson, Ryan A. – Plymouth Argyle – Torquay United; 12 Djemba-Djemba, Eric D. – Aston Villa – Burnley; 19 D'Laryea, Nathan A. – Manchester City – Macclesfield Town; 2 Doherty, Thomas – Queens Park Rangers – Wycombe Wanderers; 5 Donnelly, Ciaran – Blackpool – Southport; 5 Doyle, Nathan – Derby County – Bradford City; 19 Dugdale, Adam – Crewe Alexandra – Southport; 31 Dyer, Bruce A. – Doncaster Rovers – Bradford City; 30 Eaden, Nicholas J. – Nottingham Forest – Lincoln City; 8 Eckersley, Adam – Manchester United – Barnsley; 31 Edge, Lewis J.S. – Blackpool – Rochdale; 1 Elliott, Robert J. – Sunderland – Leeds United; 31 Elvins, Robert – West Bromwich Albion – York City; 5 Etuhu, Kelvin – Manchester City – Rochdale; 4 Evans, Jonathan – Manchester United – Sunderland; 2 Fernandez, Vincent – Nottingham Forest – Grays Athletic; 4 Ferris, Peter – Carlisle United – Kendal Town; 31 Fleetwood, Stuart K. – Hereford United – Accrington Stanley; 19 Fleming, Craig – Norwich City – Wolverhampton Wanderers; 20 Forte, Jonathan – Sheffield United – Doncaster Rovers; 12 Fortune, Clayton A. – Leyton Orient – Port Vale; 31 Fortune, Jonathan J. – Charlton Athletic – Stoke City; 1 Fortune-West, Leopold D. – Rushden & Diamonds – Shrewsbury Town; 5 Frost, Stef – Notts County – Gainsborough Trinity; 11 Gallen, Kevin A. – Queens Park Rangers – Plymouth Argyle; 19 Garner, Joseph A. – Blackburn Rovers – Carlisle United; 9 Gilbert, Peter – Sheffield Wednesday – Doncaster Rovers; 31 Gillett, Simon J. – Southampton – Blackpool; 12 Golbourne, Scott J. – Reading – Wycombe Wanderers; 1 Graham, Daniel A.W. – Middlesbrough – Carlisle United; 9 Grand, Simon – Carlisle United – Grimsby Town; 31 Grant, Gavin – Millwall – Grays Athletic; 19 Griffin, Andrew – Portsmouth – Stoke City; 26 Griffiths, Anthony J. – Doncaster Rovers – Stafford Rangers; 12 Gritton, Martin – Lincoln City – Mansfield Town; 25 Guinan, Stephen – Cheltenham Town – Hereford United; 26 Halliday, Matthew R. – Norwich City – Torquay United; 9 Harding, Benjamin S. – Milton Keynes Dons – Grays Athletic; 1 Hart, Charles J.J. – Manchester City – Tranmere Rovers; 10 Hayes, Jonathan – Reading – Milton Keynes Dons; 12 Henderson, Ian – Norwich City – Rotherham United; 12 Hennessey, Wayne R. – Wolverhampton Wanderers – Stockport County; 4 Hibbert, David J. – Preston North End – Bradford City; 31 Holgate, Ashan – Swindon Town – Macclesfield Town; 12 Holmes, Peter J. – Luton Town – Chesterfield; 31 Horsfield, Geoffrey M. – Sheffield United – Leicester City; 5 Hunt, James M. – Bristol Rovers – Grimsby Town; 31 Hurst, Kevan – Sheffield United – Scunthorpe United; 5 Ifill, Paul E. – Sheffield United – Crystal Palace; 26 Jarvis, Rossi – Norwich City – Torquay United; 31 Jennings, Steven J. – Tranmere Rovers – Hereford United; 8 Jones, Lee – Blackpool – Darlington; 8 Jones, Michael D. – Tranmere Rovers – Shrewsbury Town; 31 Joynes, Nathan – Barnsley – Boston United; 31 Kazmierczak, Przemyslaw – Bolton Wanderers – Accrington Stanley; 26 Kearns, Callum S.B. – Southend United – Chelmsford City; 12 King, Robert – Colchester United – Heybridge Swifts; 21 Krause, James – Ipswich Town – Carlisle United; 26 Laird, Marc – Manchester City – Northampton Town; 31 Lamb, Shaun A. – Bristol City – Forest Green Rovers; 22 Larrieu, Romain – Plymouth Argyle –

Gillingham; 5 Lawson, James P. – Southend United – AFC Bournemouth; 4 Leary, Michael – Luton Town – Brentford; 19 Ledgister, Joel – Southend United – Gravesend & Northfleet; 12 Lee-Barrett, Aaran – Weymouth – Coventry City; 19 Le Fondre, Adam – Stockport County – Rochdale; 11 Legzdins, Adam R. – Birmingham City – Macclesfield Town; 11 Logan, Carlos S. – Darlington – Bradford City; 5 Lowe, Keith S. – Wolverhampton Wanderers – Cheltenham Town; 19 Maidens, Michael D. – Hartlepool United – York City; 17 Mancienne, Michael I. – Chelsea – Queens Park Rangers; 26 Martin, Lee R. – Manchester United – Stoke City; 4 McDermott, David A. – Walsall – Halesowen Town; 22 McShane, Luke – Peterborough United – Gravesend & Northfleet; 31 Mears, Tyrone – West Ham United – Derby County; 24 Miller, Kevin – Southampton – Torquay United; 26 Mills, Matthew C. – Manchester City – Colchester United; 4 Murphy, John J. – Blackpool – Macclesfield Town; 18 Nicholson, Shane M. – Chesterfield – Boston United; 4 O'Cearuill, Joseph – Arsenal – Brighton & Hove Albion; 1 O'Donnell, Daniel – Liverpool – Crewe Alexandra; 1 O'Halloran, Stephen – Aston Villa – Wycombe Wanderers; 12 Oliver, Dean – Sheffield United – Hednesford Town; 1 Onibuje, Fola – Swindon Town – Wycombe Wanderers; 4 Opara, Lloyd – Peterborough United – Burton Albion; 31 Pacey, Robert – Doncaster Rovers – Gateshead; 26 Paine, Matthew S. – Colchester United – Thurrock; 4 Parker, Ben B.C. – Leeds United – Bradford City; 4 Partridge, David W. – Bristol City – Brentford; 31 Paterson, Sean P. – Blackpool – Southport; 2 Patterson, Martin – Stoke City – Grimsby Town; 31 Paynter, William P. – Southend United – Bradford City; 5 Pearce, Jason D. – Portsmouth – Woking; 11 Pollitt, Michael F. – Wigan Athletic – Burnley; 2 Price, Jamie – Birmingham City – Tamworth; 30 Prutton, David T. – Southampton – Nottingham Forest; 2 Pulis, Anthony J. – Stoke City – Grimsby Town; 26 Quigley, Damien – Bury – Hyde United; 31 Rachubka, Paul S. – Huddersfield Town – Blackpool; 16 Ravenhill, Richard J. – Grimsby Town – Darlington; 26 Reid, Reuben – Plymouth Argyle – Rochdale; 5 Rizzo, Nicholas A. – Milton Keynes Dons – Grimsby Town; 4 Roberts, Mark A. – Crewe Alexandra – Northwich Victoria; 26 Robertson, Jordan – Sheffield United – Northampton Town; 31 Rose, Daniel S. – Manchester United – Hereford United; 4 Rose, Daniel S. – Manchester United – Oxford United; 26 Ross, Ian – Sheffield United – Notts County; 29 Runstrom, Bjorn – Fulham – Luton Town; 5 Santos, George – Brighton & Hove Albion – Oxford United; 29 Shearer, Scott – Bristol Rovers – Shrewsbury Town; 29 Simpson, Daniel P. – Manchester United – Sunderland; 17 Sinclair, Scott A. – Chelsea – Plymouth Argyle; 25 Smart, Andrew J. – Macclesfield Town – Northwich Victoria; 25 Smith, Christian D. – Port Vale – Cambridge United; 4 Smith, Emmanuele – Walsall – Halesowen Town; 1 Smith, James D. – Chelsea – Queens Park Rangers; 26 Smith, Jeff – Port Vale – Carlisle United; 31 Smith, Johann – Bolton Wanderers – Carlisle United; 30 Song Billong, Alexandre D. – Arsenal – Charlton Athletic; 28 Stack, Graham – Reading – Leeds United; 4 Steele, Luke D. – West Bromwich Albion – Coventry City; 8 Stirling, Jude B. – Peterborough United – Milton Keynes Dons; 1 Strachan, Gavin D. – Hartlepool United – Peterborough United; 1 Sutton, Richard A. – Crewe Alexandra – Stafford Rangers; 31 Sweeney, Peter – Stoke City – Yeovil Town; 12 Talbot, Andrew – Sheffield Wednesday – Scunthorpe United; 31 Taylor, Andrew – Blackburn Rovers – Huddersfield Town; 5 Thomas, Bradley M. – Yeovil Town – Boston United; 3 Thomas, Sean I.S. – Queens Park Rangers – Bristol City; 31 Thompson, John – Nottingham Forest – Tranmere Rovers; 24 Thorpe, Anthony L. – Stevenage Borough – Grimsby Town; 3 Timlin, Michael – Fulham – Swindon Town; 1 Tipton, Matthew – Bury – Macclesfield Town; 4 Trotman, Neal – Oldham Athletic – Halifax Town; 2 Vaughan, Stephen J. – Chester City – Rochdale; 5 Walker, James L.N. – Charlton Athletic – Leyton Orient; 31 Ward, Nicholas – Queens Park Rangers – Brighton & Hove Albion; 26 Watt, Jerome – Northampton Town – Morecambe; 4 Webb, Daniel J. – Yeovil Town – Rushden & Diamonds; 1 Weir-Daley, Spencer J.A. – Nottingham Forest – Lincoln City; 1 Wheater, David J. – Middlesbrough – Darlington; 19 Whittington, Michael J. –

Cheltenham Town – Weston-Super-Mare; 31 Wiles, Simon P. – Blackpool – Macclesfield Town; 31 Wilkinson, Thomas – Lincoln City – Grays Athletic; 16 Wilson, Che C.A. – Southend United – Brentford; 5 Wilson, Marc D. – Portsmouth – AFC Bournemouth; 18 Windass, Dean – Braford City – Hull City; 17 Wiseman, Scott N.K. – Hull City – Rotherham United; 16 Wright, Thomas – Barnsley – Darlington; 31 Yeates, Mark – Tottenham Hotspur – Leicester City; 31 Youga, Kelly A. – Charlton Athletic – Bradford City; 30 Zakuani, Gabriel A. – Fulham – Stoke City

FEBRUARY 2007

14 Howard, Timothy M.	Manchester United	Everton

TEMPORARY TRANSFERS

22 Ainsworth, Lionel – Derby County – Wycombe Wanderers; 2 Alcock, Craig – Yeovil Town – Taunton Town; 1 Allen, Curtis L. – AFC Bournemouth – Leyton; 2 Barlow, Matthew J. – Oldham Athletic – Stalybridge Celtic; 23 Beattie, Warren S. – Preston North End – Hednesford Town; 23 Bedeau, Anthony C. – Walsall – Bury; 9 Benjamin, Trevor J. – Peterborough United – Boston United; 8 Blizzard, Dominic J. – Watford – Stockport County; 13 Camp, Lee M.J. – Derby County – Queens Park Rangers; 2 Chamberlain, Scott D. – Brighton & Hove Albion – Bognor Regis Town; 20 Charles, Anthony D. – Barnet – Aldershot Town; 9 Charles, Wesley D.D. – Brentford – Crawley Town; 2 Clarke, Tom – Yeovil Town – Taunton Town; 15 Cottrell, Adam – Millwall – Weymouth; 20 Dodds, Louis – Leicester City – Rochdale; 23 Duggan, Robert – Stoke City – Stafford Rangers; 20 Flinders, Scott L. – Crystal Palace – Brighton & Hove Albion; 17 Gilmartin, Rene – Walsall – Worcester City; 23 Harper, Kevin P. – Stoke City – Walsall; 23 Hays, Paul – Barnsley – Huddersfield Town; 23 Hinchliffe, Ben – Preston North End – Tranmere Rovers; 8 Hird, Adrian S. – Leeds United – Doncaster Rovers; 22 Hodge, Bryan – Blackburn Rovers – Mansfield Town; 16 Jarman, Nathan G. – Barnsley – Worksop Town; 16 Jarrett, Albert O. – Watford – Boston United; 8 Jarrett, Jason L. – Preston North End – Leicester City; 15 Jarvis, Ryan – Norwich City – Leyton Orient; 23 John, Alastair A. – Charlton Athletic – Torquay United; 19 Johnson, Jemal J. – Wolverhampton Wanderers – Leeds United; 9 Jones, Richard G. – Manchester United – Barnsley; 13 Kearney, Alan – Everton – Chester City; 23 Kempson, Darren – Crewe Alexandra – Bury; 16 Kerry, Lloyd – Sheffield United – Torquay United; 23 Knights, Darryl – Ipswich Town – Yeovil Town; 16 Law, Nicholas – Sheffield United – Yeovil Town; 16 Lawson, James P. – Southend United – Dagenham & Redbridge; 19 Le Fondre, Adam – Stockport County – Rochdale; 2 Malsom, Sam A. – Plymouth Argyle – Tiverton Town; 23 Martin, David E. – Liverpool – Accrington Stanley; 23 Martin, Richard W. – Brighton & Hove Albion – Folkestone Invicta; 16 McGoldrick, David J. – Southampton – AFC Bournemouth; 19 Meredith, James G. – Derby County – Chesterfield; 9 Miller, Ian – Ipswich Town – Darlington; 9 Moyo-Modise, Clive – Rochdale – Mossley; 8 Muirhead, Ben R. – Bradford City – Rochdale; 19 Nash, Carlo J. – Preston North End – Wigan Athletic; 22 Nicholls, Alex – Walsall – Burton Albion; 13 Nyatanga, Lewin J. – Derby County – Barnsley; 16 Oji, Samuel U.U. – Birmingham City – Bristol Rovers; 9 Page, Sam T. – Milton Keynes Dons – Cambridge United; 9 Pearce, Alex – Reading – Northampton Town; 15 Platt, Conal J. – AFC Bournemouth – Weymouth; 9 Richards, Gary – Colchester United – Brentford; 16 Robinson, Theo – Watford – Wealdstone; 2 Russell, James P. – Chelsea – Walton & Hersham; 1 Serrant, Ryan P. – Leeds United – Guiseley; 8 Sinclair, Frank M. – Burnley – Huddersfield Town; 2 Sleath, Danny – Mansfield Town – Alfreton Town; 25 Smart, Andrew J. – Macclesfield Town – Northwich Victoria; 16 Smith, Nicholas – Bradford City – North Ferriby United; 19 Sullivan, Neil – Leeds United – Doncaster Rovers; 23 Turnbull, Philip – Hartlepool United – Blyth Spartans; 23 Turner, Ben H. – Coventry City – Oldham Athletic; 23 Turner, Iain R. – Everton – Sheffield Wednesday; 8 Vidarsson, Bjarni T. – Everton – AFC Bournemouth; 19 Wallis, Jonathan – Hereford United –

Dagenham & Redbridge; 9 Watson, Steven C. – West Bromwich Albion – Sheffield Wednesday; 23 Whittington, Michael J. – Cheltenham Town – Mangotsfield United; 8 Wilkinson, David M. – Crystal Palace – Welling United; 16 Wright, Alan – Sheffield United – Doncaster Rovers; 9 Wroe, Nicholas – Barnsley – Bury

MARCH 2007

22 Barnes, Ashley L.	Paulton Rovers	Plymouth Argyle
12 Dickson, Christopher M.	Dulwich Hamlet	Charlton Athletic

TEMPORARY TRANSFERS

28 Alcock, Craig – Yeovil Town – Tiverton Town; 21 Aljofree, Hasney – Plymouth Arygle – Oldham Athletic; 29 Allanson, Ashley G. – Scunthorpe United – Farsley Celtic; 13 Antwi-Birago, Godwin – Liverpool – Accrington Stanley; 22 Arber, Mark A. – Peterborough United – Dagenham & Redbridge; 6 Ashikodi, Moses – Watford – Bradford City; 15 Ashton, Nathan – Charlton Athletic – Millwall; 22 Baldock, Samuel – Milton Keynes Dons – Walton & Hersham; 22 Bastians, Felix – Nottingham Forest – Gillingham; 22 Benjamin, Trevor J. – Peterborough United – Walsall; 2 Blinkhorn, Matthew D. – Blackpool – Morecambe; 22 Blizzard, Dominic J. – Watford – Milton Keynes Dons; 22 Boertien, Paul – Derby County – Chesterfield; 21 Brandon, Christopher – Huddersfield Town – Blackpool; 2 Brownlie, Royce – Swindon Town – Chester City; 18 Cadamarteri, Daniel L. – Leicester City – Doncaster Rovers; 1 Carlisle, Clarke J. – Watford – Luton Town; 22 Casement, Christopher – Ipswich Town – Millwall; 5 Chamberlain, Scott D. – Brighton & Hove Albion – Bognor Regis Town; 1 Clarke, Leon M. – Sheffield Wednesday – Oldham Athletic; 9 Clarke, Wayne J. – Darlington – Whitby Town; 22 Cole, Andrew A. – Portsmouth – Birmingham City; 19 Corr, Barry – Sheffield Wednesday – Swindon Town; 22 Coughlan, Graham – Sheffield Wednesday – Burnley; 3 Cowley, David K. – Southend United – Heybridge Swifts; 22 Cox, Simon – Reading – Northampton Town; 2 Cranie, Martin J. – Southampton – Yeovil Town; 15 Currie, Darren – Ipswich Town – Derby County; 9 Daniels, Charlie – Tottenham Hotspur – Chesterfield; 22 Dickson, Ryan A. – Plymouth Argyle – Torquay United; 22 Donnelly, Ciaran – Blackpool – Macclesfield Town; 29 Doughty, Philip M. – Blackpool – Barrow; 6 Elvins, Robert – West Bromwich Albion – York City; 9 Faulkner, James – Wycombe Wanderers – Leighton Town; 22 Ferrell, Andrew E. – Hereford United – Kidderminster Harriers; 16 Flynn, Christopher P. – Crewe Alexandra – Cambridge United; 10 Fortune, Jonathan J. – Charlton Athletic – Stoke City; 26 Gamble, Patrick J. – Nottingham Forest – York City; 15 Gleeson, Daniel E. – Notts County – Cambridge United; 21 Graham, David – Sheffield Wednesday – Torquay United; 4 Grant, Gavin – Millwall – Grays Athletic; 22 Gray, Michael – Blackburn Rovers – Leeds United; 22 Grimes, Ashley – Manchester City – Swindon Town; 4 Guinan, Stephen – Cheltenham Town – Hereford United; 3 Guthrie, Danny S. – Liverpool – Southampton; 30 Hall, Asa – Birmingham City – Ashford Town; 1 Hastings, John – Milton Keynes Dons – St Albans City; 22 Henry, James – Reading – Nottingham Forest; 22 Holmes, Peter J. – Luton Town – Lincoln City; 15 Hooper, Gary – Southend United – Leyton Orient; 21 Howarth, Christopher – Bolton Wanderers – Carlisle United; 22 Hughes, Craig – Colchester United – Cambridge United; 16 Hurst, Kevan – Sheffield United – Scunthorpe United; 10 Idiakez, Inigo – Southampton – Queens Park Rangers; 16 Idrizaj, Besian – Liverpool – Luton Town; 22 James, Craig P. – Darlington – York City; 22 James, Kevin E. – Nottingham Forest – Swindon Town; 21 Jarrett, Albert O. – Watford – Milton Keynes Dons; 13 Jarvis, Rossi – Norwich City – Rotherham United; 2 Jeffers, Francis – Blackburn Rovers – Ipswich Town; 6 Joynes, Nathan – Barnsley – Boston United; 1 Kazimierczak, Przemyslaw – Bolton Wanderers – Accrington Stanley; 1 Kennedy, Jason – Middlesbrough – Bury; 2 Kishishev, Radostin – Charlton Athletic – Leeds United; 1 Kovacs, Janos – Chesterfield – York City; 21 Laight, Ryan D. – Barnsley – Alfreton Town; 23 Laird, Scott – Plymouth Argyle – Tiverton Town; 4 Lamb,

Shaun A. – Bristol City – Forest Green Rovers; 6 Larrieu, Romain – Plymouth Argyle – Gillingham; 22 Lever, Christopher D. – Oldham Athletic – Stalybridge Celtic; 22 Lewis, Joseph – Norwich City – Stockport County; 22 Lynch, Ryan P. – Coventry City – Tamworth; 9 Marrison, Colin – Sheffield United – Hinckley United; 27 Massey, Alan – Wycombe Wanderers – Chesham United; 16 Masters, Clark J. – Brentford – AFC Wimbledon; 2 Maylett, Bradley – Boston United – Chester City; 2 McCallum, Gavin K. – Yeovil Town – Dorchester Town; 21 McNamee, Anthony – Watford – Crewe Alexandra; 22 McVeigh, Paul F. – Norwich City – Burnley; 16 Mendes, Albert J.H.A. – Notts County – Lincoln City; 9 Meynell, Rhys – Barnsley – Ossett Albion; 9 Michalik, Lubomir – Bolton Wanderers – Leeds United; 22 Mocquet, William – Sunderland – Bury; 22 Murphy, Kieran – Milton Keynes Dons – Walton & Hersham; 9 Newton, Shaun O. – West Ham United – Leicester City; 16 Nolan, Edward W. – Blackburn Rovers – Stockport County; 8 Olejnik, Robert – Aston Villa – Lincoln City; 1 Oliver, Dean – Sheffield United – Torquay United; 10 Parkin, Jonathan – Hull City – Stoke City; 22 Partridge, David W. – Bristol City – Swindon Town; 6 Paynter, William P. – Southend United – Bradford City; 16 Peltier, Lee A. – Liverpool – Hull City; 22 Peters, Ryan V. – Brentford – AFC Wimbledon; 2 Pettigrew, Adrian R.J. – Chelsea – Wycombe Wanderers; 22 Phillips, Mark I. – Millwall – Darlington; 22 Poole, Glenn S. – Grays Athletic – Rochdale; 22 Prendergast, Rory – Rochdale – Darlington; 22 Quinn, James S. – Northampton Town – Scunthorpe United; 22 Rankin, Isaiah – Grimsby Town – Macclesfield Town; 1 Rayner, Simon – Lincoln City – Torquay United; 22 Reet, Daniel – Mansfield Town – Rochdale; 22 Rehman, Zeshan – Queens Park Rangers – Brighton & Hove Albion; 22 Reid, Reuben – Plymouth Argyle – Torquay United; 9 Rhodes, Alexander – Brentford – Grays Athletic; 22 Ricketts, Rohan A. – Wolverhampton Wanderers – Queens Park Rangers; 22 Rizzo, Nicholas A. – Milton Keynes Dons – Chesterfield; 16 Rooney, Adam – Stoke City – Yeovil Town; 22 Roque, Miguel – Liverpool – Oldham Athletic; 10 Rosa, Denes – Wolverhampton Wanderers – Cheltenham Town; 2 Runstrom, Bjorn – Fulham – Luton Town; 12 Sam, Lloyd E. – Charlton Athletic – Southend United; 8 Serrant, Ryan P. – Leeds United – Farsley Celtic; 29 Sherlock, James – Lincoln City – Hinckley United; 7 Smith, Christian D. – Port Vale – Cambridge United; 21 Smith, Christian D. – Port Vale – Northwich Victoria; 21 Smith, Ryan C.M. – Derby County – Millwall; 12 Smith, Terence – Oldham Athletic – Southport; 16 Sodje, Samuel – Reading – West Bromwich Albion; 8 Songo'o, Franck S. – Portsmouth – Preston North End; 20 Summerfield, Luke – Plymouth Argyle – AFC Bournemouth; 5 Taylor, Andrew – Blackburn Rovers – Huddersfield Town; 8 Taylor, Scott J. – Milton Keynes Dons – Brentford; 20 Tonge, Dale – Barnsley – Gillingham; 2 Tonkin, Anthony – Yeovil Town – Grays Athletic; 1 Turnbull, Stephen – Hartlepool United – Rochdale; 9 Vaz Te, Ricardo J. – Bolton Wanderers – Hull City; 15 Walker, James L.N. – Charlton Athletic – Notts County; 9 Walker, Joshua – Middlesbrough – AFC Bournemouth; 2 Warner, Anthony R. – Fulham – Norwich City; 22 Watt, Jerome – Northampton Town – Salisbury City; 22 Watts, Adam – Fulham – Milton Keynes Dons; 12 Webb, Daniel J. – Yeovil Town – Woking; 22 Weir-Daley, Spencer J.A. – Nottingham Forest – Bradford City; 2 Welsh, Ishmael – Yeovil Town – Weymouth; 15 Weston, Myles – Charlton Athletic – Notts County; 2 Westwood, Ashley M. – Chester City – Swindon Town; 5 Wheater, David J. – Middlesbrough – Darlington; 20 White, Alan – Notts County – Peterborough United; 8 Wiggins-Thomas, Ruben S. – Chesterfield – Bradford Park Avenue; 6 Williams, Marvin T. – Millwall – Torquay United; 21 Williams, Robert I. – Barnsley – Blackpool; 9 Wilson, Bobby – Notts County – Hucknall Town; 22 Wilson, Che C.A. – Southend United – Rotherham United; 8 Wiseman, Scott N.K. – Hull City – Darlington; 26 Wood, Christopher H. – Mansfield Town – Ilkeston Town; 6 Worley, Harry J. – Chelsea – Doncaster Rovers; 16 Wright, Alan – Sheffield United – Nottingham Forest; 30 Wright, Nicholas – Birmingham City – Ashford Town; 8 Youga, Kelly A. – Charlton Athletic – Bradford City; 21 Zebroski, Christopher – Millwall – Oxford United

APRIL 2007

TEMPORARY TRANSFERS

8 Hart, Charles J.J. – Manchester City – Blackpool; 19 Royce, Simon E. – Queens Park Rangers – Gillingham; 21 Ruddy, John T.G. – Everton – Bristol City.

MAY 2007

29 Bale, Gareth	Southampton	Tottenham Hotspur
8 Daniel, Colin	Eastwood Town	Crewe Alexandra
29 Jackson, Matthew A.	Wigan Athletic	Watford
29 Jones, William K.	Exeter City	Crewe Alexandra
18 Jutkiewicz, Lucas I.P.	Swindon Town	Everton
18 Muamba, Fabrice	Arsenal	Birmingham City
30 Poom, Mart	Arsenal	Watford
29 Schumacher, Steven T.	Bradford City	Crewe Alexandra
21 Varney, Luke I.	Crewe Alexandra	Charlton Athletic

TEMPORARY TRANSFERS

8 Blizzard, Dominic J. – Watford – Milton Keynes Dons; 8 Currie, Darren – Ipswich Town – Derby County; 7 Eaden, Nicholas J. – Nottingham Forest – Lincoln City; 8 Hayes, Jonathan – Reading – Milton Keynes Dons; 9 Jarrett, Albert O. – Watford – Milton Keynes Dons; 14 Neal, Christopher M. – Preston North End – Morecambe; 6 Roque, Miguel – Liverpool – Oldham Athletic; 8 Watts, Adam – Fulham – Milton Keynes Dons; 10 Wright, Alan – Sheffield United – Nottingham Forest

FOREIGN TRANSFERS 2006–2007

JULY 2006	*From*	*To*
14 Assou-Ekotto, Benoit	Lens	Tottenham Hotspur
20 Aurelio, Fabio	Valencia	Liverpool
17 Ballack, Michael	Bayern Munich	Chelsea
12 Berbatov, Dimitar	Leverkusen	Tottenham Hotspur
28 Corradi, Bernardo	Valencia	Manchester City
7 Dabo, Ousmane	Lazio	Manchester City
13 Gonzalez, Mark	Albacete	Liverpool
10 Hilario	Nacional	Chelsea
13 Kalou, Salomon	Feyenoord	Chelsea
21 Landzaat, Denny	AZ	Wigan Athletic
18 Mikel, Jon O.	Manchester United/Lyn	Chelsea
6 Nade, Christopher	Troyes	Sheffield United
14 Paletta, Gabriel A.	Atletico Banfield	Liverpool
4 Shevchenko, Andriy	AC Milan	Chelsea
7 Zokora, Didier A.	St Etienne	Tottenham Hotspur

AUGUST 2006

31 Beasley, Damarcus	PSV Eindhoven	Manchester City
1 Bikey, Andre	Lokomotiv Moscow	Reading
23 Boulahrouz, Khalid	Hamburg	Chelsea
31 Denilson	Sao Paulo	Arsenal
30 Diawara, Souleymane	Sochaux	Charlton Athletic
31 Douala, Rudolphe	Sporting Lisbon	Portsmouth
30 Fernandes, Manuel	Benfica	Portsmouth, Everton
17 Isaksson, Andreas	Rennes	Manchester City
31 Julio Baptista	Real Madrid	Arsenal
31 Kranjcar, Niko	Hajduk Split	Portsmouth
18 Kuyt, Dirk	Feyenoord	Liverpool
31 Lastuvka, Jan	Shakhtar Donetsk	Fulham

25 Martins, Obafemi	Internazionale	Newcastle United
31 Mascherano, Javier	Corinthians	West Ham United
30 Mido	Roma	Tottenham Hotspur
2 McCarthy, Benni	Porto	Blackburn Rovers
10 Meite, Abdoulaye	Marseille	Bolton Wanderers
31 Nonda, Shabani	Roma	Blackburn Rovers
25 Ooijer, Andre A.M.	PSV Eindhoven	Blackburn Rovers
7 Pantsil, John	Hapoel Tel Aviv	West Ham United
30 Petrov, Stilian A.	Celtic	Aston Villa
31 Pouso, Omar	Penarol	Charlton Athletic
1 Priskin, Tamas	Gyor	Watford
7 Runstrom, Bjorn	Hammarby	Fulham
31 Tevez, Carlos	Corinthians	West Ham United
31 Teimourian, Andranik	Abu Moslem	Bolton Wanderers
10 Trabelsi, Hatem	Ajax	Manchester City
10 Valencia, Luis	Villarreal	Wigan Athletic
31 Webster, Andy	Hearts	Wigan Athletic
SEPTEMBER 2006		
12 Agathe, Didier	Celtic	Aston Villa
8 Teimourian, Andranik	Aboo Moslem	Bolton Wanderers
OCTOBER 2006		
1 El Zhar, Nabil	St Etienne	Liverpool
JANUARY 2007		
31 Aghahowa, Julius	Shakhtar Donetsk	Wigan Athletic
2 Anderson	Santander	Everton
31 Arbeloa, Alvaro	La Coruna	Liverpool
31 Avinel, Cedric	Creteil	Watford
30 Berner, Bruno	Basle	Blackburn Rovers
22 Carew, John	Lyon	Aston Villa
31 Cavalli, Johann	Istres	Watford
10 Dempsey, Clint	New England Rev	Fulham
12 Dong Fangzhou	Dalian Schide	Manchester United
31 Dong-Gook Lee	Pohang Steelers	Middlesbrough
1 Haestad, Kristofer	Start	Wigan Athletic
1 Insua, Emiliano	Boca Juniors	Liverpool
22 Kepa	Sevilla	West Ham United
31 Maloney, Shaun	Celtic	Aston Villa
25 Michalik, Lubomir	Senec	Bolton Wanderers
25 Samba, Christopher	Hertha Berlin	Blackburn Rovers
4 Montella, Vincenzo	Roma	Fulham
11 Mvuemba, Arnold	Rennes	Portsmouth
30 Onyewu, Oguchi	Standard Liege	Newcastle United
1 Padelli, Daniele	Sampdoria	Liverpool
23 Ricardo Rocha	Benfica	Tottenham Hotspur
31 Rinaldi, Douglas	Veranopolis	Watford
25 Shelton, Luton	Helsingborg	Sheffield United
2 Taarabt, Adel	Lens	Tottenham Hotspur
1 Zheng-Zhi	Shandong	Charlton Athletic
FEBRUARY 2007		
20 Cesar Martin	Levante	Bolton Wanderers
16 Mpenza, Emile	Hamburg	Manchester City

FA CUP REVIEW 2006–2007

The bare facts of the 2007 FA Cup final made more interesting reading than the reporting of a largely disappointing match itself, restored to the new Wembley. For the record Chelsea beat Manchester United 1-0 with a goal from Didier Drogba in the 116th minute during extra time. Chelsea had also won the last final at the old stadium in 2000 beating Aston Villa 1-0 with a goal from Roberto Di Matteo.

However, the final was not without its controversy. In the first half of extra time, United believed they had scored a legitimate goal. Ryan Giggs' close range shot was fielded by Petr Cech but the United captain's momentum carried him into the Chelsea goalkeeper and over the goal-line.

There was further debate over the incident because United claimed Giggs had been fouled by Michael Essien before his initial touch and a penalty should have been awarded. A free-kick for Chelsea might have been a more accurate decision. Clearly goal-line technology is a priority for the future.

Anyway it was not to be and Chelsea sealed it when John Obi Mikel fed Drogba who exchanged passes with Frank Lampard before clipping the ball over the advancing Edwin Van der Sar. It was Drogba's 33rd goal of the season and he had shaved a post earlier in the game with a free-kick.

But the final is never the entire story. The first round proper began with a goalless draw on a Friday night in November between Cheltenham Town and Scunthorpe United. The following day the remnants of the non-league grasped their opportunity, none more so than Basingstoke Town struggling at the foot of the Conference South who won 1-0 at Chesterfield.

Newly demoted Rushden & Diamonds learned the giant-killing quickly enough by beating Yeovil Town 3-1 and only Northwich Victoria shipping eight goals at Brighton & Hove Albion suffered severe damage. The following day Farsley Celtic held Milton Keynes Dons as did Weymouth against Bury before putting up a fine show in the replay before losing 4-3.

In the second round Rushden were put in their place by Tamworth and though Basingstoke held Aldershot Town they lost the home replay. But it was a Sunday best performance by Salisbury City in initially holding Nottingham Forest which captured the headlines.

Forest accounted for Charlton Athletic in the third round and Swansea City shook Sheffield United 3-0 at Bramall Lane. Chelsea were the top scorers beating Macclesfield Town 6-1 while Manchester United edged out Aston Villa 2-1. Arsenal surprised Liverpool winning 3-1 at Anfield.

The replay sensation was at Newcastle where the Magpies having drawn at Birmingham City collapsed late in the game and were beaten 5-1. Yet it was a short-lived success as City lost in round four to Reading.

A Wayne Rooney double helped United to another narrow win over Portsmouth and Chelsea took three goals off Forest without reply. Arsenal were held at the Emirates by Bolton Wanderers, before winning at Burnden Park in extra time. Middlesbrough needed penalties to dispose of Bristol City in their replay.

In the fifth round Boro found themselves unable to crack West Bromwich Albion at the Riverside in sharing four goals. Chelsea took four of their own off Norwich City and Reading held Manchester United at Old Trafford. Watford left it late prior to beating Ipswich Town and Plymouth Argyle were two goals better than Derby County. Once more Arsenal were indecisive at home and were held by Blackburn Rovers.

On the Sunday, Tottenham Hotspur won 4-0 at Fulham and Manchester City were successful 3-1 at Preston North End, but the shoot-out again proved to be Middlesbrough's replay saviour.

Three goals in the first six minutes put Manchester United in pole position at Reading who fought back to reduce their deficit to a single goal and a late effort from Blackburn ended Arsenal's involvement.

Sixth round and Boro continued their penchant for drawing. This time Manchester United earned a home replay from them. With three ties on Sunday the traditional quarter-final was unusual to say the least. Blackburn disposed of Manchester City 2-0 and Watford won at Plymouth, but Chelsea and Tottenham shared six goals at Stamford Bridge.

It took a Cristiano Ronaldo penalty to move United over Boro, but Chelsea prevailed 2-1 at White Hart Lane to surprise, surprise finding themselves missing each other in the semi-finals.

United won 4-1 against Watford, but Chelsea required extra time to overturn Blackburn. Thus to the final watched by 89,826 and remembered for the setting if little else.

THE FA CUP 2006–2007

FIRST ROUND

Cheltenham T	(0) 0	Scunthorpe U	(0) 0
Barrow	(0) 2	Bristol R	(1) 3
Bishop's Stortford	(2) 3	King's Lynn	(2) 5
Bournemouth	(2) 4	Boston U	(0) 0
Bradford C	(1) 4	Crewe Alex	(0) 0
Brentford	(0) 0	Doncaster R	(1) 1
Brighton & HA	(2) 8	Northwich Vic	(0) 0
Burton Alb	(0) 1	Tamworth	(0) 2
Chelmsford C	(0) 1	Aldershot T	(0) 1
Chesterfield	(0) 0	Basingstoke T	(1) 1
Clevedon T	(0) 1	Chester C	(1) 4
Exeter C	(1) 1	Stockport Co	(1) 2
Gainsborough T	(0) 1	Barnet	(1) 3
Gillingham	(1) 4	Bromley	(0) 1
Huddersfield T	(0) 0	Blackpool	(0) 1
Kettering T	(0) 3	Oldham Ath	(1) 4
Lewes	(0) 1	Darlington	(1) 4
Leyton Orient	(1) 2	Notts Co	(0) 1
Mansfield T	(1) 1	Accrington S	(0) 0
Morecambe	(1) 2	Kidderminster H	(0) 1
Newport Co	(0) 1	Swansea C	(3) 3
Northampton T	(0) 0	Grimsby T	(0) 0
Nottingham F	(3) 5	Yeading	(0) 0
Peterborough U	(1) 3	Rotherham U	(0) 0
Port Vale	(2) 2	Lincoln C	(0) 1
Rochdale	(0) 1	Hartlepool U	(1) 1
Rushden & D	(1) 3	Yeovil T	(0) 1
Salisbury C	(1) 3	Fleetwood T	(0) 0
Shrewsbury T	(0) 0	Hereford U	(0) 0
Stafford R	(0) 1	Maidenhead U	(0) 1
Swindon T	(1) 3	Carlisle U	(1) 1
Torquay U	(0) 2	Leatherhead	(1) 1
Tranmere R	(2) 4	Woking	(1) 2
Wrexham	(1) 1	Stevenage B	(0) 0
Wycombe W	(0) 2	Oxford U	(1) 1
York C	(0) 0	Bristol C	(0) 1
Farsley C	(0) 0	Milton Keynes D	(0) 0
Weymouth	(0) 2	Bury	(1) 2
Havant & Waterlooville	(0) 1	Millwall	(1) 2
(at Portsmouth.)			
Macclesfield T	(0) 0	Walsall	(0) 0

FIRST ROUND REPLAYS

Hartlepool U	(0) 0	Rochdale	(0) 0
(aet; Hartlepool U won 4-2 on penalties.)			
Aldershot T	(0) 2	Chelmsford C	(0) 0
Bury	(2) 4	Weymouth	(3) 3
Grimsby T	(0) 0	Northampton T	(1) 2
Hereford U	(0) 2	Shrewsbury T	(0) 0
Maidenhead U	(0) 0	Stafford R	(1) 2
Milton Keynes D	(0) 2	Farsley C	(0) 0
Scunthorpe U	(1) 2	Cheltenham T	(0) 0
Walsall	(0) 0	Macclesfield T	(0) 1

SECOND ROUND

Bradford C	(0) 0	Millwall	(0) 0
King's Lynn	(0) 0	Oldham Ath	(1) 2
Stockport Co	(1) 2	Wycombe W	(1) 1
Aldershot T	(0) 1	Basingstoke T	(1) 1
Barnet	(0) 4	Northampton T	(1) 1
Brighton & HA	(1) 3	Stafford R	(0) 0
Bristol R	(1) 1	Bournemouth	(0) 1
Bury	(0) 2	Chester C	(0) 2
Darlington	(1) 1	Swansea C	(1) 3
Hereford U	(1) 4	Port Vale	(0) 0
Macclesfield T	(1) 2	Hartlepool U	(1) 1
Mansfield T	(1) 1	Doncaster R	(0) 1
Milton Keynes D	(0) 0	Blackpool	(1) 2
Rushden & D	(0) 1	Tamworth	(1) 2
Scunthorpe U	(0) 0	Wrexham	(0) 2
Swindon T	(0) 1	Morecambe	(0) 0
Torquay U	(0) 1	Leyton Orient	(0) 1
Tranmere R	(1) 1	Peterborough U	(1) 2
Bristol C	(3) 4	Gillingham	(0) 3
Salisbury C	(0) 1	Nottingham F	(1) 1

SECOND ROUND REPLAYS

Basingstoke T	(1) 1	Aldershot T	(2) 3
Bournemouth	(0) 0	Bristol R	(0) 1
Chester C	(1) 1	Bury	(1) 3
(Chester C reinstated; Bury removed for fielding an ineligible player.)			
Doncaster R	(1) 2	Mansfield T	(0) 0
Leyton Orient	(0) 1	Torquay U	(0) 2
Millwall	(0) 1	Bradford C	(0) 0
(aet).			
Nottingham F	(0) 2	Salisbury C	(0) 0

THIRD ROUND

Bristol R	(1) 1	Hereford U	(0) 0
Stoke C	(0) 2	Millwall	(0) 0
Birmingham C	(1) 2	Newcastle U	(1) 2
Blackpool	(2) 4	Aldershot T	(1) 2
Bristol C	(3) 3	Coventry C	(2) 3
Chelsea	(2) 6	Macclesfield T	(1) 1
Chester C	(0) 0	Ipswich T	(0) 0
Crystal Palace	(1) 2	Swindon T	(0) 1
Derby Co	(1) 3	Wrexham	(0) 1
Doncaster R	(0) 0	Bolton W	(3) 4
Hull C	(0) 1	Middlesbrough	(0) 1
Leicester C	(0) 2	Fulham	(0) 2
Liverpool	(0) 1	Arsenal	(2) 3
Nottingham F	(2) 2	Charlton Ath	(0) 0
Peterborough U	(0) 1	Plymouth Arg	(0) 1
Portsmouth	(0) 2	Wigan Ath	(0) 1
Preston NE	(1) 1	Sunderland	(0) 0
QPR	(1) 2	Luton T	(1) 2
Sheffield U	(0) 0	Swansea C	(0) 3
Southend U	(0) 1	Barnsley	(0) 1
Tamworth	(0) 1	Norwich C	(2) 4
Torquay U	(0) 0	Southampton	(1) 2
WBA	(2) 3	Leeds U	(0) 1
Watford	(1) 4	Stockport Co	(1) 1
West Ham U	(0) 3	Brighton & HA	(0) 0

Wolverhampton W	(2) 2	Oldham Ath	(1) 2
Cardiff C	(0) 0	Tottenham H	(0) 0
Everton	(0) 1	Blackburn R	(3) 4
Manchester U	(0) 2	Aston Villa	(0) 1
Sheffield W	(0) 1	Manchester C	(0) 1
Barnet	(0) 2	Colchester U	(1) 1
Reading	(2) 3	Burnley	(0) 2

THIRD ROUND REPLAYS

Barnsley	(0) 0	Southend U	(1) 2
Coventry C	(0) 0	Bristol C	(1) 2
Ipswich T	(0) 1	Chester C	(0) 0
Manchester C	(1) 2	Sheffield W	(0) 1
Middlesbrough	(1) 4	Hull C	(0) 3
Oldham Ath	(0) 0	Wolverhampton W	(0) 2
Plymouth Arg	(2) 2	Peterborough U	(1) 1
Fulham	(1) 4	Leicester C	(2) 3
Newcastle U	(0) 1	Birmingham C	(2) 5
Tottenham H	(3) 4	Cardiff C	(0) 0
Luton T	(0) 1	QPR	(0) 0

FOURTH ROUND

Barnet	(0) 0	Plymouth Arg	(0) 2
Birmingham C	(0) 2	Reading	(2) 3
Blackpool	(0) 1	Norwich C	(1) 1
Bristol C	(0) 2	Middlesbrough	(2) 2
Crystal Palace	(0) 0	Preston NE	(0) 2
Derby Co	(0) 1	Bristol R	(0) 0
Fulham	(2) 3	Stoke C	(0) 0
Ipswich T	(0) 1	Swansea C	(0) 0
Luton T	(0) 0	Blackburn R	(2) 4
Manchester U	(0) 2	Portsmouth	(0) 1
Tottenham H	(1) 3	Southend U	(0) 1
West Ham U	(0) 0	Watford	(1) 1
Arsenal	(0) 1	Bolton W	(0) 1
Chelsea	(3) 3	Nottingham F	(0) 0
Manchester C	(2) 3	Southampton	(1) 1
Wolverhampton W	(0) 0	WBA	(1) 3

FOURTH ROUND REPLAYS

Middlesbrough	(0) 2	Bristol C	(1) 2
(aet; Middlesbrough won 5-4 on penalties.)			
Norwich C	(0) 3	Blackpool	(1) 2
(aet).			
Bolton W	(0) 1	Arsenal	(1) 3
(aet).			

FIFTH ROUND

Arsenal	(0) 0	Blackburn R	(0) 0
Chelsea	(1) 4	Norwich C	(0) 0
Manchester U	(1) 1	Reading	(0) 1
Middlesbrough	(2) 2	WBA	(1) 2
Plymouth Arg	(1) 2	Derby Co	(0) 0
Watford	(0) 1	Ipswich T	(0) 0
Fulham	(0) 0	Tottenham H	(1) 4
Preston NE	(1) 1	Manchester C	(1) 3

FIFTH ROUND REPLAYS

Reading	(1) 2	Manchester U	(3) 3

WBA	(1) 1	Middlesbrough	(0) 1
(aet; Middlesbrough won 5-4 on penalties.)			
Blackburn R	(0) 1	Arsenal	(0) 0

SIXTH ROUND

Middlesbrough	(1) 2	Manchester United	(1) 2
Blackburn Rovers	(1) 2	Manchester City	(0) 0
Chelsea	(1) 3	Tottenham Hotspur	(3) 3
Plymouth Arg	(0) 0	Watford	(1) 1

SIXTH ROUND REPLAYS

Manchester U	(0) 1	Middlesbrough	(0) 0
Tottenham H	(0) 1	Chelsea	(0) 2

SEMI-FINALS

Watford	(1) 1	Manchester U	(2) 4
Blackburn R	(0) 1	Chelsea	(1) 2
(aet.)			

THE FA CUP FINAL

Saturday, 19 May 2007

(at Wembley Stadium, attendance 89,826)

Chelsea (0) 1 Manchester U (0) 0

Chelsea: Cech; Paulo Ferreira, Bridge, Makelele, Terry, Essien, Wright-Phillips (Kalou), Lampard, Drogba, Mikel, Cole J (Robben) (Cole A).

Scorer: Drogba 116.

Manchester U: Van der Sar; Brown, Heinze, Carrick (O'Shea), Ferdinand, Vidic, Ronaldo, Scholes, Rooney, Fletcher (Smith), Giggs (Solskjaer).

(aet.)

Referee: S. Bennett (Kent).

PAST FA CUP FINALS

Details of one goalscorer is not available in 1878.

Year	Winner	Score	Runner-up	Score
1872	The Wanderers *Betts*	1	Royal Engineers	0
1873	The Wanderers *Kinnaird, Wollaston*	2	Oxford University	0
1874	Oxford University *Mackarness, Patton*	2	Royal Engineers	0
1875	Royal Engineers *Renny-Tailyour*	1	Old Etonians *Bonsor*	1*
Replay	Royal Engineers *Renny-Tailyour, Stafford*	2	Old Etonians	0
1876	The Wanderers *Edwards*	1	Old Etonians *Bonsor*	1*
Replay	The Wanderers *Wollaston, Hughes 2*	3	Old Etonians	0
1877	The Wanderers *Lindsay, Kenrick*	2	Oxford University *Kinnaird (og)*	1*
1878	The Wanderers *Kenrick 2, Kinnaird*	3	Royal Engineers *Unknown*	1
1879	Old Etonians *Clerke*	1	Clapham Rovers	0
1880	Clapham Rovers *Lloyd-Jones*	1	Oxford University	0
1881	Old Carthusians *Wyngard, Parry, Todd*	3	Old Etonians	0
1882	Old Etonians *Anderson*	1	Blackburn Rovers	0
1883	Blackburn Olympic *Costley, Matthews*	2	Old Etonians *Goodhart*	1*
1884	Blackburn Rovers *Sowerbutts, Forrest*	2	Queen's Park, Glasgow *Christie*	1
1885	Blackburn Rovers *Forrest, Brown*	2	Queen's Park, Glasgow	0
1886	Blackburn Rovers	0	West Bromwich Albion	0
Replay	Blackburn Rovers *Brown, Sowerbutts*	2	West Bromwich Albion	0
1887	Aston Villa *Hunter, Hodgetts*	2	West Bromwich Albion	0
1888	West Bromwich Albion *Woodhall, Bayliss*	2	Preston NE *Dewhurst*	1
1889	Preston NE *Dewhurst, J. Ross, Thompson*	3	Wolverhampton W	0
1890	Blackburn Rovers *Walton, John Southworth, Lofthouse, Townley 3*	6	Sheffield W *Bennett*	1
1891	Blackburn Rovers *Dewar, John Southworth, Townley*	3	Notts Co *Oswald*	1
1892	West Bromwich Albion *Geddes, Nicholls, Reynolds*	3	Aston Villa	0
1893	Wolverhampton W *Allen*	1	Everton	0

1894	Notts Co	4	Bolton W	1
	Watson, Logan 3		*Cassidy*	
1895	Aston Villa	1	West Bromwich Albion	0
	J. Devey			
1896	Sheffield W	2	Wolverhampton W	1
	Spiksley 2		*Black*	
1897	Aston Villa	3	Everton	2
	Campbell, Wheldon, Crabtree		*Boyle, Bell*	
1898	Nottingham F	3	Derby Co	1
	Cape 2, McPherson		*Bloomer*	
1899	Sheffield U	4	Derby Co	1
	Bennett, Beers, Almond, Priest		*Boag*	
1900	Bury	4	Southampton	0
	McLuckie 2, Wood, Plant			
1901	Tottenham H	2	Sheffield U	2
	Brown 2		*Bennett, Priest*	
Replay	Tottenham H	3	Sheffield U	1
	Cameron, Smith, Brown		*Priest*	
1902	Sheffield U	1	Southampton	1
	Common		*Wood*	
Replay	Sheffield U	2	Southampton	1
	Hedley, Barnes		*Brown*	
1903	Bury	6	Derby Co	0
	Ross, Sagar, Leeming 2, Wood, Plant			
1904	Manchester C	1	Bolton W	0
	Meredith			
1905	Aston Villa	2	Newcastle U	0
	Hampton 2			
1906	Everton	1	Newcastle U	0
	Young			
1907	Sheffield W	2	Everton	1
	Stewart, Simpson		*Sharp*	
1908	Wolverhampton W	3	Newcastle U	1
	Hunt, Hedley, Harrison		*Howey*	
1909	Manchester U	1	Bristol C	0
	A. Turnbull			
1910	Newcastle U	1	Barnsley	1
	Rutherford		*Tufnell*	
Replay	Newcastle U	2	Barnsley	0
	Shepherd 2 (1 pen)			
1911	Bradford C	0	Newcastle U	0
Replay	Bradford C	1	Newcastle U	0
	Speirs			
1912	Barnsley	0	West Bromwich Albion	0
Replay	Barnsley	1	West Bromwich Albion	0*
	Tufnell			
1913	Aston Villa	1	Sunderland	0
	Barber			
1914	Burnley	1	Liverpool	0
	Freeman			
1915	Sheffield U	3	Chelsea	0
	Simmons, Masterman, Kitchen			

Year	Winner		Runner-up	
1920	Aston Villa *Kirton*	1	Huddersfield T	0*
1921	Tottenham H *Dimmock*	1	Wolverhampton W	0
1922	Huddersfield T *Smith (pen)*	1	Preston NE	0
1923	Bolton W *Jack, J.R. Smith*	2	West Ham U	0
1924	Newcastle U *Harris, Seymour*	2	Aston Villa	0
1925	Sheffield U *Tunstall*	1	Cardiff C	0
1926	Bolton W *Jack*	1	Manchester C	0
1927	Cardiff C *Ferguson*	1	Arsenal	0
1928	Blackburn Rovers *Roscamp 2, McLean*	3	Huddersfield T *A. Jackson*	1
1929	Bolton W *Butler, Blackmore*	2	Portsmouth	0
1930	Arsenal *James, Lambert*	2	Huddersfield T	0
1931	West Bromwich Albion *W.G. Richardson 2*	2	Birmingham *Bradford*	1
1932	Newcastle U *Allen 2*	2	Arsenal *John*	1
1933	Everton *Stein, Dean, Dunn*	3	Manchester C	0
1934	Manchester C *Tilson 2*	2	Portsmouth *Rutherford*	1
1935	Sheffield W *Rimmer 2, Palethorpe, Hooper*	4	West Bromwich Albion *Boyes, Sandford*	2
1936	Arsenal *Drake*	1	Sheffield U	0
1937	Sunderland *Gurney, Carter, Burbanks*	3	Preston NE *F. O'Donnell*	1
1938	Preston NE *Mutch (pen)*	1	Huddersfield T	0*
1939	Portsmouth *Parker 2, Barlow, Anderson*	4	Wolverhampton W *Dorsett*	1
1946	Derby Co *H. Turner (og), Doherty, Stamps 2*	4	Charlton Ath *H. Turner*	1*
1947	Charlton Ath *Duffy*	1	Burnley	0*
1948	Manchester U *Rowley 2, Pearson, Anderson*	4	Blackpool *Shimwell (pen), Mortensen*	2
1949	Wolverhampton W *Pye 2, Smyth,*	3	Leicester C *Griffiths*	1
1950	Arsenal *Lewis 2*	2	Liverpool	0

1951	Newcastle U 2	Blackpool 0
	Milburn 2	
1952	Newcastle U 1	Arsenal 0
	G. Robledo	
1953	Blackpool...............................4	Bolton W 3
	Mortensen 3, Perry	*Lofthouse, Moir, Bell*
1954	West Bromwich Albion 3	Preston NE..2
	Allen 2 (1 pen), Griffin	*Morrison, Wayman*
1955	Newcastle U 3	Manchester C.......................................1
	Milburn, Mitchell, Hannah	*Johnstone*
1956	Manchester C........................3	Birmingham C.......................................1
	Hayes, Dyson, Johnstone	*Kinsey*
1957	Aston Villa 2	Manchester U 1
	McParland 2	*T. Taylor*
1958	Bolton W 2	Manchester U 0
	Lofthouse 2	
1959	Nottingham F........................2	Luton T...1
	Dwight, Wilson	*Pacey*
1960	Wolverhampton W...............3	Blackburn Rovers.................................0
	McGrath (og), Deeley 2	
1961	Tottenham H.........................2	Leicester C 0
	Smith, Dyson	
1962	Tottenham H.........................3	Burnley 1
	Greaves, Smith, Blanchflower (pen)	*Robson*
1963	Manchester U........................3	Leicester C 1
	Herd 2, Law	*Keyworth*
1964	West Ham U..........................3	Preston NE...2
	Sissons, Hurst, Boyce	*Holden, Dawson*
1965	Liverpool 2	Leeds U 1*
	Hunt, St John	*Bremner*
1966	Everton 3	Sheffield W...2
	Trebilcock 2, Temple	*McCalliog, Ford*
1967	Tottenham H.........................2	Chelsea 1
	Robertson, Saul	*Tambling*
1968	West Browmwich Albion 1	Everton 0*
	Astle	
1969	Manchester C........................1	Leicester C 0
	Young	
1970	Chelsea..................................2	Leeds U 2*
	Houseman, Hutchinson	*Charlton, Jones*
Replay	Chelsea..................................2	Leeds U 1*
	Osgood, Webb	*Jones*
1971	Arsenal..................................2	Liverpool 1*
	Kelly, George	*Heighway*
1972	Leeds U.................................1	Arsenal 0
	Clarke	
1973	Sunderland 1	Leeds U 0
	Porterfield	
1974	Liverpool 3	Newcastle 0
	Keegan 2, Heighway	
1975	West Ham U..........................2	Fulham..0
	A. Taylor 2	

1976	Southampton ....1 *Stokes*	Manchester U 0
1977	Manchester U ....2 *Pearson, J. Greenhoff*	Liverpool ....1 *Case*
1978	Ipswich T ....1 *Osborne*	Arsenal 0
1979	Arsenal ....3 *Talbot, Stapleton, Sunderland*	Manchester U ....2 *McQueen, McIlroy*
1980	West Ham U ....1 *Brooking*	Arsenal 0
1981	Tottenham H ....1 *Hutchison (og)*	Manchester C ....1* *Hutchison*
Replay	Totteham H ....3 *Villa 2, Crooks*	Manchester C ....2 *MacKenzie, Reeves (pen)*
1982	Tottenham H ....1 *Hoddle*	QPR ....1* *Fenwick*
Replay	Tottenham H ....1 *Hoddle (pen)*	QPR 0
1983	Manchester U ....2 *Stapleton, Wilkins*	Brighton & HA ....2* *Smith, Stevens*
Replay	Manchester U ....4 *Robson 2, Whiteside, Muhren (pen)*	Brighton & HA 0
1984	Everton ....2 *Sharp, Gray*	Watford 0
1985	Manchester U ....1 *Whiteside*	Everton 0*
1986	Liverpool ....3 *Rush 2, Johnston*	Everton ....1 *Lineker*
1987	Coventry C ....3 *Bennett, Houchen, Mabbutt (og)*	Tottenham H ....2* *C. Allen, Kilcline (og)*
1988	Wimbledon ....1 *Sanchez*	Liverpool 0
1989	Liverpool ....3 *Aldridge, Rush 2*	Everton ....2* *McCall 2*
1990	Manchester U ....3 *Robson, Hughes 2*	Crystal Palace ....3* *O'Reilly, Wright 2*
Replay	Manchester U ....1 *Martin*	Crystal Palace 0
1991	Tottenham H ....2 *Stewart, Walker (og)*	Nottingham F ....1* *Pearce*
1992	Liverpool ....2 *Thomas, Rush*	Sunderland 0
1993	Arsenal ....1 *Wright*	Sheffield W ....1* *Hirst*
Replay	Arsenal ....2 *Wright, Linighan*	Sheffield W ....1* *Waddle*
1994	Manchester U ....4 *Cantona 2 (2 pens), Hughes, McClair*	Chelsea 0
1995	Everton ....1 *Rideout*	Manchester U 0
1996	Manchester U ....1 *Cantona*	Liverpool 0

1997	Chelsea....................................2 *Di Matteo, Newton*	Middlesbrough....................................0
1998	Arsenal....................................2 *Overmars, Anelka*	Newcastle U 0
1999	Manchester U.........................2 *Sheringham, Scholes*	Newcastle U 0
2000	Chelsea....................................1 *Di Matteo*	Aston Villa 0
2001	Liverpool ....2 *Owen 2*	Arsenal ....1 *Ljungberg*
2002	Arsenal....................................2 *Parlour, Ljungberg*	Chelsea 0
2003	Arsenal....................................1 *Pires*	Southampton...0
2004	Manchester U.........................3 *Ronaldo, Van Nistelrooy 2 (1 pen)*	Millwall..0
2005	Arsenal....................................0 *Arsenal won 5-4 on penalties*	Manchester U 0*
2006	Liverpool ....3 *Cisse, Gerrard 2* *Liverpool won 3-1 on penalties*	West Ham U ....3* *Carragher (og), Ashton, Konchesky*
2007	Chelsea....................................1 *Drogba*	Manchester U 0*

**After extra time*

SUMMARY OF FA CUP WINNERS SINCE 1872

Club	Wins
Manchester United	11
Arsenal	10
Tottenham Hotspur	8
Aston Villa	7
Liverpool	7
Blackburn Rovers	6
Newcastle United	6
Everton	5
The Wanderers	5
West Bromwich Albion	5
Bolton Wanderers	4
Chelsea	4
Manchester City	4
Sheffield United	4
Wolverhampton Wanderers	4
Sheffield Wednesday	3
West Ham United	3
Bury	2
Nottingham Forest	2
Old Etonians	2
Preston North End	2
Sunderland	2
Barnsley	1
Blackburn Olympic	1
Blackpool	1
Bradford City	1
Burnley	1
Cardiff City	1
Charlton Athletic	1
Clapham Rovers	1
Coventry City	1
Derby County	1
Huddersfield Town	1
Ipswich Town	1
Leeds United	1
Notts County	1
Old Carthusians	1
Oxford University	1
Portsmouth	1
Royal Engineers	1
Southampton	1
Wimbledon	1

APPEARANCES IN FA CUP FINAL

Club	Appearances
Manchester United	18
Arsenal	17
Liverpool	13
Newcastle United	13
Everton	12
Aston Villa	10
West Bromwich Albion	10
Tottenham Hotspur	9
Blackburn Rovers	8
Chelsea	8
Manchester City	8
Wolverhampton Wanderers	8
Bolton Wanderers	7
Preston North End	7
Old Etonians	6
Sheffield United	6
Sheffield Wednesday	6
Huddersfield Town	5
The Wanderers	5
West Ham United	5
Derby County	4
Leeds United	4
Leicester City	4
Oxford University	4
Royal Engineers	4
Southampton	4
Sunderland	4
Blackpool	3
Burnley	3
Nottingham Forest	3
Portsmouth	3
Barnsley	2
Birmingham City	2
Bury	2
Cardiff City	2
Charlton Athletic	2
Clapham Rovers	2
Notts County	2
Queen's Park (Glasgow)	2
Blackburn Olympic	1
Bradford City	1
Brighton & Hove Albion	1
Bristol City	1
Coventry City	1
Crystal Palace	1
Fulham	1
Ipswich Town	1
Luton Town	1
Middlesbrough	1
Millwall	1
Old Carthusians	1
Queen's Park Rangers	1
Watford	1
Wimbledon	1

CARLING CUP REVIEW 2006–2007

The final minutes of the Carling Cup final sadly ensured that what had gone on beforehand would be largely forgotten. With around six minutes remaining of the Chelsea v Arsenal match at the Millennium Stadium in Cardiff, the proceedings erupted and inevitably interrupted with Chelsea leading 2-1.

John Obi Mikel tugged at Kolo Toure's shirt and then the altercation started with players involved and even the managers Jose Mourinho and Arsène Wenger doing their best to restore order.

In the end Mikel, Toure and Emmanuel Adebayor were sent off, Frank Lampard and Francesc Fabregas shown yellow cards. It took six minutes before play resumed, though only just over a couple of minutes of added time was played.

Yet it had all begun peacefully enough, Theo Walcott putting Arsenal ahead in 12 minutes, Didier Drogba equalising eight minutes later and heading the winning goal in the 84th minute.

The first round got off to an eyebrow-raising start when newly reinstalled Accrington Stanley beat Nottingham Forest. This was followed by Hereford United, from a similar background, doing even better in disposing of Coventry City with a Stuart Fleetwood hat-trick.

Six ties had to be decided by penalty kicks, four others being sorted out in extra time. Top scorers were Southampton beating Yeovil Town 5-2. Wrexham had a fine 4-1 away win to their credit at Sheffield Wednesday.

Enter the non-European Premier teams in the second round and the casualties mounted. Notts County won at Middlesbrough, Chesterfield had the better of Manchester City at Saltergate and Wycombe Wanderers won at Fulham. In addition Crewe Alexandra disposed of Wigan Athletic and only penalty kicks prevented Darlington surprising Reading at the Madejski Stadium and Accrington upsetting Watford at Vicarage Road.

The overseas contingent were paraded for the third round. Arsenal won at West Bromwich Albion, Chelsea accounted for Blackburn Rovers at Ewood Park with two goals of their own and Liverpool just edged a spirited Reading by the odd goal in seven. But Manchester United, albeit with a mixture of squad players were forced into extra time at Crewe.

Upsets were restricted to Birmingham winning at Sheffield United while Tottenham Hotspur took five goals off Milton Keynes Dons at the Hockey Stadium.

The outstanding achievement of round four concerned Manchester United with Cristiano Ronaldo and Wayne Rooney playing the full 90 minutes losing at Southend United to a Freddy Eastwood goal. One goal was enough for Arsenal at Everton and Liverpool at Birmingham, while Chelsea hit Aston Villa for four.

Chesterfield pressed Charlton Athletic the distance before succumbing to penalties and Wycombe finished Notts at Meadow Lane. Penalties enabled Newcastle United to return from Watford with relief and Spurs beat Port Vale 3-1.

Not even Christmas and the quarter-finals were completed – or nearly because fog on the Mersey caused Liverpool's tie with Arsenal to be postponed until the New Year. But there were still shocks. Wycombe won at Charlton and Southend pushed Spurs all the way at White Hart Lane into extra time. Chelsea left it late but won at Newcastle.

On Tuesday 9 January the rearranged tie at Anfield produced an astonishing feat of goalscoring, Arsenal running out winners of an incredible match 6-3. It was a personal scoring triumph for Julio Baptista who registered four of the Gunners' goals.

The following day Chelsea found themselves held in the first leg of their semi-final at Wycombe and in fact the second leg was completed even before Spurs met their north London neighbours for their first leg. This time Chelsea were four goals to the good.

Twenty-four hours later that man Julio Baptista scored a hat-trick of sorts, getting two for Arsenal and one for Tottenham with an own goal in a 2-2 draw. At the Emirates the game went into extra time before another own goal settled it for Arsenal.

Of course the Associate Members have their own competition, this time round the Johnstone's Paint Trophy with Conference teams not accepted. No extra time was to be played at all and penalties at the end of 90 minutes if the teams were level.

In the first round, five went to a shoot-out. Accrington and Blackpool shared eight goals in the second round but it still went to penalties, as did the 4-4 Northern quarter-final between Chesterfield and Chester City!

Doncaster Rovers recovered from two down against Crewe Alexandra to reach the final against Bristol Rovers who had won the Bristolian derby. In front of 59,024 at the Millennium Stadium, Rovers returned with a 3-2 win after extra time – the penalties having been excused.

CARLING CUP 2006–2007

FIRST ROUND

Accrington S	(0) 1	Nottingham F	(0) 0
Birmingham C	(0) 1	Shrewsbury T	(0) 0
Blackpool	(0) 2	Barnsley	(0) 2
(aet; Barnsley won 4-2 on penalties.)			
Bournemouth	(0) 1	Southend U	(1) 3
Bristol R	(0) 1	Luton T	(1) 1
(aet; Luton T won 5-3 on penalties.)			
Burnley	(0) 0	Hartlepool U	(0) 1
Bury	(0) 2	Sunderland	(0) 0
Cardiff C	(0) 0	Barnet	(1) 2
Carlisle U	(1) 1	Bradford C	(0) 1
(aet; Carlisle U won 4-3 on penalties.)			
Cheltenham T	(2) 2	Bristol C	(1) 1
Crystal Palace	(1) 1	Notts Co	(1) 2
Doncaster R	(0) 3	Rochdale	(1) 2
Grimsby T	(0) 0	Crewe Alex	(1) 3
Hereford U	(1) 3	Coventry C	(0) 1
Huddersfield T	(0) 0	Mansfield T	(1) 2
Hull C	(0) 2	Tranmere R	(1) 1
(aet.)			
Leeds U	(0) 1	Chester C	(0) 0
Leicester C	(1) 2	Macclesfield T	(0) 0
Millwall	(1) 2	Gillingham	(0) 1
Milton Keynes D	(0) 1	Colchester U	(0) 0
(aet.)			
Peterborough U	(1) 2	Ipswich T	(0) 2
(aet; Peterborough U won 4-2 on penalties.)			
Plymouth Arg	(0) 0	Walsall	(0) 1
QPR	(1) 3	Northampton T	(0) 2
Rotherham U	(0) 3	Oldham Ath	(1) 1
Scunthorpe U	(1) 4	Lincoln C	(0) 3
(aet.)			
Stockport Co	(0) 0	Derby Co	(1) 1
Stoke C	(1) 1	Darlington	(1) 2
Swansea C	(0) 2	Wycombe W	(0) 3
(aet.)			
Swindon T	(1) 2	Brentford	(2) 2
(aet; Brentford won 4-3 on penalties.)			
Brighton & HA	(0) 1	Boston U	(0) 0
Chesterfield	(0) 0	Wolverhampton W	(0) 0
(aet; Chesterfield won 6-5 on penalties.)			
Port Vale	(0) 2	Preston NE	(0) 1
Sheffield W	(0) 1	Wrexham	(2) 4
Southampton	(3) 5	Yeovil T	(1) 2
Torquay U	(0) 0	Norwich C	(0) 2
Leyton Orient	(0) 0	WBA	(1) 3

SECOND ROUND

Barnsley	(0) 1	Milton Keynes D	(1) 2
Birmingham C	(1) 4	Wrexham	(1) 1
Brentford	(0) 0	Luton T	(1) 3
Charlton Ath	(0) 1	Carlisle U	(0) 0
Crewe Alex	(1) 2	Wigan Ath	(0) 0
Hereford U	(0) 1	Leicester C	(1) 3

Hull C	(0) 0	Hartlepool U	(0) 0
(aet; Hull C won 3-2 on penalties.)			
Leeds U	(1) 3	Barnet	(0) 1
Mansfield T	(0) 1	Portsmouth	(2) 2
Millwall	(0) 0	Southampton	(2) 4
Peterborough U	(0) 1	Everton	(1) 2
Port Vale	(2) 3	QPR	(1) 2
Reading	(2) 3	Darlington	(2) 3
(aet; Reading won 4-2 on penalties.)			
Rotherham U	(1) 2	Norwich C	(1) 4
Sheffield U	(1) 1	Bury	(0) 0
Southend U	(0) 3	Brighton & HA	(0) 2
WBA	(0) 3	Cheltenham T	(1) 1
Walsall	(0) 1	Bolton W	(0) 3
Watford	(0) 0	Accrington Stanley	(0) 0
(aet; Watford 6-5 on penalties.)			
Chesterfield	(0) 2	Manchester C	(1) 1
Doncaster R	(2) 3	Derby Co	(0) 3
(aet; Doncaster R won 8-7 on penalties.)			
Fulham	(0) 1	Wycombe W	(2) 2
Middlesbrough	(0) 0	Notts Co	(1) 1
Scunthorpe U	(0) 1	Aston Villa	(1) 2

THIRD ROUND

Chesterfield	(0) 2	West Ham U	(1) 1
Everton	(2) 4	Luton T	(0) 0
Leeds U	(1) 1	Southend U	(2) 3
Leicester C	(1) 2	Aston Villa	(2) 3
Notts Co	(2) 2	Southampton	(0) 0
Port Vale	(0) 0	Norwich C	(0) 0
(aet; Port Vale won 3-2 on penalties.)			
Sheffield U	(1) 2	Birmingham C	(1) 4
WBA	(0) 0	Arsenal	(1) 2
Watford	(1) 2	Hull C	(0) 1
Wycombe W	(0) 2	Doncaster R	(0) 2
(aet; Wycombe W won 3-2 on penalties.)			
Blackburn R	(0) 0	Chelsea	(0) 2
Charlton Ath	(1) 1	Bolton W	(0) 0
Crewe Alex	(0) 1	Manchester U	(1) 2
Liverpool	(2) 4	Reading	(0) 3
Milton Keynes D	(0) 0	Tottenham H	(2) 5
Newcastle U	(0) 3	Portsmouth	(0) 0

FOURTH ROUND

Chesterfield	(1) 3	Charlton Ath	(1) 3
(aet; Charlton Ath won 4-3 on penalties.)			
Notts Co	(0) 0	Wycombe W	(0) 1
Southend U	(1) 1	Manchester U	(0) 0
Watford	(0) 2	Newcastle U	(1) 2
(aet; Newcastle U won 5-4 on penalties.)			
Birmingham C	(0) 0	Liverpool	(1) 1
Chelsea	(1) 4	Aston Villa	(0) 0
Everton	(0) 0	Arsenal	(0) 1
Tottenham H	(0) 3	Port Vale	(0) 1

QUARTER-FINALS

Charlton Ath	(0) 0	Wycombe W	(1) 1
Newcastle U	(0) 0	Chelsea	(0) 1
Tottenham H	(0) 1	Southend U	(0) 0

QUARTER-FINAL

Liverpool	(1) 3	Arsenal	(4) 6

SEMI-FINAL FIRST LEG

Wycombe W	(0) 1	Chelsea	(1) 1

SEMI-FINAL SECOND LEG

Chelsea	(2) 4	Wycombe W	(0) 0

SEMI-FINAL FIRST LEG

Tottenham H	(2) 2	Arsenal	(0) 2

SEMI-FINAL SECOND LEG

Arsenal *(aet.)*	(0) 3	Tottenham H	(0) 1

CARLING CUP FINAL

Sunday, 25 February 2007

(at Millennium Stadium, Cardiff, attendance 70,073)

Chelsea (1) 2 Arsenal (1) 1

Chelsea: Cech; Diarra, Bridge, Makelele (Robben), Terry (Mikel■), Ricardo Carvalho, Essien, Lampard, Drogba, Shevchenko (Kalou), Ballack.
Scorers: Drogba 20, 84.

Arsenal: Almunia; Hoyte, Traore (Eboue), Denilson, Toure■, Senderos, Walcott, Fabregas, Aliadiere (Adebayor■), Julio Baptista, Diaby (Hleb).
Scorer: Walcott 12.

Referee: H. Webb (South Yorkshire).

■ *Denotes player sent off.*

PAST LEAGUE CUP FINALS

Played as two legs up to 1966

Year	Winner	Score	Opponent	Score
1961	Rotherham U	2	Aston Villa	0
	Webster, Kirkman			
	Aston Villa	3	Rotherham U	0*
	O'Neill, Burrows, McParland			
1962	Rochdale	0	Norwich C	3
	Lythgoe 2, Punton			
	Norwich C	1	Rochdale	0
	Hill			
1963	Birmingham C	3	Aston Villa	1
	Leek 2, Bloomfield		*Thomson*	
	Aston Villa	0	Birmingham C	0
1964	Stoke C	1	Leicester C	1
	Bebbington		*Gibson*	
	Leicester C	3	Stoke C	2
	Stringfellow, Gibson, Riley		*Viollet, Kinnell*	
1965	Chelsea	3	Leicester C	2
	Tambling, Venables (pen), McCreadie		*Appleton, Goodfellow*	
	Leicester C	0	Chelsea	0
1966	West Ham U	2	WBA	1
	Moore, Byrne		*Astle*	
	WBA	4	West Ham U	1
	Kaye, Brown, Clark, Williams		*Peters*	
1967	QPR	3	WBA	2
	Morgan R, Marsh, Lazarus		*Clark C 2*	
1968	Leeds U	1	Arsenal	0
	Cooper			
1969	Swindon T	3	Arsenal	1*
	Smart, Rogers 2		*Gould*	
1970	Manchester C	2	WBA	1*
	Doyle, Pardoe		*Astle*	
1971	Tottenham H	2	Aston Villa	0
	Chivers 2			
1972	Chelsea	1	Stoke C	2
	Osgood		*Conroy, Eastham*	
1973	Tottenham H	1	Norwich C	0
	Coates			
1974	Wolverhampton W	2	Manchester C	1
	Hibbitt, Richards		*Bell*	
1975	Aston Villa	1	Norwich C	0
	Graydon			
1976	Manchester C	2	Newcastle U	1
	Barnes, Tueart		*Gowling*	
1977	Aston Villa	0	Everton	0
Replay	Aston Villa	1	Everton	1*
	Kenyon (og)		*Latchford*	

	Winner		Runner-up	
Replay	Aston Villa	3	Everton	2*
	Little 2, Nicholl		*Latchford, Lyons*	
1978	Nottingham F	0	Liverpool	0*
Replay	Nottingham F	1	Liverpool	0
	Robertson (pen)			
1979	Nottingham F	3	Southampton	2
	Birtles 2, Woodcock		*Peach, Holmes*	
1980	Wolverhampton W	1	Nottingham F	0
	Gray			
1981	Liverpool	1	West Ham U	1*
	Kennedy A		*Stewart (pen)*	
Replay	Liverpool	2	West Ham U	1
	Dalglish, Hansen		*Goddard*	
1982	Liverpool	3	Tottenham H	1*
	Whelan 2, Rush		*Archibald*	
1983	Liverpool	2	Manchester U	1*
	Kennedy A, Whelan		*Whiteside*	
1984	Liverpool	0	Everton	0*
Replay	Liverpool	1	Everton	0
	Souness			
1985	Norwich C	1	Sunderland	0
	Chisholm (og)			
1986	Oxford U	3	QPR	0
	Hebberd, Houghton, Charles			
1987	Arsenal	2	Liverpool	1
	Nicholas 2		*Rush*	
1988	Luton T	3	Arsenal	2
	Stein B 2, Wilson		*Hayes, Smith*	
1989	Nottingham F	3	Luton T	1
	Clough 2, Webb		*Harford*	
1990	Nottingham F	1	Oldham Ath	0
	Jemson			
1991	Sheffield W	1	Manchester U	0
	Sheridan			
1992	Manchester U	1	Nottingham F	0
	McClair			
1993	Arsenal	2	Sheffield W	1
	Merson, Morrow		*Harkes*	
1994	Aston Villa	3	Manchester U	1
	Atkinson, Saunders 2 (1 pen)		*Hughes*	
1995	Liverpool	2	Bolton W	1
	McManaman 2		*Thompson*	
1996	Aston Villa	3	Leeds U	0
	Milosevic, Taylor, Yorke			
1997	Leicester C	1	Middlesbrough	1*
	Heskey		*Ravanelli*	
Replay	Leicester C	1	Middlesbrough	0*
	Claridge			
1998	Chelsea	2	Middlesbrough	0*
	Sinclair, Di Matteo			

1999	Tottenham H....1 *Nielsen*	Leicester C....0
2000	Leicester C....2 *Elliott 2*	Tranmere R....1 *Kelly*
2001	Liverpool....1 *Fowler*	Birmingham C....1 *Purse (pen)*
Liverpool won 5-4 on penalties.		
2002	Blackburn....2 *Jansen, Cole*	Tottenham H....1 *Ziege*
2003	Liverpool....2 *Gerrard, Owen*	Manchester U....0
2004	Middlesbrough....2 *Job, Zenden (pen)*	Bolton W....1 *Davies*
2005	Chelsea....3 *Gerrard (og), Drogba, Kezman*	Liverpool....2* *Riise, Nunez*
2006	Manchester U....4 *Rooney 2, Saha, Ronaldo*	Wigan Ath....0
2007	Chelsea....2 *Drogba 2*	Arsenal....1 *Walcott*

**After extra time*

JOHNSTONE'S PAINT TROPHY 2006–2007

NORTHERN SECTION FIRST ROUND

Accrington S	(0) 1	Carlisle U	(1) 1
(Accrington S won 3-1 on penalties.)			
Bradford C	(0) 1	Scunthorpe U	(0) 2
Bury	(0) 0	Tranmere R	(1) 2
Hartlepool U	(2) 3	Rotherham U	(1) 1
Huddersfield T	(0) 1	Doncaster R	(1) 2
Lincoln C	(0) 0	Grimsby T	(0) 0
(Grimsby T won 5-3 on penalties.)			
Macclesfield T	(0) 0	Stockport Co	(0) 1
Wrexham	(0) 1	Rochdale	(1) 1
(Rochdale won 5-3 on penalties.)			

SOUTHERN SECTION FIRST ROUND

Brighton & HA	(1) 2	Boston U	(0) 0
Bristol R	(0) 1	Torquay U	(0) 0
Gillingham	(0) 1	Nottingham F	(1) 2
Hereford U	(0) 1	Shrewsbury T	(1) 2
Northampton T	(0) 0	Brentford	(0) 0
(Brentford won 4-2 on penalties.)			
Notts Co	(0) 0	Barnet	(1) 1
Walsall	(0) 1	Swansea C	(0) 1
(Swansea C won 4-3 on penalties.)			
Wycombe W	(1) 1	Swindon T	(0) 0

NORTHERN SECTION SECOND ROUND

Accrington S	(1) 4	Blackpool	(1) 4
(Accrington S won 4-2 on penalties.)			
Chester C	(1) 3	Stockport Co	(0) 0
Hartlepool U	(0) 1	Doncaster R	(0) 3
Mansfield T	(1) 3	Grimsby T	(0) 0
Oldham Ath	(0) 0	Chesterfield	(1) 1
Rochdale	(0) 1	Crewe Alex	(1) 1
(Crewe Alex won 2-0 on penalties.)			
Scunthorpe U	(0) 0	Port Vale	(0) 0
(Port Vale won 5-3 on penalties.)			
Tranmere R	(0) 0	Darlington	(0) 1

SOUTHERN SECTION SECOND ROUND

Brighton & HA	(2) 4	Milton Keynes D	(0) 1
Cheltenham T	(3) 3	Barnet	(1) 2
Leyton Orient	(0) 1	Bristol C	(0) 3
Millwall	(1) 2	Bournemouth	(0) 0
Nottingham F	(0) 2	Brentford	(1) 1
Peterborough U	(1) 1	Swansea C	(0) 0
Shrewsbury T	(0) 2	Yeovil T	(0) 1
Wycombe W	(0) 0	Bristol R	(1) 2

NORTHERN SECTION QUARTER-FINALS

Chesterfield	(2) 4	Chester C	(2) 4
(Chesterfield won 3-1 on penalties.)			
Darlington	(0) 1	Mansfield T	(0) 0
Doncaster R	(2) 2	Accrington S	(0) 0
Port Vale	(0) 2	Crewe Alex	(1) 3

SOUTHERN SECTION QUARTER-FINALS

Bristol R	(1) 1	Peterborough U	(0) 0
Cheltenham T	(1) 2	Shrewsbury T	(1) 3
Millwall	(1) 1	Brighton & HA	(0) 1
(Brighton & HA won 3-2 on penalties.)			
Nottingham F	(1) 2	Bristol C	(0) 2
(Bristol C won 4-2 on penalties.)			

NORTHERN SECTION SEMI-FINALS

Doncaster R	(0) 2	Darlington	(0) 0
Chesterfield	(1) 2	Crewe Alex	(1) 4

SOUTHERN SECTION SEMI-FINAL

Bristol C	(1) 2	Brighton & HA	(0) 0
Shrewsbury T	(0) 0	Bristol R	(0) 1

NORTHERN SECTION FINAL FIRST LEG

Crewe Alex	(0) 3	Doncaster R	(2) 3

NORTHERN SECTION FINAL SECOND LEG

Doncaster R	(0) 3	Crewe Alex	(2) 2

SOUTHERN SECTION FINAL FIRST LEG

Bristol C	(0) 0	Bristol R	(0) 0

SOUTHERN SECTION FINAL SECOND LEG

Bristol R	(0) 1	Bristol C	(0) 0

JOHNSTONE'S PAINT TROPHY FINAL

Sunday, 1 April 2007

(at Millennium Stadium, Cardiff, attendance 59,024)

Bristol R (0) 2 Doncaster R (2) 3

Bristol R: Phillips; Lescott, Carruthers, Campbell, Hinton, Elliott, Igoe (Sandell), Disley, Walker R (Nicholson), Lambert, Haldane (Lines).
Scorers: Walker R 49 (pen), Igoe 62.

Doncaster R: Sullivan; O'Connor, McDaid, Lockwood, Lee, Stock (Wilson), Coppinger, Green P, Heffernan, Price (Thornton), Forte (Guy).
Scorers: Forte 1, Heffernan 5, Lee 110.

(aet.)

Referee: G. Laws (Tyne & Wear).

FA CHARITY SHIELD WINNERS 1908–2006

Year	Match	Score
1908	Manchester U v QPR	4-0 after 1-1 draw
1909	Newcastle U v Northampton T	2-0
1910	Brighton v Aston Villa	1-0
1911	Manchester U v Swindon T	8-4
1912	Blackburn R v QPR	2-1
1913	Professionals v Amateurs	7-2
1920	Tottenham H v Burnley	2-0
1921	Huddersfield T v Liverpool	1-0
1922	Not played	
1923	Professionals v Amateurs	2-0
1924	Professionals v Amateurs	3-1
1925	Amateurs v Professionals	6-1
1926	Amateurs v Professionals	6-3
1927	Cardiff C v Corinthians	2-1
1928	Everton v Blackburn R	2-1
1929	Professionals v Amateurs	3-0
1930	Arsenal v Sheffield W	2-1
1931	Arsenal v WBA	1-0
1932	Everton v Newcastle U	5-3
1933	Arsenal v Everton	3-0
1934	Arsenal v Manchester C	4-0
1935	Sheffield W v Arsenal	1-0
1936	Sunderland v Arsenal	2-1
1937	Manchester C v Sunderland	2-0
1938	Arsenal v Preston NE	2-1
1948	Arsenal v Manchester U	4-3
1949	Portsmouth v Wolverhampton W	1-1*
1950	World Cup Team v Canadian Touring Team	4-2
1951	Tottenham H v Newcastle U	2-1
1952	Manchester U v Newcastle U	4-2
1953	Arsenal v Blackpool	3-1
1954	Wolverhampton W v WBA	4-4*
1955	Chelsea v Newcastle U	3-0
1956	Manchester U v Manchester C	1-0
1957	Manchester U v Aston Villa	4-0
1958	Bolton W v Wolverhampton W	4-1
1959	Wolverhampton W v Nottingham F	3-1
1960	Burnley v Wolverhampton W	2-2*
1961	Tottenham H v FA XI	3-2
1962	Tottenham H v Ipswich T	5-1
1963	Everton v Manchester U	4-0
1964	Liverpool v West Ham U	2-2*
1965	Manchester U v Liverpool	2-2*
1966	Liverpool v Everton	1-0
1967	Manchester U v Tottenham H	3-3*
1968	Manchester C v WBA	6-1
1969	Leeds U v Manchester C	2-1
1970	Everton v Chelsea	2-1
1971	Leicester C v Liverpool	1-0
1972	Manchester C v Aston Villa	1-0
1973	Burnley v Manchester C	1-0
1974	Liverpool† v Leeds U	1-1
1975	Derby Co v West Ham U	2-0
1976	Liverpool v Southampton	1-0
1977	Liverpool v Manchester U	0-0*
1978	Nottingham F v Ipswich T	5-0
1979	Liverpool v Arsenal	3-1
1980	Liverpool v West Ham U	1-0
1981	Aston Villa v Tottenham H	2-2*
1982	Liverpool v Tottenham H	1-0
1983	Manchester U v Liverpool	2-0
1984	Everton v Liverpool	1-0
1985	Everton v Manchester U	2-0
1986	Everton v Liverpool	1-1*
1987	Everton v Coventry C	1-0
1988	Liverpool v Wimbledon	2-1
1989	Liverpool v Arsenal	1-0
1990	Liverpool v Manchester U	1-1*
1991	Arsenal v Tottenham H	0-0*
1992	Leeds U v Liverpool	4-3
1993	Manchester U† v Arsenal	1-1
1994	Manchester U v Blackburn R	2-0
1995	Everton v Blackburn R	1-0
1996	Manchester U v Newcastle U	4-0
1997	Manchester U† v Chelsea	1-1
1998	Arsenal v Manchester U	3-0
1999	Arsenal v Manchester U	2-1
2000	Chelsea v Manchester U	2-0
2001	Liverpool v Manchester U	2-1
2002	Arsenal v Liverpool	1-0
2003	Manchester U† v Arsenal	1-1
2004	Arsenal v Manchester U	3-1
2005	Chelsea v Arsenal	2-1
2006	Liverpool v Chelsea	2-1

*Each club retained shield for six months. †Won on penalties.

THE FA COMMUNITY SHIELD 2006

Chelsea (1) 1, Liverpool (1) 2

At Millennium Stadium, 13 August 2006, attendance 56,275

Chelsea: Cudicini; Geremi (Bridge), Paulo Ferreira (Mikel), Essien, Terry, Ricardo Carvalho, Ballack (Kalou), Lampard, Drogba (Wright-Phillips), Shevchenko, Robben (Diarra).
Scorer: Shevchenko 43.
Liverpool: Reina; Finnan, Riise, Sissoko, Carragher, Agger, Pennant (Gerrard), Luis Garcia (Bellamy), Crouch (Sinama-Pongolle), Gonzalez (Aurelio), Zenden (Xabi Alonso).
Scorers: Riise 9, Crouch 80.
Referee: M. Atkinson (West Yorkshire).

SCOTTISH LEAGUE REVIEW 2006–2007

Celtic retained their title, the 41st championship success though Rangers arguably had the better of the second half of the season and stemmed from the dismissal of manager Paul Le Guen, with Scotland manager Walter Smith in his place. This happened early in January but it was not until 11 March that the lead of around 19 points was cut when they visited Parkhead.

A rare goal by central defender Ugo Ehiogu early in the second half was enough for three points which cut Celtic's lead to 16. A week later and the lead shrunk again as the hoops lost their third game on the trot (including Champions League) to Falkirk, reducing the advantage to 13.

Rangers were running out of games by now and though on 8 April a win at St Mirren kept them mathematically in the frame, the reality was that Celtic were going to be champions. This was confirmed on 22 April when Shunsuke Nakamura's free kick in the dying seconds at Kilmarnock gave them a 2-1 win and manager Gordon Strachan his second such honour.

Rangers did, however, achieve another satisfactory result against Celtic on 5 May when they won another Auld Firm game at Ibrox 2-0 with Kris Boyd registering his 100th Premier League goal and he finished as top scorer with 20. It was Rangers' 15th unbeaten League game. But they lost their last two.

Third place was well contested between Aberdeen and Hearts before the Dons clinched the UEFA Cup berth and the relegation place saw Dunfermline make a strenuous effort to force St Mirren into the cellar before admitting defeat. The Fifers' consolation was a Scottish Cup final pairing with Celtic and defeat no disgrace when the only goal came late on in the game.

As academic as it might have been, Kilmarnock finished their programme with three wins all by a single goal, away to Hibernian and Rangers followed by home to Hearts. Perhaps a sign of things to come in 2007–08?

At times Falkirk enjoyed some freescoring games and must have been satisfied with their performances overall in the top division. However, Hibs would have been disappointed with their finishing position, not so Inverness who kept their heads above water.

Dundee United looked in dire peril at one stage, receiving some heavy defeats, but pulled their season together well enough and Motherwell needed a crucial win over Dunfermline in late March to alleviate their concerns.

Yet, the battle to replace them from the First Division had all the hallmarks of fiction. Gretna's lead which at one time had seemed impregnable dwindled with some uncharacteristic home defeats including to the chasing St Johnstone who had plugged away stoically to give themselves a chance.

In fact, in a see-saw of the afternoon's events it needed an injury time goal for Gretna to succeed at Ross County to prevent the Saints from marching in. Even so Gretna's third promotion was unprecedented in the game and next season they will groundshare with Motherwell.

Ross were relegated along with Airdrie United who were beaten in the play-offs by Stirling Albion. Airdrie had fought off Brechin City, Stirling accounted for Raith Rovers. In Division Two, Morton had had an eight point lead to ensure automatic promotion.

At the bottom of the Second Division Forfar Athletic were doomed from early in the season. Stranraer then suffered successive demotion losing to East Fife in the play-offs.

Queen's Park from Division Three convincingly put Arbroath aside and dealt with similar efficiency in removing East Fife from the equation. Berwick Rangers were the champions of the division and accompanied the Spiders.

On the cup scene the CIS final was between Killie and Hibernian, the Hibees recording an emphatic 5-1 victory. Neither Celtic nor Rangers managed to reach the semi-finals. Rangers were beaten 2-0 at home by St Johnstone, Celtic went out on a penalty shoot-out to Falkirk in the last eight.

The Scottish League Challenge Cup was also decided on penalties with Ross County edging out Clyde on spot kicks after a 1-1 draw, what proved to be some consolation for their later relegation.

It seemed at one stage earlier in the season that East Stirling might not finish bottom of the League, thanks to a wretched start by Elgin City, but this proved to be a false dawn.

A group of First Division teams keen on a second section of the Premier League were narrowly defeated at a meeting of Scottish League clubs, but the threat remains.

SCOTTISH LEAGUE TABLES 2006–2007

Premier League	P	Home W	D	L	F	A	Away W	D	L	F	A	Total W	D	L	F	A	GD	Pts
1 Celtic	38	16	1	2	36	13	10	5	4	29	21	26	6	6	65	34	31	84
2 Rangers	38	11	6	2	35	10	10	3	6	26	22	21	9	8	61	32	29	72
3 Aberdeen	38	11	3	5	33	21	8	5	6	22	17	19	8	11	55	38	17	65
4 Hearts	38	9	4	6	26	19	8	6	5	21	16	17	10	11	47	35	12	61
5 Kilmarnock	38	7	5	6	24	22	9	2	9	23	32	16	7	15	47	54	–7	55
6 Hibernian	38	9	6	4	32	20	4	4	11	24	26	13	10	15	56	46	10	49
7 Falkirk	38	10	2	8	24	19	5	3	10	25	28	15	5	18	49	47	2	50
8 Inverness CT	38	8	6	5	25	20	3	7	9	17	28	11	13	14	42	48	–6	46
9 Dundee U	38	5	8	6	17	24	5	4	10	23	35	10	12	16	40	59	–19	42
10 Motherwell	38	5	3	11	25	34	5	5	9	16	27	10	8	20	41	61	–20	38
11 St Mirren	38	3	6	10	13	23	5	6	8	18	28	8	12	18	31	51	–20	36
12 Dunfermline Ath	38	6	4	9	17	28	2	4	13	9	27	8	8	22	26	55	–29	32

After 33 matches, the first six clubs play once against each other; bottom six likewise. Thus the finishing position of Falkirk moves them from sixth to seventh place.

First Division	P	Home W	D	L	F	A	Away W	D	L	F	A	Total W	D	L	F	A	GD	Pts
1 Gretna	36	10	4	4	35	18	9	5	4	35	22	19	9	8	70	40	30	66
2 St Johnstone	36	13	3	2	39	17	6	5	7	26	25	19	8	9	65	42	23	65
3 Dundee	36	11	2	5	27	19	5	3	10	21	23	16	5	15	48	42	6	53
4 Hamilton A	36	9	7	2	30	17	5	4	9	16	30	14	11	11	46	47	–1	53
5 Clyde	36	8	4	6	24	14	3	10	5	22	21	11	14	11	46	35	11	47
6 Livingston	36	3	7	8	20	24	8	5	5	21	22	11	12	13	41	46	–5	45
7 Partick Th	36	6	6	6	25	33	6	3	9	22	30	12	9	15	47	63	–16	45
8 Queen of the S	36	6	6	6	19	24	4	5	9	15	30	10	11	15	34	54	–20	41
9 Airdrie U	36	6	3	9	19	25	5	4	9	20	25	11	7	18	39	50	–11	40
10 Ross Co	36	6	6	6	22	25	3	4	11	18	32	9	10	17	40	57	–17	37

Second Division	P	Home W	D	L	F	A	Away W	D	L	F	A	Total W	D	L	F	A	GD	Pts
1 Morton	36	13	4	1	41	13	11	1	6	35	19	24	5	7	76	32	44	77
2 Stirling A	36	12	2	4	37	17	9	4	5	30	22	21	6	9	67	39	28	69
3 Raith R	36	7	5	6	22	18	11	3	4	28	15	18	8	10	50	33	17	62
4 Brechin C	36	9	2	7	30	24	9	4	5	31	21	18	6	12	61	45	16	60
5 Ayr U	36	7	3	8	21	23	7	5	6	25	24	14	8	14	46	47	–1	50
6 Cowdenbeath	36	7	4	7	36	35	6	2	10	23	21	13	6	17	59	56	3	45
7 Alloa Ath	36	5	6	7	24	27	6	3	9	23	43	11	9	16	47	70	–23	42
8 Peterhead	36	6	5	7	34	27	5	3	10	26	35	11	8	17	60	62	–2	41
9 Stranraer	36	8	2	8	29	38	2	7	9	16	36	10	9	17	45	74	–29	39
10 Forfar Ath	36	4	3	11	21	31	0	4	14	16	59	4	7	25	37	90	–53	19

Third Division	P	Home W	D	L	F	A	Away W	D	L	F	A	Total W	D	L	F	A	GD	Pts
1 Berwick R	36	12	3	3	29	14	12	0	6	22	15	24	3	9	51	29	22	75
2 Arbroath	36	9	4	5	27	20	13	0	5	34	13	22	4	10	61	33	28	70
3 Queen's Park	36	12	3	3	33	13	9	2	7	24	15	21	5	10	57	28	29	68
4 East Fife	36	10	4	4	26	15	10	3	5	33	22	20	7	9	59	37	22	67
5 Dumbarton	36	12	2	4	30	15	6	3	9	22	22	18	5	13	52	37	15	59
6 Albion R	36	8	2	8	30	29	6	4	8	26	32	14	6	16	56	61	–5	48
7 Stenhousemuir	36	9	1	8	36	31	4	4	10	17	32	13	5	18	53	63	–10	44
8 Montrose	36	6	2	10	20	27	5	2	11	22	35	11	4	21	42	62	–20	37
9 Elgin C	36	7	0	11	24	30	2	2	14	15	39	9	2	25	39	69	–30	29
10 East Stirling	36	3	1	14	11	37	3	2	13	16	41	6	3	27	27	78	–51	21

BANK OF SCOTLAND—PREMIER LEAGUE RESULTS 2006–2007

	Aberdeen	Celtic	Dundee U	Dunfermline Ath	Falkirk	Hearts	Hibernian	Inverness CT	Kilmarnock	Motherwell	Rangers	St Mirren
Aberdeen	—	0-1	3-1	1-0	2-1	1-3	2-1 *2-2*	1-1	3-1 *3-0*	2-1	1-2 *2-0*	2-0
	—	1-2	2-4	3-0		1-0		1-1				
Celtic	1-0 *2-1*	—	2-2	1-0	1-0	2-1 *1-3*	2-1	3-0	4-1	2-1	2-0	2-0
		—		2-1			1-0		2-0	1-0	0-1	5-1
Dundee U	3-1	1-4	—	0-0	1-2	0-1	0-3	3-1 *1-1*	1-0	1-1 *0-0*	2-1	1-0 *0-2*
		1-1	—	0-0	1-5		0-0			1-1		
Dunfermline Ath	0-3	1-2	2-1 *1-0*	—	0-3 *0-3*	1-2	0-4	0-0	3-2	0-2 *4-1*	1-1	2-1
				—		0-1	1-0		1-1		0-1	0-0
Falkirk	0-2	0-1	5-1 *2-0*	1-0	—	1-1	2-1	3-1 *1-0*	1-2	0-1	1-0	1-1 *0-2*
	1-2	1-0		1-0	—				0-2	1-2		2-0
Hearts	0-1 *1-1*	2-1	4-0	1-1	0-0	—	3-2 *2-0*	4-1	0-2	4-1	0-1	0-1
		1-2	0-4		1-0	—		1-0	1-0			1-1
Hibernian	1-1	2-2 *2-1*	2-1	2-0	0-1	2-2	—	2-0	2-2 *0-1*	3-1	2-1 *3-3*	5-1
	0-0				2-0	0-1	—			2-0	0-2	
Inverness CT	1-1	1-1	0-0	1-0 *2-1*	3-2	0-0	0-0	—	3-4	0-1 *2-0*	2-1	1-2
		1-2	1-0	1-3	1-1		3-0	—				2-1
Kilmarnock	1-0	1-2 *1-2*	0-0	5-1	2-1	0-0 *1-0*	2-1	1-1	—	1-2	2-2	1-1
	1-2		1-0				0-2	3-2	—		1-3	
Motherwell	0-2	1-1	2-3	2-1	4-2 *3-3*	0-1	1-6	1-4	5-0	—	1-2	0-0 *2-3*
	0-2			2-0		0-2		1-0	0-1	—	0-1	
Rangers	1-0	1-1 *2-0*	2-2	2-0	4-0	2-0 *2-1*	3-0	0-1	3-0 *0-1*	1-1	—	1-1
	3-0		5-0		2-1	0-0		1-1			—	
St Mirren	1-1	1-3	1-3	0-0 *0-1*	1-0	2-2	1-0	1-1 *0-1*	0-1	2-0	2-3	—
	0-2		0-1				1-1		0-2	0-0	0-1	—

BELL'S SCOTTISH LEAGUE—DIVISION ONE RESULTS 2006–2007

	Airdrie U	Clyde	Dundee	Gretna	Hamilton A	Livingston	Partick Th	Queen of the S	Ross Co	St Johnstone
Airdrie U	—	2-1	0-1	4-2	1-2	0-1	1-2	2-2	0-2	2-1
	—	1-0	0-3	0-0	1-0	3-1	1-1	0-3	0-1	1-2
Clyde	0-0	—	2-1	1-2	2-1	1-1	0-0	4-0	3-0	1-0
	0-1	—	1-1	2-0	3-0	0-1	2-0	0-1	2-4	0-1
Dundee	1-0	3-0	—	1-3	1-1	0-1	0-1	2-1	3-1	1-1
	2-1	1-4	—	0-1	1-0	2-0	3-1	1-0	3-2	2-1
Gretna	0-2	3-3	0-4	—	6-0	1-1	4-0	5-0	2-1	2-0
	0-0	0-0	1-0	—	1-0	4-1	2-0	0-3	4-1	0-2
Hamilton A	2-1	3-1	1-0	3-1	—	1-1	1-2	1-1	0-0	2-2
	3-0	1-1	1-0	0-0	—	3-0	2-1	2-2	1-0	3-4
Livingston	3-0	1-1	2-3	1-2	0-1	—	2-2	2-0	0-0	1-1
	1-3	0-0	1-3	1-1	1-2	—	0-1	0-1	1-1	3-2
Partick Th	4-2	1-1	3-1	0-6	3-1	2-3	—	1-1	3-2	1-5
	0-1	0-4	2-1	2-2	0-2	0-0	—	0-0	1-1	2-0
Queen of the S	1-1	0-2	2-0	0-3	1-1	2-0	0-2	—	2-0	0-1
	0-3	0-0	2-2	0-4	1-1	1-1	4-3	—	2-0	1-0
Ross Co	2-1	1-1	1-0	0-1	0-1	0-3	2-5	1-0	—	2-2
	1-1	2-2	0-0	2-3	4-1	0-2	2-1	1-0	—	1-1
St Johnstone	1-0	0-0	2-1	3-3	0-0	1-2	2-0	5-0	3-1	—
	4-3	2-1	2-0	2-1	4-2	1-2	2-0	3-0	2-1	—

BELL'S SCOTTISH LEAGUE—DIVISION TWO RESULTS 2006–2007

	Alloa Ath	Ayr U	Brechin C	Cowdenbeath	Forfar Ath	Morton	Peterhead	Raith R	Stirling A	Stranraer
Alloa Ath	—	0-1	2-2	2-1	2-0	3-2	1-1	1-2	1-2	1-1
	—	1-1	2-3	0-0	2-0	0-3	2-4	2-3	1-1	1-0
Ayr U	0-1	—	1-2	0-4	5-0	0-1	1-2	1-0	0-0	0-2
	4-3	—	1-1	0-2	3-1	1-0	0-0	0-2	3-2	1-0
Brechin C	2-0	0-2	—	4-2	4-2	2-3	1-0	1-0	0-1	3-0
	2-3	2-0	—	1-0	2-2	0-1	3-1	1-2	1-4	1-1
Cowdenbeath	6-1	1-1	1-3	—	3-2	1-2	4-2	1-2	2-2	4-2
	5-2	3-1	0-3	—	2-1	1-1	0-3	1-5	1-2	0-0
Forfar Ath	0-2	0-1	1-2	1-1	—	1-3	2-3	1-1	0-2	2-1
	0-2	1-1	3-2	2-0	—	0-4	1-2	1-2	0-2	5-0
Morton	4-0	0-0	1-0	1-0	1-1	—	4-2	2-0	1-1	3-0
	2-1	4-2	0-2	3-0	9-1	—	2-1	1-0	2-1	1-1
Peterhead	1-2	3-1	1-1	1-0	8-0	0-4	—	0-1	2-3	5-2
	0-0	2-2	1-4	0-2	2-2	1-2	—	0-0	2-1	5-0
Raith R	0-0	1-0	1-1	1-3	0-0	1-3	5-2	—	1-3	1-1
	3-0	0-1	1-0	1-2	2-1	2-0	2-0	—	0-1	0-0
Stirling A	5-0	1-3	2-1	1-0	3-0	2-1	2-0	1-1	—	3-3
	4-0	4-2	0-1	1-0	4-0	2-1	2-1	0-1	—	0-2
Stranraer	2-2	1-3	3-1	1-0	3-2	0-3	2-1	1-4	2-1	—
	3-4	0-3	0-2	1-6	4-1	2-1	1-1	0-2	3-1	—

BELL'S SCOTTISH LEAGUE—DIVISION THREE RESULTS 2006–2007

	Albion R	Arbroath	Berwick R	Dumbarton	East Fife	East Stirling	Elgin C	Montrose	Queen's Park	Stenhousemuir
Albion R	—	1-3	0-1	2-1	0-1	4-0	3-1	3-1	1-1	2-5
	—	0-3	0-1	0-1	0-3	2-1	6-2	2-2	2-1	2-1
Arbroath	2-3	—	0-1	0-0	1-1	1-2	2-1	3-1	1-2	2-0
	0-0	—	1-0	2-2	1-3	3-2	2-1	1-0	1-0	4-1
Berwick R	1-1	3-2	—	3-0	2-1	2-2	3-1	1-2	1-0	0-1
	3-0	1-0	—	2-1	2-0	2-0	0-0	1-0	0-2	2-1
Dumbarton	3-1	0-2	2-0	—	2-1	2-0	3-1	2-0	0-0	4-0
	3-1	1-0	1-2	—	0-2	2-1	1-0	2-1	1-2	1-1
East Fife	2-2	2-1	2-0	1-0	—	5-0	1-1	2-0	1-0	0-0
	1-3	1-2	0-2	1-0	—	0-2	3-1	2-0	1-0	1-1
East Stirling	0-1	0-2	0-1	0-2	0-4	—	2-1	0-3	2-1	5-0
	0-0	1-5	0-3	1-5	0-2	—	0-2	0-2	0-2	0-1
Elgin C	0-3	0-4	1-2	0-2	1-2	5-0	—	3-2	1-2	2-0
	3-0	0-1	2-1	0-1	2-3	2-1	—	0-2	0-3	2-1
Montrose	2-1	0-1	0-1	1-1	1-0	1-0	2-0	—	0-3	0-1
	2-3	0-1	1-2	0-5	3-3	4-0	0-1	—	0-2	3-2
Queen's Park	2-1	0-3	1-0	1-0	3-0	1-3	3-0	1-1	—	1-1
	5-0	1-0	0-2	2-0	1-1	2-1	3-0	5-0	—	1-0
Stenhousemuir	3-2	1-2	2-3	1-0	0-1	2-0	2-0	5-0	2-1	—
	0-4	1-2	2-0	5-1	3-5	1-1	3-2	2-5	1-2	—

ABERDEEN — PREMIER LEAGUE

Ground: Pittodrie Stadium, Aberdeen AB24 5QH (01224) 650400
Ground capacity: 21,421 (all seated). **Colours:** All red.
Manager: Jimmy Calderwood.
League Appearances: Anderson R 35; Brewster C 6(6); Byrne R 4(1); Clark C 37; Considine A 23(9); Crawford S 4; Daal D 1(6); Dempsey G 20(6); Diamond A 13(8); Foster R 35(2); Hart M 34; Langfield J 38; Lovell S 15(12); Mackie D 31(5); Maguire C 3(16); Miller L 25(7); Nicholson B 31; Severin S 34(2); Smith D 2(3); Smith J 20(2); Stewart J 1(3); Touzani K 6(5).
Goals – League (55): Mackie 13 (1 pen), Lovell 9, Nicholson 6 (2 pens), Miller 4, Severin 4, Crawford 3, Foster 3, Anderson 2, Considine 2, Daal 2, Dempsey 2, Clark 1, Maguire 1, Smith J 1, own goals 2.
Scottish Cup (3): Nicholson 2, Brewster 1.
CIS Cup (0).
Honours – Division 1: Champions – 1954-55, **Premier Division:** Champions – 1979-80, 1983-84, 1984-85. **Scottish Cup winners** 1947, 1970, 1982, 1983, 1984, 1986, 1990. **League Cup winners** 1956, 1977, 1986, 1990, 1996. **European Cup-Winners' Cup winners** 1983.

AIRDRIE UNITED — DIV. 2

Ground: Shyberry Excelsior Stadium, Airdrie ML6 8QZ (01236) 622000
Postal address: 60 St Enoch Square, Glasgow G1 4AG.
Ground capacity: 10,000 (all seated). **Colours:** White shirts with red diamond, white shorts.
Manager: Kenny Black.
League Appearances: Barrau X 14(1); Christie K 9(1); Harty I 7(4); Holmes G 34(1); Koudou A 3(3); Lovering P 29(1); Lukoszewski M 7(2); McDonald K 23(1); McDougall S 27(6); McGowan N 23(4); McGuire D 3(2); McKenna S 26(5); McKeown S 21(9); McLaren W 3(1); McPhee B 10(15); Potter C 3(2); Proctor D 12; Prunty B 18(8); Robertson S 36; Smyth M 29; Taylor S 23(8); Tierney G 6(8); Twigg G 27(6); Watson G 3(4).
Goals – League (39): Twigg 10, Taylor 5, Harty 3, Holmes 3, Barrau 2 (1 pen), Koudou 2, Lovering 2, McDonald 2, McPhee 2, Prunty 2, McDougall 1, McKenna 1, McKeown 1 (1 pen), Proctor 1, Smyth 1, Tierney 1.
Play-Offs (10): Harty 3 (2 pens), McDonald 2, McKeown 2, Twigg 2, Taylor 1.
Scottish Cup (0).
CIS Cup (2): McLaren 1, Prunty 1.
Challenge Cup (0).
Honours – Second Division: Champions – 2003–04; **Division II:** Champions – 1902-03, 1954-55, 1973-74. **Scottish Cup winners** 1924. **B&Q Cup winners** 1995. **Bell's League Challenge winners** 2000-01, 2001-02.

ALBION ROVERS — DIV. 3

Ground: Cliftonhill Stadium, Main Street, Coatbridge ML5 3RB (01236) 606334
Ground capacity: 1249 (seated: 489). **Colours:** Primrose yellow shirts, red shorts, red stockings.
Manager: John McCormack.
League Appearances: Bollan G 2; Bonnar M 5(3); Brown A (3); Chaplain S 35; Chisholm I 14(12); Clearie A (1); Creaney P 11(15); Donachy S (2); Donnelly C 33; Doyle J 15; Ewings J 23; Felvus B 16(11); Friel S 9; Hadden K (1); Lennon G 33; Lennox T 25(1); McBride M 5(7); McFarlane D 16(1); McGeogh J 3(3); McGhee G 4; McGoldrick J (4); Moffat G 20(3); Nicoll K 25(1); Savage J 7(1); Scott D 6;

Sichi L 3; Sim A 4(12); Smith B 28(3); Thompson L 7(3); Thomson R 9(1); Walker P 21(10); Watson P 17(1).
Goals – League (56): Chaplain 18 (3 pens), Walker 10, Chisholm 3, Creaney 3, Donnelly 3 (1 pen), Felvus 3, McFarlane 3, Lennon 2, Lennox 2, Savage 2, Doyle 1, Nicoll 1, Sim 1, Smith 1, Watson 1, own goals 2.
Scottish Cup (1): Felvus 1.
CIS Cup (1): Chaplain 1.
Challenge Cup (11): Chaplain 4, Savage 2, Chisholm 1, Donnelly 1, Higgins 1, Lennon 1, McBride 1.
Honours – Division II: Champions – 1933-34. **Second Division:** Champions 1988-89.

ALLOA ATHLETIC DIV. 2

Ground: Recreation Park, Alloa FK10 1RY (01259) 722695
Ground capacity: 3100. **Colours:** Gold shirts with black trim, black shorts with gold stripe.
Manager: Allan Maitland.
League Appearances: Bolochoweckyj M 19(8); Brown G 18(2); Caine D (1); Clark R 20(2); Coleman P 1(2); Comrie A 4(12); Coult L 6(3); Creer A 31(1); Findlay S 1(1); Forrest F 29; Grant J 30(2); Hamilton R 11(9); Hazeldine M 2(4); Johnston J (2); Kelly F (1); Mackie C 14(1); Malcolm S 23; McAnespie K 25(1); McAulay P 2(6); McCallum N 5(3); McClune D 22; McColligan B 22(3); McEwan D 4; McKeown S 30; Ovenstone J 20(3); Payo X 5(1); Sloan R 24(9); Stuart M 3(7); Thomson P (1); Thomson S 14; Townsley C 11(1).
Goals – League (47): Brown 6 (1 pen), Mackie 5, Grant 4, Hamilton 4, McKeown 4 (4 pens), Sloan 4, Bolochoweckyj 3, Clark 3, McAnespie 3, Forrest 2, McClune 2, McAulay 1, Malcolm 1, Payo 1, Townsley 1, own goals 3.
Scottish Cup (2): McAnespie 2.
CIS Cup (4): Brown 2, Forrest 1, Grant 1.
Challenge Cup (1): Townsley 1.
Honours – Division II: Champions – 1921-22. **Third Division:** Champions – 1997-98. **Bell's League Challenge winners** 1999-2000.

ARBROATH DIV. 3

Ground: Gayfield Park, Arbroath DD11 1QB (01241) 872157
Ground capacity: 8488. **Colours:** Maroon shirts with white trim, white shorts.
Manager: John McGlashan.
League Appearances: Bishop J 33; Black R 17(3); Brazil A 27(3); Cook S 2(5); Dobbins I 26(1); Doyle J 2(1); Gardiner R 4; Martin W 27(3); Masson T (2); McCulloch M 28(2); McGlashan J 1; McMullan K 26(4); Morrison S 1; Peat M 35; Raeside R 30; Reilly A 15(14); Rennie S 27(3); Savage J (3); Scott B 10(16); Sellars B 22; Smith N 17(10); Stein J 27(5); Tosh P 4(1); Voigt J (7); Watson P 11(3); Webster K 4(8).
Goals – League (61): Martin 9 (3 pens), Sellars 9, Scott 8, Reilly 7, Brazil 4, Raeside 4, Rennie 4, Bishop 3, Stein 3, Black 2, Smith 2, Webster 2, Dobbins 1, McCulloch 1, Voigt 1, Watson 1.
Play-Offs (1): Tosh 1.
Scottish Cup (2): Martin 2.
CIS Cup (0).
Challenge Cup (2): Cook 1, Rennie 1.
Honours – Nil.

AYR UNITED DIV. 2

Ground: Somerset Park, Ayr KA8 9NB (01292) 263435
Ground capacity: 10,185 (1549 seated). **Colours:** White shirts with black trim, black shorts.

Manager: Neil Watt.
League Appearances: Brown A 4; Caddis R 14(11); Campbell M 13(2); Casey M 25(2); Dunn D 29(3); Forrest E 36; Friels G 3(7); Harty I 1; Hyslop P 3(7); Johnston D (1); Logan R 2(2); Lowing D 31; McGeown M 32; McKinstry J 2; McLaren A 9; McLaren F 2(3); Miller G 14(1); Pettigrew C 9(8); Reid A (2); Reid B 15; Robertson C 28(1); Shields P 5; Stevenson R 24; Strain C 18(3); Templeton P 1(2); Vareille J 29(3); Waddell R 8(2); Walker P (9); Wardlaw G 14(10); Weaver P 25(4).
Goals – League (46): Wardlaw 7, Vareille 6, Forrest 4, Strain 4, Waddell 4, Robertson 3, Shields 3, Weaver 3, Caddis 2, Lowing 2, McLaren A 2, Stevenson 2, Friels 1, McLaren F 1, Miller 1, Pettigrew 1.
Scottish Cup (3): Dunn 1, Stevenson 1, Vareille 1.
CIS Cup (2): Caddis 1, Casey 1.
Challenge Cup (4): Robertson 1, Strain 1, Vareille 1, Weaver 1.
Honours – Division II: Champions – 1911-12, 1912-13, 1927-28, 1936-37, 1958-59, 1965-66. **Second Division:** Champions – 1987-88, 1996-97.

BERWICK RANGERS — DIV. 2

Ground: Shielfield Park, Berwick-on-Tweed TD15 2EF (01289) 307424
Ground capacity: 4131. **Colours:** Black with broad gold stripe, black shorts with white trim.
Manager: John Coughlin.
League Appearances: Britton T 7(2); Campbell N 6(6); Diack I 15(1); Flockhart C 5; Fraser S 29(1); Greenhill D 28(5); Greenhill G 20(6); Haynes K 17(5); Horn R 31; Little I 2(2); Lucas S 2(11); Manini S (1); Manson R 32(2); McCallum R 6(7); McGroarty C 15(2); McLaughlin D 5(5); McNicoll G 22(1); Noble S 24(7); Notman S 12(5); O'Connor G 31; Paliczka S 5(11); Shand C 5(3); Smith J 22; Swanson D 1(2); Thomson I 31(3); Wood G 23.
Goals – League (51): Wood 10, Diack 7, Haynes 7 (2 pens), Thomson 6, Fraser 4, Greenhill D 3, Horn 3, Manson 3, McLaughlin 2 (1 pen), McNicoll 2, Greenhill G 1, Notman 1, Paliczka 1, Smith 1.
Scottish Cup (5): Haynes 2 (1 pen), Wood 2, McLaughlin 1.
CIS Cup (0).
Challenge Cup (1): Horn 1.
Honours – Second Division: Champions – 1978-79. **Third Division:** Champions – 2006-07.

BRECHIN CITY — DIV. 2

Ground: Glebe Park, Brechin DD9 6BJ (01356) 622856
Ground capacity: 3960. **Colours:** Red with white trim.
Manager: Michael O'Neill.
League Appearances: Archibald R 15; Byers K 20(7); Callaghan S 34; Connolly P 20(12); Devlin S 3(6); Ferguson Steven 19(2); Ferguson Stuart 8(2); Flynn M 5(2); Geddes C 8(8); Hampshire S 26(5); Hillcoat J (2); Hughes C (2); Johnson G 11(1); King C 16(10); McEwan C 8(2); McManus S (2); Murie D 12; Nelson C 36; Russell I 24(9); Smith D 31; Walker R 21(7); Walker S 27(2); Ward J 22; White D 30(1).
Goals – League (61): Russell 21 (1 pen), Hampshire 7, Connolly 6, Callaghan 5 (2 pens), Smith 5, King 3, Byres 2, Geddes 2, Walker R 2, Walker S 2, Ward 2, Steven Ferguson 1, Johnson 1, White 1, own goal 1.
Play-Offs (1): Russell 1.
Scottish Cup (6): Byres 1, Callaghan 1 (pen), Connolly 1, Hampshire 1, Russell 1, own goal 1.
CIS Cup (2): Callaghan 1, Geddes 1.
Challenge Cup (1): Callaghan 1.
Honours – Second Division: Champions – 1982-83, 1989-90, 2004-05. **Third Division:** Champions – 2001-02. **C Division:** Champions – 1953-54.

CELTIC — PREMIER LEAGUE

Ground: Celtic Park, Glasgow G40 3RE (0871) 226 1888
Ground capacity: 60,355 (all seated). **Colours:** Green and white hooped shirts, white shorts.
Manager: Gordon Strachan.
League Appearances: Balde B 6; Beattie C 9(7); Bjarnason T 1; Boruc A 36; Brown M 1; Caldwell G 20(1); Camara M 1; Doumbe J 3(1); Gravesen T 18(4); Hartley P 10; Jarosik J 18(7); Kennedy J 3; Lennon N 30(1); Maloney S 7(2); Marshall D 1(1); McGeady A 22(12); McManus S 31; Miller K 20(11); Nakamura S 37; Naylor L 32; O'Dea D 9(5); Pearson S 3(9); Petrov S 3; Pressley S 14; Riordan D 6(11); Sheridan C (1); Sno E 7(11); Telfer P 20(1); Vennegoor of Hesselink 17(4); Wallace R 2; Wilson M 12; Zurawski M 19(7).
Goals – League (65): Vennegoor of Hesselink 13 (1 pen), Nakamura 9, Zurawski 7, Gravesen 6, McGeady 5, Jarosik 4, Miller 4, Riordan 4, Beattie 2, McManus 2, O'Dea 2, Petrov 2, Pearson 1, Pressley 1, Sno 1, own goals 2.
Scottish Cup (12): Vennegoor of Hesselink 4 (1 pen), Riordan 3, Zurawski 2, Miller 1, O'Dea 1, Pressley 1.
CIS Cup (3): Zurawski 2, Beattie 1.
Honours – Division I: Champions – 1892-93, 1893-94, 1895-96, 1897-98, 1904-05, 1905-06, 1906-07, 1907-08, 1908-09, 1909-10, 1913-14, 1914-15, 1915-16, 1916-17, 1918-19, 1921-22, 1925-26, 1935-36, 1937-38, 1953-54, 1965-66, 1966-67, 1967-68, 1968-69, 1969-70, 1970-71, 1971-72, 1972-73, 1973-74. **Premier Division:** Champions – 1976-77, 1978-79, 1980-81, 1981-82, 1985-86, 1987-88, 1997-98. **Premier League:** 2000-01, 2001-02, 2003–04, 2005–06, 2006–07. **Scottish Cup winners** 1892, 1899, 1900, 1904, 1907, 1908, 1911, 1912, 1914, 1923, 1925, 1927, 1931, 1933, 1937, 1951, 1954, 1965, 1967, 1969, 1971, 1972, 1974, 1975, 1977, 1980, 1985, 1988, 1989, 1995, 2001, 2004, 2005, 2007. **League Cup winners** 1957, 1958, 1966, 1967, 1968, 1969, 1970, 1975, 1983, 1998, 2000, 2001, 2004, 2006. **European Cup winners** 1967.

CLYDE — DIV. 1

Ground: Broadwood Stadium, Cumbernauld G68 9NE (01236) 451511
Ground capacity: 8200. **Colours:** White shirts with red and black trim, black shorts.
Manager: Colin Hendry.
League Appearances: Arbuckle G 24(9); Bradley K 5(10); Bryson C 33(1); Cherrie P 11; Ferguson A 10(13); Gilmore B 13; Harris R 19(5); Higgins C 34; Hunter R 4(7); Hutton D 25; Imrie D 34; MacLennan R 5(4); Malone E 18; Masterton S 19(8); McCann R 16(5); McGowan D (1); McGowan M 32(1); McGregor N 20; McHale P 18(1); McKenna S 1(7); McKeown C 30; Miller J (1); O'Donnell S 19(3); Williams A 6(7).
Goals – League (46): Arbuckle 11, Masterton 8, Imrie 6, Bryson 3, Ferguson 3, O'Donnell 3 (1 pen), McGowan M 2 (1 pen), McGregor N 2, McHale 2 (2 pens), McKeown 2, Gilmour 1, Higgins 1, Malone 1, Williams 1.
Scottish Cup (0).
CIS Cup (2): Imrie 1, O'Donnell 1 (pen).
Challenge Cup (8): McHale 2, Ferguson 1, Higgins 1, Hunter 1, Imrie 1, McGowan M 1, O'Donnell 1.
Honours – Division II: Champions – 1904-05, 1951-52, 1956-57, 1961-62, 1972-73. **Second Division:** Champions – 1977-78, 1981-82, 1992-93, 1999-2000. **Scottish Cup winners** 1939, 1955, 1958. **League Challenge Cup winners** 2006–07.

COWDENBEATH — DIV. 2

Ground: Central Park, Cowdenbeath KY4 9EY (01383) 610166
Ground capacity: 5268. **Colours:** Royal blue with white cuffs and collar, white shorts.

Manager: Brian Welsh.
League Appearances: Allison K 2(1); Armstrong D 10; Bannerman S (1); Baxter M 32(2); Bryan A (3); Buchanan L 36; Clarke P 27(5); Dalziel S 13(15); Davidson M 5; Doherty M 7(1); Ellis L 31(1); Fotheringham M 8(17); Fusco G 19(5); Gomis M 14(1); Guy G 7(7); Hannah D 14; Hay D 24(1); Hill D 27(1); Hughes C 2(2); Husband S 3(2); Kenneth G 7; Lennon D 14; Manzie G (2); McBride K 5(4); McBride M 5(4); McBride P (3); McKinlay C (1); Orr D 10; Paatelainen M 20; Ramsay I 1(2); Ritchie I 18; Scullion P 21(3); Smart C (3); Smith G 10; Weir S 4(3).
Goals – League (59): Buchanan 20 (2 pens), Clarke 13, Paatelainen 9, Dalziel 4, Ellis 3, Scullion 3, Gomis 2, Baxter 1, Doherty 1, Fotheringham 1, Hill 1, Ritchie 1.
Scottish Cup (7): Buchanan 2, Baxter 1, Clarke 1, Hill 1, Lennon 1, Paatelainen 1.
CIS Cup (4): Hughes 2, Buchanan 1, Clarke 1.
Challenge Cup (6): Clarke 2, Fotheringham 2, Dalziel 1, Paatelainen 1.
Honours – Division II: Champions – 1913-14, 1914-15, 1938-39. **Third Division:** Champions – 2005-06.

DUMBARTON — DIV. 3

Ground: Strathclyde Homes Stadium, Dumbarton G82 1JJ (01389) 762569/767864
Ground capacity: 2050. **Colours:** Gold shirts with black sleeves and black side panels, black shorts with three black side panels, black stockings.
Manager: Gerry McCabe.
League Appearances: Bagan D 25(3); Borris R 31; Boyle C 32(3); Brittain C 27(2); Canning M 32(1); Coyne T 10(6); Craig D 36; Dempsie M 1; Dillon J 18(12); Dobbie S 17; Geggan A 31(1); Gemmell J 1(4); Gentile C 8(5); Grindlay S 36; Hamilton C 12(15); Henry J 3(2); McCann K 1; McKeever J (7); McLaughlin J (1); McNaught D 25(6); McQuilken P 11(11); Quitongo J (2); Smith J 3(1); Tiernan F 6(1); Winter C 30(1).
Goals – League (52): Dobbie 10 (2 pens), Borris 6, Coyne 6 (1 pen), Winter 6, McQuilken 4, Bagan 3, Boyle 3, Gentile 3, Hamilton 2, McNaught 2, Craig 1, Dillon 1, Henry 1, Geggan 1, Quitongo 1, own goals 2.
Scottish Cup (1): Gemmell 1.
CIS Cup (4): Bagan 1, Boyle 1, Dobbie 1, Gemmell 1.
Challenge Cup (1): McNaught 1.
Honours – Division I: Champions – 1890-91 (Shared), 1891-92. **Division II:** Champions – 1910-11, 1971-72. **Second Division:** Champions – 1991-92. **Scottish Cup winners** 1883.

DUNDEE — DIV. 1

Ground: Dens Park, Dundee DD3 7JY (01382) 889966
Ground capacity: 11,760 (all seated). **Colours:** Navy shirts with white and red shoulder and sleeve flashes, white shorts with navy and red piping, navy stockings with two white hoops.
Manager: Alex Rae.
League Appearances: Boggan J (1); Campbell R 6(9); Ciani A 1(1); Clark B 2(4); Daal B 7; Davidson R 12(3); Deasley B 6(8); Dixon P 33; Forsyth C 1; Gates S 2(9); Griffin D 22(3); Hamdaoui K (4); Harpur C 1; Harris R 7(11); Higgins C (3); Johnston S (1); Lyle D 26(2); Macdonald C 2(4); Mackenzie G 19(2); Mann R 16; McDonald K 29(2); McGinty B 5(1); McHale P 12; McLaren A 10(2); Murray S (1); Rae A 24(1); Reidford C 3; Robertson S 29; Roy L 32; Shields J 19(1); Smith G 20(1); Smith K 4(4); Strong G 15(1); Swankie G 31(2).
Goals – League (48): Lyle 12 (5 pens), Swankie 7 (1 pen), Daal 5, Davidson 3 (1 pen), McLaren 3, Rae 3, Deasley 2, Harris 2, McDonald K 2, Robertson 2, Clark 1, Hamdaoui 1, McGinty 1, McHale 1, Mann 1, Smith G 1, Strong 1.
Scottish Cup (4): Lyle 3, Deasley 1.
CIS Cup (1): Swankie 1.
Challenge Cup (1): Swankie 1.

Honours – Division I: Champions – 1961-62. **First Division:** Champions – 1978-79, 1991-92, 1997-98. **Division II:** Champions – 1946-47. **Scottish Cup winners** 1910. **League Cup winners** 1952, 1953, 1974. **B&Q (Centenary) Cup winners** 1991.

DUNDEE UNITED — PREMIER LEAGUE

Ground: Tannadice Park, Dundee DD3 7JW (01382) 833166
Ground capacity: 14,223. **Colours:** Tangerine shirts, tangerine shorts.
Manager: Craig Levein.
League Appearances: Archibald A 14(2); Brewster C 1(2); Burnett G 1; Cameron G 20(5); Conway C 22(8); Daly J 10(1); Dillon S 15; Duff S 22(6); Easton W 1(6); Gomis M 9(2); Goodwillie D 3(14); Hunt N 25(3); Kalvenes C 29; Kenneth G 11; Kerr M 35(1); Mair L 17(1); McCracken D 32(1); McLean E 1; Miller L 1(2); Proctor D 9(3); Robb S 8(7); Robertson D 21(5); Robson B 29; Russell J (2); Samuel C 27(10); Smith G 4(2); Stillie D 37; Watson K (1); Wilkie L 14.
Goals – League (40): Robson 11 (2 pens), Hunt 10, Samuel 5, Robertson 3, Cameron 2, Daly 2 (1 pen), Duff 1, Kalvenes 1, Kenneth 1, McCracken 1, Mair 1, Robb 1, own goal 1.
Scottish Cup (3): Kenneth 1, Robertson 1, Robson 1.
CIS Cup (1): Robertson 1.
Honours – Premier Division: Champions – 1982-83. **Division II:** Champions – 1924-25, 1928-29. **Scottish Cup winners** 1994. **League Cup winners** 1980, 1981.

DUNFERMLINE ATHLETIC — DIV. 1

Ground: East End Park, Dunfermline KY12 7RB (01383) 724295
Ground capacity: 11,780. **Colours:** Black and white striped shirts, white shorts.
Manager: Stephen Kenny.
League Appearances: Bamba S 21(2); Burchill M 12(8); Campbell I (1); Crawford S 23(3); Daquin F 8(12); De Vries D 27; Glass S 11; Hamilton J 18(8); Hammill A 9(4); Harris J ; Labonte A 11(2); Mason G 35(1); McCunnie J 8(6); McGuire P 22(2); McIntyre J 6(4); McKenzie R 11(1); McManus T 5(2); Morrison O 12(12); Morrison S 11; Muirhead S 20(5); O'Brien J 13; Ross G 16(10); Ryan R 2(4); Shields G 29; Simmons S 23(1); Smith C (1); Tod A 5(5); Whelan M 1; Williamson K (5); Wilson C (3); Wilson S 31; Woods C 9(3); Young D 19(2).
Goals – League (26): Crawford 5 (1 pen), Glass 3 (1 pen), Hamilton 2, McIntyre 2, McManus 2, Mason 2, Simmons 2, Young 2, Hammill 1, McGuire 1, Morrison 1, O'Brien 1, Shields 1, Wilson S 1.
Scottish Cup (7): Simmons 3, Hamilton 1, McGuire 1, McIntyre 1, Wilson S 1.
CIS Cup (0).
Honours – First Division: Champions – 1988-89, 1995-96. **Division II:** Champions – 1925-26. **Second Division:** Champions – 1985-86. **Scottish Cup winners** 1961, 1968.

EAST FIFE — DIV. 3

Ground: Bayview Park, Methil, Fife KY8 3RW (01333) 426323
Ground capacity: 2000 (all seated). **Colours:** Gold and black shirts, white shorts.
Manager: David Baikie.
League Appearances: Blackadder R 29(4); Courts T 26; Crabbe S 1(8); Dair J 6; Dodds J 26; Doyle P 25; Fortune S 2(7); Gibson G 14(1); Gordon K 22(9); Hampshire P 10(4); Jablonski N 32(2); Kelly G 2(1); Linton S 13; Martin J 4(14); McBride K 13; McDonald G 12; McGowan J 10(2); Mitchell A 1(2); Nicholas S 8(6); O'Reilly C 21(10); Ritchie P 19(4); Ross D 1; Ross I 10; Smart C 12(5); Smart J 34; Smith E 26(2); Walker P 9(1); Young L 8(1).
Goals – League (59): O'Reilly 13, Jablonski 9 (1 pen), Smart J 7, Gordon 6, Blackadder 5, Ritchie 5 (1 pen), Nicholas 3, Smart C 2, Walker 2, Fortune 1, Gibson 1, Linton 1, McBride 1, McGowan 1, Martin 1, Young 1.

Play-Offs (6): O'Reilly 3, Gibson 1, McDonald 1, Young 1.
Scottish Cup (1): Jablonski 1.
CIS Cup (1): Smart C.
Challenge Cup (0).
Honours – Division II: Champions – 1947-48. **Scottish Cup winners** 1938. **League Cup winners** 1948, 1950, 1954.

EAST STIRLINGSHIRE — DIV. 3

Ground: Firs Park, Falkirk FK2 7AY (01324) 623583
Ground capacity: 1880. **Colours:** Black shirts with white hoops, black shorts with white and red stripes.
Manager: Gordon Wylde.
League Appearances: Adam S 19(6); Blair S 1(4); Boyle J 20(7); Brand A 21(2); Brownlie P 7(5); Dymock S 10(15); Galloway C 3(9); Hughes C (1); Kassim A 1(2); Learmonth S 31; Livingstone S 5(8); McAloney P 18(3); McBride P 15(6); McKenzie M 29(3); McPhee G 1; Molloy M 7(7); Nixon J 3(2); Nugent A 20; Oates S 20(1); Savage J 1; Smith A 7; Stewart P 34; Struthers K 1; Thywissen C 34; Tiropoulos R 16; Tweedie P 27(5); Ure D 28(5); Ward A 7(1); Wild C 10(2).
Goals – League (27): McKenzie 5, Stewart 4 (1 pen), Tweedie 4, Boyle 2, Dymock 2, Thywissen 2, Ure 2, Brownlie 1, McBride 1, Savage 1, own goals 3.
Scottish Cup (0).
CIS Cup (1): Thywissen.
Challenge Cup (0).
Honours – Division II: Champions – 1931-32. **C Division:** Champions – 1947-48.

ELGIN CITY — DIV. 3

Ground: Borough Briggs, Elgin IV30 1AP (01343) 551114
Ground capacity: 3927 (478 seated). **Colours:** Black and white vertical striped shirts, black shorts.
Manager: Robbie Williamson.
League Appearances: Bazie P (1); Booth M 7(2); Brewin T (2); Campbell C 34(1); Charlesworth M 19(12); Cooke S 1(1); Dempsie A 28; Dickson H 26(1); Docherty D 15(8); Easton S 5(6); Finnigan C (14); Fox C 3(1); Gardiner C 16(3); Hind D 35; Hooks N 14; Huxford R (1); Johnston M 34; Kaczan P 27(2); Kellacher S (1); Lowe S 12(1); Mackay S 34(1); McGraw A 8(3); Moffat A 28; Muir A 2; Nelson A 7(7); Niven D 6; Renton K 33; Stephen B 2(3).
Goals – League (39): Johnston 19 (3 pens), Moffat 6, Kaczan 4, Mackay 4 (1 pen), Charlesworth 3, Campbell 1, Dickson 1, Gardiner 1.
Scottish Cup (5): Johnston 3, Mackay 1, Moffat 1.
CIS Cup (0).
Challenge Cup (4): Charlesworth 2, Kaczan 1, Mackay 1.
Honours – Nil.

FALKIRK — PREMIER LEAGUE

Ground: Brockville Park, Falkirk FK1 5AX (01324) 624121
Ground capacity: 6123. **Colours:** Navy blue shirts with white seams, navy shorts.
Head Coach: John Hughes.
League Appearances: Allison B 1(2); Barr D 36; Craig L 17(10); Cregg P 32; Dodd K 14(3); Finnigan C 10(2); Gow A 34(2); Higgins S 14(1); Holden D 8(1); Lambers J 9; Latapy R 36(1); Lescinel J ; Lima V 17(5); McManus T (5); Mcstay R (4); Milne K 34; Moutinho P 14(7); O'Donnell S 20(5); Roberston D (2); Ross J 36; Schmeichel K 15; Scobbie T 16(5); Stewart J 4(14); Stokes A 16; Thomson S 17(5); Twaddle M 10(6); Uras C 8(1).
Goals – League (49): Stokes 14 (1 pen), Gow 7, Latapy 5, Finnigan 4, Cregg 3 (1

pen), Craig 2, Moutinho 2, O'Donnell 2, Thomson 2, Twaddle 2, Barr 1, Holden 1, Milne 1, Scobbie 1, own goals 2.
Scottish Cup (2): Craig 1, Gow 1.
CIS Cup (7): Moutinho 2, Stokes 2, Craig 1, Stewart 1, Twaddle 1.
Honours – Division II: Champions – 1935-36, 1969-70, 1974-75. **First Division:** Champions – 1990-91, 1993-94, 2002-03, 2004-05. **Second Division:** Champions – 1979-80. **Scottish Cup winners** 1913, 1957. **League Challenge Cup winners** 1998, 2005.

FORFAR ATHLETIC — DIV. 3

Ground: Station Park, Forfar, Angus (01307) 463576
Ground capacity: 4602. **Colours:** Sky blue shirts with navy side panels and shoulder/sleeve bands, navy shorts with sky blue trims, sky blue stockings with navy band on top.
Manager: Jim Moffat.
League Appearances: Abbot S 1; Allison M 17(1); Beith G 4(5); Coyle F 26(2); Donald B 18(2); Dunn D 10(1); Fraser G 13(13); Gates S 7; Gribben D 18(9); Kassim A 2; Keogh D 15(2); King D 21; Lombardi M 22(7); Lumsden C 18(3); Lunan P 24(1); Lynn G 18(2); Marshall C 4; McNally S 12; Montgomery R 3(1); Moon K 23(2); Murdoch S 17; Rattray A 16; Stewart W 11(3); Tade G 18(5); Tierney G 5; Tosh P 24(4); Tulloch S 3(1); Webster K 7(8); Wood A 19.
Goals – League (37): Gribben 11 (2 pens), Tosh 5, Lombardi 4, Lumsden 3, Tade 3, Donald 2, Fraser 2, Gates 2, Moon 2, Rattray 1, own goals 2.
Scottish Cup (1): Lunan 1.
CIS Cup (1): Gribben.
Challenge Cup (3): Coyle 1, Gribben 1, Lunan 1.
Honours – Second Division: Champions – 1983-84. **Third Division:** Champions – 1994-95.

GRETNA — PREMIER LEAGUE

Ground: Raydale Park, Gretna DG16 5AP (01461) 337602. Currently playing home games at Motherwell.
Ground capacity: 2200. **Colours:** Black shirt with white hoops, black shorts with white trim.
Manager: Rowan Alexander.
League Appearances: Baldacchino R (4); Barr C 13(3); Barrau X (1); Berkeley M (13); Bingham D 1(2); Birch M 4(2); Canning M 35; Cowan D 3; Deuchar K 4(4); Deverdics N 3(3); Fleming C 1(1); Grady J 16(8); Graham D 28(5); Grainger D 26(4); Hogg S 2(2); Innes C 27; Jenkins A 23(9); MacFarlane N 3(2); Main A 27; Malkowski Z 8; McGill B 6(2); McGuffie R 16(6); McMenamin C 34(1); McQuilken J 3(1); Nicholls D 19(1); O'Neil J 6(2); Paartalu E 23(3); Shields D (1); Skelton G 34; Tosh S 14; Townsley D 17(2).
Goals – League (70): McMenamin 24 (4 pens), Tosh 8, Townsley 5, Grady 4, Jenkins 4, Paartalu 4, Graham 3, Skelton 3, Deuchar 2, Grainger 2, Innes 2, McGill 2, McGuffie 2 (1 pen), Barrau 1, Berkeley 1, Canning 1, Deverdics 1, Nicholls 1.
Scottish Cup (4): Berkeley 1, Graham 1, McMenamin 1, Paartalu 1.
CIS Cup (0).
Challenge Cup (8): Deuchar 2, Graham 1, Jenkins 1, McGuffie 1, McMenamin 1, Tosh 1, Townsley 1.
Honours – First Division: Champions – 2006–07. **Second Division:** Champions – 2005–06. **Third Division:** Champions – 2004–05.

HAMILTON ACADEMICAL — DIV. 1

Ground: New Douglas Park, Cadzow Avenue, Hamilton ML3 0FT (01698) 368650
Ground capacity: 5396. **Colours:** Red and white hooped shirts, white shorts.
Manager: Billy Reid.

League Appearances: Agnew S 2(3); Di Malta D (1); Easton B 30(2); Elebert D 33; Fleming D 16; Gibson J 6(5); Gilhaney M 23(6); Jellemaa R 17(1); McArthur J 35(1); McCabe R (1); McCarthy J 14(9); McClen J 2(1); McEwan D 8(1); McJimpsey M (1); McLaughlan G 1(2); McLaughlin M 5; McLeod P 17(14); Murdoch S 11; Neil A 28(1); Offiong R 26(3); Parratt T 26(1); Payo J 2(1); Rezgane O 2; Sharp K 8; Stevenson A 15(7); Swailes C 7(1); Thomson S 1(3); Tunbridge S 5(3); Wake B 10(22); Wilson M 21(5); Winters D 25(5).
Goals – League (46): Offiong 14, Winters 6, Elebert 5, Wake 5, Gilhaney 4, McLeod 4, Stevenson 3 (3 pens), Easton 1, McArthur 1, McCarthy 1, Tunbridge 1, Wilson 1.
Scottish Cup (2): McArthur 1, McCarthy 1.
CIS Cup (1): Offiong 1.
Challenge Cup (4): Neill 1, Offiong 1, Payo 1, Tunbridge 1.
Honours – First Division: Champions – 1985-86, 1987-88. **Division II:** Champions – 1903-04. **Division III:** Champions – 2000-01. **B&Q Cup winners** 1992, 1993.

HEART OF MIDLOTHIAN — PREMIER LEAGUE

Ground: Tynecastle Park, Gorgie Road, Edinburgh EH11 2NL (0871) 663 1874
Ground capacity: 17,402. **Colours:** Maroon shirts, white shorts.
Manager: Anatoly Korobochka.
League Appearances: Aguiar B 20(5); Banks S 5; Barasa N 6(3); Bednar R 14(4); Berra C 34(1); Beslija M 2(3); Brellier J 16(6); Cesnauskis D 5(4); Costa T 1; Driver A 17(3); Elliot C 5(5); Fyssas T 18(3); Glen G (1); Goncalves J 9(2); Gordon C 34; Hartley P 18(3); Ivaskevicius K 9; Jankauskas E 8(4); Jonsson E (3); Kancelsku T 3(2); Karipidis C 10(2); Kingston L 10; Klimek A 1; Makela J 1(8); McCann N 14(7); Mikoliunas S 29(2); Mole J 7(3); Neilson R 12(2); Pilibaitis L 4(1); Pinilla M 2(1); Pospisil M 12(12); Pressley S 13; Tall I 17(6); Velicka A 23(4); Wallace L 13(4); Zaliukas M 26(1).
Goals – League (47): Velicka 10, Pospisil 6 (1 pen), Bednar 4, Mikoliunas 4, Driver 3, Hartley 3 (2 pens), Mole 3, Makela 2, Pinilla 2, Aguiar 1, Berra 1, Elliot 1, Fyssas 1, Ivaskevicius 1, Jankauskas 1, Kingston 1, Tall 1, Zaliukas 1, own goal 1.
Scottish Cup (4): Velicka 3, Bednar 1.
CIS Cup (4): Makela 3, Aguiar 1.
Honours – Division I: Champions – 1894-95, 1896-97, 1957-58, 1959-60. **First Division:** Champions – 1979-80. **Scottish Cup winners** 1891, 1896, 1901, 1906, 1956, 1998, 2006. **League Cup winners** 1955, 1959, 1960, 1963.

HIBERNIAN — PREMIER LEAGUE

Ground: Easter Road Stadium, Edinburgh EH7 5QG (0131) 661 2159
Ground capacity: 17,400. **Colours:** Green shirts with white sleeves and collar, white shorts with green stripe.
Manager: John Collins.
League Appearances: Benjelloun A 16(16); Beuzelin G 18(7); Brown Scott 30; Brown Simon 4; Campbell R 2(1); Chisholm R 5(1); Dalglish P (2); Fletcher S 24(7); Glass S 2(8); Gray D 2(1); Hogg C 15; Jones R 34; Killen C 17(1); Konde O 2(1); Konte A (1); Lynch S 2(1); Malkowski Z 19; Martis S 26; McCaffrey D 1; McCann K 7(1); McCluskey J 1(5); McNeil A 15; Murphy D 33; Shields J 3; Shiels D 13(11); Sowunmi T 2(3); Sproule I 16(16); Stevenson L 13(3); Stewart M 23(6); Thomson K 22(1); Whittaker S 34(1); Zemmama M 17(6).
Goals – League (56): Killen 13 (2 pens), Shiels 7 (1 pen), Sproule 7, Benjelloun 6, Fletcher 6, Scott Brown 5, Jones 4, Zemmama 2, Beuzelin 1, Gray 1, McCann 1, Stewart 1, Thomson 1, Whittaker 1.
Scottish Cup (11): Benjelloun 3, Fletcher 1, Jones 1, Killen 1, Murphy 1, Sowumni 1, Sproule 1, Stewart 1, own goal 1.
CIS Cup (19): Benjelloun 5, Fletcher 4, Jones 3, Scott Brown 2, Shiels 2, McCluskey 1, Murphy 1, own goal 1.

Honours – Division I: Champions – 1902-03, 1947-48, 1950-51, 1951-52. **First Division:** Champions – 1980-81, 1998-99. **Division II:** Champions – 1893-94, 1894-95, 1932-33. **Scottish Cup winners** 1887, 1902. **League Cup winners** 1973, 1992, 2007.

INVERNESS CALEDONIAN THISTLE PREMIER LEAGUE

Ground: Tulloch Caledonian Stadium, East Longman, Inverness IV1 1FF (01463) 715816
Ground capacity: 7400. **Colours:** Royal blue shirts with red and black stripes, royal blue shorts, royal blue stockings.
Manager: Charlie Christie.
League Appearances: Bayne G 29(9); Black I 22(4); Brown M 23; Dargo C 25(2); Dods D 35; Duncan R 22(6); Fraser M 15(1); Golabek S 1; Hart R 8(8); Hastings R 37; Keogh L 1(7); McAllister R 5(14); McBain R 30(2); McCaffrey S 9(4); McSwegan G 2(6); Morgan A 1(6); Munro G 36; Paatelainen M 6(5); Rankin J 32(2); Sutherland Z 1(4); Tokely R 34; Wilson B 30(4); Wyness D 14(6).
Goals – League (42): Dargo 10 (1 pen), Bayne 6, Rankin 6, Dods 4, Wilson 4, McAllister 2, Munro 2, Paatelainen 2, Tokely 2, Hastings 1, McBain 1, McCaffrey 1, Wyness 1.
Scottish Cup (8): Dargo 2, Bayne 1, Duncan 1, McBain 1, Morgan 1, Wilson 1, Wyness 1.
CIS Cup (3): Bayne 1, McAllister 1, Wyness 1.
Honours – First Division: Champions – 2003-04. **Third Division:** Champions – 1996-97. **Bell's League Challenge winners** 2004.

KILMARNOCK PREMIER LEAGUE

Ground: Rugby Park, Kilmarnock KA1 2DP (01563) 525184
Ground capacity: 18,128. **Colours:** Blue and white striped shirts, blue shorts.
Manager: Jim Jefferies.
League Appearances: Barrowman A (3); Combe A 11; Di Giacomo P 8(14); Dodds R 3(6); Fernandez D 7(1); Ford S 12(4); Fowler J 38; Gibson W 1(6); Greer G 33; Hamill J 2(1); Hay G 28(1); Invincibile D 24(1); Johnston A 25(3); Koudou A 2(3); Leven P 20(7); Lilley D 7; Locke G 4(8); Murray G 30; Murray S (9); Naismith S 35(2); Nish C 24(9); O'Leary R 5(3); Quinn R 6; Smith G 27; Syila M 10(1); Wales G 21(7); Wright F 35.
Goals – League (47): Naismith 16 (4 pens), Nish 13, Di Giacomo 6, Wales 4, Hay 2, Invincibile 2, Fernandez 1, Leven 1, Wright F 1, own goal 1.
Scottish Cup (1): Nish 1.
CIS Cup (11): Naismith 4, Wright F 3, Greer 1, Invincibile 1, Murray G 1, Wales 1.
Honours – Division I: Champions – 1964-65. **Division II:** Champions – 1897-98, 1898-99. **Scottish Cup winners** 1920, 1929, 1997.

LIVINGSTON DIV. 1

Ground: Almondvale Stadium, Alderton Road, Livingston EH54 7DN (01506) 417 000
Ground capacity: 10,024. **Colours:** Gold shirts, black shorts, white stockings.
Team Manager: Mark Proctor.
League Appearances: Adamson K 2(1); Anderson S 6; Craig S 24(3); Cuthbert S 4; Davidson M (2); Dorrans G 25(9); Fox L 11(11); Golabek S 10; Griffiths L 2(2); Hamill J 25(8); Hislop S 4(6); Kerr S (2); Mackay D 34; Makel L 28(3); McPake J 33; Millar G 8(5); Mitchell S 32; Mole J 9(3); Shields P 4(13); Smylie D 7(11); Snodgrass R 1(5); Stewart C 19; Teggart M 16(3); Thomson J 18; Torrance M 1(1); Tweed S 28; Walker A 28(3); Weir S (6); Wight J 17(1).
Goals – League (41): Craig 7, Mackay 6 (1 pen), Dorrans 5, Mitchell 4, Teggart 4,

Fox 3, McPake 3, Shields 2, Cuthbert 1, Golabek 1, Griffiths 1, Makel 1, Smylie 1, Tweed 1, Walker A 1.
Scottish Cup (5): Dorrans 2, Hamill 1, Mackay 1, Tweed 1.
CIS Cup (4): Craig 2 (1 pen), Dorrans 1, Hislop 1.
Challenge Cup (1): Craig 1.
Honours – First Division: Champions – 2000-01. **Second Division:** Champions – 1986-87, 1998-99. **Third Division:** Champions – 1995-96. **League Cup winners** 2004.

MONTROSE DIV. 3

Ground: Links Park, Montrose DD10 8QD (01674) 673200
Ground capacity: 3292. **Colours:** Royal blue shirts and shorts.
Manager: Jim Weir.
League Appearances: Adam J 8(9); Alexander J (2); Baird J 8(1); Bell C 4; Black S 7(1); Cumming S 27(4); Davidson H 22(3); Docherty M 9; Donachie B 29(3); Farquhar J 1(1); Fraser S 9(3); Gibson K 13; Henslee G 27(4); Higgins C 14; Keith S (1); Kelly D 6(2); Kerrigan S 7(11); Mackie R (1); Maitland J (2); Malcolm S 6; McKenzie S 4; McLeod C 29; Mercer J 4; Michie S 24(9); Napier P 16(13); Ndiwa K 1; Reid A 27; Reid P 1(10); Rodgers A 33; Stephen N 14; Stewart G 4(5); Stewart P 1(5); Stirling J 27(1); Tawse C 10(4); Walker P 2; Watson C 1; Woods S 1.
Goals – League (42): Rodgers 10 (3 pens), Michie 7, Baird 5 (1 pen), Black 4, Henslee 4, Stephen 4, Docherty 2, Higgins 1, Kerrigan 1, McLeod 1, Mercer 1, Stirling 1, own goal 1.
Scottish Cup (2): Henslee 1, Stirling 1.
CIS Cup (1): Rodgers 1.
Challenge Cup (2): Henslee 1, Michie 1.
Honours – Second Division: Champions – 1984-85.

MORTON DIV. 1

Ground: Cappielow Park, Greenock (01475) 723571
Ground capacity: 11,612. **Colours:** Royal blue and white hooped shirts, white shorts with royal blue panel down side.
Manager: Jim McInally.
League Appearances: Black C (1); Finlayson K 9(21); Gonet S 4; Graham B 1; Greacen S 35; Harding R 36; Keenan D 8(8); Lilley D 11(8); Linn R 2(14); MacGregor D 25(2); Mathers P 20; McAlister J 36; McGowan P 35(1); McGurn D 12(2); McKellar S (1); McLaughlin S 28(1); McLean K (4); Millar C 30(6); Russell R 1(7); Stevenson J 36; Templeman C 23(12); Walker A 10(7); Weatherson P 34.
Goals – League (76): Weatherson 15, Templeman 12, McGowan 11, Millar 8, Stevenson 8 (2 pens), McAlister 5, Greacen 4, Lilley 4 (1 pen), Linn 2, McLaughlin 2, Finlayson 1, Harding 1, Keenan 1, own goals 2.
Scottish Cup (6): Templeman 2, Greacen 1, McGowan 1, Stevenson 1, Weatherson 1.
CIS Cup (1): McGowan 1.
Challenge Cup (9): McGowan 3, Weatherson 2, Harding 1, McLaughlin 1, Millar 1, own goal 1.
Honours – First Division: Champions – 1977-78, 1983-84, 1986-87. **Division II:** Champions – 1949-50, 1963-64, 1966-67. **Second Division:** Champions – 1994-95, 2006-07. **Third Division:** Champions 2002-03. **Scottish Cup winners** 1922.

MOTHERWELL PREMIER LEAGUE

Ground: Fir Park, Motherwell ML1 2QN (01698) 333333
Ground capacity: 13,742. **Colours:** Amber shirts with claret hoop and trim, amber shorts, amber stockings with claret trim.
First Team Coach: Mark McGhee.

League Appearances: Clarkson D 19(10); Coakley A (2); Connolly K 1(1); Corrigan M 19(3); Craigan S 34; Donnelly R 2; Elliot C 10(4); Fitzpatrick M 13(11); Foran R 22(1); Hamilton J 2(1); Keegan P 4(4); Kerr B 35; Kinniburgh W 4(1); Lasley K 14; McBride K 10(7); McCormack R 6(6); McDonald S 30(2); McGarry S 22(7); McLean B 1(4); Meldrum C 15(1); Molloy T (6); Murphy D 13(1); Murphy J (1); O'Donnell P 3; Paterson J 34; Quinn P 24(2); Reynolds M 35; Smith D 12(6); Smith G 23(1); Vadocz K 11.
Goals – League (41): McDonald 15 (1 pen), Foran 7 (4 pens), Smith D 3, Clarkson 2, Elliot 2, Kerr 2, McCormack 2, Reynolds 2, Fitzpatrick 1, McGarry 1, Murphy 1, O'Donnell 1, Paterson 1, own goal 1.
Scottish Cup (4): Foran 1, Kerr 1, McCormack 1, McDonald 1.
CIS Cup (8): Foran 6, Clarkson 1, McGarry 1.
Honours – Division I: Champions – 1931-32. **First Division:** Champions – 1981-82, 1984-85. **Division II:** Champions – 1953-54, 1968-69. **Scottish Cup winners** 1952, 1991. **League Cup winners** 1951.

PARTICK THISTLE DIV. 1

Ground: Firhill Stadium, Glasgow G20 7AL (0141) 579 1971
Ground capacity: 13,141. **Colours:** Red and yellow striped shirts, red shorts.
Manager: Ian McCall.
League Appearances: Archibald A 9; Arthur K 21; Boyd S 33(3); Brady D 28(2); Campbell S 10(5); Donnelly S 24; Ferguson B 16(9); Gibson G 4(15); Gibson J 26; Gibson W 21(8); Hodge A (2); Hodge S (2); Kane J 1(2); Keogh P 16(5); Marshall C (1); McChrystal M 13(2); McConalogue S 6(15); McCulloch S 14(2); McGoldrick J (3); Morrow S 4(4); Roberts M 30(2); Robertson J 21(1); Russell A 6(8); Sives C 17; Smith B 12; Strachan A 20(6); Tuffey J 15; Young D 29.
Goals – League (47): Roberts 16 (3 pens), Donnelly 5 (1 pen), Young 5, McConalogue 4, Keogh 3, Brady 2, McCulloch 2, Strachan 2, Ferguson 1, Gibson G 1, Gibson J 1, McChrystal 1, Morrow 1, Russell 1, Sives 1, Smith 1.
Scottish Cup (2): Gibson J 1, Robertson J 1.
CIS Cup (5): Boyd 1, Brady 1, Gibson J 1, Gibson W 1, Roberts 1.
Challenge Cup (1): Ferguson 1.
Honours – First Division: Champions – 1975-76, 2001-02. **Division II:** Champions – 1896-97, 1899-1900, 1970-71. **Second Division:** Champions 2000-01. **Scottish Cup winners** 1921. **League Cup winners** 1972.

PETERHEAD DIV. 2

Ground: Balmoor Stadium, Peterhead AB42 1EU (01779) 478256
Ground capacity: 3250 (1000 seated). **Colours:** Royal blue with white shirts, royal blue shorts.
Manager: Steve Paterson.
League Appearances: Ballard D (1); Bavidge M 21(4); Buchan J 31(1); Calder J 1; Cameron D 33; Cowie D (1); Farquhar J 1(1); Gibson K 8; Gilfillan B 31(4); Good I 5; Hegarty C 11(4); Kelly G 7; Keogh L 14; Linn R 15(5); Low A 5(8); Mann R 11; Mathers P 12; McAulay K 20; McCaldon I 15; McDonald C 18(1); McGeown G 7(6); McInnes A (6); McKay S 26(9); McNally S 14(1); Perry M 18; Scott S 2(1); Shand C 3; Sharp G 29(5); Stephen N 4(1); Tully C 21(3); Wood M 11(8); Youngson A 2(10).
Goals – League (60): Bavidge 11 (2 pens), Linn 10 (1 pen), McKay 8, McAulay 6, Sharp 5, Cameron 3, Gibson 3, Tully 3, Wood 2, Gilfillan 1, Hegarty 1, Low 1, McDonald 1, McGeown 1, Mann 1, own goals 3.
Scottish Cup (0).
CIS Cup (3): Bavidge 1, Linn 1 Wood 1.
Challenge Cup (0).
Honours – None.

QUEEN OF THE SOUTH **DIV. 1**

Ground: Palmerston Park, Dumfries DG2 9BA (01387) 254853
Ground capacity: 7412 (seated: 3509). **Colours:** Royal blue shirts with white sleeves, white shorts with blue piping.
Manager: Gordon Chisholm.
League Appearances: Adams J 11; Aitken A 1(1); Barrowman A 17(7); Burns P (4); Burns P 12(3); Callaghan B 1(8); Corr B 9(1); Dobbie S 15; Gibson W 18(4); Henderson M 11(3); Henry J 1(3); Hinchcliffe C 5; Lauchlan J 32(1); McCaffrey D 11; McDonald J 14; McKenzie S 13(3); McQuilken J 15; Moon W 7(5); Mullens M 1(4); Murray S 12(2); O'Connor S 22(7); O'Neil G (1); O'Neill J 27(7); Paton E 33; Robertson S 6(5); Scally N 34(1); Scott C 8; Swift S 7(3); Thomson A 1(13); Thomson J 28(2); Tosh S 7(4); Weir G 17(11); Whorlow M (1).
Goals – League (34): O'Neill J 8 (4 pens), Dobbie 6 (3 pens), O'Connor 6, Adams 2, Murray 2, Thomson A 2, Thomson J 2, Barrowman 1, Henderson 1, Lauchlan 1, Paton 1, Weir 1, own goal 1.
Scottish Cup (7): Dobbie 3 (1 pen), O'Connor 2. Adams 1, O'Neill J 1.
CIS Cup (5): O'Neill J 2, Henderson 1, O'Connor 1, Weir 1.
Challenge Cup (3): O'Neill J 2, Lauchlan 1.
Honours – Division II: Champions – 1950-51. **Second Division:** Champions – 2001-02. **Challenge Cup winners** 2003

QUEEN'S PARK **DIV. 2**

Ground: Hampden Park, Glasgow G42 9BA (0141) 632 1275
Ground capacity: 52,000. **Colours:** Black and white hooped shirts, white shorts.
Coach: Billy Stark.
League Appearances: Agostini D 21; Boslem A 1; Bowers R 5(12); Cairney P 18(3); Cairns M 14; Canning S 28(8); Carroll F 4(13); Colquhoun C (2); Crawford D 22; Dunlop M 32; Dunlop R (1); Dunn R 14(15); Ferry M 34(1); Harty A (1); Keenan M (1); Kettlewell S 35; Molloy S 3(1); Murray T 1(6); Paton P 31; Quinn A 19(8); Reilly S 15(1); Ronald P 24(5); Sinclair R 19; Trouten A 23(3); Weatherston D 32(1); Whelan J 1(1).
Goals – League (57): Weatherston 16, Ferry 11, Trouten 8 (3 pens), Cannon 5 (1 pen), Dunn 3, Quinn 3, Kettlewell 2, Ronald 2, Bowers 1, Cairney 1, Carroll 1, Dunlop M 1, Paton 1, Reilly 1 (pen), own goal 1.
Play-Offs (11): Trouten 3, Cannon 2, Weatherston 2, Cairney 1, Carroll 1, Dunlop M 1, Paton 1.
Scottish Cup (2): Ferry 1, Ronald 1.
CIS Cup (2): Bowers 1, Cannon 1.
Challenge Cup (5): Bowers 1, Molloy 1, Paton 1, Ronald 1, own goal 1.
Second Division: Champions – 1980-81. **Third Division:** Champions – 1999-2000. **Scottish Cup winners** 1874, 1875, 1876, 1880, 1881, 1882, 1884, 1886, 1890, 1893.

RAITH ROVERS **DIV. 2**

Ground: Stark's Park, Pratt Street, Kirkcaldy KY1 1SA (01592) 263514
Ground capacity: 10,104 (all seated). **Colours:** Navy blue shirts with white sleeves, white shorts with navy blue and red edges.
Manager: John McGlynn.
League Appearances: Andrews M 22; Bannerman S (1); Barrau X (2); Batchelor B 1; Bonar S 23(5); Brown M 16; Campbell M 28; Carcary D 10(2); Ciani A (1); Currie P 6(2); Dair J 1; Darling J 1; Davidson I 28(1); Dingwall J (2); Fahey C 20(1); Fairbairn B 14(10); Fotheringham K 28(2); Halley J (1); Harty I 9(3); Hislop S 9(2); Janczyk N 3(4); Kilgannon S 9(7); Leiper C (1); Lumsden T 30; Mackie J (1); Manson S 7(6); McLaughlin D 12(4); McManus P 25(3); Neil J 6; Oné A 13(8); Pelosi M 12(5); Sargent F (1); Silvestro C 23(3); Tansey P (3); Thoraninsson H

10(1); Tulloch S 3(4); Wilson C 27.
Goals – League (50): McManus 7 (1 pen), Fotheringham 6 (1 pen), Campbell 5, Andrews 4, Fairbairn 4, Harty 4 (1 pen), Hislop 4, Oné 4, Lumsden 3, Davidson 2, McLaughlin 2, Thorarinsson 2, Bonar 1, Manson 1, Wilson 1.
Play-Offs (1): Fairbairn 1.
Scottish Cup (0).
CIS Cup (1): Oné.
Challenge Cup (1): Oné.
Honours – First Division: Champions – 1992-93, 1994-95. **Second Division:** Champions – 2002-03. **Division II:** Champions – 1907-08, 1909-10 (Shared), 1937-38, 1948-49. **League Cup winners** 1995.

RANGERS — PREMIER LEAGUE

Ground: Ibrox Stadium, Glasgow G51 2XD (0141) 580 8500
Ground capacity: 51,082. **Colours:** Royal blue shirts with red and white trim, white shorts with blue and red trim.
Manager: Walter Smith.
League Appearances: Adam C 32; Bardsley P 5; Boyd K 25(7); Buffel T 9(8); Burke C 10(12); Clement J 19; Ehiogu U 9; Ferguson B 31(1); Hemdani B 36; Hutton A 32(1); Klos S (1); Lennon S (3); Letizi L 7; Martin L 4(3); McGregor A 31; Murray I 12(1); N'Diaye M (1); Novo N 22(6); Papac S 19(2); Prso D 23(4); Rae G 3(7); Rodriguez J 12(1); Sebo F 4(20); Shinnie A (2); Sionko L 14(4); Smith S 17; Svensson K 20(1); Thomson K 8(1); Weir D 14.
Goals – League (61): Boyd 20 (5 pens), Adam 11, Novo 5 (1 pen), Ferguson 4, Prso 4, Buffel 3, Sionko 3, Burke 2, Sebo 2, Bardsley 1. Ehiogu 1, Hemdani 1, Hutton 1, Rae 1, Smith 1, own goal 1.
Scottish Cup (2): Boyd 2.
CIS Cup (2): Boyd 1, own goal 1.
Honours – Division I: Champions – 1890-91 (Shared), 1898-99, 1899-1900, 1900-01, 1901-02, 1910-11, 1911-12, 1912-13, 1917-18, 1919-20, 1920-21, 1922-23, 1923-24, 1924-25, 1926-27, 1927-28, 1928-29, 1929-30, 1930-31, 1932-33, 1933-34, 1934-35, 1936-37, 1938-39, 1946-47, 1948-49, 1949-50, 1952-53, 1955-56, 1956-57, 1958-59, 1960-61, 1962-63, 1963-64, 1974-75. **Premier Division:** Champions – 1975-76, 1977-78, 1986-87, 1988-89, 1989-90, 1990-91, 1991-92, 1992-93, 1993-94, 1994-95, 1995-96, 1996-97. **Premier League:** Champions – 1998-99, 1999-2000, 2002-03, 2004-05. **Scottish Cup winners** 1894, 1897, 1898, 1903, 1928, 1930, 1932, 1934, 1935, 1936, 1948, 1949, 1950, 1953, 1960, 1962, 1963, 1964, 1966, 1973, 1976, 1978, 1979, 1981, 1992, 1993, 1996, 1999, 2000, 2002, 2003. **League Cup winners** 1947, 1949, 1961, 1962, 1964, 1965, 1971, 1976, 1978, 1979, 1982, 1984, 1985, 1987, 1988, 1989, 1991, 1993, 1994, 1997, 1999, 2002, 2003, 2005. **European Cup-Winners' Cup winners** 1972.

ROSS COUNTY — DIV. 2

Ground: Victoria Park, Dingwall IV15 9QW (01349) 860860
Ground capacity: 6700. **Colours:** Navy blue with white and red pin stripe on collar and sleeves, white shorts with navy and red side stripe, navy stockings.
Manager: Dick Campbell.
League Appearances: Adams D 24(1); Anderson S 7(2); Ciani A 5(9); Cowie D 28; Crooks J 2(5); Dowie A 36; Gardyne M 24(8); Gunn C 7(20); Higgins S 21(7); Hooks N 1(4); Irvine G 17; Keddie A 26; McCulloch M 26(2); McKinlay K 27(3); Moore D 13(2); Morgan A 5; Niven D 6; O'Carroll D 9(6); Rezgane M (1); Robertson H 18(6); Samson C 29; Scott M 21(7); Shields D 13; Smith J 8; Tiernan F 5(3); Tomei M 7; Webb S 5(1); Wilkie L 4; Williams A 2(2); Winters D (2).
Goals – League (40): Cowie 7, Gardyne 6, Higgins 5, McKinlay 5 (2 pens), Adams 2, Dowie 2, Gunn 2, O'Carroll 2, Robertson 2, Scott 2, Ciani 1, Hooks 1, Keddie 1, own goals 2.
Scottish Cup (0).

CIS Cup (5): Cowie 2, Gunn 1, Higgins 1, McKinlay 1.
Challenge Cup (13): Gunn 3, McKinlay 3 (1 pen), Dowie 2, Higgins 2, Anderson 1, Ciani 1, Williams 1.
Honours – Third Division: Champions – 1998-99. **League Challenge Cup:** Winners – 2007.

ST JOHNSTONE — DIV. 1

Ground: McDiarmid Park, Crieff Road, Perth PH1 2SJ (01738) 459090
Ground capacity: 10,673. **Colours:** Royal blue shirts with white trim, white shorts.
Manager: Owen Coyle.
League Appearances: Anderson S 21(5); Coyle O (1); Cuthbert K 17; Doris S (1); Dyer W (1); Halliwell B 18(1); Hardie M 32; Jackson A (6); James K 22; Lawrie A 28(3); Lawson P 6(2); Lilley D (14); MacDonald P 19(17); McGovern M 1; McInnes D 16; McLaren W 14(13); McManus A 32; Mensing S 33; Milne S 15(8); Morais F 5(8); Rutkiewicz K 1; Scotland J 34(1); Sheerin P 35(1); Sheridan D 10(7); Stanik G 36; Stevenson R (2); Weir J 1; Young D (3).
Goals – League (65): Scotland 18, Hardie 12, Milne 8, Sheerin 7, MacDonald 5, Mensing 4, McLaren 3, James 2, Lawrie 2, Lawson 1, McManus 1, Morais 1, own goal 1.
Scottish Cup (8): MacDonald 3, Hardie 2, Scotland 2, James 1.
CIS Cup (13): Milne 4, Scotland 4, Hardie 1, MacDonald 1, Mensing 1, Sheerin 1, Stevenson 1.
Challenge Cup (8): Menzie 2, Milne 2, Scotland 2, James 1, MacDonald 1.
Honours – First Division: Champions – 1982-83, 1989-90, 1996-97. **Division II:** Champions – 1923-24, 1959-60, 1962-63.

ST MIRREN — PREMIER LEAGUE

Ground: St Mirren Park, Paisley PA3 2EJ (0141) 889 2558
Ground capacity: 10,866 (all seated). **Colours:** Black and white striped shirts, white shorts with black trim.
Manager: Gus MacPherson.
League Appearances: Brady G 26(3); Brittain R 26(5); Broadfoot K 37; Bullock T 17; Burke A 4(9); Corcoran M 10(17); Gemmill S (5); Kean S 21(10); Lappin S 24; Lawson P 4; Malone E 4(2); Maxwell I 16; McCay R (4); McGinn S 1(3); McGowne K 19; McKenna D 1(9); Mehmet B 11(14); Millen A 23; Molloy C 6(6); Murray H 31; O'Donnell S 5; Potter J 25(1); Reid A 20(2); Smith C 21; Sutton J 29(4); Van Zanten D 37.
Goals – League (31): Sutton 12 (1 pen), Kean 4 (1 pen), Broadfoot 3, Brady 2, Mehmet 2, Brittain 1, Corcoran 1, Lappin 1, McGinn 1, Murray 1, O'Donnell 1, Van Zanten 1, own goal 1.
Scottish Cup (2): Brittain 1, Sutton 1.
CIS Cup (3): Mehmet 2, Sutton 1.
Honours – First Division: Champions – 1976-77, 1999-2000, 2005-06. **Division II:** Champions – 1967-68. **Scottish Cup winners** 1926, 1959, 1987.
League Challenge Cup: Winners – 2005-06.

STENHOUSEMUIR — DIV. 3

Ground: Ochilview Park, Stenhousemuir FK5 4QL (01324) 562992
Ground capacity: 2654. **Colours:** Maroon shirts with dark blue trim, white shorts.
Manager: Campbell Money.
League Appearances: Aitken S 11; Baird J 17(2); Carlin A 1; Coakley A 1; Connell Graham 6; Connelly G 2(3); Cowan M 22(1); Cryans S (1); Dempster J 16; Desmond S 2(3); Diack I 8(11); Dillon S 14; Fagan S 4; Forde R 2(5); Galloway R 1; Gillies D (1); Gow A 4; Henderson D 7(1); Henderson R 13(3); Hutchison G 27(2); Johnstone S 1; MacSween I 1(2); McAlpine J 3; McBride J 19(4); McCulloch

S 13; McCulloch W 34; McEwan C 5; McKernan D (2); McLaughlin B 16(7); McLeish K 27(2); McManus S 3(8); Menzies C 15(4); Muir J (1); Murie D 16; Murphy P 23(1); Peebles R 1; Sinclair T 8(8); Templeton D 9(4); Thom G 5; Thomson A 9(1); Tyrrell M 3; Tyrrell P 27(2).
Goals – League (53): Dempster 10, Hutchison 7, McBride 7 (1 pen), Baird 5, Diack 3, McLeish 3 (1 pen), Templeton 3, Thomson 3, McManus 2, Tyrrell P 2, Fagan 1, Menzies 1, Murphy 1, Thom 1, own goals 4.
Scottish Cup (0).
CIS Cup (3): Baird 1, Sinclair 1, own goal 1.
Challenge Cup (0).
Honours – League Challenge Cup: Winners – 1996.

STIRLING ALBION — DIV. 1

Ground: Forthbank Stadium, Springkerse Industrial Estate, Stirling FK7 7UJ (01786) 450399
Ground capacity: 3808. **Colours:** Red and white halved shirts, red shorts with white piping.
Manager: Allan Moore.
League Appearances: Aitken C 28(2); Bell S 31(1); Bingham D 6(3); Cashmore I 9(15); Christie S 2(2); Coyne T 2; Cramb C 26(4); Curry D 1; Devine S 12(8); Forsyth R 30(1); Fraser J 15(5); Gibson A 1(2); Graham A 14(1); Harty I 1; Hay P 29(5); Hogarth M 34; Malseed C (1); McNally M 28; Nugent P 16; O'Brien D 21(3); Roycroft S 22; Shields D 13(4); Snodgrass R 12; Taggart N 13(18); Tomana M 25(7); Wilson D 5(15).
Goals – League (67): Cramb 14 (1 pen), Aitken 9 (4 pens), Bell 8, O'Brien 8, Shields 8, Cashmore 5, Snodgrass 5, Tomana 5, Taggart 2, Nugent 1, Roycroft 1, Wilson 1.
Play-Offs (8): Aitken 3, Snodgrass 2, Cramb 1, Devine 1, Nugent 1.
Scottish Cup (4): Bell 1, Cramb 1, O'Brien 1, Shields 1.
CIS Cup (0).
Challenge Cup (0).
Honours – Division II: Champions – 1952-53, 1957-58, 1960-61, 1964-65. **Second Division:** Champions – 1976-77, 1990-91, 1995-96.

STRANRAER — DIV. 3

Ground: Stair Park, Stranraer DG9 8BS (01776) 703271
Ground capacity: 5600. **Colours:** Blue shirts with white side panels, blue shorts with white side panels.
Manager: Gerry Britton.
League Appearances: Aitken S 10(3); Black S 26(1); Britton G (1); Burns A 17(5); Crilly M 23; Dillon S 11; Donnelly R 4; Ferguson A 3; Gaughan K 1; Gibson A 9(1); Hamilton D 34; Hodge A 7; Janczyk N 2(8); Lyle W 10(8); McAlpine J 23(3); McAusland M 1; McGrillen P 8; McGroarty C 5(5); McKinstry J 18(8); McMullan P 15(9); McPhee B 6(1); Mitchell D 5(1); Moore M 25(1); Morrison A 7; Mullen M 5(10); Nicholas S 10(8); Ramsay D 17(5); Sharp L 25(2); Snowdon W 25(2); Walker R 18(2); Wilson S 14(1); Wright K 12(3).
Goals – League (45): Moore 12, Hamilton 10 (3 pens), Mullen 6, Crilly 2, Gibson 2 (1 pen), McMullan 2, Nicholas 2 (1 pen), Wright 2, Aitken 1, Burns 1, Janczik 1, McGrillen 1, Ramsay 1, Wilson 1, own goal 1.
Play-Offs (2): McGrillen 1, Moore 1.
Scottish Cup (7): Hamilton 1, McMullan 1, Moore 1, Nicholas 1, Ramsay 1, Wilson 1, Wright 1.
CIS Cup (2): Burns 1, Moore 1.
Challenge Cup (0).
Honours – Second Division: Champions – 1993-94, 1997-98. **Third Division:** Champions – 2003–04. **League Challenge Cup winners** 1997.

SCOTTISH LEAGUE HONOURS

*On goal average (ratio)/difference. †Held jointly after indecisive play-off. ‡Won on deciding match. ††Held jointly. ¶Two points deducted for fielding ineligible player. Competition suspended 1940–45 during war; Regional Leagues operating. ‡‡Two points deducted for registration irregularities. §Not promoted after play-offs.

PREMIER LEAGUE

	First	Pts	Second	Pts	Third	Pts
			Maximum points: 108			
1998–99	Rangers	77	Celtic	71	St Johnstone	57
1999–00	Rangers	90	Celtic	69	Hearts	54
			Maximum points: 114			
2000–01	Celtic	97	Rangers	82	Hibernian	66
2001–02	Celtic	103	Rangers	85	Livingston	58
2002–03	Rangers*	97	Celtic	97	Hearts	63
2003–04	Celtic	98	Rangers	81	Hearts	68
2004–05	Rangers	93	Celtic	92	Hibernian*	61
2005–06	Celtic	91	Hearts	74	Rangers	73
2006–07	Celtic	84	Rangers	72	Aberdeen	65

PREMIER DIVISION

	First	Pts	Second	Pts	Third	Pts
			Maximum points: 72			
1975–76	Rangers	54	Celtic	48	Hibernian	43
1976–77	Celtic	55	Rangers	46	Aberdeen	43
1977–78	Rangers	55	Aberdeen	53	Dundee U	40
1978–79	Celtic	48	Rangers	45	Dundee U	44
1979–80	Aberdeen	48	Celtic	47	St Mirren	42
1980–81	Celtic	56	Aberdeen	49	Rangers*	44
1981–82	Celtic	55	Aberdeen	53	Rangers	43
1982–83	Dundee U	56	Celtic*	55	Aberdeen	55
1983–84	Aberdeen	57	Celtic	50	Dundee U	47
1984–85	Aberdeen	59	Celtic	52	Dundee U	47
1985–86	Celtic*	50	Hearts	50	Dundee U	47
			Maximum points: 88			
1986–87	Rangers	69	Celtic	63	Dundee U	60
1987–88	Celtic	72	Hearts	62	Rangers	60
			Maximum points: 72			
1988–89	Rangers	56	Aberdeen	50	Celtic	46
1989–90	Rangers	51	Aberdeen*	44	Hearts	44
1990–91	Rangers	55	Aberdeen	53	Celtic*	41
			Maximum points: 88			
1991–92	Rangers	72	Hearts	63	Celtic	62
1992–93	Rangers	73	Aberdeen	64	Celtic	60
1993–94	Rangers	58	Aberdeen	55	Motherwell	54
			Maximum points: 108			
1994–95	Rangers	69	Motherwell	54	Hibernian	53
1995–96	Rangers	87	Celtic	83	Aberdeen*	55
1996–97	Rangers	80	Celtic	75	Dundee U	60
1997–98	Celtic	74	Rangers	72	Hearts	67

DIVISION 1

	First	Pts	Second	Pts	Third	Pts
			Maximum points: 52			
1975–76	Partick Th	41	Kilmarnock	35	Montrose	30

		Maximum points: 78				
1976–77	St Mirren	62	Clydebank	58	Dundee	51
1977–78	Morton*	58	Hearts	58	Dundee	57
1978–79	Dundee	55	Kilmarnock*	54	Clydebank	54
1979–80	Hearts	53	Airdrieonians	51	Ayr U*	44
1980–81	Hibernian	57	Dundee	52	St Johnstone	51
1981–82	Motherwell	61	Kilmarnock	51	Hearts	50
1982–83	St Johnstone	55	Hearts	54	Clydebank	50
1983–84	Morton	54	Dumbarton	51	Partick Th	46
1984–85	Motherwell	50	Clydebank	48	Falkirk	45
1985–86	Hamilton A	56	Falkirk	45	Kilmarnock	44
		Maximum points: 88				
1986–87	Morton	57	Dunfermline Ath	56	Dumbarton	53
1987–88	Hamilton A	56	Meadowbank Th	52	Clydebank	49
		Maximum points: 78				
1988–89	Dunfermline Ath	54	Falkirk	52	Clydebank	48
1989–90	St Johnstone	58	Airdrieonians	54	Clydebank	44
1990–91	Falkirk	54	Airdrieonians	53	Dundee	52
		Maximum points: 88				
1991–92	Dundee	58	Partick Th*	57	Hamilton A	57
1992–93	Raith R	65	Kilmarnock	54	Dunfermline Ath	52
1993–94	Falkirk	66	Dunfermline Ath	65	Airdrieonians	54
		Maximum points: 108				
1994–95	Raith R	69	Dunfermline Ath*	68	Dundee	68
1995–96	Dunfermline Ath	71	Dundee U*	67	Morton	67
1996–97	St Johnstone	80	Airdrieonians	60	Dundee*	58
1997–98	Dundee	70	Falkirk	65	Raith R*	60
1998–99	Hibernian	89	Falkirk	66	Ayr U	62
1999–00	St Mirren	76	Dunfermline Ath	71	Falkirk	68
2000–01	Livingston	76	Ayr U	69	Falkirk	56
2001–02	Partick Th	66	Airdrieonians	56	Ayr U	52
2002–03	Falkirk	81	Clyde	72	St Johnstone	67
2003–04	Inverness CT	70	Clyde	69	St Johnstone	57
2004–05	Falkirk	75	St Mirren*	60	Clyde	60
2005–06	St Mirren	76	St Johnstone	66	Hamilton A	59
2006–07	Gretna	66	St Johnstone	65	Dundee*	53

DIVISION 2

		Maximum points: 52				
1975–76	Clydebank*	40	Raith R	40	Alloa Ath	35
		Maximum points: 78				
1976–77	Stirling A	55	Alloa Ath	51	Dunfermline Ath	50
1977–78	Clyde*	53	Raith R	53	Dunfermline Ath	48
1978–79	Berwick R	54	Dunfermline Ath	52	Falkirk	50
1979–80	Falkirk	50	East Stirling	49	Forfar Ath	46
1980–81	Queen's Park	50	Queen of the S	46	Cowdenbeath	45
1981–82	Clyde	59	Alloa Ath*	50	Arbroath	50
1982–83	Brechin C	55	Meadowbank Th	54	Arbroath	49
1983–84	Forfar Ath	63	East Fife	47	Berwick R	43
1984–85	Montrose	53	Alloa Ath	50	Dunfermline Ath	49
1985–86	Dunfermline Ath	57	Queen of the S	55	Meadowbank Th	49
1986–87	Meadowbank Th	55	Raith R*	52	Stirling A*	52
1987–88	Ayr U	61	St Johnstone	59	Queen's Park	51

1988–89	Albion R	50	Alloa Ath	45	Brechin C	43
1989–90	Brechin C	49	Kilmarnock	48	Stirling A	47
1990–91	Stirling A	54	Montrose	46	Cowdenbeath	45
1991–92	Dumbarton	52	Cowdenbeath	51	Alloa Ath	50
1992–93	Clyde	54	Brechin C*	53	Stranraer	53
1993–94	Stranraer	56	Berwick R	48	Stenhousemuir*	47

Maximum points: 108

1994–95	Morton	64	Dumbarton	60	Stirling A	58
1995–96	Stirling A	81	East Fife	67	Berwick R	60
1996–97	Ayr U	77	Hamilton A	74	Livingston	64
1997–98	Stranraer	61	Clydebank	60	Livingston	59
1998–99	Livingston	77	Inverness CT	72	Clyde	53
1999–00	Clyde	65	Alloa Ath	64	Ross County	62
2000–01	Partick Th	75	Arbroath	58	Berwick R*	54
2001–02	Queen of the S	67	Alloa Ath	59	Forfar Ath	53
2002–03	Raith R	59	Brechin C	55	Airdrie U	54
2003–04	Airdrie U	70	Hamilton A	62	Dumbarton	60
2004–05	Brechin C	72	Stranraer	63	Morton	62
2005–06	Gretna	88	Morton§	70	Peterhead*§	57
2006–07	Morton	77	Stirling A	69	Raith R§	62

DIVISION 3

Maximum points: 108

1994–95	Forfar Ath	80	Montrose	67	Ross Co	60
1995–96	Livingston	72	Brechin C	63	Caledonian T	57
1996–97	Inverness CT	76	Forfar Ath*	67	Ross Co	67
1997–98	Alloa Ath	76	Arbroath	68	Ross Co*	67
1998–99	Ross Co	77	Stenhousemuir	64	Brechin C	59
1999–00	Queen's Park	69	Berwick R	66	Forfar Ath	61
2000–01	Hamilton A*	76	Cowdenbeath	76	Brechin C	72
2001–02	Brechin C	73	Dumbarton	61	Albion R	59
2002–03	Morton	72	East Fife	71	Albion R	70
2003–04	Stranraer	79	Stirling A	77	Gretna	68
2004–05	Gretna	98	Peterhead	78	Cowdenbeath	51
2005–06	Cowdenbeath*	76	Berwick R§	76	Stenhousemuir§	73
2006–07	Berwick R	75	Arbroath§	70	Queen's Park	68

DIVISION 1 to 1974–75

Maximum points: a 36; *b* 44; *c* 40; *d* 52; *e* 60; *f* 68; *g* 76; *h* 84.

	First	*Pts*	*Second*	*Pts*	*Third*	*Pts*
1890–91*a*	Dumbarton††	29	Rangers††	29	Celtic	21
1891–92*b*	Dumbarton	37	Celtic	35	Hearts	34
1892–93*a*	Celtic	29	Rangers	28	St Mirren	20
1893–94*a*	Celtic	29	Hearts	26	St Bernard's	23
1894–95*a*	Hearts	31	Celtic	26	Rangers	22
1895–96*a*	Celtic	30	Rangers	26	Hibernian	24
1896–97*a*	Hearts	28	Hibernian	26	Rangers	25
1897–98*a*	Celtic	33	Rangers	29	Hibernian	22
1898–99*a*	Rangers	36	Hearts	26	Celtic	24
1899–1900*a*	Rangers	32	Celtic	25	Hibernian	24
1900–01*c*	Rangers	35	Celtic	29	Hibernian	25
1901–02*a*	Rangers	28	Celtic	26	Hearts	22
1902–03*b*	Hibernian	37	Dundee	31	Rangers	29
1903–04*d*	Third Lanark	43	Hearts	39	Celtic*	38
1904–05*d*	Celtic‡	41	Rangers	41	Third Lanark	35

1905–06*e*	Celtic	49	Hearts	43	Airdrieonians	38
1906–07*f*	Celtic	55	Dundee	48	Rangers	45
1907–08*f*	Celtic	55	Falkirk	51	Rangers	50
1908–09*f*	Celtic	51	Dundee	50	Clyde	48
1909–10*f*	Celtic	54	Falkirk	52	Rangers	46
1910–11*f*	Rangers	52	Aberdeen	48	Falkirk	44
1911–12*f*	Rangers	51	Celtic	45	Clyde	42
1912–13*f*	Rangers	53	Celtic	49	Hearts*	41
1913–14*g*	Celtic	65	Rangers	59	Hearts*	54
1914–15*g*	Celtic	65	Hearts	61	Rangers	50
1915–16*g*	Celtic	67	Rangers	56	Morton	51
1916–17*g*	Celtic	64	Morton	54	Rangers	53
1917–18*f*	Rangers	56	Celtic	55	Kilmarnock*	43
1918–19*f*	Celtic	58	Rangers	57	Morton	47
1919–20*h*	Rangers	71	Celtic	68	Motherwell	57
1920–21*h*	Rangers	76	Celtic	66	Hearts	50
1921–22*h*	Celtic	67	Rangers	66	Raith R	51
1922–23*g*	Rangers	55	Airdrieonians	50	Celtic	46
1923–24*g*	Rangers	59	Airdrieonians	50	Celtic	46
1924–25*g*	Rangers	60	Airdrieonians	57	Hibernian	52
1925–26*g*	Celtic	58	Airdrieonians*	50	Hearts	50
1926–27*g*	Rangers	56	Motherwell	51	Celtic	49
1927–28*g*	Rangers	60	Celtic*	55	Motherwell	55
1928–29*g*	Rangers	67	Celtic	51	Motherwell	50
1929–30*g*	Rangers	60	Motherwell	55	Aberdeen	53
1930–31*g*	Rangers	60	Celtic	58	Motherwell	56
1931–32*g*	Motherwell	66	Rangers	61	Celtic	48
1932–33*g*	Rangers	62	Motherwell	59	Hearts	50
1933–34*g*	Rangers	66	Motherwell	62	Celtic	47
1934–35*g*	Rangers	55	Celtic	52	Hearts	50
1935–36*g*	Celtic	66	Rangers*	61	Aberdeen	61
1936–37*g*	Rangers	61	Aberdeen	54	Celtic	52
1937–38*g*	Celtic	61	Hearts	58	Rangers	49
1938–39*g*	Rangers	59	Celtic	48	Aberdeen	46
1946–47*e*	Rangers	46	Hibernian	44	Aberdeen	39
1947–48*e*	Hibernian	48	Rangers	46	Partick Th	36
1948–49*e*	Rangers	46	Dundee	45	Hibernian	39
1949–50*e*	Rangers	50	Hibernian	49	Hearts	43
1950–51*e*	Hibernian	48	Rangers*	38	Dundee	38
1951–52*e*	Hibernian	45	Rangers	41	East Fife	37
1952–53*e*	Rangers*	43	Hibernian	43	East Fife	39
1953–54*e*	Celtic	43	Hearts	38	Partick Th	35
1954–55*e*	Aberdeen	49	Celtic	46	Rangers	41
1955–56*f*	Rangers	52	Aberdeen	46	Hearts*	45
1956–57*f*	Rangers	55	Hearts	53	Kilmarnock	42
1957–58*f*	Hearts	62	Rangers	49	Celtic	46
1958–59*f*	Rangers	50	Hearts	48	Motherwell	44
1959–60*f*	Hearts	54	Kilmarnock	50	Rangers*	42
1960–61*f*	Rangers	51	Kilmarnock	50	Third Lanark	42
1961–62*f*	Dundee	54	Rangers	51	Celtic	46
1962–63*f*	Rangers	57	Kilmarnock	48	Partick Th	46
1963–64*f*	Rangers	55	Kilmarnock	49	Celtic*	47
1964–65*f*	Kilmarnock*	50	Hearts	50	Dunfermline Ath	49
1965–66*f*	Celtic	57	Rangers	55	Kilmarnock	45
1966–67*f*	Celtic	58	Rangers	55	Clyde	46

1967–68*f*	Celtic	63	Rangers	61	Hibernian	45
1968–69*f*	Celtic	54	Rangers	49	DunfermlineAth	45
1969–70*f*	Celtic	57	Rangers	45	Hibernian	44
1970–71*f*	Celtic	56	Aberdeen	54	St Johnstone	44
1971–72*f*	Celtic	60	Aberdeen	50	Rangers	44
1972–73*f*	Celtic	57	Rangers	56	Hibernian	45
1973–74*f*	Celtic	53	Hibernian	49	Rangers	48
1974–75*f*	Rangers	56	Hibernian	49	Celtic	45

DIVISION 2 to 1974–75

Maximum points: a 76; *b* 72; *c* 68; *d* 52; *e* 60; *f* 36; *g* 44.

1893–94*f*	Hibernian	29	Cowlairs	27	Clyde	24
1894–95*f*	Hibernian	30	Motherwell	22	Port Glasgow	20
1895–96*f*	Abercorn	27	Leith Ath	23	Renton	21
1896–97*f*	Partick Th	31	Leith Ath	27	Kilmarnock*	21
1897–98*f*	Kilmarnock	29	Port Glasgow	25	Morton	22
1898–99*f*	Kilmarnock	32	Leith Ath	27	Port Glasgow	25
1899–1900*f*	Partick Th	29	Morton	28	Port Glasgow	20
1900–01*f*	St Bernard's	25	Airdrieonians	23	Abercorn	21
1901–02*g*	Port Glasgow	32	Partick Th	31	Motherwell	26
1902–03*g*	Airdrieonians	35	Motherwell	28	Ayr U*	27
1903–04*g*	Hamilton A	37	Clyde	29	Ayr U	28
1904–05*g*	Clyde	32	Falkirk	28	Hamilton A	27
1905–06*g*	Leith Ath	34	Clyde	31	Albion R	27
1906–07*g*	St Bernard's	32	Vale of Leven*	27	Arthurlie	27
1907–08*g*	Raith R	30	Dumbarton‡‡	27	Ayr U	27
1908–09*g*	Abercorn	31	Raith R*	28	Vale of Leven	28
1909–10*g*	Leith Ath‡	33	Raith R	33	St Bernard's	27
1910–11*g*	Dumbarton	31	Ayr U	27	Albion R	25
1911–12*g*	Ayr U	35	Abercorn	30	Dumbarton	27
1912–13*d*	Ayr U	34	Dunfermline Ath	33	East Stirling	32
1913–14*g*	Cowdenbeath	31	Albion R	27	Dunfermline Ath*	26
1914–15*d*	Cowdenbeath*	37	St Bernard's*	37	Leith Ath	37
1921–22*a*	Alloa Ath	60	Cowdenbeath	47	Armadale	45
1922–23*a*	Queen's Park	57	Clydebank ¶	50	St Johnstone ¶	45
1923–24*a*	St Johnstone	56	Cowdenbeath	55	Bathgate	44
1924–25*a*	Dundee U	50	Clydebank	48	Clyde	47
1925–26*a*	Dunfermline Ath	59	Clyde	53	Ayr U	52
1926–27*a*	Bo'ness	56	Raith R	49	Clydebank	45
1927–28*a*	Ayr U	54	Third Lanark	45	King's Park	44
1928–29*b*	Dundee U	51	Morton	50	Arbroath	47
1929–30*a*	Leith Ath*	57	East Fife	57	Albion R	54
1930–31*a*	Third Lanark	61	Dundee U	50	Dunfermline Ath	47
1931–32*a*	East Stirling*	55	St Johnstone	55	Raith R*	46
1932–33*c*	Hibernian	54	Queen of the S	49	Dunfermline Ath	47
1933–34*c*	Albion R	45	Dunfermline Ath*	44	Arbroath	44
1934–35*c*	Third Lanark	52	Arbroath	50	St Bernard's	47
1935–36*c*	Falkirk	59	St Mirren	52	Morton	48
1936–37*c*	Ayr U	54	Morton	51	St Bernard's	48
1937–38*c*	Raith R	59	Albion R	48	Airdrieonians	47
1938–39*c*	Cowdenbeath	60	Alloa Ath*	48	East Fife	48
1946–47*d*	Dundee	45	Airdrieonians	42	East Fife	31
1947–48*e*	East Fife	53	Albion R	42	Hamilton A	40
1948–49*e*	Raith R*	42	Stirling A	42	Airdrieonians*	41
1949–50*e*	Morton	47	Airdrieonians	44	Dunfermline Ath*	36
1950–51*e*	Queen of the S*	45	Stirling A	45	Ayr U*	36
1951–52*e*	Clyde	44	Falkirk	43	Ayr U	39

1952–53*e*	Stirling A	44	Hamilton A	43	Queen's Park	37
1953–54*e*	Motherwell	45	Kilmarnock	42	Third Lanark*	36
1954–55*e*	Airdrieonians	46	Dunfermline Ath	42	Hamilton A	39
1955–56*b*	Queen's Park	54	Ayr U	51	St Johnstone	49
1956–57*b*	Clyde	64	Third Lanark	51	Cowdenbeath	45
1957–58*b*	Stirling A	55	Dunfermline Ath	53	Arbroath	47
1958–59*b*	Ayr U	60	Arbroath	51	Stenhousemuir	46
1959–60*b*	St Johnstone	53	Dundee U	50	Queen of the S	49
1960–61*b*	Stirling A	55	Falkirk	54	Stenhousemuir	50
1961–62*b*	Clyde	54	Queen of the S	53	Morton	44
1962–63*b*	St Johnstone	55	East Stirling	49	Morton	48
1963–64*b*	Morton	67	Clyde	53	Arbroath	46
1964–65*b*	Stirling A	59	Hamilton A	50	Queen of the S	45
1965–66*b*	Ayr U	53	Airdrieonians	50	Queen of the S	47
1966–67*a*	Morton	69	Raith R	58	Arbroath	57
1967–68*b*	St Mirren	62	Arbroath	53	East Fife	49
1968–69*b*	Motherwell	64	Ayr U	53	East Fife*	48
1969–70*b*	Falkirk	56	Cowdenbeath	55	Queen of the S	50
1970–71*b*	Partick Th	56	East Fife	51	Arbroath	46
1971–72*b*	Dumbarton*	52	Arbroath	52	Stirling A	50
1972–73*b*	Clyde	56	Dumfermline Ath	52	Raith R*	47
1973–74*b*	Airdrieonians	60	Kilmarnock	58	Hamilton A	55
1974–75*a*	Falkirk	54	Queen of the S*	53	Montrose	53

Elected to Division 1: 1894 Clyde; 1895 Hibernian; 1896 Abercorn; 1897 Partick Th; 1899 Kilmarnock; 1900 Morton and Partick Th; 1902 Port Glasgow and Partick Th; 1903 Airdrieonians and Motherwell; 1905 Falkirk and Aberdeen; 1906 Clyde and Hamilton A; 1910 Raith R; 1913 Ayr U and Dumbarton.

SCOTTISH LEAGUE PLAY-OFFS 2006–2007

SCOTTISH DIVISION 1 SEMI-FINAL FIRST LEG

Brechin C	(0) 1	Airdrie U	(3) 3
Raith R	(0) 0	Stirling A	(0) 0

SCOTTISH DIVISION 1 SEMI-FINAL SECOND LEG

Airdrie U	(1) 3	Brechin C	(0) 0
Stirling A	(1) 3	Raith R	(1) 1

SCOTTISH DIVISION 1 FINAL FIRST LEG

Stirling A	(0) 2	Airdrie U	(2) 2

SCOTTISH DIVISION 1 FINAL SECOND LEG

Airdrie U	(1) 2	Stirling A	(2) 3

SCOTTISH DIVISION 2 SEMI-FINAL FIRST LEG

Queen's Park	(0) 2	Arbroath	(0) 0
East Fife	(3) 4	Stranraer	(0) 1

SCOTTISH DIVISION 2 SEMI-FINAL SECOND LEG

Arbroath	(0) 1	Queen's Park	(2) 2
Stranraer	(0) 1	East Fife	(0) 0

SCOTTISH DIVISION 2 FINAL FIRST LEG

Queen's Park	(2) 4	East Fife	(0) 2

SCOTTISH DIVISION 2 FINAL SECOND LEG

East Fife	(0) 0	Queen's Park	(1) 3

RELEGATED CLUBS

From Premier League

1998–99 Dunfermline Ath
1999–00 *No relegated team*
2000–01 St Mirren
2001–02 St Johnstone
2002–03 *No relegated team*
2003–04 Partick Th
2004–05 Dundee
2005–06 Livingston
2006–07 Dunfermline Ath

From Premier Division

1974–75 *No relegation due to League reorganisation*
1975–76 Dundee, St Johnstone
1976–77 Hearts, Kilmarnock
1977–78 Ayr U, Clydebank
1978–79 Hearts, Motherwell
1979–80 Dundee, Hibernian
1980–81 Kilmarnock, Hearts
1981–82 Partick Th, Airdrieonians
1982–83 Morton, Kilmarnock
1983–84 St Johnstone, Motherwell
1984–85 Dumbarton, Morton
1985–86 *No relegation due to League reorganisation*
1986–87 Clydebank, Hamilton A
1987–88 Falkirk, Dunfermline Ath, Morton
1988–89 Hamilton A
1989–90 Dundee
1990–91 None
1991–92 St Mirren, Dunfermline Ath
1992–93 Falkirk, Airdrieonians
1993–94 *See footnote, page 210*
1994–95 Dundee U
1995–96 Partick Th, Falkirk
1996–97 Raith R
1997–98 Hibernian

From Division 1

1974–75 *No relegation due to League reorganisation*
1975–76 Dunfermline Ath, Clyde
1976–77 Raith R, Falkirk
1977–78 Alloa Ath, East Fife
1978–79 Montrose, Queen of the S
1979–80 Arbroath, Clyde
1980–81 Stirling A, Berwick R
1981–82 East Stirling, Queen of the S
1982–83 Dunfermline Ath, Queen's Park
1983–84 Raith R, Alloa Ath
1984–85 Meadowbank Th, St Johnstone
1985–86 Ayr U, Alloa Ath
1986–87 Brechin C, Montrose
1987–88 East Fife, Dumbarton
1988–89 Kilmarnock, Queen of the S
1989–90 Albion R, Alloa Ath
1990–91 Clyde, Brechin C
1991–92 Montrose, Forfar Ath
1992–93 Meadowbank Th, Cowdenbeath
1993–94 *See footnote*
1994–95 Ayr U, Stranraer
1995–96 Hamilton A, Dumbarton
1996–97 Clydebank, East Fife
1997–98 Partick Th, Stirling A
1998–99 Hamilton A, Stranraer
1999–00 Clydebank
2000–01 Morton, Alloa Ath
2001–02 Raith R
2002–03 Alloa Ath, Arbroath
2003–04 Ayr U, Brechin C
2004–05 Partick Th, Raith R
2005–06 Stranraer, Brechin C
2006–07 Airdrie U, Ross Co

From Division 2

1994–95 Meadowbank Th, Brechin C
1995–96 Forfar Ath, Montrose
1996–97 Dumbarton, Berwick R
1997–98 Stenhousemuir, Brechin C
1998–99 East Fife, Forfar Ath
1999–00 Hamilton A**
2000–01 Queen's Park, Stirling A
2001–02 Morton
2002–03 Stranraer, Cowdenbeath
2003–04 East Fife, Stenhousemuir
2004–05 Arbroath, Berwick R
2005–06 Dumbarton
2006–07 Stranraer, Forfar

From Division 1 1973–74

1921–22 *Queen's Park, Dumbarton, Clydebank
1922–23 Albion R, Alloa Ath
1923–24 Clyde, Clydebank
1924–25 Third Lanark, Ayr U
1925–26 Raith R, Clydebank
1926–27 Morton, Dundee U
1927–28 Dunfermline Ath, Bo'ness
1928–29 Third Lanark, Raith R
1929–30 St Johnstone, Dundee U
1930–31 Hibernian, East Fife
1931–32 Dundee U, Leith Ath
1932–33 Morton, East Stirling
1933–34 Third Lanark, Cowdenbeath
1934–35 St Mirren, Falkirk
1935–36 Airdrieonians, Ayr U
1936–37 Dunfermline Ath, Albion R
1937–38 Dundee, Morton
1938–39 Queen's Park, Raith R
1946–47 Kilmarnock, Hamilton A
1947–48 Airdrieonians, Queen's Park
1948–49 Morton, Albion R
1949–50 Queen of the S, Stirling A
1950–51 Clyde, Falkirk
1951–52 Morton, Stirling A
1952–53 Motherwell, Third Lanark
1953–54 Airdrieonians, Hamilton A
1954–55 *No clubs relegated*
1955–56 Stirling A, Clyde
1956–57 Dunfermline Ath, Ayr U
1957–58 East Fife, Queen's Park
1958–59 Queen of the S, Falkirk
1959–60 Arbroath, Stirling A
1960–61 Ayr U, Clyde
1961–62 St Johnstone, Stirling A
1962–63 Clyde, Raith R
1963–64 Queen of the S, East Stirling
1964–65 Airdrieonians, Third Lanark
1965–66 Morton, Hamilton A
1966–67 St Mirren, Ayr U
1967–68 Motherwell, Stirling A
1968–69 Falkirk, Arbroath
1969–70 Raith R, Partick Th
1970–71 St Mirren, Cowdenbeath
1971–72 Clyde, Dunfermline Ath
1972–73 Kilmarnock, Airdrieonians
1973–74 East Fife, Falkirk

*Season 1921–22 – only 1 club promoted, 3 clubs relegated.
***15 pts deducted for failing to field a team.*

Scottish League championship wins: Rangers 51, Celtic 41, Aberdeen 4, Hearts 4, Hibernian 4, Dumbarton 2, Dundee 1, Dundee U 1, Kilmarnock 1, Motherwell 1, Third Lanark 1.

The Scottish Football League was reconstructed into three divisions at the end of the 1974–75 season, so the usual relegation statistics do not apply. Further reorganization took place at the end of the 1985–86 season. From 1986–87, the Premier and First Division had 12 teams each. The Second Division remained at 14. From 1988–89, the Premier Division reverted to 10 teams, and the First Division to 14 teams but in 1991–92 the Premier and First Division reverted to 12. At the end of the 1997–98 season, the top nine clubs in Premier Division broke away from the Scottish League to form a new competition, the Scottish Premier League, with the club promoted from Division One. At the end of the 1999–2000 season two teams were added to the Scottish League. There was no relegation from the Premier League but two promoted from the First Division and three from each of the Second and Third Divisions. One team was relegated from the First Division and one from the Second Division, leaving 12 teams in each division. In season 2002–03, Falkirk were not promoted to the Premier League due to the failure of their ground to meet League standards. Inverness CT were promoted after a previous refusal in 2003–04 because of ground sharing. At the end of 2005–06 the Scottish League introduced play-offs for the team finishing second from the bottom of Division 1 against the winners of the second, third and fourth finishing teams in Division 2 and with a similar procedure for Division 2 and Division 3.

PAST SCOTTISH LEAGUE CUP FINALS

1946–47	Rangers	4	Aberdeen	0
1947–48	East Fife	0 4	Falkirk	0* 1
1948–49	Rangers	2	Raith Rovers	0
1949–50	East Fife	3	Dunfermline	0
1950–51	Motherwell	3	Hibernian	0
1951–52	Dundee	3	Rangers	2
1952–53	Dundee	2	Kilmarnock	0
1953–54	East Fife	3	Partick Th	2
1954–55	Hearts	4	Motherwell	2
1955–56	Aberdeen	2	St Mirren	1
1956–57	Celtic	0 3	Partick Th	0 0
1957–58	Celtic	7	Rangers	1
1958–59	Hearts	5	Partick Th	1
1959–60	Hearts	2	Third Lanark	1
1960–61	Rangers	2	Kilmarnock	0
1961–62	Rangers	1 3	Hearts	1 1
1962–63	Hearts	1	Kilmarnock	0
1963–64	Rangers	5	Morton	0
1964–65	Rangers	2	Celtic	1
1965–66	Celtic	2	Rangers	1
1966–67	Celtic	1	Rangers	0
1967–68	Celtic	5	Dundee	3
1968–69	Celtic	6	Hibernian	2
1969–70	Celtic	1	St Johnstone	0
1970–71	Rangers	1	Celtic	0
1971–72	Partick Th	4	Celtic	1
1972–73	Hibernian	2	Celtic	1
1973–74	Dundee	1	Celtic	0
1974–75	Celtic	6	Hibernian	3
1975–76	Rangers	1	Celtic	0
1976–77	Aberdeen	2	Celtic	1
1977–78	Rangers	2	Celtic	1*
1978–79	Rangers	2	Aberdeen	1
1979–80	Aberdeen	0 0	Dundee U	0* 3
1980–81	Dundee	0	Dundee U	3
1981–82	Rangers	2	Dundee U	1
1982–83	Celtic	2	Rangers	1
1983–84	Rangers	3	Celtic	2
1984–85	Rangers	1	Dundee U	0
1985–86	Aberdeen	3	Hibernian	0
1986–87	Rangers	2	Celtic	1
1987–88	Rangers†	3	Aberdeen	3*
1988–89	Aberdeen	2	Rangers	3*
1989–90	Aberdeen	2	Rangers	1
1990–91	Rangers	2	Celtic	1
1991–92	Hibernian	2	Dunfermline Ath	0
1992–93	Rangers	2	Aberdeen	1*
1993–94	Rangers	2	Hibernian	1
1994–95	Raith R†	2	Celtic	2*

1995–96	Aberdeen	2	Dundee	0
1996–97	Rangers	4	Hearts	3
1997–98	Celtic	3	Dundee U	0
1998–99	Rangers	2	St Johnstone	1
1999–2000	Celtic	2	Aberdeen	0
2000–01	Celtic	3	Kilmarnock	0
2001–02	Rangers	4	Ayr U	0
2002–03	Rangers	2	Celtic	1
2003–04	Livingston	2	Hibernian	0
2004–05	Rangers	5	Motherwell	1
2005–06	Celtic	3	Dunfermline Ath	0
2006–07	Hibernian	5	Kilmarnock	1

†*Won on penalties* **After extra time*

PAST LEAGUE CHALLENGE FINALS

1990–91	Dundee	3	Ayr U	2
1991–92	Hamilton A	1	Ayr U	0
1992–93	Hamilton A	3	Morton	2
1993–94	St Mirren	9	Falkirk	3
1994–95	Airdrieonians	3	Dundee	2
1995–96	Stenhousemuir	0	Dundee U	0
	(aet; Stenhousemuir won 5-4 on penalties.)			
1996–97	Stranraer	1	St Johnstone	0
1997–98	Falkirk	1	Qeeen of the South	0
1998–99	no competition			
1999–2000	Alloa Ath	4	Inverness CT	4
	(aet; Alloa Ath won 5-4 on penalties.)			
2000–01	Airdrieonians	2	Livingston	2
	(aet; Airdrieonians won 3-2 on penalties.)			
2001–02	Airdrieonians	2	Alloa Ath	1
2002–03	Queen of the S	2	Brechin C	0
2003–04	Inverness CT	2	Airdrie U	0
2004–05	Falkirk	2	Ross Co	1
2005–06	St Mirren	2	Hamilton A	1
2006–07	Ross Co	1	Clyde	1
	(aet; Ross Co won 5-4 on penalties.)			

CIS SCOTTISH LEAGUE CUP 2006–2007

FIRST ROUND

Albion R	(1) 1	Stenhousemuir	(0) 2
Brechin C	(0) 2	Morton	(1) 1
Cowdenbeath	(4) 4	East Stirling	(0) 1
Dumbarton	(0) 3	Stirling Albion	(0) 0
Dundee	(1) 1	Partick T	(1) 3
Forfar Ath	(0) 1	Alloa Ath	(1) 2
(aet)			
Queen of the S	(4) 4	Clyde	(1) 2
Queen's Park	(1) 2	Hamilton A	(0) 1
(aet)			
Raith R	(1) 1	Airdrie U	(0) 2
Ross Co	(1) 4	Stranraer	(0) 2
St Johnstone	(0) 3	East Fife	(0) 1
Arbroath	(0) 0	Elgin C	(0) 1
Ayr U	(2) 2	Berwick R	(0) 0
Montrose	(1) 1	Peterhead	(0) 3
(aet)			

SECOND

Alloa Ath	(1) 2	Ross Co	(0) 1
Ayr U	(0) 0	Dunfermline Ath	(0) 0
(aet; Ayr U won 7-6 on penalties.)			
Brechin C	(0) 0	Livingston	(2) 3
Cowdenbeath	(0) 0	Falkirk	(1) 5
Dundee U	(0) 1	Airdrie U	(0) 0
(aet)			
Hibernian	(2) 4	Peterhead	(0) 0
Motherwell	(2) 3	Partick T	(1) 2
Queen of the S	(0) 1	Kilmarnock	(0) 2
(aet)			
Queen's Park	(0) 0	Aberdeen	(0) 0
(aet; Queen's Park won 5-3 on penalties.)			
St Johnstone	(0) 4	Elgin C	(0) 0
(aet)			
St Mirren	(3) 3	Stenhousemuir	(0) 1
Inverness CT	(1) 3	Dumbarton	(1) 1

THIRD ROUND

Celtic	(0) 2	St Mirren	(0) 0
Inverness CT	(0) 0	Falkirk	(0) 1
Kilmarnock	(0) 2	Livingston	(0) 1
(aet)			
St Johnstone	(1) 3	Dundee U	(0) 0
Alloa Ath	(0) 0	Hearts	(1) 4
Dunfermline Ath	(0) 0	Rangers	(0) 2
Hibernian	(4) 6	Gretna	(0) 0
Queen's Park	(0) 0	Motherwell	(1) 3

QUARTER-FINALS

Celtic	(0) 1	Falkirk	(0) 1
(aet; Falkirk won 5-4 on penalties.)			
Kilmarnock	(2) 3	Motherwell	(1) 2
Hibernian	(1) 1	Hearts	(0) 0
Rangers	(0) 0	St Johnstone	(0) 2

SEMI-FINALS

Kilmarnock	(1) 3	Falkirk	(0) 0
St Johnstone	(0) 1	Hibernian	(1) 3

FINAL

Kilmarnock	(0) 1	Hibernian	(1) 5

LEAGUE CHALLENGE CUP 2006–2007

FIRST ROUND

Ayr U	(1) 2	Livingston	(1) 1
Brechin C	(1) 1	Arbroath	(1) 2
Cowdenbeath	(2) 4	Stirling Albion	(0) 0
Dumbarton	(0) 1	Morton	(0) 2
(aet)			
East Stirling	(0) 0	Queen's Park	(3) 5
Forfar Ath	(0) 2	Dundee	(0) 1
Hamilton A	(1) 3	Berwick R	(1) 1
Partick T	(1) 1	Albion R	(2) 2
Queen of the S	(0) 1	Stranraer	(0) 0
St Johnstone	(1) 3	Raith R	(1) 1
(aet)			
Airdrie U	(0) 0	Gretna	(1) 3
East Fife	(0) 0	Ross Co	(1) 3
Elgin C	(0) 2	Stenhousemuir	(0) 0
Montrose	(0) 2	Peterhead	(0) 0

SECOND ROUND

Albion R	(2) 5	Elgin C	(0) 2
Forfar Ath	(1) 1	Arbroath	(1) 3
Morton	(3) 3	Cowdenbeath	(0) 2
Ross Co	(0) 2	Alloa Ath	(1) 1
(aet)			
St Johnstone	(2) 3	Queen's Park	(0) 0
Gretna	(2) 3	Hamilton A	(1) 1
Montrose	(0) 0	Clyde	(1) 3
Queen of the S	(0) 2	Ayr U	(0) 2
(aet; Ayr U won 5-4 on penalties.)			

QUARTER-FINALS

Albion R	(2) 3	Arbroath	(2) 3
(aet; Albion R won 5-3 on penalties.)			
Clyde	(0) 1	Ayr U	(0) 0
Morton	(0) 3	St Johnstone	(1) 2
Ross Co	(2) 3	Gretna	(0) 2
(aet)			

SEMI-FINALS

Clyde	(2) 3	Morton	(0) 1
Ross Co	(1) 4	Albion R	(0) 1

FINAL

Ross Co	(0) 1	Clyde	(1) 1
(aet; Ross Co won 5-4 on penalties.)			

TENNENT'S SCOTTISH CUP 2006–2007

FIRST ROUND

Arbroath	(1) 2	Albion R	(0) 1
Brechin C	(0) 1	Queen's Park	(1) 1
Deveronvale	(0) 3	Montrose	(2) 2
East Fife	(0) 1	Berwick R	(1) 3
Edinburgh University	(2) 2	Keith	(0) 1
Preston Ath	(1) 2	Stenhousemuir	(0) 0
Stranraer	(1) 4	Alloa Ath	(1) 2
East Stirling	(0) 0	Stirling Albion	(2) 2

FIRST ROUND REPLAY

Queen's Park	(1) 1	Brechin C	(0) 2

SECOND ROUND

Annan Ath	(0) 0	Morton	(3) 3
Berwick R	(1) 2	Arbroath	(0) 0
Brechin C	(1) 2	Preston Ath	(0) 1
Cowdenbeatb	(3) 5	Edinburgh University	(0) 1
Deveronvale	(1) 2	Fraserburgh	(1) 1
Edinburgh C	(0) 0	Stirling Albion	(1) 1
Elgin C	(1) 1	Buckie T	(0) 0
Peterhead	(0) 0	Ayr U	(1) 2
Raith R	(0) 0	Dumbarton	(0) 1
Stranraer	(2) 3	Forfar Ath	(0) 1

THIRD ROUND

Airdrie U	(0) 0	Motherwell	(1) 1
Berwick R	(0) 0	Falkirk	(1) 2
Celtic	(3) 4	Dumbarton	(0) 0
Clyde	(0) 0	Gretna	(1) 3
Cowdenbeath	(1) 1	Brechin C	(0) 1
Deveronvale	(4) 5	Elgin C	(1) 4
Dundee	(1) 1	Queen of the S	(1) 1
Hamilton A	(0) 2	Livingston	(1) 4
Morton	(0) 3	Kilmarnock	(0) 1
Ross Co	(0) 0	Partick T	(1) 1
St Johnstone	(0) 0	Ayr U	(0) 0
Stirling Albion	(1) 1	Inverness CT	(4) 6
Stranraer	(0) 0	Hearts	(2) 4
Dunfermline Ath	(2) 3	Rangers	(0) 2
Aberdeen	(0) 2	Hibernian	(1) 2
Dundee U	(1) 3	St Mirren	(0) 2

THIRD ROUND REPLAYS

Brechin C	(0) 0	Cowdenbeath	(1) 1
Queen of the S	(1) 3	Dundee	(0) 3
(aet; Queen of the S won 4-2 on penalties.)			
Ayr U	(0) 1	St Johnstone	(1) 2
(aet)			
Hibernian	(2) 4	Aberdeen	(1) 1

FOURTH ROUND

Deveronvale	(0) 0	Partick T	(1) 1
Dunfermline Ath	(0) 1	Hearts	(0) 0

Falkirk	(0) 0	St Johnstone	(2) 3
Hibernian	(1) 3	Gretna	(0) 1
Inverness CT	(1) 1	Dundee U	(0) 0
Motherwell	(2) 2	Morton	(0) 0
Queen of the S	(1) 2	Cowdenbeath	(0) 0
Livingston	(1) 1	Celtic	(2) 4

QUARTER-FINALS

Dunfermline Ath	(1) 2	Partick T	(0) 0
Queen of the S	(0) 1	Hibernian	(1) 2
Inverness CT	(1) 1	Celtic	(0) 2
Motherwell	(0) 1	St Johnstone	(1) 2

SEMI-FINALS

St Johnstone	(1) 1	Celtic	(1) 2
Hibernian	(0) 0	Dunfermline Ath	(0) 0

SEMI-FINAL REPLAY

Dunfermline Ath	(0) 1	Hibernian	(0) 0

FINAL

Celtic	(0) 1	Dunfermline Ath	(0) 0

PAST SCOTTISH CUP FINALS

1874	Queen's Park	2	Clydesdale	0
1875	Queen's Park	3	Renton	0
1876	Queen's Park	1 2	Third Lanark	1 0
1877	Vale of Leven	0 1 3	Rangers	0 1 2
1878	Vale of Leven	1	Third Lanark	0
1879	Vale of Leven	1	Rangers	1
	Vale of Leven awarded cup, Rangers did not appear for replay			
1880	Queen's Park	3	Thornlibank	0
1881	Queen's Park	2 3	Dumbarton	1 1
	Replayed because of protest			
1882	Queen's Park	2 4	Dumbarton	2 1
1883	Dumbarton	2 2	Vale of Leven	2 1
1884	*Queen's Park awarded cup when Vale of Leven did not appear for the final*			
1885	Renton	0 3	Vale of Leven	0 1
1886	Queen's Park	3	Renton	1
1887	Hibernian	2	Dumbarton	1
1888	Renton	6	Cambuslang	1
1889	Third Lanark	3 2	Celtic	0 1
	Replayed because of protest			
1890	Queen's Park	1 2	Vale of Leven	1 1
1891	Hearts	1	Dumbarton	0
1892	Celtic	1 5	Queen's Park	0 1
	Replayed because of protest			
1893	Queen's Park	2	Celtic	1
1894	Rangers	3	Celtic	1
1895	St Bernards	3	Renton	1
1896	Hearts	3	Hibernian	1
1897	Rangers	5	Dumbarton	1
1898	Rangers	2	Kilmarnock	0
1899	Celtic	2	Rangers	0
1900	Celtic	4	Queen's Park	3
1901	Hearts	4	Celtic	3
1902	Hibernian	1	Celtic	0
1903	Rangers	1 0 2	Hearts	1 0 0
1904	Celtic	3	Rangers	2
1905	Third Lanark	0 3	Rangers	0 1
1906	Hearts	1	Third Lanark	0
1907	Celtic	3	Hearts	0
1908	Celtic	5	St Mirren	1
1909	*After two drawn games between Celtic and Rangers, 2.2, 1.1, there was a riot and the cup was withheld*			
1910	Dundee	2 0 2	Clyde	2 0 1
1911	Celtic	0 2	Hamilton Acad	0 0
1912	Celtic	2	Clyde	0
1913	Falkirk	2	Raith R	0
1914	Celtic	0 4	Hibernian	0 1
1920	Kilmarnock	3	Albion R	2
1921	Partick Th	1	Rangers	0
1922	Morton	1	Rangers	0
1923	Celtic	1	Hibernian	0
1924	Airdrieonians	2	Hibernian	0
1925	Celtic	2	Dundee	1
1926	St Mirren	2	Celtic	0

1927	Celtic	3	East Fife	1
1928	Rangers	4	Celtic	0
1929	Kilmarnock	2	Rangers	0
1930	Rangers	0 2	Partick Th	0 1
1931	Celtic	2 4	Motherwell	2 2
1932	Rangers	1 3	Kilmarnock	1 0
1933	Celtic	1	Motherwell	0
1934	Rangers	5	St Mirren	0
1935	Rangers	2	Hamilton Acad	1
1936	Rangers	1	Third Lanark	0
1937	Celtic	2	Aberdeen	1
1938	East Fife	1 4	Kilmarnock	1 2
1939	Clyde	4	Motherwell	0
1947	Aberdeen	2	Hibernian	1
1948	Rangers	1 1	Morton	1 0
1949	Rangers	4	Clyde	1
1950	Rangers	3	East Fife	0
1951	Celtic	1	Motherwell	0
1952	Motherwell	4	Dundee	0
1953	Rangers	1 1	Aberdeen	1 0
1954	Celtic	2	Aberdeen	1
1955	Clyde	1 1	Celtic	1 0
1956	Hearts	3	Celtic	1
1957	Falkirk	1 2	Kilmarnock	1 1
1958	Clyde	1	Hibernian	0
1959	St Mirren	3	Aberdeen	1
1960	Rangers	2	Kilmarnock	0
1961	Dunfermline Ath	0 2	Celtic	0 0
1962	Rangers	2	St Mirren	0
1963	Rangers	1 3	Celtic	1 0
1964	Rangers	3	Dundee	1
1965	Celtic	3	Dunfermline Ath	2
1966	Rangers	0 1	Celtic	0 0
1967	Celtic	2	Aberdeen	0
1968	Dunfermline Ath	3	Hearts	1
1969	Celtic	4	Rangers	0
1970	Aberdeen	3	Celtic	1
1971	Celtic	1 2	Rangers	1 1
1972	Celtic	6	Hibernian	1
1973	Rangers	3	Celtic	2
1974	Celtic	3	Dundee U	0
1975	Celtic	3	Airdrieonians	1
1976	Rangers	3	Hearts	1
1977	Celtic	1	Rangers	0
1978	Rangers	2	Aberdeen	1
1979	Rangers	0 0 3	Hibernian	0 0 2
1980	Celtic	1	Rangers	0
1981	Rangers	0 4	Dundee U	0 1
1982	Aberdeen	4	Rangers	1 (aet)
1983	Aberdeen	1	Rangers	0 (aet)
1984	Aberdeen	2	Celtic	1 (aet)
1985	Celtic	2	Dundee U	1
1986	Aberdeen	3	Hearts	0
1987	St Mirren	1	Dundee U	0 (aet)
1988	Celtic	2	Dundee U	1

1989	Celtic	1	Rangers	0
1990	Aberdeen	0	Celtic	0
	(aet; Aberdeen won 9-8 on penalties)			
1991	Motherwell	4	Dundee U	3 (aet)
1992	Rangers	2	Airdrieonians	1
1993	Rangers	2	Aberdeen	1
1994	Dundee U	1	Rangers	0
1995	Celtic	1	Airdrieonians	0
1996	Rangers	5	Hearts	1
1997	Kilmarnock	1	Falkirk	0
1998	Hearts	2	Rangers	1
1999	Rangers	1	Celtic	0
2000	Rangers	4	Aberdeen	0
2001	Celtic	3	Hibernian	0
2002	Rangers	3	Celtic	2
2003	Rangers	1	Dundee	0
2004	Celtic	3	Dunfermline Ath	1
2005	Celtic	1	Dundee U	0
2006	Hearts	1	Gretna	1
	(aet; Hearts won 4-2 on penalties)			
2007	Celtic	1	Dunfermline Ath	0

SCOTS-ADS HIGHLAND LEAGUE 2006–2007

	P	*W*	*D*	*L*	*F*	*A*	*GD*	*Pts*
Keith	28	20	4	4	67	26	41	64
Inverurie Locos	28	20	4	4	62	33	29	64
Buckie Thistle	28	16	8	4	54	28	26	56
Deveronvale	28	17	4	7	77	35	42	55
Huntly	28	17	4	7	67	39	28	55
Cove Rangers	28	13	6	9	52	36	16	45
Nairn County	28	13	4	11	57	42	15	43
Fraserburgh	28	11	8	9	48	42	6	41
Clachnacuddin	28	9	6	13	43	42	1	33
Rothes	28	10	2	16	42	57	–15	32
Wick Academy	28	10	2	16	44	61	–17	32
Forres Mechanics	28	7	7	14	54	60	–6	28
Brora	28	8	2	18	38	84	–46	26
Lossiemouth	28	3	5	20	25	64	–39	14
Fort William	28	3	0	25	26	107	–81	9

WELSH LEAGUE 2006–2007

VAUXHALL MASTERFIT RETAILERS WELSH PREMIER LEAGUE

		Home					Away					Total						
	P	*W*	*D*	*L*	*F*	*A*	*W*	*D*	*L*	*F*	*A*	*W*	*D*	*L*	*F*	*A*	*GD*	*Pts*
1 The New Saints	32	14	0	2	53	12	10	4	2	28	8	24	4	4	81	20	61	76
2 Rhyl	32	10	6	0	31	11	10	3	3	36	24	20	9	3	67	35	32	69
3 Llanelli	32	9	4	3	42	18	9	5	2	30	15	18	9	5	72	33	39	63
4 Welshpool T	32	8	6	2	24	13	9	3	4	30	20	17	9	6	54	33	21	60
5 Connah's Quay N	32	9	3	4	29	21	7	5	4	20	19	16	8	8	49	40	9	56
6 Port Talbot T	32	7	3	6	22	23	8	3	5	20	16	15	6	11	42	39	3	51
7 Carmarthen T	32	8	4	4	25	18	6	4	6	32	32	14	8	10	57	50	7	50
8 Aberystwyth T	32	6	6	4	24	18	7	3	6	23	19	13	9	10	47	37	10	48
9 Bangor City	32	8	3	5	33	21	6	3	7	22	26	14	6	12	55	47	8	48
10 Haverfordwest Co	32	6	4	6	19	16	4	5	7	30	30	10	9	13	49	46	3	39
11 Porthmadog*	32	4	6	6	25	25	4	5	7	15	27	8	11	13	40	52	–12	32
12 Airbus UK	32	4	3	9	22	27	3	5	8	18	40	7	8	17	40	67	–27	29
13 NEWI Cefn Druids	32	4	4	8	26	30	3	3	10	15	36	7	7	18	41	66	–25	28
14 Caersws	32	2	5	9	15	33	4	4	8	19	26	6	9	17	34	59	–25	27
15 Caernarfon T	32	2	3	11	19	40	4	5	7	22	33	6	8	18	41	73	–32	26
16 Newtown	32	2	4	10	9	30	4	2	10	21	33	6	6	20	30	63	–33	24
17 Cwmbran Town	32	2	3	11	21	40	2	5	9	15	35	4	8	20	36	75	–39	20

**3 points deducted.*

NORTHERN IRELAND LEAGUE 2006–2007

CARNEGIE IRISH PREMIER LEAGUE

	P	*W*	*D*	*L*	*F*	*A*	*GD*	*Pts*
Linfield (C)	30	21	8	1	73	19	54	71
Glentoran	30	20	3	7	76	33	43	63
Cliftonville	30	18	7	5	47	26	21	61
Portadown	30	17	7	6	49	26	23	58
Lisburn Distillery	30	14	6	10	50	39	11	48
Crusaders	30	14	5	11	50	42	8	47
Coleraine	30	13	6	11	55	50	5	45
Dungannon Swifts	30	13	5	12	41	41	0	44
Ballymena United	30	12	7	11	46	40	6	43
Limavady United	30	10	5	15	39	54	–15	35
Armagh City	30	11	2	17	42	68	–26	35
Newry City	30	8	7	15	39	52	–13	31
Donegal Celtic	30	6	9	15	33	51	–18	27
Larne	30	7	5	18	33	60	–27	26
Glenavon (PO)	30	5	10	15	40	58	–18	25
Loughgall (R)	30	1	8	21	23	77	–54	11

EUROPEAN REVIEW 2006–2007

Another season of expectancy for English clubs ended in disappointment. Liverpool reached the final of the Champions League but were unable to repeat their performance of two years earlier. This time AC Milan gained revenge in Athens.

Yet, in the quarter-finals we had three clubs still competing: Chelsea, Manchester United plus Liverpool. Even Tottenham Hotspur were still in the UEFA Cup.

Scarcely had the World Cup ended before the new European cup season was in action, the Intertoto entering its latter rounds. The Champions League first qualifying round eliminated Linfield and The New Saints (TNS), but Cork City did well to beat the Cypriots Apollon.

The UEFA Cup was active, too, and despite the loss of Portadown, Glentoran and Rhyl – narrowly losing to Suduva – Derry City, Drogheda United and Llanelli all won their ties.

Enter Hearts for the next Champions League round and they overcame Siroki, but Red Star Belgrade proved too strong for Cork. However the Scots were on the back foot in the third qualifier losing the home leg against AEK Athens. Arsenal grabbed a 3-0 lead away at Dynamo Zagreb but Liverpool were pushed all the way at Anfield by Maccabi Haifa before taking a 2-1 lead at the death.

In the next UEFA Cup round Newcastle won away to Ventspils and Derry hit Gretna 5-1, too. Llanelli were just edged out in Odense as were Drogheda away to Start. A draw in Kiev against Haifa was enough for Liverpool, Arsenal eased to 2-1 at the Emirates against the Croatians, but Hearts departed after losing 3-0 in Athens.

Though Newcastle were held at home they qualified as did Derry. Llanelli were overwhelmed by the Danes, but Drogheda only lost on an 11-10 penalty shoot-out.

While the group stages had been reached in the Champions League, the UEFA Cup was still eliminating. Derry finished scoreless with Paris St Germain, Newcastle won in the Baltic States again, Rangers drew in Norway against Molde, Blackburn similarly in Salzburg. Spurs came back from Slavia Prague a goal to the good, but Hearts shipped in from the UEFA Cup lost at home to Sparta, the other Czechs, and West Ham United lost 1-0 at Upton Park to Palermo.

Blackburn, Newcastle, Rangers and Spurs progressed without too much of a problem, but out went Derry, West Ham and Hearts, before the UEFA Cup also became groupy.

At the halfway point in the Champions League Chelsea topped Group A after beating Barcelona 1-0 at the Bridge, Liverpool led Group C, while Manchester United and Celtic were well ahead in Group F. However, Arsenal beaten by CSKA Moscow were a point off the pace in Group G.

Six games finished and the positions remained the same for all but Arsenal who recovered to top their group on the same points total as Porto, with the Russians failing to maintain their form.

The UEFA Cup sections saw Rangers, Spurs, Blackburn and Newcastle firmly in front as the knock-out rounds returned. Slender away defeats for Blackburn, Rangers and a 3-1 lead in Belgium for Newcastle against Waregem, but Spurs' tie with Feyenoord was unplayed because the Dutch club was disqualified through crowd trouble.

Rangers and Newcastle were safely through but Blackburn went out to Leverkusen. The Champions League knock-out was in operation, Celtic being held by AC Milan, Chelsea drawing in Porto and Arsenal losing to PSV. There were excellent away wins for Liverpool and Manchester United respectively against Barcelona and Lille.

Chelsea and United completed their tasks, Celtic lost in extra time but Liverpool needed the away goals and Arsenal could only draw. Rested Spurs in the UEFA Cup won in Braga, Newcastle at home to AZ, but Osasuna held Rangers. Yet Newcastle having scored four in the first leg lost on away goals and Rangers, too, were beaten. Only Spurs carried on.

Last eight and Liverpool won 3-0 away to PSV, Roma led Manchester United 2-1 and Chelsea were held by Valencia. In the UEFA Cup Spurs were beaten 2-1 in Seville and were held at White Hart Lane. But United thrashed Roma 7-1, Chelsea won away and Liverpool eased through.

United led AC Milan 3-2 in the semi-final, Chelsea 1-0 against Liverpool. But the Italians had a comfortable 3-0 second leg victory and Chelsea lost on penalties at Anfield.

The UEFA Cup final was an all-Spanish affair Sevilla beating Espanyol on penalties, while Liverpool scored once, too little, too late in Athens to give AC Milan their seventh European Cup success, at 2-1.

UEFA CHAMPIONS LEAGUE 2006–2007

▪ *Denotes player sent off.*
* *Winner after extra time.*

FIRST QUALIFYING ROUND FIRST LEG

Birkirkara	(0) 0	B36	(2) 3
Elbasan	(0) 1	Ekranas	(0) 0
F91 Dudelange	(0) 0	Rabotnicki	(0) 1
Linfield	(0) 1	Gorica	(2) 3
Pyunik	(0) 0	Serif	(0) 0
Sioni	(0) 2	Baku	(0) 0
VMK	(0) 2	Hafnarfjordur	(1) 3
Cork City	(0) 1	Apollon	(0) 0
Metalurgs Liepaja	(1) 1	Aktobe	(0) 0
MyPa	(0) 1	TNS	(0) 0
Shakhtyor	(0) 0	Siroki	(1) 1

Tuesday, 11 July 2006

Linfield (0) 1 *(Dickson 58 (pen))*

Gorica (2) 3 *(Demirovic 14, 27, Sturm 66)* 3500

Linfield: Mannus; Ervin (Douglas 46), McShane (McCann 25), Mulgrew, Murphy, O'Kane, Thompson, Magennis (Mouncey 32), Dickson, McAreavey, Bailie.
Gorica: Pirih; Srebrnic (Jogan 84), Jokic, Zivec, Kovacevic, Dedic, Demirovic, Burgic, Sturm (Rexhay 75), Pitamic (Nikolic 63), Suler.

Wednesday, 12 July 2006

Cork City (0) 1 *(Woods 62)*

Apollon (0) 0 3000

Cork City: Devine; Murphy, Bennett, Murray D, O'Brien, Fenn, Woods, O'Donovan, Gamble, Behan (Lordan 90), Horgan.
Apollon: Chvalovsky; Barun, Alvarez, Merkis, Michalski, Andone (Machado 80), Ajeel, Solomou (Taher 65), Arig, Sosin, Hamadi (Paiva 58).

MyPa (0) 1 *(Adriano 58)*

TNS (0) 0 864

MyPa: Korhonen; Timoska, Taipale, Lindstrom, Kuparinen (Puhakainen 62), Manso, Karhu, Kangaskolkka (Pellonen 70), Miranda, Kansikas, Adriano (Leguizamon 75).
TNS: Doherty; Baker, King, Jackson, Holmes, Ruscoe (Leah 76), Hogan, Wilde (Carter 65), Beck, Ward (Toner 87), Stones.

FIRST QUALIFYING ROUND SECOND LEG

Baku	(0) 1	Sioni	(0) 0
Ekranas	(1) 3	Elbasan	(0) 0
Rabotnicki	(0) 0	F91 Dudelange	(0) 0
Serif	(1) 2	Pyunik	(0) 0
Aktobe	(1) 1	Metalurgs Liepaja	(0) 1
Apollon	(0) 1	Cork City	(0) 1
B36	(1) 2	Birkirkara	(0) 2
Gorica	(0) 2	Linfield	(0) 2
Hafnarfjordur	(0) 1	VMK	(0) 1
Siroki	(1) 1	Shakhtyor	(0) 0
TNS	(0) 0	MyPa	(1) 1

Wednesday, 19 July 2006

Apollon (0) 1 *(Sosin 51)*

Cork City (0) 1 *(Murray D 75)* 2000

Apollon: Chvalovsky; Barun (Hamadi■ 78), Alvarez, Merkis■, Michalski, Andone, Ajeel, Machado (Solomou 78), Arig, Sosin, Paiva (Taher 59).
Cork City: Devine; Murphy■, Bennett, Murray D, O'Brien, Fenn, Woods (Softic 90), O'Donovan (Lordan 90), Gamble■, Behan (Sullivan 87), Horgan.

Gorica (1) 2 *(Burgic 30, 83)*

Linfield (1) 2 *(Thompson 28, McAreavey 90)* 1250

Gorica: Pirih; Srebrnic, Jokic, Zivec (Jogan 75), Kovacevic, Dedic, Demirovic, Burgic (Matavz 85), Sturm (Rexhay 55), Nikolic, Suler.
Linfield: Mannus; Douglas (Ervin 65), McCann, Mulgrew (McAreavey 51), Murphy, O'Kane, Thompson, Kingsberry, Dickson (Garrett 82), Mouncey, Bailie.

TNS (0) 0

MyPa (1) 1 *(Puhakainen 5)* 1850

TNS: Doherty; Baker, King (Carter 61), Jackson, Holmes, Ruscoe (Toner 46), Hogan (Leah 80), Wilde, Beck, Ward, Stones.
MyPa: Korhonen; Timoska, Taipale, Lindstrom, Kuparinen, Puhakainen (Kangaskolkka 57), Manso (Huttunen 69), Leguizamon (Hernesniemi 78), Miranda, Kansikas, Adriano.

SECOND QUALIFYING ROUND FIRST LEG

Ekranas	(1) 1	Dynamo Zagreb	(2) 4
Cork City	(0) 0	Red Star Belgrade	(1) 1
Debrecen	(0) 1	Rabotnicki	(1) 1
Djurgaarden	(0) 1	Ruzomberok	(0) 0
FC Copenhagen	(0) 2	MyPa	(0) 0
Fenerbahce	(2) 4	B36	(0) 0
Gorica	(0) 0	Steaua	(0) 2
Hafjarfjordur	(0) 0	Legia	(0) 1
Hearts	(0) 3	Siroki	(0) 0
Levski	(1) 2	Sioni	(0) 0
Metalurgs Liepaja	(0) 1	Dynamo Kiev	(3) 4
Mlada Boleslav	(3) 3	Valerenga	(0) 1
Serif	(0) 1	Spartak Moscow	(0) 1
Zurich	(2) 2	Salzburg	(1) 1

Wednesday, 26 July 2006

Cork City (0) 0

Red Star Belgrade (1) 1 *(Behan 37 (og))* 5500

Cork City: Devine; Bennett, Murray D, O'Brien, Fenn, Woods, O'Donovan, Lordan (Callaghan 86), Softic, Behan (McCarthy 84), Horgan.
Red Star Belgrade: Randjelovic; Pantic (Djokic 68), Bisevac, Jankovic (Milijas 60), Perovic, Joksimovic, Kovacevic, Georgiev, Zigic (Purovic 90), Basta, Milovanovic.

Hearts (0) 3 *(Carvalho 53 (og), Tall 79, Bednar 85)*

Siroki (0) 0 28,486

Hearts: Gordon; Neilson, Fyssas, Pressley, Tall, McCann (Pospisil 56), Aguiar (Brellier 89), Jankauskas (Mikoliunas 56), Bednar, Cesnauskis, Berra.
Siroki: Basic; Anic, Silic, Pandza, Landeka, Lago, Carvalho (Papic 90), Bubalo (Doci 59), Ronelle, Karoglan (Kovacic 84), Celson.

SECOND QUALIFYING ROUND SECOND LEG

B36	(0) 0	Fenerbahce	(1) 5
Dynamo Kiev	(1) 4	Metalurgs Liepaja	(0) 0
Dynamo Zagreb	(1) 5	Ekranas	(0) 2
Legia	(1) 2	Hafnarfjordur	(0) 0
MyPa	(1) 2	FC Copenhagen	(1) 2
Rabotnicki	(3) 4	Debrecen	(1) 1
Red Star Belgrade	(2) 3	Cork City	(0) 0
Ruzomberok	(2) 3	Djurgaarden	(0) 1
Salzburg	(1) 2	Zurich	(0) 0
Sioni	(0) 0	Levski	(1) 2
Siroki	(0) 0	Hearts	(0) 0
Spartak Moscow	(0) 0	Serif	(0) 0
Steaua	(1) 3	Gorica	(0) 0
Valerenga	(0) 2	Mlada Boleslav	(1) 2

Wednesday, 2 August 2006

Red Star Belgrade (2) 3 *(Milovanovic 3, Zigic 34, 59)*

Cork City (0) 0 30,000

Red Star Belgrade: Randjelovic; Pantic, Bisevac, Djokic (Jankovic 70), Perovic (Milijas 79), Joksimovic, Kovacevic, Georgiev, Zigic (Purovic 64), Basta, Milovanovic.
Cork City: Devine; Bennett, Callaghan, O'Brien, Fenn, Woods, O'Donovan, Lordan, Softic, Behan (Sullivan 80), Horgan.

Siroki (0) 0

Hearts (0) 0 6000

Siroki: Vasilj; Anic, Silic, Lago, Papic (Studenovic 88), Pandza, Landeka, Ronelle, Kovacic (Erceg 70), Karoglan, Celson (Carvalho 75).
Hearts: Gordon; Neilson (Tall 61), Fyssas, Pressley, McCann (Mikoliunas 61), Aguiar, Pospisil, Bednar, Cesnauskis (Beslija 84), Berra, Brellier.

THIRD QUALIFYING ROUND FIRST LEG

Dynamo Zagreb	(0) 0	Arsenal	(0) 3
FK Austria	(1) 1	Benfica	(1) 1
AC Milan	(1) 1	Red Star Belgrade	(0) 0
CSKA Moscow	(0) 3	Ruzomberok	(0) 0
Dynamo Kiev	(1) 3	Fenerbahce	(0) 1
FC Copenhagen	(0) 1	Ajax	(1) 2
Galatasaray	(2) 5	Mlada Boleslav	(0) 2
Hamburg	(0) 0	Osasuna	(0) 0
Hearts	(0) 1	AEK Athens	(0) 2
Levski	(1) 2	Chievo	(0) 0
Lille	(0) 3	Rabotnicki	(0) 0
Liverpool	(1) 2	Maccabi Haifa	(1) 1
Salzburg	(0) 1	Valencia	(0) 0
Shakhtar Donetsk	(1) 1	Legia	(0) 0
Slovan Liberec	(0) 0	Spartak Moscow	(0) 0
Standard Liege	(1) 2	Steaua	(1) 2

Tuesday, 8 August 2006

Dynamo Zagreb (0) 0

Arsenal (0) 3 *(Fabregas 63, 78, Van Persie 64)* 28,500

Dynamo Zagreb: Turina; Buljat (Vukojevic 90), Cale (Carlos 90), Nowotny, Corluka, Cvitanovic, Etto, Modric, Eduardo da Silva, Mamic, Vugrinec (Agic 27).
Arsenal: Almunia; Eboue, Hoyte, Silva, Toure, Djourou, Hleb, Fabregas, Adebayor (Aliadiere 82), Rosicky (Flamini 82), Van Persie.

Wednesday, 9 August 2006

Hearts (0) 1 *(Mikoliunas 62)*

AEK Athens (0) 2 *(Kapetanos 89, Fyssas 90 (og))* 32,459

Hearts: Gordon; Neilson, Fyssas, Pressley, McCann, Aguiar■, Pospisil (Elliot 83), Bednar (Wallace 69), Mikoliunas, Berra, Karipidis (Jankauskas 55).
AEK Athens: Sorrentino; Pautasso (Tziortziopoulos 81), Dellas, Cirilo, Georgeas, Emerson, Ivic, Lagos (Lakis 65), Liberopoulos, Kapetanos, Julio Cesar (Tozser 90).

Liverpool (1) 2 *(Bellamy 32, Gonzalez 87)*

Maccabi Haifa (1) 1 *(Boccoli 29)* 40,058

Liverpool: Reina; Finnan, Riise, Xabi Alonso, Carragher, Hyypia, Pennant, Sissoko, Bellamy (Crouch 65), Gerrard (Gonzalez 86), Zenden (Luis Garcia 55).
Maccabi Haifa: Davidovich; Harazi, Anderson, Boccoli, Colautti, Masudi (Meshumar 89), Dirceu, Magrashvili, Olarra, Katan (Melikson 86), Keinan.

THIRD QUALIFYING ROUND SECOND LEG

Benfica	(2) 3	FK Austria	(0) 0
Maccabi Haifa	(0) 1	Liverpool	(0) 1
(in Kiev.)			
Osasuna	(1) 1	Hamburg	(0) 1
Red Star Belgrade	(0) 1	AC Milan	(1) 2
Valencia	(3) 3	Salzburg	(0) 0
AEK Athens	(0) 3	Hearts	(0) 0
Ajax	(0) 0	FC Copenhagen	(0) 2
Arsenal	(0) 2	Dynamo Zagreb	(1) 1
Chievo	(0) 2	Levski	(1) 2
Fenerbahce	(1) 2	Dynamo Kiev	(2) 2
Legia	(1) 2	Shakhtar Donetsk	(3) 3
Mlada Boleslav	(0) 1	Galatasaray	(0) 1
Rabotnicki	(0) 0	Lille	(1) 1
Ruzomberok	(0) 0	CSKA Moscow	(2) 2
Spartak Moscow	(1) 2	Slovan Liberec	(0) 1
Steaua	(1) 2	Standard Liege	(1) 1

Tuesday, 22 August 2006

Maccabi Haifa (0) 1 *(Colautti 63)*

Liverpool (0) 1 *(Crouch 54)* 12,500

Maccabi Haifa: Davidovich; Harazi, Magrashvili, Olarra, Keinan (Meshumar 65), Anderson (Melikson 71), Dirceu, Boccoli, Masudi (Arbeitman 80), Colautti, Katan.
Liverpool: Reina; Finnan, Warnock (Fabio Aurelio 28), Xabi Alonso, Agger, Hyypia, Pennant (Bellamy 86), Sissoko (Gerrard 67), Crouch, Luis Garcia, Gonzalez.
(in Kiev.)

Wednesday, 23 August 2006

AEK Athens (0) 3 *(Julio Cesar 79 (pen), 86, Liberopoulos 82)*

Hearts (0) 0 31,500

AEK Athens: Chiotis; Pautasso (Tozser 72), Cirilo, Dellas, Georgeas, Emerson, Ivic, Lagos (Lakis 54), Julio Cesar, Liberopoulos (Kampantais 84), Kapetanos.
Hearts: Gordon; Neilson, Pressley, Berra, Fyssas, Brellier■, Mikoliunas, McCann■, Cesnauskis (Wallace 81), Hartley (Jankauskas 61), Mole (Pinilla 89).

Arsenal (0) 2 *(Ljungberg 77, Flamini 90)*

Dynamo Zagreb (1) 1 *(Eduardo da Silva 12)* 58,418

Arsenal: Almunia; Eboue, Hoyte, Flamini, Toure, Djourou, Hleb (Silva 70), Fabregas, Adebayor (Henry 65), Van Persie (Walcott 81), Ljungberg.
Dynamo Zagreb: Turina; Corluka, Cvitanovic, Mamic, Drpic, Etto (Tomic 90), Vukojevic (Ljubojevic 89), Agic (Buljat 69), Carlos, Modric, Eduardo da Silva.

GROUP A

Barcelona	(2) 5	Levski	(0) 0
Chelsea	(1) 2	Werder Bremen	(0) 0
Levski	(0) 1	Chelsea	(1) 3
Werder Bremen	(0) 1	Barcelona	(0) 1
Chelsea	(0) 1	Barcelona	(0) 0
Werder Bremen	(1) 2	Levski	(0) 0
Barcelona	(1) 2	Chelsea	(0) 2
Levski	(0) 0	Werder Bremen	(3) 3
Levski	(0) 0	Barcelona	(1) 2
Werder Bremen	(1) 1	Chelsea	(0) 0
Barcelona	(2) 2	Werder Bremen	(0) 0
Chelsea	(1) 2	Levski	(0) 0

Tuesday, 12 September 2006

Chelsea (1) 2 *(Essien 24, Ballack 68 (pen))*

Werder Bremen (0) 0 32,135

Chelsea: Cech; Boulahrouz, Cole A, Makelele, Terry, Ricardo Carvalho, Essien, Lampard, Drogba (Kalou 86), Shevchenko (Cole J 81), Ballack (Mikel 90).
Werder Bremen: Reinke; Pasanen, Naldo, Wome, Baumann (Zidan 86), Fritz, Diego, Klose, Klasnic (Hugo Almeida 66), Frings, Borowski.

Wednesday, 27 September 2006

Levski (0) 1 *(Ognyanov 89)*

Chelsea (1) 3 *(Drogba 39, 52, 68)* 27,950

Levski: Petkov; Angelov S, Milanov, Tomasic, Topuzakov, Eromoigbe, Borimirov (Koprivarov 79), Telkiyski (Ivanov G 67), Wagner, Yovov, Bardon (Ognyanov 71).
Chelsea: Cech; Paulo Ferreira, Bridge, Essien, Terry, Ricardo Carvalho, Mikel (Kalou 63), Lampard, Drogba (Robben 70), Shevchenko (Wright-Phillips 83), Ballack.

Wednesday, 18 October 2006

Chelsea (0) 1 *(Drogba 47)*

Barcelona (0) 0 45,999

Chelsea: Hilario; Boulahrouz, Cole A, Makelele, Terry, Ricardo Carvalho, Essien, Lampard, Drogba (Kalou 90), Shevchenko (Robben 77), Ballack.
Barcelona: Valdes; Marquez, Puyol (Oleguer 74), Xavi, Gudjohnsen (Giuly 60), Zambrotta, Edmilson, Leo Messi, Ronaldinho, Deco, Van Bronckhorst (Iniesta 57).

Tuesday, 31 October 2006

Barcelona (1) 2 *(Deco 3, Gudjohnsen 58)*

Chelsea (0) 2 *(Lampard 52, Drogba 90)* 90,199

Barcelona: Valdes; Van Bronckhorst, Motta (Edmilson 57), Marquez, Puyol, Xavi (Iniesta 83), Gudjohnsen (Giuly 77), Deco, Leo Messi, Zambrotta, Ronaldinho.
Chelsea: Hilario; Boulahrouz (Cole J 75), Cole A, Makelele, Terry, Ricardo Carvalho, Essien, Lampard, Drogba, Ballack (Paulo Ferreira 90), Robben (Kalou 72).

Wednesday, 22 November 2006

Werder Bremen (1) 1 *(Mertesacker 27)*

Chelsea (0) 0 36,908

Werder Bremen: Wiese; Naldo, Wome, Fritz, Diego, Jensen (Hunt 78), Frings, Mertesacker, Borowski, Hugo Almeida (Schulz 87), Klose (Klasnic 90).
Chelsea: Cudicini; Geremi, Cole A, Makelele, Terry, Boulahrouz, Essien, Mikel (Robben 59), Drogba (Shevchenko 59), Cole J, Ballack (Wright-Phillips 77).

Tuesday, 5 December 2006

Chelsea (1) 2 *(Shevchenko 27, Wright-Phillips 83)*

Levski (0) 0 33,358

Chelsea: Hilario; Boulahrouz, Bridge, Essien, Paulo Ferreira (Diarra 58), Ricardo Carvalho, Ballack, Lampard, Drogba, Shevchenko (Kalou 69), Robben (Wright-Phillips 69).
Levski: Mitrev; Domovchiyski (Ivanov G 75), Milanov, Tomasic, Dimitrov (Baltanov 59), Eromoigbe, Borimirov, Angelov S, Bardon, Yovov (Koprivarov 70), Topuzakov.

Group A Final Table	*P*	*W*	*D*	*L*	*F*	*A*	*Pts*
Chelsea	6	4	1	1	10	4	13
Barcelona	6	3	2	1	12	4	11
Werder Bremen	6	3	1	2	7	5	10
Levski	6	0	0	6	1	17	0

GROUP B

Bayern Munich	(0) 4	Spartak Moscow	(0) 0
Sporting Lisbon	(0) 1	Internazionale	(0) 0
Internazionale	(0) 0	Bayern Munich	(0) 2
Spartak Moscow	(1) 1	Sporting Lisbon	(0) 1
Internazionale	(2) 2	Spartak Moscow	(0) 1
Sporting Lisbon	(0) 0	Bayern Munich	(1) 1
Bayern Munich	(0) 0	Sporting Lisbon	(0) 0
Spartak Moscow	(0) 0	Internazionale	(1) 1
Internazionale	(1) 1	Sporting Lisbon	(0) 0
Spartak Moscow	(1) 2	Bayern Munich	(2) 2
Bayern Munich	(0) 1	Internazionale	(0) 1
Sporting Lisbon	(1) 1	Spartak Moscow	(2) 3

Group B Final Table	*P*	*W*	*D*	*L*	*F*	*A*	*Pts*
Bayern Munich	6	3	3	0	10	3	12
Internazionale	6	3	1	2	5	5	10
Spartak Moscow	6	1	2	3	7	11	5
Sporting Lisbon	6	1	2	3	3	6	5

GROUP C

Galatasaray	(0) 0	Bordeaux	(0) 0
PSV Eindhoven	(0) 0	Liverpool	(0) 0
Bordeaux	(0) 0	PSV Eindhoven	(0) 1
Liverpool	(2) 3	Galatasaray	(0) 2
Bordeaux	(0) 0	Liverpool	(0) 1
Galatasaray	(1) 1	PSV Eindhoven	(0) 2
Liverpool	(1) 3	Bordeaux	(0) 0
PSV Eindhoven	(0) 2	Galatasaray	(0) 0
Bordeaux	(1) 3	Galatasaray	(0) 1
Liverpool	(0) 2	PSV Eindhoven	(0) 0
Galatasaray	(2) 3	Liverpool	(1) 2
PSV Eindhoven	(0) 1	Bordeaux	(3) 3

Tuesday, 12 September 2006

PSV Eindhoven (0) 0

Liverpool (0) 0 33,500

PSV Eindhoven: Gomes; Kromkamp, Alex, Reiziger, Salcido, Simons, Mendez, Afellay (Vayrynen 74), Culina (Aissati 63), Farfan, Kone.
Liverpool: Reina; Finnan, Fabio Aurelio (Gonzalez 82), Sissoko (Xabi Alonso 62), Carragher, Agger, Pennant, Zenden, Bellamy (Gerrard 72), Kuyt, Warnock.

Wednesday, 27 September 2006

Liverpool (2) 3 *(Crouch 9, 52, Luis Garcia 14)*

Galatasaray (0) 2 *(Umit K 59, 65)* 41,976

Liverpool: Reina; Finnan, Fabio Aurelio, Xabi Alonso, Carragher, Agger, Pennant (Sissoko 78), Luis Garcia, Crouch (Bellamy 90), Kuyt (Gonzalez 66), Gerrard.
Galatasaray: Mondragon; Tomas, Arda (Carrusca 86), Song, Orhan, Mehmet (Hasan Sas 46), Ayhan, Cihan (Umit K 46), Ilic, Sabri, Hakan Sukur.

Wednesday, 18 October 2006

Bordeaux (0) 0

Liverpool (0) 1 *(Crouch 58)* 31,471

Bordeaux: Rame; Henrique, Fernando, Jurietti, Laslandes (Chamakh 63), Alonso (Faubert 63), Darcheville (Perea 71), Jemmali, Micoud, Wendel, Mavuba.
Liverpool: Reina; Finnan, Riise, Xabi Alonso, Carragher, Hyypia, Luis Garcia, Zenden, Crouch (Kuyt 65), Bellamy (Warnock 87), Gonzalez (Sissoko 68).

Tuesday, 31 October 2006

Liverpool (1) 3 *(Luis Garcia 23, 76, Gerrard 72)*

Bordeaux (0) 0 41,978

Liverpool: Reina; Finnan, Riise, Xabi Alonso (Zenden 58), Carragher, Hyypia, Gerrard, Sissoko, Crouch (Pennant 73), Kuyt, Luis Garcia (Fowler 78).
Bordeaux: Rame; Cid, Chamakh (Perea 12), Faubert, Fernando■, Jemmali, Micoud (Mavuba 75), Wendel, Darcheville (Obertan 60), Ducasse, Marange.

Wednesday, 22 November 2006

Liverpool (0) 2 *(Gerrard 65, Crouch 89)*

PSV Eindhoven (0) 0 41,948

Liverpool: Reina; Finnan, Riise, Xabi Alonso (Zenden 21), Carragher, Agger, Pennant (Bellamy 79), Gerrard, Crouch, Kuyt, Gonzalez (Luis Garcia 36).
PSV Eindhoven: Gomes; Kromkamp, Afellay, Alex, Salcido, Simons, Da Costa, Farfan, Feher (Tardelli 68), Kone, Mendez (Beerens 81).

Tuesday, 5 December 2006

Galatasaray (2) 3 *(Necati 24, Okan 28, Ilic 79)*

Liverpool (1) 2 *(Fowler 22, 90)* 23,000

Galatasaray: Mondragon; Tomas, Okan, Necati (Ilic 46), Carrusca (Mehmet 75), Cihan, Emre (Tolga 46), Inamoto, Sabri, Ergun, Umit K.
Liverpool: Dudek; Paletta, Riise, Xabi Alonso (Roque 84), Carragher, Agger, Pennant, Guthrie (Luis Garcia 66), Fowler, Bellamy (Crouch 74), Peltier.

Group C Final Table	*P*	*W*	*D*	*L*	*F*	*A*	*Pts*
Liverpool	6	4	1	1	11	5	13
PSV Eindhoven	6	3	1	2	6	6	10
Bordeaux	6	2	1	3	6	7	7
Galatasaray	6	1	1	4	7	12	4

GROUP D

Olympiakos	(1) 2	Valencia	(2) 4
Roma	(0) 4	Shakhtar Donetsk	(0) 0
Shakhtar Donetsk	(1) 2	Olympiakos	(1) 2
Valencia	(2) 2	Roma	(1) 1
Olympiakos	(0) 0	Roma	(0) 1
Valencia	(2) 2	Shakhtar Donetsk	(0) 0
Roma	(0) 1	Olympiakos	(1) 1
Shakhtar Donetsk	(2) 2	Valencia	(1) 2
Shakhtar Donetsk	(0) 1	Roma	(0) 0
Valencia	(1) 2	Olympiakos	(0) 0
Olympiakos	(0) 1	Shakhtar Donetsk	(1) 1
Roma	(1) 1	Valencia	(0) 0

Group D Final Table	*P*	*W*	*D*	*L*	*F*	*A*	*Pts*
Valencia	6	4	1	1	12	6	13
Roma	6	3	1	2	8	4	10
Shakhtar Donetsk	6	1	3	2	6	11	6
Olympiakos	6	0	3	3	6	11	3

GROUP E

Dynamo Kiev	(1) 1	Steaua	(3) 4
Lyon	(2) 2	Real Madrid	(0) 0
Real Madrid	(3) 5	Dynamo Kiev	(0) 1
Steaua	(0) 0	Lyon	(1) 3
Dynamo Kiev	(0) 0	Lyon	(2) 3
Steaua	(0) 1	Real Madrid	(2) 4
Lyon	(1) 1	Dynamo Kiev	(0) 0
Real Madrid	(0) 1	Steaua	(0) 0
Real Madrid	(1) 2	Lyon	(2) 2
Steaua	(0) 1	Dynamo Kiev	(1) 1
Dynamo Kiev	(2) 2	Real Madrid	(0) 2
Lyon	(1) 1	Steaua	(1) 1

Group E Final Table	*P*	*W*	*D*	*L*	*F*	*A*	*Pts*
Lyon	6	4	2	0	12	3	14
Real Madrid	6	3	2	1	14	8	11
Steaua	6	1	2	3	7	11	5
Dynamo Kiev	6	0	2	4	5	16	2

GROUP F

FC Copenhagen	(0) 0	Benfica	(0) 0
Manchester United	(2) 3	Celtic	(2) 2
Benfica	(0) 0	Manchester United	(0) 1
Celtic	(1) 1	FC Copenhagen	(0) 0
Celtic	(0) 3	Benfica	(0) 0
Manchester United	(1) 3	FC Copenhagen	(0) 0
Benfica	(2) 3	Celtic	(0) 0
FC Copenhagen	(0) 1	Manchester United	(0) 0
Benfica	(3) 3	FC Copenhagen	(0) 1
Celtic	(0) 1	Manchester United	(0) 0
FC Copenhagen	(2) 3	Celtic	(0) 1
Manchester United	(1) 3	Benfica	(1) 1

Wednesday, 13 September 2006

Manchester United (2) 3 *(Saha 30 (pen), 40, Solskjaer 47)*

Celtic (2) 2 *(Vennegoor of Hesselink 21, Nakamura 43)* 74,031

Manchester United: Van der Sar; Neville, Silvestre, Carrick, Ferdinand, Brown, Fletcher, Scholes (O'Shea 80), Saha, Rooney (Richardson 86), Giggs (Solskjaer 33).
Celtic: Boruc; Wilson (Telfer 52), Naylor, Nakamura, McManus, Caldwell, Lennon, Gravesen, McGeady (Maloney 70), Vennegoor of Hesselink, Jarosik (Miller 56).

Tuesday, 26 September 2006

Benfica (0) 0

Manchester United (0) 1 *(Saha 60)* 61,000

Benfica: Quim; Anderson (Mantorras 82), Alcides, Luisao, Leo, Petit, Simao Sabrosa, Katsouranis, Nuno Gomes, Karagounis (Nuno Assis 62), Paulo Jorge (Miccoli 65).
Manchester United: Van der Sar; Neville, Heinze, Carrick, Ferdinand, Vidic, Ronaldo, Scholes, Saha (Smith 85), Rooney (Fletcher 85), O'Shea.

Celtic (1) 1 *(Miller 36 (pen))*

FC Copenhagen (0) 0 57,598

Celtic: Boruc; Telfer, Naylor, Gravesen, Caldwell, Nakamura, Zurawski (Beattie 73), Lennon, Miller (Maloney 82), McGeady (Pearson 88), McManus.
FC Copenhagen: Christiansen; Jacobsen, Bergdolmo (Thomassen 75), Norregaard, Hangeland, Linderoth, Hutchinson, Silberbauer, Berglund (Kvist 55), Gravgaard, Allback.

Tuesday, 17 October 2006

Celtic (0) 3 *(Miller 56, 66, Pearson 90)*

Benfica (0) 0 58,313

Celtic: Boruc; Telfer, Naylor, Lennon, Caldwell, Sno (Pearson 88), Zurawski (Jarosik 84), Nakamura, Miller, Maloney, McManus.
Benfica: Quim; Nuno Assis, Ricardo Rocha, Luisao, Leo, Petit, Katsouranis (Nelson 72), Alcides, Simao Sabrosa, Nuno Gomes (Kikin 78), Miccoli.

Manchester United (1) 3 *(Scholes 39, O'Shea 46, Richardson 83)*

FC Copenhagen (0) 0 72,020

Manchester United: Van der Sar; O'Shea, Evra, Carrick (Solskjaer 60), Brown, Vidic, Fletcher, Scholes (Richardson 76), Saha (Smith 60), Rooney, Ronaldo.
FC Copenhagen: Christiansen; Jacobsen, Norregaard (Kvist 57), Hangeland, Linderoth, Silberbauer (Bergvold 82), Berglund (Pimpong 57), Allback, Hutchinson, Gravgaard, Wendt.

Wednesday, 1 November 2006

Benfica (2) 3 *(Caldwell 10 (og), Nuno Gomes 22, Karyaka 76)*

Celtic (0) 0 49,000

Benfica: Quim; Luisao, Leo, Petit (Beto 84), Katsouranis, Simao Sabrosa, Nuno Gomes (Mantorras 89), Nelson, Nuno Assis, Miccoli (Karyaka 67), Ricardo Rocha.
Celtic: Boruc; Telfer, Naylor, Sno (Zurawski 72), Caldwell, Maloney (McGeady 65), McManus, Lennon, Miller, Nakamura, Pearson.

FC Copenhagen (0) 1 *(Allback 73)*
Manchester United (0) 0 40,308

FC Copenhagen: Christiansen; Jacobsen, Norregaard, Hangeland, Linderoth, Silberbauer (Kvist 71), Hutchinson, Gravgaard, Allback (Thomassen 89), Wendt, Bergvold (Berglund 68).
Manchester United: Van der Sar; Heinze (Evra 80), Silvestre, O'Shea, Brown, Vidic (Ferdinand 46), Ronaldo, Carrick, Solskjaer, Rooney, Fletcher (Scholes 71).

Tuesday, 21 November 2006

Celtic (0) 1 *(Nakamura 81)*
Manchester United (0) 0 60,632

Celtic: Boruc; Telfer, Naylor, Sno (Jarosik 46), McMannus, Balde, Zurawski (Maloney 46), Gravesen, Vennegoor of Hesselink, Nakamura (Miller 85), Lennon.
Manchester United: Van der Sar; Neville, Heinze (Evra 87), Carrick (O'Shea 87), Ferdinand, Vidic, Ronaldo, Scholes, Saha, Rooney, Giggs.

Wednesday, 6 December 2006

FC Copenhagen (2) 3 *(Hutchinson 2, Gronkjaer 27, Allback 57)*
Celtic (0) 1 *(Jarosik 75)* 38,647

FC Copenhagen: Christiansen; Jacobsen (Norregaard 56), Hangeland, Linderoth, Silberbauer, Gronkjaer (Berglund 90), Allback (Bergvold 81), Hutchinson, Gravgaard, Wendt, Kvist.
Celtic: Boruc; McManus (O'Dea 73), Naylor, Wilson, McGeady (Pearson 69), Balde, Zurawski, Lennon, Miller, Gravesen (Nakamura 69), Jarosik.

Manchester United (1) 3 *(Vidic 45, Giggs 61, Saha 75)*
Benfica (1) 1 *(Nelson 27)* 74,955

Manchester United: Van der Sar; Neville, Evra (Heinze 67), Carrick, Ferdinand, Vidic, Ronaldo, Scholes (Solskjaer 79), Saha, Rooney, Giggs (Fletcher 74).
Benfica: Quim; Luisao, Leo, Petit, Katsouranis, Simao Sabrosa, Nuno Gomes, Nelson, Nuno Assis (Karagounis 73), Miccoli (Paulo Jorge 64), Ricardo Rocha.

Group F Final Table	*P*	*W*	*D*	*L*	*F*	*A*	*Pts*
Manchester United	6	4	0	2	10	5	12
Celtic	6	3	0	3	8	9	9
Benfica	6	2	1	3	7	8	7
FC Copenhagen	6	2	1	3	5	8	7

GROUP G

Hamburg	(0) 1	Arsenal	(1) 2
Porto	(0) 0	CSKA Moscow	(0) 0
Arsenal	(1) 2	Porto	(0) 0
CSKA Moscow	(0) 1	Hamburg	(0) 0
CSKA Moscow	(1) 1	Arsenal	(0) 0
Porto	(2) 4	Hamburg	(0) 1
Arsenal	(0) 0	CSKA Moscow	(0) 0
Hamburg	(0) 1	Porto	(1) 3
Arsenal	(0) 3	Hamburg	(1) 1
CSKA Moscow	(0) 0	Porto	(1) 2
Hamburg	(1) 3	CSKA Moscow	(1) 2
Porto	(0) 0	Arsenal	(0) 0

Wednesday, 13 September 2006

Hamburg (0) 1 *(Sanogo 90)*

Arsenal (1) 2 *(Silva 12 (pen), Rosicky 53)* 50,389

Hamburg: Kirschstein■; Demel (Mahdavikia 54), Reinhardt, Kompany, Mathijsen, Jarolim, De Jong, Wicky (Wachter 12), Trochowski, Sanogo, Ljuboja (Guerrero 82).
Arsenal: Lehmann; Eboue, Gallas, Silva, Toure (Hoyte 29), Djourou, Hleb (Flamini 70), Fabregas, Adebayor, Van Persie (Julio Baptista 70), Rosicky.

Tuesday, 26 September 2006

Arsenal (1) 2 *(Henry 38, Hleb 48)*

Porto (0) 0 59,861

Arsenal: Lehmann; Eboue, Hoyte, Silva, Toure, Gallas (Song 90), Hleb (Walcott 86), Fabregas, Van Persie (Ljungberg 74), Henry, Rosicky.
Porto: Helton; Ricardo Costa (Raul Meireles 46), Pepe, Bruno Alves, Marek Cech, Paulo Assuncao, Ricardo Quaresma, Lucho Gonzalez, Helder Postiga (Lisandro Lopez 46), Anderson (Adriano 66), Bosingwa.

Tuesday, 17 October 2006

CSKA Moscow (1) 1 *(Daniel Carvalho 24)*

Arsenal (0) 0 28,800

CSKA Moscow: Akinfeev; Semberas, Berezutski V, Ignashevich, Berezutski A, Daniel Carvalho (Taranov 89), Zhirkov, Dudu, Vagner Love (Olic 86), Aldonin (Krasic 90), Rahimic.
Arsenal: Lehmann; Hoyte, Gallas, Silva, Toure, Djourou (Clichy 75), Hleb, Fabregas, Van Persie (Adebayor 68), Henry, Rosicky (Walcott 80).

Wednesday, 1 November 2006

Arsenal (0) 0

CSKA Moscow (0) 0 60,003

Arsenal: Lehmann; Hoyte, Clichy, Silva, Toure, Gallas, Hleb (Walcott 71), Fabregas (Flamini 89), Van Persie (Aliadiere 82), Henry, Rosicky.
CSKA Moscow: Akinfeev; Semberas, Berezutski V, Ignashevich, Rahimic, Berezutski A, Daniel Carvalho (Taranov 90), Zhirkov, Dudu, Krasic (Aldonin 40), Vagner Love (Olic 85).

Tuesday, 21 November 2006

Arsenal (0) 3 *(Van Persie 52, Eboue 83, Julio Baptista 88)*

Hamburg (1) 1 *(Van der Vaart 4)* 59,962

Arsenal: Lehmann; Eboue, Clichy, Flamini, Toure, Senderos, Hleb (Julio Baptista 81), Fabregas, Van Persie (Adebayor 70), Henry, Ljungberg (Walcott 75).
Hamburg: Wachter; Fillinger, Atouba (Ljuboja 67), Reinhardt, Mathijsen, Wicky (Lauth 87), Mahdavikia (Feilhaber 46), Trochowski, Sanogo, Benjamin, Van der Vaart.

Wednesday, 6 December 2006

Porto (0) 0

Arsenal (0) 0 41,500

Porto: Helton; Pepe, Ricardo Quaresma, Lucho Gonzalez, Lisandro Lopez, Bosingwa, Fucile, Bruno Alves, Raul Meireles (Ibson 86), Paulo Assuncao, Helder Postiga (Bruno Moraes 81).
Arsenal: Lehmann; Eboue, Clichy, Silva, Toure, Djourou, Hleb, Fabregas, Adebayor (Van Persie 79), Ljungberg, Flamini.

Group G Final Table	P	W	D	L	F	A	Pts
Arsenal	6	3	2	1	7	3	11
Porto	6	3	2	1	9	4	11
CSKA Moscow	6	2	2	2	4	5	8
Hamburg	6	1	0	5	7	15	3

GROUP H

AC Milan	(2) 3	AEK Athens	(0) 0
Anderlecht	(1) 1	Lille	(0) 1
AEK Athens	(1) 1	Anderlecht	(1) 1
Lille	(0) 0	AC Milan	(0) 0
Anderlecht	(0) 0	AC Milan	(0) 1
Lille	(0) 3	AEK Athens	(0) 1
AC Milan	(2) 4	Anderlecht	(0) 1
AEK Athens	(0) 1	Lille	(0) 0
AEK Athens	(1) 1	AC Milan	(0) 0
Lille *(at Lens.)*	(1) 2	Anderlecht	(1) 2
AC Milan	(0) 0	Lille	(1) 2
Anderlecht	(1) 2	AEK Athens	(0) 2

Group H Final Table	P	W	D	L	F	A	Pts
AC Milan	6	3	1	2	8	4	10
Lille	6	2	3	1	8	5	9
AEK Athens	6	2	2	2	6	9	8
Anderlecht	6	0	4	2	7	11	4

KNOCK-OUT STAGE

KNOCK-OUT ROUND FIRST LEG

Celtic	(0) 0	AC Milan	(0) 0
Lille *(at Lens.)*	(0) 0	Manchester United	(0) 1
PSV Eindhoven	(0) 1	Arsenal	(0) 0
Real Madrid	(3) 3	Bayern Munich	(1) 2
Barcelona	(1) 1	Liverpool	(1) 2
Internazionale	(1) 2	Valencia	(0) 2
Porto	(1) 1	Chelsea	(1) 1
Roma	(0) 0	Lyon	(0) 0

Tuesday, 20 February 2007

Celtic (0) 0

AC Milan (0) 0 58,785

Celtic: Boruc; Wilson, Naylor, Sno, McManus, O'Dea, Lennon (Gravesen 81), Nakamura, Vennegoor of Hesselink, Miller (Jarosik 63), McGeady.
AC Milan: Kalac; Oddo, Jankulovski, Gattuso, Kaladze (Bonera 63), Maldini, Gourcuff, Pirlo, Gilardino (Oliveira 77), Kaka, Ambrosini.

Lille (0) 0

Manchester United (0) 1 *(Giggs 83)* 31,680

Lille: Sylva; Chalme, Tafforeau, Bodmer, Plestan, Tavlaridis, Debuchy, Makoun, Fauvergue (Cabaye 57), Odemwingie (Audel 75), Obraniak (Bastos 90).
Manchester United: Van der Sar; Neville, Evra, Carrick, Ferdinand, Vidic, Ronaldo (Saha 67), Scholes (O'Shea 90), Larsson, Rooney, Giggs.
at Lens.

PSV Eindhoven (0) 1 *(Mendez 61)*

Arsenal (0) 0 35,100

PSV Eindhoven: Gomes; Kromkamp, Salcido, Cocu, Alex, Da Costa (Sun 66), Culina, Simons, Tardelli (Vayrynen 75), Kone, Mendez.
Arsenal: Lehmann; Gallas, Clichy, Silva, Toure, Senderos, Hleb (Julio Baptista 75), Fabregas, Adebayor, Henry, Rosicky.

Wednesday, 21 February 2007

Barcelona (1) 1 *(Deco 14)*

Liverpool (1) 2 *(Bellamy 43, Riise 74)* 93,641

Barcelona: Valdes; Belletti, Zambrotta, Xavi (Giuly 65), Puyol, Marquez, Motta (Iniesta 54), Deco, Saviola (Gudjohnsen 82), Ronaldinho, Messi.
Liverpool: Reina; Arbeloa, Riise, Xabi Alonso, Carragher, Agger, Finnan, Sissoko (Zenden 84), Bellamy (Pennant 80), Kuyt (Crouch 90), Gerrard.

Porto (1) 1 *(Raul Meireles 12)*

Chelsea (1) 1 *(Shevchenko 16)* 50,216

Porto: Helton; Bosingwa, Fucile (Bruno Moraes 65), Paulo Assuncao, Pepe, Bruno Alves, Gonzalez, Raul Meireles (Cech 56), Helder Postiga (Adriano 77), Quaresma, Lopez.
Chelsea: Cech; Diarra, Bridge, Makelele, Terry (Robben 13) (Mikel 46), Ricardo Carvalho, Essien, Lampard, Drogba, Shevchenko (Kalou 88), Ballack.

KNOCK-OUT ROUND SECOND LEG

Chelsea	(0) 2	Porto	(1) 1
Liverpool	(0) 0	Barcelona	(0) 1
Lyon	(0) 0	Roma	(2) 2
Valencia	(0) 0	Internazionale	(0) 0
AC Milan*	(0) 1	Celtic	(0) 0
Arsenal	(0) 1	PSV Eindhoven	(0) 1
Bayern Munich	(1) 2	Real Madrid	(0) 1
Manchester United	(0) 1	Lille	(0) 0

Tuesday, 6 March 2007

Chelsea (0) 2 *(Robben 48, Ballack 79)*

Porto (1) 1 *(Quaresma 15)* 39,041

Chelsea: Cech; Diarra (Paulo Ferreira 65), Cole A, Makelele (Mikel 46), Essien, Ricardo Carvalho, Ballack, Lampard, Drogba, Shevchenko (Kalou), Robben.
Porto: Helton; Fucile, Cech (Ibson 55), Ricardo Costa, Pepe, Bruno Alves, Gonzalez, Paulo Assuncao, Lopez (Bruno Moraes 82), Quaresma, Raul Meireles (Adriano 55).

Liverpool (0) 0

Barcelona (0) 1 *(Gudjohnsen 75)* 42,579

Liverpool: Reina; Finnan, Arbeloa, Xabi Alonso, Carragher, Agger, Gerrard, Sissoko, Bellamy (Pennant 67), Kuyt (Crouch 89), Riise (Fabio Aurelio 77).
Barcelona: Valdes; Thuram (Gudjohnsen 71), Oleguer, Xavi, Puyol, Marquez, Iniesta, Deco, Eto'o (Giuly 61), Ronaldinho, Messi.

Wednesday, 7 March 2007

AC Milan (0) 1 *(Kaka 93)*

Celtic (0) 0 52,918

AC Milan: Dida; Oddo (Simic 116), Jankulovski, Pirlo, Bonera, Maldini, Gattuso (Brocchi 79), Ambrosini, Inzaghi (Gilardino 73), Kaka, Seedorf.
Celtic: Boruc; Telfer, Naylor, Sno (Beattie 97), McManus, O'Dea, Nakamura (Miller 106), Lennon, Vennegoor of Hesselink, Jarosik (Gravesen 62), McGeady.
(aet.)

Arsenal (0) 1 *(Alex 58 (og))*

PSV Eindhoven (0) 1 *(Alex 83)* 60,073

Arsenal: Lehmann; Toure, Clichy (Walcott 85), Silva, Gallas, Denilson, Hleb, Fabregas, Adebayor, Julio Baptista (Henry 66), Ljungberg (Diaby 75).
PSV Eindhoven: Gomes; Salcido, Sun, Mendez (Vayrynen 90), Alex, Feher, Culina, Simons, Kone (Afellay 41), Cocu, Farfan (Addo 89).

Manchester United (0) 1 *(Larsson 72)*

Lille (0) 0 75,182

Manchester United: Van der Sar; Neville, Silvestre, O'Shea, Ferdinand, Vidic, Ronaldo (Richardson), Carrick, Larsson (Smith 74), Rooney (Park 82), Scholes.
Lille: Sylva; Chalme, Tafforeau, Dumont (Fauvergue 74), Tavlaridis, Plestan, Makoun, Keita, Odemwingie (Mirallas 74), Michel Bastos (Debuchy 46), Obraniak.

QUARTER-FINALS FIRST LEG

AC Milan	(1) 2	Bayern Munich	(0) 2
PSV Eindhoven	(0) 0	Liverpool	(1) 3
Chelsea	(0) 1	Valencia	(1) 1
Roma	(1) 2	Manchester United	(0) 1

Tuesday, 3 April 2007

PSV Eindhoven (0) 0

Liverpool (1) 3 *(Gerrard 27, Riise 49, Crouch 63)* 36,500

PSV Eindhoven: Gomes; Kromkamp (Feher 68), Da Costa, Simons, Salcido, Mendez (Kluivert 51), Vayrynen, Cocu, Culina, Farfan (Sun 46), Tardelli.
Liverpool: Reina; Finnan, Riise (Zenden 65), Mascherano, Carragher, Agger, Gerrard, Xabi Alonso, Crouch (Pennant 85), Kuyt, Fabio Aurelio (Gonzalez 75).

Wednesday, 4 April 2007

Chelsea (0) 1 *(Drogba 53)*

Valencia (1) 1 *(Silva 30)* 38,065

Chelsea: Cech; Diarra, Cole A, Mikel (Cole J 74), Terry, Ricardo Carvalho, Kalou (Wright-Phillips 74), Lampard, Drogba, Shevchenko, Ballack.
Valencia: Canizares; Miguel, Del Horno, Albelda, Ayala, Moretti, Vicente (Angulo 57), Albiol, Silva, David Villa (Jorge Lopez 90), Joaquin (Hugo Viana 86).

Roma (1) 2 *(Taddei 44, Vucinic 67)*

Manchester United (0) 1 *(Rooney 60)* 75,000

Roma: Doni; Panucci, Mexes, Chivu, Cassetti, Wilhelmsson (Vucinic 62), Taddei (Rosi 82), De Rossi, Perrotta, Mancini, Totti.
Manchester United: Van der Sar; Brown, Heinze, Carrick, Ferdinand, O'Shea, Ronaldo, Scholes■, Solskjaer (Fletcher 72), Rooney, Giggs (Saha 77).

QUARTER-FINALS SECOND LEG

Manchester United	(4) 7	Roma	(0) 1
Valencia	(1) 1	Chelsea	(0) 2
Bayern Munich	(0) 0	AC Milan	(2) 2
Liverpool	(0) 1	PSV Eindhoven	(0) 0

Tuesday, 10 April 2007

Manchester United (4) 7 *(Carrick 12, 60, Smith 17, Rooney 19, Ronaldo 44, 49, Evra 81)*

Roma (0) 1 *(Di Rossi 69)* 74,476

Manchester United: Van der Sar; Brown, O'Shea (Evra 52), Carrick (Richardson 73), Ferdinand, Heinze, Ronaldo, Fletcher, Smith, Rooney, Giggs (Solskjaer 61).
Roma: Doni; Panucci, Cassetti, De Rossi (Faty 80), Mexes, Chivu, Wilhelmsson (Rosi 88), Vucinic, Mancini (Okaka Chuka 90), Totti, Pizarro.

Valencia (1) 1 *(Morientes 32)*

Chelsea (0) 2 *(Shevchenko 52, Essien 90)* 53,000

Valencia: Canizares; Miguel, Del Horno, Albelda, Ayala, Moretti, Joaquin, Albiol (Hugo Viana 72), David Villa, Morientes (Angulo 65), Silva.
Chelsea: Cech; Diarra (Cole J 46), Cole A, Mikel, Terry, Ricardo Carvalho, Essien, Lampard (Makele 90), Drogba, Shevchenko (Kalou 90), Ballack.

Wednesday, 11 April 2007

Liverpool (0) 1 *(Crouch 68)*

PSV Eindhoven (0) 0 41,447

Liverpool: Reina; Arbeloa, Riise, Xabi Alonso (Gonzalez 72), Agger (Paletta 78), Hyypia, Pennant, Sissoko, Crouch, Bellamy (Fowler 17), Zenden.
PSV Eindhoven: Gomes; Marcellis■, Salcido, Cocu, Simons, Addo, Feher (Sun 62), Vayrynen, Farfan (Kluivert 62), Kone (Van Eijden 71), Culina.

SEMI-FINAL FIRST LEG

Manchester United	(1) 3	AC Milan	(2) 2
Chelsea	(1) 1	Liverpool	(0) 0

Tuesday, 24 April 2007

Manchester United (1) 3 *(Ronaldo 6, Rooney 59, 90)*

AC Milan (2) 2 *(Kaka 22, 37)* 73,820

Manchester United: Van der Sar; O'Shea, Evra, Carrick, Heinze, Brown, Fletcher, Scholes, Ronaldo, Rooney, Giggs.
AC Milan: Dida; Oddo, Jankulovski, Ambrosini, Nesta, Maldini (Bonera 46), Pirlo, Gattuso (Brocchi 52), Gilardino (Gourcuff 84), Kaka, Seedorf.

Wednesday, 25 April 2007

Chelsea (1) 1 *(Cole J 29)*

Liverpool (0) 0 39,483

Chelsea: Cech; Paulo Ferreira, Cole A, Makelele, Terry, Ricardo Carvalho, Mikel, Lampard, Drogba, Shevchenko (Kalou 76), Cole J (Wright-Phillips 84).
Liverpool: Reina; Arbeloa, Riise, Xabi Alonso (Pennant 83), Carragher, Agger, Gerrard, Mascherano, Bellamy (Crouch 52), Kuyt, Zenden.

SEMI-FINAL SECOND LEG

Liverpool	(1) 1	Chelsea	(0) 0
(aet; Liverpool won 4-1 on penalties.)			
AC Milan	(2) 3	Manchester United	(0) 0

Tuesday, 1 May 2007

Liverpool (1) 1 *(Agger 22)*

Chelsea (0) 0 42,554

Liverpool: Reina; Finnan, Riise, Mascherano (Fowler 118), Carragher, Agger, Pennant (Xabi Alonso 78), Gerrard, Crouch (Bellamy 106), Kuyt, Zenden.
Chelsea: Cech; Paulo Ferreira, Cole A, Makelele (Geremi 118), Terry, Essien, Mikel, Lampard, Drogba, Kalou (Wright-Phillips 107), Cole J (Robben 98).
(aet; Liverpool won 4-1 on penalties.)

Wednesday, 2 May 2007

AC Milan (2) 3 *(Kaka 11, Seedorf 30, Gilardino 78)*

Manchester United (0) 0 67,500

AC Milan: Dida; Oddo, Jankulovski, Ambrosini, Nesta, Kaladze, Pirlo, Gattuso (Cafu 84), Inzaghi (Gilardino 66), Kaka (Favalli 86), Seedorf.
Manchester United: Van der Sar; O'Shea (Saha 77), Heinze, Carrick, Brown, Vidic, Fletcher, Scholes, Ronaldo, Rooney, Giggs.

UEFA CHAMPIONS LEAGUE FINAL 2007

Wednesday, 23 May 2007

AC Milan (1) 2 *(Inzaghi 45, 82)* **Liverpool (0) 1** *(Kuyt 89)*

(in Athens, 74,000)

AC Milan: Dida; Oddo, Jankulovski (Kaladze 79), Gattuso, Nesta, Maldini, Pirlo, Ambrosini, Inzaghi (Gilardino 88), Kaka, Seedorf (Favalli 90).

Liverpool: Reina; Finnan (Arbeloa 88), Riise, Mascherano (Crouch 78), Carragher, Agger, Pennant, Xabi Alonso, Gerrard, Kuyt, Zenden (Kewell 59).

Referee: Fandel (Germany).

INTERTOTO CUP 2006

FIRST ROUND, FIRST LEG
Achnas 4, Partizani 2
Araz 1, Tiraspol 0
Dinaburg 1, HB 1
Keflavik 4, Dungannon 1
Kilikia 1, Dinamo Tbilisi 5
Nitra 6, Grevenmacher 2
Pobeda 2, Farul 2
Sant Julia 0, Maribor 3
Shakhtyor 1, MTZ-RIPO 5
Tampere 5, Carmarthen Town 0
Trans 1, Kalmar 6
Vetra 0, Shelbourne 1
Zrinjski 3, Marsaxlokk 0

FIRST ROUND, SECOND LEG
Carmarthen Town 1, Tampere 3
Dungannon 0, Keflavik 0
Dinamo Tbilisi 3, Kilikia 0
Farul 2, Pobeda 0
Grevenmacher 0, Nitra 6
HB 0, Dinaburg 1
Kalmar 2, Trans 0
Maribor 5, Sant Julia 0
Marsaxlokk 1, Zrinjski 1
MTZ-RIPO 1, Shakhtyor 3
Partizani 2, Achnas 1
Shelbourne 4, Vetra 0
Tiraspol 2, Araz 0

SECOND ROUND, FIRST LEG
Farul 2, Lokomotiv Plovdiv 1
Grasshoppers 2, Teplice 0
Hibernian 5, Dinaburg 0
Lillestrom 4, Keflavik 1
Maccabi Petah Tikva 1, Zrinjski 1
Moscow FK 2, MTZ-RIPO 0
Nitra 2, Dnepr 1
Odense 3, Shelbourne 0
Osijek 2, Achnas 2
Ried 3, Dinamo Tbilisi 1
Sopron 3, Kayseri 3
Tampere 1, Kalmar 2
Tiraspol 1, Lech 0
Zeta 0, Maribor 3

SECOND ROUND, SECOND LEG
Achnas 0, Osijek 0
Dinaburg 0, Hibernian 3
Dnepr 2, Nitra 0
Dinamo Tbilisi 0, Ried 1
Kalmar 3, Tampere 2
Kayseri 1, Sopron 0
Keflavik 2, Lillestrom 2
Lech 1, Tiraspol 3
Lokomotiv Plovdiv 1, Farul 1
Maribor 2, Zeta 0
MTZ-RIPO 0, Moscow FK 1
Shelbourne 1, Odense 0
Teplice 0, Grasshoppers 2
Zrinjski 1, Maccabi Petah Tikva 3

THIRD ROUND, FIRST LEG
Auxerre 4, Farul 1
Grasshoppers 2, Gent 1
Hertha Berlin 0, Moscow FK 0
Kalmar 1, Twente 0
Larissa 0, Kayseri 0
Maccabi Petah Tikva 0, Achnas 2
Marseille 0, Dnepr 0
Newcastle United 1, Lillestrom 1
Odense 1, Hibernian 0
Ried 3, Tiraspol 1
Villarreal 1, Maribor 2

THIRD ROUND, SECOND LEG
Achnas 2, Maccabi Petah Tikva 3
Dnepr 2, Marseille 2
Farul 1, Auxerre 0
Gent 1, Grasshoppers 1
Hibernian 2, Odense 1
Kayseri 2, Larissa 0
Lillestrom 0, Newcastle United 3
Maribor 1, Villarreal 1
Moscow FK 0, Hertha Berlin 2
Tiraspol 1, Ried 1
Twente 3, Kalmar 1
Eleven winners qualify for the UEFA Cup.

Newcastle U (0) 1 *(Luque 50)*

Lillestrom (1) 1 *(Koren 21)* 31,059
Newcastle U: Given; Carr, Babayaro, Parker, Taylor, Bramble, Solano, Emre, Milner (Ameobi 65), Luque (O'Brien 81), N'Zogbia.

Lillestrom (0) 0

Newcastle U (2) 3 *(Ameobi 29, 36, Emre 90)* 8742

Newcastle U: Given; Carr, Babayaro (Moore 69), Parker, Taylor, Bramble, Solano, Emre, Milner, Ameobi (Butt 79), N'Zogbia (Pattison 86).

UEFA CUP 2006–2007

▪ *Denotes player sent off.*
* *Winner after extra time. †Winner after extra time and penalties*

FIRST QUALIFYING ROUND FIRST LEG

Ameri	(0) 0	Banants	(1) 1
Apoel	(1) 3	Murata	(0) 1
Artmedia	(1) 2	WIT	(0) 0
Atvidaberg	(2) 4	Etzella	(0) 0
BATE Borisov	(0) 2	Otaci	(0) 0
Basle	(1) 3	Tobol	(0) 1
Brondby	(3) 3	Valur	(0) 1
Dinamo Tirana	(0) 0	CSKA Sofia	(0) 1
Fehervar	(1) 1	Kairat	(0) 0
Hibernians	(0) 0	Dinamo Bucharest	(1) 4
Jeunesse Esch	(0) 0	Skonto Riga	(0) 2
Karvan	(0) 1	Spartak Trnava	(0) 0
Koper	(0) 0	Litex	(1) 1
Levadia	(2) 2	Haka	(0) 0
Lokomotiv Sofia	(0) 2	Makedonia	(0) 0
Lyn	(1) 1	Flora	(0) 1
Mika	(0) 1	Young Boys	(1) 3
Orasje	(0) 0	Domzale	(2) 2
Randers	(0) 1	IA Akranes	(0) 0
Rapid Bucharest	(5) 5	Sliema Wanderers	(0) 0
Rijeka	(1) 2	Omonia	(1) 2
Sarajevo	(3) 3	Ranger's	(0) 0
Skala	(0) 0	Start	(1) 1
Ujpest	(0) 0	Vaduz	(2) 4
Vardar	(1) 1	Roeselare	(2) 2
Varteks	(0) 1	SK Tirana	(1) 1
Ventspils	(1) 2	GI Gotu	(1) 1
Zaglebie	(0) 1	Dynamo Minsk	(0) 1
Zimbru	(0) 1	Karabakh	(0) 1
Gefle	(1) 1	Llanelli	(0) 2
Glentoran	(0) 0	Brann	(0) 1
HJK Helsinki	(0) 1	Drogheda United	(1) 1
IFK Gothenburg	(0) 0	Derry City	(0) 1
Portadown	(0) 1	Kaunas	(2) 3
Rhyl	(0) 0	Suduva	(0) 0

Thursday, 13 July 2006

Gefle (1) 1 *(Viikmae 20)*

Llanelli (0) 2 *(Griffiths 82, Mingorance 87)* 839

Gefle: Hugosson; Hedlund, Karlsson P, Viikmae, Claesson, Bernhardsson, Woxlin, Wikstrom M, Bapupa (Ericsson 69), Mattsson (Westlin 76), Makondele.
Llanelli: Roberts; Phillips (Harrhy 46), Lloyd, Thomas N, Thomas D, Appleby (Mingorance 46), Griffiths, Corbisiero, Belle, Fernandez, Williams (Maxwell 90).

Glentoran (0) 0

Brann (0) 1 *(Memelli 69)* 1743

Glentoran: Morris (McLaughlin 60); Nixon, Holmes, Walker, Simpson, Halliday (Hamilton 81), McDonagh, Berry, Neill, Morgan (Tolan 73), Hill.
Brann: Thorbjornsen; Dahl (Miller 46), Zavrl, Sigurdsson, Hanstveit, Knudsen, Monkam▪, Haugen, Moen (Kalvenes 70), Saeternes (Bjarnason 67), Memelli.

HJK Helsinki (0) 1 *(Halsti 83)*

Drogheda United (1) 1 *(Robinson 41)* 2467

HJK Helsinki: Wallen; Marjamaa, Aalto I, Pohja, Ghazi (Savolainen 87), Lampi, Nurmela, Parikka (Zeneli E 69), Hakanpaa (Oravainen 72), Halsti, Sorsa.
Drogheda United: Connor; Lynch, Webb, Gavin, Gartland, Robinson, Whelan, Grant (Barrett 75), Shelly, Zayed (Ristila 57), Keegan.

IFK Gothenburg (0) 0

Derry City (0) 1 *(Hargan 79)* 3316

IFK Gothenburg: Andersson; Bjarsmyr, Alexandersson, Kihlberg, Selakovic (Mourad 65), Johansson A, Johansson M, Jonsson H, Wernbloom, Berg (Wallerstedt 73), Vasques (Wowoah 83).
Derry City: Forde; McCallion, Hargan, Hutton, Higgins (Martyn 90), Beckett (O'Flynn 86), McHugh (McGlynn 89), Brennan, Deery, Molloy, Kelly.

Portadown (0) 1 *(McCutcheon 63)*

Kaunas (2) 3 *(Ivaskevicius 2, Manchkhava 9, Velicka 47)* 500

Portadown: Dougherty; Convery, Marks (MacNerney 86), Boyle, McCutcheon, Kennedy, Tiggart, Devenney (McCann 58), Smart (Baker 79), O'Hara, Clarke.
Kaunas: Kurskis; Radzius, Kancelskis, Manchkhava, Barevicius (Kunevicius 82), Velicka, Baguzis, Ivaskevicius, Pilibaitis (Pacevicius 88), Zaliukas, Pehlic (Klimek 58).

Rhyl (0) 0

Suduva (0) 0 1479

Rhyl: Whitfield; Powell M, Brewerton, Connelly, Horan, Edwards, Wilson, Moran (Rafferty 76), Hunt (Sharp 66), Murtagh, Hay.
Suduva: Padimanskas; Chigladze D, Gvildys, Grigas, Mikuckis, Miklinevicius, Cordeiro, Adomaitus (Samusiovas 46), Urbsys (Uselis 72), Maciulis, Braga (Abramenko 89).

FIRST QUALIFYING ROUND SECOND LEG

Banants	(1) 1	Ameri	(0) 2
CSKA Sofia	(1) 4	Dinamo Tirana	(1) 1
Dinamo Bucharest	(0) 5	Hibernians	(0) 1
Dynamo Minsk	(0) 0	Zaglebie	(0) 0
Domzale	(3) 5	Orasje	(0) 0
Etzella	(0) 0	Atvidaberg	(0) 3
Flora	(0) 0	Lyn	(0) 0
GI Gotu	(0) 0	Ventspils	(0) 2
Haka	(1) 1	Levadia	(0) 0
IA Akranes	(1) 2	Randers	(1) 1
Kairat	(0) 2	Fehervar	(1) 1
Karabakh	(1) 1	Zimbru*	(0) 2
Litex	(1) 5	Koper	(0) 0
Makedonia	(1) 1	Lokomotiv Sofia	(0) 1
Murata	(0) 0	Apoel	(3) 4
Omonia	(0) 2	Rijeka	(0) 1
Otaci	(0) 0	BATE Borisov	(1) 1
Ranger's	(0) 0	Sarajevo	(2) 2
Roeselare	(3) 5	Vardar	(0) 1
Skonto Riga	(2) 3	Jeunesse Esch	(0) 0
Sliema Wanderers	(0) 0	Rapid Bucharest	(1) 1
Spartak Trnava	(0) 0	Karvan	(1) 1
Start	(1) 3	Skala	(0) 0
SK Tirana	(1) 2	Varteks	(0) 0
Tobol	(0) 0	Basle	(0) 0
Vaduz	(0) 0	Ujpest	(0) 1

Valur	(0) 0	Brondby	(0) 0
WIT	(1) 2	Artmedia	(0) 1
Young Boys	(0) 1	Mika	(0) 0
Brann	(0) 1	Glentoran	(0) 0
Derry City	(1) 1	IFK Gothenburg	(0) 0
Kaunas	(1) 1	Portadown	(0) 0
Drogheda United*	(0) 3	HJK Helsinki	(1) 1
Suduva	(2) 2	Rhyl	(0) 1

Thursday, 27 July 2006

Llanelli (0) 0

Gefle (0) 0 3000

Llanelli: Roberts; Lloyd, Thomas N, Thomas W, Mingorance (Harrhy 65), Griffiths, Corbisiero, Belle, Fernandez, Maxwell (Appleby 89), Williams.
Gefle: Hugosson; Hedlund■, Karlsson P, Ericsson (Wikstrom A 37), Viikmae (Bapupa 56), Claesson, Bernhardsson, Woxlin, Wikstrom M, Westlin (Mattsson 78), Makondele.

Brann (0) 1 *(Bjarnason 85 (pen))*

Glentoran (0) 0 3547

Brann: Thorbjornsen; Knudsen, Sigurdsson (Bjarnason 46), Kalvenes, Hanstveit, Huseklepp, Zavrl (Misje 86), Haugen, Winters, Miller (Ludvigsen 46), Memelli.
Glentoran: Morris; Nixon, Neill, Simpson (Leeman 25), Smyth, Berry, Hill, McDonagh, Morgan (Tolan 56), Hamilton (Halliday 86), Lockhart.

Derry City (1) 1 *(O'Flynn 32 (pen))*

IFK Gothenburg (0) 0 2400

Derry City: Forde; McCallion, Hargan, Hutton, Higgins (Oman 83), Beckett, McHugh (McGlynn 83), Deery, Molloy, O'Flynn (Martyn 86), Kelly.
IFK Gothenburg: Andersson; Bjarsmyr, Johansson A, Kihlberg, Šelakovic (Berg 60), Alexandersson, Jonsson H (Johansson M 74), Mourad, Wernbloom, Jonsson D, Vasques.

Kaunas (1) 1 *(Ivaskevicius 43)*

Portadown (0) 0 2000

Kaunas: Kurskis; Radzius, Kancelskis, Manchkhava, Barevicius (Juska 64), Velicka, Baguzis, Ivaskevicius (Kunevicius 77), Pilibaitis, Zaliukas, Pehlic (Klimek 64).
Portadown: Dougherty; Convery, Marks, Boyle, McCutcheon, Kennedy, Tiggart, Devenney (McCann 56), Smart, O'Hara, Clarke.

Drogheda United (0) 3 *(Gartland 57, Lynch 96, 114)*

HJK Helsinki (1) 1 *(Ghazi 36)* 3000

Drogheda United: Connor; Lynch, Webb, Gavin, Gartland, Robinson, Whelan (Gray 117), Fitzpatrick (Zayed 58), Grant (Barrett 78), Shelly, Keegan.
HJK Helsinki: Wallen; Aalto I, Pohja, Ghazi, Lampi, Nurmela (Marjamaa 88), Aho■, Hakanpaa (Savolainen 103), Halsti, Zeneli E (Oravainen 74), Sorsa.
(aet.)

Suduva (2) 2 *(Maciulevicius 18 (pen), Mikuckis 25)*

Rhyl (0) 1 *(Grigas 80 (og))* 2500

Suduva: Padimanskas; Grigas, Klevinskas, Mikuckis, Chigladze D, Miklinevicius, Maciulis (Chigladze B 46), Maciulevicius (Cordeiro 90), Urbsys, Abramenko, Braga (Jasaitis 61).
Rhyl: Whitfield; Powell M, Graves, Connelly, Horan, Edwards (Hay 45), Wilson■, Moran, Hunt (Sharp 63) (Orlick 70), Murtagh, Brewerton.

SECOND QUALIFYING ROUND FIRST LEG

Apoel	(1) 1	Trabzonspor	(0) 1
Artmedia	(0) 2	Dynamo Minsk	(1) 1
Basle	(0) 1	Vaduz	(0) 0
Bnei Yehuda	(0) 0	Lokomotiv Sofia	(1) 2
Brann	(2) 3	Atvidaberg	(1) 3
Chornomorets	(0) 0	Plock	(0) 0
CSKA Sofia	(0) 0	Kula	(0) 0
Dinamo Bucharest	(0) 1	Beitar	(0) 0
Fehervar	(0) 1	Grasshoppers	(0) 1
Flora	(0) 0	Brondby	(0) 0
Hapoel Tel Aviv	(1) 1	Domzale	(0) 2
Hertha Berlin	(0) 1	Ameri	(0) 0
Karvan	(0) 0	Slavia Prague	(1) 2
Mattersburg	(1) 1	Wisla	(1) 1
Molde	(0) 0	Skonto Riga	(0) 0
OFK Belgrade	(1) 1	Auxerre	(0) 0
Omonia	(0) 0	Litex	(0) 0
Partizan Belgrade	(2) 2	Maribor	(0) 1
Randers	(0) 3	Kaunas	(0) 1
Ried	(0) 0	Sion	(0) 0
Roeselare	(1) 2	Ethnikos Achnas	(0) 1
Rubin	(1) 3	BATE Borisov	(0) 0
Sarajevo	(0) 1	Rapid Bucharest	(0) 0
Suduva	(0) 0	FC Brugge	(1) 2
SK Tirana	(0) 0	Kayseri	(2) 2
Twente	(0) 1	Levadia	(1) 1
Young Boys	(1) 3	Marseille	(2) 3
Zimbru	(0) 0	Metallurg Zapor	(0) 0
Gretna	(1) 1	Derry City	(1) 5
Odense	(1) 1	Llanelli	(0) 0
Start	(0) 1	Drogheda United	(0) 0
Ventspils	(0) 0	Newcastle United	(0) 1

Thursday, 10 August 2006

Gretna (1) 1 *(McGuffie 12)*

Derry City (1) 5 *(Kelly 23, Deery 54, 56, Martyn 63, 75)*
(at Motherwell). 6040

Gretna: Main; Canning, Innes, Townsley (Jenkins 57), McGill (O'Neil 46), McGuffie, Tosh, Skelton, McQuilken, Deuchar (Graham 79), Grady.
Derry City: Forde; McCallion, Hargan, Hutton, Martyn, Beckett (McGlynn 84), McHugh, Deery, Molloy (Higgins 76), O'Flynn (McCourt 73), Kelly.

Odense (1) 1 *(Bechara 29)*

Llanelli (0) 0 2744

Odense: Onyszko; Ophaug, Laursen, Fevang, Christensen, Bechara (Larsen 63), Hansen, Sorensen, Jensen, Borre, Borring.
Llanelli: Roberts; Lloyd, Thomas N, Thomas D, Mingorance (Williams 58), Griffiths R, Corbisiero, Belle, Fernandez, Griffiths D (Harrhy 73), Legg.

Start (0) 1 *(Stromstad 66)*

Drogheda United (0) 0 1433

Start: Nilssen; Paulsen K, Pedersen S, Engedal, Johnson, Stromstad, Aarsheim, Haestad (Fevang 85), Barlin (Nielsen 19) (Borgersen 85), Valencia, Jonsson.
Drogheda United: Connor; Lynch, Gartland, Jason, Webb, Robertson, Keegan, Bradley (Whelan 82), Shelley, Barrett (Keddy 90), Fitzpatrick (Grant 87).

Ventspils (0) 0

Newcastle United (0) 1 *(Bramble 67)* 6000

Ventspils: Vanins; Ndeki, Gorkss, Kacanovs, Bicka, Zangareev, Dubenskiy(Kosmacovs 89), Vukovic, Kolesnicenko (Pokarynin 84), Butriks, Slesarcuks (Zizilevs 16).
Newcastle United: Given; Carr, Babayaro (Ramage 90), Butt, Moore, Bramble, Solano (Milner 84), Emre (N'Zogbia 79), Ameobi, Parker, Duff.

SECOND QUALIFYING ROUND SECOND LEG

Ameri	(1) 2	Hertha Berlin	(1) 2
Atvidaberg	(1) 1	Brann	(0) 1
Auxerre	(2) 5	OFK Belgrade	(1) 1
BATE Borisov	(0) 0	Rubin	(2) 2
Beitar Jerusalem	(1) 1	Dinamo Bucharest	(1) 1
Brondby	(0) 4	Flora	(0) 0
FC Brugge	(2) 5	Suduva	(0) 2
Domzale	(0) 0	Hapoel Tel Aviv	(0) 3
Dynamo Minsk	(0) 2	Artmedia	(2) 3
Ethnikos Achnas	(2) 5	Roeselare	(0) 0
Grasshoppers	(2) 2	Fehervar	(0) 0
Hajduk Kula	(0) 1	CSKA Sofia	(0) 1
Kaunas	(0) 1	Randers	(0) 0
Kayseri	(2) 3	SK Tirana	(0) 1
Levadia	(1) 1	Twente	(0) 0
Litex	(2) 2	Omonia	(1) 1
Lokomotiv Sofia	(2) 4	Bnei Yehuda	(0) 0
Maribor	(0) 1	Partizan Belgrade	(1) 1
Marseille	(0) 0	Young Boys	(0) 0
Metallurg Zapor	(1) 3	Zimbru	(0) 0
Plock	(0) 1	Chornomorets	(1) 1
Rapid Bucharest	(1) 2	Sarajevo	(0) 0
Sion	(1) 1	Ried	(0) 0
Skonto Riga	(0) 1	Molde	(1) 2
Slavia Prague	(0) 0	Karvan	(0) 0
Trabzonspor	(0) 1	Apoel	(0) 0
Vaduz	(0) 2	Basle	(0) 1
Wisla	(1) 1	Mattersburg	(0) 0
Derry City	(1) 2	Gretna	(1) 2
Drogheda United	(0) 1	Start†	(0) 0
Llanelli	(1) 1	Odense	(2) 5
Newcastle United	(0) 0	Ventspils	(0) 0

Thursday, 24 August 2006

Derry City (1) 2 *(Farren 37, Oman 69)*

Gretna (1) 2 *(Graham 17, Baldacchino 77)* 2850

Derry City: Forde; McCallion, Hargan, Higgins (Deery 59), McHugh (Martyn 74), Oman, McGlynn, Molloy, Farren, O'Flynn (Beckett 61), Kelly.
Gretna: Main; Birch, Grady, Skelton, Canning, Graham, Deuchar, McGuffie (Jenkins 73), Tosh (O'Neil 53), Townsley, Granger.

Drogheda United (0) 1 *(Zayed 84)*

Start (0) 0 4154

Drogheda United: Connor; Lynch, Webb, Gavin, Gartland, Robinson, Keddy (Whelan 71), Bradley, Keegan, Ristila (Zayed 57), Barrett (Gray 96).
Start: Nilssen; Pedersen S (Paulsen K 90), Haland, Borgersen, Johnson, Fevang (Stromstad 83), Aarsheim, Haestad, Valencia, Nielsen (Barlin 71), Garba.
(aet; Start won 11-10 on penalties.)

Llanelli (1) 1 *(Corbisiero 10)*

Odense (2) 5 *(Timm 15, Hansen 34, Christensen 59, Ophaug 65, Bechara 90)* 2759

Llanelli: Roberts; Lloyd, Thomas N, Jones (Griffiths D 60), Thomas W, Griffiths R, Corbisiero, Harrhy (Mingorance 57), Belle, Williams C, Legg (Lewis 64).
Odense: Onyszko; Ophaug (Larsen 86), Laursen, Christensen, Timm (Bechara 78), Grahn, Hansen, Sorensen, Jensen, Borre, Borring.

Newcastle United (0) 0

Ventspils (0) 0 30,498

Newcastle United: Harper; Carr, Babayaro, Parker, Bramble, Taylor, Duff, Emre, Milner, Luque, N'Zogbia.
Ventspils: Vanins; Kacanovs, Ndeki, Gorkss, Pokarynin, Vukovic, Dubenskiy, Bicka, Zizilevs, Rimkus (Stukalinas 90), Kolesnicenko (Kosmacovs 86).

FIRST ROUND FIRST LEG

Artmedia	(2) 2	Espanyol	(1) 2
Atromitos	(0) 1	Sevilla	(2) 2
Atvidaberg	(0) 0	Grasshoppers	(2) 3
AZ	(2) 3	Kayseri	(1) 2
Basle	(4) 6	Rabotnicki	(0) 2
Besiktas	(0) 2	CSKA Sofia	(0) 0
Braga	(1) 2	Chievo	(0) 0
Chornomorets	(0) 0	Hapoel Tel Aviv	(0) 1
Dynamo Zagreb	(0) 1	Auxerre	(1) 2
Eintracht Frankfurt	(0) 4	Brondby	(0) 0
Ethnikos Achnas	(0) 0	Lens	(0) 0
Fenerbahce	(1) 2	Randers	(1) 1
Hertha Berlin	(1) 2	Odense	(1) 2
Legia	(1) 1	FK Austria	(1) 1
Liberec	(1) 2	Red Star Belgrade	(0) 0
Livorno	(1) 2	Pasching	(0) 0
Lokomotiv Moscow	(1) 2	Waregem	(0) 1
Lokomotiv Sofia	(2) 2	Feyenoord	(1) 2
Maccabi Haifa	(1) 1	Litex	(0) 1
(at Nijmegen.)			
Marseille	(1) 1	Mlada Boleslav	(0) 0
Panathinaikos	(1) 1	Metallurg Zapor	(0) 1
Partizan Belgrade	(3) 4	Groningen	(0) 2
Rapid Bucharest	(1) 1	Nacional	(0) 0
Rubin	(0) 0	Parma	(0) 1
Ruzomberok	(0) 0	FC Brugge	(1) 1
Schalke	(0) 1	Nancy	(0) 0
Sion	(0) 0	Leverkusen	(0) 0
Standard Liege	(0) 0	Celta Vigo	(1) 1
Start	(1) 2	Ajax	(2) 5
Trabzonspor	(0) 2	Osasuna	(1) 2
(Behind closed doors.)			
Setubal	(0) 0	Heerenveen	(0) 3
Wisla	(0) 0	Iraklis	(1) 1
Xanthi	(2) 3	Dinamo Bucharest	(3) 4
Derry City	(0) 0	Paris St Germain	(0) 0
Hearts	(0) 0	Sparta Prague	(1) 2
Levadia	(0) 0	Newcastle United	(1) 1
Molde	(0) 0	Rangers	(0) 0
Salzburg	(1) 2	Blackburn Rovers	(2) 2
Slavia Prague	(0) 0	Tottenham Hotspur	(1) 1
West Ham United	(0) 0	Palermo	(1) 1

Thursday, 14 September 2006

Derry City (0) 0

Paris St Germain (0) 0 3000

Derry City: Forde; McCallion, Hargan, Martyn, McHugh, Brennan (Farren 80), Oman, Kelly, McCourt (Beckett 57), Molloy, Deery.
Paris St Germain: Landreau; Paulo Cesar, Armand, Baning (Chantome 84), Diane (Pauleta 71), Drame, Frau, Hellebuyck, Pancrate (Kalou 80), Rozehnal, Traore.

Hearts (0) 0

Sparta Prague (1) 2 *(Kolar 34, Matusovic 71)* 27,255

(at Murrayfield).

Hearts: Gordon; Neilson, Pressley, Bednar, Beslija (Tall 63), Pinilla (Cesnauskis 63), Berra, Mole, Wallace, Aguiar, Hartley.
Sparta Prague: Blazek; Repka, Sivok, Dosek, Kolar (Hasek 75), Simak (Matusovic 63), Sylvestre (Lustrinelli 85), Kisel, Pospech, Homola, Kadlec.

Levadia (0) 0

Newcastle United (1) 1 *(Sibierski 10)* 7917

Levadia: Kotenko; Cepauskas, Lemsalu, Sisov, Kalimullin, Nahk, Dmitrijev (Kink 82), Vassiljev, Dovydenas (Puri 71), Andreev (Purje 66), Voskoboinikov.
Newcastle United: Given; Carr, Ramage, Parker, Moore, Bramble (Milner 36), Duff, Emre, Martins, Sibierski (Luque 80), N'Zogbia (Butt 73).

Molde (0) 0

Rangers (0) 0 6569

Molde: Larsen; Andreasson, Kallio, Hestad, Hoseth, Ohr, Rudi, Rindaroy (Strande 71), Grande, Mavric, Konate (Diouf 83).
Rangers: McGregor; Buffel (Burke 66), Ferguson (Clement 75), Hemdani, Sionko (Prso 64), Boyd, Bardsley, Svensson, Smith, Rodriguez, Martin.

Salzburg (1) 2 *(Zickler 30, Janko 90)*

Blackburn Rovers (2) 2 *(Savage 32, McCarthy 39)* 17,000

Salzburg: Ochs; Bodnar, Dudic, Linke, Carboni, Kovac, Zickler, Jezek (Vonlanthen 63), Tiffert (Pitak 63), Meyer, Janocko (Janko 46).
Blackburn Rovers: Friedel; Emerton, Neill, Tugay, Khizanishvili, Ooijer, Bentley, Savage, Gallagher (Peter 81), McCarthy (Nonda 87), Pedersen.

Slavia Prague (0) 0

Tottenham Hotspur (1) 1 *(Jenas 37)* 14,869

Slavia Prague: Vorel (Kozacik 28); Hubacek, Svec, Latka, Vlcek, Gaucho (Fort 63), Janda (Necas 72), Suchy, Svento, Jarolim, Hrdlicka.
Tottenham Hotspur: Robinson; Chimbonda, Assou-Ekotto, Huddlestone (Davids 71), Dawson, King, Zokora, Jenas, Mido, Defoe (Keane 78), Tainio.

West Ham United (0) 0

Palermo (1) 1 *(Caracciolo 45)* 32,222

West Ham United: Carroll; Mears, Konchesky, Gabbidon, Ferdinand, Mascherano, Bowyer (Etherington 59), Reo-Coker, Zamora (Cole 77), Tevez (Harewood 77), Benayoun.
Palermo: Fontana; Zaccardo, Diana Aimo, Caracciolo, Cassani, Di Michele (Capuano 79), Parravicini (Guana 54), Bresciano (Biava 90), Pisano, Simplicio, Barzagli.

FIRST ROUND SECOND LEG

Ajax	(3) 4	Start	(0) 0
FK Austria	(0) 1	Legia	(0) 0
Auxerre	(2) 3	Dynamo Zagreb	(0) 1
Brondby	(1) 2	Eintracht Frankfurt	(1) 2
FC Brugge	(0) 1	Ruzomberok	(1) 1
Celta Vigo	(1) 3	Standard Liege	(0) 0
Chievo	(1) 2	Braga*	(0) 1
CSKA Sofia	(0) 2	Besiktas*	(0) 2
Dynamo Bucharest	(2) 4	Xanthi	(0) 1
Espanyol	(1) 3	Artmedia	(1) 1
Feyenoord	(0) 0	Lokomotiv Sofia	(0) 0
Grasshoppers	(2) 5	Atvidaberg	(0) 0
Groningen	(0) 1	Partizan Belgrade	(0) 0
Hapoel Tel Aviv	(1) 3	Chornomorets	(0) 1
Heerenveen	(0) 0	Setubal	(0) 0
Iraklis	(0) 0	Wisla*	(0) 2
Kayseri	(1) 1	AZ	(0) 1
Lens	(1) 3	Ethnikos Achnas	(0) 1
Leverkusen	(0) 3	Sion	(0) 1
Litex	(1) 1	Maccabi Haifa	(2) 3
Metallurg Zapor	(0) 0	Panathinaikos	(1) 1
Mlada Boleslav	(1) 4	Marseille	(1) 2
Nacional	(1) 1	Rapid Bucharest*	(0) 2
Nancy	(2) 3	Schalke	(0) 1
Odense	(0) 1	Hertha Berlin	(0) 0
Osasuna	(0) 0	Trabzonspor	(0) 0
Parma	(0) 1	Rubin	(0) 0
Pasching	(0) 0	Livorno	(0) 1
Rabotnicki	(0) 0	Basle	(0) 1
Randers	(0) 0	Fenerbahce	(0) 3
Red Star Belgrade	(1) 1	Liberec	(1) 2
Sevilla	(3) 4	Atromitos	(0) 0
Waregem	(0) 2	Lokomotiv Moscow	(0) 0
Blackburn Rovers	(1) 2	Salzburg	(0) 0
Newcastle United	(0) 2	Levadia	(0) 1
Paris St Germain	(2) 2	Derry City	(0) 0
Palermo	(1) 3	West Ham United	(0) 0
Rangers	(2) 2	Molde	(0) 0
Sparta Prague	(0) 0	Hearts	(0) 0
Tottenham Hotspur	(0) 1	Slavia Prague	(0) 0

Thursday, 28 September 2006

Blackburn Rovers (1) 2 *(McCarthy 32, Bentley 56)*

Salzburg (0) 0 18,888

Blackburn Rovers: Friedel; Emerton, Neill, Tugay (Gallagher 83), Khizanishvili, Ooijer, Bentley, Savage (Mokoena 60), Nonda, McCarthy (Jeffers 83), Pedersen.
Salzburg: Ochs; Bodnar, Dudic, Linke, Carboni, Kovac (Aufhauser 68), Zickler (Janocko 64), Tiffert (Jezek 58), Vonlanthen, Janko, Vargas.

Newcastle United (0) 2 *(Martins 47, 50)*

Levadia (0) 1 *(Zelinski 65)* 27,012

Newcastle United: Harper; Carr, Taylor, Butt, Bramble, Ramage, Milner, Emre (Parker 81), Martins (Luque 70), Sibierski, N'Zogbia (Duff 70).
Levadia: Kotenko; Lemsalu, Sisov, Cepauskas, Kalimullin, Nahk, Dovydenas (Puri 55), Dmitrijev (Kink 63), Vassilijev, Voskoboinikov (Zelinski 63), Purje.

Paris St Germain (2) 2 *(Cisse 7, Pauleta 42)*
Derry City (0) 0 7000

Paris St Germain: Landreau; Rozehnal, Mendy, Cisse, Pauleta (Rodriguez 66), Frau, Kalou (Pancrate 66), Traore, Armand, Drame, Paulo Cesar.
Derry City: Forde; McCallion, Hargan (O'Flynn 82), Deery, Molloy, Kelly, McCourt (McHugh 61), Martyn, Beckett (Farren 61), Brennan, Oman.

Palermo (1) 3 *(Simplicio 35, 62, Di Michele 67)*
West Ham United (0) 0 19,264

Palermo: Fontana; Zaccardo, Corini (Guana 79), Diana Aimo (Della Fiore 89), Caracciolo, Cassani, Di Michele (Brienza 86), Bresciano, Pisano, Simplicio, Barzagli.
West Ham United: Carroll; Spector, Konchesky, Gabbidon, Collins, Mascherano (Benayoun 68), Bowyer, Reo-Coker, Harewood (Sheringham 68), Cole (Zamora 60), Tevez.

Rangers (2) 2 *(Buffel 12, Ferguson 45)*
Molde (0) 0 48,024

Rangers: McGregor; Bardsley, Adam, Buffel, Sionko (N'Diaye 90), Ferguson, Hemdani, Smith, Prso (Sebo 81), Boyd (Rae 67), Rodriguez.
Molde: Larsen; Andreasson (Gjerde 65), Kallio, Hestad, Hoseth, Ohr (Moster 70), Rudi, Rindaroy, Grande (Konate 85), Baldvinsson, Mavric.

Sparta Prague (0) 0
Hearts (0) 0 16,505

Sparta Prague: Blazek; Repka, Kadlec, Homola, Pospech, Sivok, Simak (Matusovic 62), Sylvestre, Kisel, Dosek (Lustrinelli 74), Kolar (Jun 86).
Hearts: Gordon; Neilson (Tall 65), Berra, Pressley, Cesnauskis, Pinilla (Aguiar 83), Brellier, Mole (Bednar 55), Hartley, Wallace, Mikoliunas.

Tottenham Hotspur (0) 1 *(Keane 79)*
Slavia Prague (0) 0 35,191

Tottenham Hotspur: Robinson; Chimbonda, Lee, Zokora, Dawson, Davenport, Murphy (Ghaly 70), Jenas, Mido, Keane, Ziegler (Tainio 61).
Slavia Prague: Kozacik; Fort (Necid 79), Svento, Hubacek, Svec, Latka, Krajcik, Jarolim, Hrdlicka (Kalivoda 74), Janda (Vlcek 63), Suchy.

GROUP STAGE

GROUP A

Livorno	(1) 2	Rangers	(3) 3
Maccabi Haifa	(1) 3	Auxerre	(1) 1
Partizan Belgrade	(0) 1	Livorno	(0) 1
Rangers	(1) 2	Maccabi Haifa	(0) 0
Auxerre	(1) 2	Rangers	(0) 2
Maccabi Haifa	(1) 1	Partizan Belgrade	(0) 0
Livorno	(1) 1	Maccabi Haifa	(0) 1
Partizan Belgrade	(1) 1	Auxerre	(3) 4
Auxerre	(0) 0	Livorno	(0) 1
Rangers	(0) 1	Partizan Belgrade	(0) 0

Thursday, 19 October 2006

Livorno (1) 2 *(Lucarelli 34 (pen), 90)*
Rangers (3) 3 *(Adam 27, Boyd 30 (pen), Novo 35)* 13,200

Livorno: Amelia; Galante, Vidigal, Vigiani (Bakayoko 78), Kuffour, Rezaei (Morrone 57), Pasquale, Passoni, Cesar Prates (Balleri 46), Danilevicius, Lucarelli.
Rangers: Letizi; Svensson, Hutton, Ferguson, Rodriguez, Adam, Hemdani, Buffel (Rae 89), Novo (Prso 87), Boyd (Sebo 82), Smith.

Thursday, 2 November 2006

Rangers (1) 2 *(Novo 5, Adam 89 (pen))*

Maccabi Haifa (0) 0 43,062

Rangers: McGregor; Hutton, Hemdani, Svensson, Smith, Novo, Ferguson, Clement, Adam (Rae 90), Prso (Buffel 66), Boyd (Sebo 66).
Maccabi Haifa: Davidovich; Harazi (Meshumar 85), Keinan, Olarra, Magrashvili, Dirceu, Anderson, Boccoli (Melikson 60), Katan, Masudi (Arbeitman 81), Colautti.

Thursday, 23 November 2006

Auxerre (1) 2 *(Jelen 31, Niculae 75)*

Rangers (0) 2 *(Novo 62, Boyd 84)* 8305

Auxerre: Cool; Jaures, Kalabane, Kaboul, Sagna, Pedretti (Niculae 75), Cheyrou, Akale, Thomas, Pieroni, Jelen (Ba 80).
Rangers: McGregor; Svensson, Hutton, Smith (Rodrigues 20), Adam, Ferguson, Hemdani, Clement, Prso (Sionko 67), Novo (Sebo 81), Boyd.

Thursday, 14 December 2006

Rangers (0) 1 *(Hutton 55)*

Partizan Belgrade (0) 0 45,129

Rangers: McGregor; Hutton (Lowing 75), Rodriguez, Svensson, Smith, Hemdani, N'Diaye, Buffel (Stanger 80), Rae, Sebo, Novo (Sionko 64).
Partizan Belgrade: Asprogenis; Rnic, Mihajlov, Djordjevic, Lomic, Zajic, Smiljanic, Tomic, Nebojsa Marinkovic (Vukelia 69), Bosancic (Nenad Marinkovic 67), Mirosavljevic (Gulan 89).

Group A Final Table	*P*	*W*	*D*	*L*	*F*	*A*	*Pts*
Rangers	4	3	1	0	8	4	10
Maccabi Haifa	4	2	1	1	5	4	7
Livorno	4	1	2	1	5	5	5
Auxerre	4	1	1	2	7	7	4
Partizan Belgrade	4	0	1	3	2	7	1

GROUP B

Besiktas	(0) 0	Tottenham H	(1) 2
FC Brugge	(0) 1	Leverkusen	(1) 1
Dinamo Bucharest	(1) 2	Besiktas	(0) 1
Tottenham Hotspur	(1) 3	FC Brugge	(1) 1
FC Brugge	(0) 1	Dinamo Bucharest	(1) 1
Leverkusen	(0) 0	Tottenham Hotspur	(1) 1
Besiktas	(1) 2	FC Brugge	(1) 1
Dinamo Bucharest	(1) 2	Leverkusen	(1) 1
Leverkusen	(0) 2	Besiktas	(0) 1
Tottenham Hotspur	(2) 3	Dinamo Bucharest	(0) 1

Thursday, 19 October 2006

Besiktas (0) 0

Tottenham H (1) 2 *(Ghali 32, Berbatov 63)* 26,800

Besiktas: Vedran; Serdar, Mehmet (Deivson 46), Gokhan, Burak, Baki, Marcio Nobre, Ricardinho, Ibrahim U, Fahri (Ibrahim A 66), Ibrahim T.
Tottenham H: Robinson; Chimbonda, Assou-Ekotto, Huddlestone, Dawson, King, Ghali (Lennon 83), Jenas, Berbatov, Keane, Murphy (Ziegler 80).

Thursday, 2 November 2006

Tottenham Hotspur (1) 3 *(Berbatov 17, 73, Keane 63)*

FC Brugge (1) 1 *(Ibrahim 14)* 35,716

Tottenham Hotspur: Robinson; Chimbonda, Assou-Ekotto, Zokora, Dawson, King, Lennon (Murphy 80), Jenas, Berbatov (Mido 80), Keane, Ghali.
FC Brugge: Stijnen; Pedersen, Clement, Maertens (Vandelannoite 80), Gvozdenovic, Yulu-Matondo, Vermant, Blondel, Englebert, Ibrahim, Balaban (Ishiaku 90).

Thursday, 23 November 2006

Leverkusen (0) 0

Tottenham Hotspur (1) 1 *(Berbatov 36)* 22,500

Leverkusen: Butt; Madouni, Juan, Ramelow (De Wit 80), Schneider, Rolfes, Barnetta (Schwegler 15), Barbarez, Castro, Voronin, Kiessling (Freier 46).
Tottenham Hotspur: Robinson; Chimbonda, Assou-Ekotto, Zokora, Dawson, King, Lennon, Malbranque (Huddlestone 68), Berbatov (Mido 76), Keane, Tainio.

Thursday, 14 December 2006

Tottenham Hotspur (2) 3 *(Berbatov 16, Defoe 39, 50)*

Dinamo Bucharest (0) 1 *(Mendy 90)* 34,004

Tottenham Hotspur: Robinson; Chimbonda (Stalteri 76), Assou-Ekotto, Zokora, Dawson, King (Davenport 68), Lennon, Huddlestone (Malbranque 68), Berbatov, Defoe, Ghali.
Dinamo Bucharest: Hayeu; Mihut, Radu, Moti, Pulhac, Cristea, Margaritescu (Blay 65), Ropotan, Munteanu (Goian 57), Danciulescu (Mendy 77), Ganea I.

Group B Final Table	*P*	*W*	*D*	*L*	*F*	*A*	*Pts*
Tottenham Hotspur	4	4	0	0	9	2	12
Dinamo Bucharest	4	2	1	1	6	6	7
Leverkusen	4	1	1	2	4	5	4
Besiktas	4	1	0	3	4	7	3
FC Brugge	4	0	2	2	4	7	2

GROUP C

AZ	(1) 3	Braga	(0) 0
Slovan Liberec	(0) 0	Sevilla	(0) 0
Braga	(2) 4	Slovan Liberec	(0) 0
Grasshoppers	(1) 2	AZ	(0) 5
Sevilla	(1) 2	Braga	(0) 0
Slovan Liberec	(2) 4	Grasshoppers	(1) 1
AZ	(0) 2	Slovan Liberec	(1) 2
Grasshoppers	(0) 0	Sevilla	(1) 4
Braga	(0) 2	Grasshoppers	(0) 0
Sevilla	(0) 1	AZ	(0) 2

Group C Final Table	*P*	*W*	*D*	*L*	*F*	*A*	*Pts*
AZ	4	3	1	0	12	5	10
Sevilla	4	2	1	1	7	2	7
Braga	4	2	0	2	6	5	6
Slovan Liberec	4	1	2	1	6	7	5
Grasshoppers	4	0	0	4	3	15	0

GROUP D

Odense	(1) 1	Parma	(1) 2
Osasuna	(0) 0	Heerenveen	(0) 0
Heerenveen	(0) 0	Odense	(1) 2
Lens	(1) 3	Osasuna	(0) 1

Odense	(0) 1	Lens	(0) 1
Parma	(1) 2	Heerenveen	(1) 1
Lens	(1) 1	Parma	(0) 2
Osasuna	(1) 3	Odense	(0) 1
Heerenveen	(0) 1	Lens	(0) 0
Parma	(0) 0	Osasuna	(2) 3

Group D Final Table	*P*	*W*	*D*	*L*	*F*	*A*	*Pts*
Parma	4	3	0	1	6	6	9
Osasuna	4	2	1	1	7	4	7
Lens	4	1	1	2	5	5	4
Odense	4	1	1	2	5	6	4
Heerenveen	4	1	1	2	2	4	4

GROUP E

Basle	(0) 1	Feyenoord	(0) 1
Wisla	(1) 1	Blackburn R	(0) 2
Blackburn Rovers	(0) 3	Basle	(0) 0
Nancy	(1) 2	Wisla	(1) 1
Basle	(1) 2	Nancy	(2) 2
Feyenoord	(0) 0	Blackburn Rovers	(0) 0
Nancy	(2) 3	Feyenoord	(0) 0
Wisla	(1) 3	Basle	(1) 1
Blackburn Rovers	(0) 1	Nancy	(0) 0
Feyenoord	(2) 3	Wisla	(1) 1

Thursday, 19 October 2006

Wisla (1) 1 *(Cantoro 28)*

Blackburn R (0) 2 *(Savage 56, Bentley 90)* 14,000

Wisla: Dolha; Baszczynski, Dudka, Cleber, Mijailovic, Blaszczykowski, Sobolewski, Cantoro, Zienczuk (Piotr Brozek 66), Paulista, Radovanovic (Kryszalowicz 83).
Blackburn R: Friedel; Emerton, Neill, Tugay, Khizanishvili, Ooijer, Bentley, Savage (Mokoena 87), Nonda, McCarthy, Pedersen (Roberts 74).

Thursday, 2 November 2006

Blackburn Rovers (0) 3 *(Tugay 75, Jeffers 89 (pen), McCarthy 90)*

Basle (0) 0 13,789

Blackburn Rovers: Friedel; Neill, Gray, Tugay (Gallagher 84), Khizanishvili, Ooijer, Bentley, Savage (Mokoena 38), Nonda (Jeffers 83), McCarthy, Pedersen.
Basle: Costanzo; Zanni, Majstorovic, Papa Malik, Chipperfield, Rakitic (Cristiano 55), Kuzmanovic, Sterjovski, Eduardo (Buckley 64), Ergic, Petric.

Thursday, 23 November 2006

Feyenoord (0) 0

Blackburn Rovers (0) 0 35,000

Feyenoord: Timmer; Tiendalli, Bahia, Greene, Drenthe, Buijs, Hofs (De Guzman 77), Lucius, Kolkka (Boussaboun 65), Charisteas, Huysegems.
Blackburn Rovers: Friedel; Emerton, Gray, Tugay (Mokoena 81), Khizanishvili, Ooijer, Bentley, Savage, Nonda (Jeffers 69), McCarthy (Peter 90), Pedersen.

Wednesday, 13 December 2006

Blackburn Rovers (0) 1 *(Neill 90)*

Nancy (0) 0 12,568

Blackburn Rovers: Friedel; Neill, McEveley, Mokoena, Todd (Nolan 28), Ooijer, Bentley, Savage, Gallagher (McCarthy 67), Derbyshire, Peter (Pedersen 67).
Nancy: Lapeyre; Lecluse, Diakhate, Puygrenier, Chretien, Berenguer, Andre Luiz, Gavanon, Biancalani (Sauget 73), Kim (Curbelo 76), Dia (Nguemo 64).

Group E Final Table	*P*	*W*	*D*	*L*	*F*	*A*	*Pts*
Blackburn Rovers	4	3	1	0	6	1	10
Nancy	4	2	1	1	7	4	7
Feyenoord*	4	1	2	1	4	5	5
Wisla	4	1	0	3	6	8	3
Basle	4	0	2	2	4	9	2

**Feyenoord fined then removed from the competition for crowd trouble at Nancy; Tottenham Hotspur received a bye.*

GROUP F

FK Austria	(1) 1	Waregem	(1) 4
Sparta Prague	(0) 0	Espanyol	(1) 2
Ajax	(1) 3	FK Austria	(0) 0
Waregem	(2) 3	Sparta Prague	(0) 1
Espanyol	(4) 6	Waregem	(1) 2
Sparta Prague	(0) 0	Ajax	(0) 0
Ajax	(0) 0	Espanyol	(1) 2
FK Austria	(0) 0	Sparta Prague	(1) 1
Espanyol	(0) 1	FK Austria	(0) 0
Waregem	(0) 0	Ajax	(1) 3

Group F Final Table	*P*	*W*	*D*	*L*	*F*	*A*	*Pts*
Espanyol	4	4	0	0	11	2	12
Ajax	4	2	1	1	6	2	7
Waregem	4	2	0	2	9	11	6
Sparta Prague	4	1	1	2	2	5	4
FK Austria	4	0	0	4	1	9	0

GROUP G

Panathinaikos	(0) 2	Hapoel Tel Aviv	(0) 0
(Behind closed doors.)			
Rapid Bucharest	(0) 0	Paris St Germain	(0) 0
Hapoel Tel Aviv	(2) 2	Rapid Bucharest	(1) 2
Mlada Boleslav	(0) 0	Panathinaikos	(0) 1
Paris St Germain	(2) 2	Hapoel Tel Aviv	(3) 4
Rapid Bucharest	(0) 1	Mlada Boleslav	(1) 1
Mlada Boleslav	(0) 0	Paris St Germain	(0) 0
Panathinaikos	(0) 0	Rapid Bucharest	(0) 0
Hapoel Tel Aviv	(1) 1	Mlada Boleslav	(1) 1
Paris St Germain	(1) 4	Panathinaikos	(0) 0

Group G Final Table	*P*	*W*	*D*	*L*	*F*	*A*	*Pts*
Panathinaikos	4	2	1	1	3	4	7
Paris St Germain	4	1	2	1	6	4	5
Hapoel Tel Aviv	4	1	2	1	7	7	5
Rapid Bucharest	4	0	4	0	3	3	4
Mlada Boleslav	4	0	3	1	2	3	3

GROUP H

Eintracht Frankfurt	(1) 1	Palermo	(0) 2
Newcastle United	(0) 1	Fenerbahce	(0) 0
Celta Vigo	(1) 1	Eintracht Frankfurt	(1) 1

Palermo	(0) 0	Newcastle United	(1) 1
Fenerbahce	(1) 3	Palermo	(0) 0
Newcastle United	(1) 2	Celta Vigo	(1) 1
Celta Vigo	(0) 1	Fenerbahce	(0) 0
Eintracht Frankfurt	(0) 0	Newcastle United	(0) 0
Fenerbahce	(0) 2	Eintracht Frankfurt	(1) 2
Palermo	(0) 1	Celta Vigo	(0) 1

Thursday, 19 October 2006

Newcastle United (0) 1 *(Sibierski 79)*

Fenerbahce (0) 0 30,035

Newcastle United: Harper; Carr, Taylor, Parker, Ramage, Emre (Butt 54), Milner, Sibierski, Martins (Ameobi 75), Duff, N'Zogbia (Solano 64).
Fenerbahce: Rustu; Onder, Lugano, Edu, Umit O (Deivid 81), Mehmet (Ugur 69), Appiah, Marco Aurelio, Tuncay, Kezman, Alex.

Thursday, 2 November 2006

Palermo (0) 0

Newcastle United (1) 1 *(Luque 37)* 16,904

Palermo: Fontana; Dellafiore, Cassani, Barzagli (Biava 46), Pisano, Tedesco (Simplicio 66), Guana (Di Michele 66), Parravicini, Munari, Brienza, Caracciolo.
Newcastle United: Krul; Ramage, Taylor, Butt, Moore, Bramble, Solano (Carroll 90), Emre, Luque (Pattison 77), Milner, N'Zogbia (Sibierski 68).

Thursday, 23 November 2006

Newcastle United (1) 2 *(Sibierski 37, Taylor 86)*

Celta Vigo (1) 1 *(Canobbio 9)* 25,079

Newcastle United: Given; Solano, Ramage, Butt (Parker 65), Taylor, Bramble, Milner, Emre (Martins 70), Luque, Sibierski, N'Zogbia.
Celta Vigo: Esteban; Angel, Yago, Contreras, Placente, Jonathan, Iriney, Borja Oubina, Nene (Gustavo Lopez 74), Baiano (Perera 61), Canobbio (Jorge 86).

Thursday, 30 November 2006

Eintracht Frankfurt (0) 0

Newcastle United (0) 0 47,000

Eintracht Frankfurt: Proll; Vasoski, Kyrgiakos, Spycher, Rehmer (Ochs 64), Streit, Huggel, Weissenberger, Takahara, Amanatidis (Fink 78), Kohler.
Newcastle United: Given; Solano, Ramage, Butt, Taylor, Bramble, Milner, Emre, Luque (Martins 59), Sibierski, N'Zogbia.

Group H Final Table	*P*	*W*	*D*	*L*	*F*	*A*	*Pts*
Newcastle United	4	3	1	0	4	1	10
Celta Vigo	4	1	2	1	4	4	5
Fenerbahce	4	1	1	2	5	4	4
Palermo	4	1	1	2	3	6	4
Eintracht Frankfurt	4	0	3	1	4	5	3

KNOCK-OUT STAGE

THIRD ROUND FIRST LEG

AEK Athens	(0) 0	Paris St Germain	(1) 2
Benfica	(0) 1	Dinamo Bucharest	(0) 0
Bordeaux	(0) 0	Osasuna	(0) 0
CSKA Moscow	(0) 0	Maccabi Haifa	(0) 0

(in Vladikavkaz.)

Fenerbahce	(1) 3	AZ	(1) 3
Hapoel Tel Aviv	(1) 2	Rangers	(0) 1
Leverkusen	(2) 3	Blackburn R	(1) 2
Livorno	(0) 1	Espanyol	(1) 2
(Behind closed doors.)			
Shakhtar Donetsk	(0) 1	Nancy	(0) 1
Werder Bremen	(0) 3	Ajax	(0) 0
Braga	(0) 1	Parma	(0) 0
Lens	(0) 3	Panathinaikos	(0) 1
Spartak Moscow	(0) 1	Celta Vigo	(1) 1
Steaua	(0) 0	Sevilla	(1) 2
Waregem	(0) 1	Newcastle United	(0) 3

Tottenham H bye after Feyenoord removed

Wednesday, 14 February 2007

Hapoel Tel Aviv (1) 2 *(Toema 43, Dego 76)*

Rangers (0) 1 *(Novo 53)* 13,000

Hapoel Tel Aviv: Elimelech; Abuksis (Chen 83), Ogbona (Vermouth 87), Antebi, Badir, Bondarv, Barda, Dego, Doani, Wellington (De Bruno 67), Toema.
Rangers: McGregor; Hutton, Svensson, Weir, Rae, Ferguson, Hemdani, Novo (Sionko 79), Burke (Adam 84), Murray, Boyd.

Leverkusen (2) 3 *(Callsen-Bracker 18, Ramelow 43, Schneider 56)*

Blackburn R (1) 2 *(Bentley 39, Nonda 86)* 22,500

Leverkusen: Butt; Haggui, Callsen-Bracker, Rolfes, Castro, Schneider, Barbarez, Ramelow, Babic, Voronin, Kiessling (Freier 85).
Blackburn R: Friedel; Emerton, Warnock, Tugay, Nelsen, Henchoz, Bentley, Mokoena (Todd 90), Roberts (Nonda 69), McCarthy, Dunn (Peter 65).

Thursday, 15 February 2007

Waregem (0) 1 *(D'Haene 69)*

Newcastle United (0) 3 *(Dindeleux 47 (og), Martins 59 (pen), Sibierski 76)* 8015

Waregem: Merlier; De Brul (Van Steenbrugghe 81), D'Haene, Dindeleux, Leleu, Reina, Meert (Buysse 85), Sergeant, Vandendreissche (Vandemarliere 85), Verschuere, Matthys.
Newcastle United: Harper; Solano, Babayaro, Butt, Taylor, Bramble, Milner, Sibierski, Martins (Luque 85), Dyer, Duff.

THIRD ROUND SECOND LEG

AZ	(0) 2	Fenerbahce	(2) 2
Ajax	(1) 3	Werder Bremen	(1) 1
Blackburn Rovers	(0) 0	Leverkusen	(0) 0
Celta Vigo	(1) 2	Spartak Moscow	(0) 1
Dinamo Bucharest	(1) 1	Benfica	(0) 2
Espanyol	(1) 2	Livorno	(0) 0
Maccabi Haifa	(1) 1	CSKA Moscow	(0) 0
Nancy	(0) 0	Shakhtar Donetsk	(0) 1
Newcastle United	(0) 1	Waregem	(0) 0
Osasuna*	(0) 1	Bordeaux	(0) 0
Panathinaikos	(0) 0	Lens	(0) 0
Paris St Germain	(1) 2	AEK Athens	(0) 0
Parma	(0) 0	Braga	(0) 1
Rangers	(2) 4	Hapoel Tel Aviv	(0) 0
Sevilla	(1) 1	Steaua	(0) 0

Thursday, 22 February 2007

Blackburn Rovers (0) 0

Leverkusen (0) 0 25,124

Blackburn Rovers: Friedel; Emerton, Warnock, Tugay (Nonda 71), Nelsen, Khizanishvili (Roberts 86), Bentley, Dunn, Derbyshire, McCarthy, Pedersen.
Leverkusen: Butt; Babic, Castro, Rolfes, Juan, Haggui (Callsen-Bracker 59), Ramelow, Freier (Barnetta 73), Schneider, Voronin (Madouni 88), Barbarez.

Newcastle United (0) 1 *(Martins 68)*

Waregem (0) 0 30,083

Newcastle United: Harper; Solano, Babayaro (Huntington 46), Butt (Pattison 65), Taylor, Bramble, Milner, Dyer, Martins, Luque (Carroll 65), Duff.
Waregem: Bossut; Minne (Reina 76), Buysse, Van Steenbrugge, D'Haene, Dindeleux, Vandermarliere, Van Nieuwenhuyse, Vandendriessche (Sergeant 56), Siani (Matthys 56), Meert.

Rangers (2) 4 *(Ferguson 24, 73, Boyd 35, Adam 90)*

Hapoel Tel Aviv (0) 0 46,213

Rangers: McGregor▪; Hutton, Murray, Ferguson, Weir, Hemdani (Adam 90), Rae, Thomson, Boyd (Prso 64), Novo (Klos 75), Burke.
Hapoel Tel Aviv: Elimelech; Bondarv, Badir, Abuksis (Vermouth 65), Doani, Antebi, Dego (De Bruno 46), Wellington (Jolic 80), Ogbona, Barda, Toema.

FOURTH ROUND FIRST LEG

Braga	(0) 2	Tottenham H	(0) 3
Celta Vigo	(0) 0	Werder Bremen	(0) 1
Lens	(1) 2	Leverkusen	(0) 1
Maccabi Haifa	(0) 0	Espanyol	(0) 0
Newcastle United	(4) 4	AZ	(1) 2
Paris St Germain	(2) 2	Benfica	(1) 1
Rangers	(0) 1	Osasuna	(1) 1
Sevilla	(1) 2	Shakhtar Donetsk	(1) 2

Braga (0) 2 *(Paulo Jorge 76, Ze Carlos 81)*

Tottenham H (0) 3 *(Keane 57, 90, Malbranque 72)* 24,500

Braga: Paulo Santos; Luis Filipe, Andrade, Castanheira, Paulo Jorge, Rodriguez, Carlos Fernandes, Joao Pinto (Maciel 80), Wender (Diego 69), Ze Carlos, Bruno Gama (Cesinha 69).
Tottenham H: Robinson; Chimbonda, Lee, Zokora, Dawson, Gardner, Lennon, Malbranque, Berbatov, Keane, Tainio (Huddlestone 74).

Newcastle United (4) 4 *(Steinsson 8 (og), Dyer 22, Martins 23, 37)*

AZ (1) 2 *(Arveladze 31, Koevermans 73)* 28,452

Newcastle United: Given; Solano, Carr, Parker, Taylor, Bramble, Dyer, Butt, Martins, Sibierski (Milner 65), Duff (Emre 77).
AZ: Waterman; Steinsson, Jaliens, Opdam, De Cler, Jenner (Lens 65), De Zeeuw, Martens (Dembele 59), Boukhari (Luirink 83), Koevermans, Arveladze.

Rangers (0) 1 *(Hemdani 90)*

Osasuna (1) 1 *(Raul Garcia 17)* 50,290

Rangers: Klos; Weir, Hutton, Ferguson, Ehogiou, Murray, Thomson (Prso 66), Hemdani, Boyd (Sebo 87), Adam (Novo 46), Burke.
Osasuna: Ricardo; Izquierdo, Miguel Flano, Cuellar, Monreal, Raul Garcia, David Lopez, Juanlu (Juanfran 77), Munoz, Nekounam, Webo (Romeo 82).

FOURTH ROUND SECOND LEG

Leverkusen	(1) 3	Lens	(0) 0
Osasuna	(0) 1	Rangers	(0) 0
Tottenham H	(2) 3	Braga	(1) 2
Werder Bremen	(0) 2	Celta Vigo	(0) 0
AZ	(1) 2	Newcastle United	(0) 0
Benfica	(2) 3	Paris St Germain	(1) 1
Espanyol	(0) 4	Maccabi Haifa	(0) 0
Shakhtar Donetsk	(0) 2	Sevilla*	(0) 3

Wednesday, 14 March 2007

Osasuna (0) 1 *(Webo 71)*

Rangers (0) 0 19,126

Osasuna: Ricardo; Cruchaga, Josetxo, Azpilicueta (David Lopez 66), Javier Flano, Corrales, Punal, Juanlu (Juanfran 82), Romeo (Raul Garcia 74), Webo, Nekounam.
Rangers: McGregor; Weir, Hutton, Thomson (Burke 53), Ehiogu, Murray, Adam, Rae (Boyd 73), Novo, Sebo (Prso 64), Hemdani.

Tottenham H (2) 3 *(Berbatov 28, 42, Malbranque 76)*

Braga (1) 2 *(Huddlestone 24 (og), Andrade 61)* 33,761

Tottenham H: Cerny; Stalteri, Lee, Zokora, Dawson, Chimbonda, Lennon (Ghaly 81), Huddlestone, Berbatov, Keane (Defoe 66), Malbranque.
Braga: Paulo Santos; Luis Filipe, Carlos Fernandes, Madrid, Paulo Jorge, Rodriguez (Nem 40), Frechaut, Andrade, Wender, Ze Carlos (Maciel 74), Joao Pinto (Cesinha 74).

Thursday, 15 March 2007

AZ (1) 2 *(Arveladze 14, Koevermans 56)*

Newcastle United (0) 0 16,401

AZ: Waterman; Jaliens, De Zeeuw, Dembele, De Cler, Steinsson, Donk, Martens (Boukhari 90), Arveladze, Jenner (Lens 80), Koevermans (Opdam 84).
Newcastle United: Given; Solano, Huntington (N'Zogbia 86), Parker, Taylor, Bramble, Dyer, Butt, Martins, Sibierski, Duff (Emre 59).

QUARTER-FINALS FIRST LEG

AZ	(0) 0	Werder Bremen	(0) 0
Espanyol	(2) 3	Benfica	(0) 2
Leverkusen	(0) 0	Osasuna	(1) 3
Sevilla	(2) 2	Tottenham Hotspur	(1) 1

Thursday, 5 April 2007

Sevilla (2) 2 *(Kanoute 19 (pen), Kerzhakov 35)*

Tottenham Hotspur (1) 1 *(Keane 2)* 32,000

Sevilla: Palop; Javi Navarro, David (Dragutinovic 68), Daniel Alves, Escude, Renato (Marti 60), Poulsen, Adriano Correia, Kerzhakov, Kanoute, Jesus Navas.
Tottenham Hotspur: Robinson; Stalteri, Lee, Zokora, Dawson, Chimbonda, Lennon (Malbranque 80), Jenas, Berbatov, Keane, Tainio (Ghaly 84).

QUARTER-FINALS SECOND LEG

Benfica	(0) 0	Espanyol	(0) 0
Osasuna	(0) 1	Leverkusen	(0) 0
Tottenham Hotspur	(0) 2	Sevilla	(2) 2
Werder Bremen	(2) 4	AZ	(1) 1

Thursday, 12 April 2007

Tottenham Hotspur (0) 2 *(Defoe 65, Lennon 67)*

Sevilla (2) 2 *(Malbranque 3 (og), Kanoute 8)* 35,284

Tottenham Hotspur: Robinson; Tainio■, Chimbonda, Zokora (Defoe 65), Dawson, King, Lennon, Jenas, Berbatov, Keane, Malbranque.
Sevilla: Cobeno; Hinkel, Puerta, Poulsen, Javi Navarro, Escude, Daniel Alves (Renato 55), Marti, Kerzhakov (Maresca 82), Kanoute, Adriano Correia (Aitor Ocio 69).

SEMI-FINALS FIRST LEG

Espanyol	(1) 3	Werder Bremen	(0) 0
Osasuna	(0) 1	Sevilla	(0) 0

SEMI-FINALS SECOND LEG

Sevilla	(1) 2	Osasuna	(0) 0
Werder Bremen	(1) 1	Espanyol	(0) 2

UEFA CUP FINAL 2007

Wednesday, 16 May 2007
(at Hampden Park, Glasgow, 50,670)

Espanyol (1) 2 *(Riera 28, Jonatas 115)*

Sevilla (1) 2 *(Adriano Correia 18, Kanoute 105)*

Espanyol: Iraizoz; David Garcia, Jarque, Zabaleta, Moises Hurtado■, Torrejon, De la Pena (Jonatas 87), Luis Garcia, Tamudo (Lacruz 72), Rufete (Pandiani 56), Riera.

Sevilla: Palop; Javi Navarro, Adriano Correia (Renato 76), Daniel Alves, Dragutinovic, Poulsen, Puerta, Luis Fabiano (Kerzhakov 64), Kanoute, Marti, Maresca (Jesus Navas 46).
(aet; Sevilla won 3-1 on penalties.)

Referee: Busacca (Switzerland).

PAST EUROPEAN CUP FINALS

Year	Winner	Score	Runner-up	Score
1956	Real Madrid	4	Stade de Rheims	3
1957	Real Madrid	2	Fiorentina	0
1958	Real Madrid*	3	AC Milan	2
1959	Real Madrid	2	Stade de Rheims	0
1960	Real Madrid	7	Eintracht Frankfurt	3
1961	Benfica	3	Barcelona	2
1962	Benfica	5	Real Madrid	3
1963	AC Milan	2	Benfica	1
1964	Internazionale	3	Real Madrid	1
1965	Internazionale	1	SL Benfica	0
1966	Real Madrid	2	Partizan Belgrade	1
1967	Celtic	2	Internazionale	1
1968	Manchester U*	4	Benfica	1
1969	AC Milan	4	Ajax	1
1970	Feyenoord*	2	Celtic	1
1971	Ajax	2	Panathinaikos	0
1972	Ajax	2	Internazionale	0
1973	Ajax	1	Juventus	0
1974	Bayern Munich	1 4	Atletico Madrid	1 0
1975	Bayern Munich	2	Leeds U	0
1976	Bayern Munich	1	St Etienne	0
1977	Liverpool	3	Borussia Moenchengladbach	1
1978	Liverpool	1	FC Brugge	0
1979	Nottingham F	1	Malmö	0
1980	Nottingham F	1	Hamburg	0
1981	Liverpool	1	Real Madrid	0
1982	Aston Villa	1	Bayern Munich	0
1983	Hamburg	1	Juventus	0
1984	Liverpool†	1	Roma	1
1985	Juventus	1	Liverpool	0
1986	Steaua Bucharest†	0	Barcelona	0
1987	Porto	2	Bayern Munich	1
1988	PSV Eindhoven†	0	Benfica	0
1989	AC Milan	4	Steaua Bucharest	0
1990	AC Milan	1	Benfica	0
1991	Red Star Belgrade†	0	Marseille	0
1992	Barcelona	1	Sampdoria	0

PAST UEFA CHAMPIONS LEAGUE FINALS

Year	Winner	Score	Runner-up	Score
1993	Marseille	1	AC Milan	0
(Marseille subsequently stripped of title)				
1994	AC Milan	4	Barcelona	0
1995	Ajax	1	AC Milan	0
1996	Juventus†	1	Ajax	1
1997	Borussia Dortmund	3	Juventus	1
1998	Real Madrid	1	Juventus	0
1999	Manchester U	2	Bayern Munich	1
2000	Real Madrid	3	Valencia	0
2001	Bayern Munich†	1	Valencia	1
2002	Real Madrid	2	Leverkusen	1
2003	AC Milan†	0	Juventus	0
2004	Porto	3	Monaco	0
2005	Liverpool†	3	AC Milan	3
2006	Barcelona	2	Arsenal	1
2007	AC Milan	2	Liverpool	1

*† aet; won on penalties. * aet.*

PAST UEFA CUP FINALS

Year	Team	Score	Team	Score
1972	Tottenham H	2 1	Wolverhampton W	1 1
1973	Liverpool	3 0	Borussia Moenchengladbach	0 2
1974	Feyenoord	2 2	Tottenham H	2 0
1975	Borussia Moenchengladbach	0 5	Twente Enschede	0 1
1976	Liverpool	3 1	FC Brugge	2 1
1977	Juventus**	1 1	Athletic Bilbao	0 2
1978	PSV Eindhoven	0 3	SEC Bastia	0 0
1979	Borussia Moenchengladbach	1 1	Red Star Belgrade	1 0
1980	Borussia Moenchengladbach	3 0	Eintracht Frankfurt**	2 1
1981	Ipswich T	3 2	AZ 67 Alkmaar	0 4
1982	IFK Gothenburg	1 3	SV Hamburg	0 0
1983	Anderlecht	1 1	Benfica	0 1
1984	Tottenham H†	1 1	RSC Anderlecht	1 1
1985	Real Madrid	3 0	Videoton	0 1
1986	Real Madrid	5 0	Cologne	1 2
1987	IFK Gothenburg	1 1	Dundee U	0 1
1988	Bayer Leverkusen†	0 3	Espanol	0 3
1989	Napoli	2 3	Stuttgart	1 3
1990	Juventus	3 0	Fiorentina	1 0
1991	Internazionale	2 0	AS Roma	0 1
1992	Ajax**	0 2	Torino	0 2
1993	Juventus	3 3	Borussia Dortmund	1 0
1994	Internazionale	1 1	Salzburg	0 0
1995	Parma	1 1	Juventus	0 1
1996	Bayern Munich	2 3	Bordeaux	0 1
1997	Schalke*†	1 0	Internazionale	0 1
1998	Internazionale	3	Lazio	0
1999	Parma	3	Marseille	0
2000	Galatasaray†	0	Arsenal	0
2001	Liverpool§	5	Alaves	4
2002	Feyenoord	3	Borussia Dortmund	2
2003	Porto*	3	Celtic	2
2004	Valencia	2	Marseille	0
2005	CSKA Moscow	3	Sporting Lisbon	1
2006	Sevilla	4	Middlesbrough	0
2007	Sevilla*†	2	Espanyol	2

**After extra time* ***Won on away goals* †*Won on penalties* §*Won on sudden death.*

UEFA CHAMPIONS LEAGUE 2007–2008

PARTICIPATING CLUBS

AC Milan (holders); Real Madrid CF; FC Barcelona; Sevilla FC; Valencia CF; FC Internazionale Milano; AS Roma; S.S. Lazio; Manchester United; Chelsea FC; Liverpool FC; Arsenal FC; Olympique Lyonnais; Olympique de Marseille; Toulouse FC; VfB Stuttgart; FC Schalke 04; Werder Bremen; FC Porto; Sporting Clube de Portugal; SL Benfica; PSV Eindhoven; AFC Ajax; Olympiacos CFP; AEK Athens FC; PFC CSKA Moskva; FC Spartak Moskva; FC Dinamo 1948 Bucuresti; FC Steaua Bucuresti; Celtic FC; Rangers FC; RSC Anderlecht; KRC Genk; FC Dynamo Kyiv; FC Shakhtar Donetsk; AC Sparta Praha; SK Slavia Praha; Fenerbahçe SK; Beşiktaş JK; FC Zürich; PFC Levski Sofia; Beitar Jerusalem FC; Rosenborg BK; FC Salzburg; FK Crvena Zvezda; Zagłębie Lubin; FC København; Debreceni VSC; NK Dinamo Zagreb; IF Elfsborg; MŠK Žilina; APOEL FC; NK Domžale; FK Sarajevo; Tampere United; Ventspils; FC Sheriff; FC Olimpi Rustavi; FBK Kaunas; FK Pobeda; FH Hafnarfjördur; FC BATE Borisov; Derry City FC*; KF Tirana; FC Pyunik; FC Levadia Tallinn; Marsaxlokk FC; The New Saints FC; Linfield FC; FK Khazar Lenkoran; F91 Dudelange; FK Astana; HB Tórshavn; FK Zeta; FC Rànger's; S.S. Murata.

* Shelbourne FC won the title but did not apply to enter the UEFA Champions League after being relegated for financial reasons. Derry City FC inherited their place in the competition as Irish runners-up.

UEFA CUP 2007–2008

PARTICIPATING CLUBS

Villarreal CF; Real Zaragoza; Getafe CF[5]; US Città di Palermo ; ACF Fiorentina ; Empoli FC ; Tottenham Hotspur FC; Everton FC ; Bolton Wanderers FC; FC Sochaux-Montbéliard[1]; Stade Rennais FC; FC Girondins de Bordeaux[3]; 1. FC Nürnberg[1]; FC Bayern München; Bayer 04 Leverkusen; SC Braga; CF Os Belenenses; FC Paços de Ferreira; AZ Alkmaar; FC Twente; SC Heerenveen; FC Groningen; Larissa FC[1]; Panathinaikos FC; Aris Thessaloniki FC; Panionios NFC; FC Lokomotiv Moskva[1]; FC Zenit St. Petersburg; AFC Rapid Bucuresti[1]; CFR Economax Cluj-Napoca; Aberdeen FC; Dunfermline Athletic FC[2]; Club Brugge KV[1]; R. Standard de Liège; FC Metalist Kharkiv; FC Dnipro Dnipropetrovsk; FK Mladá Boleslav; FK Jablonec 97[2]; Galatasaray SK; Kayseri Erciyesspor[2]; FC Basel 1893[1]; FC Sion; BSC Young Boys; PFC CSKA Sofia; PFC Lokomotiv Sofia; PFC Litex Lovech[2]; Hapoel Tel-Aviv FC[1]; Maccabi Netanya FC; Maccabi Tel-Aviv FC; Fredrikstad FK[1]; Lillestrøm SK[4]; SK Brann; Vålerenga IF; FK Austria Wien; SV Ried; SV Mattersburg; FK Partizan; FK Vojvodina; FK Bezanija; Groclin Grozisk Wielkopolski[1]; GKS Bełchatów; Odense BK[1]; FC Midtjylland; Budapest Honvéd FC[1]; MTK Budapest; HNK Hajduk Split; NK Slaven Koprivnica[2]; BK Hacken[4]; Helsingborgs IF[1]; AIK Solna; FC Vion Zlaté Moravce[1]; FC Artmedia Petržalka; Anorthosis Famagusta FC[1]; AC Omonia; FC Koper[1]; NK Gorica; NK Široki Brijeg[1]; NK Zrinjski; Myllykosken Pallo-47[4]; HJK Helsinki[1]; FC Haka; SK Liepājas Metalurgs[1]; Skonto FC; CSF Zimbru Chisinau[1]; FC Nistru Otaci; FC Ameri Tbilisi[1]; FC Dinamo Tbilisi; FK Sūduva[1]; FK Ekranas; FK Vardar[1]; FK Rabotnicki; Keflavík[1]; KR Reykjavík; FC Vaduz[1]; FC Dinamo Brest[1]; FC Dinamo Minsk; Drogheda United FC; Saint Patrick's Athletic FC[2]; KS Besa[1]; KS Teuta; FC Banants[1]; FC MIKA; JK Trans Narva; FC Flora; Hibernians FC[1]; Sliema Wanderers FC; Carmarthen Town AFC[1]; Rhyl FC; Glentoran FC; Dungannon Swifts[2]; PFC Neftchi; MKT Araz[2]; FC Etzella Ettelbrück; UN Kaerjeng 97[2]; FC Alma-Ata[1]; FK Aktobe; B36 Tórshavn[1]; EB/Streymur; FK Rudar Pljevlja[1]; FK Buducnost Podgorica; FC Santa Coloma[1]; SP Libertas[2]; 11 Teams as winners of UEFA Intertoto Cup.

[1]domestic cup winners, [2]losing domestic cup finalists, [3]domestic league cup winners, [4]national domestic title winners, [5]Fair Play winners.

EUROPEAN CHAMPIONSHIPS 2008 REVIEW

Have improved, but can and must do better. That must be the appraisal of England's performance thus far in the qualifying competition.

It began with a canter against Andorra and a win in Macedonia, but they were held in the return against the eastern Europeans and worse followed four days later with defeat in Croatia. Then came a draw in Israel, but some encouragement has come from comfortable victories in Andorra and Estonia.

With four of the last five matches at the new Wembley, surely the odds on England reaching the final stages have shortened. Yet since their three main rivals, Croatia, Israel and Russia, all with more points, are among the visitors, a draw would probably suit each and every one of them.

Worryingly, too, eastern European opposition frequently achieved a draw at the old arena and cost England in other competitions. In addition England go to Russia. Neither Estonia nor Andorra have managed a point between them in Group E.

As far as the other UK countries are concerned, Scotland in Group B with France and Italy sitting above them will have at least to beat the Italians at Hampden Park in the last crucial fixture to edge into the finals.

The Scots, now under new management with Alex McLeish taking over from Walter Smith, began by hitting the Faeroes for six, won in Lithuania and then managed to beat the French at Hampden. Defeats in the Ukraine and Italy sandwiched a win in Georgia and the latest came from completing the double over the Faeroes.

Northern Ireland, themselves with a new head man in Nigel Worthington after Lawrie Sanchez surprisingly decided club management was the better option and went to Fulham, were understandably unhappy over UEFA's decision to award Sweden a statutory 3-0 win over Denmark following the abandonment of the game in Copenhagen when a Danish supporter attacked the refereee. The 3-3 result was annulled. This gave the Swedes 18 points.

Even so, it had begun badly for Northern Ireland with a 3-0 defeat at Windsor Park against Iceland. All credit to them four days later they pulled off a deserved 3-2 victory over the Spaniards, arguably one of their finest performances.

A useful goalless draw in Denmark followed by wins over Latvia, Liechtenstein and crucially Sweden placed them handily with a game in hand. All this before UEFA stepped in of course.

The Irish have to go to Spain in their last game which again could decide whether they achieve the goal of a place in the final tournament from Group F.

Sadly Wales in Group D are trailing behind the front runners led by Germany, who look certainties to qualify and their 13-0 away win over San Marino broke the competition's previous highest score.

Wales losing away to the Czech Republic and at home to Slovakia was not the manner for potential qualifiers, expected wins over Cyprus and San Marino were offset by a reverse in Dublin against the Republic squeezed in between. The Czechs drew in Cardiff, too. Germany have to be faced twice!

However, the Republic of Ireland still have a chance of ousting the Czech Republic from second place, providing they do not lose when they visit them in the second match of the 2007–08 season. This and the Germans' trip to Croke Park which will be bursting at the seams again, are the key encounters.

Such optimism when you realise they started disastrously with an understandable defeat in Germany, but amazingly 5-2 in Cyprus, probably the worst result in the country's competitive history. Improvement came from a draw with the Czechs, two wins over San Marino, the victory over Wales mentioned earlier and another home success against Slovakia.

The heavily subscribed Group A has Poland in first place even though they have suffered two defeats. But having played two more matches than their three nearest rivals Serbia, Portugal and Finland – all on the same points – this is unlikely to be the ultimate outcome.

Moreover defeat in Erevan against Armenia has not helped the Polish situation and they have to travel to the trio previously mentioned.

In Group C the holders Greece have made a recovery from their World Cup qualifying disappointments and should make it. The next three Bosnia, Turkey and Norway each have the same points total.

However, Group G still has three unbeaten teams, Romania, Bulgaria and Holland, thanks to the number of drawn matches. Of this trio, Romania have the easier run-in and should finish second at least.

EUROPEAN CHAMPIONSHIPS 2008

▪ *Denotes player sent off.*

GROUP A

Belgium	(0) 0	Kazakhstan	(0) 0
Poland	(0) 1	Finland	(0) 3
Serbia	(0) 1	Azerbaijan	(0) 0
Armenia	(0) 0	Belgium	(1) 1
Azerbaijan	(1) 1	Kazakhstan	(1) 1
Finland	(1) 1	Portugal	(1) 1
Poland	(1) 1	Serbia	(0) 1
Armenia	(0) 0	Finland	(0) 0
Kazakhstan	(0) 0	Poland	(0) 1
Portugal	(2) 3	Azerbaijan	(0) 0
Serbia	(0) 1	Belgium	(0) 0
Belgium	(1) 3	Azerbaijan	(0) 0
Kazakhstan	(0) 0	Finland	(1) 2
Poland	(2) 2	Portugal	(0) 1
Serbia	(0) 3	Armenia	(0) 0
Belgium	(0) 0	Poland	(1) 1
Finland	(1) 1	Armenia	(0) 0
Portugal	(2) 3	Kazakhstan	(0) 0
Kazakhstan	(0) 2	Serbia	(0) 1
Poland	(3) 5	Azerbaijan	(0) 0
Portugal	(0) 4	Belgium	(0) 0
Azerbaijan	(0) 1	Finland	(0) 0
Poland	(1) 1	Armenia	(0) 0
Serbia	(1) 1	Portugal	(1) 1
Azerbaijan	(1) 1	Poland	(0) 3
Belgium	(0) 1	Portugal	(1) 2
Finland	(0) 0	Serbia	(1) 2
Kazakhstan	(0) 1	Armenia	(2) 2
Armenia	(0) 1	Poland	(0) 0
Finland	(1) 2	Belgium	(0) 0
Kazakhstan	(0) 1	Azerbaijan	(1) 1

Group A Table	*P*	*W*	*D*	*L*	*F*	*A*	*Pts*
Poland	9	6	1	2	15	7	19
Serbia	7	4	2	1	10	4	14
Portugal	7	4	2	1	15	5	14
Finland	8	4	2	2	9	5	14
Belgium	8	2	1	5	5	10	7
Armenia	7	2	1	4	3	7	7
Kazakhstan	8	1	3	4	5	11	6
Azerbaijan	8	1	2	5	4	17	5

GROUP B

Faeroes	(0) 0	Georgia	(3) 6
Georgia	(0) 0	France	(2) 3
Italy	(1) 1	Lithuania	(1) 1
Scotland	(5) 6	Faeroes	(0) 0
France	(2) 3	Italy	(1) 1
Lithuania	(0) 1	Scotland	(0) 2
Ukraine	(1) 3	Georgia	(1) 2
Faeroes	(0) 0	Lithuania	(0) 1
Italy	(0) 2	Ukraine	(0) 0
Scotland	(0) 1	France	(0) 0
France	(2) 5	Faeroes	(0) 0
Georgia	(1) 1	Italy	(1) 3

Ukraine	(0) 2	Scotland	(0) 0
Faeroes	(0) 0	Ukraine	(1) 2
Lithuania	(0) 0	France	(0) 1
Scotland	(1) 2	Georgia	(1) 1
Georgia	(2) 3	Faeroes	(0) 1
Italy	(1) 2	Scotland	(0) 0
Ukraine	(0) 1	Lithuania	(0) 0
Faeroes	(0) 1	Italy	(1) 2
France	(0) 2	Ukraine	(0) 0
Lithuania	(0) 1	Georgia	(0) 0
Faeroes	(0) 0	Scotland	(2) 2
France	(1) 1	Georgia	(0) 0
Lithuania	(0) 0	Italy	(2) 2

Celtic Park, 2 September 2006, 50,059

Scotland (5) 6 *(Fletcher 7, McFadden 10, Boyd 24 (pen), 38, Miller 30 (pen), O'Connor 85)*

Faeroes (0) 0

Scotland: Gordon; Dailly, Weir, Pressley, Naysmith, Fletcher (Teale 46), Hartley, Quashie (Severin 84), Miller (O'Connor 61), Boyd, McFadden.
Faeroes: Mikkelsen; Hansen P, Johannesen O, Danielsen, Joensen J, Benjaminsen, Johnsson (Samuelsen S 76), Borg, Fredriksberg (Thorleifson 60), Jacobsen C, Jacobsen R (Nielsen 84).
Referee: Yegorov (Russia).

Kaunas, 6 September 2006, 6500

Lithuania (0) 1 *(Miceika 85)*

Scotland (0) 2 *(Dailly 46, Miller 62)*

Lithuania: Karcemarskas; Stankevicius, Dziaukstas, Skerla, Zvirgzdauskas, Savenas (Tamosauskas 50), Kalonas, Mikoliunas (Labukas 66), Preiksaitis (Miceika 81), Poskus, Danilevicius.
Scotland: Gordon; Dailly, Weir, Caldwell G, Naysmith, Pressley, Fletcher, Quashie (Boyd 43), McFadden (Alexander G 21), Hartley (Severin 88), Miller.
Referee: Hrinek (Slovakia).

Glasgow, 7 October 2006, 57,000

Scotland (0) 1 *(Caldwell G 67)*

France (0) 0

Scotland: Gordon; Dailly, Alexander G, Pressley, Weir, Ferguson B, Fletcher, Caldwell G, McFadden (O'Connor 72), Hartley, McCulloch (Teale 58).
France: Coupet; Abidal, Thuram, Boumsong, Sagnol, Ribery (Wiltord 74), Vieira, Makelele, Malouda, Trezeguet (Saha 62), Henry.
Referee: Busacca (Switzerland).

Kiev, 11 October 2006, 55,000

Ukraine (0) 2 *(Kucher 60, Shevchenko 90 (pen))*

Scotland (0) 0

Ukraine: Shovkovskyi; Nesmachni, Sviderskyi, Kucher, Rusol, Tymoschuk, Shelayev, Gusev (Milevski 62), Kalynychenko (Vorobei 76), Shevchenko, Voronin (Shershun 90).
Scotland: Gordon; Neilson (McManus 89), Alexander G, Ferguson B, Weir, Pressley■, Fletcher, Caldwell G, Miller, Hartley, McFadden (Boyd 73).
Referee: Hansson (Sweden).

Glasgow, 24 March 2007, 50,850

Scotland (1) 2 *(Boyd 11, Beattie 89)*

Georgia (1) 1 *(Arveladze 41)*

Scotland: Gordon; Alexander G, Naysmith, Ferguson B, Weir, McManus, Teale (Brown 60), Hartley, Boyd (Beattie 76), Miller (Maloney 90), McCulloch.
Georgia: Lomaia; Shashiashvili, Khizanishvili, Sulukvadze, Eliava, Burduli (Siradze 57), Tskitishvili (Mujiri 90), Menteshashvili (Gogua 46), Kobiashvili, Demetradze, Arveladze.
Referee: Vollquartz (Denmark).

Bari, 28 March 2007, 37,500

Italy (1) 2 *(Toni 12, 70)*

Scotland (0) 0

Italy: Buffon; Oddo, Cannavaro, Materazzi, Zambrotta, Gattuso, De Rossi, Camoranesi, Perrotta (Pirlo 77), Di Natale (Del Piero 66), Toni (Quagliarella 87).
Scotland: Gordon; Alexander G, Naysmith, Weir, McManus, Ferguson B, Teale (Maloney 66), Hartley, Brown (Beattie 86), McCulloch (Boyd 81), Miller.
Referee: De Bleeckere (Belgium).

Toftir, 6 June 2007, 4100

Faeroes (0) 0

Scotland (2) 2 *(Maloney 31, O'Connor 35)*

Faeroes: Mikkelsen; Danielsen, Jacobsen J, Johannesen O (Djurhuss 36) (Samuelsen S 77), Benjaminsen, Thomassen, Borg (Flotum 82), Olsen, Jacobsen R, Jacobsen C, Holst.
Scotland: Gordon; Alexander G, Weir, McManus, Naysmith, Hartley, Ferguson B, Fletcher (Teale 68), Maloney (Adam 77), O'Connor, Boyd (Naismith 83).
Referee: Germanakos (Greece).

Group B Table	*P*	*W*	*D*	*L*	*F*	*A*	*Pts*
France	7	6	0	1	15	2	18
Italy	7	5	1	1	13	6	16
Scotland	7	5	0	2	13	6	15
Ukraine	6	4	0	2	8	6	12
Lithuania	7	2	1	4	4	7	7
Georgia	8	2	0	6	13	14	6
Faeroes	8	0	0	8	2	27	0

GROUP C

Hungary	(0) 1	Norway	(3) 4
Malta	(1) 2	Bosnia	(3) 5
Moldova	(0) 0	Greece	(0) 1
Bosnia	(0) 1	Hungary	(1) 3
Norway	(0) 2	Moldova	(0) 0
Turkey	(0) 2	Malta	(0) 0
(Played behind closed doors in Frankfurt.)			
Greece	(1) 1	Norway	(0) 0
Hungary	(0) 0	Turkey	(1) 1
Moldova	(2) 2	Bosnia	(0) 2
Bosnia	(0) 0	Greece	(1) 4
Malta	(1) 2	Hungary	(1) 1
Turkey	(3) 5	Moldova	(0) 0
(Played behind closed doors in Frankfurt.)			
Greece	(1) 1	Turkey	(1) 4
Moldova	(0) 1	Malta	(0) 1
Norway	(0) 1	Bosnia	(2) 2

Hungary	(1) 2	Moldova	(0) 0
Malta	(0) 0	Greece	(0) 1
Turkey	(0) 2	Norway	(2) 2

(Played behind closed doors in Frankfurt.)

Bosnia	(2) 3	Turkey	(2) 2
Greece	(2) 2	Hungary	(0) 0
Norway	(1) 4	Malta	(0) 0
Bosnia	(1) 1	Malta	(0) 0
Greece	(1) 2	Moldova	(0) 1
Norway	(1) 4	Hungary	(0) 0

Group C Table	*P*	*W*	*D*	*L*	*F*	*A*	*Pts*
Greece	7	6	0	1	12	5	18
Bosnia	7	4	1	2	14	14	13
Turkey	6	4	1	1	16	6	13
Norway	7	4	1	2	17	6	13
Hungary	7	2	0	5	7	14	6
Malta	7	1	1	5	5	15	4
Moldova	7	0	2	5	4	15	2

GROUP D

Czech Republic	(0) 2	Wales	(0) 1
Germany	(0) 1	Republic of Ireland	(0) 0
Slovakia	(3) 6	Cyprus	(0) 1
San Marino	(0) 0	Germany	(6) 13
Slovakia	(0) 0	Czech Republic	(2) 3
Cyprus	(2) 5	Republic of Ireland	(2) 2
Czech Republic	(4) 7	San Marino	(0) 0
Wales	(1) 1	Slovakia	(3) 5
Republic of Ireland	(0) 1	Czech Republic	(0) 0
Slovakia	(0) 1	Germany	(3) 4
Wales	(2) 3	Cyprus	(0) 1
Cyprus	(1) 1	Germany	(1) 1
Republic of Ireland	(3) 5	San Marino	(0) 0
San Marino	(0) 1	Republic of Ireland	(0) 2
Cyprus	(1) 1	Slovakia	(0) 3
Czech Republic	(0) 1	Germany	(1) 2
Republic of Ireland	(1) 1	Wales	(0) 0
Czech Republic	(1) 1	Cyprus	(0) 0
Republic of Ireland	(1) 1	Slovakia	(0) 0
Wales	(2) 3	San Marino	(0) 0
Germany	(1) 6	San Marino	(0) 0
Wales	(0) 0	Czech Republic	(0) 0
Germany	(2) 2	Slovakia	(1) 1

Teplice, 2 September 2006, 16,204

Czech Republic (0) 2 *(Lafata 76, 89)*

Wales (0) 1 *(Jiranek 85 (og))*

Czech Republic: Cech; Ujfalusi, Jiranek, Rozehnal, Jankulovski, Stajner (Sionko 46), Galasek (Kovac R 87), Rosicky, Plasil, Kulic (Lafata 75), Koller.
Wales: Jones P; Delaney (Cotterill 78), Ricketts (Earnshaw 79), Robinson, Gabbidon, Collins J, Davies S, Fletcher (Ledley 47), Bellamy, Nyatanga, Giggs.
Referee: Eriksson (Sweden).

Stuttgart, 2 September 2006, 53,198

Germany (0) 1 *(Podolski 57)*

Republic of Ireland (0) 0

Germany: Lehmann; Lahm, Friedrich A, Friedrich M, Jansen, Schneider (Borowski 83), Frings, Ballack, Schweinsteiger, Podolski (Neuville 76), Klose.
Republic of Ireland: Given; Carr, Finnan, Andy O'Brien, Dunne, O'Shea, Duff (McGeady 77), Reid S, Robbie Keane, Doyle K (Elliott 79), Kilbane (Alan O'Brien 83).
Referee: Kantalejo (Spain).

Nicosia, 7 October 2006, 12,000

Cyprus (2) 5 *(Konstantinou M 10, 50 (pen), Garpozis 16, Charalambides 60, 75)*

Republic of Ireland (2) 2 *(Ireland 8, Dunne 44)*

Cyprus: Morfis; Satsias, Lambrou, Louka, Theodotou, Michael (Charalambides 46), Garpozis (Charalambous 77), Makrides, Okkas (Yiasoumis 86), Konstantinou M, Aloneftis.
Republic of Ireland: Kenny; Finnan, O'Shea, Andy O'Brien (Lee 71), Dunne■, Kilbane, McGeady (Alan O'Brien 80), Ireland (Douglas 83), Morrison, Robbie Keane, Duff.
Referee: Batista (Portugal).

Cardiff, 7 October 2006, 28,493

Wales (1) 1 *(Bale 37)*

Slovakia (3) 5 *(Svento 14, Mintal 32, 38, Karhan 51, Vittek 59)*

Wales: Jones P; Duffy, Bale, Gabbidon, Nyatanga, Robinson, Edwards (Ledley 58), Koumas, Davies S (Cotterill 88), Bellamy, Earnshaw (Parry 46).
Slovakia: Contofalsky; Kozak, Kratochvil, Petras M, Varga, Karhan (Krajcik 67), Mintal (Hodur 71), Vittek (Holosko 77), Petras P, Svento, Durica.
Referee: Egmond (Holland).

Dublin, 11 October 2006, 35,500

Republic of Ireland (0) 1 *(Kilbane 62)*

Czech Republic (0) 0

Republic of Ireland: Henderson; Kelly, Finnan, O'Shea, McShane, Carsley, Reid A (Quinn 72), Douglas, Robbie Keane, Kilbane (Alan O'Brien 79), Duff.
Czech Republic: Cech; Polak, Ujfalusi, Kovac R, Jankulovski, Jiranek, Rosicky, Plasil (Grygera 85), Rozehnal, Koller, Baros (Jarolim 82).
Referee: Layec (France).

Cardiff, 11 October 2006, 20,456

Wales (2) 3 *(Koumas 33, Earnshaw 39, Bellamy 72)*

Cyprus (0) 1 *(Okkas 83)*

Wales: Price; Duffy (Edwards 78), Bale, Gabbidon, Nyatanga, Robinson, Morgan, Koumas (Ledley 76), Earnshaw, Bellamy (Parry 90), Davies S.
Cyprus: Morfis; Theodotou, Lambrou, Louka, Satsias (Yiasoumis 84), Michael (Charalambides 46), Garpozis (Charalambous 46), Makrides, Aloneftis, Konstantinou M, Okkas.
Referee: Granat (Poland).

Dublin, 15 November 2006, 34,018

Republic of Ireland (3) 5 *(Simoncini D 7 (og), Doyle K 24, Robbie Keane 31, 58 (pen), 85)*

San Marino (0) 0

Republic of Ireland: Given; Finnan, O'Shea, Dunne, McShane, Carsley (Douglas 50), Reid A, Doyle K (McGeady 63), Robbie Keane, Duff, Kilbane (Lee 79).
San Marino: Valentini F; Bugli, Albani, Bacciocchi, Simoncini D (Bonini 81), Vannucci (Crescentini 72), Valentini C, Andreini, Mariotti (Michele Marani 59), Manuel Marani, Selva A.
Referee: Isaksen (Faeroes).

Serravalle, 7 February 2007, 3294

San Marino (0) 1 *(Manuel Marani 86)*

Republic of Ireland (0) 2 *(Kilbane 49, Ireland 90)*

San Marino: Simoncini A; Valentini C, Manuel Marani, Albani, Simoncini D, Muccioli, Bonini (Vannucci 76), Domeniconi (Bugli 88), Michele Marani, Selva A, Gasperoni A (Andreini 66).
Republic of Ireland: Henderson; Finnan, Harte (Hunt 74), Dunne, O'Shea (McShane 46), Carsley, Duff, Ireland, Keane, Long (Stokes 80), Kilbane.
Referee: Rasmussen (Denmark).

Dublin, 24 March 2007, 72,539

Republic of Ireland (1) 1 *(Ireland 39)*

Wales (0) 0

Republic of Ireland: Given; Finnan, O'Shea, Dunne, McShane, Carsley, Douglas (Hunt 80), Ireland (Doyle K 59), Robbie Keane (McGeady 89), Kilbane, Duff.
Wales: Coyne; Ricketts, Bale (Collins D 74), Collins J, Evans S, Nyatanga, Ledley (Fletcher 46), Robinson (Easter 90), Davies S, Bellamy, Giggs.
Referee: Hauge (Norway).

Dublin, 28 March 2007, 71,297

Republic of Ireland (1) 1 *(Doyle 12)*

Slovakia (0) 0

Republic of Ireland: Given; O'Shea, Finnan, McShane, Dunne, Carsley, Ireland (Hunt 70), McGeady (Quinn A 87), Kilbane, Duff, Doyle K (Long 74).
Slovakia: Contofalsky; Singlar (Sestak 80), Skrtel, Klimpl, Gresko, Svento (Michalik 86), Zofcak, Borbely, Sapara (Holosko 72), Vittek, Jakubko.
Referee: Baskakov (Russia).

Cardiff, 28 March 2007, 18,752

Wales (2) 3 *(Giggs 3, Bale 20, Koumas 63 (pen))*

San Marino (0) 0

Wales: Coyne; Ricketts, Evans S (Nyatanga 63), Collins J, Bale, Fletcher, Koumas, Davies S, Giggs (Parry 73), Bellamy, Easter (Cotterill 46).
San Marino: Simoncini A; Valentini C (Toccaceli 85), Andreini, Albani, Muccioli, Bacciocchi, Negri (Nanni 79), Domeniconi (Bugli 67), Manuel Marani, Selva A, Gasperoni A.
Referee: Tchagharyan (Armenia).

Cardiff, 2 June 2007, 30,714

Wales (0) 0

Czech Republic (0) 0

Wales: Hennessey; Ricketts, Nyatanga, Gabbidon, Collins J, Robinson, Ledley, Koumas, Davies S, Giggs (Earnshaw 89), Bellamy.
Czech Republic: Cech; Ujfalusi, Kovac R, Rozehnal, Jankulovski, Polak (Jarolim 65), Sivok (Matejovsky 83), Rosicky, Plasil, Koller, Baros (Kulic 46).
Referee: Allaerts (Belgium).

Group D Table	*P*	*W*	*D*	*L*	*F*	*A*	*Pts*
Germany	7	6	1	0	29	4	19
Czech Republic	7	4	2	1	15	4	14
Republic of Ireland	7	4	1	2	12	8	13
Slovakia	7	3	0	4	16	13	9
Wales	6	2	1	3	8	9	7
Cyprus	6	1	1	4	9	16	4
San Marino	6	0	0	6	1	36	0

GROUP E

Estonia	(0) 0	Macedonia	(0) 1
England	(3) 5	Andorra	(0) 0
Estonia	(0) 0	Israel	(1) 1
Israel	(3) 4	Andorra	(0) 1
Macedonia	(0) 0	England	(0) 1
Russia	(0) 0	Croatia	(0) 0
Croatia	(2) 7	Andorra	(0) 0
England	(0) 0	Macedonia	(0) 0
Russia	(1) 1	Israel	(0) 1
Andorra	(0) 0	Macedonia	(3) 3
Croatia	(0) 2	England	(0) 0
Russia	(0) 2	Estonia	(0) 0
Israel	(1) 3	Croatia	(2) 4
Macedonia	(0) 0	Russia	(2) 2
Croatia	(0) 2	Macedonia	(1) 1
Estonia	(0) 0	Russia	(0) 2
Israel	(0) 0	England	(0) 0
Andorra	(0) 0	England	(0) 3
Israel	(2) 4	Estonia	(0) 0
Estonia	(0) 0	Croatia	(1) 1
Macedonia	(1) 1	Israel	(2) 2
Russia	(2) 4	Andorra	(0) 0
Andorra	(0) 0	Israel	(1) 2
Croatia	(0) 0	Russia	(0) 0
Estonia	(0) 0	England	(1) 3

Old Trafford, 2 September 2006, 56,290

England (3) 5 *(Crouch 5, 66, Gerrard 13, Defoe 38, 47)*

Andorra (0) 0

England: Robinson; Neville P (Lennon 65), Cole A, Hargreaves, Terry, Brown, Gerrard, Lampard, Crouch, Defoe (Johnson A 71), Downing (Richardson 64).
Andorra: Koldo; Lima A, Txema, Ayala, Sonejee, Javi Sanchez (Juli Sanchez 46), Sivera (Garcia 77), Vieira, Silva, Pujol (Jimenez 49), Ruiz.
Referee: Brugger (Austria).

Skopje, 6 September 2006, 16,500

Macedonia (0) 0

England (0) 1 *(Crouch 46)*

Macedonia: Nikolovski; Noveski, Petrov, Sedloski, Mitreski I, Lazarevski, Jancevski (Tasevski 52), Sumulikoski, Naumoski (Sakiri 74), Maznov (Stojkov 56), Pandev.
England: Robinson; Neville P, Cole A, Hargreaves, Terry, Ferdinand, Gerrard, Lampard (Carrick 84), Crouch (Johnson A 87), Defoe (Lennon 76), Downing.
Referee: Layec (France).

Old Trafford, 7 October 2006, 72,062

England (0) 0

Macedonia (0) 0

England: Robinson; Neville G, Cole A, Carrick, Terry, King, Gerrard, Lampard, Crouch, Rooney (Defoe 74), Downing (Wright-Phillips 70).
Macedonia: Nikolovski; Noveski, Petrov, Sedloski, Lazarevski, Mitreski I, Mitreski A, Sumulikoski, Maznov, Naumoski (Stojkov 46), Pandev (Tasevski 83).
Referee: Merk (Germany).

Zagreb, 11 October 2006, 38,000

Croatia (0) 2 *(Eduardo 61, Neville G 69 (og))*

England (0) 0

Croatia: Pletikosa; Simic, Simunic, Kovac R, Corluka, Rapaic (Olic 76), Kovac N, Modric, Kranjcar (Babic 89), Eduardo (Leko J 81), Petric.
England: Robinson; Neville G, Cole A, Ferdinand, Terry, Carragher (Wright-Phillips 73), Carrick, Lampard, Crouch (Richardson 72), Rooney, Parker (Defoe 72).
Referee: Rosetti (Italy).

Tel Aviv, 24 March 2007, 35,000

Israel (0) 0

England (0) 0

Israel: Awat; Ben Haim, Gershon, Ziv, Benado, Shpungin, Badir, Benayoun, Ben Shushan (Alberman 87), Tamuz Temile (Barda 75), Balali (Sahar 69).
England: Robinson; Neville P (Richards 72), Carragher, Gerrard, Ferdinand, Terry, Hargreaves, Lampard, Johnson A (Defoe 80), Rooney, Lennon (Downing 83).
Referee: Ovrebo (Norway).

Barcelona, 28 March 2007, 12,800

Andorra (0) 0

England (0) 3 *(Gerrard 54, 76, Nugent 90)*

Andorra: Koldo; Sonejee, Lima A, Ayala, Bernaus, Escura, Vieira, Garcia, Ruiz (Fernandez 88), Jimenez (Martinez 69), Toscano (Moreno 90).
England: Robinson; Richards (Dyer 61), Cole A, Hargreaves, Terry, Ferdinand, Lennon, Gerrard, Johnson A (Nugent 79), Rooney (Defoe 61), Downing.
Referee: Paixao (Portugal).

Tallinn, 6 June 2007, 11,000

Estonia (0) 0

England (1) 3 *(Cole J 37, Crouch 54, Owen 62)*

Estonia: Poom; Jaager, Stepanov, Kruglov, Klavan, Dmitrijev, Lindpere, Vassilijev, Konsa (Neemelo 46), Voskoboinikov, Terehhov (Kink 64).
England: Robinson; Brown, Bridge, Gerrard, Terry, King, Beckham (Dyer 68), Lampard, Crouch, Owen (Jenas 88), Cole J (Downing 75).
Referee: Gilewski (Poland).

Group E Table	*P*	*W*	*D*	*L*	*F*	*A*	*Pts*
Croatia	7	5	2	0	16	4	17
Israel	8	5	2	1	17	7	17
Russia	7	4	3	0	11	1	15
England	7	4	2	1	12	2	14
Macedonia	7	2	1	4	6	7	7
Estonia	7	0	0	7	0	14	0
Andorra	7	0	0	7	1	28	0

GROUP F

Latvia	(0) 0	Sweden	(1) 1
Northern Ireland	(0) 0	Iceland	(3) 3
Spain	(2) 4	Liechtenstein	(0) 0
Iceland	(0) 0	Denmark	(2) 2
Northern Ireland	(1) 3	Spain	(1) 2
Sweden	(1) 3	Liechtenstein	(1) 1
Denmark	(0) 0	Northern Ireland	(0) 0
Latvia	(3) 4	Iceland	(0) 0
Sweden	(1) 2	Spain	(0) 0
Iceland	(1) 1	Sweden	(1) 2
Liechtenstein	(0) 0	Denmark	(2) 4
Northern Ireland	(1) 1	Latvia	(0) 0
Liechtenstein	(0) 1	Northern Ireland	(0) 4
Spain	(2) 2	Denmark	(0) 1
Liechtenstein	(1) 1	Latvia	(0) 0
Northern Ireland	(1) 2	Sweden	(1) 1
Spain	(0) 1	Iceland	(0) 0
Denmark	(1) 3	Sweden	(3) 3

(Match abandoned 89 minutes; match awarded to Sweden 3-0.)

Iceland	(1) 1	Liechtenstein	(0) 1
Latvia	(0) 0	Spain	(1) 2
Latvia	(0) 0	Denmark	(2) 2
Liechtenstein	(0) 0	Spain	(2) 2
Sweden	(3) 5	Iceland	(0) 0

Belfast, 2 September 2006, 14,500

Northern Ireland (0) 0

Iceland (3) 3 *(Thorvaldsson 13, Hreidarsson 20, Gudjohnsen E 37)*

Northern Ireland: Maik Taylor; Baird, Capaldi (Duff 76), Davis, Hughes A, Craigan, Gillespie, Clingan, Quinn (Feeney 83), Healy, Elliott (Lafferty 63).
Iceland: Arason; Steinsson, Sigurdsson I, Ingimarsson, Hreidarsson, Gunnarsson B (Gislason 75), Arnason (Danielsson 55), Gudjonsson J, Gudjohnsen E, Sigurdsson H (Jonsson 64), Thorvaldsson.
Referee: Skjerven (Norway).

Belfast, 6 September 2006, 14,500

Northern Ireland (1) 3 *(Healy 20, 64, 80)*

Spain (1) 2 *(Xavi 14, David Villa 52)*

Northern Ireland: Carroll (Maik Taylor 12); Duff, Hughes A, Craigan, Evans, Gillespie, Clingan, Davis, Baird, Healy (Feeney 85), Lafferty (Quinn 54).
Spain: Casillas; Sergio Ramos (Michel Salgado 46), Puyol, Pablo, Antonio Lopez, Albelda (Fabregas 29), Xavi, Xabi Alonso, Fernando Torres (Luis Garcia 63), David Villa, Raul.
Referee: De Bleeckere (Belgium).

Copenhagen, 7 October 2006, 41,482

Denmark (0) 0

Northern Ireland (0) 0

Denmark: Sorensen (Christiansen 68); Jacobsen, Gravgaard, Agger, Jensen N (Bendtner 73), Jensen D, Poulsen, Kahlenberg, Tomasson, Jorgensen, Lovenkrands (Jensen C 55).
Northern Ireland: Maik Taylor; Duff, Hughes A, Craigan, Baird, Clingan (Johnson 56), Davis, Evans, Gillespie, Lafferty (Jones 63), Healy (Feeney 84).
Referee: Plautz (Austria).

Belfast, 11 October 2006, 14,500

Northern Ireland (1) 1 *(Healy 35)*

Latvia (0) 0

Northern Ireland: Maik Taylor; Baird, Evans, Craigan, Hughes A, Davis, Gillespie, Johnson, Lafferty (Quinn 88), Healy (Feeney 90), Clingan.
Latvia: Kolinko; Stepanovs, Astafjevs, Zirnis, Laizans, Kacanovs, Solonicins (Visnakovs 85), Smirnovs (Gorkss 46), Verpakovskis (Kalnins 78), Karlsons, Pahars.
Referee: Fleischer (Germany).

Vaduz, 24 March 2007, 4340

Liechtenstein (0) 1 *(Burgmeier 89)*

Northern Ireland (0) 4 *(Healy 52, 75, 83, McCann 90)*

Liechtenstein: Jehle; Oehri (Telser 68), Martin Stocklasa, Ritter, Michael Stocklasa, Buchel M, Buchel R (Frick D 88), Burgmeier, Beck T, Frick M, Rohrer (Buchel S 84).
Northern Ireland: Maik Taylor; Duff, Johnson, Evans, Hughes A, Craigan, Brunt (McCann 68), Davis, Lafferty (Feeney 56), Healy (Jones 84), Gillespie.
Referee: Oriekhov (Ukraine).

Belfast, 28 March 2007, 14,500

Northern Ireland (1) 2 *(Healy 31, 58)*

Sweden (1) 1 *(Elmander 26)*

Northern Ireland: Maik Taylor; Duff, Hughes A, Craigan, Evans, Johnson, McCann, Davis, Brunt (Sproule 90), Healy (Webb 89), Feeney (Lafferty 79).
Sweden: Isaksson; Nilsson, Mellberg (Majstorovic 69), Hansson, Edman, Alexandersson (Wilhelmsson 61), Andersson D, Anders Svensson (Kallstrom 46), Ljungberg, Ibrahimovic, Elmander.
Referee: Braamhaar (Holland).

Group F Table	*P*	*W*	*D*	*L*	*F*	*A*	*Pts*
Sweden	7	6	0	1	17	4	18
Spain	7	5	0	2	13	6	15
Northern Ireland	6	4	1	1	10	7	13
Denmark	6	3	1	2	9	5	10
Liechtenstein	7	1	1	5	4	18	4
Iceland	7	1	1	5	5	15	4
Latvia	6	1	0	5	4	7	3

GROUP G

Belarus	(2) 2	Albania	(1) 2
Luxembourg	(0) 0	Holland	(1) 1
Romania	(1) 2	Bulgaria	(0) 2
Albania	(0) 0	Romania	(0) 2
Bulgaria	(0) 3	Slovenia	(0) 0
Holland	(1) 3	Belarus	(0) 0
Bulgaria	(1) 1	Holland	(0) 1
Romania	(2) 3	Belarus	(1) 1
Slovenia	(2) 2	Luxembourg	(0) 0
Belarus	(1) 4	Slovenia	(2) 2
Holland	(2) 2	Albania	(0) 1
Luxembourg	(0) 0	Bulgaria	(1) 1
Albania	(0) 0	Slovenia	(0) 0
Holland	(0) 0	Romania	(0) 0
Luxembourg	(0) 1	Belarus	(1) 2
Bulgaria	(0) 0	Albania	(0) 0
Romania	(1) 3	Luxembourg	(0) 0
Slovenia	(0) 0	Holland	(0) 1
Albania	(1) 2	Luxembourg	(0) 0
Belarus	(0) 0	Bulgaria	(1) 2
Slovenia	(0) 1	Romania	(0) 2
Bulgaria	(2) 2	Belarus	(1) 1
Luxembourg	(0) 0	Albania	(2) 3
Romania	(1) 2	Slovenia	(0) 0

Group G Table	*P*	*W*	*D*	*L*	*F*	*A*	*Pts*
Romania	7	5	2	0	14	4	17
Bulgaria	7	4	3	0	11	4	15
Holland	6	4	2	0	8	2	14
Albania	7	2	3	2	8	6	9
Belarus	7	2	1	4	10	15	7
Slovenia	7	1	1	5	5	12	4
Luxembourg	7	0	0	7	1	14	0

EUROPEAN CHAMPIONSHIPS 2008
REMAINING FIXTURES

Top two from each group qualify for finals; Austria and Switzerland qualify as co-hosts.
Final Tournament 7 to 29 June 2008.

GROUP A

22.08.07 Armenia v Portugal; Belgium v Serbia; Finland v Kazakhstan
08.09.07 Azerbaijan v Armenia; Portugal v Poland; Serbia v Finland
12.09.07 Armenia v Azerbaijan; Finland v Poland; Kazakhstan v Belgium
21.09.07 Portugal v Serbia
13.10.07 Armenia v Serbia; Azerbaijan v Portugal; Belgium v Finland; Poland v Kazakhstan
17.10.07 Azerbaijan v Serbia; Belgium v Armenia; Kazakhstan v Poland
17.11.07 Finland v Azerbaijan; Poland v Belgium; Portugal v Armenia; Serbia v Kazakhstan
21.11.07 Armenia v Kazakhstan; Azerbaijan v Belgium; Portugal v Finland; Serbia v Poland

GROUP B

22.08.07 Faeroes v Ukraine
08.09.07 Georgia v Ukraine; Italy v France; Scotland v Lithuania
12.09.07 France v Scotland; Lithuania v Faeroes; Ukraine v Italy
13.10.07 Faeroes v France; Italy v Georgia; Scotland v Ukraine
17.10.07 France v Lithuania; Scotland v Georgia; Ukraine v Faeroes; Lithuania v Ukraine; Scotland v Italy
21.11.07 Georgia v Lithuania; Italy v Faeroes; Ukraine v France

GROUP C

08.09.07 Hungary v Bosnia; Malta v Turkey; Moldova v Norway
12.09.07 Bosnia v Moldova; Norway v Greece; Turkey v Hungary
13.10.07 Greece v Bosnia; Hungary v Malta; Moldova v Turkey
17.10.07 Bosnia v Norway; Malta v Moldova; Turkey v Greece
17.11.07 Greece v Malta; Moldova v Hungary; Norway v Turkey
21.11.07 Hungary v Greece; Malta v Norway; Turkey v Bosnia

GROUP D

22.08.07 San Marino v Cyprus
08.09.07 San Marino v Czech Republic; Slovakia v Republic of Ireland; Wales v Germany
12.09.07 Cyprus v San Marino; Czech Republic v Republic of Ireland; Slovakia v Wales
13.10.07 Cyprus v Wales; Republic of Ireland v Germany; Slovakia v San Marino
17.10.07 Germany v Czech Republic; Republic of Ireland v Cyprus; San Marino v Wales
17.11.07 Czech Republic v Slovakia; Czech Republic v Slovakia; Germany v Cyprus; Wales v Republic of Ireland
21.11.07 Cyprus v Czech Republic; Germany v Wales; San Marino v Slovakia

GROUP E
22.08.07 Estonia v Andorra
08.09.07 Croatia v Estonia; England v Israel; Russia v Macedonia
12.09.07 Andorra v Croatia; England v Russia; Macedonia v Estonia
13.10.07 England v Estonia
17.10.07 Croatia v Russia; Macedonia v Andorra; Russia v England
17.11.07 Andorra v Estonia; Israel v Russia; Macedonia v Croatia
21.11.07 Andorra v Russia; England v Croatia; Israel v Macedonia

GROUP F
22.08.07 Northern Ireland v Liechtenstein
08.09.07 Iceland v Spain; Latvia v Northern Ireland; Sweden v Denmark
12.09.07 Denmark v Liechtenstein; Iceland v Northern Ireland; Spain v Latvia
13.10.07 Denmark v Spain; Iceland v Latvia; Liechtenstein v Sweden
17.10.07 Denmark v Latvia; Liechtenstein v Iceland; Sweden v Northern Ireland
17.11.07 Latvia v Liechtenstein; Northern Ireland v Denmark; Spain v Sweden
21.11.07 Denmark v Iceland; Spain v Northern Ireland; Sweden v Latvia

GROUP G
08.09.07 Belarus v Romania; Luxembourg v Slovenia; Holland v Bulgaria
12.09.07 Albania v Holland; Bulgaria v Luxembourg; Slovenia v Belarus
13.10.07 Belarus v Luxembourg; Romania v Holland; Slovenia v Albania
17.10.07 Albania v Bulgaria; Luxembourg v Romania; Holland v Slovenia
17.11.07 Albania v Belarus; Bulgaria v Romania; Holland v Luxembourg
21.11.07 Belarus v Holland; Romania v Albania; Slovenia v Bulgaria

PAST EUROPEAN CHAMPIONSHIP FINALS

Year	*Winners*		*Runners-up*		*Venue*	*Attendance*
1960	USSR	2	Yugoslavia	1	Paris	17,966
1964	Spain	2	USSR	1	Madrid	120,000
1968	Italy	2	Yugoslavia	0	Rome	60,000
	(After 1-1 draw)					75,000
1972	West Germany	3	USSR	0	Brussels	43,437
1976	Czechoslovakia	2	West Germany	2	Belgrade	45,000
	(Czechoslovakia won on penalties)					
1980	West Germany	2	Belgium	1	Rome	47,864
1984	France	2	Spain	0	Paris	48,000
1988	Holland	2	USSR	0	Munich	72,308
1992	Denmark	2	Germany	0	Gothenburg	37,800
1996	Germany	2	Czech Republic	1	Wembley	73,611
	(Germany won on sudden death)					
2000	France	2	Italy	1	Rotterdam	50,000
	(France won on sudden death)					
2004	Greece	1	Portugal	0	Lisbon	62,865

PAST WORLD CUP FINALS

Year	**Winners**		**Runners-up**		**Venue**	**Att.**	**Referee**
1930	Uruguay	4	Argentina	2	Montevideo	90,000	Langenus (B)
1934	Italy*	2	Czechoslovakia	1	Rome	50,000	Eklind (Se)
1938	Italy	4	Hungary	2	Paris	45,000	Capdeville (F)
1950	Uruguay	2	Brazil	1	Rio de Janeiro	199,854	Reader (E)
1954	West Germany	3	Hungary	2	Berne	60,000	Ling (E)
1958	Brazil	5	Sweden	2	Stockholm	49,737	Guigue (F)
1962	Brazil	3	Czechoslovakia	1	Santiago	68,679	Latychev (USSR)
1966	England*	4	West Germany	2	Wembley	93,802	Dienst (Sw)
1970	Brazil	4	Italy	1	Mexico City	107,412	Glockner (EG)
1974	West Germany	2	Holland	1	Munich	77,833	Taylor (E)
1978	Argentina*	3	Holland	1	Buenos Aires	77,000	Gonella (I)
1982	Italy	3	West Germany	1	Madrid	90,080	Coelho (Br)
1986	Argentina	3	West Germany	2	Mexico City	114,580	Filho (Br)
1990	West Germany	1	Argentina	0	Rome	73,603	Mendez (Mex)
1994	Brazil*	0	Italy	0	Los Angeles	94,194	Puhl (H)
	(Brazil won 3-2 on penalties)						
1998	France	3	Brazil	0	St-Denis	75,000	Belqola (Mor)
2002	Brazil	2	Germany	0	Yokohama	69,029	Collina (I)
2006	Italy*	1	France	1	Berlin	69,000	Elizondo (Arg)
	(Italy won 5-3 on penalties)						

**After extra time.*

FIFA CLUB WORLD CUP 2006–2007

Formerly known as the FIFA Club World Championship, this tournament is played annually between the champion clubs from all 6 continental confederations, although since 2007 the champions of Oceania must play a qualifying play-off against the champion club of the permanent host country Japan.

QUARTER-FINALS

Auckland City (0) 0, Al Ahly (0) 2 *(Flavio 51, Aboutrika 73)*
att: 29,912 in Toyota.

Jeonbuk Motors (0) 0, Club America (0) 1 *(Rojas 79)*
att: 34,197 in Tokyo.

SEMI-FINALS

Al Ahly (0) 1 *(Flavio 54),* **Internacional (1) 2** *(Alexandre Pato 23, Luiz Adriano 72)*
att: 33,690 in Tokyo.

Club America (0) 0, Barcelona (2) 4 *(Gudjohnsen 11, Marquez 30, Ronaldinho 65, Deco 85)*
att: 62,316 in Yokohama.

MATCH FOR 5TH PLACE

Auckland City (0) 0, Jeonbuk Motors (2) 3 *(Lee 17, Kim 31, Zecarlo 73 (pen))*
att: 23,258 in Tokyo.

MATCH FOR 3RD PLACE

Al Ahly (1) 2 *(Aboutrika 42, 79),* **Club America (0) 1** *(Cabanas 59)*
att: 51,641 in Yokohama.

FIFA CLUB WORLD CUP FINAL 2006

in Yokohama (attendance 67,128)

Internacional (0) 1 *(Adriano 82)*

Barcelona (0) 0

Internacional: Clemer; Ceara, Indio, Fabiano Eller, Wellington Monteiro, Alex (Vargas 46), Edinho, Fernandao (Adriano 76), Iarley, Alexandre Pato (Luiz Adriano 61), Rubens Cardoso.

Barcelona: Valdes; Motta (Xavi 59), Marquez, Puyol, Gudjohnsen (Ezquerro 88), Giuly, Ronaldinho, Zambrotta (Belletti 46), Van Bronckhorst, Deco, Iniesta.

Previous Matches

2000 Corinthians beat Vaso de Gama 4-3 on penalties after 0-0 draw
2005 Sao Paulo béat Liverpool 1-0
2006 Internacional beat Barcelona 1-0

WORLD CLUB CHAMPIONSHIP

Played annually up to 1974 and intermittently since then between the winners of the European Cup and the winners of the South American Champions Cup — known as the Copa Libertadores. In 1980 the winners were decided by one match arranged in Tokyo in February 1981 which remained the venue until 2004, after which the match was superseded by the FIFA World Club Championship. AC Milan replaced Marseille who had been stripped of their European Cup title in 1993.

1960 Real Madrid beat Penarol 0-0, 5-1
1961 Penarol beat Benfica 0-1, 5-0, 2-1
1962 Santos beat Benfica 3-2, 5-2
1963 Santos beat AC Milan 2-4, 4-2, 1-0
1964 Inter-Milan beat Independiente 0-1, 2-0, 1-0
1965 Inter-Milan beat Independiente 3-0, 0-0
1966 Penarol beat Real Madrid 2-0, 2-0
1967 Racing Club beat Celtic 0-1, 2-1, 1-0
1968 Estudiantes beat Manchester United 1-0, 1-1
1969 AC Milan beat Estudiantes 3-0, 1-2
1970 Feyenoord beat Estudiantes 2-2, 1-0
1971 Nacional beat Panathinaikos* 1-1, 2-1
1972 Ajax beat Independiente 1-1, 3-0
1973 Independiente beat Juventus* 1-0
1974 Atlético Madrid* beat Independiente 0-1, 2-0
1975 Independiente and Bayern Munich could not agree dates; no matches.
1976 Bayern Munich beat Cruzeiro 2-0, 0-0
1977 Boca Juniors beat Borussia Moenchengladbach* 2-2, 3-0
1978 Not contested
1979 Olimpia beat Malmö* 1-0, 2-1
1980 Nacional beat Nottingham Forest 1-0
1981 Flamengo beat Liverpool 3-0
1982 Penarol beat Aston Villa 2-0
1983 Gremio Porto Alegre beat SV Hamburg 2-1
1984 Independiente beat Liverpool 1-0
1985 Juventus beat Argentinos Juniors 4-2 on penalties after a 2-2 draw
1986 River Plate beat Steaua Bucharest 1-0
1987 FC Porto beat Penarol 2-1 after extra time
1988 Nacional (Uru) beat PSV Eindhoven 7-6 on penalties after 1-1 draw
1989 AC Milan beat Atletico Nacional (Col) 1-0 after extra time
1990 AC Milan beat Olimpia 3-0
1991 Red Star Belgrade beat Colo Colo 3-0
1992 Sao Paulo beat Barcelona 2-1
1993 Sao Paulo beat AC Milan 3-2
1994 Velez Sarsfield beat AC Milan 2-0
1995 Ajax beat Gremio Porto Alegre 4-3 on penalties after 0-0 draw
1996 Juventus beat River Plate 1-0
1997 Borussia Dortmund beat Cruzeiro 2-0
1998 Real Madrid beat Vasco da Gama 2-1
1999 Manchester U beat Palmeiras 1-0
2000 Boca Juniors beat Real Madrid 2-1
2001 Bayern Munich beat Boca Juniors 1-0 after extra time
2002 Real Madrid beat Olimpia 2-0
2003 Boca Juniors beat AC Milan 3-1 on penalties after 1-1 draw
2004 Porto beat Once Caldas 8-7 on penalties afer 0-0 draw

**European Cup runners-up; winners declined to take part.*

EUROPEAN SUPER CUP

Played annually between the winners of the European Champions' Cup and the European Cup-Winners' Cup (UEFA Cup from 2000). AC Milan replaced Marseille in 1993–94.

EUROPEAN SUPER CUP 2006–07

25 August 2006, Monaco (attendance 18,500)

Barcelona (0) 0

Sevilla (2) 3 *(Renato 7, Kanoute 45, Maresca 90 (pen))*

Barcelona: Valdes; Belletti, Motta (Gudjohnsen 57), Marquez, Puyol, Xavi (Iniesta 57), Eto'o, Ronaldinho, Sylvinho (Giuly 72), Messi, Deco.

Sevilla: Palop; Javi Navarro, Castedo, Daniel Alves, Adriano (Puerta 81), Poulsen, Luis Fabiano (Marti 46), Renato, Kanoute, Escude, Jesus Navas (Maresca 75).

Referee: S. Farina (Italy).

Previous Matches

1972 Ajax beat Rangers 3-1, 3-2
1973 Ajax beat AC Milan 0-1, 6-0
1974 Not contested
1975 Dynamo Kiev beat Bayern Munich 1-0, 2-0
1976 Anderlecht beat Bayern Munich 4-1, 1-2
1977 Liverpool beat Hamburg 1-1, 6-0
1978 Anderlecht beat Liverpool 3-1, 1-2
1979 Nottingham F beat Barcelona 1-0, 1-1
1980 Valencia beat Nottingham F 1-0, 1-2
1981 Not contested
1982 Aston Villa beat Barcelona 0-1, 3-0
1983 Aberdeen beat Hamburg 0-0, 2-0
1984 Juventus beat Liverpool 2-0
1985 Juventus v Everton not contested due to UEFA ban on English clubs
1986 Steaua Bucharest beat Dynamo Kiev 1-0
1987 FC Porto beat Ajax 1-0, 1-0
1988 KV Mechelen beat PSV Eindhoven 3-0, 0-1
1989 AC Milan beat Barcelona 1-1, 1-0
1990 AC Milan beat Sampdoria 1-1, 2-0
1991 Manchester U beat Red Star Belgrade 1-0
1992 Barcelona beat Werder Bremen 1-1, 2-1
1993 Parma beat AC Milan 0-1, 2-0
1994 AC Milan beat Arsenal 0-0, 2-0
1995 Ajax beat Zaragoza 1-1, 4-0
1996 Juventus beat Paris St Germain 6-1, 3-1
1997 Barcelona beat Borussia Dortmund 2-0, 1-1
1998 Chelsea beat Real Madrid 1-0
1999 Lazio beat Manchester U 1-0
2000 Galatasaray beat Real Madrid 2-1
(aet; Galatasaray won on sudden death.)
2001 Liverpool beat Bayern Munich 3-2
2002 Real Madrid beat Feyenoord 3-1
2003 AC Milan beat Porto 1-0
2004 Valencia beat Porto 2-1
2005 Liverpool beat CSKA Moscow 3-1
2006 Sevilla beat Barcelona 3-0

OTHER BRITISH AND IRISH INTERNATIONAL MATCHES 2006–2007

Old Trafford, 16 August 2006, 45,864

England (4) 4 *(Terry 14, Lampard 30, Crouch 35, 42)*

Greece (0) 0

England: Robinson (Kirkland 46); Neville G (Carragher 78), Cole A (Bridge 80), Hargreaves, Terry, Ferdinand, Gerrard (Bent D 78), Lampard, Crouch, Defoe (Richardson 69), Downing (Lennon 69).
Greece: Nikopolidis; Fyssas (Lagos 29), Dellas (Anatolakis 64), Katsouranis, Antzas (Kyrgiakos 46), Vyntra, Zagorakis (Basinas 46), Karagounis, Giannakopoulos (Salpigidis 46), Samaras (Amanatidis 46), Charisteas.
Referee: Stark (Germany).

Amsterdam, 15 November 2006, 44,000

Holland (0) 1 *(Van der Vaart 86)*

England (1) 1 *(Rooney 37)*

Holland: Timmer (Stekelenburg 46); Boulahrouz (Jaliens 61), Emanuelson, Landzaat, Mathijsen, Ooijer (Vennegoor of Hesselink 83), Schaars, Seedorf, Van der Vaart, Kuyt (Huntelaar 61), Robben.
England: Robinson; Richards, Cole A, Carrick, Ferdinand, Terry, Gerrard, Lampard, Johnson A (Wright-Phillips 73), Rooney, Cole J (Richardson 77).
Referee: Michel (Slovakia).

Old Trafford, 7 February 2007, 58,247

England (0) 0

Spain (0) 1 *(Iniesta 63)*

England: Foster; Neville G (Richards 64), Neville P (Downing 74), Carrick, Ferdinand, Woodgate (Carragher 64), Wright-Phillips (Defoe 70), Lampard (Barton 78), Crouch, Dyer, Gerrard (Barry 46).
Spain: Casillas; Sergio Ramos (Angel 46), Capdevila, Xavi, Puyol (Javi Navarro 46), Pablo, Angulo (Iniesta 56), Silva (Arizmendi 65), Albelda, David Villa (Fabregas 74), Morientes (Torres 46).
Referee: Weiner (Germany).

Wembley, 1 June 2007, 88,745

England (0) 1 *(Terry 68)*

Brazil (0) 1 *(Diego 90)*

England: Robinson; Carragher, Shorey, Gerrard, Terry (Brown 72), King, Beckham (Jenas 77), Lampard (Carrick 88), Smith (Dyer 62), Owen (Crouch 83), Cole J (Downing 62).
Brazil: Helton; Daniel (Maicon 65), Gilberto, Silva, Naldo, Juan, Ronaldinho, Mineiro (Edmilson 63), Robinho (Diego 74), Kaka (Alves 71), Vagner Love.
Referee: Merk (Germany).

Dublin, 16 August 2006, 42,400

Republic of Ireland (0) 0

Holland (2) 4 *(Huntelaar 25, 53, Robben 41, Van Persie 70)*

Republic of Ireland: Kenny; Carr (Alan O'Brien 46), Finnan (Kelly 63), Andy O'Brien, Kavanagh (Douglas 46), O'Shea, McGeady, Reid S (Miller 46), Morrison (Doyle K 46), Elliott, Kilbane.
Holland: Van der Sar; Heitinga, Mathijsen, Ooijer (Jaliens 77), De Cler (Emanuelson 60), Landzaat (De Jong 46), Schaars (Janssen 63), Van der Vaart, Van Persie, Huntelaar, Robben (Kuyt 46).
Referee: Ovrebo (Norway).

New Jersey, 23 May 2007, 20,823

Ecuador (1) 1 *(Benitez 13)*

Republic of Ireland (1) 1 *(Doyle K 44)*

Ecuador: Elizaga; Montano, Castro, Campos, Bagui, Caicedo, Urrutia, Quiroz (Salas 66) (Palacios 77), Ayovi, Kaviedes, Benitez.
Republic of Ireland: Doyle C; Kelly, O'Halloran (O'Cearuill 73), Potter, Bennett, Bruce, Murphy D (Lapira 85), Hunt (Stokes 69), Keogh (Gamble 69), Doyle K (Long 60), Kilbane (Gleeson 79).
Referee: Marrufo (USA).

Boston, 26 May 2007

Bolivia (1) 1 *(Hoyos 14)*

Republic of Ireland (1) 1 *(Long 12)*

Bolivia: Suarez; Hoyos, Mendez, Pena, Alvarez, Garcia (Lima 61), Moijca, Reyes, Vaca (Galindo 74), Moreno (Cabrera 46), Arce (Pinedo 69).
Republic of Ireland: Colgan (Henderson 46); O'Cearuill, Kelly, Gamble (Murphy D 46), Bennett, Murphy P (O'Halloran 46), Andy O'Brien (Gleeson 77), Potter, Stokes, Long (Doyle K 54), Kilbane (Hunt 66).
Referee: Vaugh (USA).

Helsinki, 16 August 2006, 12,500

Finland (0) 1 *(Vayrynen 74)*

Northern Ireland (1) 2 *(Healy 34, Lafferty 64)*

Finland: Jaaskelainen; Kallio, Hyypia (Pasoja 81), Tihinen, Pasanen, Kolkka (Lagerblom 74), Ilola (Wiss 46), Nurmela (Johansson 74), Riihilahti (Vayrynen 46), Eremenko Jr, Forssell (Kuqi 57).
Northern Ireland: Maik Taylor (Carroll 46); Baird, Capaldi, Hughes A (Duff 67), Craigan, Clingan, Gillespie (Jones 46), McCann, Healy (Feeney 46), Quinn (Lafferty 52), Elliott (Sproule 65).
Referee: Svendsen (Denmark).

Swansea, 15 August 2006, 8200

Wales (0) 0

Bulgaria (0) 0

Wales: Jones P; Delaney (Duffy 60), Ricketts (Vaughan 69), Gabbidon (Edwards 74), Collins J, Robinson, Bellamy (Parry 72), Earnshaw, Fletcher (Ledley 53), Davies S, Giggs (Nyatanga 53).
Bulgaria: Petkov G (Ivankov 46); Kishishev (Todorov Y 73), Kirilov, Tomasic, Wagner, Angelov S (Illiev 81), Berbatov, Peev (Georgiev 55), Lankovic (Todorov S 64), Petrov M (Lazarov 55), Petrov S.
Referee: Attard (Malta).

White Hart Lane, 5 September 2006, 22,008

Wales (0) 0

Brazil (0) 2 *(Marcelo 61, Vagner Love 74)*

Wales: Jones P; Duffy (Edwards 64), Bale (Ledley 46), Gabbidon, Collins J, Nyatanga, Bellamy, Earnshaw (Cotterill 77), Robinson (Fletcher 53), Davies S (Vaughan 68), Giggs (Ricketts 46).
Brazil: Gomes; Maicon (Cicinho 59), Luisao, Alex, Edmilson (Silva 46), Marcelo (Gilberto 74), Cearense, Kaka (Elano 72), Vagner Love, Ronaldinho (Robinho 67), Julio Baptista (Rafael Sobis 78).
Referee: Riley (West Yorkshire).

Wrexham, 14 November 2006, 8752

Wales (2) 4 *(Koumas 9, 15, Bellamy 78, Llewellyn 90)*

Liechtenstein (0) 0

Wales: Brown; Duffy (Fletcher 46), Ricketts, Nyatanga, Evans S, Robinson (Crofts 80), Bellamy, Earnshaw (Llewellyn 59), Koumas (Craig Davies 87), Davies S (Mark Jones 69), Giggs (Ledley 56).
Liechtenstein: Jehle; Telser, Hasler, Ritter, Ritzberger (Frick D 59), Martin Stocklasa, Buchel M, Burgmeier, Beck T (Kieber 88), Frick M (Buchel R 83), D'Elia (Rohrer 59).
Referee: Wilmes (Luxembourg).

Belfast, 6 February 2007, 14,000

Northern Ireland (0) 0

Wales (0) 0

Northern Ireland: Maik Taylor (Ingham 46); Duff, Capaldi, Hughes A, Craigan (Webb 78), Clingan (McCann 61), Gillespie, Davis, Sproule (Thompson 68), Lafferty (Shiels 68), Brunt.
Wales: Coyne; Duffy (Cotterill 46) (Easter 70), Evans S, Collins D, Nyatanga, Davies S, Koumas, Robinson, Parry (Crofts 83), Vaughan (Ricketts 46), Bellamy.
Referee: C. Richmond (Scotland).

26 May 2007, 7819

Wales (2) 2 *(Bellamy 18, 38)*

New Zealand (2) 2 *(Smeltz 2, 24)*

Wales: Coyne (Hennessey 46); Gunter (Evans S 46), Collins J, Gabbidon, Ricketts, Davies S (Crofts 76), Fletcher (Ledley 46), Robinson, Giggs (Llewellyn 76), Bellamy, Earnshaw (Nardiello 64).
New Zealand: Paston; Pritchett, Boyens, Sigmund, Lochhead, Christie (Barron 58), Brown, Oughton, Bertos (Campbell 60), James, Smeltz.
Referee: Skjerven (Norway).

Vienna, 30 May 2007, 13,200

Austria (0) 0

Scotland (0) 1 *(O'Connor 59)*

Austria: Payer; Standfest, Hiden, Patocka (Prodl 89), Fuchs (Katzer 74), Ivanschitz, Aufhauser (Sariyar 74), Saumel, Leitgeb, Linz, Haas (Kuljic 60).
Scotland: McGregor (Gordon 46); Alexander G (Hutton 71), Weir (Hartley 46), Caldwell G, Naysmith, Maloney (Adam 67), Fletcher, Ferguson B, McCulloch (Dailly 46), O'Connor (McManus 87), Boyd.
Referee: Szabo (Hungary).

ENGLAND UNDER-21 TEAMS 2006–2007

▪*Denotes player sent off.*

Ipswich, 15 August 2006, 13,556

England (1) 2 *(Walcott 3, Nugent 76)*

Moldova (0) 2 *(Alexeev 75, Zislis 86)*

England: Carson; Richards, Baines, Taylor S, Ferdinand, Huddlestone, Reo-Coker, Routledge, Walcott (Jerome 67), Nugent, Bentley (Ambrose 78).

Lucerne, 6 September 2006, 8500

Switzerland (1) 2 *(Vonlanthen 29 (pen), Barnetta 70)*

England (2) 3 *(Walcott 13, Nugent 18, Milner 88)*

England: Carson; Hoyte, Baines, Taylor S, Ferdinand, Huddlestone, Reo-Coker, Bentley (Milner 46), Walcott, Nugent (Jerome 69), Routledge (Young 78).

Coventry, 6 October 2006, 30,919

England (0) 1 *(Baines 77)*

Germany (0) 0

England: Carson; Richards, Baines, Taylor S, Ferdinand, Huddlestone, Reo-Coker, Milner, Walcott (Young 66), Nugent (Watson 81), Routledge (Agbonlahor 71).

Leverkusen, 10 October 2006, 20,800

Germany (0) 0 *Brzenska*▪

England (0) 2 *(Walcott 84, 90)*

England: Carson; Richards, Baines, Taylor S▪, Ferdinand, Huddlestone, Reo-Coker, Milner, Agbonlahor (Walcott 76), Nugent (Hoyte 66), Young (Jerome 90).

Alkmaar, 14 November 2006, 15,000

Holland (0) 0

England (1) 1 *(Hoyte 12)*

England: Carson; Hoyte, Baines (Rosenior 46), Davies, Kilgallon, Huddlestone, Routledge (Welsh 78), Milner (Whittingham 65), Nugent (Onuoha 85), Young, Walcott (Jerome 83).

Derby, 6 February 2007, 28,295

England (0) 2 *(Nugent 50, Lita 79)*

Spain (2) 2 *(Soldado 34, Jurado 45)*

England: Carson (Hart 82); Hoyte, Andrew D Taylor (Rosenior 62), Huddlestone (Richardson 52), Davies, Taylor S, Bentley, Reo-Coker, Young (Walcott 46), Nugent, Milner (Lita 62).

Wembley, 24 March 2007, 55,700

England (1) 3 *(Bentley 30, Routledge 52, Derbyshire 58)*

Italy (1) 3 *(Pazzini 1, 53, 68)*

England: Camp; Rosenior (Hoyte 57), Baines, Reo-Coker, Ferdinand, Cahill, Bentley (Young 87), Lita, Richardson (Huddlestone 79), Agbonlahor (Derbyshire 46), Routledge (Milner 57).

Norwich, 5 June 2007, 20,193

England (1) 5 *(Richardson 35 (pen), Reo-Coker 61, Taylor S 77, Huddlestone 82, Lita 84)*

Slovakia (0) 0

England: Hart; Onuoha (Baines 46), Hoyte (Rosenior 71), Huddlestone, Taylor S, Cahill, Reo-Coker (Lita 62), Milner (Routledge 46), Nugent (Derbyshire 71), Young (Whittingham 78), Richardson (Noble 46).

Arnhem, 11 June 2007

Czech Republic (0) 0

England (0) 0

England: Carson; Hoyte, Baines, Cahill, Reo-Coker, Richardson (Routledge 57), Nugent, Young, Milner (Lita 64), Huddlestone (Noble 82), Onuoha.

Arnhem, 14 June 2007, 17,103

Italy (1) 2 *(Chiellini 35, Aquilani 69)*

England (2) 2 *(Nugent 24, Lita 26)*

England: Carson; Hoyte, Baines, Taylor S, Reo-Coker (Richardson 90), Nugent (Whittingham 69), Young, Milner, Lita (Vaughan 84), Noble, Onuoha.

Nijmegen, 17 June 2007

Serbia (0) 0

England (1) 2 *(Lita 5, Derbyshire 77)*

England: Carson; Hoyte, Baines, Taylor S, Reo-Coker (Huddlestone■ 88), Richardson (Routledge 80), Nugent, Milner, Lita (Derbyshire 70), Noble, Onuoha.

Heerenveen, 20 June 2007, 23,467

Holland (0) 1 *(Rigters 89)*

England (1) 1 *(Lita 39)*

England: Carson; Hoyte, Baines (Rosenior 46), Taylor S, Reo-Coker, Nugent (Derbyshire 78), Young, Milner, Lita (Ferdinand 87), Noble, Onuoha.

aet; Holland won 13-12 on penalties:- Young scored; Babel scored; Milner scored; Drenthe hit post; Noble scored; Janssen scored; Hoyte saved; Beerens scored; Derbyshire scored; Maduro scored; Ferdinand scored; De Ridder scored; Carson scored; Zuiverloon scored; Rosenior scored; Rigters scored; Reo-Coker saved; Kruiswijk missed; Taylor scored; Waterman scored; Young scored; Beerens scored; Milner scored; Drenthe scored; Noble scored; Maduro scored; Hoyte scored; Janssen scored; Derbyshire saved; De Ridder saved; Ferdinand hit bar; Zuiverloon scored.

ENGLAND B INTERNATIONAL

England (2) 3 *(Smith 34, Downing 37, 58)*

Albania (1) 1 (Berisha 44)

England: Carson; Neville P (Jagielka 46), Shorey (Lescott 73), Jenas, Dawson, King, Bentley (Defoe 72), Lennon (Downing 10), Smith (Dyer 64), Owen, Barry (Taylor S 64).
Albania: Beqaj (Hidi 78); Vangeli, Dede, Rrustemi, Haxhi (Ahmataj 79), Bulku, Skela (Hyka 75), Duro (Vrapi 65), Berisha, Muka (Murati 46), Bushi (Sinani 72).

POST-WAR INTERNATIONAL APPEARANCES

As at July 2007 *(Season of first cap given)*

ENGLAND

A'Court, A. (5) 1957/8 Liverpool
Adams, T. A. (66) 1986/7 Arsenal
Allen, C. (5) 1983/4 QPR, Tottenham H
Allen, R. (5) 1951/2 WBA
Allen, T. (3) 1959/60 Stoke C
Anderson, S. (2) 1961/2 Sunderland
Anderson, V. (30) 1978/9 Nottingham F, Arsenal, Manchester U
Anderton, D. R. (30) 1993/4 Tottenham H
Angus, J. (1) 1960/1 Burnley
Armfield, J. (43) 1958/9 Blackpool
Armstrong, D. (3) 1979/80 Middlesbrough, Southampton
Armstrong, K. (1) 1954/5 Chelsea
Astall, G. (2) 1955/6 Birmingham C
Astle, J. (5) 1968/9 WBA
Aston, J. (17) 1948/9 Manchester U
Atyeo, J. (6) 1955/6 Bristol C

Bailey, G. R. (2) 1984/5 Manchester U
Bailey, M. (2) 1963/4 Charlton
Baily, E. (9) 1949/50 Tottenham H
Baker, J. (8) 1959/60 Hibernian, Arsenal
Ball, A. (72) 1964/5 Blackpool, Everton, Arsenal
Ball, M. J. (1) 2000/01 Everton
Banks, G. (73) 1962/3 Leicester C, Stoke C
Banks, T. (6) 1957/8 Bolton W
Bardsley, D. (2) 1992/3 QPR
Barham, M. (2) 1982/3 Norwich C
Barlow, R. (1) 1954/5 WBA
Barmby, N. J. (23) 1994/5 Tottenham H, Middlesbrough, Everton, Liverpool
Barnes, J. (79) 1982/3 Watford, Liverpool
Barnes, P. (22) 1977/8 Manchester C, WBA, Leeds U
Barrass, M. (3) 1951/2 Bolton W
Barrett, E. D. (3) 1990/1 Oldham Ath, Aston Villa
Barry, G. (9) 1999/00 Aston Villa
Barton, J. (1) 2006/07 Manchester C
Barton, W. D. (3) 1994/5 Wimbledon, Newcastle U
Batty, D. (42) 1990/1 Leeds U, Blackburn R, Newcastle U, Leeds U
Baynham, R. (3) 1955/6 Luton T
Beardsley, P. A. (59) 1985/6 Newcastle U, Liverpool, Newcastle U
Beasant, D. J. (2) 1989/90 Chelsea
Beattie, J. S. (5) 2002/03 Southampton
Beattie, T. K. (9) 1974/5 Ipswich T
Beckham, D. R. J. (96) 1996/7 Manchester U, Real Madrid
Bell, C. (48) 1967/8 Manchester C
Bent, D. A. (2) 2005/06 Charlton Ath
Bentley, R. (12) 1948/9 Chelsea
Berry, J. (4) 1952/3 Manchester U
Birtles, G. (3) 1979/80 Nottingham F
Blissett, L. (14) 1982/3 Watford, AC Milan
Blockley, J. (1) 1972/3 Arsenal
Blunstone, F. (5) 1954/5 Chelsea
Bonetti, P. (7) 1965/6 Chelsea
Bould, S. A. (2) 1993/4 Arsenal
Bowles, S. (5) 1973/4 QPR
Bowyer, L. D. (1) 2002/03 Leeds U
Boyer, P. (1) 1975/6 Norwich C
Brabrook, P. (3) 1957/8 Chelsea
Bracewell, P. W. (3) 1984/5 Everton
Bradford, G. (1) 1955/6 Bristol R
Bradley, W. (3) 1958/9 Manchester U
Bridge, W. M. (25) 2001/02 Southampton, Chelsea
Bridges, B. (4) 1964/5 Chelsea
Broadbent, P. (7) 1957/8 Wolverhampton W
Broadis, I. (14) 1951/2 Manchester C, Newcastle U
Brooking, T. (47) 1973/4 West Ham U
Brooks, J. (3) 1956/7 Tottenham H
Brown, A. (1) 1970/1 WBA
Brown, K. (1) 1959/60 West Ham U
Brown, W. M. (12) 1998/9 Manchester U
Bull, S. G. (13) 1988/9 Wolverhampton W
Butcher, T. (77) 1979/80 Ipswich T, Rangers
Butt, N. (39) 1996/7 Manchester U, Newcastle U
Byrne, G. (2) 1962/3 Liverpool
Byrne, J. (11) 1961/2 Crystal P, West Ham U
Byrne, R. (33) 1953/4 Manchester U

Callaghan, I. (4) 1965/6 Liverpool
Campbell, S. (69) 1995/6 Tottenham H, Arsenal

Carragher, J. L. (34) 1998/9 Liverpool
Carrick, M. (13) 2000/01 West Ham U, Tottenham H, Manchester U
Carter, H. (7) 1946/7 Derby Co
Chamberlain, M. (8) 1982/3 Stoke C
Channon, M. (46) 1972/3 Southampton, Manchester C
Charles, G. A. (2) 1990/1 Nottingham F
Charlton, J. (35) 1964/5 Leeds U
Charlton, R. (106) 1957/8 Manchester U
Charnley, R. (1) 1962/3 Blackpool
Cherry, T. (27) 1975/6 Leeds U
Chilton, A. (2) 1950/1 Manchester U
Chivers, M. (24) 1970/1 Tottenham H
Clamp, E. (4) 1957/8 Wolverhampton W
Clapton, D. (1) 1958/9 Arsenal
Clarke, A. (19) 1969/70 Leeds U
Clarke, H. (1) 1953/4 Tottenham H
Clayton, R. (35) 1955/6 Blackburn R
Clemence, R (61) 1972/3 Liverpool, Tottenham H
Clement, D. (5) 1975/6 QPR
Clough, B. (2) 1959/60 Middlesbrough
Clough, N. H. (14) 1988/9 Nottingham F
Coates, R. (4) 1969/70 Burnley, Tottenham H
Cockburn, H. (13) 1946/7 Manchester U
Cohen, G. (37) 1963/4 Fulham
Cole, Andy (15) 1994/5 Manchester U
Cole, Ashley (58) 2000/01 Arsenal, Chelsea
Cole, J. J. (40) 2000/01 West Ham U, Chelsea
Collymore, S. V. (3) 1994/5 Nottingham F, Aston Villa
Compton, L. (2) 1950/1 Arsenal
Connelly, J. (20) 1959/60 Burnley, Manchester U
Cooper, C. T. (2) 1994/5 Nottingham F
Cooper, T. (20) 1968/9 Leeds U
Coppell, S. (42) 1977/8 Manchester U
Corrigan, J. (9) 1975/6 Manchester C
Cottee, A. R. (7) 1986/7 West Ham U, Everton
Cowans, G. (10) 1982/3 Aston Villa, Bari, Aston Villa
Crawford, R. (2) 1961/2 Ipswich T
Crouch, P. J. (19) 2004/05 Southampton, Liverpool
Crowe, C. (1) 1962/3 Wolverhampton W
Cunningham, L. (6) 1978/9 WBA, Real Madrid
Curle, K. (3) 1991/2 Manchester C
Currie, A. (17) 1971/2 Sheffield U, Leeds U

Daley, A. M. (7) 1991/2 Aston Villa
Davenport, P. (1) 1984/5 Nottingham F
Deane, B. C. (3) 1990/1 Sheffield U
Deeley, N. (2) 1958/9 Wolverhampton W
Defoe, J. C. (24) 2003/04 Tottenham H
Devonshire, A. (8) 1979/80 West Ham U
Dickinson, J. (48) 1948/9 Portsmouth
Ditchburn, E. (6) 1948/9 Tottenham H
Dixon, K. M. (8) 1984/5 Chelsea
Dixon, L. M. (22) 1989/90 Arsenal
Dobson, M. (5) 1973/4 Burnley, Everton
Dorigo, A. R. (15) 1989/90 Chelsea, Leeds U
Douglas, B. (36) 1957/8 Blackburn R
Downing, S. (14) 2004/05 Middlesbrough
Doyle, M. (5) 1975/6 Manchester C
Dublin, D. (4) 1997/8 Coventry C, Aston Villa
Dunn, D. J. I. (1) 2002/03 Blackburn R
Duxbury, M. (10) 1983/4 Manchester U
Dyer, K. C. (32) 1999/00 Newcastle U

Eastham, G. (19) 1962/3 Arsenal
Eckersley, W. (17) 1949/50 Blackburn R
Edwards, D. (18) 1954/5 Manchester U
Ehiogu, U. (4) 1995/6 Aston Villa, Middlesbrough
Ellerington, W. (2) 1948/9 Southampton
Elliott, W. H. (5) 1951/2 Burnley

Fantham, J. (1) 1961/2 Sheffield W
Fashanu, J. (2) 1988/9 Wimbledon
Fenwick, T. (20) 1983/4 QPR, Tottenham H
Ferdinand, L. (17) 1992/3 QPR, Newcastle U, Tottenham H
Ferdinand, R. G. (59) 1997/8 West Ham U, Leeds U, Manchester U
Finney, T. (76) 1946/7 Preston NE
Flowers, R. (49) 1954/5 Wolverhampton W
Flowers, T. (11) 1992/3 Southampton, Blackburn R
Foster, B. (1) 2006/07 Manchester U
Foster, S. (3) 1981/2 Brighton
Foulkes, W. (1) 1954/5 Manchester U

Fowler, R. B. (26) 1995/6 Liverpool, Leeds U
Francis, G. (12) 1974/5 QPR
Francis, T. (52) 1976/7 Birmingham C, Nottingham F, Manchester C, Sampdoria
Franklin, N. (27) 1946/7 Stoke C
Froggatt, J. (13) 1949/50 Portsmouth
Froggatt, R. (4) 1952/3 Sheffield W

Gardner, A. (1) 2003/04 Tottenham H
Garrett, T. (3) 1951/2 Blackpool
Gascoigne, P. J. (57) 1988/9 Tottenham H, Lazio, Rangers, Middlesbrough
Gates, E. (2) 1980/1 Ipswich T
George, F. C. (1) 1976/7 Derby Co
Gerrard, S. G. (57) 1999/00 Liverpool
Gidman, J. (1) 1976/7 Aston Villa
Gillard, I. (3) 1974/5 QPR
Goddard, P. (1) 1981/2 West Ham U
Grainger, C. (7) 1955/6 Sheffield U, Sunderland
Gray, A. A. (1) 1991/2 Crystal P
Gray, M. (3) 1998/9 Sunderland
Greaves, J. (57) 1958/9 Chelsea, Tottenham H
Green, R. P. (1) 2004/05 Norwich C
Greenhoff, B. (18) 1975/6 Manchester U, Leeds U
Gregory, J. (6) 1982/3 QPR
Guppy, S. (1) 1999/00 Leicester C

Hagan, J. (1) 1948/9 Sheffield U
Haines, J. (1) 1948/9 WBA
Hall, J. (17) 1955/6 Birmingham C
Hancocks, J. (3) 1948/9 Wolverhampton W
Hardwick, G. (13) 1946/7 Middlesbrough
Harford, M. G. (2) 1987/8 Luton T
Hargreaves, O. (39) 2001/02 Bayern Munich
Harris, G. (1) 1965/6 Burnley
Harris, P. (2) 1949/50 Portsmouth
Harvey, C. (1) 1970/1 Everton
Hassall, H. (5) 1950/1 Huddersfield T, Bolton W
Hateley, M. (32) 1983/4 Portsmouth, AC Milan, Monaco, Rangers
Haynes, J. (56) 1954/5 Fulham
Hector, K. (2) 1973/4 Derby Co
Hellawell, M. (2) 1962/3 Birmingham C
Hendrie, L. A. (1) 1998/9 Aston Villa
Henry, R. (1) 1962/3 Tottenham H
Heskey, E. W. (43) 1998/9 Leicester C, Liverpool, Birmingham C
Hill, F. (2) 1962/3 Bolton W
Hill, G. (6) 1975/6 Manchester U
Hill, R. (3) 1982/3 Luton T
Hinchcliffe, A. G. (7) 1996/7 Everton, Sheffield W
Hinton, A. (3) 1962/3 Wolverhampton W, Nottingham F
Hirst, D. E. (3) 1990/1 Sheffield W
Hitchens, G. (7) 1960/1 Aston Villa, Internazionale
Hoddle, G. (53) 1979/80 Tottenham H, Monaco
Hodge, S. B. (24) 1985/6 Aston Villa, Tottenham H, Nottingham F
Hodgkinson, A. (5) 1956/7 Sheffield U
Holden, D. (5) 1958/9 Bolton W
Holliday, E. (3) 1959/60 Middlesbrough
Hollins, J. (1) 1966/7 Chelsea
Hopkinson, E. (14) 1957/8 Bolton W
Howe, D. (23) 1957/8 WBA
Howe, J. (3) 1947/8 Derby Co
Howey, S. N. (4) 1994/5 Newcastle U
Hudson, A. (2) 1974/5 Stoke C
Hughes, E. (62) 1969/70 Liverpool, Wolverhampton W
Hughes, L. (3) 1949/50 Liverpool
Hunt, R. (34) 1961/2 Liverpool
Hunt, S. (2) 1983/4 WBA
Hunter, N. (28) 1965/6 Leeds U
Hurst, G. (49) 1965/6 West Ham U

Ince, P. (53) 1992/3 Manchester U, Internazionale, Liverpool, Middlesbrough

James, D. B. (34) 1996/7 Liverpool, Aston Villa, West Ham U, Manchester C
Jeffers, F. (1) 2002/03 Arsenal
Jenas, J. A. (17) 2002/03 Newcastle U, Tottenham H
Jezzard, B. (2) 1953/4 Fulham
Johnson, A. (7) 2004/05 Crystal P, Everton
Johnson, D. (8) 1974/5 Ipswich T, Liverpool
Johnson, G. M. C. (5) 2003/04 Chelsea
Johnson, S. A. M. (1) 2000/01 Derby Co
Johnston, H. (10) 1946/7 Blackpool
Jones, M. (3) 1964/5 Sheffield U, Leeds U
Jones, R. (8) 1991/2 Liverpool
Jones, W. H. (2) 1949/50 Liverpool

Kay, A. (1) 1962/3 Everton

Keegan, K. (63) 1972/3 Liverpool, SV Hamburg, Southampton
Kennedy, A. (2) 1983/4 Liverpool
Kennedy, R. (17) 1975/6 Liverpool
Keown, M. R. (43) 1991/2 Everton, Arsenal
Kevan, D. (14) 1956/7 WBA
Kidd, B. (2) 1969/70 Manchester U
King, L. B. (19) 2001/02 Tottenham H
Kirkland, C. E. (1) 2006/07 Liverpool
Knight, Z. (2) 2004/05 Fulham
Knowles, C. (4) 1967/8 Tottenham H
Konchesky, P. M. (2) 2002/03 Charlton Ath, West Ham U

Labone, B. (26) 1962/3 Everton
Lampard, F. J. (55) 1999/00 West Ham U, Chelsea
Lampard, F. R. G. (2) 1972/3 West Ham U
Langley, J. (3) 1957/8 Fulham
Langton, R. (11) 1946/7 Blackburn R, Preston NE, Bolton W
Latchford, R. (12) 1977/8 Everton
Lawler, C. (4) 1970/1 Liverpool
Lawton, T. (15) 1946/7 Chelsea, Notts Co
Lee, F. (27) 1968/9 Manchester C
Lee, J. (1) 1950/1 Derby C
Lee, R. M. (21) 1994/5 Newcastle U
Lee, S. (14) 1982/3 Liverpool
Lennon, A. J. (9) 2005/06 Tottenham H
Le Saux, G. P. (36) 1993/4 Blackburn R, Chelsea
Le Tissier, M. P. (8) 1993/4 Southampton
Lindsay, A. (4) 1973/4 Liverpool
Lineker, G. (80) 1983/4 Leicester C, Everton, Barcelona, Tottenham H
Little, B. (1) 1974/5 Aston Villa
Lloyd, L. (4) 1970/1 Liverpool, Nottingham F
Lofthouse, N. (33) 1950/1 Bolton W
Lowe, E. (3) 1946/7 Aston Villa

Mabbutt, G. (16) 1982/3 Tottenham H
Macdonald, M. (14) 1971/2 Newcastle U
Madeley, P. (24) 1970/1 Leeds U
Mannion, W. (26) 1946/7 Middlesbrough
Mariner, P. (35) 1976/7 Ipswich T, Arsenal
Marsh, R. (9) 1971/2 QPR, Manchester C
Martin, A. (17) 1980/1 West Ham U
Martyn, A. N. (23) 1991/2 Crystal P, Leeds U
Marwood, B. (1) 1988/9 Arsenal
Matthews, R. (5) 1955/6 Coventry C
Matthews, S. (37) 1946/7 Stoke C, Blackpool
McCann, G. P. (1) 2000/01 Sunderland
McDermott, T. (25) 1977/8 Liverpool
McDonald, C. (8) 1957/8 Burnley
McFarland, R. (28) 1970/1 Derby C
McGarry, W. (4) 1953/4 Huddersfield T
McGuinness, W. (2) 1958/9 Manchester U
McMahon, S. (17) 1987/8 Liverpool
McManaman, S. (37) 1994/5 Liverpool, Real Madrid
McNab, R. (4) 1968/9 Arsenal
McNeil, M. (9) 1960/1 Middlesbrough
Meadows, J. (1) 1954/5 Manchester C
Medley, L. (6) 1950/1 Tottenham H
Melia, J. (2) 1962/3 Liverpool
Merrick, G. (23) 1951/2 Birmingham C
Merson, P. C. (21) 1991/2 Arsenal, Middlesbrough, Aston Villa
Metcalfe, V. (2) 1950/1 Huddersfield T
Milburn, J. (13) 1948/9 Newcastle U
Miller, B. (1) 1960/1 Burnley
Mills, D. J. (19) 2000/01 Leeds U
Mills, M. (42) 1972/3 Ipswich T
Milne, G. (14) 1962/3 Liverpool
Milton, C. A. (1) 1951/2 Arsenal
Moore, R. (108) 1961/2 West Ham U
Morley, A. (6) 1981/2 Aston Villa
Morris, J. (3) 1948/9 Derby Co
Mortensen, S. (25) 1946/7 Blackpool
Mozley, B. (3) 1949/50 Derby Co
Mullen, J. (12) 1946/7 Wolverhampton W
Mullery, A. (35) 1964/5 Tottenham H
Murphy, D. B. (9) 2001/02 Liverpool

Neal, P. (50) 1975/6 Liverpool
Neville, G. A. (85) 1994/5 Manchester U
Neville, P. J. (56) 1995/6 Manchester U, Everton
Newton, K. (27) 1965/6 Blackburn R, Everton
Nicholls, J. (2) 1953/4 WBA
Nicholson, W. (1) 1950/1 Tottenham H
Nish, D. (5) 1972/3 Derby Co
Norman, M. (23) 1961/2 Tottenham H
Nugent, D. J. (1) 2006/07 Preston NE

O'Grady, M. (2) 1962/3 Huddersfield T, Leeds U
Osgood, P. (4) 1969/70 Chelsea

Osman, R. (11) 1979/80 Ipswich T
Owen, M. J. (82) 1997/8 Liverpool, Real Madrid, Newcastle U
Owen, S. (3) 1953/4 Luton T

Paine, T. (19) 1962/3 Southampton
Pallister, G. (22) 1987/8 Middlesbrough, Manchester U
Palmer, C. L. (18) 1991/2 Sheffield W
Parker, P. A. (19) 1988/9 QPR, Manchester U
Parker, S. M. (3) 2003/04 Charlton Ath, Chelsea, Newcastle U
Parkes, P. (1) 1973/4 QPR
Parlour, R. (10) 1998/9 Arsenal
Parry, R. (2) 1959/60 Bolton W
Peacock, A. (6) 1961/2 Middlesbrough, Leeds U
Pearce, S. (78) 1986/7 Nottingham F, West Ham U
Pearson, Stan (8) 1947/8 Manchester U
Pearson, Stuart (15) 1975/6 Manchester U
Pegg, D. (1) 1956/7 Manchester U
Pejic, M. (4) 1973/4 Stoke C
Perry, W. (3) 1955/6 Blackpool
Perryman, S. (1) 1981/2 Tottenham H
Peters, M. (67) 1965/6 West Ham U, Tottenham H
Phelan, M. C. (1) 1989/90 Manchester U
Phillips, K. (8) 1998/9 Sunderland
Phillips, L. (3) 1951/2 Portsmouth
Pickering, F. (3) 1963/4 Everton
Pickering, N. (1) 1982/3 Sunderland
Pilkington, B. (1) 1954/5 Burnley
Platt, D. (62) 1989/90 Aston Villa, Bari, Juventus, Sampdoria, Arsenal
Pointer, R. (3) 1961/2 Burnley
Powell, C. G. (5) 2000/01 Charlton Ath
Pye, J. (1) 1949/50 Wolverhampton W

Quixall, A. (5) 1953/4 Sheffield W

Radford, J. (2) 1968/9 Arsenal
Ramsey, A. (32) 1948/9 Southampton, Tottenham H
Reaney, P. (3) 1968/9 Leeds U
Redknapp, J. F. (17) 1995/6 Liverpool
Reeves, K. (2) 1979/80 Norwich C, Manchester C
Regis, C. (5) 1981/2 WBA, Coventry C
Reid, P. (13) 1984/5 Everton
Revie, D. (6) 1954/5 Manchester C
Richards, J. (1) 1972/3 Wolverhampton W
Richards, M. (4) 2006/07 Manchester C
Richardson, K. (1) 1993/4 Aston Villa
Richardon, K. E. (8) 2004/05 Manchester U
Rickaby, S. (1) 1953/4 WBA
Ricketts, M. B. (1) 2001/02 Bolton W
Rimmer, J. (1) 1975/6 Arsenal
Ripley, S. E. (2) 1993/4 Blackburn R
Rix, G. (17) 1980/1 Arsenal
Robb, G. (1) 1953/4 Tottenham H
Roberts, G. (6) 1982/3 Tottenham H
Robinson, P. W. (36) 2002/03 Leeds U, Tottenham H
Robson, B. (90) 1979/80 WBA, Manchester U
Robson, R. (20) 1957/8 WBA
Rocastle, D. (14) 1988/9 Arsenal
Rooney, W. (38) 2002/03 Everton, Manchester U
Rowley, J. (6) 1948/9 Manchester U
Royle, J. (6) 1970/1 Everton, Manchester C
Ruddock, N. (1) 1994/5 Liverpool

Sadler, D. (4) 1967/8 Manchester U
Salako, J. A. (5) 1990/1 Crystal P
Sansom, K. (86) 1978/9 Crystal P, Arsenal
Scales, J. R. (3) 1994/5 Liverpool
Scholes, P. (66) 1996/7 Manchester U
Scott, L. (17) 1946/7 Arsenal
Seaman, D. A. (75) 1988/9 QPR, Arsenal
Sewell, J. (6) 1951/2 Sheffield W
Shackleton, L. (5) 1948/9 Sunderland
Sharpe, L. S. (8) 1990/1 Manchester U
Shaw, G. (5) 1958/9 Sheffield U
Shearer, A. (63) 1991/2 Southampton, Blackburn R, Newcastle U
Shellito, K. (1) 1962/3 Chelsea
Sheringham, E. (51) 1992/3 Tottenham H, Manchester U, Tottenham H
Sherwood, T. A. (3) 1998/9 Tottenham H
Shilton, P. (125) 1970/1 Leicester C, Stoke C, Nottingham F, Southampton, Derby Co
Shimwell, E. (1) 1948/9 Blackpool
Shorey, N, (1) 2006/07 Reading
Sillett, P. (3) 1954/5 Chelsea
Sinclair, T. (12) 2001/02 West Ham U, Manchester C
Sinton, A. (12) 1991/2 QPR, Sheffield W
Slater, W. (12) 1954/5 Wolverhampton W
Smith, A. (17) 2000/01 Leeds U, Mancheser U
Smith, A. M. (13) 1988/9 Arsenal
Smith, L. (6) 1950/1 Arsenal

Smith, R. (15) 1960/1 Tottenham H
Smith, Tom (1) 1970/1 Liverpool
Smith, Trevor (2) 1959/60 Birmingham C
Southgate, G. (57) 1995/6 Aston Villa, Middlesbrough
Spink, N. (1) 1982/3 Aston Villa
Springett, R. (33) 1959/60 Sheffield W
Staniforth, R. (8) 1953/4 Huddersfield T
Statham, D. (3) 1982/3 WBA
Stein, B. (1) 1983/4 Luton T
Stepney, A. (1) 1967/8 Manchester U
Sterland, M. (1) 1988/9 Sheffield W
Steven, T. M. (36) 1984/5 Everton, Rangers, Marseille
Stevens, G. A. (7) 1984/5 Tottenham H
Stevens, M. G. (46) 1984/5 Everton, Rangers
Stewart, P. A. (3) 1991/2 Tottenham H
Stiles, N. (28) 1964/5 Manchester U
Stone, S. B. (9) 1995/6 Nottingham F
Storey-Moore, I. (1) 1969/70 Nottingham F
Storey, P. (19) 1970/1 Arsenal
Streten, B. (1) 1949/50 Luton T
Summerbee, M. (8) 1967/8 Manchester C
Sunderland, A. (1) 1979/80 Arsenal
Sutton, C. R. (1) 1997/8 Blackburn R
Swan, P. (19) 1959/60 Sheffield W
Swift, F. (19) 1946/7 Manchester C

Talbot, B. (6) 1976/7 Ipswich T, Arsenal
Tambling, R. (3) 1962/3 Chelsea
Taylor, E. (1) 1953/4 Blackpool
Taylor, J. (2) 1950/1 Fulham
Taylor, P. H. (3) 1947/8 Liverpool
Taylor, P. J. (4) 1975/6 Crystal P
Taylor, T. (19) 1952/3 Manchester U
Temple, D. (1) 1964/5 Everton
Terry, J. G. (39) 2002/03 Chelsea
Thomas, Danny (2) 1982/3 Coventry C
Thomas, Dave (8) 1974/5 QPR
Thomas, G. R. (9) 1990/1 Crystal P
Thomas, M. L. (2) 1988/9 Arsenal
Thompson, A. (1) 2003/04 Celtic
Thompson, P. (16) 1963/4 Liverpool
Thompson, P. B. (42) 1975/6 Liverpool
Thompson, T. (2) 1951/2 Aston Villa, Preston NE
Thomson, R. (8) 1963/4 Wolverhampton W
Todd, C. (27) 1971/2 Derby Co
Towers, T. (3) 1975/6 Sunderland
Tueart, D. (6) 1974/5 Manchester C

Ufton, D. (1) 1953/4 Charlton Ath
Unsworth, D. G. (1) 1994/5 Everton
Upson, M. J. (7) 2002/03 Birmingham C

Vassell, D. (22) 2001/02 Aston Villa
Venables, T. (2) 1964/5 Chelsea
Venison, B. (2) 1994/5 Newcastle U
Viljoen, C. (2) 1974/5 Ipswich T
Viollet, D. (2) 1959/60 Manchester U

Waddle, C. R. (62) 1984/5 Newcastle U, Tottenham H, Marseille
Waiters, A. (5) 1963/4 Blackpool
Walcott, T. J. (1) 2005/06 Arsenal
Walker, D. S. (59) 1988/9 Nottingham F, Sampdoria, Sheffield W
Walker, I. M. (4) 1995/6 Tottenham H, Leicester C
Wallace, D. L. (1) 1985/6 Southampton
Walsh, P. (5) 1982/3 Luton T
Walters, K. M. (1) 1990/1 Rangers
Ward, P. (1) 1979/80 Brighton
Ward, T. (2) 1947/8 Derby C
Watson, D. (12) 1983/4 Norwich C, Everton
Watson, D. V. (65) 1973/4 Sunderland, Manchester C, Werder Bremen, Southampton, Stoke C
Watson, W. (4) 1949/50 Sunderland
Webb, N. (26) 1987/8 Nottingham F, Manchester U
Weller, K. (4) 1973/4 Leicester C
West, G. (3) 1968/9 Everton
Wheeler, J. (1) 1954/5 Bolton W
White, D. (1) 1992/3 Manchester C
Whitworth, S. (7) 1974/5 Leicester C
Whymark, T. (1) 1977/8 Ipswich T
Wignall, F. (2) 1964/5 Nottingham F
Wilcox, J. M. (3) 1995/6 Blackburn R, Leeds U
Wilkins, R. (84) 1975/6 Chelsea, Manchester U, AC Milan
Williams, B. (24) 1948/9 Wolverhampton W
Williams, S. (6) 1982/3 Southampton
Willis, A. (1) 1951/2 Tottenham H
Wilshaw, D. (12) 1953/4 Wolverhampton W
Wilson, R. (63) 1959/60 Huddersfield T, Everton
Winterburn, N. (2) 1989/90 Arsenal
Wise, D. F. (21) 1990/1 Chelsea
Withe, P. (11) 1980/1 Aston Villa
Wood, R. (3) 1954/5 Manchester U
Woodcock, A. (42) 1977/8 Nottingham F, FC Cologne, Arsenal

Woodgate, J. S. (6) 1998/9 Leeds U, Newcastle U, Real Madrid
Woods, C. C. E. (43) 1984/5 Norwich C, Rangers, Sheffield W
Worthington, F. (8) 1973/4 Leicester C
Wright, I. E. (33) 1990/1 Crystal P, Arsenal, West Ham U
Wright, M. (45) 1983/4 Southampton, Derby C, Liverpool
Wright, R. I. (2) 1999/00 Ipswich T, Arsenal
Wright, T. (11) 1967/8 Everton
Wright, W. (105) 1946/7 Wolverhampton W
Wright-Phillips, S. C. (12) 2004/05 Manchester C, Chelsea

Young, G. (1) 1964/5 Sheffield W
Young, L. P. (7) 2004/05 Charlton Ath

NORTHERN IRELAND

Aherne, T. (4) 1946/7 Belfast Celtic, Luton T
Anderson, T. (22) 1972/3 Manchester U, Swindon T, Peterborough U
Armstrong, G. (63) 1976/7 Tottenham H, Watford, Real Mallorca, WBA, Chesterfield

Baird, C. P. (25) 2002/03 Southampton
Barr, H. (3) 1961/2 Linfield, Coventry C
Best, G. (37) 1963/4 Manchester U, Fulham
Bingham, W. (56) 1950/1 Sunderland, Luton T, Everton, Port Vale
Black, K. (30) 1987/8 Luton T, Nottingham F
Blair, R. (5) 1974/5 Oldham Ath
Blanchflower, D. (54) 1949/50 Barnsley, Aston Villa, Tottenham H
Blanchflower, J. (12) 1953/4 Manchester U
Blayney, A. (1) 2005/06 Doncaster R
Bowler, G. (3) 1949/50 Hull C
Braithwaite, R. (10) 1961/2 Linfield, Middlesbrough
Brennan, R. (5) 1948/9 Luton T, Birmingham C, Fulham
Briggs, R. (2) 1961/2 Manchester U, Swansea
Brotherston, N. (27) 1979/80 Blackburn R
Bruce, W. (2) 1960/1 Glentoran
Brunt, C. (10) 2004/05 Sheffield W

Campbell, A. (2) 1962/3 Crusaders
Campbell, D. A. (10) 1985/6 Nottingham F, Charlton Ath
Campbell, J. (2) 1950/1 Fulham
Campbell, R. M. (2) 1981/2 Bradford C
Campbell, W. (6) 1967/8 Dundee
Capaldi, A. C. (21) 2003/04 Plymouth Arg
Carey, J. (7) 1946/7 Manchester U
Carroll, R. E. (19) 1996/7 Wigan Ath, Manchester U, West Ham U
Casey, T. (12) 1954/5 Newcastle U, Portsmouth
Caskey, A. (8) 1978/9 Derby C, Tulsa Roughnecks
Cassidy, T. (24) 1970/1 Newcastle U, Burnley
Caughey, M. (2) 1985/6 Linfield
Clarke, C. J. (38) 1985/6 Bournemouth, Southampton, Portsmouth
Cleary, J. (5) 1981/2 Glentoran
Clements, D. (48) 1964/5 Coventry C, Sheffield W, Everton, New York Cosmos
Clingan, S. G. (8) 2005/06 Nottingham F
Clyde, M.G. (3) 2004/05 Wolverhampon W
Cochrane, D. (10) 1946/7 Leeds U
Cochrane, T. (26) 1975/6 Coleraine, Burnley, Middlesbrough, Gillingham
Connell, T. E. (1) 1977/8 Coleraine
Coote, A. (6) 1998/9 Norwich C
Cowan, J. (1) 1969/70 Newcastle U
Coyle, F. (4) 1955/6 Coleraine, Nottingham F
Coyle, L. (1) 1988/9 Derry C
Coyle, R. (5) 1972/3 Sheffield W
Craig, D. (25) 1966/7 Newcastle U
Craigan, S. (29) 2002/03 Partick T, Motherwell
Crossan, E. (3) 1949/50 Blackburn R
Crossan, J. (24) 1959/60 Sparta Rotterdam, Sunderland, Manchester C, Middlesbrough
Cunningham, W. (30) 1950/1 St Mirren, Leicester C, Dunfermline Ath

Cush, W. (26) 1950/1 Glentoran, Leeds U, Portadown

D'Arcy, S. (5) 1951/2 Chelsea, Brentford
Davis, S. (20) 2004/05 Aston Villa
Davison, A. J. (3) 1995/6 Bolton W, Bradford C, Grimsby T
Dennison, R. (18) 1987/8 Wolverhampton W
Devine, J. (1) 1989/90 Glentoran
Dickson, D. (4) 1969/70 Coleraine
Dickson, T. (1) 1956/7 Linfield
Dickson, W. (12) 1950/1 Chelsea, Arsenal
Doherty, L. (2) 1984/5 Linfield
Doherty, P. (6) 1946/7 Derby Co, Huddersfield T, Doncaster R
Doherty, T. E. (9) 2002/03 Bristol C
Donaghy, M. (91) 1979/80 Luton T, Manchester U, Chelsea
Dougan, D. (43) 1957/8 Portsmouth, Blackburn R, Aston Villa, Leicester C, Wolverhampton W
Douglas, J. P. (1) 1946/7 Belfast Celtic
Dowd, H. (3) 1973/4 Glenavon, Sheffield W
Dowie, I. (59) 1989/90 Luton T, West Ham U, Southampton, Crystal P, West Ham U, QPR
Duff, M. J. (17) 2001/02 Cheltenham T, Burnley
Dunlop, G. (4) 1984/5 Linfield

Eglington, T. (6) 1946/7 Everton
Elder, A. (40) 1959/60 Burnley, Stoke C
Elliott, S. (36) 2000/01 Motherwell, Hull C
Evans, J. G. (5) 2006/07 Manchester U

Farrell, P. (7) 1946/7 Everton
Feeney, J. (2) 1946/7 Linfield, Swansea T
Feeney, W. (1) 1975/6 Glentoran
Feeney, W. J. (18) 2001/02 Bournemouth, Luton T
Ferguson, G. (5) 1998/9 Linfield
Ferguson, W. (2) 1965/6 Linfield
Ferris, R. (3) 1949/50 Birmingham C
Fettis, A. (25) 1991/2 Hull C, Nottingham F, Blackburn R
Finney, T. (14) 1974/5 Sunderland, Cambridge U
Fleming, J. G. (31) 1986/7 Nottingham F, Manchester C, Barnsley
Forde, T. (4) 1958/9 Ards

Gallogly, C. (2) 1950/1 Huddersfield T
Garton, R. (1) 1968/9 Oxford U
Gillespie, K. R. (75) 1994/5 Manchester U, Newcastle U, Blackburn R, Leicester C, Sheffield U
Gorman, W. (4) 1946/7 Brentford
Graham, W. (14) 1950/1 Doncaster R
Gray, P. (26) 1992/3 Luton T, Sunderland, Nancy, Luton T, Burnley, Oxford U
Gregg, H. (25) 1953/4 Doncaster R, Manchester U
Griffin, D. J. (29) 1995/6 St Johnstone, Dundee U, Stockport Co

Hamill, R. (1) 1998/9 Glentoran
Hamilton, B. (50) 1968/9 Linfield, Ipswich T, Everton, Millwall, Swindon T
Hamilton, G. (5) 2002/03 Portadown
Hamilton, W. (41) 1977/8 QPR, Burnley, Oxford U
Harkin, T. (5) 1967/8 Southport, Shrewsbury T
Harvey, M. (34) 1960/1 Sunderland
Hatton, S. (2) 1962/3 Linfield
Healy, D. J. (56) 1999/00 Manchester U, Preston NE, Leeds U
Healy, P. J. (4) 1981/2 Coleraine, Glentoran
Hegan, D. (7) 1969/70 WBA, Wolverhampton W
Hill, C. F. (27) 1989/90 Sheffield U, Leicester C, Trelleborg, Northampton T
Hill, J. (7) 1958/9 Norwich C, Everton
Hinton, E. (7) 1946/7 Fulham, Millwall
Holmes, S. P. (1) 2001/02 Wrexham
Horlock, K. (32) 1994/5 Swindon T, Manchester C
Hughes, A. W. (54) 1997/8 Newcastle U, Aston Villa
Hughes, J, (2) 2005/06 Lincoln C
Hughes, M. A. (2) 2005/06 Oldham Ath
Hughes, M. E. (71) 1991/2 Manchester C, Strasbourg, West Ham U, Wimbledon, Crystal P
Hughes, P. (3) 1986/7 Bury
Hughes, W. (1) 1950/1 Bolton W
Humphries, W. (14) 1961/2 Ards, Coventry C, Swansea T
Hunter, A. (53) 1969/70 Blackburn R, Ipswich T
Hunter, B. V. (15) 1994/5 Wrexham, Reading
Hunter, V. (2) 1961/2 Coleraine

Ingham, M. G. (3) 2004/05 Sunderland, Wrexham
Irvine, R. (8) 1961/2 Linfield, Stoke C
Irvine, W. (23) 1962/3 Burnley, Preston NE, Brighton & HA

Jackson, T. (35) 1968/9 Everton, Nottingham F, Manchester U
Jamison, A. (1) 1975/6 Glentoran
Jenkins, I. (6) 1996/7 Chester C, Dundee U
Jennings, P. (119) 1963/4 Watford, Tottenham H, Arsenal, Tottenham H
Johnson, D. M. (46) 1998/9 Blackburn R, Birmingham C
Johnston, W. (2) 1961/2 Glenavon, Oldham Ath
Jones, J. (3) 1955/6 Glenavon
Jones, S. G. (27) 2002/03 Crewe Alex, Burnley

Keane, T. (1) 1948/9 Swansea T
Kee, P. V. (9) 1989/90 Oxford U, Ards
Keith, R. (23) 1957/8 Newcastle U
Kelly, H. (4) 1949/50 Fulham, Southampton
Kelly, P. (1) 1949/50 Barnsley
Kennedy, P. H. (20) 1998/9 Watford, Wigan Ath
Kirk, A. R. (8) 1999/00 Heart of Midlothian, Boston U, Northampton T

Lafferty, K. (10) 2005/06 Burnley
Lawther, I. (4) 1959/60 Sunderland, Blackburn R
Lennon, N. F. (40) 1993/4 Crewe Alex, Leicester C, Celtic
Lockhart, N. (8) 1946/7 Linfield, Coventry C, Aston Villa
Lomas, S. M. (45) 1993/4 Manchester C, West Ham U
Lutton, B. (6) 1969/70 Wolverhampton W, West Ham U

Magill, E. (26) 1961/2 Arsenal, Brighton & HA
Magilton, J. (52) 1990/1 Oxford U, Southampton, Sheffield W, Ipswich T
Mannus, A. (1) 2003/04 Linfield
Martin, C. (6) 1946/7 Glentoran, Leeds U, Aston Villa
McAdams, W. (15) 1953/4 Manchester C, Bolton W, Leeds U
McAlinden, J. (2) 1946/7 Portsmouth, Southend U
McAuley, G. (5) 2004/05 Lincoln C
McBride, S. (4) 1990/1 Glenavon
McCabe, J. (6) 1948/9 Leeds U
McCann, G. S. (15) 2001/02 West Ham U, Cheltenham T, Barnsley
McCarthy, J. D. (18) 1995/6 Port Vale, Birmingham C
McCartney, G. (20) 2001/02 Sunderland
McCavana, T. (3) 1954/5 Coleraine
McCleary, J. W. (1) 1954/5 Cliftonville
McClelland, J. (6) 1960/1 Arsenal, Fulham
McClelland, J. (53) 1979/80 Mansfield T, Rangers, Watford, Leeds U
McCourt, F. (6) 1951/2 Manchester C
McCourt, P. J. (1) 2001/02 Rochdale
McCoy, R. (1) 1986/7 Coleraine
McCreery, D. (67) 1975/6 Manchester U, QPR, Tulsa Roughnecks, Newcastle U, Heart of Midlothian
McCrory, S. (1) 1957/8 Southend U
McCullough, W. (10) 1960/1 Arsenal, Millwall
McCurdy, C. (1) 1979/80 Linfield
McDonald, A. (52) 1985/6 QPR
McElhinney, G. (6) 1983/4 Bolton W
McEvilly, L. R. (1) 2001/02 Rochdale
McFaul, I. (6) 1966/7 Linfield, Newcastle U
McGarry, J. K. (3) 1950/1 Cliftonville
McGaughey, M. (1) 1984/5 Linfield
McGibbon, P. C. G. (7) 1994/5 Manchester U, Wigan Ath
McGrath, R. (21) 1973/4 Tottenham H, Manchester U
McIlroy, J. (55) 1951/2 Burnley, Stoke C
McIlroy, S. B. (88) 1971/2 Manchester U, Stoke C, Manchester C
McKeag, W. (2) 1967/8 Glentoran
McKenna, J. (7) 1949/50 Huddersfield T
McKenzie, R. (1) 1966/7 Airdrieonians
McKinney, W. (1) 1965/6 Falkirk
McKnight, A. (10) 1987/8 Celtic, West Ham U
McLaughlin, J. (12) 1961/2 Shrewsbury T, Swansea T
McLean, B. S. (1) 2005/06 Rangers
McMahon, G. J. (17) 1994/5 Tottenham H, Stoke C
McMichael, A. (39) 1949/50 Newcastle U
McMillan, S. (2) 1962/3 Manchester U
McMordie, E. (21) 1968/9 Middlesbrough

McMorran, E. (15) 1946/7 Belfast Celtic, Barnsley, Doncaster R
McNally, B. A. (5) 1985/6 Shrewsbury T
McParland, P. (34) 1953/4 Aston Villa, Wolverhampton W
McVeigh, P. (20) 1998/9 Tottenham H, Norwich C
Montgomery, F. J. (1) 1954/5 Coleraine
Moore, C. (1) 1948/9 Glentoran
Moreland, V. (6) 1978/9 Derby Co
Morgan, S. (18) 1971/2 Port Vale, Aston Villa, Brighton & HA, Sparta Rotterdam
Morrow, S. J. (39) 1989/90 Arsenal, QPR
Mullan, G. (4) 1982/3 Glentoran
Mulryne, P. P. (27) 1996/7 Manchester U, Norwich C, Cardiff C
Murdock, C. J. (34) 1999/00 Preston NE, Hibernian, Crewe Alex, Rotherham U

Napier, R. (1) 1965/6 Bolton W
Neill, T. (59) 1960/1 Arsenal, Hull C
Nelson, S. (51) 1969/70 Arsenal, Brighton & HA
Nicholl, C. (51) 1974/5 Aston Villa, Southampton, Grimsby T
Nicholl, J. M. (73) 1975/6 Manchester U, Toronto Blizzard, Sunderland, Rangers, WBA
Nicholson, J. (41) 1960/1 Manchester U, Huddersfield T
Nolan, I. R. (18) 1996/7 Sheffield W, Bradford C, Wigan Ath

O'Boyle, G. (13) 1993/4 Dunfermline Ath, St Johnstone
O'Doherty, A. (2) 1969/70 Coleraine
O'Driscoll, J. (3) 1948/9 Swansea T
O'Kane, L. (20) 1969/70 Nottingham F
O'Neill, C. (3) 1988/9 Motherwell
O'Neill, H. M. (64) 1971/2 Distillery, Nottingham F, Norwich C, Manchester C, Norwich C, Notts Co
O'Neill, J. (1) 1961/2 Sunderland
O'Neill, J. P. (39) 1979/80 Leicester C
O'Neill, M. A. (31) 1987/8 Newcastle U, Dundee U, Hibernian, Coventry C

Parke, J. (13) 1963/4 Linfield, Hibernian, Sunderland
Patterson, D. J. (17) 1993/4 Crystal P, Luton T, Dundee U
Peacock, R. (31) 1951/2 Celtic, Coleraine
Penney, S. (17) 1984/5 Brighton & HA
Platt, J. A. (23) 1975/6 Middlesbrough, Ballymena U, Coleraine

Quinn, J. M. (46) 1984/5 Blackburn R, Swindon T, Leicester, Bradford C, West Ham U, Bournemouth, Reading
Quinn, S. J. (50) 1995/6 Blackpool, WBA, Willem II, Sheffield W, Peterborough U, Northampton T

Rafferty, P. (1) 1979/80 Linfield
Ramsey, P. (14) 1983/4 Leicester C
Rice, P. (49) 1968/9 Arsenal
Robinson, S. (6) 1996/7 Bournemouth, Luton T
Rogan, A. (18) 1987/8 Celtic, Sunderland, Millwall
Ross, E. (1) 1968/9 Newcastle U
Rowland, K. (19) 1994/5 West Ham U, QPR
Russell, A. (1) 1946/7 Linfield
Ryan, R. (1) 1949/50 WBA

Sanchez, L. P. (3) 1986/7 Wimbledon
Scott, J. (2) 1957/8 Grimsby T
Scott, P. (10) 1974/5 Everton, York C, Aldershot
Sharkey, P. (1) 1975/6 Ipswich T
Shields, J. (1) 1956/7 Southampton
Shiels, D. (4) 2005/06 Hibernian
Simpson, W. (12) 1950/1 Rangers
Sloan, D. (2) 1968/9 Oxford
Sloan, T. (3) 1978/9 Manchester U
Sloan, W. (1) 1946/7 Arsenal
Smith, A. W. (18) 2002/03 Glentoran, Preston NE
Smyth, S. (9) 1947/8 Wolverhampton W, Stoke C
Smyth, W. (4) 1948/9 Distillery
Sonner, D. J. (13) 1997/8 Ipswich T, Sheffield W, Birmingham C, Nottingham F, Peterborough U
Spence, D. (29) 1974/5 Bury, Blackpool, Southend U
Sproule, I. (8) 2005/06 Hibernian
Stevenson, A. (3) 1946/7 Everton
Stewart, A. (7) 1966/7 Glentoran, Derby
Stewart, D. (1) 1977/8 Hull C
Stewart, I. (31) 1981/2 QPR, Newcastle U
Stewart, T. (1) 1960/1 Linfield

Taggart, G. P. (51) 1989/90 Barnsley, Bolton W, Leicester C
Taylor, M. S. (60) 1998/9 Fulham, Birmingham C
Thompson, P. (5) 2005/06 Linfield
Todd, S. (11) 1965/6 Burnley, Sheffield W
Toner, C. (2) 2002/03 Leyton Orient
Trainor, D. (1) 1966/7 Crusaders
Tully, C. (10) 1948/9 Celtic

Uprichard, N. (18) 1951/2 Swindon T, Portsmouth

Vernon, J. (17) 1946/7 Belfast Celtic, WBA

Walker, J. (1) 1954/5 Doncaster R
Walsh, D. (9) 1946/7 WBA
Walsh, W. (5) 1947/8 Manchester C
Watson, P. (1) 1970/1 Distillery
Webb, S. M. (4) 2005/06 Ross Co
Welsh, S. (4) 1965/6 Carlisle U
Whiteside, N. (38) 1981/2 Manchester U, Everton
Whitley, Jeff (20) 1996/7 Manchester C, Sunderland, Cardiff C
Whitley, Jim (3) 1997/8 Manchester C
Williams, M. S. (36) 1998/9 Chesterfield, Watford, Wimbledon, Stoke C, Wimbledon, Milton Keynes D
Williams, P. (1) 1990/1 WBA
Wilson, D. J. (24) 1986/7 Brighton & HA, Luton, Sheffield W
Wilson, K. J. (42) 1986/7 Ipswich T, Chelsea, Notts C, Walsall
Wilson, S. (12) 1961/2 Glenavon, Falkirk, Dundee
Wood, T. J. (1) 1995/6 Walsall
Worthington, N. (66) 1983/4 Sheffield W, Leeds U, Stoke C
Wright, T. J. (31) 1988/9 Newcastle U, Nottingham F, Manchester C

SCOTLAND

Adam, C. G. (2) 2006/07 Rangers
Aird, J. (4) 1953/4 Burnley
Aitken, G. G. (8) 1948/9 East Fife, Sunderland
Aitken, R. (57) 1979/80 Celtic, Newcastle U, St Mirren
Albiston, A. (14) 1981/2 Manchester U
Alexander, G. (30) 2001/02 Preston NE
Alexander, N. (3) 2005/06 Cardiff C
Allan, T. (2) 1973/4 Dundee
Anderson, J. (1) 1953/4 Leicester C
Anderson, R. (9) 2002/03 Aberdeen
Archibald, S. (27) 1979/80 Aberdeen, Tottenham H, Barcelona
Auld, B. (3) 1958/9 Celtic

Baird, H. (1) 1955/6 Airdrieonians
Baird, S. (7) 1956/7 Rangers
Bannon, E. (11) 1979/80 Dundee U
Bauld, W. (3) 1949/50 Heart of Midlothian
Baxter, J. (34) 1960/1 Rangers, Sunderland
Beattie, C. (4) 2005/06 Celtic
Bell, W. (2) 1965/6 Leeds U
Bernard, P. R. (2) 1994/5 Oldham Ath
Bett, J. (25) 1981/2 Rangers, Lokeren, Aberdeen
Black, E. (2) 1987/8 Metz
Black, I. (1) 1947/8 Southampton
Blacklaw, A. (3) 1962/3 Burnley
Blackley, J. (7) 1973/4 Hibernian
Blair, J. (1) 1946/7 Blackpool
Blyth, J. (2) 1977/8 Coventry C
Bone, J. (2) 1971/2 Norwich C
Booth, S. (21) 1992/3 Aberdeen, Borussia Dortmund, Twente
Bowman, D. (6) 1991/2 Dundee U
Boyd, K. (9) 2005/06 Rangers
Boyd, T. (72) 1990/1 Motherwell, Chelsea, Celtic
Brand, R. (8) 1960/1 Rangers
Brazil, A. (13) 1979/80 Ipswich T, Tottenham H
Bremner, D. (1) 1975/6 Hibernian
Bremner, W. (54) 1964/5 Leeds U
Brennan, F. (7) 1946/7 Newcastle U
Brogan, J. (4) 1970/1 Celtic
Brown, A. (14) 1949/50 East Fife, Blackpool
Brown, H. (3) 1946/7 Partick Th
Brown, J. (1) 1974/5 Sheffield U
Brown, R. (3) 1946/7 Rangers
Brown, S. (3) 2005/06 Hibernian
Brown, W. (28) 1957/8 Dundee, Tottenham H
Brownlie, J. (7) 1970/1 Hibernian
Buchan, M. (34) 1971/2 Aberdeen, Manchester U
Buckley, P. (3) 1953/4 Aberdeen
Burchill, M. J. (6) 1999/00 Celtic
Burke, C. (2) 2005/06 Rangers

Burley, C. W. (46) 1994/5 Chelsea, Celtic, Derby Co
Burley, G. (11) 1978/9 Ipswich T
Burns, F. (1) 1969/70 Manchester U
Burns, K. (20) 1973/4 Birmingham C, Nottingham F
Burns, T. (8) 1980/1 Celtic

Calderwood, C. (36) 1994/5 Tottenham H, Aston Villa
Caldow, E. (40) 1956/7 Rangers
Caldwell, G. (24) 2001/02 Newcastle U, Hibernian, Celtic
Caldwell, S. (9) 2000/01 Newcastle U, Sunderland
Callaghan, W. (2) 1969/70 Dunfermline
Cameron, C. (28) 1998/9 Heart of Midlothian, Wolverhampton W
Campbell, R. (5) 1946/7 Falkirk, Chelsea
Campbell, W. (5) 1946/7 Morton
Canero, P. (1) 2003/04 Leicester C
Carr, W. (6) 1969/70 Coventry C
Chalmers, S. (5) 1964/5 Celtic
Clark, J. (4) 1965/6 Celtic
Clark, R. (17) 1967/8 Aberdeen
Clarke, S. (6) 1987/8 Chelsea
Collins, J. (58) 1987/8 Hibernian, Celtic, Monaco, Everton
Collins, R. (31) 1950/1 Celtic, Everton, Leeds U
Colquhoun, E. (9) 1971/2 Sheffield U
Colquhoun, J. (2) 1987/8 Heart of Midlothian
Combe, R. (3) 1947/8 Hibernian
Conn, A. (1) 1955/6 Heart of Midlothian
Conn, A. (2) 1974/5 Tottenham H
Connachan, E. (2) 1961/2 Dunfermline Ath
Connelly, G. (2) 1973/4 Celtic
Connolly, J. (1) 1972/3 Everton
Connor, R. (4) 1985/6 Dundee, Aberdeen
Cooke, C. (16) 1965/6 Dundee, Chelsea
Cooper, D. (22) 1979/80 Rangers, Motherwell
Cormack, P. (9) 1965/6 Hibernian, Nottingham F
Cowan, J. (25) 1947/8 Morton
Cowie, D. (20) 1952/3 Dundee
Cox, C. (1) 1947/8 Heart of Midlothian
Cox, S. (24) 1947/8 Rangers
Craig, J. (1) 1976/7 Celtic
Craig, J. P. (1) 1967/8 Celtic
Craig, T. (1) 1975/6 Newcastle U
Crainey, S. (6) 2001/02 Celtic, Southampton
Crawford, S. (25) 1994/5 Raith R, Dunfermline Ath, Plymouth Arg
Crerand, P. (16) 1960/1 Celtic, Manchester U
Cropley, A. (2) 1971/2 Hibernian
Cruickshank, J. (6) 1963/4 Heart of Midlothian
Cullen, M. (1) 1955/6 Luton T
Cumming, J. (9) 1954/5 Heart of Midlothian
Cummings. W. (1) 2001/02 Chelsea
Cunningham, W. (8) 1953/4 Preston NE
Curran, H. (5) 1969/70 Wolverhampton W

Dailly, C. (65) 1996/7 Derby Co, Blackburn R, West Ham U
Dalglish, K. (102) 1971/2 Celtic, Liverpool
Davidson, C. I. (17) 1998/9 Blackburn R, Leicester C
Davidson, J. (8) 1953/4 Partick Th
Dawson, A. (5) 1979/80 Rangers
Deans, D. (2) 1974/5 Celtic
Delaney, J. (4) 1946/7 Manchester U
Devlin, P. J. (10) 2002/03 Birmingham C
Dick, J. (1) 1958/9 West Ham U
Dickov, P. (10) 2000/01 Mancheser C, Leicester C, Blackburn R
Dickson, W. (5) 1969/70 Kilmarnock
Dobie, R. S. (6) 2001/02 WBA
Docherty, T. (25) 1951/2 Preston NE, Arsenal
Dodds, D. (2) 1983/4 Dundee U
Dodds, W. (26) 1996/7 Aberdeen, Dundee U, Rangers
Donachie, W. (35) 1971/2 Manchester C
Donnelly, S. (10) 1996/7 Celtic
Dougall, C. (1) 1946/7 Birmingham C
Dougan, R. (1) 1949/50 Heart of Midlothian
Douglas, R. (19) 2001/02 Celtic, Leicester C
Doyle, J. (1) 1975/6 Ayr U
Duncan, A. (6) 1974/5 Hibernian
Duncan, D. (3) 1947/8 East Fife
Duncanson, J. (1) 1946/7 Rangers
Durie, G. S. (43) 1987/8 Chelsea, Tottenham H, Rangers
Durrant, I. (20) 1987/8 Rangers, Kilmarnock

Elliott, M. S. (18) 1997/8 Leicester C

Evans, A. (4) 1981/2 Aston Villa
Evans, R. (48) 1948/9 Celtic, Chelsea
Ewing, T. (2) 1957/8 Partick Th

Farm, G. (10) 1952/3 Blackpool
Ferguson, B. (39) 1998/9 Rangers, Blackburn R, Rangers
Ferguson, Derek (2) 1987/8 Rangers
Ferguson, Duncan (7) 1991/2 Dundee U, Everton
Ferguson, I. (9) 1988/9 Rangers
Ferguson, R. (7) 1965/6 Kilmarnock
Fernie, W. (12) 1953/4 Celtic
Flavell, R. (2) 1946/7 Airdrieonians
Fleck, R. (4) 1989/90 Norwich C
Fleming, C. (1) 1953/4 East Fife
Fletcher, D. B. (29) 2003/04 Manchester U
Forbes, A. (14) 1946/7 Sheffield U, Arsenal
Ford, D. (3) 1973/4 Heart of Midlothian
Forrest, J. (1) 1957/8 Motherwell
Forrest, J. (5) 1965/6 Rangers, Aberdeen
Forsyth, A. (10) 1971/2 Partick Th, Manchester U
Forsyth, C. (4) 1963/4 Kilmarnock
Forsyth, T. (22) 1970/1 Motherwell, Rangers
Fraser, D. (2) 1967/8 WBA
Fraser, W. (2) 1954/5 Sunderland
Freedman, D. A. (2) 2001/02 Crystal P

Gabriel, J. (2) 1960/1 Everton
Gallacher, K. W. (53) 1987/8 Dundee U, Coventry C, Blackburn R, Newcastle U
Gallacher, P. (8) 2001/02 Dundee U
Gallagher, P. (1) 2003/04 Blackburn R
Galloway, M. (1) 1991/2 Celtic
Gardiner, W. (1) 1957/8 Motherwell
Gemmell, T. (2) 1954/5 St Mirren
Gemmell, T. (18) 1965/6 Celtic
Gemmill, A. (43) 1970/1 Derby Co, Nottingham F, Birmingham C
Gemmill, S. (26) 1994/5 Nottingham F, Everton
Gibson, D. (7) 1962/3 Leicester C
Gillespie, G. T. (13) 1987/8 Liverpool
Gilzean, A. (22) 1963/4 Dundee, Tottenham H
Glass, S. (1) 1998/9 Newcastle U
Glavin, R. (1) 1976/7 Celtic
Glen, A. (2) 1955/6 Aberdeen
Goram, A. L. (43) 1985/6 Oldham Ath, Hibernian, Rangers
Gordon, C. S. (23) 2003/04 Heart of Midlothian
Gough, C. R. (61) 1982/3 Dundee U, Tottenham H, Rangers
Gould, J. (2) 1999/00 Celtic
Govan, J. (6) 1947/8 Hibernian
Graham, A. (11) 1977/8 Leeds U
Graham, G. (12) 1971/2 Arsenal, Manchester U
Grant, J. (2) 1958/9 Hibernian
Grant, P. (2) 1988/9 Celtic
Gray, A. (20) 1975/6 Aston Villa, Wolverhampton W, Everton
Gray, A. D. (2) 2002/03 Bradford C
Gray, E. (12) 1968/9 Leeds U
Gray F. (32) 1975/6 Leeds U, Nottingham F, Leeds U
Green, A. (6) 1970/1 Blackpool, Newcastle U
Greig, J. (44) 1963/4 Rangers
Gunn, B. (6) 1989/90 Norwich C

Haddock, H. (6) 1954/5 Clyde
Haffey, F. (2) 1959/60 Celtic
Hamilton, A. (24) 1961/2 Dundee
Hamilton, G. (5) 1946/7 Aberdeen
Hamilton, W. (1) 1964/5 Hibernian
Hammell, S. (1) 2004/05 Motherwell
Hansen, A. (26) 1978/9 Liverpool
Hansen, J. (2) 1971/2 Partick Th
Harper, J. (4) 1972/3 Aberdeen, Hibernian, Aberdeen
Hartford, A. (50) 1971/2 WBA, Manchester C, Everton, Manchester C
Hartley, P. J. (15) 2004/05 Heart of Midlothian, Celtic
Harvey, D. (16) 1972/3 Leeds U
Haughney, M. (1) 1953/4 Celtic
Hay, D. (27) 1969/70 Celtic
Hegarty, P. (8) 1978/9 Dundee U
Henderson, J. (7) 1952/3 Portsmouth, Arsenal
Henderson, W. (29) 1962/3 Rangers
Hendry, E. C. J. (51) 1992/3 Blackburn R, Rangers, Coventry C, Bolton W
Herd, D. (5) 1958/9 Arsenal
Herd, G. (5) 1957/8 Clyde
Herriot, J. (8) 1968/9 Birmingham C
Hewie, J. (19) 1955/6 Charlton Ath
Holt, D. D. (5) 1962/3 Heart of Midlothian
Holt, G. J. (10) 2000/01 Kilmarnock, Norwich C
Holton, J. (15) 1972/3 Manchester U
Hope, R. (2) 1967/8 WBA
Hopkin, D. (7) 1996/7 Crystal P, Leeds U

Houliston, W. (3) 1948/9 Queen of the South
Houston, S. (1) 1975/6 Manchester U
Howie, H. (1) 1948/9 Hibernian
Hughes, J. (8) 1964/5 Celtic
Hughes, R. D. (5) 2003/04 Portsmouth
Hughes, W. (1) 1974/5 Sunderland
Humphries, W. (1) 1951/2 Motherwell
Hunter, A. (4) 1971/2 Kilmarnock, Celtic
Hunter, W. (3) 1959/60 Motherwell
Husband, J. (1) 1946/7 Partick Th
Hutchison, D. (26) 1998/9 Everton, Sunderland, West Ham U
Hutchison, T. (17) 1973/4 Coventry C
Hutton, A. (1) 2006/07 Rangers

Imlach, S. (4) 1957/8 Nottingham F
Irvine, B. (9) 1990/1 Aberdeen

Jackson, C. (8) 1974/5 Rangers
Jackson, D. (28) 1994/5 Hibernian, Celtic
Jardine, A. (38) 1970/1 Rangers
Jarvie, A. (3) 1970/1 Airdrieonians
Jess, E. (18) 1992/3 Aberdeen, Coventry C, Aberdeen
Johnston, A. (18) 1998/9 Sunderland, Rangers, Middlesbrough
Johnston, M. (38) 1983/4 Watford, Celtic, Nantes, Rangers
Johnston, L. (2) 1947/8 Clyde
Johnston, W. (22) 1965/6 Rangers, WBA
Johnstone, D. (14) 1972/3 Rangers
Johnstone, J. (23) 1964/5 Celtic
Johnstone, R. (17) 1950/1 Hibernian, Manchester C
Jordan, J. (52) 1972/3 Leeds U, Manchester U, AC Milan

Kelly, H. (1) 1951/2 Blackpool
Kelly, J. (2) 1948/9 Barnsley
Kennedy, Jim (6) 1963/4 Celtic
Kennedy, John (1) 2003/04 Celtic
Kennedy, S. (5) 1974/5 Rangers
Kennedy, S. (8) 1977/8 Aberdeen
Kerr, A. (2) 1954/5 Partick Th
Kerr, B. (3) 2002/03 Newcastle U
Kyle, K. (9) 2001/02 Sunderland

Lambert, P. (40) 1994/5 Motherwell, Borussia Dortmund, Celtic
Law, D. (55) 1958/9 Huddersfield T, Manchester C, Torino, Manchester U, Manchester C
Lawrence, T. (3) 1962/3 Liverpool
Leggat, G. (18) 1955/6 Aberdeen, Fulham
Leighton, J. (91) 1982/3 Aberdeen, Manchester U, Hibernian, Aberdeen
Lennox, R. (10) 1966/7 Celtic
Leslie, L. (5) 1960/1 Airdrieonians
Levein, C. (16) 1989/90 Heart of Midlothian
Liddell, W. (28) 1946/7 Liverpool
Linwood, A. (1) 1949/50 Clyde
Little, R. J. (1) 1952/3 Rangers
Logie, J. (1) 1952/3 Arsenal
Long, H. (1) 1946/7 Clyde
Lorimer, P. (21) 1969/70 Leeds U

Macari, L. (24) 1971/2 Celtic, Manchester U
Macaulay, A. (7) 1946/7 Brentford, Arsenal
MacDougall, E. (7) 1974/5 Norwich C
Mackay, D. (22) 1956/7 Heart of Midlothian, Tottenham H
Mackay, G. (4) 1987/8 Heart of Midlothian
Mackay, M. (5) 2003/04 Norwich C
Maloney, S. R. (6) 2005/06 Celtic, Aston Villa
Malpas, M. (55) 1983/4 Dundee U
Marshall, D. J. (2) 2004/05 Celtic
Marshall, G. (1) 1991/2 Celtic
Martin, B. (2) 1994/5 Motherwell
Martin, F. (6) 1953/4 Aberdeen
Martin, N. (3) 1964/5 Hibernian, Sunderland
Martis, J. (1) 1960/1 Motherwell
Mason, J. (7) 1948/9 Third Lanark
Masson, D. (17) 1975/6 QPR, Derby C
Mathers, D. (1) 1953/4 Partick Th
Matteo, D. (6) 2000/01 Leeds U
McAllister, B. (3) 1996/7 Wimbledon
McAllister, G. (57) 1989/90 Leicester C, Leeds U, Coventry C
McAllister, J. R. (1) 2003/04 Livingston
McAvennie, F. (5) 1985/6 West Ham U, Celtic
McBride, J. (2) 1966/7 Celtic
McCall, S. M. (40) 1989/90 Everton, Rangers
McCalliog, J. (5) 1966/7 Sheffield W, Wolverhampton W
McCann, N. D. (26) 1998/9 Heart of Midlothian, Rangers, Southampton
McCann, R. (5) 1958/9 Motherwell
McClair, B. (30) 1986/7 Celtic, Manchester U
McCloy, P. (4) 1972/3 Rangers

McCoist, A. (61) 1985/6 Rangers, Kilmarnock
McColl, I. (14) 1949/50 Rangers
McCreadie, E. (23) 1964/5 Chelsea
McCulloch, L. (11) 2004/05 Wigan Ath
MacDonald, A. (1) 1975/6 Rangers
McDonald, J. (2) 1955/6 Sunderland
McFadden, J. (31) 2001/02 Motherwell, Everton
McFarlane, W. (1) 1946/7 Heart of Midlothian
McGarr, E. (2) 1969/70 Aberdeen
McGarvey, F. (7) 1978/9 Liverpool, Celtic
McGhee, M. (4) 1982/3 Aberdeen
McGinlay, J. (13) 1993/4 Bolton W
McGrain, D. (62) 1972/3 Celtic
McGregor, A. (1) 2006/07 Rangers
McGrory, J. (3) 1964/5 Kilmarnock
McInally, A. (8) 1988/9 Aston Villa, Bayern Munich
McInally, J. (10) 1986/7 Dundee U
McInnes, D. (2) 2002/03 WBA
MacKay, D. (14) 1958/9 Celtic
McKean, R. (1) 1975/6 Rangers
MacKenzie, J. (9) 1953/4 Partick Th
McKimmie, S. (40) 1988/9 Aberdeen
McKinlay, T. (22) 1995/6 Celtic
McKinlay, W. (29) 1993/4 Dundee U, Blackburn R
McKinnon, Rob (3) 1993/4 Motherwell
McKinnon, Ronnie (28) 1965/6 Rangers
McLaren, Alan (24) 1991/2 Heart of Midlothian, Rangers
McLaren, Andy (4) 1946/7 Preston NE
McLaren, Andy (1) 2000/01 Kilmarnock
McLean, G. (1) 1967/8 Dundee
McLean, T. (6) 1968/9 Kilmarnock
McLeish, A. (77) 1979/80 Aberdeen
McLeod, J. (4) 1960/1 Hibernian
MacLeod, M. (20) 1984/5 Celtic, Borussia Dortmund, Hibernian
McLintock, F. (9) 1962/3 Leicester C, Arsenal
McManus, S. (5) 2006/07 Celtic
McMillan, I. (6) 1951/2 Airdrieonians, Rangers
McNamara, J. (33) 1996/7 Celtic, Wolverhampton W
McNamee, D. (4) 2003/04 Livingston
McNaught, W. (5) 1950/1 Raith R
McNaughton, K. (3) 2001/02 Aberdeen
McNeill, W. (29) 1960/1 Celtic
McPhail, J. (5) 1949/50 Celtic
McPherson, D. (27) 1988/9 Heart of Midlothian, Rangers
McQueen, G. (30) 1973/4 Leeds U, Manchester U
McStay, P. (76) 1983/4 Celtic
McSwegan, G. (2) 1999/00 Heart of Midlothian
Millar, J. (2) 1962/3 Rangers
Miller, C. (1) 2000/01 Dundee U
Miller, K. (31) 2000/01 Rangers, Wolverhampton W, Celtic
Miller, L. (1) 2005/06 Dundee U
Miller, W. (6) 1946/7 Celtic
Miller, W. (65) 1974/5 Aberdeen
Mitchell, R. (2) 1950/1 Newcastle U
Mochan, N. (3) 1953/4 Celtic
Moir, W. (1) 1949/50 Bolton W
Moncur, R. (16) 1967/8 Newcastle U
Morgan, W. (21) 1967/8 Burnley, Manchester U
Morris, H. (1) 1949/50 East Fife
Mudie, J. (17) 1956/7 Blackpool
Mulhall, G. (3) 1959/60 Aberdeen, Sunderland
Munro, F. (9) 1970/1 Wolverhampton W
Munro, I. (7) 1978/9 St Mirren
Murdoch, R. (12) 1965/6 Celtic
Murray, I. (6) 2002/03 Hibernian, Rangers
Murray, J. (5) 1957/8 Heart of Midlothian
Murray, S. (1) 1971/2 Aberdeen
Murty, G. S. (3) 2003/04 Reading

Naismith, S. J. (1) 2006/07 Kilmarnock
Narey, D. (35) 1976/7 Dundee U
Naysmith, G. A. (36) 1999/00 Heart of Midlothian, Everton
Neilson, R. (1) 2006/07 Heart of Midlothian
Nevin, P. K. F. (28) 1985/6 Chelsea, Everton, Tranmere R
Nicholas, C. (20) 1982/3 Celtic, Arsenal, Aberdeen
Nicholson, B. (3) 2000/01 Dunfermline Ath
Nicol, S. (27) 1984/5 Liverpool

O'Connor, G. (11) 2001/02 Hibernian, Lokomotiv Moscow
O'Donnell, P. (1) 1993/4 Motherwell
O'Hare, J. (13) 1969/70 Derby Co
O'Neil, B. (7) 1995/6 Celtic, Wolfsburg, Derby Co, Preston NE
O'Neil, J. (1) 2000/01 Hibernian
Ormond, W. (6) 1953/4 Hibernian
Orr, T. (2) 1951/2 Morton

Parker, A. (15) 1954/5 Falkirk, Everton
Parlane, D. (12) 1972/3 Rangers
Paton, A. (2) 1951/2 Motherwell
Pearson, S. P. (6) 2003/04 Motherwell, Celtic
Pearson, T. (2) 1946/7 Newcastle U
Penman, A. (1) 1965/6 Dundee
Pettigrew, W. (5) 1975/6 Motherwell
Plenderleith, J. (1) 1960/1 Manchester C
Pressley, S. J. (32) 1999/00 Heart of Midlothian
Provan, David (10) 1979/80 Celtic
Provan, Davie (5) 1963/4 Rangers

Quashie, N. F. (14) 2003/04 Portsmouth, Southampton, WBA
Quinn, P. (4) 1960/1 Motherwell

Rae, G. (11) 2000/01 Dundee, Rangers
Redpath, W. (9) 1948/9 Motherwell
Reilly, L. (38) 1948/9 Hibernian
Ring, T. (12) 1952/3 Clyde
Rioch, B. (24) 1974/5 Derby Co, Everton, Derby Co
Riordan, D. G. (1) 2005/06 Hibernian
Ritchie, P. S. (7) 1998/9 Heart of Midlothian, Bolton W, Walsall
Ritchie, W. (1) 1961/2 Rangers
Robb, D. (5) 1970/1 Aberdeen
Robertson, A. (5) 1954/5 Clyde
Robertson, D. (3) 1991/2 Rangers
Robertson, H. (1) 1961/2 Dundee
Robertson, J. (16) 1990/1 Heart of Midlothian
Robertson, J. G. (1) 1964/5 Tottenham H
Robertson, J. N. (28) 1977/8 Nottingham F, Derby Co
Robinson, B. (4) 1973/4 Dundee
Ross, M. (13) 2001/02 Rangers
Rough, A. (53) 1975/6 Partick Th, Hibernian
Rougvie, D. (1) 1983/4 Aberdeen
Rutherford, E. (1) 1947/8 Rangers

St John, I. (21) 1958/9 Motherwell, Liverpool
Schaedler, E. (1) 1973/4 Hibernian
Scott, A. (16) 1956/7 Rangers, Everton
Scott, Jimmy (1) 1965/6 Hibernian
Scott, Jocky (2) 1970/1 Dundee
Scoular, J. (9) 1950/1 Portsmouth
Severin, S. D. (15) 2001/02 Heart of Midlothian, Aberdeen
Sharp, G. M. (12) 1984/5 Everton
Shaw, D. (8) 1946/7 Hibernian
Shaw, J. (4) 1946/7 Rangers
Shearer, D. (7) 1993/4 Aberdeen
Shearer, R. (4) 1960/1 Rangers
Simpson, N. (4) 1982/3 Aberdeen
Simpson, R. (5) 1966/7 Celtic
Sinclair, J. (1) 1965/6 Leicester C
Smith, D. (2) 1965/6 Aberdeen, Rangers
Smith, E. (2) 1958/9 Celtic
Smith, G. (18) 1946/7 Hibernian
Smith, H. G. (3) 1987/8 Heart of Midlothian
Smith, J. (4) 1967/8 Aberdeen, Newcastle U
Smith, J. (2) 2002/03 Celtic
Souness, G. (54) 1974/5 Middlesbrough, Liverpool, Sampdoria
Speedie, D. R. (10) 1984/5 Chelsea, Coventry C
Spencer, J. (14) 1994/5 Chelsea, QPR
Stanton, P. (16) 1965/6 Hibernian
Steel, W. (30) 1946/7 Morton, Derby C, Dundee
Stein, C. (21) 1968/9 Rangers, Coventry C
Stephen, J. (2) 1946/7 Bradford PA
Stewart, D. (1) 1977/8 Leeds U
Stewart, J. (2) 1976/7 Kilmarnock, Middlesbrough
Stewart, M. J. (3) 2001/02 Manchester U
Stewart, R. (10) 1980/1 West Ham U
Stockdale, R. K. (5) 2001/02 Middlesbrough
Strachan, G. (50) 1979/80 Aberdeen, Manchester U, Leeds U
Sturrock, P. (20) 1980/1 Dundee U
Sullivan, N. (28) 1996/7 Wimbledon, Tottenham H

Teale, G. (8) 2005/06 Wigan Ath
Telfer, P. N. (1) 1999/00 Coventry C
Telfer, W. (1) 1953/4 St Mirren
Thompson, S. (16) 2001/02 Dundee U, Rangers
Thomson, W. (7) 1979/80 St Mirren
Thornton, W. (7) 1946/7 Rangers
Toner, W. (2) 1958/9 Kilmarnock
Turnbull, E. (8) 1947/8 Hibernian

Ure, I. (11) 1961/2 Dundee, Arsenal

Waddell, W. (17) 1946/7 Rangers
Walker, A. (3) 1987/8 Celtic
Walker, J. N. (2) 1992/3 Heart of Midlothian, Partick Th
Wallace, I. A. (3) 1977/8 Coventry C

Wallace, W. S. B. (7) 1964/5 Heart of Midlothian, Celtic
Wardhaugh, J. (2) 1954/5 Heart of Midlothian
Wark, J. (29) 1978/9 Ipswich T, Liverpool
Watson, J. (2) 1947/8 Motherwell, Huddersfield T
Watson, R. (1) 1970/1 Motherwell
Webster, A. (22) 2002/03 Heart of Midlothian
Weir, A. (6) 1958/9 Motherwell
Weir, D. G. (56) 1996/7 Heart of Midlothian, Everton, Rangers
Weir, P. (6) 1979/80 St Mirren, Aberdeen
White, J. (22) 1958/9 Falkirk, Tottenham H
Whyte, D. (12) 1987/8 Celtic, Middlesbrough, Aberdeen
Wilkie, L. (11) 2001/02 Dundee
Williams, G. (5) 2001/02 Nottingham F
Wilson, A. (1) 1953/4 Portsmouth
Wilson, D. (22) 1960/1 Rangers
Wilson, I. A. (5) 1986/7 Leicester C, Everton
Wilson, P. (1) 1974/5 Celtic
Wilson, R. (2) 1971/2 Arsenal
Winters, R. (1) 1998/9 Aberdeen
Wood, G. (4) 1978/9 Everton, Arsenal
Woodburn, W. (24) 1946/7 Rangers
Wright, K. (1) 1991/2 Hibernian
Wright, S. (2) 1992/3 Aberdeen
Wright, T. (3) 1952/3 Sunderland

Yeats, R. (2) 1964/5 Liverpool
Yorston, H. (1) 1954/5 Aberdeen
Young, A. (8) 1959/60 Heart of Midlothian, Everton
Young, G. (53) 1946/7 Rangers
Younger, T. (24) 1954/5 Hibernian, Liverpool

WALES

Aizlewood, M. (39) 1985/6 Charlton Ath, Leeds U, Bradford C, Bristol C, Cardiff C
Allchurch, I. (68) 1950/1 Swansea T, Newcastle U, Cardiff C, Swansea T
Allchurch, L. (11) 1954/5 Swansea T, Sheffield U
Allen, B. (2) 1950/1 Coventry C
Allen, M. (14) 1985/6 Watford, Norwich C, Millwall, Newcastle U

Baker, C. (7) 1957/8 Cardiff C
Baker, W. (1) 1947/8 Cardiff C
Bale, G. (6) 2005/06 Southampton
Barnard, D. S. (22) 1997/8 Barnsley, Grimsby T
Barnes, W. (22) 1947/8 Arsenal
Bellamy, C. D. (46) 1997/8 Norwich C, Coventry C, Newcastle U, Blackburn R, Liverpool
Berry, G. (5) 1978/9 Wolverhampton W, Stoke C
Blackmore, C. G. (39) 1984/5 Manchester U, Middlesbrough
Blake, N. (29) 1993/4 Sheffield U, Bolton W, Blackburn R, Wolverhampton W
Bodin, P. J. (23) 1989/90 Swindon T, Crystal P, Swindon T
Bowen, D. (19) 1954/5 Arsenal
Bowen, J. P. (2) 1993/4 Swansea C, Birmingham C
Bowen, M. R. (41) 1985/6 Tottenham H, Norwich C, West Ham U
Boyle, T. (2) 1980/1 Crystal P
Brown, J. R. (2) 2005/06 Gillingham, Blackburn R
Browning, M. T. (5) 1995/6 Bristol R, Huddersfield T
Burgess, R. (32) 1946/7 Tottenham H
Burton, O. (9) 1962/3 Norwich C, Newcastle U

Cartwright, L. (7) 1973/4 Coventry C, Wrexham
Charles, J. (38) 1949/50 Leeds U, Juventus, Leeds U, Cardiff C
Charles, J. M. (19) 1980/1 Swansea C, QPR, Oxford U
Charles, M. (31) 1954/5 Swansea T, Arsenal, Cardiff C
Clarke, R. (22) 1948/9 Manchester C
Coleman, C. (32) 1991/2 Crystal P, Blackburn R, Fulham
Collins, D. L. (6) 2004/05 Sunderland
Collins, J. M. (19) 2003/04 Cardiff C, West Ham U
Cornforth, J. M. (2) 1994/5 Swansea C
Cotterill, D. R. G. B. (8) 2005/06 Bristol C, Wigan Ath
Coyne, D. (15) 1995/6 Tranmere R, Grimsby T, Leicester C, Burnley
Crofts, A. L. (6) 2005/06 Gillingham
Crossley, M. G. (8) 1996/7 Nottingham F, Middlesbrough, Fulham

Crowe, V. (16) 1958/9 Aston Villa
Curtis, A. (35) 1975/6 Swansea C, Leeds U, Swansea C, Southampton, Cardiff C

Daniel, R. (21) 1950/1 Arsenal, Sunderland
Davies, A. (13) 1982/3 Manchester U, Newcastle U, Swansea C, Bradford C
Davies. A. R. (1) 2005/06 Yeovil T
Davies, C. (1) 1971/2 Charlton Ath
Davies, C. M. (4) 2005/06 Oxford U, Verona
Davies, D. (52) 1974/5 Everton, Wrexham, Swansea C
Davies, G. (16) 1979/80 Fulham, Manchester C
Davies, R. Wyn (34) 1963/4 Bolton W, Newcastle U, Manchester C, Manchester U, Blackpool
Davies, Reg (6) 1952/3 Newcastle U
Davies, Ron (29) 1963/4 Norwich C, Southampton, Portsmouth
Davies, S. (41) 2000/01 Tottenham H, Everton, Fulham
Davies, S. I. (1) 1995/6 Manchester U
Davis, G. (3) 1977/8 Wrexham
Deacy, N. (12) 1976/7 PSV Eindhoven, Beringen
Delaney, M. A. (36) 1999/00 Aston Villa
Derrett, S. (4) 1968/9 Cardiff C
Dibble, A. (3) 1985/6 Luton T, Manchester C
Duffy, R. M. (12) 2005/06 Portsmouth
Durban, A. (27) 1965/6 Derby C
Dwyer, P. (10) 1977/8 Cardiff C

Earnshaw, R. (34) 2001/02 Cardiff C, WBA, Norwich C
Easter, J. M. (3) 2006/07 Wycombe W
Edwards, C. N. H. (1) 1995/6 Swansea C
Edwards, G. (12) 1946/7 Birmingham C, Cardiff C
Edwards, I. (4) 1977/8 Chester, Wrexham
Edwards, R. O. (15) 2002/03 Aston Villa, Wolverhampton W
Edwards, R. W. (4) 1997/8 Bristol C
Edwards, T. (2) 1956/7 Charlton Ath
Emanuel, J. (2) 1972/3 Bristol C
England, M. (44) 1961/2 Blackburn R, Tottenham H
Evans, B. (7) 1971/2 Swansea C, Hereford U
Evans, I. (13) 1975/6 Crystal P
Evans, P. S. (2) 2001/02 Brentford, Bradford C
Evans, R. (1) 1963/4 Swansea T
Evans, S. J. (5) 2006/07 Wrexham

Felgate, D. (1) 1983/4 Lincoln C
Fletcher, C. N. (22) 2003/04 Bournemouth, West Ham U, Crystal P
Flynn, B. (66) 1974/5 Burnley, Leeds U, Burnley
Ford, T. (38) 1946/7 Swansea T, Aston Villa, Sunderland, Cardiff C
Foulkes, W. (11) 1951/2 Newcastle U
Freestone, R. (1) 1999/00 Swansea C

Gabbidon, D. L. (33) 2001/02 Cardiff C, West Ham U
Garner, G. (1) 2005/06 Leyton Orient
Giggs, R. J. (64) 1991/2 Manchester U
Giles, D. (12) 1979/80 Swansea C, Crystal P
Godfrey, B. (3) 1963/4 Preston NE
Goss, J. (9) 1990/1 Norwich C
Green, C. (15) 1964/5 Birmingham C
Green, R. M. (2) 1997/8 Wolverhampton W
Griffiths, A. (17) 1970/1 Wrexham
Griffiths, H. (1) 1952/3 Swansea T
Griffiths, M. (11) 1946/7 Leicester C
Gunter, C. R. (1) 2006/07 Cardiff C

Hall, G. D. (9) 1987/8 Chelsea
Harrington, A. (11) 1955/6 Cardiff C
Harris, C. (24) 1975/6 Leeds U
Harris, W. (6) 1953/4 Middlesbrough
Hartson, J. (51) 1994/5 Arsenal, West Ham U, Wimbledon, Coventry C, Celtic
Haworth, S. O. (5) 1996/7 Cardiff C, Coventry C
Hennessey, T. (39) 1961/2 Birmingham C, Nottingham F, Derby Co
Hennessey, W. R. (2) 2006/07 Wolverhampton W
Hewitt, R. (5) 1957/8 Cardiff C
Hill, M. (2) 1971/2 Ipswich T
Hockey, T. (9) 1971/2 Sheffield U, Norwich C, Aston Villa
Hodges, G. (18) 1983/4 Wimbledon, Newcastle U, Watford, Sheffield U
Holden, A. (1) 1983/4 Chester C
Hole, B. (30) 1962/3 Cardiff C, Blackburn R, Aston Villa, Swansea C
Hollins, D. (11) 1961/2 Newcastle U
Hopkins, J. (16) 1982/3 Fulham, Crystal P

Hopkins, M. (34) 1955/6 Tottenham H
Horne, B. (59) 1987/8 Portsmouth, Southampton, Everton, Birmingham C
Howells, R. (2) 1953/4 Cardiff C
Hughes, C. M. (8) 1991/2 Luton T, Wimbledon
Hughes, I. (4) 1950/1 Luton T
Hughes, L. M. (72) 1983/4 Manchester U, Barcelona, Manchester U, Chelsea, Southampton
Hughes, W. (3) 1946/7 Birmingham C
Hughes, W. A. (5) 1948/9 Blackburn R
Humphreys, J. (1) 1946/7 Everton

Jackett, K. (31) 1982/3 Watford
James, G. (9) 1965/6 Blackpool
James, L. (54) 1971/2 Burnley, Derby C, QPR, Burnley, Swansea C, Sunderland
James, R. M. (47) 1978/9 Swansea C, Stoke C, QPR, Leicester C, Swansea C
Jarvis, A. (3) 1966/7 Hull C
Jenkins, S. R. (16) 1995/6 Swansea C, Huddersfield T
Johnson, A. J. (15) 1998/9 Nottingham F, WBA
Johnson, M. (1) 1963/4 Swansea T
Jones, A. (6) 1986/7 Port Vale, Charlton Ath
Jones, Barrie (15) 1962/3 Swansea T, Plymouth Argyle, Cardiff C
Jones, Bryn (4) 1946/7 Arsenal
Jones, C. (59) 1953/4 Swansea T, Tottenham H, Fulham
Jones, D. (8) 1975/6 Norwich C
Jones, E. (4) 1947/8 Swansea T, Tottenham H
Jones, J. (72) 1975/6 Liverpool, Wrexham, Chelsea, Huddersfield T
Jones, K. (1) 1949/50 Aston Villa
Jones, M. A. (1) 2006/07 Wrexham
Jones, M. G. (13) 1999/00 Leeds U, Leicester C
Jones, P. L. (2) 1996/7 Liverpool, Tranmere R
Jones, P. S. (50) 1996/7 Stockport Co, Southampton, Wolverhampton W, QPR
Jones, R. (1) 1993/4 Sheffield W
Jones, T. G. (13) 1946/7 Everton
Jones, V. P. (9) 1994/5 Wimbledon
Jones, W. (1) 1970/1 Bristol R

Kelsey, J. (41) 1953/4 Arsenal
King, J. (1) 1954/5 Swansea T
Kinsey, N. (7) 1950/1 Norwich C, Birmingham C
Knill, A. R. (1) 1988/9 Swansea C
Koumas, J. (23) 2000/01 Tranmere R, WBA
Krzywicki, R. (8) 1969/70 WBA, Huddersfield T

Lambert, R. (5) 1946/7 Liverpool
Law, B. J. (1) 1989/90 QPR
Lea, C. (2) 1964/5 Ipswich T
Ledley, J. C. (12) 2005/06 Cardiff C
Leek, K. (13) 1960/1 Leicester C, Newcastle U, Birmingham C, Northampton T
Legg, A. (6) 1995/6 Birmingham C, Cardiff C
Lever, A. (1) 1952/3 Leicester C
Lewis, D. (1) 1982/3 Swansea C
Llewellyn, C. M. (6) 1997/8 Norwich C, Wrexham
Lloyd, B. (3) 1975/6 Wrexham
Lovell, S. (6) 1981/2 Crystal P, Millwall
Lowndes, S. (10) 1982/3 Newport Co, Millwall, Barnsley
Lowrie, G. (4) 1947/8 Coventry C, Newcastle U
Lucas, M. (4) 1961/2 Leyton Orient
Lucas, W. (7) 1948/9 Swansea T

Maguire, G. T. (7) 1989/90 Portsmouth
Mahoney, J. (51) 1967/8 Stoke C, Middlesbrough, Swansea C
Mardon, P. J. (1) 1995/6 WBA
Margetson, M. W. (1) 2003/04 Cardiff C
Marriott, A. (5) 1995/6 Wrexham
Marustik, C. (6) 1981/2 Swansea C
Medwin, T. (30) 1952/3 Swansea T, Tottenham H
Melville, A. K. (65) 1989/90 Swansea C, Oxford U, Sunderland, Fulham, West Ham U
Mielczarek, R. (1) 1970/1 Rotherham U
Millington, A. (21) 1962/3 WBA, Crystal P, Peterborough U, Swansea C
Moore, G. (21) 1959/60 Cardiff C, Chelsea, Manchester U, Northampton T, Charlton Ath
Morgan, C. (1) 2006/07 Milton Keynes D
Morris, W. (5) 1946/7 Burnley

Nardiello, D. (2) 1977/8 Coventry C
Nardiello, D. A. (1) 2006/07 Barnsley

Neilson, A. B. (5) 1991/2 Newcastle U, Southampton
Nicholas, P. (73) 1978/9 Crystal P, Arsenal, Crystal P, Luton T, Aberdeen, Chelsea, Watford
Niedzwiecki, E. A. (2) 1984/5 Chelsea
Nogan, L. M. (2) 1991/2 Watford, Reading
Norman, A. J. (5) 1985/6 Hull C
Nurse, M. T. G. (12) 1959/60 Swansea T, Middlesbrough
Nyatanga, L. J. (12) 2005/06 Derby Co

O'Sullivan, P. (3) 1972/3 Brighton & HA
Oster, J. M. (13) 1997/8 Everton, Sunderland

Page, M. (28) 1970/1 Birmingham C
Page, R. J. (41) 1996/7 Watford, Sheffield U, Cardiff C, Coventry C
Palmer, D. (3) 1956/7 Swansea T
Parry, J. (1) 1950/1 Swansea T
Parry, P. I. (11) 2003/04 Cardiff C
Partridge, D. W. (7) 2004/05 Motherwell, Bristol C
Pascoe, C. (10) 1983/4 Swansea C, Sunderland
Paul, R. (33) 1948/9 Swansea T, Manchester C
Pembridge, M. A. (54) 1991/2 Luton T, Derby C, Sheffield W, Benfica, Everton, Fulham
Perry, J. (1) 1993/4 Cardiff C
Phillips, D. (62) 1983/4 Plymouth Argyle, Manchester C, Coventry C, Norwich C, Nottingham F
Phillips, J. (4) 1972/3 Chelsea
Phillips, L. (58) 1970/1 Cardff C, Aston Villa, Swansea C, Charlton Ath
Pipe, D. R. (1) 2002/03 Coventry C
Pontin, K. (2) 1979/80 Cardiff C
Powell, A. (8) 1946/7 Leeds U, Everton, Birmingham C
Powell, D. (11) 1967/8 Wrexham, Sheffield U
Powell, I. (8) 1946/7 QPR, Aston Villa
Price, L. P. (3) 2005/06 Ipswich T
Price, P. (25) 1979/80 Luton T, Tottenham H
Pring, K. (3) 1965/6 Rotherham U
Pritchard, H. K. (1) 1984/5 Bristol C

Rankmore, F. (1) 1965/6 Peterborough U
Ratcliffe, K. (59) 1980/1 Everton, Cardiff C
Ready, K. (5) 1996/7 QPR
Reece, G. (29) 1965/6 Sheffield U, Cardiff C
Reed, W. (2) 1954/5 Ipswich T
Rees, A. (1) 1983/4 Birmingham C
Rees, J. M. (1) 1991/2 Luton T
Rees, R. (39) 1964/5 Coventry C, WBA, Nottingham F
Rees, W. (4) 1948/9 Cardiff C, Tottenham H
Richards, S. (1) 1946/7 Cardiff C
Ricketts, S. (19) 2004/05 Swansea C, Hull C
Roberts, A. M. (2) 1992/3 QPR
Roberts, D. (17) 1972/3 Oxford U, Hull C
Roberts, G. W. (9) 1999/00 Tranmere R
Roberts, I. W. (15) 1989/90 Watford, Huddersfield T, Leicester C, Norwich C
Roberts, J. G. (22) 1970/1 Arsenal, Birmingham C
Roberts, J. H. (1) 1948/9 Bolton W
Roberts, N. W. (4) 1999/00 Wrexham, Wigan Ath
Roberts, P. (4) 1973/4 Portsmouth
Roberts, S. W. (1) 2004/05 Wrexham
Robinson, C. P. (39) 1999/00 Wolverhampton W, Portsmouth, Sunderland, Norwich C, Toronto Lynx
Robinson, J. R. C. (30) 1995/6 Charlton Ath
Rodrigues, P. (40) 1964/5 Cardiff C, Leicester C, Sheffield W
Rouse, V. (1) 1958/9 Crystal P
Rowley, T. (1) 1958/9 Tranmere R
Rush, I. (73) 1979/80 Liverpool, Juventus, Liverpool

Saunders, D. (75) 1985/6 Brighton & HA, Oxford U, Derby C, Liverpool, Aston Villa, Galatasaray, Nottingham F, Sheffield U, Benfica, Bradford C
Savage, R. W. (39) 1995/6 Crewe Alexandra, Leicester C, Birmingham C
Sayer, P. (7) 1976/7 Cardiff C
Scrine, F. (2) 1949/50 Swansea T
Sear, C. (1) 1962/3 Manchester C
Sherwood, A. (41) 1946/7 Cardiff C, Newport C
Shortt, W. (12) 1946/7 Plymouth Argyle
Showers, D. (2) 1974/5 Cardiff C
Sidlow, C. (7) 1946/7 Liverpool

Slatter, N. (22) 1982/3 Bristol R, Oxford U
Smallman, D. (7) 1973/4 Wrexham, Everton
Southall, N. (92) 1981/2 Everton
Speed, G. A. (85) 1989/90 Leeds U, Everton, Newcastle U, Bolton W
Sprake, G. (37) 1963/4 Leeds U, Birmingham C
Stansfield, F. (1) 1948/9 Cardiff C
Stevenson, B. (15) 1977/8 Leeds U, Birmingham C
Stevenson, N. (4) 1981/2 Swansea C
Stitfall, R. (2) 1952/3 Cardiff C
Sullivan, D. (17) 1952/3 Cardiff C
Symons, C. J. (37) 1991/2 Portsmouth, Manchester C, Fulham, Crystal P

Tapscott, D. (14) 1953/4 Arsenal, Cardiff C
Taylor, G. K. (15) 1995/6 Crystal P, Sheffield U, Burnley, Nottingham F
Thatcher, B. D. (7) 2003/04 Leicester C, Manchester C
Thomas, D. (2) 1956/7 Swansea T
Thomas, M. (51) 1976/7 Wrexham, Manchester U, Everton, Brighton & HA, Stoke C, Chelsea, WBA
Thomas, M. R. (1) 1986/7 Newcastle U
Thomas, R. (50) 1966/7 Swindon T, Derby C, Cardiff C
Thomas, S. (4) 1947/8 Fulham
Toshack, J. (40) 1968/9 Cardiff C, Liverpool, Swansea C
Trollope, P. J. (9) 1996/7 Derby Co, Fulham, Coventry C, Northampton T

Van Den Hauwe, P. W. R. (13) 1984/5 Everton
Vaughan, D. O. (10) 2002/03 Crewe Alex
Vaughan, N. (10) 1982/3 Newport Co, Cardiff C
Vearncombe, G. (2) 1957/8 Cardiff C
Vernon, R. (32) 1956/7 Blackburn R, Everton, Stoke C
Villars, A. (3) 1973/4 Cardiff C

Walley, T. (1) 1970/1 Watford
Walsh, I. (18) 1979/80 Crystal P, Swansea C
Ward, D. (2) 1958/9 Bristol R, Cardiff C
Ward, D. (5) 1999/00 Notts Co, Nottingham F
Webster, C. (4) 1956/7 Manchester U
Weston, R. D. (7) 1999/00 Arsenal, Cardiff C
Williams, A. (13) 1993/4 Reading, Wolverhampton W, Reading
Williams, A. P. (2) 1997/8 Southampton
Williams, D. G. 1987/8 13, Derby Co, Ipswich T
Williams, D. M. (5) 1985/6 Norwich C
Williams, G. (1) 1950/1 Cardiff C
Williams, G. E. (26) 1959/60 WBA
Williams, G. G. (5) 1960/1 Swansea T
Williams, G. J. (2) 2005/06 West Ham U, Ipswich T
Williams, H. (4) 1948/9 Newport Co, Leeds U
Williams, Herbert (3) 1964/5 Swansea T
Williams, S. (43) 1953/4 WBA, Southampton
Witcomb, D. (3) 1946/7 WBA, Sheffield W
Woosnam, P. (17) 1958/9 Leyton Orient, West Ham U, Aston Villa

Yorath, T. (59) 1969/70 Leeds U, Coventry C, Tottenham H, Vancouver Whitecaps
Young, E. (21) 1989/90 Wimbledon, Crystal P, Wolverhampton W

REPUBLIC OF IRELAND

Aherne, T. (16) 1945/6 Belfast Celtic, Luton T
Aldridge, J. W. (69) 1985/6 Oxford U, Liverpool, Real Sociedad, Tranmere R
Ambrose, P. (5) 1954/5 Shamrock R
Anderson, J. (16) 1979/80 Preston NE, Newcastle U

Babb, P. (35) 1993/4 Coventry C, Liverpool, Sunderland
Bailham, E. (1) 1963/4 Shamrock R
Barber, E. (2) 1965/6 Shelbourne, Birmingham C
Barrett, G. (6) 2002/03 Arsenal, Coventry C
Beglin, J. (15) 1983/4 Liverpool
Bennett, A. J. (2) 2006/07 Reading
Bonner, P. (80) 1980/1 Celtic
Braddish, S. (1) 1977/8 Dundalk
Brady, T. R. (6) 1963/4 QPR

Brady, W. L. (72) 1974/5 Arsenal, Juventus, Sampdoria, Internazionale, Ascoli, West Ham U
Branagan, K. G. (1) 1996/7 Bolton W
Breen, G. (63) 1995/6 Birmingham C, Coventry C, West Ham U, Sunderland
Breen, T. (3) 1946/7 Shamrock R
Brennan, F. (1) 1964/5 Drumcondra
Brennan, S. A. (19) 1964/5 Manchester U, Waterford
Browne, W. (3) 1963/4 Bohemians
Bruce, A. (1) 2006/07 Ipswich T
Buckley, L. (2) 1983/4 Shamrock R, Waregem
Burke, F. (1) 1951/2 Cork Ath
Butler, P. J. (1) 1999/00 Sunderland
Butler, T. (2) 2002/03 Sunderland
Byrne, A. B. (14) 1969/70 Southampton
Byrne, J. (23) 1984/5 QPR, Le Havre, Brighton & HA, Sunderland, Millwall
Byrne, J. (2) 2003/04 Shelbourne
Byrne, P. (8) 1983/4 Shamrock R

Campbell, A. (3) 1984/5 Santander
Campbell, N. (11) 1970/1 St Patrick's Ath, Fortuna Cologne
Cantwell, N. (36) 1953/4 West Ham U, Manchester U
Carey, B. P. (3) 1991/2 Manchester U, Leicester C
Carey, J. J. (21) 1945/6 Manchester U
Carolan, J. (2) 1959/60 Manchester U
Carr, S. (43) 1998/9 Tottenham H, Newcastle U
Carroll, B. (2) 1948/9 Shelbourne
Carroll, T. R. (17) 1967/8 Ipswich T, Birmingham C
Carsley, L. K. (34) 1997/8 Derby Co, Blackburn R, Coventry C, Everton
Cascarino, A. G. (88) 1985/6 Gillingham, Millwall, Aston Villa, Celtic, Chelsea, Marseille, Nancy
Chandler, J. (2) 1979/80 Leeds U
Clarke, C. R. (2) 2003/04 Stoke C
Clarke, J. (1) 1977/8 Drogheda U
Clarke, K. (2) 1947/8 Drumcondra
Clarke, M. (1) 1949/50 Shamrock R
Clinton, T. J. (3) 1950/1 Everton
Coad, P. (11) 1946/7 Shamrock R
Coffey, T. (1) 1949/50 Drumcondra
Colfer, M. D. (2) 1949/50 Shelbourne
Colgan, N. (9) 2001/02 Hibernian, Barnsley
Conmy, O. M. (5) 1964/5 Peterborough U
Connolly, D. J. (41) 1995/6 Watford, Feyenoord, Wolverhampton W, Excelsior, Wimbledon, West Ham U, Wigan Ath
Conroy, G. A. (27) 1969/70 Stoke C
Conway, J. P. (20) 1966/7 Fulham, Manchester C
Corr, P. J. (4) 1948/9 Everton
Courtney, E. (1) 1945/6 Cork U
Coyle, O. (1) 1993/4 Bolton W
Coyne, T. (22) 1991/2 Celtic, Tranmere R, Motherwell
Crowe, G. (2) 2002/03 Bohemians
Cummins, G. P. (19) 1953/4 Luton T
Cuneen, T. (1) 1950/1 Limerick
Cunningham, K. (72) 1995/6 Wimbledon, Birmingham C
Curtis, D. P. (17) 1956/7 Shelbourne, Bristol C, Ipswich T, Exeter C
Cusack, S. (1) 1952/3 Limerick

Daish, L. S. (5) 1991/2 Cambridge U, Coventry C
Daly, G. A. (48) 1972/3 Manchester U, Derby C, Coventry C, Birmingham C, Shrewsbury T
Daly, M. (2) 1977/8 Wolverhampton W
Daly, P. (1) 1949/50 Shamrock R
Deacy, E. (4) 1981/2 Aston Villa
Delap, R. J. (11) 1997/8 Derby Co, Southampton
De Mange, K. J. P. P. (2) 1986/7 Liverpool, Hull C
Dempsey, J. T. (19) 1966/7 Fulham, Chelsea
Dennehy, J. (11) 1971/2 Cork Hibernian, Nottingham F, Walsall
Desmond, P. (4) 1949/50 Middlesbrough
Devine, J. (13) 1979/80 Arsenal, Norwich C
Doherty, G. M. T. (34) 1999/00 Luton T, Tottenham H, Norwich C
Donovan, D. C. (5) 1954/5 Everton
Donovan, T. (1) 1979/80 Aston Villa
Douglas, J. (7) 2003/04 Blackburn R, Leeds U
Doyle, C. (1) 1958/9 Shelbourne
Doyle, Colin (1) 2006/07 Birmingham C
Doyle, K. E. (9) 2005/06 Reading
Doyle, M. P. (1) 2003/04 Coventry C
Duff, D. A. (66) 1997/8 Blackburn R, Chelsea, Newcastle U
Duffy, B. (1) 1949/50 Shamrock R
Dunne, A. P. (33) 1961/2 Manchester U, Bolton W
Dunne, J. C. (1) 1970/1 Fulham

Dunne, P. A. J. (5) 1964/5 Manchester U
Dunne, R. P. (35) 1999/00 Everton, Manchester C
Dunne, S. (15) 1952/3 Luton T
Dunne, T. (3) 1955/6 St Patrick's Ath
Dunning, P. (2) 1970/1 Shelbourne
Dunphy, E. M. (23) 1965/6 York C, Millwall
Dwyer, N. M. (14) 1959/60 West Ham U, Swansea T

Eccles, P. (1) 1985/6 Shamrock R
Eglington, T. J. (24) 1945/6 Shamrock R, Everton
Elliott, S. W. (9) 2004/05 Sunderland
Evans, M. J. (1) 1997/8 Southampton

Fagan, E. (1) 1972/3 Shamrock R
Fagan, F. (8) 1954/5 Manchester C, Derby C
Fairclough, M. (2) 1981/2 Dundalk
Fallon, S. (8) 1950/1 Celtic
Farrell, P. D. (28) 1945/6 Shamrock R, Everton
Farrelly, G. (6) 1995/6 Aston Villa, Everton, Bolton W
Finnan, S. (46) 1999/00 Fulham, Liverpool
Finucane, A. (11) 1966/7 Limerick
Fitzgerald, F. J. (2) 1954/5 Waterford
Fitzgerald, P. J. (5) 1960/1 Leeds U, Chester
Fitzpatrick, K. (1) 1969/70 Limerick
Fitzsimons, A. G. (26) 1949/50 Middlesbrough, Lincoln C
Fleming, C. (10) 1995/6 Middlesbrough
Fogarty, A. (11) 1959/60 Sunderland, Hartlepool U
Foley, D. J. (6) 1999/00 Watford
Foley, T. C. (9) 1963/4 Northampton T
Fullam, J. 1960/1 Preston NE, Shamrock R

Gallagher, C. (2) 1966/7 Celtic
Gallagher, M. (1) 1953/4 Hibernian
Galvin, A. (29) 1982/3 Tottenham H, Sheffield W, Swindon T
Gamble, J. (2) 2006/07 Cork C
Gannon, E. (14) 1948/9 Notts Co, Sheffield W, Shelbourne K
Gannon, M. (1) 1971/2 Shelbourne
Gavin, J. T. (7) 1949/50 Norwich C, Tottenham H, Norwich C
Gibbons, A. (4) 1951/2 St Patrick's Ath
Gilbert, R. (1) 1965/6 Shamrock R
Giles, C. (1) 1950/1 Doncaster R
Giles, M. J. (59) 1959/60 Manchester U, Leeds U, WBA, Shamrock R
Given, S. J. J. (80) 1995/6 Blackburn R, Newcastle U
Givens, D. J. (56) 1968/9 Manchester U, Luton T, QPR, Birmingham C, Neuchatel Xamax
Gleeson, S. M. (2) 2006/07 Wolverhampton W
Glynn, D. (2) 1951/2 Drumcondra
Godwin, T. F. (13) 1948/9 Shamrock R, Leicester C, Bournemouth
Goodman, J. (4) 1996/7 Wimbledon
Goodwin, J. (1) 2002/03 Stockport Co
Gorman, W. C. (2) 1946/7 Brentford
Grealish, A. (45) 1975/6 Orient, Luton T, Brighton & HA, WBA
Gregg, E. (8) 1977/8 Bohemians
Grimes, A. A. (18) 1977/8 Manchester U, Coventry C, Luton T

Hale, A. (13) 1961/2 Aston Villa, Doncaster R, Waterford
Hamilton, T. (2) 1958/9 Shamrock R
Hand, E. K. (20) 1968/9 Portsmouth
Harte, I. P. (64) 1995/6 Leeds U, Levante
Hartnett, J. B. (2) 1948/9 Middlesbrough
Haverty, J. (32) 1955/6 Arsenal, Blackburn R, Millwall, Celtic, Bristol R, Shelbourne
Hayes, A. W. P. (1) 1978/9 Southampton
Hayes, W. E. (2) 1946/7 Huddersfield T
Hayes, W. J. (1) 1948/9 Limerick
Healey, R. (2) 1976/7 Cardiff C
Healy, C. (13) 2001/02 Celtic, Sunderland
Heighway, S. D. (34) 1970/1 Liverpool, Minnesota Kicks
Henderson, B. (2) 1947/8 Drumcondra
Henderson, W. C. P. (5) 2005/06 Brighton & HA, Preston NE
Hennessy, J. (5) 1964/5 Shelbourne, St Patrick's Ath
Herrick, J. (3) 1971/2 Cork Hibernians, Shamrock R
Higgins, J. (1) 1950/1 Birmingham C
Holland, M. R. (49) 1999/00 Ipswich T, Charlton Ath
Holmes, J. (30) 1970/1 Coventry C, Tottenham H, Vancouver Whitecaps
Houghton, R. J. (73) 1985/6 Oxford U, Liverpool, Aston Villa, Crystal P, Reading
Howlett, G. (1) 1983/4 Brighton & HA

Hughton, C. (53) 1979/80 Tottenham H, West Ham U
Hunt, S. P. (5) 2006/07 Reading
Hurley, C. J. (40) 1956/7 Millwall, Sunderland, Bolton W

Ireland, S. J. (5) 2005/06 Manchester C
Irwin, D. J. (56) 1990/1 Manchester U

Kavanagh, G. A. (16) 1997/8 Stoke C, Cardiff C, Wigan Ath
Keane, R. D. (72) 1997/8 Wolverhampton W, Coventry C, Internazionale, Leeds U, Tottenham H
Keane, R. M. (67) 1990/1 Nottingham F, Manchester U
Keane, T. R. (4) 1948/9 Swansea T
Kearin, M. (1) 1971/2 Shamrock R
Kearns, F. T. (1) 1953/4 West Ham U
Kearns, M. (18) 1969/70 Oxford U, Walsall, Wolverhampton W
Kelly, A. T. (34) 1992/3 Sheffield U, Blackburn R
Kelly, D. T. (26) 1987/8 Walsall, West Ham U, Leicester C, Newcastle U, Wolverhampton W, Sunderland, Tranmere R
Kelly, G. (52) 1993/4 Leeds U
Kelly, J. A. (48) 1956/7 Drumcondra, Preston NE
Kelly, J. P. V. (5) 1960/1 Wolverhampton W
Kelly, M. J. (4) 1987/8 Portsmouth
Kelly, N. (1) 1953/4 Nottingham F
Kelly, S. M. (5) 2005/06 Tottenham H, Birmingham C
Kenna, J. J. (27) 1994/5 Blackburn R
Kennedy, M. (34) 1995/6 Liverpool, Wimbledon, Manchester C, Wolverhampton W
Kennedy, M. F. (2) 1985/6 Portsmouth
Kenny, P. (7) 2003/04 Sheffield U
Keogh, A. D. (1) 2006/07 Wolverhampton W
Keogh, J. (1) 1965/6 Shamrock R
Keogh, S. (1) 1958/9 Shamrock R
Kernaghan, A. N. (22) 1992/3 Middlesbrough, Manchester C
Kiely, D. L. (8) 1999/00 Charlton Ath
Kiernan, F. W. (5) 1950/1 Shamrock R, Southampton
Kilbane, K. D. (80) 1997/8 WBA, Sunderland, Everton, Wigan Ath
Kinnear, J. P. (26) 1966/7 Tottenham H, Brighton & HA
Kinsella, M. A. (48) 1997/8 Charlton Ath, Aston Villa, WBA

Langan, D. (26) 1977/8 Derby Co, Birmingham C, Oxford U
Lapira, J. (1) 2006/07 Notre Dame
Lawler, J. F. (8) 1952/3 Fulham
Lawlor, J. C. (3) 1948/9 Drumcondra, Doncaster R
Lawlor, M. (5) 1970/1 Shamrock R
Lawrenson, M. (39) 1976/7 Preston NE, Brighton & HA, Liverpool
Lee, A. L. (10) 2002/03 Rotherham U, Cardiff C, Ipswich T
Leech, M. (8) 1968/9 Shamrock R
Long, S. P. (4) 2006/07 Reading
Lowry, D. (1) 1961/2 St Patrick's Ath

McAlinden, J. (2) 1945/6 Portsmouth
McAteer, J. W. (52) 1993/4 Bolton W, Liverpool, Blackburn R, Sunderland
McCann, J. (1) 1956/7 Shamrock R
McCarthy, M. (57) 1983/4 Manchester C, Celtic, Lyon, Millwall
McConville, T. (6) 1971/2 Dundalk, Waterford
McDonagh, Jim (25) 1980/1 Everton, Bolton W, Notts C
McDonagh, Jacko (3) 1983/4 Shamrock R
McEvoy, M. A. (17) 1960/1 Blackburn R
McGeady, A. (10) 2003/04 Celtic
McGee, P. (15) 1977/8 QPR, Preston NE
McGoldrick, E. J. (15) 1991/2 Crystal P, Arsenal
McGowan, D. (3) 1948/9 West Ham U
McGowan, J. (1) 1946/7 Cork U
McGrath, M. (22) 1957/8 Blackburn R, Bradford Park Avenue
McGrath, P. (83) 1984/5 Manchester U, Aston Villa, Derby C
McLoughlin, A. F. (42) 1989/90 Swindon T, Southampton, Portsmouth
McMillan, W. (2) 1945/6 Belfast Celtic
McNally, J. B. (3) 1958/9 Luton T
McPhail, S. (10) 1999/00 Leeds U
McShane, P. D. (5) 2006/07 WBA
Macken, A. (1) 1976/7 Derby Co
Macken, J. P. (1) 2004/05 Manchester C
Mackey, G. (3) 1956/7 Shamrock R
Mahon, A. J. (2) 1999/00 Tranmere R
Malone, G. (1) 1948/9 Shelbourne
Mancini, T. J. (5) 1973/4 QPR, Arsenal
Martin, C. J. (30) 1945/6 Glentoran, Leeds U, Aston Villa
Martin, M. P. (52) 1971/2 Bohemians, Manchester U, WBA, Newcastle U

Maybury, A. (10) 1997/8 Leeds U, Heart of Midlothian, Leicester C
Meagan, M. K. (17) 1960/1 Everton, Huddersfield T, Drogheda
Miller, L. W. P. (13) 2003/04 Celtic, Manchester U
Milligan, M. J. (1) 1991/2 Oldham Ath
Mooney, J. (2) 1964/5 Shamrock R
Moore, A. (8) 1995/6 Middlesbrough
Moran, K. (71) 1979/80 Manchester U, Sporting Gijon, Blackburn R
Moroney, T. (12) 1947/8 West Ham U, Evergreen U
Morris, C. B. (35) 1987/8 Celtic, Middlesbrough
Morrison, C. H. (36) 2001/02 Crystal P, Birmingham C, Crystal P
Moulson, G. B. (3) 1947/8 Lincoln C
Mucklan, C. (1) 1977/8 Drogheda
Mulligan, P. M. (50) 1968/9 Shamrock R, Chelsea, Crystal P, WBA, Shamrock R
Munroe, L. (1) 1953/4 Shamrock R
Murphy, A. (1) 1955/6 Clyde
Murphy, B. (1) 1985/6 Bohemians
Murphy, D. (2) 2006/07 Sunderland
Murphy, Jerry (1) 1979/80 Crystal P
Murphy, Joe (1) 2003/04 WBA
Murphy, P. M. (1) 2006/07 Carlisle U
Murray, T. (1) 1949/50 Dundalk

Newman, W. (1) 1968/9 Shelbourne
Nolan, R. (10) 1956/7 Shamrock R

O'Brien, A. (5) 2006/07 Newcastle U
O'Brien, A. J. (26) 2000/01 Newcastle U, Portsmouth
O'Brien, F. (3) 1979/80 Philadelphia Fury
O'Brien, J. M. (1) 2005/06 Bolton W
O'Brien, L. (16) 1985/6 Shamrock R, Manchester U, Newcastle U, Tranmere R
O'Brien, R. (5) 1975/6 Notts Co
O'Byrne, L. B. (1) 1948/9 Shamrock R
O'Callaghan, B. R. (6) 1978/9 Stoke C
O'Callaghan, K. (21) 1980/1 Ipswich T, Portsmouth
O'Cearuill, J. (2) 2006/07 Arsenal
O'Connnell, A. (2) 1966/7 Dundalk, Bohemians
O'Connor, T. (4) 1949/50 Shamrock R
O'Connor, T. (7) 1967/8 Fulham, Dundalk, Bohemians
O'Driscoll, J. F. (3) 1948/9 Swansea T
O'Driscoll, S. (3) 1981/2 Fulham
O'Farrell, F. (9) 1951/2 West Ham U, Preston NE
O'Flanagan, K. P. (3) 1946/7 Arsenal
O'Flanagan, M. (1) 1946/7 Bohemians
O'Halloran, S. E. (2) 2006/07 Aston Villa
O'Hanlon, K. G. (1) 1987/8 Rotherham U
O'Keefe, E. (5) 1980/1 Everton, Port Vale
O'Leary, D. (68) 1976/7 Arsenal
O'Leary, P. (7) 1979/80 Shamrock R
O'Neill, F. S. (20) 1961/2 Shamrock R
O'Neill, J. (17) 1951/2 Everton
O'Neill, J. (1) 1960/1 Preston NE
O'Neill, K. P. (13) 1995/6 Norwich C, Middlesbrough
O'Regan, K. (4) 1983/4 Brighton & HA
O'Reilly, J. (2) 1945/6 Cork U
O'Shea, J. F. (38) 2001/02 Manchester U

Peyton, G. (33) 1976/7 Fulham, Bournemouth, Everton
Peyton, N. (6) 1956/7 Shamrock R, Leeds U
Phelan, T. (42) 1991/2 Wimbledon, Manchester C, Chelsea, Everton, Fulham
Potter, D. M. (2) 2006/07 Wolverhampton W

Quinn, A. (8) 2002/03 Sheffield W, Sheffield U
Quinn, B. S. (4) 1999/00 Coventry C
Quinn, N. J. (91) 1985/6 Arsenal, Manchester C, Sunderland

Reid, A. M. (22) 2003/04 Nottingham F, Tottenham H, Charlton Ath
Reid, S. J. (20) 2001/02 Millwall, Blackburn R
Richardson, D. J. (3) 1971/2 Shamrock R, Gillingham
Ringstead, A. (20) 1950/1 Sheffield U
Robinson, M. (24) 1980/1 Brighton & HA, Liverpool, QPR
Roche, P. J. (8) 1971/2 Shelbourne, Manchester U
Rogers, E. (19) 1967/8 Blackburn R, Charlton Ath
Rowlands, M. C. (3) 2003/04 QPR
Ryan, G. (18) 1977/8 Derby Co, Brighton & HA
Ryan, R. A. (16) 1949/50 WBA, Derby C

Sadlier, R. T. (1) 2001/02 Millwall
Savage, D. P. T. (5) 1995/6 Millwall

Saward, P. (18) 1953/4 Millwall, Aston Villa, Huddersfield T
Scannell, T. (1) 1953/4 Southend U
Scully, P. J. (1) 1988/9 Arsenal
Sheedy, K. (46) 1983/4 Everton, Newcastle U
Sheridan, J. J. (34) 1987/8 Leeds U, Sheffield W
Slaven, B. (7) 1989/90 Middlesbrough
Sloan, J. W. (2) 1945/6 Arsenal
Smyth, M. (1) 1968/9 Shamrock R
Stapleton, F. (71) 1976/7 Arsenal, Manchester U, Ajax, Le Havre, Blackburn R
Staunton, S. (102) 1988/9 Liverpool, Aston Villa, Liverpool, Aston Villa
Stevenson, A. E. (6) 1946/7 Everton
Stokes, A. (3) 2006/07 Sunderland
Strahan, F. (5) 1963/4 Shelbourne
Swan, M. M. G. (1) 1959/60 Drumcondra
Synott, N. (3) 1977/8 Shamrock R

Taylor T. (1) 1958/9 Waterford
Thomas, P. (2) 1973/4 Waterford
Thompson, J. (1) 2003/04 Nottingham F
Townsend, A. D. (70) 1988/9 Norwich C, Chelsea, Aston Villa, Middlesbrough
Traynor, T. J. (8) 1953/4 Southampton
Treacy, R. C. P. (42) 1965/6 WBA, Charlton Ath, Swindon T, Preston NE, WBA, Shamrock R
Tuohy, L. (8) 1955/6 Shamrock R, Newcastle U, Shamrock R
Turner, P. (2) 1962/3 Celtic

Vernon, J. (2) 1945/6 Belfast Celtic

Waddock, G. (21) 1979/80 QPR, Millwall
Walsh, D. J. (20) 1945/6 Linfield, WBA, Aston Villa
Walsh, J. (1) 1981/2 Limerick
Walsh, M. (21) 1975/6 Blackpool, Everton, QPR, Porto
Walsh, M. (4) 1981/2 Everton
Walsh, W. (9) 1946/7 Manchester C
Waters, J. (2) 1976/7 Grimsby T
Whelan, R. (2) 1963/4 St Patrick's Ath
Whelan, R. (53) 1980/1 Liverpool, Southend U
Whelan, W. (4) 1955/6 Manchester U
Whittaker, R. (1) 1958/9 Chelsea

REPUBLIC OF IRELAND LEAGUE 2006

	P	*W*	*D*	*L*	*F*	*A*	*Pts*
Shelbourne	30	18	8	4	60	27	62
Derry City	30	18	8	4	46	20	62
Drogheda United	30	16	10	4	37	23	58
Cork City	30	15	11	4	37	15	56
Sligo Rovers	30	11	7	12	33	42	40
UCD	30	9	11	10	26	26	38
St Patrick's Ath	30	9	10	11	32	29	37
Longford Town	30	8	10	12	23	27	34
Bohemians	30	9	5	16	29	34	29
Bray Wanderers	30	3	8	19	22	64	17
Waterford United†	30	2	6	22	20	58	12
Dublin City*	17	4	3	10	11	24	15

Dublin City withdrew after 17 matches; Bohemians deducted three points for fielding a suspended player.
**relegated; †relegated after play-off.*

BRITISH ISLES INTERNATIONAL GOALSCORERS SINCE 1946

ENGLAND

Name	Goals
A'Court, A.	1
Adams, T.A.	5
Allen, R.	2
Anderson, V.	2
Anderton, D.R.	7
Astall, G.	1
Atyeo, P.J.W.	5
Baily, E.F.	5
Baker, J.H.	3
Ball, A.J.	8
Barnes, J.	11
Barnes, P.S.	4
Barmby, N.J.	4
Beardsley, P.A.	9
Beattie, J.K.	1
Beckham, D.R.J.	17
Bell, C.	9
Bentley, R.T.F.	9
Blissett, L.	3
Bowles, S.	1
Bradford, G.R.W.	1
Bradley, W.	2
Bridge, W.M.	1
Bridges, B.J.	1
Broadbent, P.F.	2
Broadis, I.A.	8
Brooking, T.D.	5
Brooks, J.	2
Bull, S.G.	4
Butcher, T.	3
Byrne, J.J.	8
Campbell, S.J.	1
Carter, H.S.	5
Chamberlain, M.	1
Channon, M.R.	21
Charlton, J.	6
Charlton, R.	49
Chivers, M.	13
Clarke, A.J.	10
Cole, A.	1
Cole, J.J.	7
Connelly, J.M.	7
Coppell, S.J.	7
Cowans, G.	2
Crawford, R.	1
Crouch, P.J.	12
Currie, A.W.	3
Defoe, J.C.	3
Dixon, L.M.	1
Dixon, K.M.	4
Douglas, B.	11
Eastham, G.	2
Edwards, D.	5
Ehiogu, U.	1
Elliott, W.H.	3
Ferdinand, L.	5
Ferdinand, R.G.	1
Finney, T.	30
Flowers, R.	10
Fowler, R.B.	7
Francis, G.C.J.	3
Francis, T.	12
Froggatt, J.	2
Froggatt, R.	2
Gascoigne, P.J.	10
Gerrard, S.G.	12
Goddard, P.	1
Grainger, C.	3
Greaves, J.	44
Haines, J.T.W.	2
Hancocks, J.	2
Hassall, H.W.	4
Hateley, M.	9
Haynes, J.N.	18
Heskey, E.W.	5
Hirst, D.E.	1
Hitchens, G.A.	5
Hoddle, G.	8
Hughes, E.W.	1
Hunt, R.	18
Hunter, N.	2
Hurst, G.C.	24
Ince P.E.C.	2
Jeffers, F.	1
Johnson, D.E.	6
Kay, A.H.	1
Keegan, J.K.	21
Kennedy, R.	3
Keown, M.R.	2
Kevan, D.T.	8
Kidd, B.	1
King, L.B.	1
Lampard, F.J.	12
Langton, R.	1
Latchford, R.D.	5
Lawler, C.	1
Lawton, T.	16
Lee, F.	10
Lee, J.	1
Lee, R.M.	2
Lee, S.	2
Le Saux, G.P.	1
Lineker, G.	48
Lofthouse, N.	30
Mabbutt, G.	1
McDermott, T.	3
Macdonald, M.	6
McManaman, S.	3
Mannion, W.J.	11
Mariner, P.	13
Marsh, R.W.	1
Matthews, S.	3
Medley, L.D.	1
Melia, J.	1
Merson, P.C.	3
Milburn, J.E.T.	10
Moore, R.F.	2
Morris, J.	3
Mortensen, S.H.	23
Mullen, J.	6
Mullery, A.P.	1
Murphy, D.B.	1
Neal, P.G.	5
Nicholls, J.	1
Nicholson, W.E.	1
Nugent, D.J.	1
O'Grady, M.	3
Owen, M.J.	37
Own goals	20
Paine, T.L.	7
Palmer, C.L.	1
Parry, R.A.	1
Peacock, A.	3
Pearce, S.	5
Pearson, J.S.	5
Pearson, S.C.	5
Perry, W.	2
Peters, M.	20
Pickering, F.	5

Platt, D.	27
Pointer, R.	2
Ramsay, A.E.	3
Redknapp, J.F.	1
Revie, D.G.	4
Richardson, K.E.	2
Robson, B.	26
Robson, R.	4
Rooney, W.	12
Rowley, J.F.	6
Royle, J.	2
Sansom, K.	1
Scholes, P.	14
Sewell, J.	3
Shackleton, L.F.	1
Shearer, A.	30
Sheringham, E.P.	11
Smith, A.	1
Smith, A.M.	2
Smith, R.	13
Southgate, G.	2
Steven, T.M.	4
Stiles, N.P.	1
Stone, S.B.	2
Summerbee, M.G.	1
Tambling, R.V.	1
Taylor, P.J.	2
Taylor, T.	16
Terry, J.G.	3
Thompson, P.B.	1
Tueart, D.	2
Vassell, D.	6
Viollet, D.S.	1
Waddle, C.R.	6
Wallace, D.L.	1
Walsh, P.	1
Watson, D.V.	4
Webb, N.	4
Weller, K.	1
Wignall, F.	2
Wilkins, R.G.	3
Wilshaw, D.J.	10
Wise, D.F.	1
Withe, P.	1
Woodcock, T.	16
Worthington, F.S.	2
Wright, I.E.	9
Wright, M.	1
Wright, W.A.	3
Wright-Phillips, S.C.	1

SCOTLAND

Aitken, R.	1
Archibald, S.	4
Baird, S.	2
Bannon, E.	1
Bauld, W.	2
Baxter, J.C.	3
Beattie, C.	1
Bett, J.	1
Bone, J.	1
Booth, S.	6
Boyd, K.	5
Boyd, T.	1
Brand, R.	8
Brazil, A.	1
Bremner, W.J.	3
Brown, A.D.	6
Buckley, P.	1
Burke, C.	2
Burley, C.W.	3
Burns, K.	1
Caldwell, G.	2
Calderwood, C.	1
Caldow, E.	4
Cameron, C.	2
Campbell, R.	1
Chalmers, S.	3
Collins, J.	12
Collins, R.V.	10
Combe, J.R.	1
Conn, A.	1
Cooper, D.	6
Craig, J.	1
Crawford, S.	4
Curran, H.P.	1
Dailly, C.	6
Dalglish, K.	30
Davidson, J.A.	1
Dickov, P.	1
Dobie, R.S.	1
Docherty, T.H.	1
Dodds, D.	1
Dodds, W.	7
Duncan, D.M.	1
Durie, G.S.	7
Elliott, M.S.	1
Ferguson, B.	2
Fernie, W.	1
Flavell, R.	2
Fleming, C.	2
Fletcher, D.	4
Freedman, D.A.	1

Gallacher, K.W.	9
Gemmell, T.K *(St Mirren)*	1
Gemmell, T.K *(Celtic)*	1
Gemmill, A.	8
Gemmill, S.	1
Gibson, D.W.	3
Gilzean, A.J.	12
Gough, C.R.	6
Graham, A.	2
Graham, G.	3
Gray, A.	7
Gray, E.	3
Gray, F.	1
Greig, J.	3
Hamilton, G.	4
Harper, J.M.	2
Hartford, R.A.	4
Hartley, P.J.	1
Henderson, J.G.	1
Henderson, W.	5
Hendry, E.C.J.	3
Herd, D.G.	3
Herd, G.	1
Hewie, J.D.	2
Holt, G.J.	1
Holton, J.A.	2
Hopkin, D.	2
Houliston, W.	2
Howie, H.	1
Hughes, J.	1
Hunter, W.	1
Hutchison, D.	6
Hutchison, T.	1
Jackson, C.	1
Jackson, D.	4
Jardine, A.	1
Jess, E.	2
Johnston, A.	2
Johnston, L.H.	1
Johnston, M.	14
Johnstone, D.	2
Johnstone, J.	4
Johnstone, R.	10
Jordan, J.	11
Kyle, K.	1
Lambert, P.	1
Law, D.	30
Leggat, G.	8
Lennox, R.	3
Liddell, W.	6
Linwood, A.B.	1
Lorimer, P.	4

Macari, L.	5
MacDougall, E.J.	3
MacKay, D.C.	4
Mackay, G.	1
MacKenzie, J.A.	1
MacLeod, M.	1
McAllister, G.	5
McAvennie, F.	1
McCall, S.M.	1
McCalliog, J.	1
McCann, N.	3
McClair, B.	2
McCoist, A.	19
McFadden, J.	9
McGhee, M.	2
McGinlay, J.	3
McInally, A.	3
McKimmie, S.I.	1
McKinlay, W.	4
McKinnon, R.	1
McLaren, A.	4
McLean, T.	1
McLintock, F.	1
McMillan, I.L.	2
McNeill, W.	3
McPhail, J.	3
McQueen, G.	5
McStay, P.	9
McSwegan, G.J.	1
Maloney, S.	1
Mason, J.	4
Masson, D.S.	5
Miller, K.	9
Miller, W.	1
Mitchell, R.C.	1
Morgan, W.	1
Morris, H.	3
Mudie, J.K.	9
Mulhall, G.	1
Murdoch, R.	5
Murray, J.	1
Narey, D.	1
Naysmith, G.A.	1
Nevin, P.K.F.	5
Nicholas, C.	5
O'Connor, G.	4
O'Hare, J.	5
Ormond, W.E.	2
Orr, T.	1
Own goals	10
Parlane, D.	1
Pettigrew, W.	2
Provan, D.	1
Quashie, N.F.	1
Quinn, J.	7
Quinn, P.	1
Reilly, L.	22
Ring, T.	2
Rioch, B.D.	6
Ritchie, P.S.	1
Robertson, A.	2
Robertson, J.	3
Robertson, J.N.	8
St John, I.	9
Scott, A.S.	5
Sharp, G.	1
Shearer, D.	2
Smith, G.	4
Souness, G.J.	4
Steel, W.	12
Stein, C.	10
Stewart, R.	1
Strachan, G.	5
Sturrock, P.	3
Thompson, S.	3
Thornton, W.	1
Waddell, W.	6
Wallace, I.A.	1
Wark, J.	7
Webster, A.	1
Weir, A.	1
Weir, D.	1
White, J.A.	3
Wilkie, L.	1
Wilson, D.	9
Young, A.	2

WALES

Allchurch, I.J.	23
Allen, M.	3
Bale, G.	2
Barnes, W.	1
Bellamy, C.D.	13
Blackmore, C.G.	1
Blake, N.A.	4
Bodin, P.J.	3
Bowen, D.I.	3
Bowen, M.	2
Boyle, T.	1
Burgess, W.A.R.	1
Charles, J.	1
Charles, M.	6
Charles, W.J.	15
Clarke, R.J.	5
Coleman, C.	4
Curtis, A.	6
Davies, G.	2
Davies, R.T.	9
Davies, R.W.	6
Davies, Simon	5
Deacy, N.	4
Durban, A.	2
Dwyer, P.	2
Earnshaw, R.	12
Edwards, G.	2
Edwards, R.I.	4
England, H.M.	4
Evans, I.	1
Flynn, B.	7
Ford, T.	23
Foulkes, W.J.	1
Giggs, R.J.	12
Giles, D.	2
Godfrey, B.C.	2
Griffiths, A.T.	6
Griffiths, M.W.	2
Harris, C.S.	1
Hartson, J.	14
Hewitt, R.	1
Hockey, T.	1
Hodges, G.	2
Horne, B.	2
Hughes, L.M.	16
James, L.	10
James, R.	7
Jones, A.	1
Jones, B.S.	2
Jones, Cliff	16
Jones, D.E.	1
Jones, J.P.	1
Koumas, J.	5
Kryzwicki, R.I.	1
Leek, K.	5
Llewelyn, C.M	1
Lovell, S.	1
Lowrie, G.	2
Mahoney, J.F.	1
Medwin, T.C.	6
Melville, A.K.	3
Moore, G.	1
Nicholas, P.	2

O'Sullivan, P.A. 1
Own goals 6

Palmer, D. 1
Parry, P.I. 1
Paul, R. 1
Pembridge, M.A. 6
Phillips, D. 2
Powell, A. 1
Powell, D. 1
Price, P. 1

Reece, G.I. 2
Rees, R.R. 3
Roberts, P.S. 1
Robinson, C.P. 1
Robinson, J.R.C. 3
Rush, I. 28

Saunders, D. 22
Savage R.W. 2
Slatter, N. 2
Smallman, D.P. 1
Speed, G.A. 7
Symons, C.J. 2

Tapscott, D.R. 4
Taylor, G.J. 1
Thomas, M. 4
Toshack, J.B. 12

Vernon, T.R. 8

Walsh, I. 7
Williams, A. 1
Williams, G.E. 1
Williams, G.G. 1
Woosnam, A.P. 3

Yorath, T.C. 2
Young, E. 1

NORTHERN IRELAND

Anderson, T. 4
Armstrong, G. 12

Barr, H.H. 1
Best, G. 9
Bingham, W.L. 10
Black, K. 1
Blanchflower, D. 2
Blanchflower, J. 1
Brennan, R.A. 1
Brotherston, N. 3

Campbell, W.G. 1
Casey, T. 2
Caskey, W. 1
Cassidy, T. 1
Clarke, C.J. 13
Clements, D. 2
Cochrane, T. 1
Crossan, E. 1
Crossan, J.A. 10
Cush, W.W. 5

Davis, S. 1
D'Arcy, S.D. 1
Doherty, I. 1
Doherty, P.D. 2
Dougan, A.D. 8
Dowie, I. 12

Elder, A.R. 1
Elliott, S. 4

Feeney, W. 1
Feeney, W.J. 2
Ferguson, W. 1
Ferris, R.O. 1
Finney, T. 2

Gibson, W. 1
Gillespie, K.R. 2
Gray, P. 6
Griffin, D.J. 1

Hamilton, B. 4
Hamilton, W. 5
Harkin, J.T. 2
Harvey, M. 3
Healy, D.J. 29
Hill, C.F. 1
Humphries, W. 1
Hughes, M.E. 5
Hunter, A. 1
Hunter, B.V. 1

Irvine, W.J. 8

Johnston, W.C. 1
Jones, J. 1
Jones, S. 1

Lafferty, K. 1
Lennon, N.F. 2
Lockhart, N. 3
Lomas, S.M. 3

Magilton, J. 5
McAdams, W.J. 7
McCann, G.S. 1
McCartney, G. 1
McClelland, J. 1
McCrory, S. 1
McCurdy, C. 1
McDonald, A. 3
McGarry, J.K. 1
McGrath, R.C. 4
McIlroy, J. 10
McIlroy, S.B. 5
McLaughlin, J.C. 6
McMahon, G.J. 2
McMordie, A.S. 3
McMorran, E.J. 4
McParland, P.J. 10
Moreland, V. 1
Morgan, S. 3
Morrow, S.J. 1
Mulryne, P.P. 3
Murdoch, C.J. 1

Neill, W.J.T. 2
Nelson, S. 1
Nicholl, C.J. 3
Nicholl, J.M. 1
Nicholson, J.J. 6

O'Boyle, G. 1
O'Kane, W.J. 1
O'Neill, J. 2
O'Neill, M.A. 4
O'Neill, M.H. 8
Own goals 17

Patterson, D.J. 1
Peacock, R. 2
Penney, S. 2

Quinn, J.M. 12
Quinn, S.J. 4

Rowland, K. 1

Simpson, W.J. 5
Smyth, S. 5
Spence, D.W. 3
Sproule, I. 1
Stewart, I. 2

Taggart, G.P. 7
Tully, C.P. 3

Walker, J. 1
Walsh, D.J. 5
Welsh, E. 1
Whiteside, N. 9
Whitley, Jeff 2
Williams, M.S. 1
Wilson, D.J. 1
Wilson, K.J. 6
Wilson, S.J. 7

EIRE

Player	Goals
Aldridge, J.	19
Ambrose, P.	1
Anderson, J.	1
Barrett, G.	2
Brady, L.	9
Breen, G.	7
Byrne, J.	4
Cantwell, J.	14
Carey, J.	3
Carroll, T.	1
Cascarino, A.	19
Coad, P.	3
Connolly, D.J.	9
Conroy, T.	2
Conway, J.	3
Coyne, T.	6
Cummins, G.	5
Curtis, D.	8
Daly, G.	13
Dempsey, J.	1
Dennehy, M.	2
Doherty, G.M.T.	4
Doyle, K.E.	3
Duff, D.A.	7
Duffy, B.	1
Dunne, R.P.	5
Eglinton, T.	2
Elliott, S.W.	1
Fagan, F.	5
Fallon, S.	2
Farrell, P.	3
Finnan, S.	1
Fitzgerald, J.	1
Fitzgerald, P.	2
Fitzsimons, A.	7
Fogarty, A.	3
Foley, D.	2
Fullam, J.	1
Galvin, A.	1
Gavin, J.	2
Giles, J.	5
Givens, D.	19
Glynn, D.	1
Grealish, T.	8
Grimes, A.A.	1
Hale, A.	2
Hand, E.	2
Harte, I.P.	11
Haverty, J.	3
Healy, C.	1
Holland, M.R.	5
Holmes, J.	1
Houghton, R.	6
Hughton, C.	1
Hurley, C.	2
Ireland, S.J.	3
Irwin, D.	4
Kavanagh, G.A.	1
Keane, R.D.	29
Keane, R.M.	9
Kelly, D.	9
Kelly, G.	2
Kennedy, M.	4
Kernaghan, A.	1
Kilbane, K.D.	7
Kinsella, M.A.	3
Lawrenson, M.	5
Leech, M.	2
Long, S.P.	1
McAteer, J.W.	3
McCann, J.	1
McCarthy, M.	2
McEvoy, A.	6
McGee, P.	4
McGrath, P.	8
McLoughlin, A.	2
McPhail, S.	1
Mancini, T.	1
Martin, C.	6
Martin, M.	4
Miller, L.W.P.	1
Mooney, J.	1
Moran, K.	6
Moroney, T.	1
Morrison, C.H.	9
Mulligan, P.	1
O'Brien, A.J.	1
O'Callaghan, K.	1
O'Connor, T.	2
O'Farrell, F.	2
O'Keefe, E.	1
O'Leary, D.A.	1
O'Neill, F.	1
O'Neill, K.P.	4
O'Reilly, J.	1
O'Shea, J.F.	1
Own goals	10
Quinn, N.	21
Reid, A.M.	4
Reid, S.J.	2
Ringstead, A.	7
Robinson, M.	4
Rogers, E.	5
Ryan, G.	1
Ryan, R.	3
Sheedy, K.	9
Sheridan, J.	5
Slaven, B.	1
Sloan, J.	1
Stapleton, F.	20
Staunton, S.	7
Strahan, F.	1
Townsend, A.D.	7
Treacy, R.	5
Tuohy, L.	4
Waddock, G.	3
Walsh, D.	5
Walsh, M.	3
Waters, J.	1
Whelan, R.	3

UEFA UNDER-21 CHAMPIONSHIP 2006–07

Qualifying competition

PRELIMINARY ROUND
Malta 1, Georgia 2
Liechtenstein 1, Northern Ireland 4
Luxembourg 0, Macedonia 3
Georgia 2, Malta 1
Macedonia 2, Luxembourg 0
Andorra 0, Iceland 0
Estonia 0, Wales 2
Northern Ireland 4, Liechtenstein 0
Azerbaijan 0, Republic of Ireland 3
San Marino 3, Armenia 0
Republic of Ireland 3, Azerbaijan 0
Wales 5, Estonia 1
Iceland 2, Andorra 0
Armenia 4, San Marino 0
Kazakhstan 0, Moldova 0
Moldova 1, Kazakhstan 0

QUALIFYING ROUND
GROUP 1
Bosnia 3, Armenia 2
Armenia 1, Norway 0
Norway 1, Bosnia 1

GROUP 2
Slovakia 0, Albania 0
Albania 0, Spain 3
Spain 4, Slovakia 2

GROUP 3
Lithuania 1, Georgia 0
Georgia 1, Serbia 3
Serbia 2, Lithuania 0

GROUP 4
Greece 0, Republic of Ireland 2
Republic of Ireland 0, Belgium 1
Belgium 2, Greece 1

GROUP 5
Austria 0, Iceland 0
Iceland 0, Italy 1
Italy 1, Austria 0

GROUP 6
Hungary 5, Finland 0
Finland 1, Russia 5
Russia 3, Hungary 1

GROUP 7
Poland 3, Latvia 1
Latvia 1, Portugal 2
Portugal 2, Poland 0

GROUP 8
England 2, Moldova 2
Moldova 1, Switzerland 3
Switzerland 2, England 3

GROUP 9
Belarus 1, Cyprus 0
Cyprus 0, Czech Republic 2
Czech Republic 2, Belarus 1

GROUP 10
Romania 3, Northern Ireland 0
Northern Ireland 2, Germany 3
Germany 5, Romania 1

GROUP 11
Sweden 3, Macedonia 1
Macedonia 0, Denmark 3
Denmark 0, Sweden 2

GROUP 12
Ukraine 0, Bulgaria 3
Bulgaria 2, Croatia 1
Croatia 1, Ukraine 2

GROUP 13
Israel 3, Wales 2
Wales 0, Turkey 0
Turkey 0, Israel 0

GROUP 14
Slovenia 1, Scotland 0
Scotland 1, France 3
France 2, Slovenia 0

PLAY-OFFS FOR FINAL TOURNAMENT FIRST LEG
Serbia 0, Sweden 3
Czech Republic 2, Bosnia 1
England 1, Germany 0
Italy 0, Spain 0
Belgium 1, Bulgaria 1
France 1, Israel 1
Russia 4, Portugal 1

PLAY-OFFS FOR FINAL TOURNAMENT SECOND LEG
Bosnia 1, Czech Republic 1
Sweden 0, Serbia 5
Germany 0, England 2
Spain 1, Italy 2
Bulgaria 1, Belgium 4
Israel 1, France 0
Portugal 3, Russia 0

Finals in Holland

GROUP A
Holland 1, Israel 0
Portugal 0, Belgium 0
Israel 0, Belgium 1
Holland 2, Portugal 1
Israel 0, Portugal 4
Belgium 2, Holland 2

GROUP B
Czech Republic 0, England 0
Serbia 1, Italy 0
Czech Republic 0, Serbia 1
England 2, Italy 2
England 2, Serbia 0
Italy 3, Czech Republic 1

SEMI-FINALS
Serbia 2, Belgium 0
Holland 1, England 1
Holland won 13-12 on penalties.

OLYMPIC QUALIFYING PLAY-OFF
Portugal 0, Italy 0
aet; Italy won 4-3 on penalties.

UEFA UNDER-21 CHAMPIONSHIP 2006–07 FINAL

Holland (1) 4 *(Bakkal 17, Babel 60, Rigters 67, Bruins 87)*
Serbia (0) 1 *(Mrdja 79)* 19,800

Holland: Waterman; Zuiverloon, Kruiswijk, Pieters (Jong-A-Pin 89), Maduro, Drenthe (Beerens 78), Babel, De Ridder, Rigters (Bruins 69), Donk, Bakkal.
Serbia: Kahriman; Ivanovic, Rukavina, Kolarov■, Smiljanic, Jankovic, Rakic (Mrdja 73), Milovanovic, Tosic D, Drincic (Tosic Z 65), Basta (Babovic 73).
Referee: Skomina (Slovenia).

UEFA UNDER-19 CHAMPIONSHIP 2007

Finals in Poland

GROUP A
Czech Republic 2, Poland 0
Austria 4, Belgium 1
Poland 4, Belgium 1
Austria 1, Czech Republic 3
Poland 0, Austria 1
Belgium 4, Czech Republic 2

GROUP B
Portugal 1, Spain 1
Turkey 2, Scotland 3
Scotland 0, Spain 4
Portugal 4, Turkey 4
Spain 5, Turkey 3
Scotland 2, Portugal 2

SEMI-FINALS
Czech Republic 0, Scotland 1
Spain 5, Austria 0

FINAL
Scotland 1, Spain 2

UEFA UNDER-17 CHAMPIONSHIP 2007

Finals in Belgium

GROUP A
Spain 0, Germany 0
Ukraine 2, France 2
France 2, Germany 1
Spain 3, Ukraine 1
Germany 2, Ukraine 0
France 0, Spain 2

GROUP B
Belgium 5, Iceland 1
England 4, Holland 2
Holland 3, Iceland 0
Belgium 1, England 1
Holland 2, Belgium 2
Iceland 0, England 2

SEMI-FINALS
Spain 1, Belgium 1
Spain won 7-6 on penalties.
England 1, France 0

FIFTH PLACE PLAY-OFF
Germany 3, Holland 2

FINAL *(in Tournai)*
Spain 1, England 0

NATIONWIDE CONFERENCE 2006–2007

		Home					Away					Total						
	P	*W*	*D*	*L*	*F*	*A*	*W*	*D*	*L*	*F*	*A*	*W*	*D*	*L*	*F*	*A*	*GD*	*Pts*
1 Dagenham & R	46	16	4	3	50	20	12	7	4	43	28	28	11	7	93	48	45	95
2 Oxford U	46	11	9	3	33	16	11	6	6	33	17	22	15	9	66	33	33	81
3 Morecambe	46	11	7	5	29	20	12	5	6	35	26	23	12	11	64	46	18	81
4 York C	46	10	6	7	29	22	13	5	5	36	23	23	11	12	65	45	20	80
5 Exeter C	46	14	7	2	39	19	8	5	10	28	29	22	12	12	67	48	19	78
6 Burton Alb	46	13	3	7	28	21	9	6	8	24	26	22	9	15	52	47	5	75
7 Gravesend & N	46	12	6	5	33	25	9	5	9	30	31	21	11	14	63	56	7	74
8 Stevenage B	46	12	4	7	46	30	8	6	9	30	36	20	10	16	76	66	10	70
9 Aldershot T	46	11	7	5	40	31	7	4	12	24	31	18	11	17	64	62	2	65
10 Kidderminster H	46	7	5	11	19	26	10	7	6	24	24	17	12	17	43	50	–7	63
11 Weymouth	46	12	6	5	35	26	6	3	14	21	47	18	9	19	56	73	–17	63
12 Rushden & D	46	10	5	8	34	24	7	6	10	24	30	17	11	18	58	54	4	62
13 Northwich Vic	46	9	2	12	26	33	9	2	12	25	36	18	4	24	51	69	–18	58
14 Forest Green R	46	10	5	8	34	33	3	13	7	25	31	13	18	15	59	64	–5	57
15 Woking	46	8	8	7	34	26	7	4	12	22	35	15	12	19	56	61	–5	57
16 Halifax T	46	12	8	3	40	22	3	2	18	15	40	15	10	21	55	62	–7	55
17 Cambridge U	46	8	4	11	34	33	7	6	10	23	33	15	10	21	57	66	–9	55
18 Crawley T*	46	10	6	7	27	20	7	6	10	25	32	17	12	17	52	52	0	53
19 Grays Ath	46	8	9	6	29	21	5	4	14	27	34	13	13	20	56	55	1	52
20 Stafford R	46	7	4	12	25	33	7	6	10	24	38	14	10	22	49	71	–22	52
21 Altrincham	46	9	4	10	28	32	4	8	11	25	35	13	12	21	53	67	–14	51
22 Tamworth	46	8	6	9	24	27	5	3	15	19	34	13	9	24	43	61	–18	48
23 Southport	46	7	4	12	29	30	4	10	9	28	37	11	14	21	57	67	–10	47
24 St Albans C	46	5	5	13	28	49	5	5	13	29	40	10	10	26	57	89	–32	40

**Deducted 10 points for entering administration.*

Leading Goalscorers 2006–07

	League	*FA Cup*	*Trophy*	*Total*
Paul Benson *(Dagenham & R)*	28	0	2	30
Charlie MacDonald *(Gravesend & N)*	27	0	2	29
Clayton Donaldson *(York C)*	24	1	1	26
Steve Morison *(Stevenage B)*	23	2	8	33
Simeon Jackson *(Rushden & D)*	19	1	0	20
Robert Duffy *(Oxford U)*	18	1	2	21
John Grant *(Aldershot T)*	17	5	1	23
Robbie Simpson *(Cambridge U)*	17	0	0	17
Daryl Clare *(Burton Alb)*	16	2	0	18
Craig McAllister *(Woking)*	15	1	1	17
Craig Mackail–Smith *(Dagenham & R)*	15	0	1	16
Neil Grayson *(Stafford R)*	13	0	0	13
Aaron McLean *(Grays Ath)*	13	0	0	13

NATIONWIDE CONFERENCE RESULTS 2006–2007

	Aldershot T	Altrincham	Burton A	Cambridge U	Crawley T	Dagenham & R	Exeter C	Forest Green R	Gravesend & N	Grays Ath	Halifax T	Kidderminster H	Morecambe	Northwich V	Oxford U	Rushden & D	Southport	St Albans C	Stafford R	Stevenage B	Tamworth	Weymouth	Woking	York C
Aldershot T	—	0-0	3-2	0-1	0-2	1-1	3-2	2-1	3-2	1-0	1-0	4-2	0-1	1-3	1-1	2-2	2-2	2-0	4-2	4-0	3-3	1-0	2-2	0-2
Altrincham	0-0	—	2-3	5-0	1-1	0-5	1-2	2-2	0-2	1-0	1-0	0-1	0-2	3-0	0-3	2-1	2-1	2-0	0-1	2-1	2-0	0-0	2-3	0-4
Burton A	1-3	2-1	—	2-1	2-1	0-2	1-0	1-0	0-1	3-0	1-0	1-1	2-1	2-0	1-2	1-2	0-1	1-0	0-0	2-1	1-0	1-1	2-1	1-2
Cambridge U	2-0	2-2	1-2	—	1-2	4-2	1-3	1-1	3-0	2-0	1-2	1-1	1-3	0-1	0-3	0-1	2-2	0-2	0-1	1-0	1-0	7-0	3-0	0-5
Crawley T	1-2	1-1	1-0	1-1	—	0-0	0-3	3-1	1-1	0-1	2-0	0-0	4-0	0-2	0-1	1-0	2-1	2-1	1-2	3-0	1-0	0-3	0-0	3-0
Dagenham & R	2-1	4-1	3-0	2-0	2-1	—	4-1	1-1	2-1	0-0	1-0	1-3	2-1	5-0	0-1	1-2	0-0	4-2	1-1	2-0	4-0	4-1	3-2	2-1
Exeter C	0-0	2-1	3-0	2-0	1-1	3-2	—	1-0	1-3	2-1	4-1	1-1	1-0	1-1	2-1	0-0	2-1	4-2	1-2	1-1	1-0	4-0	1-0	1-1
Forest Green R	3-0	2-2	1-0	1-1	1-0	0-1	2-1	—	0-1	0-0	2-0	2-1	1-3	2-1	1-5	0-2	1-2	2-2	2-1	4-4	2-0	3-2	2-3	0-1
Gravesend & N	1-1	3-1	0-0	2-0	1-0	0-0	2-2	1-1	—	2-0	2-0	1-3	2-1	3-0	1-0	1-0	0-4	3-2	1-4	1-1	4-1	1-3	1-0	0-1
Grays Ath	1-2	1-1	0-1	1-1	0-0	0-1	2-2	1-1	0-2	—	1-0	3-0	0-1	1-0	2-2	3-1	4-0	2-1	1-1	0-2	1-0	2-2	3-0	0-0
Halifax Town	2-0	1-1	1-2	1-0	2-1	3-1	2-1	2-2	1-1	0-2	—	2-0	1-1	0-2	1-1	0-0	1-1	4-1	3-1	2-1	3-1	4-1	3-0	1-1
Kidderminster H	0-0	3-2	0-0	1-0	0-1	1-4	0-2	2-2	1-2	2-1	1-0	—	0-1	0-1	0-0	0-0	2-0	1-3	2-0	1-2	0-2	0-1	0-1	2-1
Morecambe	2-1	0-1	0-1	2-2	1-0	1-1	2-2	1-1	1-0	1-0	4-0	0-1	—	2-1	0-3	1-0	0-0	2-0	1-0	3-3	0-0	2-0	2-0	1-3
Northwich V	1-3	1-1	0-3	0-4	2-1	2-0	1-0	2-0	1-2	0-3	3-2	0-1	0-2	—	1-0	4-1	3-1	0-3	4-0	0-0	0-1	0-1	0-2	1-2
Oxford U	2-0	1-1	0-0	1-1	1-1	2-2	1-0	0-2	1-0	1-1	2-0	0-1	0-0	5-1	—	0-1	2-2	2-1	2-0	2-0	2-1	4-1	0-0	2-0
Rushden & D	0-1	3-0	1-2	3-1	1-1	2-3	3-0	2-0	0-0	1-3	0-1	0-1	2-2	1-0	1-0	—	2-3	1-0	2-1	2-2	1-1	4-1	2-0	0-1
Southport	1-0	2-1	3-1	1-2	3-1	1-4	0-1	1-2	2-2	3-1	1-1	0-1	1-2	1-2	0-1	1-2	—	1-1	5-1	1-2	1-0	0-1	0-0	0-1
St Albans C	3-5	1-5	0-1	0-0	2-2	1-2	1-2	0-0	2-3	0-6	3-2	1-1	0-2	1-3	0-2	3-2	2-2	—	0-3	2-3	1-0	1-0	0-1	4-2
Stafford R	0-3	1-0	1-1	1-2	0-1	1-2	0-1	0-1	3-1	4-2	2-3	1-2	1-3	2-0	0-1	1-1	1-0	2-2	—	1-3	0-4	2-0	1-0	0-0
Stevenage B	3-2	0-1	2-1	4-1	2-3	1-2	0-0	3-3	3-0	1-0	2-1	1-2	3-3	0-2	2-2	1-0	3-1	1-2	6-0	—	3-0	1-0	3-2	1-2
Tamworth	2-0	1-0	0-1	0-1	0-1	0-2	1-0	1-1	2-1	4-2	1-0	0-0	0-1	0-1	1-3	1-4	1-1	1-1	0-0	2-1	—	1-3	3-1	2-2
Weymouth	1-0	1-2	1-1	2-1	3-2	1-1	2-1	1-0	2-1	3-2	1-0	1-1	2-1	1-1	1-1	1-1	2-0	2-1	1-2	0-1	3-1	—	2-3	1-2
Woking	2-0	2-0	0-0	0-1	1-2	2-2	0-2	3-3	2-2	1-0	2-2	3-0	1-1	3-2	1-0	3-0	1-1	1-2	1-1	0-1	0-2	4-0	—	1-2
York C	1-0	1-0	3-2	1-2	5-0	2-3	0-0	0-0	0-2	2-2	2-0	1-0	2-3	2-1	1-0	3-1	2-2	0-0	0-0	0-1	0-2	1-0	0-1	—

APPEARANCES AND GOALSCORERS 2006–2007

ALDERSHOT TOWN
Goals: *League (64):* John Grant 17, Williams 9 (1 pen), Dixon 8, Gayle 7, Barnard 4 (2 pens), Hudson 4, Day 3, Joel Grant 3, Soares 3, Beckford 1, Molesley 1, Pritchard 1, Scott 1, Winfield 1, own goal 1.
FA Cup (13): John Grant 5, Barnard 3 (1 pen), Soares 3, Pritchard 1, own goal 1.
Trophy (1): John Grant 1.
League Appearances: Anderson, 6+6; Barnard, 40+1; Beckford, 10+9; Bull, 46; Charles, 13; Day, 36+1; Dixon, 21+1; Edwards, 15+2; Gayle, 18+6; Joel Grant 8+6; John Grant 39+2; Harding, 8+8; Hudson, 9+17; Hylton, 0+1; Lee, 9+3; Molesley, 33; Newman, 37; Okuonghae, 2; Osano, 9+1; Pritchard, 2+21; Scott, 18+14; Smith, 36+5; Soares, 32+8; Wells, 0+1; Williams, 45+1; Winfield, 14+8.

ALTRINCHAM TOWN
Goals: *League (53):* Little 12, Chalmers 6, O'Neill 6, Aspinall 5 (5 pens), Lawton 5, Thornley 4, Owen 3, Senior 3, Peyton 2, Bushell 1, Lugsden 1, Munroe 1, Talbot 1, Thompson 1, own goals 2.
FA Cup (0).
Trophy (1): Little 1.
League Appearances: Acton, 10+1; Aspinall, 29+6; Band, 34+3; Bowler, 0+7; Bushell, 34+1; Chalmers, 40+5; Coburn, 36; Hendley, 0+8; Hussin, 0+3; Lawton, 46; Little, 34; Lugsden, 1+4; McFadden, 1+19; Munroe, 37+2; O'Neill, 41+3; Owen, 28+1; Peyton, 45+1; Potts, 8+3; Rose, 25+3; Scott, A. 5+1; Scott, G. 20+6; Senior, 8+7; Talbot, 10+11; Thompson, 2+6; Thornley, 12+20.

BURTON ALBION
Goals: *League (52):* Clare 16 (2 pens), Webster 8 (2 pens), Corbett 4, Ducros 4, Shaw 4, Fowler 2, Holmes 2, Stride 2, Brayford 1, Carden 1, Gilroy 1, Goodfellow 1, Hall 1, Harrad 1, Rowett 1, Scoffham 1, own goals 2.
FA Cup (2): Clare 2.
Trophy (5): Shaw 2, Ducros 1, Harrad 1, own goal 1.
League Appearances: Austin, 33+4; Bell, 9+3; Brayford, 21+4; Brown, 4; Carden, 27+1; Clare, 41; Corbett, 43+2; Ducros, 25+5; Fowler, 20+2; Gilroy, 20+5; Goodfellow, 2+4; Hall, 7+5; Harrad, 13+28; Henshaw, 1+8; Holmes, 21+12; Liversage, 0+1; Nicholls, 14; Opara, 1; Poole, 46; Rowett, 26; Scoffham, 4+6; Shaw, 23+13; Stride, 36+3; Tinson, 33+2; Webster, 36.

CAMBRIDGE UNITED
Goals: *League (57):* Simpson R 17 (3 pens), Chillingworth 5, Brady 3, Bridges 3, Carey-Bertram 3 (1 pen), Marum 3, Pitt 3, Richardson 3 (1 pen), Gash 2, Peters 2, Smith S 2, Ademeno 1, Brown 1, Duncan 1, Gleeson 1, Holdsworth 1, Jaszczun 1, Morrison 1, Sedgemore 1, Smith C 1, Wolleaston 1, own goal 1.
FA Cup (0).
Trophy (0).
League Appearances: Ademeno, 1+5; Bloomer, 16+2; Brady, 31+4; Bridges, 19+12; Brown, 24; Carey-Bertram, 8+9; Chillingworth, 15+1; Collins, A. 10+1; Collins, J. 6+1; Crichton, 33; Davies, 1; Duncan, 20; Flynn, 1; Gash, 7+9; Gier, 15+2; Gill, 3+1; Gleeson, 8; Gordon, 1; Hanlon, 11+2; Herbert, 13; Holdsworth, 3; Hooper, 2+1; Hughes, 0+5; Hyem, 0+1; Jaszczun, 10+1; Lawrence, 0+1; Marum, 7+9; Meredith, 1; Morrison, 46; Page, 6+2; Peters, 19+4; Pitt, 40+3; Purser, 5+5; Quinton, 3+4; Richardson, 17+3; Robinson, 7+2; Sedgemore, 3+1; Simpson, J. 11+8; Simpson, R. 28+5; Smith, C. 5+1; Smith, S. 16+7; Wolleaston, 34+3.

CRAWLEY TOWN
Goals: *League (52):* Rendell 11 (3 pens), Scully 7, Blackburn 4, Bulman 4 (1 pen), Strevens 4 (2 pens), Woozley 4, Benyon 3, Bostwick 2, Bull 2, Edwards 2, Evans 2, Okuonghae 2, Richardson 2, Judge 1, Peters 1, Wright 1.
FA Cup (2): Bostwick 1, Rendell 1.
Trophy (0).
League Appearances: Baker, 0+1; Benjamin, 0+3; Benyon, 12+3; Berry, 6+2; Blackburn, 39+2; Blackman, 9+7; Bostwick, 24; Brown, 13+1; Bull, 16+1; Bulman, 36+1; Charles, 5+1; Dadson, 0+1; Edwards, 16+5; England, 2+1; Evans, 14+2; Hamer, 45; Hiley, 42+2; Judge, 29+1; Kember, 1; Lovegrove, 4+1; Macleod, 5+6; Marshall, 3+12; McCallum, 2; Mills, 17+4; Nayee, 0+2; Obersteller, 0+1; Okuonghae, 21; Peters, 3; Rendell, 26+16; Richardson, 11+7; Rowaye, 0+1; Sappleton, 2+7; Scully, 36+4; Strevens, 13+2; Suliaman, 0+2; Tolfrey, 1+1; Townsend, 0+1; Woozley, 44+1; Wright, 9.

DAGENHAM & REDBRIDGE
Goals: *League (93):* Benson 28, Mackail-Smith 15, Rainford 11 (3 pens), Sloma 8, Southam 7 (2 pens), Strevens 6, Akurang 3 (1 pen), Boardman 3, Moore 3 (1 pen), Saunders 3, Uddin 3, Taylor 1, own goals 2.
FA Cup (0).
Trophy (4): Benson 2, Mackail-Smith 1, Sloma 1.
League Appearances: Akurang, 10+17; Arber, 6; Atieno, 0+3; Batt, 0+4; Benson, 45+1; Blackett, 17; Boardman, 9; Bruce, 1+12; Cole, 3+1; Eyre, 1; Foster, 45; Griffiths, 44+1; Hogan, 0+1; Lawson, 0+3; Leberl, 28+9; Lettejallon, 0+3; Mackail-Smith, 27+1; Moore, 6+9; Olayle, 2; Rainford, 40; Roberts, 45; Saunders, 37+5; Sloma, 40+4; Southam, 42+1; Strevens, 10+10; Taylor, 2+2; Uddin, 42+1; Vernazza, 4+6; Wallis, 0+2.

EXETER CITY
Goals: *League (67):* Jones B 10 (4 pens), Challinor 9, Stansfield 9, Elam 7, Carlisle 5,

Mackie 5, Logan 4 (1 pen), Phillips 4, Buckle 3, Moxey 2, Cozic 1, Edwards 1, Gill 1, Seaborne 1, Todd 1, own goals 4.
FA Cup (3): Challinor 1, Phillips 1, Taylor 1.
Trophy (3): Cozic 1, Gill 1, Jones B 1.
Play-Offs (3): Phillips 2, Stansfield 1.
League Appearances: Ada, 5+1; Buckle, 26+3; Carlisle, 21+3; Challinor, 32+10; Clay, 2+3; Cozic, 15+15; Edwards, 43; Elam, 19+1; Friend, 0+2; Gill, 46; Jones, B. 46; Jones, P. 21; Logan, 10+7; Mackie, 22+18; Moxey, 11+12; Phillips, 21+15; Rice, 25+1; Richardson, 13+6; Seaborne, 3+1; Stansfield, 26+12; Taylor, 26+4; Todd, 35; Tully, 17; Woodards, 21+1.

FOREST GREEN ROVERS
Goals: *League (59):* Carey-Bertram 7, Clist 7, Nicholson 6 (3 pens), Rigoglioso 6, Beesley 5, Russell 5, Afful 2, Brough 2, Butler 2, Giles 2, Hardiker 2, Meechan 2, Stonehouse 2, Dodgson 1, Griffin 1, Lawless 1, Pitman 1, Preece 1, Robinson M 1, Williams D 1, own goals 2.
FA Cup (1): Nicholson 1.
Trophy (0).
League Appearances: Afful, 25+16; Beesley, 24+7; Brough, 39+1; Butler, 6+3; Carey-Bertram, 14+6; Clist, 44+1; Dodgson, 4+9; Edwards, 9+1; Giles, 22+1; Griffin, 5+9; Hardiker, 23; Harrison, 2+1; Ipoua, 2+5; Jones, 40; Lamb, 1+4; Lawless, 33+5; Meechan, 26+3; Nicholson, 44; Pitman, 23+9; Preece, 19+11; Rigoglioso, 9+2; Robinson, M. 11+1; Robinson, R. 18; Russell, 15+5; Stonehouse, 8+18; Wanless, 3+5; Williams, D. 11+7; Williams, S. 26; Zarczynski, 0+3.

GRAVESEND & NORTHFLEET
Goals: *League (63):* MacDonald 27 (7 pens), Sodje 9, Moore 7, De Bolla 6, Smith R 3, Ledgister 2, Slatter 2, Varney 2, Coleman 1, Eribenne 1, Hawkins 1, Long 1, McCarthy 1.
FA Cup (0).
Trophy (4): MacDonald 2 (1 pen), De Bolla 1, Long 1.
League Appearances: Anderson, 0+1; Coleman, 10+20; Cronin, 43; De Bolla, 25+6; Ekoku, 1+5; Eribenne, 9+1; Hawkins, 29+4; Howe, 0+1; Keeling, 26+11; Ledgister, 6+7; Long, 27+2; MacDonald, 41; McCarthy, 38; McKenna, 0+1; McShane, 3; Moore, 30+8; Opinel, 31+1; Purcell, 1+9; Quinn, 42; Ricketts, 26+5; Roberts, 0+1; Slatter, 38+3; Smith, J. 22+2; Smith, R. 42; Sodje, 14+25; Varney, 2+2.

GRAYS ATHLETIC
Goals: *League (56):* McLean 13, Kightly 10, Poole 6, O'Connor 4, Boylan 3, Grant 3, Oli 3, Green 2, Griffiths 2, Slabber 2, Stuart 2, Thurgood 2 (2 pens), Downer 1, Harding 1, Rhodes 1, Williamson 1.
FA Cup (1): Boylan 1.
Trophy (13): Martin 5, Turner 2, Boylan 1, Cadamarteri 1, Grant 1, Poole 1, Rhodes 1, Thurgood 1.
League Appearances: Barness, 3+3; Bayes, 36; Bodkin, 9+3; Boylan, 16+5; Bull, 3; Cadamarteri, 1; Comyn-Platt, 4; Coutts, 0+1; Cowan, 8; Downer, 9; El Kholti, 4+2; Eribenne, 2+2; Fernandez, 1+1; Grant, 7; Green, 17+1; Griffiths, 6+7; Harding, 11+8; Howell, 3+6; Joseph-Dubois, 0+1; Kamara, 2+2; Kemp, 4; Kightly, 18; Knowles, 10+1; Martin, 31+5; Mawer, 8+2; McLean, 17; Molango, 1+1; Nicholls, 33+2; O'Connor, 14+1; Oli, 31+5; Plummer, 3; Poole, 30+6; Rhodes, 6+6; Richards, 5; Sambrook, 36; Sangere, 6+2; Slabber, 2+10; Smith, 20+2; Stuart, 46; Thurgood, 20+3; Tonkin, 11+1; Turner, 1+10; Williamson, 11+7.

HALIFAX TOWN
Goals: *League (55):* Forrest 7, Torpey 7, Sugden 5, Bastians 4, Campbell 4, Stamp 4, Joynes 3, Killeen 3, Uhlenbeek 3, Atkinson 2, Quinn 2, Smeltz 2, Trotman 2, Wright 2, Ainsworth 1, Roberts 1, Senior 1, Strong 1, own goal 1.
FA Cup (0).
Trophy (11): Killeen 2, Smeltz 2, Stamp 2, Atkinson 1, Foster 1 (pen), Joynes 1, Senior 1, Trotman 1.
League Appearances: Ainsworth, 2; Atkinson, 4; Bastians, 8+1; Billy, 10+3; Campbell, 12+10; Cresswell, 14+1; Doughty, 29+4; Forrest, 38+2; Foster, 20+3; Fry, 2+2; Gray, 2+5; Haslam, 20; Joynes, 5+2; Kearney, 28+2; Killeen, 39+4; Matthews, 3; Mawson, 46; Parke, 0+3; Quinn, 31+1; Roberts, 12+1; Senior, 4+14; Smeltz, 13+18; Stamp, 14+4; Strong, 7+1; Sugden, 16+7; Thompson, 33+5; Torpey, 17+10; Toulson, 11+4; Trotman, 11; Uhlenbeek, 23+7; Wright, 22+5; Young, 10+1.

KIDDERMINSTER HARRIERS
Goals: *League (43):* Christie 9 (4 pens), Constable 6, Penn 5, Harkness 4, Russell 4, Hurren 3, Reynolds 3, Blackwood 2, Reid 2, White 2, Kenna 1, Smikle 1, own goal 1.
FA Cup (6): White 2, Christie 1, Hurren 1, Nelthorpe 1, Penn 1.
Trophy (21): Constable 9, Christie 2, Hurren 2, Penn 2, Russell 2, Blackwood 1, Creighton 1, Reynolds 1, White 1.
League Appearances: Bevan, 40; Bignot, 3; Blackwood, 38+6; Brady, 6+3; Christie, 32+2; Constable, 21+2; Cowan, 5; Craven, 0+1; Creighton, 46; Davies, 4; Eaton, 1+1; Ferrell, 1; Harkness, 29+2; Hay, 3+7; Hurren, 34+5; Kenna, 29; Lee, 5; McClen, 5; McGrath, 7+6; Nelthorpe, 4; Penn, 40+1; Reid, 6; Reynolds, 12+28; Russell, 34+8; Sedgemore, 23+7; Smikle, 11+17; Sturridge, 2+4; Taylor, B. 4+2; Taylor, S. 2+1; White, 10+16; Whitehead, 43; Wilson, 6.

MORECAMBE
Goals: *League (64):* Thompson 11 (1 pen), Twiss 10, Blinkhorn 8, Carlton 7, Curtis 6 (1 pen), Blackburn 3, Lloyd 3, McNiven 3, Sorvel 2, Stanley 2, Yates 2, Bentley 1, McLachlan 1, Meadowcroft 1, own goals 4.
FA Cup (4): Curtis 1 (pen), McNiven 1, Stanley 1, Twiss 1.

Trophy (8): Twiss 3, Curtis 1, Howard 1, Hunter 1, Thompson 1 (pen), Walker 1.
Play-Offs (4): Curtis 2, Carlton 1, Thompson 1.
League Appearances: Adams, 16; Bentley, 31; Blackburn, 39+1; Blinkhorn, 12; Brannan, 17+14; Burns, 4+10; Carlton, 27+5; Curtis, 28+2; Davies, 1+2; Drench, 41; Howard, 31+1; Hunter, 27+7; Lloyd, 4+4; McLachlan, 10+5; McNiven, 13+14; Meadowcroft, 7+5; Perkins, 20; Platt, 1+3; Rigoglioso, 7+3; Robinson, 4; Shaw, 0+4; Sorvel, 19; Stanley, 37+6; Thompson, 35; Twiss, 30; Walker, 1+4; Walmsley, 0+1; Watt, 1+2; Yates, 43+1.

NORTHWICH VICTORIA
Goals: *League (51):* Brayson 12, Byrne 7 (1 pen), Allan 5, Carr 5 (1 pen), Dean 4, Dodds 3, Townson 3, Mayman 2, Bastians 1, Charnock 1, Elliott 1 (pen), Gallimore 1, Griffiths 1, Roberts 1, Roca 1, Shaw 1, Smart 1, own goal 1.
FA Cup (2): Brayson 1, Carr 1.
Trophy (12): Brayson 3, Carr 2 (1 pen), Roca 2, Shaw 2, Allan 1, Battersby 1, Griffiths 1.
League Appearances: Allan, 21+1; Barwick, 14+7; Bastians, 3+1; Battersby, 34+5; Beaumont, 5; Brayson, 33+7; Brown, 21+2; Byrne, 26+12; Carr, 37+1; Charnock, 42; Connett, 20; Dean, 15+5; Dodds, 6; Elliott, 25+1; Gallimore, 12+1; Griffiths, 25+3; Mayman, 24+2; McCarthy, 17+11; Payne, 11+4; Roberts, 22+1; Roca, 15+13; Rutter, 0+2; Sale, 2+7; Senior, 26; Shaw, 9+4; Smart, 17+1; Smith, 3; Townson, 15+17; Warburton, 0+2; Williams, 3+3; Young, 3.

OXFORD UNITED
Goals: *League (66):* Duffy 18 (7 pens), Odubade 11, Burgess 6 (2 pens), Day 5, Hargreaves 5, Basham 4, Anaclet 3, Robinson 3, Zebroski 2, Corcoran 1, Foster L 1, Gilchrist 1, Johnson 1, Pettefer 1, Quinn 1, Rose 1, own goals 2.
FA Cup (2): Duffy 1, Johnson 1.
Trophy (4): Duffy 2 (1 pen), Robinson 1, Rose 1.
Play-Offs (2): Odubade 1, own goal 1.
League Appearances: Anaclet, 41+3; Basham, 17+3; Brevett, 19+2; Burgess, 32+7; Coombes, 1; Corcoran, 16; Day, 21+16; Dempster, 8+9; Duffy, 33+3; Foster, L. 7+2; Foster, M. 13; Gilchrist, 36; Grebis, 3+1; Gunn, 1+2; Hargreaves, 30+8; Hutchinson, 8+10; Johnson, 23+7; Kennet, 0+1; Odubade, 19+25; Pettefer, 34+4; Quinn, 40+1; Robinson, 10+11; Rose, 19+1; Santos, 3; Slabber, 2+1; Tardif, 4+1; Turley, 42; Willmott, 17; Zebroski, 7+1.

RUSHDEN & DIAMONDS
Goals: *League (58):* Jackson 19, Rankine 7, Kelly 5, Tomlin 4, Woodhouse 4, Hope 3, Ashton 2 (1 pen), Beardsley 2, Chillingworth 2, Watson 2 (1 pen), Albrighton 1, Cook 1, Hatswell 1, Maamria 1, Savage 1, Williams 1, own goals 2.
FA Cup (7): Rankine 2, Shaw 2, Hope 1, Jackson 1, Tomlin 1.
Trophy (5): Ashton 1, Chillingworth 1, Rankine 1, Tomlin 1, Woodhouse 1.
League Appearances: Albrighton, 16+1; Ashton, 40; Baker, 6; Beardsley, 5+7; Beecroft, 0+1; Berry, 14+9; Bostwick, 5+3; Chillingworth, 12+5; Cook, 7+1; Eyre, 19; Fortune-West, 2+4; Ghaichem, 0+1; Goodlife, 5+2; Grainger, 2+1; Hatswell, 34+1; Hope, 45; Jackson, 35+10; Kelly, 33+1; Lambley, 1+5; Maamria, 3+1; Mills, 15+2; Pearson, 3+4; Perpetuini, 3+2; Plummer, 2; Rankine, 32+8; Rigby, 2; Savage, 25+10; Sedgemore, 1; Shaw, 14+6; Tomlin, 10+15; Tynan, 21; Watson, 37+3; Webb, 1; Williams, 12; Wilson, 27+4; Woodhouse, 15+1; Wright, 2+1.

ST ALBANS CITY
Goals: *League (57):* Clarke 9 (2 pens), Hakim 9, Archer 6, Benyon 6, Davis 5 (3 pens), Marwa 4, Theobald 3, Batt D 2, Cracknell 2, Flynn 2, Sangare 2, Elphick 1, Hann 1, Jackman 1, Martin B 1, McBean 1, Walshe 1, Watters 1.
FA Cup (1): Davis 1 (pen).
Trophy (2): Clarke 1, own goal 1.
League Appearances: Ada, 11; Archer, 15+2; Basse, 0+3; Bastock, 44; Batt, D. 22; Batt, S. 2; Benyon, 10+2; Buari, 9+4; Clarke, 39+5; Cousins, 5; Cracknell, 18+11; Davis, 39+1; Deen, 15; Elphick, 36+1; Flynn, 16+4; Hakim, 21+2; Hann, 30+8; Hastings, 5+1; Husnu, 1; Jackman, 3+3; Lewis, 1; Lopez, 5+5; Martin, B. 2+6; Martin, S. 5+9; Marwa, 23+6; McBean, 2; Nicolas, 6; Norris, 2+7; Okuonghae, 15+4; Perks, 2; Roddis, 0+2; Sangare, 16+1; Seeby, 40+3; Simpson, 2+2; Sozzo, 2+4; Theobald, 22; Walshe, 6; Watters, 7+4; Wilde, 7+3.

SOUTHPORT
Goals: *League (57):* Baker 11 (3 pens), Gray 9, Maamria 8 (1 pen), Blakeman 6, Boyd 4, Duffy 4, Paterson 3, Powell 2, Tait 2, Birch 1, Doherty 1, Donnelly 1, Fowler 1, Hoolickin 1, Newby 1, Smith A 1, own goal 1.
FA Cup (0).
Trophy (2): Baker 1, Gray 1.
League Appearances: Baker, 36+4; Barlow, 0+1; Barry, 0+3; Birch, 19; Blakeman, 24+10; Booth, 4+3; Boyd, 35+6; Clancy, 6+5; Doherty, 6; Donnelly, 11; Douglas, 0+5; Dubourdeau, 3; Duffy, 15+2; Dugdale, 7+1; Fowler, 5+13; Gray, 26+8; Harrison, 17+2; Hocking, 14; Holland, 17; Hoolickin, 22+3; Jackson, 7+2; Kirkup, 11+1; Lane, 29+4; Lee, 32; Maamria, 26+1; Martin, 6+1; Newby, 7+4; Olsen, 12+7; Owen, 0+1; Paterson, 4+10; Powell, 28+10; Robinson, 16; Rowland, 32+2; Smith, A. 10; Smith, T. 10; Tait, 6+9; Ventre, 3.

STAFFORD RANGERS
Goals: *League (49):* Grayson 13 (3 pens), Madjo 12, McNiven 9, Olaoye 4, Gibson R 3, McAughtrie 3, Edwards 1, Reid 1, Street 1, Talbott 1, own goal 1.
FA Cup (6): Madjo 2, Murray 2, Daniel 1, McAughtrie 1.
Trophy (0).

League Appearances: Alcock, 23+1; Bailey, 2; Barlow, 1+1; Basham, 3; Dacres, 1+1; Daniel, 46; Downes, 11+1; Duggan, 14; Edwards, 5+17; Gibson, A. 3+1; Gibson, R. 37+6; Grayson, 38+6; Griffith, 20; Lorougnon, 0+4; Lovatt, 30+6; Madjo, 37+5; McAughtrie, 38+1; McNiven, 8+1; Murphy, 34+4; Murray, 18+2; Olaoye, 5+12; Oldfield, 5+7; Quailey, 4+8; Reid, 10+3; Ridgeway, 1+1; Robinson, 2; Street, 20; Sutton, 37; Talbott, 43; White, 1+5; Williams, 9.

STEVENAGE BOROUGH

Goals: *League (76):* Morison 23, Boyd 11, Nurse 8, Nutter 6 (5 pens), Miller 5 (1 pen), Dobson 4, Beard 3, Binns 2, Cole 2, Hakim 2, Hughes 2, Oliver 2, Fuller 1, Guppy 1, Henry 1, Lee 1, own goals 2.

FA Cup (4): Morison 2, Boyd 1, Miller 1.

Trophy (23): Morison 8, Boyd 4, Dobson 2, Slabber 2, Cole 1, Gaia 1, Guppy 1, McMahon 1, Miller 1, Nurse 1, Oliver 1.

League Appearances: Batt, 5+3; Beard, 37+2; Binns, 3+6; Boyd, 25; Bradshaw, 0+1; Bulman, 1; Cole, 14+5; Deen, 2+5; Dobson, 23+15; Fuller, 38; Gaia, 38+1; Goodliffe, 7+1; Guppy, 25+2; Hakim, 5+7; Hatton, 0+1; Henry, 37+3; Hicks, 4; Hughes, 8+2; Johnson, 4; Julian, 42+1; Lee, 10+2; Lewis, 3+5; McMahon, 12; Miller, 24+5; Morison, 42+1; Nurse, 23+9; Nutter, 46; Oliver, 19+9; Potter, 4; Scaley, 0+1; Slabber, 2+2; Stamp, 1+3; Sullivan, 0+6; Thorpe, 2+2.

TAMWORTH

Goals: *League (43):* Atieno 12, Edwards 7, Williams 5, Taylor 4, Burton 3 (1 pen), McGrath 3, Thomas 2, Heslop 1, Law 1 (pen), Smith 1, Stevenson 1, Storer 1, Weaver 1, own goal 1.

FA Cup (8): McGrath 2, Atieno 1, Burton 1, Stevenson 1, Storer 1, Williams 1, own goal 1.

Trophy (4): Edwards 1, Heslop 1, Stevenson 1, Taylor 1.

League Appearances: Atieno, 37+2; Bains, 21; Bampton, 3+6; Belford, C. 1; Belford, D. 0+1; Birch, 1; Bowles, 15+1; Bradley, 2; Briscoe, 15+2; Burton, 12+14; Cooper, 0+1; Da Viega, 28; Deakin, 5; Devlin, 1+3; Dormand, 1; Edwards, 20+1; Friars, 19+2; Ghent, 1; Harban, 4; Heslop, 24+3; Kemp, 20+1; Kendrick, 9+6; Laight, 12+1; Law, 23+5; Lynch, 3; McCallum, 12+1; McGrath, 41+1; Moore, 3+2; Neilson, 4+3; Price, 1+1; Quistin, 0+9; Redmile, 2; Smith, 35+1; Stevenson, 13+14; Storer, 22+8; Taylor, 21+2; Thomas, 11; Touhy, 4+5; Ujah, 1; Ward, 5+5; Weaver, 36+2; Williams, 18+14.

WEYMOUTH

Goals: *League (56):* Smith 10, Beavon 7, Nade 6, Logan 5 (1 pen), Crittenden 4, Coutts 3, Eribenne 3 (1 pen), James 3 (3 pens), Purser 3, Downer 2, Elam 2, Weatherstone 2, Matthews 1, Tindall 1 (pen), Tully 1, own goals 3.

FA Cup (8): Purser 2, Downer 1, Elam 1, Logan 1, O'Brien 1, Tully 1, Weatherstone 1.

Trophy (1): Logan 1 (pen).

League Appearances: Beavon, 18+2; Bell, 0+3; Bernard, 9+3; Challis, 17+5; Cottrell, 16+1; Coutts, 16+5; Crawley, 2+3; Crittenden, 30+2; Dixon, 1+2; Downer, 15+2; Dutton, 7+7; El Kholti, 23; Elam, 23; Eribenne, 16+8; Hartman, 3+1; Howell, 11+6; Ironside, 0+1; James, 26+7; Jones, 2; Lee-Barrett, 19; Logan, 14+9; Matthews, 25; Nade, 32+5; O'Brien, 15+4; Phillips, 7+4; Platt, 6+5; Purser, 7+5; Rink, 0+1; Robinson, 10+2; Ross-Jennings, 0+1; Smith, 25; Tindall, 5+13; Tully, 23+2; Vickers, 26+4; Weatherstone, 38+4; Welsh, 9; Wilkinson, 10+5; Williams, 0+2.

WOKING

Goals: *League (56):* McAllister 15 (2 pens), Sole 12, Hutchinson 6, Lambu 3, Marum 3, Berquez 2, Ferguson 2, Murray 2, Nurse 2, Smith 2, Bunce 1, Evans 1, Pearce 1, Sharpling 1, Taylor 1, Webb 1, own goal 1.

FA Cup (5): Smith 2, Jackson 1, McAllister 1, Sole 1.

Trophy (1): McAllister 1.

League Appearances: Barrett, 6+1; Berquez, 17+11; Bittner, 12; Bunce, 34+2; Cockerill, L. 2; Cockerill, S. 1+3; El-Salahi, 12+3; Evans, 14+3; Ferguson, 7+16; Gier, 7; Gindre, 8; Green, 15+2; Hutchinson, 34; Jackson, 11+5; Jalal, 23; Lambu, 31+8; MacDonald, 28; Marum, 6+8; McAllister, 44; Murray, 42+1; Nurse, 8; Osano, 13+1; Oyedele, 9+10; Pearce, 16+3; Poke, 3; Ruby, 8+1; Sankoh, 1+15; Selley, 3+3; Sharpling, 2+1; Smith, 40+1; Sole, 33+9; Taylor, 9+2; Webb, 7+1.

YORK CITY

Goals: *League (65):* Donaldson 24 (4 pens), Farrell 10, Woolford 8, Bowey 7, Bishop 3, Panther 3, Convery 2, Peat 2, Brodie 1, Goodliffe 1, Kovacs 1, McMahon 1, own goals 2.

FA Cup (1): Donaldson 1 (pen).

Trophy (1): Donaldson 1.

Play-Offs (1): Bowey 1 (pen).

League Appearances: Bell, 0+1; Bishop, 42+3; Bowey, 42; Brodie, 3+9; Convery, 15+9; Craddock, 32+3; Donaldson, 43; Dudgeon, 9+4; Elvins, 4+5; Evans, 45; Farrell, 44+2; Foster, 4+1; Goodliffe, 11; Greenwood, 2+10; James, 8; Kovacs, 8; Lloyd, 23+7; Maidens, 1+2; McGurk, 38; McMahon, 8+11; Panther, 42+2; Parslow, 21+3; Peat, 22+3; Purkiss, 7+1; Reid, 1+1; Stamp, 5+5; Webster, 0+2; Woolford, 26+14.

CONFERENCE NATIONAL PLAY-OFFS 2006–2007

CONFERENCE SEMI-FINAL FIRST LEG

Exeter C	(0) 0	Oxford U	(1) 1
York C	(0) 0	Morecambe	(0) 0

CONFERENCE SEMI-FINAL SECOND LEG

Morecambe	(1) 2	York C	(1) 1
Oxford U	(1) 1	Exeter C	(1) 2

CONFERENCE FINAL (at Wembley)

Sunday, 20 May 2007

Exeter C (1) 1 *(Phillips 8)*

Morecambe (1) 2 *(Thompson 42, Carlton 82)* 40,043

Exeter C: Jones P; Tully, Jones B, Gill■, Edwards, Todd, Carlisle (Logan), Taylor, Phillips (Stansfield), Challinor, Elam (Mackie).
Morecambe: Davies; Yates, Adams, Stanley, Bentley, Blackburn, Thompson (Brannan), Sorvel, Twiss (Hunter), Carlton (McNiven), Curtis.
Referee: M. Oliver (Ashington).

ATTENDANCES BY CLUB 2006–2007

	Aggregate 2006–07	*Average 2006–07*	*Highest Attendance 2006–07*
Oxford United	145,634	6,332	11,065 v Woking
Exeter City	83,427	3,627	6,670 v Southport
York City	65,764	2,859	5,378 v Oxford United
Cambridge United	64,747	2,815	6,021 v Tamworth
Aldershot Town	54,284	2,360	3,621 v Oxford United
Stevenage Borough	48,898	2,126	3,058 v Exeter City
Rushden & Diamonds	47,028	2,045	3,270 v Oxford United
Weymouth	45,269	1,968	5,244 v Oxford United
Burton Albion	43,045	1,872	2,910 v Rushden & Diamonds
Woking	40,808	1,774	3,725 v Aldershot Town
Dagenham & Redbridge	40,390	1,756	4,044 v Aldershot Town
Halifax Town	38,138	1,658	2,515 v Stevenage Borough
Kidderminster Harriers	37,345	1,624	2,264 v Oxford United
Morecambe	36,763	1,598	2,412 v Halifax Town
Tamworth	29,282	1,273	2,411 v Altrincham
Southport	27,593	1,200	3,206 v York City
Forest Green Rovers	27,258	1,185	3,021 v Oxford United
Stafford Rangers	27,164	1,181	1,795 v Oxford United
Altrincham	26,818	1,166	2,330 v Northwich Victoria
Gravesend & Northfleet	26,804	1,165	2,019 v Oxford United
Crawley Town	26,638	1,158	2,101 v Oxford United
St Albans City	26,300	1,143	2,878 v Stevenage Borough
Grays Athletic	24,772	1,077	1,759 v Oxford United
Northwich Victoria	22,352	972	1,552 v Oxford United

CONFERENCE SECOND DIVISION NORTH 2006–2007

FINAL LEAGUE TABLE

	Home						Away					Total						
	P	*W*	*D*	*L*	*F*	*A*	*W*	*D*	*L*	*F*	*A*	*W*	*D*	*L*	*F*	*A*	*GD*	*Pts*
1 Droylsden	42	16	4	1	54	25	7	5	9	31	30	23	9	10	85	55	30	78
2 Kettering T	42	11	6	4	41	27	9	7	5	34	31	20	13	9	75	58	17	73
3 Workington	42	12	5	4	33	17	8	5	8	28	29	20	10	12	61	46	15	70
4 Hinckley U	42	10	8	3	40	24	9	4	8	28	30	19	12	11	68	54	14	69
5 Farsley Celtic	42	10	5	6	27	21	9	6	6	31	30	19	11	12	58	51	7	68
6 Harrogate T	42	8	8	5	27	18	10	5	6	31	23	18	13	11	58	41	17	67
7 Blyth Spartans	42	10	5	6	30	21	9	4	8	26	29	19	9	14	56	50	6	66
8 Hyde U	42	12	5	4	47	24	6	6	9	32	38	18	11	13	79	62	17	65
9 Worcester C	42	9	8	4	41	28	7	6	8	26	26	16	14	12	67	54	13	62
10 Nuneaton Borough	42	8	9	4	19	13	7	6	8	35	32	15	15	12	54	45	9	60
11 Moor Green	42	8	6	7	30	23	8	5	8	23	28	16	11	15	53	51	2	59
12 Gainsborough T	42	9	5	7	30	26	6	6	9	21	31	15	11	16	51	57	–6	56
13 Hucknall T	42	8	4	9	40	37	7	5	9	29	32	15	9	18	69	69	0	54
14 Alfreton T	42	8	6	7	24	21	6	6	9	20	29	14	12	16	44	50	–6	54
15 Vauxhall Motors	42	6	6	9	29	31	6	9	6	33	33	12	15	15	62	64	–2	51
16 Barrow	42	7	6	8	23	23	5	8	8	24	25	12	14	16	47	48	–1	50
17 Leigh RMI	42	9	4	8	31	32	4	6	11	16	29	13	10	19	47	61	–14	49
18 Stalybridge Celtic	42	7	6	8	38	45	6	4	11	26	36	13	10	19	64	81	–17	49
19 Redditch U	42	6	7	8	32	35	5	8	8	30	32	11	15	16	62	67	–5	48
20 Scarborough*	42	6	6	9	21	21	7	10	4	29	24	13	16	13	50	45	5	45
21 Worksop T	42	6	6	9	24	29	6	3	12	20	33	12	9	21	44	62	–18	45
22 Lancaster C*	42	0	2	19	10	49	2	3	16	17	61	2	5	35	27	110	–83	1

**Deducted 10 points for entering administration.*

CONFERENCE SECOND DIVISION NORTH PLAY-OFFS

SEMI-FINAL FIRST LEG
Hinckley United 0, Workington 0
Farsley Celtic 1 *(Reeves 17)*, Kettering Town 1 *(Solkhon 75)*

SEMI-FINAL SECOND LEG
Kettering Town 0, Farsley Celtic 0
aet; Farsley Celtic won 4-2 on penalties.
Workington 1 *(Hewson 87)*, Hinckley United 2 *(Jackson 43, Marrison 47)*

FINAL
Farsley Celtic 4 *(Grant 15, Reeves 79, 89 (pen), Crossley 87)*, Hinckley United 3 *(Shilton 19, Cartwright 21, 83)*

CONFERENCE SECOND DIVISION NORTH RESULTS 2006–2007

	Alfreton Town	Barrow	Blyth Spartans	Droylsden	Farsley Celtic	Gainsborough Trinity	Harrogate Town	Hinckley United	Hucknall Town	Hyde United	Kettering Town	Lancaster City	Leigh RMI	Moor Green	Nuneaton Borough	Redditch United	Scarborough	Stalybridge Celtic	Vauxhall Motors	Worcester City	Workington	Worksop Town
Alfreton Town	—	1-0	0-1	1-3	0-1	3-1	0-0	0-1	2-1	2-2	1-1	2-1	1-0	3-0	0-3	0-0	1-1	1-2	2-0	0-2	1-1	3-0
Barrow	1-1	—	0-2	2-1	2-2	3-0	2-3	1-0	1-0	1-2	0-1	3-0	2-0	1-1	0-1	0-4	1-1	2-1	0-0	0-1	0-0	1-2
Blyth Spartans	3-0	1-0	—	0-3	4-1	2-0	0-0	3-1	2-2	0-0	2-2	3-0	1-0	0-1	1-2	1-2	2-0	1-0	1-2	2-2	0-2	2-0
Droylsden	1-1	2-1	0-0	—	4-1	2-1	2-0	3-1	5-3	4-2	1-1	6-1	2-2	1-0	4-2	2-1	1-3	6-1	1-0	2-1	2-1	3-2
Farsley Celtic	1-1	2-2	3-0	0-3	—	1-0	1-0	0-2	1-0	1-1	2-1	3-1	1-1	0-1	0-1	4-0	0-2	1-1	3-2	1-0	1-2	1-0
Gainsborough Trinity	4-0	1-0	0-2	3-2	0-0	—	1-3	1-0	2-3	2-3	2-3	1-0	0-0	1-0	1-1	2-2	3-1	2-0	1-2	1-3	1-0	1-1
Harrogate Town	0-1	1-1	1-2	1-1	1-0	1-1	—	2-0	1-1	1-2	2-3	3-0	2-1	1-1	1-1	2-2	0-1	0-0	1-0	1-0	4-0	1-0
Hinckley United	2-2	1-1	2-1	2-1	2-1	1-1	0-1	—	1-1	2-0	3-1	5-0	3-1	2-0	2-2	3-1	1-1	2-3	1-1	3-3	2-1	0-1
Hucknall Town	0-2	1-3	1-2	2-2	0-1	3-3	0-3	1-2	—	4-2	1-2	5-0	1-3	3-2	2-1	2-2	0-1	2-1	2-2	4-2	2-1	4-0
Hyde United	2-1	1-1	5-1	2-1	3-4	3-0	4-0	2-0	1-0	—	3-5	5-0	2-0	4-1	3-2	0-2	1-1	3-1	1-1	0-0	1-1	1-2
Kettering Town	0-1	3-2	1-1	1-0	3-2	4-2	3-1	1-2	0-0	1-0	—	3-3	4-0	1-1	3-2	3-1	3-1	2-1	0-1	1-1	2-3	2-2
Lancaster City	0-2	0-2	0-2	1-2	1-2	0-1	0-2	1-4	0-1	2-3	0-1	—	0-0	0-3	0-4	1-2	1-5	0-1	2-2	0-2	1-5	0-3
Leigh RMI	2-0	0-3	3-1	2-2	1-3	2-0	1-3	2-3	4-3	2-0	1-2	0-1	—	2-2	1-0	0-0	1-1	1-3	0-3	2-1	2-0	2-1
Moor Green	2-0	0-0	0-2	5-2	1-1	2-1	0-1	0-1	1-2	1-1	1-2	3-1	0-0	—	1-1	1-1	1-2	2-1	5-2	3-1	1-0	0-1
Nuneaton Borough	1-0	3-0	1-1	1-0	1-1	0-1	0-0	0-1	2-1	0-0	2-1	1-0	0-1	0-1	—	1-0	1-1	3-2	1-1	1-1	0-0	0-0
Redditch United	3-2	1-1	0-2	0-0	1-4	1-1	2-1	1-3	1-2	2-1	4-4	2-2	2-1	0-1	2-0	—	1-1	1-2	3-3	1-2	4-1	0-1
Scarborough	0-1	1-1	0-1	1-0	0-0	0-0	1-1	3-0	1-2	1-2	1-1	1-2	1-1	3-0	1-3	3-2	—	0-1	0-1	1-0	0-1	2-1
Stalybridge Celtic	3-2	0-4	3-2	1-2	0-2	0-2	0-2	2-2	2-2	3-7	0-0	3-1	2-1	2-3	4-3	3-2	2-2	—	3-3	1-1	1-2	3-0
Vauxhall Motors	1-2	0-1	2-0	2-3	1-2	0-1	1-5	2-2	1-2	1-0	1-1	4-1	2-1	1-1	1-3	1-1	1-1	2-2	—	2-0	1-2	2-0
Worcester City	0-0	3-0	3-2	3-1	0-1	1-1	2-3	3-1	2-0	2-2	2-0	4-1	1-2	0-1	3-3	1-1	3-2	1-1	3-3	—	2-2	2-1
Workington	1-1	1-1	3-0	0-0	3-0	1-2	3-2	1-1	1-0	3-1	2-0	1-1	0-1	3-2	2-0	1-0	0-1	2-1	2-0	0-1	—	3-2
Worksop Town	2-0	2-0	1-1	0-2	2-2	1-2	0-0	1-1	1-3	3-1	0-2	3-1	2-0	0-1	0-0	2-3	0-0	2-1	1-4	0-2	1-3	—

CONFERENCE SECOND DIVISION SOUTH 2006–2007

FINAL LEAGUE TABLE

		Home					*Away*					*Total*						
	P	*W*	*D*	*L*	*F*	*A*	*W*	*D*	*L*	*F*	*A*	*W*	*D*	*L*	*F*	*A*	*GD*	*Pts*
1 Histon	42	18	0	3	47	20	12	4	5	38	24	30	4	8	85	44	41	94
2 Salisbury C	42	10	7	4	26	14	11	5	5	39	23	21	12	9	65	37	28	75
3 Braintree T	42	9	7	5	27	19	12	4	5	24	19	21	11	10	51	38	13	74
4 Havant & Waterlooville	42	15	4	2	52	20	5	9	7	23	26	20	13	9	75	46	29	73
5 Bishop's Stortford	42	11	7	3	37	26	10	3	8	35	35	21	10	11	72	61	11	73
6 Newport Co	42	15	1	5	52	24	6	6	9	31	33	21	7	14	83	57	26	70
7 Eastbourne Borough	42	11	8	2	29	15	7	7	7	29	27	18	15	9	58	42	16	69
8 Welling U	42	11	3	7	37	23	10	3	8	28	28	21	6	15	65	51	14	69
9 Lewes	42	11	7	3	41	25	4	10	7	26	27	15	17	10	67	52	15	62
10 Fisher Athletic	42	11	5	5	49	33	4	6	11	29	47	15	11	16	78	80	–2	56
11 Farnborough T*	42	14	4	3	36	20	5	4	12	23	32	19	8	15	59	52	7	55
12 Bognor Regis T	42	6	10	5	29	23	7	3	11	27	39	13	13	16	56	62	–6	52
13 Cambridge C	42	8	4	9	25	21	7	3	11	19	31	15	7	20	44	52	–8	52
14 Sutton U	42	8	8	5	30	26	6	1	14	28	37	14	9	19	58	63	–5	51
15 Eastleigh	42	8	6	7	26	26	3	9	9	22	27	11	15	16	48	53	–5	48
16 Yeading	42	6	9	6	27	28	6	0	15	29	50	12	9	21	56	78	–22	45
17 Dorchester T	42	6	2	13	26	44	5	10	6	23	33	11	12	19	49	77	–28	45
18 Thurrock	42	6	6	9	34	41	5	5	11	27	39	11	11	20	61	80	–19	44
19 Basingstoke T	42	4	6	11	18	26	5	10	6	28	32	9	16	17	46	58	–12	43
20 Hayes	42	5	4	12	25	37	6	6	9	22	36	11	10	21	47	73	–26	43
21 Weston-Super-Mare	42	4	4	13	25	45	4	7	10	24	32	8	11	23	49	77	–28	35
22 Bedford Town	42	5	5	11	25	36	3	2	16	18	46	8	7	27	43	82	–39	31

**Deducted 10 points for entering administration.*

CONFERENCE SECOND DIVISION SOUTH PLAY-OFFS

SEMI-FINAL FIRST LEG

Havant & Waterlooville 1 *(Louis 88)*, Braintree Town 1 *(Baker 45)*
Bishop's Stortford 1 *(Pearson 54)*, Salisbury City 1 *(Matthews 64)*

SEMI-FINAL SECOND LEG

Braintree Town 1 *(Hawes 75)*, Havant & Waterlooville 1 *(Collins 89 (pen))*
aet; Braintree Town won 4-2 on penalties.
Salisbury City 3 *(Tubbs 18, Matthews 100, Fowler 118)*, Bishop's Stortford 1 *(Porter 34)*

FINAL

Braintree Town 0, Salisbury City 1 *(Tubbs 84)*

CONFERENCE SECOND DIVISION SOUTH RESULTS 2006–2007

	Basingstoke Town	Bedford Town	Bishop's Stortford	Bognor Regis Town	Braintree Town	Cambridge City	Dorchester Town	Eastbourne Borough	Eastleigh	Farnborough Town	Fisher Athletic	Havant & Waterlooville	Hayes	Histon	Lewes	Newport County	Salisbury City	Sutton United	Thurrock	Welling United	Weston-Super-Mare	Yeading
Basingstoke Town	—	0-1	1-0	4-0	1-2	0-0	2-2	0-1	0-1	0-2	2-1	2-1	1-1	1-2	0-0	0-1	1-1	0-2	1-1	1-3	0-1	1-3
Bedford Town	0-0	—	3-1	2-3	1-2	0-1	1-1	1-1	1-1	0-2	1-4	2-1	1-2	0-2	0-2	0-2	1-2	2-0	3-1	2-2	2-1	2-5
Bishop's Stortford	3-1	2-2	—	0-1	0-2	2-1	4-3	1-0	1-1	2-1	2-2	1-0	3-1	0-0	3-0	2-2	1-1	3-2	2-1	1-3	2-2	2-0
Bognor Regis Town	1-2	1-0	2-4	—	1-2	0-1	3-0	1-1	0-0	1-1	1-1	0-0	5-1	0-0	1-1	1-1	1-1	0-4	3-0	1-1	3-1	3-1
Braintree Town	1-0	2-0	3-1	1-2	—	2-1	3-1	1-1	1-1	2-1	2-2	0-0	0-1	1-1	1-1	2-1	0-0	0-1	0-1	2-1	0-1	3-1
Cambridge City	0-1	0-0	0-1	2-0	1-0	—	0-1	1-0	2-0	1-1	0-0	3-0	2-2	0-1	1-0	2-1	1-3	2-3	2-3	0-1	2-3	3-0
Dorchester Town	1-2	1-3	0-1	0-1	0-0	3-1	—	0-0	1-0	4-1	1-3	1-3	0-2	1-2	1-5	0-4	0-3	5-4	3-1	0-1	1-5	3-2
Eastbourne Borough	1-1	0-3	2-1	2-0	1-2	2-1	1-1	—	0-0	0-0	3-1	1-1	0-0	1-1	2-1	2-1	1-0	2-0	3-1	0-0	3-0	2-0
Eastleigh	3-1	2-0	1-1	0-4	0-3	0-1	1-1	1-1	—	3-1	4-0	0-1	2-1	1-0	0-0	3-1	0-1	1-0	1-1	1-3	1-1	1-4
Farnborough Town	1-1	3-2	3-1	3-1	2-1	2-1	1-1	1-0	1-0	—	2-0	2-1	1-3	2-3	1-1	1-0	0-1	4-0	2-1	2-1	0-0	2-1
Fisher Athletic	3-3	3-0	0-1	3-0	3-0	3-0	1-1	0-3	3-1	3-0	—	3-3	3-0	1-4	5-1	3-3	1-4	2-1	3-5	2-1	1-1	3-1
Havant & Waterlooville	1-0	4-0	5-4	2-2	1-1	2-3	2-0	2-1	1-1	2-0	1-3	—	6-0	2-1	1-1	3-1	3-1	1-0	3-0	4-0	2-1	4-0
Hayes	1-1	3-1	1-2	2-3	2-3	0-1	4-0	1-1	2-1	1-1	4-3	0-1	—	1-3	1-4	0-1	0-4	0-4	1-1	0-1	1-0	0-1
Histon	4-2	1-0	0-2	2-1	2-0	2-1	3-0	1-2	1-0	2-1	2-1	4-0	5-0	—	3-2	1-0	4-2	2-1	3-1	1-0	3-2	1-2
Lewes	2-2	5-1	2-3	1-1	0-1	1-1	2-2	1-1	0-3	1-0	2-0	1-1	2-0	3-1	—	2-0	1-0	3-1	1-1	4-2	4-2	3-2
Newport County	3-0	2-0	4-1	3-1	0-1	1-2	0-1	4-0	3-1	3-4	4-2	1-0	2-0	5-1	1-1	—	4-3	3-1	1-3	3-1	1-0	4-1
Salisbury City	0-0	3-1	3-1	2-1	0-1	2-0	1-1	1-2	1-0	0-1	3-0	1-1	0-0	0-3	1-1	2-1	—	1-0	0-0	1-0	0-0	4-0
Sutton United	3-3	3-1	1-1	3-2	0-0	2-2	0-0	3-1	2-2	1-0	2-2	0-1	1-0	1-0	0-2	1-1	0-1	—	2-1	1-2	3-1	1-3
Thurrock	2-2	2-1	0-3	1-1	0-1	1-0	2-3	2-4	1-1	1-4	5-1	1-1	0-1	0-4	3-2	2-2	1-5	3-0	—	1-2	2-2	1-0
Welling United	0-2	5-0	2-3	3-0	4-1	1-0	1-2	1-0	2-1	1-0	2-0	1-1	1-1	2-4	0-0	2-3	1-2	1-0	1-2	—	1-0	5-1
Weston-Super-Mare	1-3	2-1	1-2	1-3	0-0	0-1	1-2	2-4	3-3	2-1	0-1	1-5	0-5	1-2	1-1	3-4	1-1	0-2	2-1	1-2	—	2-1
Yeading	1-1	2-1	1-1	2-0	0-1	5-0	0-0	2-5	1-4	2-1	1-1	1-1	1-1	1-3	1-0	1-1	1-3	2-2	2-1	0-1	0-0	—

UNIBOND LEAGUE 2006–2007

Premier Division

		Home					*Away*					*Total*						
	P	*W*	*D*	*L*	*F*	*A*	*W*	*D*	*L*	*F*	*A*	*W*	*D*	*L*	*F*	*A*	*GD*	*Pts*
1 Burscough*	42	15	5	1	50	14	8	7	6	30	23	23	12	7	80	37	43	80
2 Witton Albion	42	14	4	3	57	25	10	4	7	33	23	24	8	10	90	48	42	80
3 AFC Telford U	42	9	10	2	41	23	12	5	4	31	17	21	15	6	72	40	32	78
4 Marine	42	12	5	4	36	23	10	3	8	34	30	22	8	12	70	53	17	74
5 Matlock Town	42	12	4	5	38	20	9	5	7	32	23	21	9	12	70	43	27	72
6 Guiseley	42	10	7	4	43	25	9	5	7	28	24	19	12	11	71	49	22	69
7 Hednesford Town	42	9	8	4	26	17	9	6	6	23	24	18	14	10	49	41	8	68
8 Fleetwood Town	42	13	3	5	41	21	6	7	8	30	39	19	10	13	71	60	11	67
9 Gateshead	42	11	5	5	41	30	6	9	6	34	27	17	14	11	75	57	18	65
10 Ossett Town	42	9	6	6	33	27	9	4	8	28	25	18	10	14	61	52	9	64
11 Whitby Town	42	13	3	5	39	26	5	3	13	24	52	18	6	18	63	78	–15	60
12 Ilkeston Town	42	7	6	8	29	29	9	5	7	37	33	16	11	15	66	62	4	59
13 North Ferriby U	42	10	3	8	30	30	5	6	10	24	31	15	9	18	54	61	–7	54
14 Prescot Cables	42	8	8	5	30	24	5	6	10	22	32	13	14	15	52	56	–4	53
15 Lincoln United	42	5	10	6	18	22	7	5	9	22	36	12	15	15	40	58	–18	51
16 Frickley Athletic	42	8	6	7	27	27	5	4	12	23	42	13	10	19	50	69	–19	49
17 Leek Town	42	7	5	9	21	25	6	4	11	28	36	13	9	20	49	61	–12	48
18 Ashton United	42	10	3	8	33	37	3	6	12	19	35	13	9	20	52	72	–20	48
19 Kendal Town	42	8	4	9	28	35	4	7	10	31	44	12	11	19	59	79	–20	47
20 Mossley	42	5	2	14	24	40	5	3	13	24	39	10	5	27	48	79	–31	35
21 Radcliffe Borough	42	4	5	12	19	36	3	6	12	20	35	7	11	24	39	71	–32	32
22 Grantham Town	42	3	3	15	16	44	0	5	16	23	50	3	8	31	39	94	–55	17

**Deducted 1 point for fielding an ineligible player.*

SOUTHERN LEAGUE 2006–2007

British Gas Business Premier Division

		Home					*Away*					*Total*						
	P	*W*	*D*	*L*	*F*	*A*	*W*	*D*	*L*	*F*	*A*	*W*	*D*	*L*	*F*	*A*	*GD*	*Pts*
1 Bath City	42	13	5	3	43	15	14	5	2	41	14	27	10	5	84	29	55	91
2 Team Bath	42	14	3	4	39	19	9	6	6	27	23	23	9	10	66	42	24	78
3 King's Lynn	42	15	3	3	37	12	7	7	7	32	28	22	10	10	69	40	29	76
4 Maidenhead U	42	11	6	4	31	17	9	4	8	27	19	20	10	12	58	36	22	70
5 Hemel Hempstead T	42	12	6	3	44	22	7	6	8	35	38	19	12	11	79	60	19	69
6 Halesowen Town	42	11	6	4	43	30	7	7	7	23	23	18	13	11	66	53	13	67
7 Chippenham Town	42	11	6	4	35	20	8	3	10	26	36	19	9	14	61	56	5	66
8 Stamford	42	10	4	7	31	23	6	7	8	34	39	16	11	15	65	62	3	59
9 Mangotsfield U	42	5	11	5	21	22	8	8	5	23	23	13	19	10	44	45	–1	58
10 Gloucester City	42	6	6	9	28	40	9	7	5	39	30	15	13	14	67	70	–3	58
11 Hitchin Town	42	11	3	7	31	28	5	6	10	24	40	16	9	17	55	68	–13	57
12 Merthyr Tydfil	42	10	7	4	28	15	4	7	10	19	30	14	14	14	47	45	2	56
13 Banbury United	42	6	6	9	33	33	9	4	8	27	31	15	10	17	60	64	–4	55
14 Yate Town	42	7	7	7	41	36	7	5	9	18	35	14	12	16	59	71	–12	54
15 Tiverton Town	42	10	3	8	30	26	4	5	12	26	41	14	8	20	56	67	–11	50
16 Cheshunt	42	10	3	8	34	29	4	4	13	22	42	14	7	21	56	71	–15	49
17 Rugby Town	42	10	2	9	31	32	5	2	14	26	47	15	4	23	57	79	–22	49
18 Clevedon Town	42	6	7	8	32	30	6	5	10	28	31	12	12	18	60	61	–1	48
19 Wealdstone	42	8	6	7	38	36	5	3	13	31	46	13	9	20	69	82	–13	48
20 Corby Town	42	5	6	10	27	33	5	3	13	25	36	10	9	23	52	69	–17	39
21 Cirencester Town	42	6	6	9	29	36	3	6	12	17	40	9	12	21	46	76	–30	39
22 Northwood	42	4	4	13	23	37	4	6	11	21	37	8	10	24	44	74	–30	34

RYMAN LEAGUE 2006–2007

Premier Division		Home					Away					Total						
	P	W	D	L	F	A	W	D	L	F	A	W	D	L	F	A	GD	Pts
1 Hampton & RB	42	11	6	4	39	32	13	4	4	38	21	24	10	8	77	53	24	82
2 Bromley	42	13	3	5	44	28	10	8	3	39	15	23	11	8	83	43	40	80
3 Chelmsford City	42	15	4	2	63	23	8	4	9	33	28	23	8	11	96	51	45	77
4 Billericay Town	42	15	5	1	40	9	7	6	8	31	33	22	11	9	71	42	29	77
5 AFC Wimbledon*	42	11	7	3	45	18	10	8	3	31	19	21	15	6	76	37	39	75
6 Margate	42	11	6	4	34	17	9	5	7	45	31	20	11	11	79	48	31	71
7 Boreham Wood	42	9	5	7	38	29	10	7	4	33	20	19	12	11	71	49	22	69
8 Horsham	42	8	9	4	39	30	10	5	6	31	27	18	14	10	70	57	13	68
9 Ramsgate	42	12	4	5	35	24	8	1	12	28	39	20	5	17	63	63	0	65
10 Heybridge Swifts	42	9	6	6	26	18	8	7	6	31	22	17	13	12	57	40	17	64
11 Tonbridge Angels	42	9	3	9	43	40	11	1	9	31	32	20	4	18	74	72	2	64
12 Staines Town	42	8	8	5	31	27	7	4	10	33	37	15	12	15	64	64	0	57
13 Carshalton Athletic	42	9	5	7	32	28	5	7	9	22	31	14	12	16	54	59	–5	54
14 Hendon	42	8	4	9	25	27	8	2	11	27	36	16	6	20	52	63	–11	54
15 Leyton	42	8	4	9	30	40	5	6	10	24	36	13	10	19	54	76	–22	49
16 East Thurrock U	42	6	2	13	22	37	8	4	9	34	33	14	6	22	56	70	–14	48
17 Ashford Town	42	8	6	7	34	26	3	7	11	25	45	11	13	18	59	71	–12	46
18 Folkestone Invicta	42	6	5	10	23	35	6	5	10	22	31	12	10	20	45	66	–21	46
19 Harrow Borough	42	8	2	11	32	35	5	4	12	29	36	13	6	23	61	71	–10	45
20 Worthing	42	6	4	11	26	36	2	7	12	31	46	8	11	23	57	82	–25	35
21 Walton & Hersham	42	8	5	8	26	31	1	1	19	12	52	9	6	27	38	83	–45	33
22 Slough Town	42	1	3	17	8	58	3	3	15	18	65	4	6	32	26	123	–97	18

**Deducted 3 points for fielding an ineligible player.*

CUP FINALS 2006–2007

UNIBOND LEAGUE

CHALLENGE CUP FINAL 2006–07
Fleetwood Town 1, Matlock Town 0

PRESIDENT'S CUP FINAL
Buxton 3, Wakefield 1

CHAIRMAN'S CUP FINAL
Guiseley 2, Cammell Laird 1

PETER SWALES MEMORIAL
Burscough 3, Buxton 1

PREMIER PLAY-OFF FINAL
Witton Albion 1, AFC Telford United 3

FIRST DIVISION PLAY-OFF FINAL
Cammell Laird 1, Eastwood Town 2

SOUTHERN LEAGUE

PLAY-OFF FINALS
PREMIER DIVISION
Team Bath 0, Maidenhead United 1

DIVISION ONE MIDLANDS
Bromsgrove Rovers 2, Willenhall Town 1
aet.

DIVISION ONE SOUTHERN & WEST
Swindon Supermarine 2, Taunton Town 1

ERREA SOUTHERN LEAGUE CUP

Final First Leg
Tiverton Town 1,
Hemel Hempstead Town 0

Final Second Leg
Hemel Hempstead Town 2,
Tiverton Town 2

RYMAN LEAGUE

PREMIER DIVISION PLAY-OFF FINAL
Bromley 1, Billericay Town 1
Bromley won 4-2 on penalties.

DIVISION ONE NORTH PLAY-OFF FINAL
Harlow Town 2, AFC Sudbury 2
Harlow Town won 5-3 on penalties.

DIVISION ONE SOUTH PLAY-OFF FINAL
Tooting & Mitcham United 0,
Hastings United 2

WESTVIEW LEAGUE CUP FINAL
Ashford Town (Middlesex) 4,
Dover Athletic 1
(at Bromley).

PONTIN'S HOLIDAYS LEAGUE 2006–2007

DIVISION ONE CENTRAL

	P	*W*	*D*	*L*	*F*	*A*	*GD*	*Pts*
Birmingham C	22	13	5	4	38	21	+17	44
Nottingham F	22	13	4	5	44	23	+21	43
Walsall	22	12	4	6	41	23	+18	40
Sheffield W	22	12	4	6	36	25	+11	40
WBA	22	11	3	8	36	30	+6	36
Leeds U	22	7	7	8	33	35	–2	28
Barnsley	22	7	5	10	44	47	–3	26
Stoke C	22	6	7	9	25	37	–12	25
Huddersfield T	22	6	6	10	25	32	–7	24
Port Vale	22	6	5	11	25	35	–10	23
Shrewsbury T	22	5	5	12	29	44	–15	20
Bradford C	22	4	5	13	19	43	–24	17

DIVISION ONE WEST

	P	*W*	*D*	*L*	*F*	*A*	*GD*	*Pts*
Oldham Ath	20	10	7	3	39	18	+21	37
Preston NE	20	11	2	7	48	32	+16	35
Bury	20	10	5	5	43	32	+11	35
Accrington S	20	9	3	8	38	36	+2	30
Tranmere R	20	9	2	9	30	31	–1	29
Blackpool	20	9	1	10	32	34	–2	28
Manchester C	20	7	5	8	26	32	–6	26
Rochdale	20	8	1	11	32	39	–7	25
Wrexham	20	7	4	9	21	33	–12	25
Carlisle U	20	6	4	10	28	38	–10	22
Chester C	20	6	2	12	21	33	–12	20

DIVISION ONE EAST

	P	*W*	*D*	*L*	*F*	*A*	*GD*	*Pts*
Rotherham U	18	12	3	3	46	23	+23	39
Grimsby T	18	12	2	4	35	22	+13	38
Hartlepool U	18	10	6	2	40	17	+23	36
Hull C	18	11	1	6	35	22	+13	34
York C	18	6	7	5	32	21	+11	25
Sheffield U	18	6	4	8	28	33	–5	22
Scunthorpe U	18	6	2	10	24	32	–8	20
Doncaster R	18	4	3	11	19	46	–27	15
Darlington	18	3	3	12	14	33	–19	12
Lincoln C	18	3	3	12	14	38	–24	12

PONTIN'S HOLIDAYS COMBINATION 2006–2007

CENTRAL DIVISION

	P	*W*	*D*	*L*	*Pts*
Brighton & HA	14	12	1	1	37
Southampton	14	12	0	2	36
Crystal Palace	14	7	1	6	22
QPR	14	6	2	6	20
Millwall	14	4	3	7	15
Bournemouth	14	4	2	8	14
Wycombe W	14	4	1	9	13
Aldershot T	14	1	2	11	5

WALES AND WEST DIVISION

	P	*W*	*D*	*L*	*Pts*
Cheltenham T	18	11	5	2	38
Bristol C	18	8	6	4	30
Cardiff C	18	7	7	4	28
Bristol R	18	8	4	6	28
Plymouth Arg	18	7	5	6	26
Exeter C	18	7	3	8	24
Swindon T	18	6	4	8	22
Yeovil T	18	6	3	9	21
Swansea C	18	4	4	10	16
Weymouth	18	4	3	11	15

EAST DIVISION

	P	*W*	*D*	*L*	*Pts*
Ipswich T	18	13	2	3	41
Colchester U	18	8	8	2	32
Luton T	18	9	3	6	30
Southend U	18	9	2	7	29
Leyton Orient	18	6	8	4	26
Northampton T	18	7	4	7	25
Norwich C	18	8	6	6	24
Milton Keynes D	18	7	2	9	23
Stevenage B	18	2	5	11	11
Oxford U	18	1	4	13	7

FA ACADEMY UNDER-18 LEAGUE 2006–2007

GROUP A	P	W	D	L	F	A	GD	Pts
Arsenal	28	20	5	3	75	38	37	65
West Ham U	28	17	6	5	50	36	14	57
Chelsea	28	16	5	7	46	30	16	53
Southampton	28	16	2	10	66	44	22	50
Crystal Palace	28	14	8	6	60	45	15	50
Ipswich T	28	10	8	10	48	47	1	38
Charlton Ath	28	9	7	12	47	50	–3	34
Millwall	28	7	8	13	38	56	–18	29
Norwich C	28	7	1	20	26	51	–25	22
Fulham	28	4	7	17	32	62	–30	19

GROUP B	P	W	D	L	F	A	GD	Pts
Leicester C	28	21	3	4	93	36	57	66
Reading	28	20	4	4	51	24	27	64
Tottenham H	28	13	10	5	50	38	12	49
Aston Villa	28	13	9	6	51	32	19	48
Watford	28	9	8	11	45	48	–3	35
Bristol C	28	10	5	13	49	61	–12	35
Birmingham C	28	9	3	16	37	64	–27	30
Coventry C	28	8	4	16	31	45	–14	28
Cardiff C	28	5	4	19	30	55	–25	19
Milton Keynes D	28	5	1	22	30	72	–42	16

GROUP C	P	W	D	L	F	A	GD	Pts
Manchester C	28	21	3	4	63	28	35	66
Bolton W	28	14	6	8	38	26	12	48
Blackburn R	28	13	7	8	47	34	13	46
Manchester U	28	12	4	12	51	42	9	40
WBA	28	12	2	14	44	45	–1	38
Everton	28	6	13	9	38	38	0	31
Crewe Alex	28	9	3	16	44	57	–13	30
Liverpool	28	7	8	13	29	37	–8	29
Wolverhampton W	28	6	7	15	30	52	–22	25
Stoke C	28	3	5	20	14	53	–39	14

GROUP D	P	W	D	L	F	A	GD	Pts
Sunderland	28	15	9	4	54	32	22	54
Nottingham F	28	15	7	6	54	30	24	52
Leeds U	28	16	4	8	50	37	13	52
Newcastle U	28	15	4	9	57	41	16	49
Derby Co	28	12	7	9	53	42	11	43
Sheffield W	28	9	7	12	30	40	–10	34
Sheffield U	28	9	6	13	25	43	–18	33
Barnsley	28	7	6	15	35	60	–25	27
Huddersfield T	28	7	4	17	32	55	–23	25
Middlesbrough	28	5	8	15	39	56	–17	23

FA PREMIER RESERVE LEAGUES 2006–2007

NORTH SECTION

	P	W	D	L	F	A	Pts
Bolton W	18	10	3	5	21	16	33
Manchester U	18	9	4	5	24	17	31
Middlesbrough	18	9	3	6	31	25	30
Manchester C	18	9	2	7	27	24	29
Liverpool	18	8	2	8	24	19	26
Blackburn R	18	7	5	6	16	15	26
Sheffield U	18	8	2	8	23	23	26
Newcastle U	18	6	5	7	29	29	23
Everton	18	3	7	8	18	25	16
Wigan Ath	18	2	5	11	8	28	11

Leading Goalscorers

Graham D (Middlesbrough)	8
Carroll A (Newcastle U)	8
Evans C (Manchester C)	6
Lindfield C (Liverpool)	5
Marsh P (Manchester U)	5
Christie M (Middlesbrough)	5
Craddock T (Middlesbrough)	5
Johansson A (Wigan Ath)	5
Hughes M (Everton)	4
McFadden J (Everton)	4
Idrizaj B (Liverpool)	4
Marshall P (Manchester C)	4
Burns A (Manchester U)	4
Finnigan C (Newcastle U)	4
Quinn S (Sheffield U)	4

SOUTH SECTION

	P	W	D	L	F	A	Pts
Reading	18	12	2	4	45	15	38
Watford	18	11	2	5	26	20	35
Chelsea	18	10	3	5	26	11	33
Aston Villa	18	9	3	6	38	26	30
Tottenham H	18	8	6	4	22	18	30
Charlton Ath	18	7	4	7	28	24	25
West Ham U	18	5	3	10	18	28	18
Fulham	18	4	5	9	16	30	17
Arsenal	18	4	4	10	15	29	16
Portsmouth	18	2	4	12	12	45	10

Leading Goalscorers

Long S (Reading)	14
Moore L (Aston Villa)	7
Dickinson C (Charlton Ath)	7
Sinclair S (Chelsea)	7
Sahar B (Chelsea)	7
Aliadiere J (Arsenal)	5
Baros M (Aston Villa)	5
Lisbie K (Charlton Ath)	5
Bangura A (Watford)	5
McGurk A (Aston Villa)	4
Younghusband P (Chelsea)	4
Brown W (Fulham)	4
Henry J (Reading)	4
Cox S (Reading)	4
Sears F (West Ham U)	4

WOMEN'S FOOTBALL 2006–2007

PREMIER LEAGUE

NATIONAL DIVISION

	P	W	D	L	F	A	GD	Pts
Arsenal	22	22	0	0	119	10	109	66
Everton	22	17	1	4	56	15	41	52
Charlton Athletic	22	16	2	4	63	32	31	50
Bristol Academy	22	13	1	8	53	41	12	40
Leeds United	22	12	1	9	50	44	6	37
Blackburn Rovers	22	10	2	10	37	36	1	32
Birmingham City	22	8	4	10	34	29	5	28
Chelsea	22	8	4	10	33	34	–1	28
Doncaster R Belles	22	7	2	13	29	54	–25	23
Cardiff City	22	3	3	16	26	64	–38	12
Sunderland	22	3	2	17	15	72	–57	11
Fulham	22	1	2	19	12	96	–84	5

NORTHERN DIVISION

	P	W	D	L	F	A	GD	Pts
Liverpool	22	16	2	4	56	17	39	50
Lincoln City	22	13	6	3	50	23	27	45
Nottingham Forest	22	11	3	8	41	36	5	36
Crewe Alexandra	22	10	4	8	33	38	–5	34
Preston North End	22	9	6	7	36	41	–5	33
Tranmere Rovers	22	9	4	9	41	34	7	31
Newcastle United	22	8	5	9	37	34	3	29
Stockport County	22	8	4	10	34	36	–2	28
Aston Villa	22	6	6	10	36	43	–7	24
Manchester City	22	6	6	10	27	35	–8	24
Wolverhampton W.	22	5	6	11	26	44	–18	21
Curzon Ashton	22	4	2	16	24	60	–36	14

SOUTHERN DIVISION

	P	W	D	L	F	A	GD	Pts
Watford	22	19	0	3	99	35	64	57
Portsmouth	22	14	5	3	60	32	28	47
Millwall Lionesses	22	13	3	6	61	35	26	42
Barnet	22	11	4	7	52	33	19	37
Keynsham Town	22	11	4	7	52	46	6	37
Bristol City	22	9	5	8	44	37	7	32
Reading Royals	22	10	1	11	36	34	2	31
Crystal Palace	22	7	5	10	48	48	0	26
Brighton & Hove A	22	7	2	13	39	65	–26	23
West Ham United	22	6	3	13	25	44	–19	21
AFC Wimbledon	22	5	2	15	26	61	–35	17
Southampton Saints	22	1	4	17	21	93	–72	7

WOMEN'S CUP FINAL 2006–2007

Tuesday, 8 May 2007
(at Nottingham Forest)

Arsenal 4 *(Smith 6, 81, Ludlow 14, 45)*

Charlton Athletic 1 *(Holtham 2)* 24,529

Arsenal: Byrne; Ludlow, Grant, Smith, Sanderson (Carney 64), Fleeting (Davison 79), Yankey, Scott, Chapman, Asante, Phillip.

Charlton Athletic: Wayne; Stoney, Holtham (Hughes 85), Hills, Bertelli, Murphy, Aluko, Dowie (Heatherson 85), Potter, Smith (Hincks 71), Boyer.

Referee: A. Bates (Staffordshire).

ENGLAND WOMEN'S INTERNATIONAL MATCHES 2006–2007

31 August 2006 *(at Charlton)*
England 4 *(Smith K 9, 25, 50, Yankey 67)* **Holland 0** 7931
England: Brown; Scott A, Unitt, Chapman, Asante, Phillip, Carny, Williams, Aluko (Handley 84), Smith K (Scott J 82), Yankey (Smith S 74).

30 September 2006 *(in Rennes)*
France 1 *(Diquelman 89)* **England 1** *(Lattaf 64 (og))* 19,215
England: Brown; Scott A, Unitt (Stoney 46), Chapman, Asante, Philip, Carny (Johnson 90), Williams, Aluko, Smith K, Yankey (Smith S 78).

25 October 2006 *(in Aalen)*
Germany 5 *(Stegemann 28, Smisek 36, Prinz 66, Muller 75, De Mbabi 86)*
England 1 *(Scott A 26)* 11,161
England: Brown (Chamberlain 56); Scott A, Stoney, Williams (Aluko 77), Asante, Philip, Carny (Johnson 46), Exley, Handley, Smith K (Scott J 61), Yankey (Smith S 68).

THE CHINA CUP 26 January 2007 *(in Guangzhou)*
China 2 *(Zhang Ying 4, Han Duan 45)* **England 0**
England: Chamberlain; Scott A, Stoney (Unitt 87), Chapman, Asante, Philip, Carny (Johnson 46), Williams, Handley (Sanderson 73), Smith K (Westwood 62), Smith S.

THE CHINA CUP 28 January 2007 *(in Guandong)*
England 1 *(Scott A 47)* **USA 1** *(O'Reilly 17)*
England: Brown; Scott A, Stoney, Asante, Westwood (Unitt 79), Chapman (Exley 83), Williams, Smith K, Carny, Aluko (Scott J 59), Yankey.

THE CHINA CUP 30 January 2007 *(in Guandong)*
Germany 0 **England 0**
England: Brown; Scott A, Unitt, Scott J (Exley 66), Philip (Asante 29), Westwood, Williams (Chapman 55), Smith K, Carny (Johnson 46), Aluko (Sanderson 46), Yankey.

8 March 2007 *(in Milton Keynes)*
England 6 *(Scott A 10, Aluko 15, Carny 25, Smith K 41, Yankey 64, Stoney 80).*
Russia 0 5421
England: Brown; Scott A (Johnson 57), Stoney, Chapman (Exley 86), Asante (Bassett 86), Westwood (Houghton 73), Carny, Williams (Scott J 73), Aluko (Handley 46). Smith K, Yankey.

11 March 2007 *(at Wycombe)*
England 1 *(Williams 30)* **Scotland 0** 2066
England: Chamberlain (Telford 46); Houghton, Unitt (Yorston 78), Scott J, Bassett, Philip, Scott A (Johnson 78), Williams, Sanderson (Barr 58), Smith K (Chapman 46), Smith S (Potter 58).

14 March 2007 *(at Swindon)*
England 0 **Holland 1** *(Melis 78)* 5957
England: Brown; Scott A, Stoney, Chapman, Asante, Westwood, Carny (Houghton 79), Williams, Aluko, Smith K, Yankey (Potter 69).

13 May 2007 *(at Gillingham)*
England 4 *(Smith K 52, Harkin 66 (og), Chapman 72, Sanderson 76)*
Northern Ireland 0
England: Brown; Houghton (Carny 46), Unitt, Chapman, Asante, Phillip, Scott A, Williams, Sanderson (Barr 77), Smith K (White 73), Smith S.

17 May 2007 *(at Southend)*
England 4 *(Yankey 23, Chapman 45, 69, Smith K 64)*
Iceland 0 7606
England: Brown; Scott A (Johnson 46), Stoney, Chapman (Houghton 79), Asante, Phillip (White 46), Carney (Smith S 69), Williams (Scott J 46), Handley, Smith K (Sanderson 84), Yankey (Potter 46).

THE FA TROPHY 2006–2007

FINAL (at Wembley) – Saturday, 12 May 2007

Kidderminster Harriers (2) 2 *(Constable 31, 37)*

Stevenage Borough (0) 3 *(Cole 51, Dobson 74, Morison 88)* 53,262

Kidderminster Harriers: Bevan; Kenna, Blackwood, Hurren, Creighton, Whitehead, Russell, Penn, Christie (White 76), Constable, Smikle (Reynolds 90).
Stevenage Borough: Julian; Fuller, Nutter, Miller, Gaia, Oliver, Henry, Beard, Morison, Guppy (Dobson 63), Cole.
Referee: C. Foy (Merseyside).

THE FA VASE 2006–2007

FINAL (at Wembley) – Sunday, 13 May 2007

AFC Totton (1) 1 *(Potter 28)*

Truro City (1) 3 *(Wills 45, 57, Broad 84)* 27,754

AFC Totton: Brunnschweiler; Reacord, Troon (Stevens 61), Potter (Gregory 82), Bottomley, Austen, Roden, Gosney, Hamodu (Goss 89), Osman, Byres.
Truro City: Stevenson; Ash, Power, Smith, Martin (Pope 86), Broad, Wills, Gosling, Yetton, Watkins, Walker (Ludlam 90).
Referee: P. Joslin (Nottinghamshire).

THE FA YOUTH CUP 2006–2007

FINAL (First Leg) – Monday, 16 April 2007

Liverpool (1) 1 *(Lindfield 16)*

Manchester United (0) 2 *(Threlfall 49 (og), Hewson 74 (pen))* 19,518

Liverpool: Hansen; Darby, Burns, Spearing, Threlfall, Barnett, Ryan, Flynn, Lindfield, Woodward (Eccleston 68), Putterill.
Manchester United: Zieler; Eckersley, Evans, Strickland, Chester, Drinkwater (Bryan 75), Welbeck, Hewson, Brandy (James 90), Fagan, Galbraith.
Referee: M. Clattenburg (Tyne & Wear).

FINAL (Second Leg) – Thursday, 26 April 2007

Manchester United (0) 0

Liverpool (0) 1 *(Threlfall 51)* 24,347

Manchester United: Zieler; Eckersley, Evans (Moffatt 99), Strickland, Chester, Drinkwater (Bryan 72), Welbeck (Eikrem 87), Hewson, Brandy, Fagan, Galbraith.
Liverpool: Roberts; Darby, Burns, Spearing, Threlfall, Barnett, Ryan (Woodward 95), Ajdarevic (Irwin 81), Lindfield, Flynn, Putterill.
aet; Liverpool won 4-3 on penalties.
Referee: M. Clattenburg (Tyne & Wear).

THE FA SUNDAY CUP 2006–2007

FINAL (at Liverpool FC)

Coundon Conservative Club 5 *(Ellison, Thompson 2, Johnson 2)*

Lebeq Tavern Courage 0 1289

THE FA COUNTY YOUTH CUP 2006–2007

FINAL (at Bradford City FC)

West Riding (0) 1 *(Oxey 50)*

Suffolk (0) 1 *(Chaplin 75)* 546

aet; West Riding won 4-3 on penalties.

NATIONAL LIST OF REFEREES FOR SEASON 2007–2008

Armstrong, P (Paul) – Berkshire
Atkinson, M (Martin) – W. Yorkshire
Attwell, SB (Stuart) – Warwickshire
Bates, A (Tony) – Staffordshire
Beeby, RJ (Richard) – Northamptonshire
Bennett, SG (Steve) – Kent
Booth, RJ (Russell) – Nottinghamshire
Boyeson, C (Carl) – E. Yorkshire
Bratt, SJ (Steve) – West Midlands
Clattenburg, M (Mark) – Tyne & Wear
Cook, SD (Steven) – Surrey
Crossley, PT (Phil) – Kent
Deadman, D (Darren) – Cambridgeshire
Dean, ML (Mike) – Wirral
Dorr, SJ (Steve) – Worcestershire
Dowd, P (Phil) – Staffordshire
Drysdale, D (Darren) – Lincolnshire
D'Urso, AP (Andy) – Essex
East, R (Roger) – Wiltshire
Evans, KG (Karl) – Gtr Manchester
Foster, D (David) – Tyne & Wear
Foy, CJ (Chris) – Merseyside
Friend, KA (Kevin) – Leicestershire
Graham F (Fred) – Essex
Haines, A (Andy) – Tyne & Wear
Hall, AR (Andy) – W. Midlands
Halsey, MR (Mark) – Lancashire
Haywood, M (Mark) – W. Yorkshire
Hegley, GK (Grant) – Hertfordshire
Hill, KD (Keith) – Hertfordshire
Horwood, GD (Graham) – Bedfordshire
Ilderton, EL (Eddie) – Tyne & Wear
Jones, MJ (Michael) – Cheshire
Joslin, PJ (Phil) – Nottinghamshire
Kettle, TM (Trevor) – Rutland
Knight, B (Barry) – Kent
Laws, G (Graham) – Tyne & Wear
Lee, R (Ray) – Essex
Lewis, GJ (Gary) – Cambridgeshire
Lewis, RL (Rob) – Shropshire
McDermid, D (Danny) – London
Marriner, AM (Andre) – W. Midlands
Mason, LS (Lee) – Lancashire
Mathieson, SW (Scott) – Cheshire
Mellin, PW (Paul) – Surrey
Miller, NS (Nigel) – Durham
Miller, P (Pat) – Bedfordshire
Moss, J (Jon) – W. Yorkshire
Oliver, CW (Clive) – Northumberland
Oliver, M (Michael) – Northumberland
Penn, AM (Andy) – W. Midlands
Penton, C (Clive) – Sussex
Pike, MS (Mike) – Cumbria
Probert, LW (Lee) – Wiltshire
Rennie, UD (Uriah) – S. Yorkshire
Riley, MA (Mike) – W. Yorkshire
Russell, MP (Mike) – Hertfordshire
Salisbury, G (Graham) – Lancashire
Shoebridge, RL (Rob) – Derbyshire
Singh, J (Jarnail) – Middlesex
Stroud, KP (Keith) – Hampshire
Styles, R (Rob) – Hampshire
Swarbrick, ND (Neil) – Lancashire
Tanner, SJ (Steve) – Somerset
Taylor, A (Anthony) – Gtr Manchester
Taylor, P (Paul) – Hertfordshire
Thorpe, M (Mike) – Suffolk
Walton, P (Peter) – Northamptonshire
Ward, GL (Gavin) – Surrey
Webb, HM (Howard) – S. Yorkshire
Webster, CH (Colin) – Tyne & Wear
Whitestone, D (Dean) – Northamptonshire
Wiley, AG (Alan) – Staffordshire
Williamson, IG (Iain) – Berkshire
Woolmer, KA (Andy) – Northamptonshire
Wright, KK (Kevin) – Cambridgeshire

ENGLISH LEAGUE FIXTURES 2006–2007

**Sky Sports*

Saturday, 11 August 2007

Barclays Premier League
Aston Villa v Liverpool
Bolton W v Newcastle U
Derby Co v Portsmouth
Everton v Wigan Ath
Middlesbrough v Blackburn R
Sunderland v Tottenham H* (12.45)
West Ham U v Manchester C

Coca-Cola Football League Championship
Barnsley v Coventry C
Bristol C v QPR
Burnley v WBA
Cardiff C v Stoke C
Charlton Ath v Scunthorpe U
Hull C v Plymouth Arg
Ipswich T v Sheffield W
Leicester C v Blackpool
Preston NE v Norwich C
Sheffield U v Colchester U
Southampton v Crystal Palace
Wolverhampton W v Watford* (5.20)

Coca-Cola Football League One
Cheltenham T v Gillingham
Crewe Alex v Brighton & HA
Doncaster R v Millwall
Huddersfield T v Yeovil T
Luton T v Hartlepool U
Northampton T v Swindon T
Nottingham F v Bournemouth
Oldham Ath v Swansea C
Port Vale v Bristol R
Southend U v Leyton Orient
Tranmere R v Leeds U
Walsall v Carlisle U

Coca-Cola Football League Two
Bradford C v Macclesfield T
Brentford v Mansfield T
Chester C v Chesterfield
Darlington v Wrexham
Grimsby T v Notts Co
Hereford U v Rotherham U
Lincoln C v Shrewsbury T
Milton Keynes Dons v Bury
Morecambe v Barnet
Peterborough U v Rochdale
Stockport Co v Dagenham & R
Wycombe W v Accrington S

Sunday, 12 August 2007

Barclays Premier League
Arsenal v Fulham
Chelsea v Birmingham C* (1.30)
Manchester U v Reading* (4.00)

Tuesday, 14 August 2007

Barclays Premier League
Birmingham C v Sunderland
Tottenham H v Everton* (8.00)

Wednesday, 15 August 2007

Barclays Premier League
Blackburn R v Aston Villa
Fulham v Bolton W
Liverpool v Arsenal *(postponed)*
Manchester C v Derby Co
Newcastle U v Liverpool *(postponed)*
Portsmouth v Manchester U
Reading v Chelsea
Wigan Ath v Middlesbrough* (8.00)

Saturday, 18 August 2007

Barclays Premier League
Birmingham C v West Ham U
Blackburn R v Arsenal
Fulham v Middlesbrough
Newcastle U v Aston Villa
Portsmouth v Bolton W* (12.45)
Reading v Everton
Tottenham H v Derby Co
Wigan Ath v Sunderland

Coca-Cola Football League Championship
Blackpool v Bristol C
Colchester U v Barnsley
Coventry C v Hull C
Crystal Palace v Leicester C
Norwich C v Southampton
Plymouth Arg v Ipswich T
QPR v Cardiff C
Scunthorpe U v Burnley
Stoke C v Charlton Ath* (5.20)
Watford v Sheffield U
WBA v Preston NE

Coca-Cola Football League One
Bournemouth v Huddersfield T
Brighton & HA v Northampton T
Bristol R v Crewe Alex
Carlisle U v Oldham Ath

Gillingham v Tranmere R
Hartlepool U v Doncaster R
Leeds U v Southend U
Leyton Orient v Walsall
Millwall v Cheltenham T
Swansea C v Nottingham F
Swindon T v Luton T
Yeovil T v Port Vale

Coca-Cola Football League Two
Accrington S v Darlington
Barnet v Hereford U
Bury v Grimsby T
Chesterfield v Stockport Co
Dagenham & R v Wycombe W
Macclesfield T v Milton Keynes Dons
Mansfield T v Lincoln C
Notts Co v Brentford
Rochdale v Chester C
Shrewsbury T v Bradford C
Wrexham v Morecambe

Sunday, 19 August 2007

Barclays Premier League
Liverpool v Chelsea* (4.00)
Manchester C v Manchester U* (1.30)

Coca-Cola Football League Championship
Sheffield W v Wolverhampton W

Coca-Cola Football League Two
Rotherham U v Peterborough U

Saturday, 25 August 2007

Barclays Premier League
Arsenal v Manchester C
Aston Villa v Fulham
Bolton W v Reading
Chelsea v Portsmouth
Derby Co v Birmingham C
Everton v Blackburn R
Sunderland v Liverpool* (12.45)
West Ham U v Wigan Ath

Coca-Cola Football League Championship
Barnsley v Plymouth Arg
Bristol C v Scunthorpe U
Burnley v QPR
Cardiff C v Coventry C
Charlton Ath v Sheffield W
Hull C v Norwich C
Ipswich T v Crystal Palace
Leicester C v Watford
Preston NE v Colchester U
Sheffield U v WBA* (5.20)
Southampton v Stoke C
Wolverhampton W v Blackpool

Coca-Cola Football League One
Cheltenham T v Swindon T
Crewe Alex v Leyton Orient
Doncaster R v Bournemouth
Huddersfield T v Carlisle U
Luton T v Gillingham
Northampton T v Yeovil T
Nottingham F v Leeds U
Oldham Ath v Bristol R
Port Vale v Hartlepool U
Southend U v Millwall
Tranmere R v Brighton & HA
Walsall v Swansea C

Coca-Cola Football League Two
Bradford C v Wrexham
Brentford v Barnet
Chester C v Dagenham & R
Darlington v Notts Co
Grimsby T v Macclesfield T
Hereford U v Rochdale
Lincoln C v Accrington S
Milton Keynes Dons v Shrewsbury T
Morecambe v Mansfield T
Peterborough U v Chesterfield
Stockport Co v Rotherham U
Wycombe W v Bury

Sunday, 26 August 2007

Barclays Premier League
Manchester U v Tottenham H* (4.00)
Middlesbrough v Newcastle U

Saturday, 1 September 2007

Barclays Premier League
Blackburn R v Manchester C
Bolton W v Everton
Fulham v Tottenham H
Liverpool v Derby Co
Manchester U v Sunderland
Middlesbrough v Birmingham C
Newcastle U v Wigan Ath
Reading v West Ham U

Coca-Cola Football League Championship
Colchester U v Burnley
Coventry C v Preston NE* (5.20)
Crystal Palace v Charlton Ath
Norwich C v Cardiff C
Plymouth Arg v Leicester C
QPR v Southampton
Scunthorpe U v Sheffield U
Sheffield W v Bristol C
Stoke C v Wolverhampton W
Watford v Ipswich T
WBA v Barnsley

Coca-Cola Football League One
Bournemouth v Port Vale
Brighton & HA v Southend U
Bristol R v Nottingham F
Carlisle U v Cheltenham T
Gillingham v Walsall
Hartlepool U v Oldham Ath
Leeds U v Luton T
Leyton Orient v Northampton T
Millwall v Huddersfield T
Swansea C v Doncaster R
Swindon T v Crewe Alex
Yeovil T v Tranmere R

Coca-Cola Football League Two
Accrington S v Peterborough U
Barnet v Bradford C
Bury v Brentford
Chesterfield v Wycombe W
Dagenham & R v Lincoln C
Macclesfield T v Darlington
Mansfield T v Stockport Co
Notts Co v Morecambe
Rochdale v Milton Keynes Dons
Rotherham U v Chester C
Shrewsbury T v Grimsby T
Wrexham v Hereford U

Sunday, 2 September 2007
Barclays Premier League
Arsenal v Portsmouth* (1.30)
Aston Villa v Chelsea* (4.00)

Monday, 3 September 2007
Coca-Cola Football League Championship
Blackpool v Hull C* (7.45)

Friday, 7 September 2007
Coca-Cola Football League One
Brighton & HA v Millwall
Cheltenham T v Swansea C
Northampton T v Doncaster R

Coca-Cola Football League Two
Chester C v Morecambe
Chesterfield v Bury
Lincoln C v Bradford C
Milton Keynes Dons v Notts Co

Saturday, 8 September 2007
Coca-Cola Football League One
Carlisle U v Tranmere R
Crewe Alex v Huddersfield T
Leeds U v Hartlepool U
Leyton Orient v Bournemouth
Luton T v Bristol R
Nottingham F v Oldham Ath
Southend U v Gillingham
Walsall v Port Vale

Coca-Cola Football League Two
Accrington S v Grimsby T
Dagenham & R v Barnet
Hereford U v Macclesfield T
Peterborough U v Mansfield T
Rochdale v Wrexham
Rotherham U v Darlington
Stockport Co v Shrewsbury T

Sunday, 9 September 2007
Coca-Cola Football League One
Swindon T v Yeovil T* (4.00)

Coca-Cola Football League Two
Wycombe W v Brentford* (1.30)

Friday, 14 September 2007
Coca-Cola Football League One
Bristol R v Leeds U
Swansea C v Carlisle U
Tranmere R v Luton T

Saturday, 15 September 2007
Barclays Premier League
Birmingham C v Bolton W
Chelsea v Blackburn R
Everton v Manchester U
Portsmouth v Liverpool* (12.45)
Sunderland v Reading
Tottenham H v Arsenal
West Ham U v Middlesbrough
Wigan Ath v Fulham

Coca-Cola Football League Championship
Barnsley v Scunthorpe U
Burnley v Blackpool
Colchester U v Charlton Ath
Coventry C v Bristol C
Hull C v Stoke C
Leicester C v QPR
Norwich C v Crystal Palace
Plymouth Arg v Cardiff C* (5.20)
Preston NE v Sheffield W
Sheffield U v Wolverhampton W
Watford v Southampton
WBA v Ipswich T

Coca-Cola Football League One
Bournemouth v Northampton T
Gillingham v Brighton & HA
Hartlepool U v Swindon T
Huddersfield T v Cheltenham T
Millwall v Walsall
Oldham Ath v Southend U
Port Vale v Nottingham F
Yeovil T v Leyton Orient

Coca-Cola Football League Two
Barnet v Rochdale
Bradford C v Peterborough U
Brentford v Milton Keynes Dons
Bury v Chester C
Darlington v Lincoln C
Grimsby T v Stockport Co
Macclesfield T v Wycombe W
Mansfield T v Chesterfield
Morecambe v Hereford U
Notts Co v Dagenham & R
Shrewsbury T v Accrington S
Wrexham v Rotherham U

Sunday, 16 September 2007
Barclays Premier League
Manchester C v Aston Villa* (4.00)

Coca-Cola Football League One
Doncaster R v Crewe Alex

Monday, 17 September 2007
Barclays Premier League
Derby Co v Newcastle U

Tuesday, 18 September 2007
Coca-Cola Football League Championship
Blackpool v Sheffield U
Bristol C v WBA
Cardiff C v Watford
Charlton Ath v Norwich C
Crystal Palace v Coventry C
Ipswich T v Leicester C
QPR v Plymouth Arg
Scunthorpe U v Preston NE
Sheffield W v Burnley
Southampton v Colchester U
Stoke C v Barnsley
Wolverhampton W v Hull C

Saturday, 22 September 2007
Barclays Premier League
Arsenal v Derby Co
Blackburn R v Portsmouth
Fulham v Manchester C
Liverpool v Birmingham C
Middlesbrough v Sunderland
Reading v Wigan Ath

Coca-Cola Football League Championship
Blackpool v Colchester U
Bristol C v Burnley
Cardiff C v Preston NE
Charlton Ath v Leicester C
Crystal Palace v Sheffield U
Ipswich T v Coventry C* (5.20)
QPR v Watford
Scunthorpe U v WBA
Sheffield W v Hull C
Southampton v Barnsley
Stoke C v Plymouth Arg
Wolverhampton W v Norwich C

Coca-Cola Football League One
Brighton & HA v Yeovil T
Carlisle U v Bristol R
Cheltenham T v Tranmere R
Crewe Alex v Millwall
Leeds U v Swansea C
Leyton Orient v Hartlepool U
Luton T v Port Vale
Northampton T v Huddersfield T
Nottingham F v Gillingham
Southend U v Doncaster R
Swindon T v Bournemouth
Walsall v Oldham Ath

Coca-Cola Football League Two
Accrington S v Mansfield T
Chester C v Brentford
Chesterfield v Barnet
Dagenham & R v Bury
Hereford U v Bradford C
Lincoln C v Grimsby T
Milton Keynes Dons v Darlington
Peterborough U v Morecambe
Rochdale v Macclesfield T
Rotherham U v Notts Co
Stockport Co v Wrexham
Wycombe W v Shrewsbury T

Sunday, 23 September 2007
Barclays Premier League
Aston Villa v Everton
Bolton W v Tottenham H
Manchester U v Chelsea* (4.00)
Newcastle U v West Ham U* (1.30)

Saturday, 29 September 2007
Barclays Premier League
Birmingham C v Manchester U
Chelsea v Fulham
Derby Co v Bolton W
Manchester C v Newcastle U* (12.45)
Portsmouth v Reading
Sunderland v Blackburn R
West Ham U v Arsenal
Wigan Ath v Liverpool

Coca-Cola Football League Championship
Barnsley v Cardiff C
Burnley v Crystal Palace
Colchester U v Scunthorpe U
Coventry C v Charlton Ath
Hull C v Ipswich T
Leicester C v Stoke C
Norwich C v Sheffield W* (5.20)
Plymouth Arg v Wolverhampton W
Preston NE v Bristol C
Sheffield U v Southampton
Watford v Blackpool
WBA v QPR

Coca-Cola Football League One
Bournemouth v Carlisle U
Bristol R v Leyton Orient
Doncaster R v Cheltenham T
Gillingham v Leeds U
Hartlepool U v Walsall
Huddersfield T v Luton T
Millwall v Swindon T
Oldham Ath v Crewe Alex
Port Vale v Southend U
Swansea C v Brighton & HA
Tranmere R v Northampton T
Yeovil T v Nottingham F

Coca-Cola Football League Two
Barnet v Rotherham U
Bradford C v Wycombe W
Brentford v Stockport Co
Bury v Accrington S
Darlington v Peterborough U
Grimsby T v Hereford U
Macclesfield T v Chester C
Mansfield T v Dagenham & R
Morecambe v Milton Keynes Dons
Notts Co v Chesterfield
Shrewsbury T v Rochdale
Wrexham v Lincoln C

Sunday, 30 September 2007
Barclays Premier League
Everton v Middlesbrough* (4.00)

Monday, 1 October 2007

Barclays Premier League

Tottenham H v Aston Villa

Tuesday, 2 October 2007

Coca-Cola Football League Championship

Barnsley v Bristol C
Burnley v Ipswich T
Colchester U v QPR
Coventry C v Blackpool
Hull C v Charlton Ath
Leicester C v Wolverhampton W
Norwich C v Scunthorpe U
Plymouth Arg v Crystal Palace
Preston NE v Southampton
Sheffield U v Cardiff C
Watford v Sheffield W
WBA v Stoke C

Coca-Cola Football League One

Bournemouth v Brighton & HA
Bristol R v Southend U
Doncaster R v Walsall
Gillingham v Leyton Orient
Hartlepool U v Carlisle U
Huddersfield T v Nottingham F
Millwall v Northampton T
Oldham Ath v Leeds U
Port Vale v Cheltenham T
Swansea C v Swindon T
Tranmere R v Crewe Alex
Yeovil T v Luton T

Coca-Cola Football League Two

Barnet v Wycombe W
Bradford C v Accrington S
Brentford v Dagenham & R
Bury v Lincoln C
Darlington v Rochdale
Grimsby T v Chester C
Macclesfield T v Rotherham U
Mansfield T v Milton Keynes Dons
Morecambe v Stockport Co
Notts Co v Hereford U
Shrewsbury T v Peterborough U
Wrexham v Chesterfield

Saturday, 6 October 2007

Barclays Premier League

Aston Villa v West Ham U
Blackburn R v Birmingham C
Manchester U v Wigan Ath* (12.45)

Coca-Cola Football League Championship

Blackpool v Plymouth Arg
Bristol C v Sheffield U* (5.20)
Cardiff C v Burnley
Charlton Ath v Barnsley
Crystal Palace v Hull C
Ipswich T v Preston NE
Scunthorpe U v Watford
Sheffield W v Leicester C
Southampton v WBA
Stoke C v Colchester U
Wolverhampton W v Coventry C

Coca-Cola Football League One

Brighton & HA v Bristol R
Carlisle U v Millwall
Cheltenham T v Oldham Ath
Crewe Alex v Bournemouth
Leeds U v Yeovil T
Leyton Orient v Swansea C
Luton T v Doncaster R
Northampton T v Port Vale
Nottingham F v Hartlepool U
Southend U v Tranmere R
Swindon T v Gillingham
Walsall v Huddersfield T

Coca-Cola Football League Two

Accrington S v Wrexham
Chesterfield v Macclesfield T
Dagenham & R v Darlington
Hereford U v Brentford
Lincoln C v Morecambe
Milton Keynes Dons v Bradford C
Peterborough U v Grimsby T
Rochdale v Bury
Rotherham U v Mansfield T
Stockport Co v Barnet
Wycombe W v Notts Co

Sunday, 7 October 2007

Barclays Premier League

Arsenal v Sunderland
Bolton W v Chelsea
Fulham v Portsmouth* (4.10)
Liverpool v Tottenham H
Manchester C v Middlesbrough
Newcastle U v Everton
Reading v Derby Co* (2.00)

Coca-Cola Football League Two

Chester C v Shrewsbury T

Monday, 8 October 2007

Coca-Cola Football League Championship

QPR v Norwich C* (7.45)

Friday, 12 October 2007

Coca-Cola Football League One

Hartlepool U v Bristol R

Coca-Cola Football League Two

Brentford v Rotherham U
Chester C v Hereford U
Grimsby T v Rochdale
Morecambe v Bradford C

Saturday, 13 October 2007

Coca-Cola Football League One

Bournemouth v Swansea C
Cheltenham T v Nottingham F
Gillingham v Millwall
Leeds U v Leyton Orient
Port Vale v Brighton & HA
Southend U v Crewe Alex
Tranmere R v Walsall
Yeovil T v Carlisle U

Coca-Cola Football League Two
Barnet v Mansfield T
Dagenham & R v Accrington S
Darlington v Stockport Co
Macclesfield T v Wrexham
Notts Co v Bury
Peterborough U v Wycombe W
Shrewsbury T v Chesterfield

Sunday, 14 October 2007
Coca-Cola Football League One
Doncaster R v Huddersfield T* (4.00)
Oldham Ath v Swindon T

Coca-Cola Football League Two
Milton Keynes Dons v Lincoln C* (1.30)

Monday, 15 October 2007
Coca-Cola Football League One
Luton T v Northampton T* (7.45)

Saturday, 20 October 2007
Barclays Premier League
Arsenal v Bolton W
Aston Villa v Manchester U
Blackburn R v Reading
Everton v Liverpool* (12.45)
Fulham v Derby Co
Manchester C v Birmingham C
Middlesbrough v Chelsea
Wigan Ath v Portsmouth

Coca-Cola Football League Championship
Barnsley v Burnley
Blackpool v Crystal Palace
Colchester U v WBA
Norwich C v Bristol C
Plymouth Arg v Coventry C
QPR v Ipswich T
Scunthorpe U v Leicester C* (5.20)
Sheffield U v Preston NE
Southampton v Cardiff C
Stoke C v Sheffield W
Watford v Hull C
Wolverhampton W v Charlton Ath

Coca-Cola Football League One
Brighton & HA v Leeds U
Bristol R v Yeovil T
Carlisle U v Gillingham
Crewe Alex v Luton T
Huddersfield T v Oldham Ath
Leyton Orient v Port Vale
Millwall v Bournemouth
Northampton T v Cheltenham T
Nottingham F v Doncaster R
Swansea C v Hartlepool U
Swindon T v Tranmere R
Walsall v Southend U

Coca-Cola Football League Two
Accrington S v Macclesfield T
Bradford C v Darlington
Bury v Shrewsbury T
Chesterfield v Dagenham & R
Hereford U v Milton Keynes Dons
Lincoln C v Peterborough U
Mansfield T v Notts Co
Rochdale v Brentford
Rotherham U v Morecambe
Stockport Co v Chester C
Wrexham v Barnet
Wycombe W v Grimsby T

Sunday, 21 October 2007
Barclays Premier League
West Ham U v Sunderland* (4.00)

Monday, 22 October 2007
Barclays Premier League
Newcastle U v Tottenham H

Coca-Cola Football League Championship
Hull C v Barnsley* (7.45)

Tuesday, 23 October 2007
Coca-Cola Football League Championship
Bristol C v Southampton
Burnley v Norwich C
Cardiff C v Wolverhampton W
Charlton Ath v Plymouth Arg
Coventry C v Watford
Crystal Palace v Stoke C
Ipswich T v Colchester U
Leicester C v Sheffield U
Preston NE v QPR
Sheffield W v Scunthorpe U
WBA v Blackpool

Friday, 26 October 2007
Coca-Cola Football League One
Tranmere R v Huddersfield T

Saturday, 27 October 2007
Barclays Premier League
Birmingham C v Wigan Ath
Chelsea v Manchester C
Derby Co v Everton
Manchester U v Middlesbrough
Portsmouth v West Ham U
Reading v Newcastle U
Sunderland v Fulham
Tottenham H v Blackburn R

Coca-Cola Football League Championship
Bristol C v Stoke C
Burnley v Southampton* (5.20)
Cardiff C v Scunthorpe U
Charlton Ath v QPR
Coventry C v Colchester U
Crystal Palace v Watford
Hull C v Sheffield U
Ipswich T v Wolverhampton W
Leicester C v Barnsley
Preston NE v Plymouth Arg
Sheffield W v Blackpool
WBA v Norwich C

Coca-Cola Football League One
Bournemouth v Walsall

Cheltenham T v Crewe Alex
Gillingham v Bristol R
Hartlepool U v Brighton & HA
Leeds U v Millwall
Luton T v Nottingham F
Oldham Ath v Northampton T
Port Vale v Swindon T
Southend U v Carlisle U
Yeovil T v Swansea C

Coca-Cola Football League Two
Barnet v Accrington S
Brentford v Lincoln C
Chester C v Wycombe W
Dagenham & R v Rotherham U
Darlington v Chesterfield
Grimsby T v Bradford C
Macclesfield T v Bury
Milton Keynes Dons v Stockport Co
Morecambe v Rochdale
Notts Co v Wrexham
Peterborough U v Hereford U
Shrewsbury T v Mansfield T

Sunday, 28 October 2007

Barclays Premier League
Bolton W v Aston Villa* (1.30)
Liverpool v Arsenal* (4.00)

Coca-Cola Football League One
Doncaster R v Leyton Orient

Friday, 2 November 2007

Coca-Cola Football League Two
Lincoln C v Chester C

Saturday, 3 November 2007

Barclays Premier League
Arsenal v Manchester U* (12.45)
Aston Villa v Derby Co
Blackburn R v Liverpool
Everton v Birmingham C
Fulham v Reading
Middlesbrough v Tottenham H
Newcastle U v Portsmouth
Wigan Ath v Chelsea

Coca-Cola Football League Championship
Barnsley v Preston NE
Blackpool v Cardiff C
Colchester U v Leicester C* (5.20)
Plymouth Arg v Sheffield W
QPR v Hull C
Scunthorpe U v Crystal Palace
Sheffield U v Burnley
Southampton v Charlton Ath
Stoke C v Coventry C
Watford v WBA
Wolverhampton W v Bristol C

Coca-Cola Football League One
Brighton & HA v Luton T
Bristol R v Bournemouth
Carlisle U v Leeds U
Crewe Alex v Yeovil T
Huddersfield T v Port Vale
Leyton Orient v Oldham Ath
Millwall v Hartlepool U
Northampton T v Southend U
Nottingham F v Tranmere R
Swansea C v Gillingham
Swindon T v Doncaster R
Walsall v Cheltenham T

Coca-Cola Football League Two
Accrington S v Notts Co
Bradford C v Brentford
Bury v Barnet
Chesterfield v Morecambe
Hereford U v Darlington
Mansfield T v Macclesfield T
Rochdale v Dagenham & R
Rotherham U v Grimsby T
Stockport Co v Peterborough U
Wycombe W v Milton Keynes Dons

Sunday, 4 November 2007

Barclays Premier League
West Ham U v Bolton W* (4.00)

Coca-Cola Football League Championship
Norwich C v Ipswich T

Coca-Cola Football League Two
Wrexham v Shrewsbury T

Monday, 5 November 2007

Barclays Premier League
Manchester C v Sunderland

Tuesday, 6 November 2007

Coca-Cola Football League Championship
Barnsley v Blackpool
Bristol C v Charlton Ath
Burnley v Hull C
Cardiff C v Crystal Palace
Colchester U v Plymouth Arg
Norwich C v Watford
Preston NE v Leicester C
QPR v Coventry C
Scunthorpe U v Stoke C
Sheffield U v Ipswich T
Southampton v Wolverhampton W
WBA v Sheffield W

Coca-Cola Football League One
Bournemouth v Leeds U
Brighton & HA v Walsall
Cheltenham T v Yeovil T
Gillingham v Doncaster R
Huddersfield T v Hartlepool U
Luton T v Carlisle U
Millwall v Swansea C
Northampton T v Bristol R
Nottingham F v Southend U
Port Vale v Crewe Alex
Swindon T v Leyton Orient
Tranmere R v Oldham Ath

Coca-Cola Football League Two
Barnet v Notts Co
Bradford C v Chester C
Darlington v Shrewsbury T
Hereford U v Mansfield T
Lincoln C v Chesterfield
Macclesfield T v Brentford
Milton Keynes Dons v Grimsby T
Morecambe v Accrington S
Peterborough U v Dagenham & R
Rochdale v Stockport Co
Rotherham U v Bury

Wednesday, 7 November 2007

Coca-Cola Football League Two
Wrexham v Wycombe W

Saturday, 10 November 2007

Barclays Premier League
Bolton W v Middlesbrough
Chelsea v Everton
Derby Co v West Ham U
Liverpool v Fulham
Manchester U v Blackburn R
Sunderland v Newcastle U* (12.45)
Tottenham H v Wigan Ath

Coca-Cola Football League Championship
Blackpool v Scunthorpe U
Charlton Ath v Cardiff C
Crystal Palace v QPR
Hull C v Preston NE
Ipswich T v Bristol C
Leicester C v Burnley
Plymouth Arg v Norwich C
Sheffield W v Southampton
Stoke C v Sheffield U* (5.20)
Watford v Colchester U
Wolverhampton W v Barnsley

Sunday, 11 November 2007

Barclays Premier League
Birmingham C v Aston Villa* (1.00)
Portsmouth v Manchester C* (4.00)

Monday, 12 November 2007

Barclays Premier League
Reading v Arsenal

Coca-Cola Football League Championship
Coventry C v WBA* (7.45)

Friday, 16 November 2007

Coca-Cola Football League One
Swansea C v Huddersfield T

Saturday, 17 November 2007

Coca-Cola Football League One
Bristol R v Millwall
Crewe Alex v Northampton T
Doncaster R v Tranmere R
Hartlepool U v Bournemouth
Leeds U v Swindon T
Leyton Orient v Brighton & HA
Oldham Ath v Port Vale
Southend U v Cheltenham T
Walsall v Luton T

Coca-Cola Football League Two
Accrington S v Rotherham U
Brentford v Darlington
Bury v Peterborough U
Chester C v Milton Keynes Dons
Chesterfield v Rochdale
Dagenham & R v Bradford C
Grimsby T v Morecambe
Mansfield T v Wrexham
Notts Co v Macclesfield T
Shrewsbury T v Barnet
Stockport Co v Hereford U
Wycombe W v Lincoln C

Sunday, 18 November 2007

Coca-Cola Football League One
Carlisle U v Nottingham F* (4.00)
Yeovil T v Gillingham* (1.30)

Saturday, 24 November 2007

Barclays Premier League
Arsenal v Wigan Ath
Birmingham C v Portsmouth
Bolton W v Manchester U
Derby Co v Chelsea
Everton v Sunderland
Manchester C v Reading
Middlesbrough v Aston Villa
Newcastle U v Liverpool* (12.45)

Coca-Cola Football League Championship
Barnsley v Watford
Bristol C v Leicester C
Burnley v Stoke C
Cardiff C v Ipswich T
Colchester U v Crystal Palace
Norwich C v Coventry C
Preston NE v Charlton Ath* (5.20)
QPR v Sheffield W
Scunthorpe U v Hull C
Sheffield U v Plymouth Arg
Southampton v Blackpool
WBA v Wolverhampton W

Coca-Cola Football League One
Bournemouth v Oldham Ath
Brighton & HA v Carlisle U
Cheltenham T v Leeds U
Gillingham v Hartlepool U
Huddersfield T v Leyton Orient
Luton T v Southend U
Millwall v Yeovil T
Northampton T v Walsall
Nottingham F v Crewe Alex
Port Vale v Doncaster R
Swindon T v Bristol R
Tranmere R v Swansea C

Coca-Cola Football League Two
Barnet v Grimsby T
Bradford C v Stockport Co
Darlington v Wycombe W

Hereford U v Accrington S
Lincoln C v Notts Co
Macclesfield T v Dagenham & R
Milton Keynes Dons v Chesterfield
Morecambe v Bury
Peterborough U v Brentford
Rochdale v Mansfield T
Rotherham U v Shrewsbury T

Sunday, 25 November 2007

Barclays Premier League
Fulham v Blackburn R* (4.00)
West Ham U v Tottenham H* (1.30)

Coca-Cola Football League Two
Wrexham v Chester C

Tuesday, 27 November 2007

Coca-Cola Football League Championship
Blackpool v Norwich C
Charlton Ath v Sheffield U
Coventry C v Scunthorpe U
Crystal Palace v Preston NE
Hull C v Bristol C
Ipswich T v Southampton
Leicester C v Cardiff C
Plymouth Arg v WBA
Sheffield W v Barnsley
Stoke C v QPR
Watford v Burnley

Wednesday, 28 November 2007

Coca-Cola Football League Championship
Wolverhampton W v Colchester U

Saturday, 1 December 2007

Barclays Premier League
Aston Villa v Arsenal
Blackburn R v Newcastle U
Chelsea v West Ham U
Liverpool v Bolton W
Manchester U v Fulham
Portsmouth v Everton
Reading v Middlesbrough
Sunderland v Derby Co
Tottenham H v Birmingham C
Wigan Ath v Manchester C

Coca-Cola Football League Championship
Blackpool v QPR
Charlton Ath v Burnley
Coventry C v Sheffield U
Crystal Palace v WBA
Hull C v Cardiff C
Ipswich T v Barnsley
Leicester C v Southampton
Plymouth Arg v Scunthorpe U
Sheffield W v Colchester U
Stoke C v Norwich C
Watford v Bristol C
Wolverhampton W v Preston NE

Tuesday, 4 December 2007

Coca-Cola Football League Championship
Barnsley v Wolverhampton W
Bristol C v Ipswich T
Burnley v Leicester C
Cardiff C v Charlton Ath
Colchester U v Watford
Norwich C v Plymouth Arg
Preston NE v Hull C
QPR v Crystal Palace
Scunthorpe U v Blackpool
Sheffield U v Stoke C
Southampton v Sheffield W
WBA v Coventry C

Coca-Cola Football League One
Carlisle U v Swindon T
Crewe Alex v Gillingham
Doncaster R v Brighton & HA
Hartlepool U v Tranmere R
Leeds U v Port Vale
Leyton Orient v Millwall
Oldham Ath v Luton T
Swansea C v Northampton T
Walsall v Nottingham F
Yeovil T v Bournemouth

Coca-Cola Football League Two
Brentford v Morecambe
Bury v Wrexham
Chester C v Barnet
Dagenham & R v Milton Keynes Dons
Grimsby T v Darlington
Mansfield T v Bradford C
Notts Co v Peterborough U
Shrewsbury T v Macclesfield T
Stockport Co v Lincoln C
Wycombe W v Hereford U

Wednesday, 5 December 2007

Coca-Cola Football League One
Bristol R v Cheltenham T
Southend U v Huddersfield T

Coca-Cola Football League Two
Accrington S v Rochdale
Chesterfield v Rotherham U

Friday, 7 December 2007

Coca-Cola Football League One
Brighton & HA v Nottingham F

Saturday, 8 December 2007

Barclays Premier League
Aston Villa v Portsmouth
Blackburn R v West Ham U
Bolton W v Wigan Ath
Chelsea v Sunderland
Everton v Fulham
Manchester U v Derby Co
Middlesbrough v Arsenal
Newcastle U v Birmingham C
Reading v Liverpool
Tottenham H v Manchester C

Coca-Cola Football League Championship
Barnsley v Crystal Palace
Cardiff C v Colchester U

Charlton Ath v Ipswich T
Leicester C v WBA
Norwich C v Sheffield U
Plymouth Arg v Bristol C
Preston NE v Blackpool
Scunthorpe U v QPR
Sheffield W v Coventry C
Southampton v Hull C
Stoke C v Watford
Wolverhampton W v Burnley

Coca-Cola Football League One
Bristol R v Swansea C
Crewe Alex v Walsall
Gillingham v Port Vale
Leeds U v Huddersfield T
Leyton Orient v Cheltenham T
Luton T v Millwall
Northampton T v Carlisle U
Oldham Ath v Doncaster R
Southend U v Swindon T
Tranmere R v Bournemouth
Yeovil T v Hartlepool U

Coca-Cola Football League Two
Barnet v Macclesfield T
Brentford v Grimsby T
Chester C v Peterborough U
Chesterfield v Bradford C
Dagenham & R v Wrexham
Hereford U v Lincoln C
Mansfield T v Bury
Milton Keynes Dons v Accrington S
Morecambe v Darlington
Notts Co v Shrewsbury T
Rotherham U v Rochdale
Stockport Co v Wycombe W

Friday, 14 December 2007
Coca-Cola Football League One
Cheltenham T v Luton T

Saturday, 15 December 2007
Barclays Premier League
Arsenal v Chelsea
Birmingham C v Reading
Derby Co v Middlesbrough
Fulham v Newcastle U
Liverpool v Manchester U
Manchester C v Bolton W
Portsmouth v Tottenham H
Sunderland v Aston Villa
West Ham U v Everton
Wigan Ath v Blackburn R

Coca-Cola Football League Championship
Blackpool v Stoke C
Bristol C v Cardiff C
Burnley v Preston NE
Colchester U v Norwich C
Coventry C v Southampton
Crystal Palace v Sheffield W
Hull C v Leicester C
Ipswich T v Scunthorpe U
QPR v Wolverhampton W
Sheffield U v Barnsley
Watford v Plymouth Arg
WBA v Charlton Ath

Coca-Cola Football League One
Bournemouth v Gillingham
Carlisle U v Leyton Orient
Hartlepool U v Crewe Alex
Huddersfield T v Bristol R
Millwall v Oldham Ath
Nottingham F v Northampton T
Port Vale v Tranmere R
Swansea C v Southend U
Swindon T v Brighton & HA
Walsall v Leeds U

Coca-Cola Football League Two
Accrington S v Chesterfield
Bradford C v Rotherham U
Bury v Hereford U
Darlington v Chester C
Grimsby T v Mansfield T
Lincoln C v Barnet
Macclesfield T v Stockport Co
Peterborough U v Milton Keynes Dons
Rochdale v Notts Co
Shrewsbury T v Dagenham & R
Wrexham v Brentford
Wycombe W v Morecambe

Sunday, 16 December 2007
Coca-Cola Football League One
Doncaster R v Yeovil T

Friday, 21 December 2007
Coca-Cola Football League One
Brighton & HA v Gillingham
Northampton T v Bournemouth

Coca-Cola Football League Two
Chesterfield v Mansfield T
Milton Keynes Dons v Brentford

Saturday, 22 December 2007
Barclays Premier League
Arsenal v Tottenham H
Aston Villa v Manchester C
Blackburn R v Chelsea
Bolton W v Birmingham C
Fulham v Wigan Ath
Liverpool v Portsmouth
Manchester U v Everton
Middlesbrough v West Ham U
Newcastle U v Derby Co
Reading v Sunderland

Coca-Cola Football League Championship
Blackpool v Coventry C
Bristol C v Barnsley
Cardiff C v Sheffield U
Charlton Ath v Hull C
Crystal Palace v Plymouth Arg
Ipswich T v Burnley
QPR v Colchester U

Scunthorpe U v Norwich C
Sheffield W v Watford
Southampton v Preston NE
Stoke C v WBA
Wolverhampton W v Leicester C

Coca-Cola Football League One
Carlisle U v Swansea C
Cheltenham T v Huddersfield T
Crewe Alex v Doncaster R
Leeds U v Bristol R
Leyton Orient v Yeovil T
Luton T v Tranmere R
Nottingham F v Port Vale
Southend U v Oldham Ath
Swindon T v Hartlepool U
Walsall v Millwall

Coca-Cola Football League Two
Accrington S v Shrewsbury T
Chester C v Bury
Dagenham & R v Notts Co
Hereford U v Morecambe
Lincoln C v Darlington
Peterborough U v Bradford C
Rochdale v Barnet
Rotherham U v Wrexham
Stockport Co v Grimsby T
Wycombe W v Macclesfield T

Wednesday, 26 December 2007

Barclays Premier League
Birmingham C v Middlesbrough
Chelsea v Aston Villa
Derby Co v Liverpool
Everton v Bolton W
Manchester C v Blackburn R
Portsmouth v Arsenal
Sunderland v Manchester U
Tottenham H v Fulham
West Ham U v Reading
Wigan Ath v Newcastle U

Coca-Cola Football League Championship
Barnsley v Stoke C
Burnley v Sheffield W
Colchester U v Southampton
Coventry C v Crystal Palace
Hull C v Wolverhampton W
Leicester C v Ipswich T
Norwich C v Charlton Ath
Plymouth Arg v QPR
Preston NE v Scunthorpe U
Sheffield U v Blackpool
Watford v Cardiff C
WBA v Bristol C

Coca-Cola Football League One
Bournemouth v Leyton Orient
Bristol R v Luton T
Doncaster R v Northampton T
Gillingham v Southend U
Hartlepool U v Leeds U
Huddersfield T v Crewe Alex
Millwall v Brighton & HA
Oldham Ath v Nottingham F
Port Vale v Walsall
Swansea C v Cheltenham T
Tranmere R v Carlisle U
Yeovil T v Swindon T

Coca-Cola Football League Two
Barnet v Dagenham & R
Bradford C v Lincoln C
Brentford v Wycombe W
Bury v Chesterfield
Darlington v Rotherham U
Grimsby T v Accrington S
Macclesfield T v Hereford U
Mansfield T v Peterborough U
Morecambe v Chester C
Notts Co v Milton Keynes Dons
Shrewsbury T v Stockport Co
Wrexham v Rochdale

Saturday, 29 December 2007

Barclays Premier League
Birmingham C v Fulham
Chelsea v Newcastle U
Derby Co v Blackburn R
Everton v Arsenal
Manchester C v Liverpool
Portsmouth v Middlesbrough
Sunderland v Bolton W
Tottenham H v Reading
West Ham U v Manchester U
Wigan Ath v Aston Villa

Coca-Cola Football League Championship
Barnsley v Southampton
Burnley v Bristol C
Colchester U v Blackpool
Coventry C v Ipswich T
Hull C v Sheffield W
Leicester C v Charlton Ath
Norwich C v Wolverhampton W
Plymouth Arg v Stoke C
Preston NE v Cardiff C
Sheffield U v Crystal Palace
Watford v QPR
WBA v Scunthorpe U

Coca-Cola Football League One
Bournemouth v Swindon T
Bristol R v Carlisle U
Doncaster R v Southend U
Gillingham v Nottingham F
Hartlepool U v Leyton Orient
Huddersfield T v Northampton T
Millwall v Crewe Alex
Oldham Ath v Walsall
Port Vale v Luton T
Swansea C v Leeds U
Tranmere R v Cheltenham T
Yeovil T v Brighton & HA

Coca-Cola Football League Two
Barnet v Chesterfield

Bradford C v Hereford U
Brentford v Chester C
Bury v Dagenham & R
Darlington v Milton Keynes Dons
Grimsby T v Lincoln C
Macclesfield T v Rochdale
Mansfield T v Accrington S
Morecambe v Peterborough U
Notts Co v Rotherham U
Shrewsbury T v Wycombe W
Wrexham v Stockport Co

Tuesday, 1 January 2008

Barclays Premier League
Arsenal v West Ham U
Aston Villa v Tottenham H
Blackburn R v Sunderland
Bolton W v Derby Co
Fulham v Chelsea
Liverpool v Wigan Ath
Manchester U v Birmingham C
Middlesbrough v Everton
Newcastle U v Manchester C
Reading v Portsmouth

Coca-Cola Football League Championship
Blackpool v Burnley
Bristol C v Coventry C
Cardiff C v Plymouth Arg
Charlton Ath v Colchester U
Crystal Palace v Norwich C
Ipswich T v WBA
QPR v Leicester C
Scunthorpe U v Barnsley
Sheffield W v Preston NE
Southampton v Watford
Stoke C v Hull C
Wolverhampton W v Sheffield U

Coca-Cola Football League One
Brighton & HA v Bournemouth
Carlisle U v Hartlepool U
Crewe Alex v Tranmere R
Leeds U v Oldham Ath
Leyton Orient v Gillingham
Luton T v Yeovil T
Northampton T v Millwall
Nottingham F v Huddersfield T
Southend U v Bristol R
Swindon T v Swansea C
Walsall v Doncaster R

Coca-Cola Football League Two
Accrington S v Bradford C
Chester C v Grimsby T
Chesterfield v Wrexham
Dagenham & R v Brentford
Hereford U v Notts Co
Lincoln C v Bury
Milton Keynes Dons v Mansfield T
Peterborough U v Shrewsbury T
Rochdale v Darlington
Rotherham U v Macclesfield T
Stockport Co v Morecambe
Wycombe W v Barnet

Wednesday, 2 January 2008

Coca-Cola Football League One
Cheltenham T v Port Vale

Saturday, 5 January 2008

Coca-Cola Football League One
Bournemouth v Luton T
Brighton & HA v Cheltenham T
Bristol R v Doncaster R
Carlisle U v Port Vale
Gillingham v Oldham Ath
Hartlepool U v Southend U
Leeds U v Northampton T
Leyton Orient v Tranmere R
Millwall v Nottingham F
Swansea C v Crewe Alex
Swindon T v Huddersfield T
Yeovil T v Walsall

Coca-Cola Football League Two
Accrington S v Chester C
Barnet v Darlington
Bury v Bradford C
Chesterfield v Grimsby T
Dagenham & R v Hereford U
Macclesfield T v Morecambe
Mansfield T v Wycombe W
Notts Co v Stockport Co
Rochdale v Lincoln C
Rotherham U v Milton Keynes Dons
Shrewsbury T v Brentford
Wrexham v Peterborough U

Friday, 11 January 2008

Coca-Cola Football League One
Tranmere R v Bristol R

Saturday, 12 January 2008

Barclays Premier League
Arsenal v Birmingham C
Aston Villa v Reading
Bolton W v Blackburn R
Chelsea v Tottenham H
Derby Co v Wigan Ath
Everton v Manchester C
Manchester U v Newcastle U
Middlesbrough v Liverpool
Sunderland v Portsmouth
West Ham U v Fulham

Coca-Cola Football League Championship
Barnsley v Norwich C
Bristol C v Colchester U
Burnley v Plymouth Arg
Cardiff C v Sheffield W
Charlton Ath v Blackpool
Hull C v WBA
Ipswich T v Stoke C
Leicester C v Coventry C
Preston NE v Watford
Sheffield U v QPR
Southampton v Scunthorpe U
Wolverhampton W v Crystal Palace

Coca-Cola Football League One
Cheltenham T v Bournemouth
Crewe Alex v Leeds U
Doncaster R v Carlisle U
Huddersfield T v Gillingham
Luton T v Swansea C
Northampton T v Hartlepool U
Nottingham F v Leyton Orient
Oldham Ath v Brighton & HA
Port Vale v Millwall
Southend U v Yeovil T
Walsall v Swindon T

Coca-Cola Football League Two
Bradford C v Notts Co
Brentford v Chesterfield
Chester C v Mansfield T
Darlington v Bury
Grimsby T v Wrexham
Lincoln C v Rotherham U
Milton Keynes Dons v Barnet
Morecambe v Dagenham & R
Peterborough U v Macclesfield T
Stockport Co v Accrington S
Wycombe W v Rochdale

Sunday, 13 January 2008

Coca-Cola Football League Two
Hereford U v Shrewsbury T

Friday, 18 January 2008

Coca-Cola Football League One
Hartlepool U v Cheltenham T

Saturday, 19 January 2008

Barclays Premier League
Birmingham C v Chelsea
Blackburn R v Middlesbrough
Fulham v Arsenal
Liverpool v Aston Villa
Manchester C v West Ham U
Newcastle U v Bolton W
Portsmouth v Derby Co
Reading v Manchester U
Tottenham H v Sunderland
Wigan Ath v Everton

Coca-Cola Football League Championship
Blackpool v Ipswich T
Colchester U v Hull C
Coventry C v Burnley
Crystal Palace v Bristol C
Norwich C v Leicester C
Plymouth Arg v Southampton
QPR v Barnsley
Scunthorpe U v Wolverhampton W
Sheffield W v Sheffield U
Stoke C v Preston NE
Watford v Charlton Ath
WBA v Cardiff C

Coca-Cola Football League One
Bournemouth v Southend U
Brighton & HA v Huddersfield T
Bristol R v Walsall
Carlisle U v Crewe Alex
Gillingham v Northampton T
Leeds U v Doncaster R
Leyton Orient v Luton T
Millwall v Tranmere R
Swansea C v Port Vale
Swindon T v Nottingham F
Yeovil T v Oldham Ath

Coca-Cola Football League Two
Accrington S v Brentford
Barnet v Peterborough U
Bury v Stockport Co
Chesterfield v Hereford U
Dagenham & R v Grimsby T
Macclesfield T v Lincoln C
Mansfield T v Darlington
Notts Co v Chester C
Rochdale v Bradford C
Rotherham U v Wycombe W
Shrewsbury T v Morecambe
Wrexham v Milton Keynes Dons

Friday, 25 January 2008

Coca-Cola Football League One
Cheltenham T v Carlisle U
Northampton T v Leyton Orient

Saturday, 26 January 2008

Coca-Cola Football League One
Crewe Alex v Swindon T
Doncaster R v Swansea C
Huddersfield T v Millwall
Luton T v Leeds U
Nottingham F v Bristol R
Oldham Ath v Hartlepool U
Port Vale v Bournemouth
Southend U v Brighton & HA
Tranmere R v Yeovil T
Walsall v Gillingham

Coca-Cola Football League Two
Bradford C v Barnet
Brentford v Bury
Chester C v Rotherham U
Darlington v Macclesfield T
Grimsby T v Shrewsbury T
Hereford U v Wrexham
Lincoln C v Dagenham & R
Milton Keynes Dons v Rochdale
Morecambe v Notts Co
Peterborough U v Accrington S
Stockport Co v Mansfield T
Wycombe W v Chesterfield

Tuesday, 29 January 2008

Barclays Premier League
Arsenal v Newcastle U
Bolton W v Fulham
Derby Co v Manchester C
Middlesbrough v Wigan Ath
Sunderland v Birmingham C
West Ham U v Liverpool

Coca-Cola Football League Championship
Barnsley v Colchester U
Bristol C v Blackpool
Burnley v Scunthorpe U
Cardiff C v QPR
Charlton Ath v Stoke C
Hull C v Coventry C
Ipswich T v Plymouth Arg
Leicester C v Crystal Palace
Preston NE v WBA
Sheffield U v Watford
Southampton v Norwich C
Wolverhampton W v Sheffield W

Coca-Cola Football League One
Cheltenham T v Millwall
Crewe Alex v Bristol R
Doncaster R v Hartlepool U
Huddersfield T v Bournemouth
Luton T v Swindon T
Northampton T v Brighton & HA
Nottingham F v Swansea C
Oldham Ath v Carlisle U
Port Vale v Yeovil T
Southend U v Leeds U
Tranmere R v Gillingham
Walsall v Leyton Orient

Coca-Cola Football League Two
Bradford C v Shrewsbury T
Brentford v Notts Co
Chester C v Rochdale
Darlington v Accrington S
Grimsby T v Bury
Hereford U v Barnet
Lincoln C v Mansfield T
Milton Keynes Dons v Macclesfield T
Morecambe v Wrexham
Peterborough U v Rotherham U
Stockport Co v Chesterfield
Wycombe W v Dagenham & R

Wednesday, 30 January 2008

Barclays Premier League
Aston Villa v Blackburn R
Chelsea v Reading
Everton v Tottenham H
Manchester U v Portsmouth

Saturday, 2 February 2008

Barclays Premier League
Birmingham C v Derby Co
Blackburn R v Everton
Fulham v Aston Villa
Liverpool v Sunderland
Manchester C v Arsenal
Newcastle U v Middlesbrough
Portsmouth v Chelsea
Reading v Bolton W
Tottenham H v Manchester U
Wigan Ath v West Ham U

Coca-Cola Football League Championship
Blackpool v Leicester C
Colchester U v Sheffield U
Coventry C v Barnsley
Crystal Palace v Southampton
Norwich C v Preston NE
Plymouth Arg v Hull C
QPR v Bristol C
Scunthorpe U v Charlton Ath
Sheffield W v Ipswich T
Stoke C v Cardiff C
Watford v Wolverhampton W
WBA v Burnley

Coca-Cola Football League One
Bournemouth v Nottingham F
Brighton & HA v Crewe Alex
Bristol R v Port Vale
Carlisle U v Walsall
Gillingham v Cheltenham T
Hartlepool U v Luton T
Leeds U v Tranmere R
Leyton Orient v Southend U
Millwall v Doncaster R
Swansea C v Oldham Ath
Swindon T v Northampton T
Yeovil T v Huddersfield T

Coca-Cola Football League Two
Accrington S v Wycombe W
Barnet v Morecambe
Bury v Milton Keynes Dons
Chesterfield v Chester C
Dagenham & R v Stockport Co
Macclesfield T v Bradford C
Mansfield T v Brentford
Notts Co v Grimsby T
Rochdale v Peterborough U
Rotherham U v Hereford U
Shrewsbury T v Lincoln C
Wrexham v Darlington

Saturday, 9 February 2008

Barclays Premier League
Arsenal v Blackburn R
Aston Villa v Newcastle U
Bolton W v Portsmouth
Chelsea v Liverpool
Derby Co v Tottenham H
Everton v Reading
Middlesbrough v Fulham
Sunderland v Wigan Ath
West Ham U v Birmingham C

Coca-Cola Football League Championship
Barnsley v WBA
Bristol C v Sheffield W
Burnley v Colchester U
Cardiff C v Norwich C
Charlton Ath v Crystal Palace
Hull C v Blackpool
Ipswich T v Watford
Leicester C v Plymouth Arg
Preston NE v Coventry C
Sheffield U v Scunthorpe U
Southampton v QPR
Wolverhampton W v Stoke C

Coca-Cola Football League One
Cheltenham T v Brighton & HA
Crewe Alex v Swansea C
Doncaster R v Bristol R
Huddersfield T v Swindon T
Luton T v Bournemouth
Northampton T v Leeds U
Nottingham F v Millwall
Oldham Ath v Gillingham
Port Vale v Carlisle U
Southend U v Hartlepool U
Tranmere R v Leyton Orient
Walsall v Yeovil T

Coca-Cola Football League Two
Bradford C v Bury
Brentford v Shrewsbury T
Chester C v Accrington S
Darlington v Barnet
Grimsby T v Chesterfield
Hereford U v Dagenham & R
Lincoln C v Rochdale
Milton Keynes Dons v Rotherham U
Morecambe v Macclesfield T
Peterborough U v Wrexham
Stockport Co v Notts Co
Wycombe W v Mansfield T

Sunday, 10 February 2008

Barclays Premier League
Manchester U v Manchester C

Tuesday, 12 February 2008

Coca-Cola Football League Championship
Blackpool v Wolverhampton W
Colchester U v Preston NE
Coventry C v Cardiff C
Crystal Palace v Ipswich T
Norwich C v Hull C
Plymouth Arg v Barnsley
QPR v Burnley
Scunthorpe U v Bristol C
Sheffield W v Charlton Ath
Stoke C v Southampton
Watford v Leicester C
WBA v Sheffield U

Coca-Cola Football League One
Bournemouth v Doncaster R
Brighton & HA v Tranmere R
Bristol R v Oldham Ath
Carlisle U v Huddersfield T
Gillingham v Luton T
Hartlepool U v Port Vale
Leeds U v Nottingham F
Leyton Orient v Crewe Alex
Millwall v Southend U
Swansea C v Walsall
Swindon T v Cheltenham T
Yeovil T v Northampton T

Coca-Cola Football League Two
Accrington S v Lincoln C
Barnet v Brentford
Bury v Wycombe W
Dagenham & R v Chester C
Macclesfield T v Grimsby T
Mansfield T v Morecambe
Notts Co v Darlington
Rochdale v Hereford U
Rotherham U v Stockport Co
Shrewsbury T v Milton Keynes Dons
Wrexham v Bradford C

Wednesday, 13 February 2008

Coca-Cola Football League Two
Chesterfield v Peterborough U

Saturday, 16 February 2008

Coca-Cola Football League Championship
Barnsley v QPR
Bristol C v Crystal Palace
Burnley v Coventry C
Cardiff C v WBA
Charlton Ath v Watford
Hull C v Colchester U
Ipswich T v Blackpool
Leicester C v Norwich C
Preston NE v Stoke C
Sheffield U v Sheffield W
Southampton v Plymouth Arg
Wolverhampton W v Scunthorpe U

Coca-Cola Football League One
Cheltenham T v Hartlepool U
Crewe Alex v Carlisle U
Doncaster R v Leeds U
Huddersfield T v Brighton & HA
Luton T v Leyton Orient
Northampton T v Gillingham
Nottingham F v Swindon T
Oldham Ath v Yeovil T
Port Vale v Swansea C
Southend U v Bournemouth
Tranmere R v Millwall
Walsall v Bristol R

Coca-Cola Football League Two
Bradford C v Rochdale
Brentford v Accrington S
Chester C v Notts Co
Darlington v Mansfield T
Grimsby T v Dagenham & R
Hereford U v Chesterfield
Lincoln C v Macclesfield T
Milton Keynes Dons v Wrexham
Morecambe v Shrewsbury T
Peterborough U v Barnet
Stockport Co v Bury
Wycombe W v Rotherham U

Friday, 22 February 2008

Coca-Cola Football League One
Hartlepool U v Northampton T
Swansea C v Luton T

Coca-Cola Football League Two
Wrexham v Grimsby T

Saturday, 23 February 2008

Barclays Premier League
Birmingham C v Arsenal
Blackburn R v Bolton W
Fulham v West Ham U
Liverpool v Middlesbrough
Manchester C v Everton
Newcastle U v Manchester U
Portsmouth v Sunderland
Reading v Aston Villa
Tottenham H v Chelsea
Wigan Ath v Derby Co

Coca-Cola Football League Championship
Blackpool v Charlton Ath
Colchester U v Bristol C
Coventry C v Leicester C
Crystal Palace v Wolverhampton W
Norwich C v Barnsley
Plymouth Arg v Burnley
QPR v Sheffield U
Scunthorpe U v Southampton
Sheffield W v Cardiff C
Stoke C v Ipswich T
Watford v Preston NE
WBA v Hull C

Coca-Cola Football League One
Bournemouth v Cheltenham T
Brighton & HA v Oldham Ath
Bristol R v Tranmere R
Carlisle U v Doncaster R
Gillingham v Huddersfield T
Leeds U v Crewe Alex
Leyton Orient v Nottingham F
Millwall v Port Vale
Swindon T v Walsall
Yeovil T v Southend U

Coca-Cola Football League Two
Accrington S v Stockport Co
Barnet v Milton Keynes Dons
Bury v Darlington
Chesterfield v Brentford
Dagenham & R v Morecambe
Macclesfield T v Peterborough U
Mansfield T v Chester C
Notts Co v Bradford C
Rochdale v Wycombe W
Rotherham U v Lincoln C
Shrewsbury T v Hereford U

Friday, 29 February 2008

Coca-Cola Football League One
Cheltenham T v Southend U

Saturday, 1 March 2008

Barclays Premier League
Arsenal v Aston Villa
Birmingham C v Tottenham H
Bolton W v Liverpool
Derby Co v Sunderland
Everton v Portsmouth
Fulham v Manchester U
Manchester C v Wigan Ath
Middlesbrough v Reading
Newcastle U v Blackburn R
West Ham U v Chelsea

Coca-Cola Football League Championship
Barnsley v Sheffield W
Bristol C v Hull C
Burnley v Watford
Cardiff C v Leicester C
Colchester U v Wolverhampton W
Norwich C v Blackpool
Preston NE v Crystal Palace
QPR v Stoke C
Scunthorpe U v Coventry C
Sheffield U v Charlton Ath
Southampton v Ipswich T
WBA v Plymouth Arg

Coca-Cola Football League One
Bournemouth v Hartlepool U
Brighton & HA v Leyton Orient
Gillingham v Yeovil T
Huddersfield T v Swansea C
Luton T v Walsall
Millwall v Bristol R
Northampton T v Crewe Alex
Nottingham F v Carlisle U
Port Vale v Oldham Ath
Swindon T v Leeds U
Tranmere R v Doncaster R

Coca-Cola Football League Two
Barnet v Shrewsbury T
Bradford C v Dagenham & R
Darlington v Brentford
Hereford U v Stockport Co
Lincoln C v Wycombe W
Macclesfield T v Notts Co
Milton Keynes Dons v Chester C
Morecambe v Grimsby T
Peterborough U v Bury
Rochdale v Chesterfield
Rotherham U v Accrington S
Wrexham v Mansfield T

Tuesday, 4 March 2008

Coca-Cola Football League Championship
Blackpool v Barnsley
Charlton Ath v Bristol C
Coventry C v QPR
Crystal Palace v Cardiff C
Hull C v Burnley
Ipswich T v Sheffield U
Leicester C v Preston NE
Plymouth Arg v Colchester U
Sheffield W v WBA
Stoke C v Scunthorpe U
Watford v Norwich C
Wolverhampton W v Southampton

Coca-Cola Football League One
Bristol R v Northampton T

Saturday, 8 March 2008

Barclays Premier League
Aston Villa v Middlesbrough
Blackburn R v Fulham
Chelsea v Derby Co
Liverpool v Newcastle U
Manchester U v Bolton W
Portsmouth v Birmingham C
Reading v Manchester C
Sunderland v Everton
Tottenham H v West Ham U
Wigan Ath v Arsenal

Coca-Cola Football League Championship
Blackpool v Southampton
Charlton Ath v Preston NE
Coventry C v Norwich C
Crystal Palace v Colchester U
Hull C v Scunthorpe U
Ipswich T v Cardiff C
Leicester C v Bristol C
Plymouth Arg v Sheffield U
Sheffield W v QPR
Stoke C v Burnley
Watford v Barnsley
Wolverhampton W v WBA

Coca-Cola Football League One
Bristol R v Swindon T
Carlisle U v Brighton & HA
Crewe Alex v Nottingham F
Doncaster R v Port Vale
Hartlepool U v Gillingham
Leeds U v Bournemouth
Leyton Orient v Huddersfield T
Oldham Ath v Tranmere R
Southend U v Luton T
Swansea C v Millwall
Walsall v Northampton T
Yeovil T v Cheltenham T

Coca-Cola Football League Two
Accrington S v Hereford U
Brentford v Macclesfield T
Bury v Morecambe
Chesterfield v Lincoln C
Dagenham & R v Peterborough U
Grimsby T v Milton Keynes Dons
Mansfield T v Rochdale
Notts Co v Barnet
Shrewsbury T v Rotherham U
Stockport Co v Bradford C
Wycombe W v Darlington

Sunday, 9 March 2008

Coca-Cola Football League Two
Chester C v Wrexham

Tuesday, 11 March 2008

Coca-Cola Football League Championship
Barnsley v Ipswich T
Bristol C v Watford
Burnley v Charlton Ath
Cardiff C v Hull C
Colchester U v Sheffield W
Norwich C v Stoke C
Preston NE v Wolverhampton W
QPR v Blackpool
Scunthorpe U v Plymouth Arg
Sheffield U v Coventry C
Southampton v Leicester C
WBA v Crystal Palace

Coca-Cola Football League One
Carlisle U v Luton T
Crewe Alex v Port Vale
Doncaster R v Gillingham
Hartlepool U v Huddersfield T
Leeds U v Cheltenham T
Leyton Orient v Swindon T
Oldham Ath v Bournemouth
Southend U v Nottingham F
Swansea C v Tranmere R
Walsall v Brighton & HA
Yeovil T v Millwall

Coca-Cola Football League Two
Brentford v Peterborough U
Bury v Rotherham U
Dagenham & R v Macclesfield T
Grimsby T v Barnet
Mansfield T v Hereford U
Notts Co v Lincoln C
Shrewsbury T v Darlington
Stockport Co v Rochdale
Wycombe W v Wrexham

Wednesday, 12 March 2008

Coca-Cola Football League Two
Accrington S v Morecambe
Chester C v Bradford C
Chesterfield v Milton Keynes Dons

Saturday, 15 March 2008

Barclays Premier League
Arsenal v Middlesbrough
Birmingham C v Newcastle U
Derby Co v Manchester U
Fulham v Everton
Liverpool v Reading
Manchester C v Tottenham H
Portsmouth v Aston Villa
Sunderland v Chelsea
West Ham U v Blackburn R
Wigan Ath v Bolton W

Coca-Cola Football League Championship
Blackpool v Preston NE
Bristol C v Plymouth Arg
Burnley v Wolverhampton W
Colchester U v Cardiff C
Coventry C v Sheffield W
Crystal Palace v Barnsley
Hull C v Southampton
Ipswich T v Charlton Ath
QPR v Scunthorpe U
Sheffield U v Norwich C
Watford v Stoke C
WBA v Leicester C

Coca-Cola Football League One
Bournemouth v Yeovil T
Brighton & HA v Doncaster R
Cheltenham T v Bristol R
Gillingham v Crewe Alex
Huddersfield T v Southend U
Luton T v Oldham Ath
Millwall v Leyton Orient
Northampton T v Swansea C
Nottingham F v Walsall
Port Vale v Leeds U
Swindon T v Carlisle U
Tranmere R v Hartlepool U

Coca-Cola Football League Two
Barnet v Chester C
Bradford C v Mansfield T
Darlington v Grimsby T
Hereford U v Wycombe W
Lincoln C v Stockport Co
Macclesfield T v Shrewsbury T
Milton Keynes Dons v Dagenham & R
Morecambe v Brentford
Peterborough U v Notts Co
Rochdale v Accrington S
Rotherham U v Chesterfield
Wrexham v Bury

Friday, 21 March 2008
Coca-Cola Football League One
Northampton T v Nottingham F
Yeovil T v Doncaster R

Saturday, 22 March 2008
Barclays Premier League
Aston Villa v Sunderland
Blackburn R v Wigan Ath
Bolton W v Manchester C
Chelsea v Arsenal
Everton v West Ham U
Manchester U v Liverpool
Middlesbrough v Derby Co
Newcastle U v Fulham
Reading v Birmingham C
Tottenham H v Portsmouth

Coca-Cola Football League Championship
Barnsley v Sheffield U
Cardiff C v Bristol C
Charlton Ath v WBA
Leicester C v Hull C
Norwich C v Colchester U
Plymouth Arg v Watford
Preston NE v Burnley
Scunthorpe U v Ipswich T
Sheffield W v Crystal Palace
Southampton v Coventry C
Stoke C v Blackpool
Wolverhampton W v QPR

Coca-Cola Football League One
Brighton & HA v Swindon T
Bristol R v Huddersfield T
Crewe Alex v Hartlepool U
Gillingham v Bournemouth
Leeds U v Walsall
Leyton Orient v Carlisle U
Luton T v Cheltenham T
Oldham Ath v Millwall
Southend U v Swansea C
Tranmere R v Port Vale

Coca-Cola Football League Two
Barnet v Lincoln C
Brentford v Wrexham
Chester C v Darlington
Chesterfield v Accrington S
Dagenham & R v Shrewsbury T
Hereford U v Bury
Mansfield T v Grimsby T
Milton Keynes Dons v Peterborough U
Morecambe v Wycombe W
Notts Co v Rochdale
Rotherham U v Bradford C
Stockport Co v Macclesfield T

Monday, 24 March 2008
Coca-Cola Football League One
Bournemouth v Tranmere R
Carlisle U v Northampton T
Cheltenham T v Leyton Orient
Doncaster R v Oldham Ath
Hartlepool U v Yeovil T
Millwall v Luton T
Nottingham F v Brighton & HA
Port Vale v Gillingham
Swansea C v Bristol R
Swindon T v Southend U
Walsall v Crewe Alex

Coca-Cola Football League Two
Accrington S v Milton Keynes Dons
Bradford C v Chesterfield
Bury v Mansfield T
Darlington v Morecambe
Grimsby T v Brentford
Lincoln C v Hereford U
Macclesfield T v Barnet
Peterborough U v Chester C
Rochdale v Rotherham U
Shrewsbury T v Notts Co
Wrexham v Dagenham & R
Wycombe W v Stockport Co

Tuesday, 25 March 2008
Coca-Cola Football League One
Huddersfield T v Leeds U

Friday, 28 March 2008
Coca-Cola Football League One
Doncaster R v Nottingham F
Tranmere R v Swindon T

Saturday, 29 March 2008
Barclays Premier League
Birmingham C v Manchester C
Bolton W v Arsenal
Chelsea v Middlesbrough

Derby Co v Fulham
Liverpool v Everton
Manchester U v Aston Villa
Portsmouth v Wigan Ath
Reading v Blackburn R
Sunderland v West Ham U

Coca-Cola Football League Championship
Bristol C v Norwich C
Burnley v Barnsley
Cardiff C v Southampton
Charlton Ath v Wolverhampton W
Coventry C v Plymouth Arg
Crystal Palace v Blackpool
Hull C v Watford
Ipswich T v QPR
Leicester C v Scunthorpe U
Preston NE v Sheffield U
Sheffield W v Stoke C
WBA v Colchester U

Coca-Cola Football League One
Bournemouth v Millwall
Cheltenham T v Northampton T
Gillingham v Carlisle U
Hartlepool U v Swansea C
Leeds U v Brighton & HA
Luton T v Crewe Alex
Oldham Ath v Huddersfield T
Port Vale v Leyton Orient
Southend U v Walsall
Yeovil T v Bristol R

Coca-Cola Football League Two
Barnet v Wrexham
Brentford v Rochdale
Chester C v Stockport Co
Dagenham & R v Chesterfield
Darlington v Bradford C
Grimsby T v Wycombe W
Macclesfield T v Accrington S
Milton Keynes Dons v Hereford U
Morecambe v Rotherham U
Notts Co v Mansfield T
Peterborough U v Lincoln C
Shrewsbury T v Bury

Sunday, 30 March 2008
Barclays Premier League
Tottenham H v Newcastle U

Friday, 4 April 2008
Coca-Cola Football League Two
Lincoln C v Milton Keynes Dons

Saturday, 5 April 2008
Barclays Premier League
Arsenal v Liverpool
Aston Villa v Bolton W
Blackburn R v Tottenham H
Fulham v Sunderland
Manchester C v Chelsea
Middlesbrough v Manchester U
Newcastle U v Reading
West Ham U v Portsmouth
Wigan Ath v Birmingham C

Coca-Cola Football League Championship
Barnsley v Hull C
Blackpool v WBA
Colchester U v Ipswich T
Norwich C v Burnley
Plymouth Arg v Charlton Ath
QPR v Preston NE
Scunthorpe U v Sheffield W
Sheffield U v Leicester C
Southampton v Bristol C
Stoke C v Crystal Palace
Watford v Coventry C
Wolverhampton W v Cardiff C

Coca-Cola Football League One
Brighton & HA v Port Vale
Bristol R v Hartlepool U
Carlisle U v Yeovil T
Crewe Alex v Southend U
Huddersfield T v Doncaster R
Leyton Orient v Leeds U
Millwall v Gillingham
Northampton T v Luton T
Nottingham F v Cheltenham T
Swansea C v Bournemouth
Swindon T v Oldham Ath
Walsall v Tranmere R

Coca-Cola Football League Two
Accrington S v Dagenham & R
Bradford C v Morecambe
Bury v Notts Co
Chesterfield v Shrewsbury T
Hereford U v Chester C
Mansfield T v Barnet
Rochdale v Grimsby T
Rotherham U v Brentford
Stockport Co v Darlington
Wrexham v Macclesfield T
Wycombe W v Peterborough U

Sunday, 6 April 2008
Barclays Premier League
Everton v Derby Co

Saturday, 12 April 2008
Barclays Premier League
Birmingham C v Everton
Bolton W v West Ham U
Chelsea v Wigan Ath
Derby Co v Aston Villa
Liverpool v Blackburn R
Manchester U v Arsenal
Portsmouth v Newcastle U
Reading v Fulham
Sunderland v Manchester C
Tottenham H v Middlesbrough

Coca-Cola Football League Championship
Bristol C v Wolverhampton W
Burnley v Sheffield U
Cardiff C v Blackpool

Charlton Ath v Southampton
Coventry C v Stoke C
Crystal Palace v Scunthorpe U
Hull C v QPR
Leicester C v Colchester U
Preston NE v Barnsley
Sheffield W v Plymouth Arg
WBA v Watford

Coca-Cola Football League One
Bournemouth v Bristol R
Cheltenham T v Walsall
Doncaster R v Swindon T
Gillingham v Swansea C
Hartlepool U v Millwall
Leeds U v Carlisle U
Luton T v Brighton & HA
Oldham Ath v Leyton Orient
Port Vale v Huddersfield T
Southend U v Northampton T
Tranmere R v Nottingham F
Yeovil T v Crewe Alex

Coca-Cola Football League Two
Barnet v Bury
Brentford v Bradford C
Chester C v Lincoln C
Dagenham & R v Rochdale
Darlington v Hereford U
Grimsby T v Rotherham U
Macclesfield T v Mansfield T
Milton Keynes Dons v Wycombe W
Morecambe v Chesterfield
Notts Co v Accrington S
Peterborough U v Stockport Co

Sunday, 13 April 2008
Coca-Cola Football League Championship
Ipswich T v Norwich C

Coca-Cola Football League Two
Shrewsbury T v Wrexham

Saturday, 19 April 2008
Barclays Premier League
Arsenal v Reading
Blackburn R v Manchester U
Everton v Chelsea
Fulham v Liverpool
Manchester C v Portsmouth
Middlesbrough v Bolton W
Newcastle U v Sunderland
West Ham U v Derby Co
Wigan Ath v Tottenham H

Coca-Cola Football League Championship
Barnsley v Leicester C
Blackpool v Sheffield W
Colchester U v Coventry C
Norwich C v WBA
Plymouth Arg v Preston NE
QPR v Charlton Ath
Scunthorpe U v Cardiff C
Sheffield U v Hull C
Southampton v Burnley
Stoke C v Bristol C
Watford v Crystal Palace
Wolverhampton W v Ipswich T

Coca-Cola Football League One
Brighton & HA v Hartlepool U
Bristol R v Gillingham
Carlisle U v Southend U
Crewe Alex v Cheltenham T
Huddersfield T v Tranmere R
Leyton Orient v Doncaster R
Millwall v Leeds U
Northampton T v Oldham Ath
Nottingham F v Luton T
Swansea C v Yeovil T
Swindon T v Port Vale
Walsall v Bournemouth

Coca-Cola Football League Two
Accrington S v Barnet
Bradford C v Grimsby T
Bury v Macclesfield T
Chesterfield v Darlington
Hereford U v Peterborough U
Lincoln C v Brentford
Mansfield T v Shrewsbury T
Rochdale v Morecambe
Rotherham U v Dagenham & R
Stockport Co v Milton Keynes Dons
Wrexham v Notts Co
Wycombe W v Chester C

Sunday, 20 April 2008
Barclays Premier League
Aston Villa v Birmingham C

Saturday, 26 April 2008
Barclays Premier League
Birmingham C v Liverpool
Chelsea v Manchester U
Derby Co v Arsenal
Everton v Aston Villa
Manchester C v Fulham
Portsmouth v Blackburn R
Sunderland v Middlesbrough
Tottenham H v Bolton W
West Ham U v Newcastle U
Wigan Ath v Reading

Coca-Cola Football League Championship
Barnsley v Charlton Ath
Burnley v Cardiff C
Colchester U v Stoke C
Coventry C v Wolverhampton W
Hull C v Crystal Palace
Leicester C v Sheffield W
Norwich C v QPR
Plymouth Arg v Blackpool
Preston NE v Ipswich T
Sheffield U v Bristol C
Watford v Scunthorpe U
WBA v Southampton

Coca-Cola Football League One
Bournemouth v Crewe Alex
Bristol R v Brighton & HA
Doncaster R v Luton T
Gillingham v Swindon T
Hartlepool U v Nottingham F
Huddersfield T v Walsall
Millwall v Carlisle U
Oldham Ath v Cheltenham T
Port Vale v Northampton T
Swansea C v Leyton Orient
Tranmere R v Southend U
Yeovil T v Leeds U

Coca-Cola Football League Two
Barnet v Stockport Co
Bradford C v Milton Keynes Dons
Brentford v Hereford U
Bury v Rochdale
Darlington v Dagenham & R
Grimsby T v Peterborough U
Macclesfield T v Chesterfield
Mansfield T v Rotherham U
Morecambe v Lincoln C
Notts Co v Wycombe W
Shrewsbury T v Chester C
Wrexham v Accrington S

Saturday, 3 May 2008
Barclays Premier League
Arsenal v Everton
Aston Villa v Wigan Ath
Blackburn R v Derby Co
Bolton W v Sunderland
Fulham v Birmingham C
Liverpool v Manchester C
Manchester U v West Ham U
Middlesbrough v Portsmouth
Newcastle U v Chelsea
Reading v Tottenham H

Coca-Cola Football League One
Brighton & HA v Swansea C
Carlisle U v Bournemouth
Cheltenham T v Doncaster R
Crewe Alex v Oldham Ath
Leeds U v Gillingham
Leyton Orient v Bristol R
Luton T v Huddersfield T
Northampton T v Tranmere R
Nottingham F v Yeovil T
Southend U v Port Vale
Swindon T v Millwall
Walsall v Hartlepool U

Coca-Cola Football League Two
Accrington S v Bury
Chester C v Macclesfield T
Chesterfield v Notts Co
Dagenham & R v Mansfield T
Hereford U v Grimsby T
Lincoln C v Wrexham
Milton Keynes Dons v Morecambe
Peterborough U v Darlington
Rochdale v Shrewsbury T
Rotherham U v Barnet
Stockport Co v Brentford
Wycombe W v Bradford C

Sunday, 4 May 2008
Coca-Cola Football League Championship
Blackpool v Watford
Bristol C v Preston NE
Cardiff C v Barnsley
Charlton Ath v Coventry C
Crystal Palace v Burnley
Ipswich T v Hull C
QPR v WBA
Scunthorpe U v Colchester U
Sheffield W v Norwich C
Southampton v Sheffield U
Stoke C v Leicester C
Wolverhampton W v Plymouth Arg

Sunday, 11 May 2008
Barclays Premier League
Birmingham C v Blackburn R
Chelsea v Bolton W
Derby Co v Reading
Everton v Newcastle U
Middlesbrough v Manchester C
Portsmouth v Fulham
Sunderland v Arsenal
Tottenham H v Liverpool
West Ham U v Aston Villa
Wigan Ath v Manchester U

BLUE SQUARE PREMIER FIXTURES 2006–2007

Saturday, 11 August 2007
Altrincham T v Exeter C
Crawley T v Stevenage B
Droylsden v Salisbury C
Ebbsfleet U v Northwich Vic
Farsley Celtic v Stafford R
Histon v Burton Alb
Kidderminster H v Aldershot T
Oxford U v Forest Green R
Torquay U v Grays Ath
Weymouth v Halifax T
Woking v Rushden & D'monds
York C v Cambridge U

Tuesday, 14 August 2007
Aldershot T v Torquay U
Burton Alb v York C
Cambridge U v Oxford U
Exeter C v Crawley T
Forest Green R v Weymouth
Grays Ath v Woking
Halifax T v Altrincham T
Northwich Vic v Droylsden

Rushden & D'monds v Farsley Celtic
Salisbury C v Ebbsfleet U
Stafford R v Kidderminster H
Stevenage B v Histon

Saturday, 18 August 2007
Aldershot T v Droylsden
Burton Alb v Oxford U
Cambridge U v Farsley Celtic
Exeter C v York C
Forest Green R v Altrincham T
Grays Ath v Kidderminster H
Halifax T v Histon
Northwich Vic v Torquay U
Rushden & D'monds v Ebbsfleet U
Salisbury C v Crawley T
Stafford R v Woking
Stevenage B v Weymouth

Friday, 24 August 2007
Histon v Aldershot T

Saturday, 25 August 2007
Altrincham T v Grays Ath
Crawley T v Northwich Vic
Droylsden v Exeter C
Ebbsfleet U v Halifax T
Farsley Celtic v Salisbury C
Kidderminster H v Stevenage B
Oxford U v Stafford R
Torquay U v Rushden & D'monds
Weymouth v Burton Alb
Woking v Cambridge U
York C v Forest Green R

Monday, 27 August 2007
Aldershot T v Crawley T
Burton Alb v Farsley Celtic
Cambridge U v Ebbsfleet U
Exeter C v Weymouth
Forest Green R v Torquay U
Grays Ath v Histon
Halifax T v Droylsden
Northwich Vic v York C
Rushden & D'monds v Kidderminster H
Salisbury C v Woking
Stafford R v Altrincham T
Stevenage B v Oxford U

Friday, 31 August 2007
Weymouth v Cambridge U

Saturday, 1 September 2007
Altrincham T v Aldershot T
Crawley T v Burton Alb
Droylsden v Grays Ath
Ebbsfleet U v Stevenage B
Farsley Celtic v Northwich Vic
Histon v Salisbury C
Kidderminster H v Exeter C
Oxford U v Halifax T
Torquay U v Stafford R
Woking v Forest Green R
York C v Rushden & D'monds

Tuesday, 4 September 2007
Cambridge U v Grays Ath
Droylsden v Stevenage B
Ebbsfleet U v Histon
Farsley Celtic v Kidderminster H
Forest Green R v Aldershot T
Northwich Vic v Burton Alb
Oxford U v Exeter C
Rushden & D'monds v Crawley T
Stafford R v Halifax T
Torquay U v Salisbury C
Woking v Weymouth
York C v Altrincham T

Saturday, 8 September 2007
Aldershot T v Northwich Vic
Altrincham T v Oxford U
Burton Alb v Torquay U
Crawley T v Droylsden
Exeter C v Cambridge U
Grays Ath v Forest Green R
Halifax T v Woking
Histon v Farsley Celtic
Kidderminster H v York C
Salisbury C v Rushden & D'monds
Stevenage B v Stafford R
Weymouth v Ebbsfleet U

Saturday, 15 September 2007
Cambridge U v Crawley T
Droylsden v Weymouth
Ebbsfleet U v Kidderminster H
Farsley Celtic v Exeter C
Forest Green R v Salisbury C
Northwich Vic v Histon
Oxford U v Aldershot T
Rushden & D'monds v Burton Alb
Stafford R v Grays Ath
Torquay U v Halifax T
Woking v Altrincham T
York C v Stevenage B

Tuesday, 18 September 2007
Aldershot T v York C
Altrincham T v Cambridge U
Burton Alb v Ebbsfleet U
Crawley T v Woking
Exeter C v Forest Green R
Grays Ath v Oxford U
Halifax T v Northwich Vic
Histon v Torquay U
Kidderminster H v Droylsden
Salisbury C v Stafford R
Stevenage B v Farsley Celtic
Weymouth v Rushden & D'monds

Friday, 21 September 2007
Histon v Oxford U

Saturday, 22 September 2007
Aldershot T v Farsley Celtic
Altrincham T v Droylsden
Burton Alb v Woking
Crawley T v Forest Green R
Exeter C v Ebbsfleet U

Grays Ath v York C
Halifax T v Rushden & D'monds
Kidderminster H v Torquay U
Salisbury C v Northwich Vic
Stevenage B v Cambridge U
Weymouth v Stafford R

Tuesday, 25 September 2007
Cambridge U v Aldershot T
Droylsden v Burton Alb
Ebbsfleet U v Crawley T
Farsley Celtic v Altrincham T
Forest Green R v Stevenage B
Northwich Vic v Kidderminster H
Oxford U v Salisbury C
Rushden & D'monds v Grays Ath
Stafford R v Histon
Torquay U v Weymouth
Woking v Exeter C
York C v Halifax T

Saturday, 29 September 2007
Aldershot T v Exeter C
Crawley T v Altrincham T
Farsley Celtic v Ebbsfleet U
Forest Green R v Cambridge U
Grays Ath v Stevenage B
Halifax T v Burton Alb
Histon v Weymouth
Northwich Vic v Woking
Oxford U v York C
Rushden & D'monds v Stafford R
Salisbury C v Kidderminster H
Torquay U v Droylsden

Saturday, 6 October 2007
Altrincham T v Rushden & D'monds
Burton Alb v Salisbury C
Cambridge U v Halifax T
Droylsden v Oxford U
Ebbsfleet U v Torquay U
Exeter C v Grays Ath
Kidderminster H v Crawley T
Stafford R v Forest Green R
Stevenage B v Aldershot T
Weymouth v Northwich Vic
Woking v Farsley Celtic
York C v Histon

Tuesday, 9 October 2007
Aldershot T v Ebbsfleet U
Altrincham T v Burton Alb
Cambridge U v Rushden & D'monds
Crawley T v Histon
Droylsden v Farsley Celtic
Exeter C v Salisbury C
Forest Green R v Northwich Vic
Grays Ath v Weymouth
Kidderminster H v Halifax T
Oxford U v Torquay U
Stevenage B v Woking
York C v Stafford R

Friday, 12 October 2007
Weymouth v Crawley T

Saturday, 13 October 2007
Burton Alb v Aldershot T
Ebbsfleet U v Droylsden
Farsley Celtic v Oxford U
Halifax T v Grays Ath
Histon v Kidderminster H
Northwich Vic v Exeter C
Rushden & D'monds v Forest Green R
Salisbury C v Altrincham T
Stafford R v Cambridge U
Torquay U v Stevenage B
Woking v York C

Saturday, 20 October 2007
Aldershot T v Halifax T
Altrincham T v Ebbsfleet U
Cambridge U v Salisbury C
Crawley T v Stafford R
Droylsden v Histon
Exeter C v Rushden & D'monds
Forest Green R v Farsley Celtic
Grays Ath v Northwich Vic
Kidderminster H v Weymouth
Oxford U v Woking
Stevenage B v Burton Alb
York C v Torquay U

Saturday, 3 November 2007
Burton Alb v Kidderminster H
Ebbsfleet U v Forest Green R
Farsley Celtic v York C
Halifax T v Crawley T
Histon v Altrincham T
Northwich Vic v Stevenage B
Rushden & D'monds v Oxford U
Salisbury C v Grays Ath
Stafford R v Exeter C
Torquay U v Cambridge U
Weymouth v Aldershot T
Woking v Droylsden

Saturday, 17 November 2007
Aldershot T v Rushden & D'monds
Altrincham T v Weymouth
Cambridge U v Northwich Vic
Crawley T v Torquay U
Droylsden v Stafford R
Exeter C v Burton Alb
Forest Green R v Histon
Grays Ath v Farsley Celtic
Kidderminster H v Woking
Oxford U v Ebbsfleet U
Stevenage B v Halifax T
York C v Salisbury C

Saturday, 24 November 2007
Aldershot T v Grays Ath
Burton Alb v Cambridge U
Crawley T v Farsley Celtic
Droylsden v Forest Green R
Ebbsfleet U v Stafford R
Halifax T v Salisbury C
Histon v Exeter C
Kidderminster H v Oxford U

Northwich Vic v Rushden & D'monds
Stevenage B v Altrincham T
Torquay U v Woking
Weymouth v York C

Saturday, 1 December 2007
Altrincham T v Kidderminster H
Cambridge U v Droylsden
Exeter C v Stevenage B
Farsley Celtic v Torquay U
Forest Green R v Halifax T
Grays Ath v Burton Alb
Oxford U v Weymouth
Rushden & D'monds v Histon
Salisbury C v Aldershot T
Stafford R v Northwich Vic
Woking v Ebbsfleet U
York C v Crawley T

Saturday, 8 December 2007
Aldershot T v Stafford R
Burton Alb v Forest Green R
Crawley T v Grays Ath
Droylsden v Rushden & D'monds
Ebbsfleet U v York C
Halifax T v Exeter C
Histon v Woking
Kidderminster H v Cambridge U
Northwich Vic v Oxford U
Stevenage B v Salisbury C
Torquay U v Altrincham T
Weymouth v Farsley Celtic

Wednesday, 26 December 2007
Altrincham T v Northwich Vic
Cambridge U v Histon
Exeter C v Torquay U
Farsley Celtic v Halifax T
Forest Green R v Kidderminster H
Grays Ath v Ebbsfleet U
Oxford U v Crawley T
Rushden & D'monds v Stevenage B
Salisbury C v Weymouth
Stafford R v Burton Alb
Woking v Aldershot T
York C v Droylsden

Saturday, 29 December 2007
Altrincham T v Stevenage B
Cambridge U v Burton Alb
Exeter C v Histon
Farsley Celtic v Crawley T
Forest Green R v Droylsden
Grays Ath v Aldershot T
Oxford U v Kidderminster H
Rushden & D'monds v Northwich Vic
Salisbury C v Halifax T
Stafford R v Ebbsfleet U
Woking v Torquay U
York C v Weymouth

Tuesday, 1 January 2008
Aldershot T v Woking
Burton Alb v Stafford R
Crawley T v Oxford U
Droylsden v York C
Ebbsfleet U v Grays Ath
Halifax T v Farsley Celtic
Histon v Cambridge U
Kidderminster H v Forest Green R
Northwich Vic v Altrincham T
Stevenage B v Rushden & D'monds
Torquay U v Exeter C
Weymouth v Salisbury C

Saturday, 5 January 2008
Cambridge U v Exeter C
Droylsden v Crawley T
Ebbsfleet U v Weymouth
Farsley Celtic v Histon
Forest Green R v Grays Ath
Northwich Vic v Aldershot T
Oxford U v Altrincham T
Rushden & D'monds v Salisbury C
Stafford R v Stevenage B
Torquay U v Burton Alb
Woking v Halifax T
York C v Kidderminster H

Saturday, 19 January 2008
Aldershot T v Forest Green R
Altrincham T v York C
Burton Alb v Northwich Vic
Crawley T v Rushden & D'monds
Exeter C v Oxford U
Grays Ath v Cambridge U
Halifax T v Stafford R
Histon v Ebbsfleet U
Kidderminster H v Farsley Celtic
Salisbury C v Torquay U
Stevenage B v Droylsden
Weymouth v Woking

Saturday, 26 January 2008
Cambridge U v Altrincham T
Droylsden v Kidderminster H
Ebbsfleet U v Burton Alb
Farsley Celtic v Stevenage B
Forest Green R v Exeter C
Northwich Vic v Halifax T
Oxford U v Grays Ath
Rushden & D'monds v Weymouth
Stafford R v Salisbury C
Torquay U v Histon
Woking v Crawley T
York C v Aldershot T

Saturday, 2 February 2008
Aldershot T v Oxford U
Altrincham T v Woking
Burton Alb v Rushden & D'monds
Crawley T v Cambridge U
Exeter C v Farsley Celtic
Grays Ath v Stafford R
Halifax T v Torquay U
Histon v Northwich Vic
Kidderminster H v Ebbsfleet U
Salisbury C v Forest Green R
Stevenage B v York C
Weymouth v Droylsden

Saturday, 9 February 2008
Cambridge U v Stevenage B
Droylsden v Altrincham T
Ebbsfleet U v Exeter C
Farsley Celtic v Aldershot T
Forest Green R v Crawley T
Northwich Vic v Salisbury C
Oxford U v Histon
Rushden & D'monds v Halifax T
Stafford R v Weymouth
Torquay U v Kidderminster H
Woking v Burton Alb
York C v Grays Ath

Tuesday, 12 February 2008
Aldershot T v Cambridge U
Altrincham T v Farsley Celtic
Burton Alb v Droylsden
Crawley T v Ebbsfleet U
Exeter C v Woking
Grays Ath v Rushden & D'monds
Halifax T v York C
Histon v Stafford R
Kidderminster H v Northwich Vic
Salisbury C v Oxford U
Stevenage B v Forest Green R
Weymouth v Torquay U

Saturday, 16 February 2008
Aldershot T v Stevenage B
Crawley T v Kidderminster H
Farsley Celtic v Woking
Forest Green R v Stafford R
Grays Ath v Exeter C
Halifax T v Cambridge U
Histon v York C
Northwich Vic v Weymouth
Oxford U v Droylsden
Rushden & D'monds v Altrincham T
Salisbury C v Burton Alb
Torquay U v Ebbsfleet U

Saturday, 23 February 2008
Altrincham T v Crawley T
Burton Alb v Halifax T
Cambridge U v Forest Green R
Droylsden v Torquay U
Ebbsfleet U v Farsley Celtic
Exeter C v Aldershot T
Kidderminster H v Salisbury C
Stafford R v Rushden & D'monds
Stevenage B v Grays Ath
Weymouth v Histon
Woking v Northwich Vic
York C v Oxford U

Saturday, 1 March 2008
Aldershot T v Kidderminster H
Burton Alb v Histon
Cambridge U v York C
Exeter C v Altrincham T
Forest Green R v Oxford U
Grays Ath v Torquay U
Halifax T v Weymouth
Northwich Vic v Ebbsfleet U
Rushden & D'monds v Woking
Salisbury C v Droylsden
Stafford R v Farsley Celtic
Stevenage B v Crawley T

Tuesday, 4 March 2008
Altrincham T v Halifax T
Crawley T v Exeter C
Droylsden v Northwich Vic
Ebbsfleet U v Salisbury C
Farsley Celtic v Rushden & D'monds
Histon v Stevenage B
Kidderminster H v Stafford R
Oxford U v Cambridge U
Torquay U v Aldershot T
Weymouth v Forest Green R
Woking v Grays Ath
York C v Burton Alb

Saturday, 8 March 2008
Altrincham T v Forest Green R
Crawley T v Salisbury C
Droylsden v Aldershot T
Ebbsfleet U v Rushden & D'monds
Farsley Celtic v Cambridge U
Histon v Halifax T
Kidderminster H v Grays Ath
Oxford U v Burton Alb
Torquay U v Northwich Vic
Weymouth v Stevenage B
Woking v Stafford R
York C v Exeter C

Saturday, 15 March 2008
Aldershot T v Histon
Burton Alb v Weymouth
Cambridge U v Woking
Exeter C v Droylsden
Forest Green R v York C
Grays Ath v Altrincham T
Halifax T v Ebbsfleet U
Northwich Vic v Crawley T
Rushden & D'monds v Torquay U
Salisbury C v Farsley Celtic
Stafford R v Oxford U
Stevenage B v Kidderminster H

Saturday, 22 March 2008
Aldershot T v Altrincham T
Burton Alb v Crawley T
Cambridge U v Weymouth
Exeter C v Kidderminster H
Forest Green R v Woking
Grays Ath v Droylsden
Halifax T v Oxford U
Northwich Vic v Farsley Celtic
Rushden & D'monds v York C
Salisbury C v Histon
Stafford R v Torquay U
Stevenage B v Ebbsfleet U

Monday, 24 March 2008
Altrincham T v Stafford R
Crawley T v Aldershot T

Droylsden v Halifax T
Ebbsfleet U v Cambridge U
Farsley Celtic v Burton Alb
Histon v Grays Ath
Kidderminster H v Rushden & D'monds
Oxford U v Stevenage B
Torquay U v Forest Green R
Weymouth v Exeter C
Woking v Salisbury C
York C v Northwich Vic

Saturday, 29 March 2008
Altrincham T v Torquay U
Cambridge U v Kidderminster H
Exeter C v Halifax T
Farsley Celtic v Weymouth
Forest Green R v Burton Alb
Grays Ath v Crawley T
Oxford U v Northwich Vic
Rushden & D'monds v Droylsden
Salisbury C v Stevenage B
Stafford R v Aldershot T
Woking v Histon
York C v Ebbsfleet U

Saturday, 5 April 2008
Aldershot T v Salisbury C
Burton Alb v Grays Ath
Crawley T v York C
Droylsden v Cambridge U
Ebbsfleet U v Woking
Halifax T v Forest Green R
Histon v Rushden & D'monds
Kidderminster H v Altrincham T
Northwich Vic v Stafford R
Stevenage B v Exeter C
Torquay U v Farsley Celtic
Weymouth v Oxford U

Tuesday, 8 April 2008
Burton Alb v Altrincham T
Ebbsfleet U v Aldershot T
Farsley Celtic v Droylsden
Halifax T v Kidderminster H
Histon v Crawley T
Northwich Vic v Forest Green R
Rushden & D'monds v Cambridge U
Salisbury C v Exeter C
Stafford R v York C
Torquay U v Oxford U
Weymouth v Grays Ath
Woking v Stevenage B

Saturday, 12 April 2008
Aldershot T v Burton Alb
Altrincham T v Salisbury C
Cambridge U v Stafford R
Crawley T v Weymouth
Droylsden v Ebbsfleet U
Exeter C v Northwich Vic
Forest Green R v Rushden & D'monds
Grays Ath v Halifax T
Kidderminster H v Histon
Oxford U v Farsley Celtic
Stevenage B v Torquay U
York C v Woking

Saturday, 19 April 2008
Burton Alb v Stevenage B
Ebbsfleet U v Altrincham T
Farsley Celtic v Forest Green R
Halifax T v Aldershot T
Histon v Droylsden
Northwich Vic v Grays Ath
Rushden & D'monds v Exeter C
Salisbury C v Cambridge U
Stafford R v Crawley T
Torquay U v York C
Weymouth v Kidderminster H
Woking v Oxford U

Saturday, 26 April 2008
Aldershot T v Weymouth
Altrincham T v Histon
Cambridge U v Torquay U
Crawley T v Halifax T
Droylsden v Woking
Exeter C v Stafford R
Forest Green R v Ebbsfleet U
Grays Ath v Salisbury C
Kidderminster H v Burton Alb
Oxford U v Rushden & D'monds
Stevenage B v Northwich Vic
York C v Farsley Celtic

Saturday, 3 May 2008
Burton Alb v Exeter C
Ebbsfleet U v Oxford U
Farsley Celtic v Grays Ath
Halifax T v Stevenage B
Histon v Forest Green R
Northwich Vic v Cambridge U
Rushden & D'monds v Aldershot T
Salisbury C v York C
Stafford R v Droylsden
Torquay U v Crawley T
Weymouth v Altrincham T
Woking v Kidderminster H

OTHER FIXTURES — SEASON 2007–2008

AUGUST 2007

Wed 1 UEFA Champions League 2Q (1)
Thu 2 UEFA Cup 1Q (2)
Sun 5 The FA Community Shield
Tue 7 UEFA Champions League 2Q (2)
Wed 8 UEFA Champions League 2Q (2)
Sat 11 Start of Premier and Football League
Tue 14 UEFA Champions League 3Q (1)
Wed 15 UEFA Champions League 3Q (1)
FL Carling Cup 1
Thu 16 UEFA Cup 2Q (1)
Sat 18 The FA Cup sponsored by E.ON – EP
North Korea v England – FIFA U17 World Cup – South Korea
Tue 21 New Zealand v England – FIFA U17 World Cup – South Korea
England v Romania – U21 Friendly International
Wed 22 England v Germany – Friendly International
Fri 24 England v Brazil – FIFA U17 World Cup – South Korea
Mon 27 Bank Holiday
Tue 28 UEFA Champions League 3Q (2)
Wed 29 UEFA Champions League 3Q (2)
FL Carling Cup 2
Thu 30 UEFA Cup 2Q (2)
Fri 31 UEFA Super Cup

SEPTEMBER 2007

Sat 1 The FA Cup sponsored by E.ON – P
Sun 2 The FA Women's Cup sponsored by E.ON – P
Wed 5 FL Johnstone's Paint Trophy 1
Fri 7 Montenegro v England – U21 European Championship Qualifier
Sat 8 The FA Carlsberg Vase – 1Q
England v Israel – European Championship Qualifier
Mon 10 The FA Youth Cup sponsored by E.ON – P**
Tue 11 Bulgaria v England – U21 European Championship Qualifier
England v Japan – FIFA Women's World Cup – Shanghai, China
Wed 12 England v Russia – European Championship Qualifier
Fri 14 England v Germany – FIFA Women's World Cup – Shanghai, China
Sat 15 The FA Cup sponsored by E.ON – 1Q
Sun 16 The FA Women's Cup sponsored by E.ON – 1Q
Tue 18 UEFA Champions League MD 1
England v Argentina – FIFA Women's World Cup – Chengdu, China
Wed 19 UEFA Champions League MD 1
Wed 19–23 England v Denmark – Women's U17 Friendly International
Thu 20 UEFA Cup 1 (1)
Sat 22 The FA Carlsberg Vase – 2Q
FIFA Women's World Cup – China – Quarter Finals
Sun 23 The FA Carlsberg Sunday Cup – P
FIFA Women's World Cup – China – Quarter Finals
Mon 24 The FA Youth Cup sponsored by E.ON – 1Q**
Wed 26 FL Carling Cup 3
FIFA Women's World Cup – China – Semi-Final
Thu 27 FIFA Women's World Cup – China – Semi-Final
Thu 27–2 Oct UEFA Women's U19 Championship Round 1 – Lithuania
Sat 29 The FA Cup sponsored by E.ON – 2Q
The FA Carlsberg National League System Cup – 1*
Sun 30 FIFA Women's World Cup – China – Final

OCTOBER 2007

Tue 2 UEFA Champions League MD 2
Wed 3 UEFA Champions League MD 2
Thu 4 UEFA Cup 1 (2)
Sat 6 The FA Carlsberg Trophy – P
The FA Carlsberg Vase – 1P
Sun 7 The FA County Youth Cup – 1*
The FA Women's Cup sponsored by E.ON – 2Q
Mon 8 The FA Youth Cup sponsored by E.ON – 2Q**
Wed 10 FL Johnstone's Paint Trophy 2
Fri 12 England v Montenegro – U21 European Championship Qualifier
England v Iceland – U19 European Championship Qualifier
Sat 13 The FA Cup sponsored by E.ON – 3Q
England v Estonia – European Championship Qualifier
Sun 14 The FA Carlsberg Sunday Cup – 1
Romania v England – U19 European Championship Qualifier
Tue 16 Republic of Ireland v England – U21 European Championship Qualifier
Wed 17 Russia v England – European Championship Qualifier
England v Belgium – U19 European Championship Qualifier
Sat 20 The FA Carlsberg Trophy – 1Q
Sun 21 England v Malta – U17 European Championship Qualifier – Estonia
Mon 22 The FA Youth Cup sponsored by E.ON – 3Q**

Mon 22–28 UEFA Women's U17 Championship Round 1 – Georgia
Tue 23 UEFA Champions League MD 3
England v Estonia – U17 European Championship Qualifier – Estonia
Wed 24 UEFA Champions League MD 3
Thu 25 UEFA Cup MD 1
Fri 26 Portugal v England – U17 European Championship Qualifier – Estonia
Sat 27 The FA Cup sponsored by E.ON – 4Q
England v Belarus – UEFA Women's Championship Qualifier
Sun 28 The FA Women's Cup sponsored by E.ON – 1P
Tue 30 England v France – Women's U19 Friendly International
Wed 31 FL Carling Cup 4

NOVEMBER 2007

Sat 3 The FA Carlsberg Trophy – 2Q
Sun 4 The FA County Youth Cup – 2*
The FA Carlsberg Sunday Cup – 2
Tue 6 UEFA Champions League MD 4
Wed 7 UEFA Champions League MD 4
Thu 8 UEFA Cup MD 2
Sat 10 The FA Cup sponsored by E.ON – 1P
The FA Youth Cup sponsored by E.ON – 1P*
Sun 11 The FA Women's Cup sponsored by E.ON – 2P
Wed 14 FL Johnstone's Paint Trophy AQF
Germany v England – U19 Friendly International
Fri 16 England v Bulgaria – U21 European Championship Qualifier
Sat 17 The FA Carlsberg Vase – 2P
International – European Championship Qualifier
Tue 20 Portugal v England – U21 European Championship Qualifier
Wed 21 The FA Cup sponsored by E.ON – 1P-R
England v Croatia – European Championship Qualifier
Sat 24 The FA Carlsberg Trophy – 3Q
The FA Youth Cup sponsored by E.ON – 2P*
Sun 25 The FA Carlsberg Sunday Cup – 3
England v Spain – UEFA Women's Championship Qualifier
Tue 27 UEFA Champions League MD 5
Wed 28 UEFA Champions League MD 5
Thu 29 UEFA Cup MD 3

DECEMBER 2007

Sat 1 The FA Cup sponsored by E.ON – 2P
The FA Carlsberg National League System Cup – 2*
Sun 2 The FA Women's Cup sponsored by E.ON – 3P
Tue 4 UEFA Champions League MD 6 *(for the 2006–07 UEFA CL Title Holders' group)*
Wed 5 UEFA Cup MD 4 *(English Clubs seeded "bye" in UEFA Cup)*
Thu 6 UEFA Cup MD 4 *(English Clubs seeded "bye" in UEFA Cup)*
Sat 8 The FA Carlsberg Vase – 3P
Sun 9 The FA County Youth Cup – 3*
Tue 11 UEFA Champions League MD 6
Wed 12 The FA Cup sponsored by E.ON – 2P-R
UEFA Champions League MD 6
Sat 15 The FA Carlsberg Trophy – 1P
The FA Youth Cup sponsored by E.ON – 3P*
Wed 19 UEFA Cup MD 5
FL Carling Cup 5
Thu 20 UEFA Cup MD 5
Mon 24 Christmas Eve
Tue 25 Christmas Day
Wed 26 Boxing Day

JANUARY 2008

Tue 1 New Year's Day
Sat 5 The FA Cup sponsored by E.ON – 3P
Sun 6 The FA Women's Cup sponsored by E.ON – 4P
Wed 9 FL Carling Cup SF (1)
FL Johnstone's Paint Trophy ASF
Sat 12 The FA Carlsberg Trophy – 2P
Sun 13 The FA Carlsberg Sunday Cup – 4
Wed 16 The FA Cup sponsored by E.ON – 3P-R
Sat 19 The FA Carlsberg Vase – 4P
The FA Youth Cup sponsored by E.ON – 4P*
Wed 23 FL Carling Cup SF (2)
Sat 26 The FA Cup sponsored by E.ON – 4P
Sun 27 The FA County Youth Cup – 4*
The FA Women's Cup sponsored by E.ON – 5P

FEBRUARY 2008

Sat 2 The FA Carlsberg Trophy – 3P
The FA Youth Cup sponsored by E.ON – 5P*
Tue 5 England v Republic of Ireland – U21 European Championship Qualifier
Wed 6 The FA Cup sponsored by E.ON – 4P-R (prov)
International – Friendly
Sat 9 The FA Cup sponsored by E.ON – 4P-R (prov)
The FA Carlsberg Vase – 5P
Sun 10 The FA Women's Cup sponsored by E.ON – 6P
Mon 11 The FA Cup sponsored by E.ON – 4P-R (prov)
Wed 13 UEFA Cup 32 (1)
Thu 14 UEFA Cup 32 (1)

Sat 16 The FA Cup sponsored by E.ON – 5P
The FA Youth Cup sponsored by E.ON – 6P*
The FA Carlsberg National League System Cup – 3*
Tue 19 UEFA Champions League 16 (1)
Wed 20 UEFA Champions League 16 (1)
FL Johnstone's Paint Trophy AF (1)
Thu 21 UEFA Cup 32 (2)
Sat 23 The FA Carlsberg Trophy – 4P
Sun 24 The FA Carlsberg Sunday Cup – 5
FL Carling Cup – Final
Wed 27 The FA Cup sponsored by E.ON – 5P-R
FL Johnstone's Paint Trophy AF (2)

MARCH 2008

Sat 1 The FA Carlsberg Vase – 6P
Sun 2 The FA County Youth Cup – SF*
Tue 4 UEFA Champions League 16 (2)
Wed 5 UEFA Champions League 16 (2)
Thu 6 UEFA Cup 16 (1)
Northern Ireland v England – UEFA Women's Championship Qualifier
Sat 8 The FA Cup sponsored by E.ON – 6P
The FA Carlsberg Trophy – SF (1)
The FA Youth Cup sponsored by E.ON – SF (1)*
Sun 9 The FA Women's Cup sponsored by E.ON – SF
Wed 12 UEFA Cup 16 (2)
Thu 13 UEFA Cup 16 (2)
Sat 15 The FA Carlsberg Trophy – SF (2)
Sun 16 The FA Carlsberg Sunday Cup – SF
Wed 19 The FA Cup sponsored by E.ON – 6P-R
Thu 20 England v Czech Republic – UEFA Women's Championship Qualifier
Fri 21 Good Friday
Sat 22 The FA Carlsberg Vase – SF (1)
The FA Youth Cup sponsored by E.ON – SF (2)*
Mon 24 Easter Monday
Tue 25 U21 Friendly International
Wed 26 International – Friendly
Sat 29 The FA Carlsberg Vase – SF (2)
Sun 30 FL Johnstone's Paint Trophy – Final

APRIL 2008

Tue 1 UEFA Champions League QF (1)
Wed 2 UEFA Champions League QF (1)
Thu 3 UEFA Cup QF (1)
Sat 5 The FA Cup sponsored by E.ON – SF
Sun 6 The FA Cup sponsored by E.ON – SF
Tue 8 UEFA Champions League QF (2)
Wed 9 UEFA Champions League QF (2)
Thu 10 UEFA Cup QF (2)
Sat 12 The FA Carlsberg National League System Cup – SF*
Sat 19
Tue 22 UEFA Champions League SF (1)
Wed 23 UEFA Champions League SF (1)
Thu 24 UEFA Cup SF (1)
Sat 26 The FA County Youth Cup – Final (prov)
Sun 27 The FA Carlsberg Sunday Cup – Final (prov)
Tue 29 UEFA Champions League SF (2)
Wed 30 UEFA Champions League SF (2)

MAY 2008

Thu 1 UEFA Cup SF (2)
Sat 3 Football League Season Ends
The FA County Youth Cup – Final (prov)
Sun 4 The FA Carlsberg Sunday Cup – Final (prov)
Mon 5 Bank Holiday
The FA Women's Cup sponsored by E.ON – Final
Thu 8 Belarus v England – UEFA Women's Championship Qualifier
Sat 10 The FA Carlsberg Trophy – Final
Premier League Season Ends
Sun 11 The FA Carlsberg Vase – Final
Wed 14 UEFA Cup Final
Sat 17 The FA Cup sponsored by E.ON – Final
Wed 21 UEFA Champions League Final
Sat 24 Championship Play-off Final
Sun 25 League 1 Play-off Final
Mon 26 Bank Holiday
League 2 Play-off Final

JUNE 2008

7–29 European Championship Finals

SEPTEMBER 2008

Sun 7 Czech Republic v England – UEFA Women's Championship Qualifier

OCTOBER 2008

Thu 2 Spain v England – UEFA Women's Championship Qualifier

DATES TO BE CONFIRMED

The FA Youth Cup sponsored by E.ON – Final (1)
The FA Youth Cup sponsored by E.ON – Final (2)
The FA Carlsberg National League System Cup – Final
* closing date of round
** ties to be played in the week commencing

STOP PRESS

Summer transfers completed and pending:

Premier Division: Arsenal: Eduardo da Silva (Dynamo Zagreb) undisclosed; Lukasz Fabianski (Legia Warsaw) undisclosed; Bakari Sagna (Auxerre) undisclosed. **Aston Villa:** Nigel Reo-Coker (West Ham U) £8,500,000. **Birmingham C:** Daniel de Ridder (Celta Vigo) Free; Olivier Kapo (Juventus) £3,000,000; Richard Kingson (Hammarby) Free; Fabrice Muamba (Arsenal) undisclosed; Garry O'Connor (Lokomotiv Moscow) £2,700,000; Stuart Parnaby (Middlesbrough) Free; Rafael Schmitz (Lille) Loan. **Blackburn R:** Gunnar Nielsen (Frem) undisclosed; Maceo Rigters (NAC Breda) undisclosed. **Bolton W:** Gerald Cid (Bordeaux) Free; Blerim Dzemaili (Zurich) Free; Danny Guthrie (Liverpool) Loan; Gavin McCann (Aston Villa) £1,000,000; J Lloyd Samuel (Aston Villa) Free. **Chelsea:** Tal Ben Haim (Bolton W) Free; Claudio Pizarro (Bayern Munich) Free; Steve Sidwell (Reading) Free; Florent Malouda (Lyon) undisclosed; **Derby Co:** Robert Earnshaw (Norwich C) £3,500,000; Tyrone Mears (West Ham U) £1,000,000; Andy Todd (Blackburn R) undisclosed. **Everton:** Phil Jagielka (Sheffield U) £4,000,000. **Fulham:** Chris Baird (Southampton) £3,025,000; Steven Davis (Aston Villa) undisclosed; Aaron Hughes (Aston Villa) £1,000,000; Diomansy Kamara (WBA) £6,000,000. **Liverpool:** Ryan Babel (Ajax) £11,500,000; Yossi Benayoun (West Ham U) £5,000,000; Lucas Leiva (Gremio) undisclosed; Fernando Torres (Atletico Madrid) £20,000,000; Andriy Voronin (Leverkusen) Free; Ryan Crowther (Stockport Co) undisclosed; Krisztian Nemeth (MTK) undisclosed; Andras Simon (MTK) undisclosed. **Manchester C:** Rolando Bianchi (Reggina) £8,800,000. **Manchester U:** Anderson (Porto) £18,000,000; Owen Hargreaves (Bayern Munich) undisclosed; Tomasz Kuszczak (WBA) undisclosed; Nani (Sporting Lisbon) £17,000,000. **Middlesbrough:** Jeremie Aliadiere (Arsenal) £2,000,000; Tuncay (Fenerbahce) Free; Jonathan Woodgate (Real Madrid) £7,000,000. **Newcastle U:** Joey Barton (Manchester C) £5,800,000; Geremi (Chelsea) Free; David Rozehnal (Paris St Germain) £2,900,000; Mark Viduka (Middlesbrough) Free. **Portsmouth:** Martin Cranie (Southampton) undisclosed; Paris Cowan-Hall (Rushden & D) undisclosed; Sylvain Distin (Manchester C) Free; Hermann Hreidarsson (Charlton Ath) Free; Sulley Muntari (Udinese) £7,000,000; David Nugent (Preston NE) £6,000,000; Callum Reynolds (Rushden & D) undisclosed; John Utaka (Rennes) £7,000,000. **Reading:** Kalifa Cisse (Boavista) undisclosed. **Sunderland:** Russell Anderson (Aberdeen) £1,000,000; Michael Chopra (Cardiff C) undisclosed; Greg Halford (Reading) £3,000,000. **Tottenham H:** Gareth Bale (Southampton) £5,000,000; Darren Bent (Charlton Ath) £16,500,000; Younes Kaboul (Auxerre) undisclosed; Adel Taarabt (Lens) undisclosed. **West Ham U:** Craig Bellamy (Liverpool) £7,500,000; Julien Faubert (Bordeaux) £6,100,000; Scott Parker (Newcastle U) £7,000,000; Richard Wright (Everton) Free. **Wigan Ath:** Titus Bramble (Newcastle U) Free; Andreas Granqvist (Helsingborg) Free; Jason Koumas (WBA) £5,300,000; Mario Melchiot (Rennes) Free; Carlo Nash (Preston NE) £300,000; Antoine Sibierski (Newcastle U) Free.

Football League Championship: Barnsley: Marciano Bruma (Sparta Rotterdam); Andy Johnson (Leicester C); Kayode Odejayi (Cheltenham T). **Blackpool:** John Hills (Sheffield W); Robbie Williams (Barnsley). **Bristol C:** Ivan Sproule (Hibernian). **Burnley:** Besart Berisha (Hamburg); Gabor Kiraly (Crystal Palace). **Cardiff C:** Steven MacLean (Sheffield W); Gavin Rae (Rangers); Tony Capaldi (Plymouth Arg); Trevor Sinclair (Mànchester C). **Charlton Ath:** Svetoslav Todorov (Portsmouth); Nicky Weaver (Manchester C); Jose Vitor Semedo (Sporting Lisbon); Yassin Moutaouakil (Chatearoux); Patrick McCarthy (Leicester C); Chris Iwelumo (Colchester U); Luke Varney (Crewe Alex). **Colchester U:** Danny Granville (Crystal Palace); Matthew Connolly (Arsenal) Loan; Luke Guttridge (Leyton Orient); Teddy Sheringham (West Ham U); Clive Platt (Milton Keynes D); Mark Yeates (Tottenham H). **Coventry C:** Michael Hughes (Crystal Palace); Leon Best (Southampton); Gary Borrowdale (Crystal Palace); Ellery Cairo (Hertha Berlin); Arjan De Zeeuw (Wigan Ath); Dimitrios Konstantopoulos (Hartlepool U); Julian Gray (Birmingham C). **Crystal Palace:** Jeff Hughes (Lincoln C); Tony Craig (Millwall). **Hull C:** Richard Garcia (Colchester U); Bryan Hughes (Charlton Ath); Dean Windass (Bradford C). **Leicester C:** Shaun Newton (West Ham U); Hossein Kaebi (Persepolis); Jonathan Hayes (Reading); James Chambers (Watford); Radostin Kishishev (Charlton Ath); Bruno N'Gotty (Birmingham C); Jimmy Nielsen (Aalborg). **Norwich C:** David Marshall (Celtic); Julien Brellier (Hearts); Jon Otsemobor (Crewe Alex); Jamie Cureton (Colchester U); Matthew Gilks (Rochdale). **Preston NE:** Karl Hawley (Carlisle U); Billy Jones (Crewe Alex). **QPR:** John Curtis (Nottingham F); Daniel Nardiello (Barnsley); Chris Barker (Cardiff C). **Scunthorpe U:** Jonathan Forte (Sheffield U); Martin Paterson (Stoke C); Ezomo Iriekpen (Swansea

C); Paul Hayes (Barnsley). **Sheffield U:** Gary Naysmith (Everton); Billy Sharp (Scunthorpe U). **Sheffield W:** Robert Burch (Tottenham H); Richard Hinds (Scunthorpe U); Steve Watson (WBA). **Stoke C:** Jonathan Parkin (Hull C). **Watford:** Botond Antal (Ujpest); Jobi McAnuff (Crystal Palace); Mart Poom (Arsenal); Matt Jackson (Wigan Ath). **WBA:** Craig Beattie (Celtic); Shelton Martis (Hibernian). **Wolverhampton W:** Freddy Eastwood (Southend U) £1,500,000; Darren Ward (Crystal Palace); Matthew Jarvis (Gillingham).

Football League 1: Bournemouth: Jo Osei-Kuffour (Brentford). **Brighton & HA:** Nicky Forster (Hull C). **Bristol R:** Joe Jacobson (Cardiff C); Andy Williams (Herefored U). **Carlisle U:** Marc Bridge-Wilkinson (Bradford C); Danny Carlton (Morecambe); Danny Graham (Middlesbrough). **Cheltenham T:** Lee Ridley (Scunthorpe U); Andy Lindegaard (Yeovil T). **Crewe Alex:** Chris McCready (Tranmere R); Billy Jones (Exeter C); Steven Schumacher (Bradford C). **Doncaster R:** Richard Wellens (Oldham Ath); Sam Hird (Leeds U); Martin Woods (Rotherham U). **Gillingham:** Craig Armstrong (Cheltenham T); Aaron Brown (Swindon T); Barry Cogan (Barnet); Delroy Facey (Rotherham U); Simon King (Barnet). **Hartlepool U:** Robbie Elliott (Leeds U); Arran Lee-Barrett (Coventry C); Godwin Antwi-Birago (Liverpool); Jan Budtz (Doncaster R); Jamie McCunnie (Dunfermline Ath); Ian Moore (Leeds U). **Huddersfield T:** Malvin Kamara (Port Vale). **Leyton Orient:** Sean Thornton (Doncaster R); Stuart Nelson (Brentford); Tamika Mkandawire (Hereford U); JJ Melligan (Cheltenham T); Stephen Purches (Bournemouth). **Luton T:** Chris Perry (WBA); Paul Furlong (QPR); Darren Currie (Ipswich T); David Edwards (Shrewsbury T). **Millwall:** Daniel Spiller (Gillingham). **Northampton T:** Giles Coke (Mansfield T); Colin Larkin (Chesterfield); Danny Jackman (Gillingham). **Nottingham F:** Arron Davies (Yeovil T); Chris Cohen (Yeovil T); Matthew Lockwood (Leyton Orient); Neil Lennon (Celtic). **Oldham Ath:** Mark Allott (Chesterfield); Jean-Paul Kamudimba Kala (Yeovil T); Craig Davies (Verona); John Thompson (Nottingham F); Mark Crossley (Fulham). **Port Vale:** Paul Edwards (Oldham Ath); Keith Lowe (Wolverhampton W); Craig Rocastle (Oldham Ath); Justin Miller (Leyton Orient); Shane Tudor (Leyton Orient). **Southend U:** Nick Bailey (Barnet); Tommy Black (Crystal Palace); Charlie MacDonald (Gravesend & N). **Swansea C:** Darryl Duffy (Hull C) £200,000; Dorus de Vries (Dunfermline Ath); Ferry Bodde (Den Haag); Matty Collins (Fulham); Jason Scotland (St Johnstone). **Swindon T:** Hasney Aljofree (Plymouth Arg); Barry Corr (Sheffield W). **Tranmere R:** Antony Kay (Barnsley); Adrian Ahmed (Huddersfield T). **Walsall:** Tommy Mooney (Wycombe W); Danny Sonner (Port Vale). **Yeovil T:** Lloyd Owusu (Brentford); Jerahl Hughes (Crystal Palace); Peter Sweeney (Stoke C); Gary Dempsey (Aberdeen).

Football League 2: Accrington S: Roscoe Dsane (AFC Wimbledon); Kenny Arthur (Partick T); Paul Carden (Burton Alb); John Miles (Macclesfield T). **Barnet:** Neal Bishop (York C). **Bradford C:** Barry Conlon (Mansfield T); Peter Thorne (Norwich C). **Brentford:** Lee Thorpe (Torquay U); Alan Connell (Hereford U); Glenn Poole (Grays Ath); John Mackie (Leyton Orient). **Bury:** Ben Futcher (Peterborough U); Paul Morgan (Lincoln C); Steven Haslam (Halifax T). **Chester C:** Kevin Ellison (Tranmere R); Ritchie Partridge (Rotherham U); Nathan Lowndes (Port Vale). **Chesterfield:** Steven Fletcher (Bournemouth); Gregor Robertson (Rotherham U); Jack Lester (Nottingham F). **Dagenham & R:** Richard Graham (Barnet); Shane Huke (Peterborough U). **Darlington:** Pawel Abbott (Swansea C) £100,000; Rob Purdie (Hereford U); Andy Oakes (Swansea C); John Brackstone (Hartlepool U); Kevin McBride (Motherwell); Scott Wiseman (Hull C). **Hereford U:** Karl Broadhurst (Bournemouth); John McCombe (Huddersfield T). **Lincoln C:** Stephen Torpey (Scunthorpe U). **Macclesfield T:** Francis Green (Boston U); Danny Thomas (Hereford U). **Mansfield T:** Martin McIntosh (Huddersfield T); Daniel Martin (Notts Co); John McAliskey (Huddersfield T). **Milton Keynes D:** Kevin Gallen (Plymouth Arg). **Morecambe:** Chris Neal (Preston NE). **Notts Co:** Neil MacKenzie (Scunthorpe U); Paul Mayo (Lincoln C). **Peterborough U:** Kieran Charnock (Northwich Vic); Rene Howe (Kettering T); Charlie Lee (Tottenham H). **Rochdale:** Nathan D'Laryea (Manchester C); Tom Kennedy (Bury); Ben Muirhead (Bradford C); James Spencer (Stockport Co). **Rotherham U:** Marc Joseph (Blackpool); Mark Hudson (Huddersfield T); Danny Harrison (Tranmere R); Dale Tonge (Barnsley); Andrew Todd (Accrington S). **Shrewsbury T:** Dave Hibbert (Preston NE); Darren Moss (Crewe Alex). **Wrexham:** Eifion Williams (Hartlepool U); Richard Hope (Shrewsbury T); Michael Proctor (Hartlepool U); Anthony Williams (Carlisle U). **Wycombe W:** Craig Woodman (Bristol C); Gary Holt (Nottingham F).